The
DYNAMICS of
ORGANIZATIONAL
CHANGE in
EDUCATION

·

Edited by

J. Victor Baldridge
University of California, Los Angeles

and

Terrence Deal
Harvard University

with the assistance of

Cynthia Ingols

·

McCutchan Publishing Corporation
2526 Grove Street
Berkeley, California 94704

ISBN 0-8211-0134-X
Library of Congress Catalog Card Number 82-62033

Cover design by Terry Down, Griffin Graphics
Typesetting composition by Delmas

Contributors

J. Victor Baldridge, University of California, Los Angeles
Warren Bennis, University of Southern California
William Lowe Boyd, University of Rochester
Burton Clark, University of California, Los Angeles
David Cohen, Harvard University
Michael D. Cohen, Stanford University
Margaret Davis, Stanford University
John DeSantis, Massachusetts Department of Education
Terrence Deal, Harvard University
Eleanor Farrar, The Huron Institute
Elisabeth Hansot, Kenyon College
Susan Moore Johnson, Harvard University
Michael Kirst, Stanford University
James March, Stanford University
John Meyer, Stanford University
Samuel Nutt, Harvard University
Johan P. Olsen, University of Bergen, Norway
Bella Rosenberg
Brian Rowan, Far West Educational Laboratory
Irene S. Rubin, University of Maryland
W. Richard Scott, Stanford University
Lee S. Sproull, Carnegie-Mellon University
E. Anne Stackhouse, Stanford University
David Tyack, Stanford University
Karl Weick, Cornell University

Stephen Weiner, University of California, Berkeley
Arthur Wise, Educational Policy Research Institute, Educational
    Testing Service
Martha Stone Wiske, Harvard University
David Wolf

Contents

Preface

This book is a collection of twenty-four carefully selected and edited articles about educational change, innovation, and organizational dynamics. The editors compiled an earlier, very successful book entitled *Managing Change in Educational Organizations*. This volume is a new, updated collection of current research, scholarship, and practical experience, and it covers many educational settings: elementary, secondary, and higher education.

A note about the editors: J. Victor Baldridge is senior research sociologist at the Graduate School of Education at the University of California, Los Angeles. Terrence Deal is on the faculty of the Graduate School of Education at Harvard University. Both have written extensively about organizational change in educational settings—Dr. Deal primarily on elementary and secondary schools and Dr. Baldridge primarily on colleges and universities.

Part I of the book is entitled "Characteristics of Educational Organizations." In the last few years much attention has focused on how educational organizations are similar to—or different from—other organizations. Our understanding of how institutional organizations change must be solidly founded on how they are organized. The literature argues that educational organizations have many unique features when compared to government agencies and businesses. For example, "loosely coupled systems" is a term widely applied to educational organizations, and these organizations have patterns of change significantly different from business organizations as a consequence. Part I discusses this link between *organizational structure* and *change*.

Part II, "Complications of the Rational Approach to Change," presents case studies that provide a real-life commentary on the limits of theories of rational change. The case studies are reminders of how things often turn

ix

out. Much literature of the preceding two decades written on organizational change focused on planned, rational change. There were several components to this rational orientation: (1) psychological "human-relation" strategies to improve organizational morale, (2) program planning and evalution, and (3) reform by social groups through legal mandates and pressure-group activities. These approaches shared a rational, "planning-can-work" philosophy, and overlaid on that philosophy was a social science "planning-and-evaluation" model. But those rationalistic approaches to change have worn thin, battered by the winds of environmental, political, and economic trends.

Part III, "Politics and the Environment," turns to the environmental and political themes of change. Both social scientists and managers of education know that the primary stimulus for change comes from the environment: economic conditions, competition with other institutions for students and funds, governmental regulation, and many other social forces. Organizations survey the environment regularly to find out what they should be doing to survive and to continue receiving support. Organizations participate in a constant dance with the environment, and the dance is a major impetus for changes.

This part also examines the politics of change. Politics and conflict are synonymous with change: one person's change is another's loss. Individuals and groups fight to protect their interests and form coalitions to promote or resist changes. Conflict, interest-group in-fighting, control over scarce resources, are the political dynamics that constitute some of the most critical aspects of change.

"Process Descriptions of Change" is the title of Part IV. The articles show the unfolding of change dynamics in "loosely coupled" educational organizations. In organizations where preferences and goals are unclear, the decision process is ambiguous. Under these conditions, decisions and changes attract people, problems, and solutions. Decisions about changes, like other decisions, are reached by a complex set of organizational dynamics, not simply by the rational choices of selected decision makers. To use one interesting metaphor, change is a "garbage can" that attracts whatever is littering an organization at the time. Change attracts issues and releases tensions. These process descriptions of change are the subject matter of Part IV.

Part V is entitled "Drama and Culture: The Symbolic Aspects of Change." We often think of change as pragmatic, goal oriented, and highly rational. But practical experience and recent sociological research suggest that there is a symbolic, cultural aspect to change dynamics. Organizational change often seems to be more theater than science, more symbolic than rational, more a cultural statement of values than a pragmatic program. We call this the "dramaturgical" aspect of change. Change often seems to be theater, playing to audiences inside and outside organizational boundaries. Organizations are held together by values and beliefs. Change is a ritual that reinforces traditional beliefs and values, or creates and profiles new ones. The drama of changing follows a script, has a plot and actions, and unfolds on a stage appropriate to a particular setting. Part V describes this cultural, theatrical aspect of organizational change.

We want to thank all those who helped in this process. At UCLA, Terri Weiner was enormously helpful in pulling together and reviewing material. At Harvard, Cynthia Ingols contributed to the introduction, and she and Betty Barnes shouldered many tasks that facilitated the book's production. At McCutchan Publishing, John McCutchan and Kim Sharrar handled the project and carried the book through the production process. A hearty thanks goes to all these helping hands.

In addition, we would like to acknowledge the intellectual contributions of Lee Bolman, who co-teaches with Terry Deal a course on organizational theory and behavior at Harvard. A book synthesizing in greater detail four perspectives on organizations is nearly completed and will soon be published, but it is impossible to keep a few Bolman-Deal ideas from infiltrating our work on change processes. Lee Bolman is a gifted theoretician and consultant. We recognize his indirect contributions to this book.

J. Victor Baldridge
Malibu, California

Terrence Deal
Concord, Massachusetts

August 1982

1

The Basics of Change in Educational Organizations

J. Victor Baldridge and Terrence E. Deal

The Shifting Sands of Organizational Life

The most stable fact about organizations, including schools and colleges, is that they change. You can count on it—if you leave an organization for a few years and return, it will be different. The differences may not be radical; some are so subtle that they are noticed only by those who leave for awhile. Think of the graduate who returns to the ivy-walled alma mater noticing—and often resenting—changes that evolved so slowly they escaped the attention of faculty or administrators. Or, by contrast, differences may be widely and readily recognized because they are dramatic shifts in the organization's foundation. Imagine a former teacher from an urban high school who returns after five years abroad to find what was a conventional college preparatory program now a modern mix of specialists, vocational programs, and federally financed efforts to upgrade basic skills. But whether changes are minute or monumental in scope, the constant in our modern society is that organizations are always shifting, changing, transforming, and realigning. Like the landscape of a windswept desert, the topography of organizations, including their various species of flora and fauna, is never stationary.

The people in organizations change. When you go back to an organization that you once knew, you're always shocked that the old-timers aren't there anymore: new faces, new personalities, and new egos run the place. The people you thought were utterly indispensable were not: the faculty have changed, the students have come and gone, and the administrative positions have been turned over a half dozen times.

Institutional purposes change, too. New programs, fresh projects, new twists to old themes emerge—the organization seems to rock along with its old purposes, but new objectives are always entering on the stage to play for a while. Today's emphasis might be on opening access for new clients; tomorrow's concern might be on improving the quality of service to people the organization already serves. Yesterday's push for growth may have settled into today's penny-pinching concern for decline. The times are indeed changing!

The relationship between the organization and its environment is like an ever-changing kaleidoscope. The environment is a complex mixture of political support and control, competing organizations trying to steal clients or funds, supporters trying to build the organization up, and detractors working to tear it down. Government policies are generous one minute and stingy the next. Every organization faces a bewildering whirlwind of environmental changes, environmental demands, and environmental controls.

New technologies come and go. About the time we became accustomed to individualized instruction, microcomputers became the rage. When we finally embraced modern management techniques, we were faced with the idea that organizational culture matters more and that some old-fashioned ideas will work better. And, of course, the structure of most organizations is always in flux. Reorganizing—changing roles, responsibilities, job titles, and channels of communication—is the knee-jerk reaction of organizations to almost any problem or opportunity. The organizational chart of today is tomorrow's forgotten artifact. Although people often raise questions about the real payoff of tinker-toy strategies that produce an endless series of new structural forms, there is little doubt that such changes involve an enormous amount of time and energy.

If anything in an organization is stable, it's the culture—the values, symbols, and rituals of the work place. Cultures evolve slowly over time through trial and error and grow from people talking and discovering new meaning in the work place. The culture acts as a counterbalance to keep people, goals, and roles from changing too fast. But in many modern organizations, cultures are weak or place a premium on innovation, which means that even the stabilizing forces of custom and history give way to a focus on changing—the "hype" of innovation. The culture of educational organizations often acts as a brake to slow the momentum of changes in people, purposes, and structures. But it's often alumni, parents, and other custodians in the outside environment—not the professionals inside the organization—who provide the conservative impulse.

Change can be a major overhaul or a cosmetic afterthought, a substantive renovation or a lively ritual, a response to crisis or an opportunity for excitement and adventure. But whatever its scope, motivation, or result, change as a noun or verb is a major part of any modern organization's language. As an activity, changing takes a sizable chunk of any workday—both for those who are trying to promote change and for others who are working to maintain the status quo. In short, change is the name of the game in organizations today.

Change in Educational Organizations

This book concerns change in educational organizations. As editors of the book, we believe that there are basic organizational ties between elementary, secondary, and post-secondary institutions: their similarities often outweigh their differences. We wanted, therefore, to examine the change processes that occur throughout the educational network; consequently, we have written and compiled articles that deal with elementary schools, high schools, school districts, and colleges and universities. This book is dedicated to the countless educational administrators and faculty members who are constantly grappling with their changing organizations, constantly trying to make those organizations work better, and constantly trying to adapt to a rapidly changing environment.

To set the stage for the book, we will consider a few basic assumptions. First, as already noted, organizational change is natural and fundamental. Much of the older literature in this field assumed the opposite: that organizations had to be forced to change. "Change agents" were seen as providing the needed force, but these noble innovators would predictably meet enormous resistance from stuffy bureaucracies where the valued status quo was entrenched. We assume just the opposite. We believe organizations are changing all the time for many reasons that force the organization to respond—trial and error, shifting environments that cause new demands, changes in technology that raise new opportunities, shifts in the economy that cause feast or famine, changes in demographic patterns that cause bulges or declines in markets or clientele. True enough, it is sometimes very difficult to make organizations change the way we would like them to. But that is not the same as saying they never change. The empirical evidence clearly suggests that change is one of the most stable features of organizational behavior.

Second, we assume that most important organizational change is largely unplanned, at least from the perspective of the people inside the organization. A decade ago, the literature on organizational change, especially in education, assumed that change was a deliberate enterprise, a conscious effort by people to make an organization different—maybe even better. That literature focused on issues like the role of "change agents," the power of administrators to make change, and the importance of parent groups in educational change. Both practical administrators and organizational theorists soon learned that such optimistic assumptions were belied by reality. Most important changes are unplanned, governed by a serendipitous flow of events, people, and karma. They come as a result of large-scale social forces, new laws, the economy, and other factors beyond the control of administrators, faculty, and students.

Third, we assume that there is no such thing as a special theory of change. Good organizational change theory is simply good organizational theory; good organizational change management practices are simply good management. Since change and transformation is a constant in organizational life, there is no need for a special "change theory." In many ways this book is not so much about educational change as about educational management. When we learn important lessons about organizational change we have also learned important lessons about organizational management in general—or vice versa. Most of the ideas in this book directly apply to all the facets of managing a complex organization. But since changing—or figuring out how not to—occupies such an important place in any administrator's daily routine, this book emphasizes change rather than other management issues.

The Changing Context of Educational Change: From Growth to Decline

In 1975, we published a collection of readings entitled *Managing Change in Educational Organizations*. Relying on current state-of-the-art organizational theory, that collection emphasized several points about educational change in an atmosphere of growth and innovation:

—research on change processes can be especially useful to administrators who typically "fly by the seat of their pants."

—research on change is useful only if it focuses on organizational factors as well as on individual factors, highlights things that administrators can control, and pays attention to policy implications.

—organizations are interlocking subsystems of people, goals, formal roles, technologies, and information systems.

—when something changes in one subsystem, it creates the need for changes in others.

—planned change is very difficult to produce, often results in intense political conflicts, and usually ends far from where its originators intended.

Managing Change brought the literature on planned change to the attention of organizational administrators. That book was divided into three parts: (1) *theories* to help administrators think differently about change; (2) *case studies* to provide opportunities for administrators to learn important lessons secondhand; and (3) *strategies*, such as planning, evaluation, and leadership, for changing organizations.

Since 1975, a lot has happened in the educational world. Most changes are immediately apparent to administrators who have directly felt the shift. And the alterations have profound implications for the context in which administrators take action to change things or merely to survive.

Shifts in the Causes of Change

The first set of shifts is the factors that promote change. Several trends are apparent:

1. *The pressure for change has shifted from inside to outside educational organizations.* In the 1960s and 1970s many changes in education were initiated by professionals inside schools, colleges, or universities. Behind the changes was the profound hope that better education could cure many social ills. Administrators thought they had a vision of necessary improvements and how those changes could be made: administrators and faculty could be change agents—innovators with grand ideas. Since that time, pressures for change have drifted to outside constituencies. The pressures are to "reform" educational organizations—particularly to make them more accountable and efficient.

2. *The incentives for change have shifted from voluntary improvements to mandatory requirements.* Many earlier innovations were either voluntary actions at the local level or projects encouraged by state or federal funds. Title III and IV of the Higher Education Act made monies available to post-secondary institutions wanting new ventures. Similar titles in elementary and secondary legislation gave funds to innovative local schools and school districts. A few urban and rural districts received large sums over an extended period to restructure comprehensively. Over time, however, voluntary incentives have been replaced by requirements. Courts have ordered desegregation. States have mandated competency testing for teachers and students and have specified criteria for evaluation. The federal government has developed regulations for special education, against sexual discrimination, and for the education of bilingual children. Colleges and universities have not been able to escape outside influence on issues such as admissions policies and racial discrimination.

3. *Changes in response to growth—new programs, expanding clientele, and optimism—have decreased, while changes in response to decline have increased.* Terminating programs, shrinking markets, pessimism, and

frustration are now the common denominator in many educational organizations. Administrators in the preceding two decades could often count on constructing buildings, hiring personnel, and planning exciting new programs. They can now count on closing schools, firing people (many of whom they originally hired), dropping and consolidating programs, and searching for new markets and funds. Creating is exciting; terminating is depressing. Most administrators have learned that tough decisions, widespread anxiety, and pessimism come with the territory.

Shifts in Administrative Behavior

Not only are the causes of change different, but administrative behavior has been transformed.

1. *The task of administration has shifted from management to survival in many situations.* The main problem of administering educational organizations in the past was to manage people and resources effectively. Administrators could usually count on their authority and their powers of persuasion to help the enterprise. But in the intervening years the task of management often became the task of survival. Administrators can no longer count on either their authority or their charisma. Persuasion has changed to politics, and nearly everyone has an interest to protect. Administrators are one force in a constellation of interest groups—and often they are not the most powerful. Survival for many administrators is a top-priority item.

2. *Administrative arrogance has been replaced by a humility.* Educational administrators were once an arrogant bunch (ourselves included). There was a superior air about them and an eagerness to make things work. Changes were needed to bring education into the modern era, and administrators believed they were the ones who could pull the strings. As it became apparent that administrators were not puppeteers, arrogance gave way to a more humble conception of their role. Most administrators realize now that educational organizations are not easy to control; many have given up.

3. *Simple conceptions of change have given way to complex ideas.* Early change models were linear and predictable chains of activity. Innovations were invented—usually in universities. Ideas were developed, packaged, and later installed in local sites. The pathway between planning and implementation was seen as relatively straightforward. Once in place, changes could be evaluated according to merit—the good ones were kept and those that did not measure up were eliminated. We now know that the pathway between planning and implementation is rocky: new ideas are buffeted by nearly everyone, and they are terribly difficult to evaluate. Organizations are more complex than most administrators imagined.

When changes are introduced, those organizations become even more complex.

In many ways, the environment surrounding educational change—or, for that matter, educational administration—has shifted substantially. Consequently, there is a need to update our knowledge about change; we need to make it relevant to new circumstances and challenges.

Changes in Organization Theory: From Rational Systems to Organized Anarchies

Managing Change brought to educational administrators the literature on organizations as it existed in the 1970s. It was a solid and impressive literature—and it still is. But the accumulated changes in education present administrators with a world different from a decade ago. And, during the 1970s, organization theory has gone through its own equally impressive evolution. Although the field today hardly offers any universal laws or unequivocal answers to the pressing issues of today's administrators, it offers an expanded set of ideas—metaphors if you will—to put the problems in perspective.

Most notably, organization theory has relaxed its assumptions of rationality. Earlier theories emphasized logical connections between various parts of an organization and assumed a fairly tight connection between goals, structures, activities, and outcomes. People were seen as rational actors whose behavior would and should be guided by what was best for the collective welfare. But one by one, these assumptions have been called into question by substantial evidence that there may be a gap between theoretical "truth" and organizational "facts."

The disjunction between theory and reality was particularly evident as rational ideas were applied to management—particularly to strategies for changing organizations. Earlier attempts to manage or to change organizations were guided by norms of rationality. People thought that goals should be clear and believed that the linkage between means and ends was logical and straightforward. As the experience of changing organizations began to accumulate, it soon became apparent that people and organizations are not very rational—or at least that they operate from a logic very different from that of theorists and administrators. Efforts to clarify goals produced more confusion, and results never seemed to follow from the activities designed to produce them. As changes were carried out, administrators were often surprised by reactions and results. More often than not, their plans to improve educational organizations—to implement bold new visions—ended in various forms of disappointment:

Status Quo: "The more things change, the more they stay the
                   same."
Conflict: "Now you see it, now you don't."
Symbolic   "If you look hard and wish upon a star, you can see
Change: our impressive new program."
Administrative   "Where did that change agent—old what's-his-
Turnover: name—go after he left here?"

As we enter a new era, the canons of rationality are not very strong; in
fact, that rationality is open to serious challenge. For this reason, as well as
the changing context of educational administration, many of the ideas and
assumptions in the previous volume need updating. We still believe that
research and theory can be helpful, but the literature needs to be expanded
and brought up to date. We do not believe that everything needs to be tossed
away or that we must start anew. In fact, the two of us in our administrative,
teaching, or consulting practices still frequently turn to many of the
articles in the 1975 edition of *Managing Change* for information and new
ideas. But we do believe that several emerging assumptions in the field of
organization theory require some careful administrative attention.

This new volume emphasizes the following four areas:

1. *Administrative experience is important.* "Flying by the seat of one's
pants" is often an accurate description of administrative action.
Intuition—the subtle voice from one's soul—needs to be heeded. Research
is helpful to challenge, reinforce, or supplement intuition, but theory and
research can never replace the wisdom of a seasoned administrator. Much of
the theory and research in this volume supports and extols administrative
judgment derived from open-minded reflection on practice and experience.

2. *Organizations are subsystems of parts.* But the parts are often loosely
connected. Goals and roles, intentions and outcomes, structure and
activity, operate quasi-independently. Each serves a purpose; but often the
purposes are political or symbolic rather than instrumental. Reorganizing
signals new ideas and values even when it makes very little difference in
day-to-day efficiency. Hiring a new superintendent—or firing a college
president—kindles new hope and encourages a belief that things will
improve. A chaotic meeting about the new curriculum may not solve a
problem, but it provides an arena for rival forces to lock horns and convenes
a dialogue that may lead to a merger of new and old ideas—maybe even a
shared understanding—about where to go next. The image of
organizations in this volume is much more flexible than was the systems
logic of the 1975 work.

3. *The environment around schools, colleges, and universities has
always been and will continue to be the most powerful source of change in*

educational organizations. But the relationship between an organization and its environment is even more complex than our 1975 work suggested. Educational organizations do not merely respond to tangible pressures for change and reform. They are also sensitive to and will adjust to local myths and expectations. They adapt to fit internal needs and agenda—they even pretend to conform to outside pressures in order to protect their stable identity. Organizations and their environment engage in a continual dance, each adjusting to the rhythm, tempo, and movement of the other. The conception in this volume of how educational organizations interact with various constituencies in the environment is very complex; it stresses the interplay between rational, political, and symbolic needs.

4. *The concept of rational, planned change is challenged.* A focal point of this volume is the debate over the concept and value of rationality. Our 1975 work centered on another debate: Do individuals or organizations provide the main forces that cause, resist, and underline change? The position of that book was to provide a counterweight to the prevailing "psychological fallacy" that individuals are the prime movers or barriers in changing organizations. We stressed organizational dynamics—the interplay between goals, roles, technologies, and the environment—as the primary forces in initiating or impeding change. Another position, the fallacy of rationality, seems to have gained an undue advantage in conceptions of how and why organizations change, and in this book we challenge that position, even though we were once among its advocates.

Most of our articles echo the concern that the literature on organization has become overly rational, overly plan-oriented, overly pseudo-scientific. This book represents a shift in our former thinking—an altered direction influenced heavily by the changing context in which educational administrators work and by emerging trends in the field of organizational studies.

Metaphors and Symbols in Organizational Change

We believe that much of what administrators do, and how they think about themselves and their role, is based on their implicit metaphors— their images of how the world of education works. These metaphors evolve from experience, but are much influenced by metaphors embedded in formal theories of organization and administration.[1]

---

[1]These metaphors are adopted in part from a more in-depth presentation of conceptual perspectives on organizations: Lee Bolman and Terrence E. Deal, "Four Organizational Frames for Administrative Thought and Action." Unpublished manuscript. Harvard University, 1981.

In the early approaches to administration and change, the prevailing metaphor—in both theory and practice—was the *revival tent.* This was the psychological approach—change the individual and you will change the organization. Administrators were the crusaders, bringing the word of modern ways to the "heathen" in an attempt to convert them from their wicked and primitive ways. Through preaching and persuasion, the chosen tried to whip up enthusiasm and zeal. Many people often came forward to renounce their old ways for the new spirit. Sometimes no one came forward at all. In either case, the crusaders stayed only a short while and then struck their tents to move on to new missions. We call this process the "psychological fallacy."

As systems theory began to influence theorist and administrator, a new metaphor began to emerge—the *erector set.* Administrators became engineers whose primary task was to tinker with the structure of organizations in the hope of producing more efficient and effective forms. Prototypes were often constructed by the engineers. But they underestimated the materials needed to apply the models to a real and very human social collective. The materials are not rigid and predictable; they are flexible, and their performance is impossible to predict from specifications. Just as the Queen of Hearts in *Alice In Wonderland* had trouble with the flamingo, a croquet mallet with a perverse mind of its own, administrators found that people don't always understand or accept their role in a new game. The erector set mentality left in its wake a number of projects that were never completed and even more that collapsed under their own weight.

Lurking in the background all the while was the metaphor of the *jungle.* Politics—power, conflict, and manipulation—is a game as old as the human species. It was articulated well by Machiavelli and represented a strategy followed by many of our successful leaders and statesmen. In the jungle metaphor, the administrators were often seen as lions, and their kingdoms were shaped as they saw fit. But as their turf was invaded, other jungle creatures bonded together to drive out the lion—or the snake as the administrator was often recast. In contests of power in changing educational organizations, it was sometimes the administrator who lost and left. Often, the struggle left the entire jungle in ruins—the inhabitants shocked and suspicious.

Our 1975 book was a reaction to the revival tent metaphor of the individual school, and the imagery of the erector set and jungle is interspersed throughout the work. As we review case studies of innovation and change and talk with educational organizations—principals, superintendents, deans, and presidents—it is not difficult to see that these three metaphors have played a powerful role in shaping our approaches to organizational change. They have been useful, but none has been sufficient to help administrators understand—let alone manage—change in organizations.

The flaw lies in a common feature of all three: they are metaphors of control. As crusader, engineer, or king of the jungle, the administrator is cast in a role at odds with the circumstances in most of today's elementary, secondary, and post-secondary institutions. As James March has noted in Chapter 18, educational administrators are given responsibility to control skidding cars or ships without rudders. As a consequence, we think that additional metaphors are needed, particularly those that convey images of organizations with limits on rationality and control. Alternative metaphors are embedded in emerging theories of organization. To think of change—or management itself—as a magnet, a sponge, a garbage can, or a theater is to expand the possibilities of administrative behavior.

Organizations are always changing, but in very unpredictable ways. Administrative action is guided best—in today's world at least—by humility, sensitivity, and a profound appreciation for serendipity, ambiguity, and implicit controls. The norms of rationality, and the control emphasis of the earlier literature, is supplemented in this volume by an emphasis on politics, symbolism, environmental impact, and behavior that is not always "rational" in the narrow sense of the word.

PART I
Characteristics of Educational Organizations

How special are educational organizations? For several years, scholars of organizations have noted the differences between schools, colleges, or universities and business organizations, factories, or even hospitals. The unique function of educational organizations and their relation to changing political winds seem to encourage the development of roles and relationships that deviate from the classic textbook image. But are these quirks a source of strength and stability or does this dominant pattern reduce the ability of educational organizations to perform at satisfactory levels?

It is fashionable to assume that educational organizations are poorly organized, and efforts abound to put schools and universities on more of a "business footing." But the actual impact of these proposed reforms—as we discuss in detail in the next part—raises deeper questions about the formal structure of schools and universities. What purposes may be served by departing from conventional patterns of coordination and control? Are schools and institutions of higher education really that much different from private corporations?

These questions are more than just academic. No administrator can change or manage an organization without knowing its unique characteristics and natural rhythm. To impose a new vision without an accurate image of the existing order and underlying logic is to create chaos and cause an unnecessary waste of human energy.

In this part, three articles provide a comprehensive introduction to and a general profile of educational organizations.

Chapter 2, Karl Weick's classic article, provides one of the first official recognitions of the unusual structure of educational organizations. Rather than being tightly controlled by rule and command, these organizations are "loosely coupled," and Weick notes the variety of manifestations of loose

13

coupling. But looseness is not necessarily a sin to be redeemed—Weick acknowledges the drawbacks and virtues of looseness in educational organizations. Structural looseness provides a number of internal blessings. In tightening the structure of a school or university, administrators often quickly see that the existing patterns have hidden benefits as well as obvious drawbacks.

In Chapter 3 Baldridge focuses on the organizational characteristics of colleges and universities. Like elementary and secondary schools, institutions of higher education are politically vulnerable and organizationally loose, but colleges and universities have other characteristics that make them slightly different from elementary or secondary schools. Baldridge addresses these differences in considerable detail.

Meyer and Rowan take a different slant in Chapter 4 on the loose coupling ideas; they argue that schools are controlled by society's myths, not by formal structure. A school or university must meet several visible requirements to be viewed as legitimate. It must provide: (1) a place recognizable as an educational institution, which conforms to expectations and contains classrooms, libraries, and administrative offices; (2) roles that are certified by degrees, licensing procedures, or appropriate titles, and teachers, professors, administrators, and students who are classified by appropriate labels; and (3) topics that are sanctified by a curriculum, formally adopted and accredited. These categories are used to determine the integrity and effectiveness of an educational organization. Inside these boundaries, participants go about their business without formal control or inspection. Educational organizations operate with a logic of confidence that assumes everything is working as it should, and their structure reflects society's beliefs of what a school should be. Day-to-day activities are loosely linked so that everyone's expectations can be met without conflict or formal coordination.

These three readings document characteristics of schools that depart significantly from the rational norms prominent in conventional organizational theory. Whether these characteristics distinguish schools and universities from other organizations is open to question. It seems clear that schools and universities are a unique organizational species if viewed along traditional lines, but it is less clear that the unusual characteristics of schools are not shared by many businesses or factories. Nonetheless, educational administrators need to understand the nature of the organizations they are supposed to manage. Without such intimate knowledge—unencumbered by normative theories that advocate what organizations should be like—administrators will make mistakes in trying to make things different. The case studies in Part II will highlight some of the more common errors.

2

Educational Organizations as Loosely Coupled Systems

Karl Weick

Imagine that you're either the referee, coach, player, or spectator at an unconventional soccer match: the field for the game is round; there are several goals scattered haphazardly around the circular field; people can enter and leave the game whenever they want to; they can throw balls in whenever they want to; they can say "that's my goal" whenever they want to, as many times as they want to, and for as many goals as they want to; the

This paper is the result of a conference held at La Jolla, California, February 2–4, 1975 with support from the National Institute of Education (NIE). Participants in the conference were, in addition to the author, W.W. Charters, Center for Educational Policy and Management, University of Oregon; Craig Lundberg, School of Business, Oregon State University; John Meyer, Dept. of Sociology, Stanford University; Miles Meyers, Dept. of English, Oakland (Calif.) High School; Karlene Roberts, School of Business, University of California, Berkeley; Gerald Salancik, Dept. of Business Administration, University of Illinois; and Robert Wentz, Superintendent of Schools, Pomona (Calif.) Unified School District. James G. March, School of Education, Stanford University, a member of the National Council on Educational Research, and members of the NIE staff were present as observers. This conference was one of several on organizational processes in education which will lead to a report that will be available from the National Institute of Education, Washington, D.C. 20208. The opinions expressed in this paper do not necessarily reflect the position or policy of the National Institute of Education or the Department of Health, Education, and Welfare.

Reprinted, by permission, from *Administrative Science Quarterly* 23 (December 1978): 541–52.

entire game takes place on a sloped field; and the game is played as if it makes sense (March, personal communication).

If you now substitute in that example principals for referees, teachers for coaches, students for players, parents for spectators, and schooling for soccer, you have an equally unconventional depiction of school organizations. The beauty of this depiction is that it captures a different set of realities within educational organizations than are caught when these same organizations are viewed through the tenets of bureaucratic theory.

Consider the contrast in images. For some time people who manage organizations and people who study this managing have asked, "How does an organization go about doing what it does and with what consequences for its people, processes, products, and persistence?" And for some time they've heard the same answers. In paraphrase, the answers say essentially that an organization does what it does because of plans, intentional selection of means that get the organization to agree upon goals, and all of this is accomplished by such rationalized procedures as cost-benefit analyses, division of labor, specified areas of discretion, authority invested in the office, job descriptions, and a consistent evaluation and reward system. The only problem with that portrait is that it is rare in nature. People in organizations, including educational organizations, find themselves hard pressed either to find actual instances of those rational practices, or to find rationalized practices whose outcomes have been as beneficent as predicted, or to feel that those rational occasions explain much of what goes on within the organization. Parts of some organizations are heavily rationalized but many parts also prove intractable to analysis through rational assumptions.

It is this substantial unexplained remainder that is the focus of this paper. Several people in education have expressed dissatisfaction with the prevailing ideas about organizations supplied by organizational theorists. Fortunately they have also made some provocative suggestions about newer, more unconventional ideas about organizations that should be given serious thought. A good example of this is the following observation by John M. Stephens:

[There is a] remarkable constancy of educational results in the face of widely differing deliberate approaches. Every so often we adopt new approaches or new methodologies and place our reliance on new panaceas. At the very least we seem to chorus new slogans. Yet the academic growth within the classroom continues at about the same rate, stubbornly refusing to cooperate with the bright new dicta emanating from the conference room...[These observations suggest that] we would be making a great mistake in regarding the management of schools as similar to the process of constructing a building or operating a factory. In these latter processes deliberate decisions play a crucial part, and the enterprise advances or stands still in proportion to the amount of deliberate effort exerted. If we must use a metaphor or model in seeking to understand the process of schooling, we should look to agriculture rather than to the factory. In agriculture we do not start from scratch, and we do not direct our efforts to inert and passive materials. We start, on the contrary, with a complex and ancient process, and we organize our efforts around what seeds, plants, and insects are likely to do anyway. . . . The crop, once planted, may undergo some development even while the farmer sleeps or loafs. No matter what he does, some aspects of the outcome will remain constant. When teachers and pupils foregather, some education may proceed even while the Superintendent disports himself in Atlantic City [1967, pp. 9-11].

It is crucial to highlight what is important in the examples of soccer and schooling viewed as agriculture. To view these examples negatively and dismiss them by observing that "the referee should tighten up those rules," "superintendents don't do that," "schools are more sensible than that," or "these are terribly sloppy organizations" is to miss the point. The point is researchers don't know what these kinds of structures are like but [they] do know [these structures] exist and that each of the negative judgments expressed above makes sense only if the observer assumes that organizations are constructed and managed according to rational assumptions and therefore are scrutable only when rational analyses are applied to them. This paper attempts to expand and enrich the set of ideas available to people when they try to make sense out of their organizational life. From this standpoint, it is unproductive to observe that fluid participation in schools and soccer is absurd. But it can be more interesting and productive to ask, How can it be that even though the activities in both situations are only modestly connected, the situations are still recognizable and nameable? The goals, player movements, and trajectory of the ball are still recognizable and can be labeled "soccer." And despite variations in class size, format, locations, and architecture, the results are still recognized and can be labeled "schools." How can such loose assemblages retain sufficient similarity and permanence across time that they can be recognized, labeled, and dealt with? The prevailing ideas in organization theory do not shed much light on how such "soft" structures develop, persist, and impose crude orderliness among their elements.

The basic premise here is that concepts such as loose coupling serve as sensitizing devices. They sensitize the observer to notice and question things that had previously been taken for granted. It is the intent of the program described here to develop a language that may highlight features that have previously gone unnoticed. The guiding principle is a reversal of the common assertion, "I'll believe it when I see it" and presumes an epistemology that asserts, "I'll see it when I believe it." Organizations as loosely coupled systems may not have been seen before because nobody believed in them or could afford to believe in them. It is conceivable that preoccupation with rationalized, tidy, efficient, coordinated structures has blinded many practitioners as well as researchers to some of the attractive and unexpected properties of less rationalized and less tightly related clusters of events. This paper intends to eliminate such blindspots.

The Concept of Coupling

The phrase "loose coupling" has appeared in the literature (Glassman 1973; March and Olsen 1975), and it is important to highlight the connotation that is captured by this phrase and by no other. It might seem that the word "coupling" is synonymous with words like connection, link, or interdependence, yet each of these latter terms misses a crucial nuance.

By loose coupling, the author intends to convey the image that coupled events are responsive, but that each event also preserves its own identity and some evidence of its physical or logical separateness. Thus, in the case of an educational organization, it may be the case that the counselor's office is loosely coupled to the principal's office. The image is that the principal and the counselor are somehow attached, but that each retains some identity and separateness and that their attachment may be circumscribed, infrequent, weak in its mutual affects, unimportant, and/or slow to respond. Each of those connotations would be conveyed if the qualifier "loosely" were attached to the word coupled. Loose coupling also carries connotations of impermanence, dissolvability, and tacitness, all of which are potentially crucial properties of the "glue" that holds organizations together.

Glassman (1973) categorizes the degree of coupling between two systems on the basis of the activity of the variables which the two systems share. To the extent that two systems either have few variables in common or share weak variables, they are independent of each other. Applied to the educational situation, if the principal-vice-principal-superintendent is regarded as one system and the teacher-classroom-pupil-parent-curriculum as another system, then, by Glassman's argument, if we did not find many variables in the teacher's world to be shared in the world of a principal and/or if the variables held in common were unimportant relative to the other variables, then the principal can be regarded as being loosely coupled with the teacher.

A final advantage of coupling imagery is that it suggests the idea of building blocks that can be grafted onto an organization or severed with relatively little disturbance to either the blocks or the organization. Simon (1969) has argued for the attractiveness of this feature in that most complex systems can be decomposed into stable subassemblies and that these are the crucial elements in any organization or system. Thus, the coupling imagery gives researchers access to one of the more powerful ways of talking about complexity now available.

But if the concept of loose coupling highlights novel images heretofore unseen in organizational theory, what is it about these images that is worth seeing?

Coupled Elements

There is no shortage of potential coupling elements, but neither is the population infinite.

At the outset the two most commonly discussed coupling mechanisms are the technical core of the organization and the authority of office. The relevance of those two mechanisms for the issue of identifying elements is that in the case of technical couplings, each element is some kind of technology, task, subtask, role, territory and person, and the couplings are task-induced. In the case of authority as the coupling mechanism, the elements include positions, offices, responsibilities, opportunities, rewards, and sanctions, and it is the couplings among these elements that presumably hold the organization together. A compelling argument can be made that neither of these coupling mechanisms is prominent in educational organizations found in the United States. This leaves one with the question: What does hold an educational organization together?

A short list of potential elements in educational organizations will provide background for subsequent propositions. March and Olsen (1975) utilize the elements of intention and action. There is a developing position in psychology which argues that intentions are a poor guide for action, intentions often follow rather than precede action, and that intentions and action are loosely coupled. Unfortunately, organizations continue to think that planning is a good thing, they spend much time on planning, and actions are assessed in terms of their fit with plans. Given a potential loose coupling between the intentions and actions of organizational members, it should come as no surprise that administrators are baffled and angered when things never happen the way they were supposed to.

Additional elements may consist of events like yesterday and tomorrow (what happened yesterday may be tightly or loosely coupled with what happens tomorrow) or hierarchical positions, like top and bottom, line and staff, or administrators and teachers. An interesting set of elements that lends itself to the loose coupling imagery is means and ends. Frequently, several different means lead to the same outcome. When this happens, it can be argued that any one means is loosely coupled to the end in the sense that there are alternative pathways to achieve that same end. Other elements that might be found in loosely coupled educational systems are teachers-materials, voters-school board, administrators-classroom, process-outcome, teacher-teacher, parent-teacher, and teacher-pupil.

While all of these elements are obvious, it is not a trivial matter to specify which elements are coupled. As the concept of coupling is crucial because of its ability to highlight the identity and separateness of elements that are momentarily attached, that conceptual asset puts pressure on the investigator to specify clearly the identity, separateness, and boundaries of the elements coupled. While there is some danger of reification when that kind of pressure is exerted, there is the even greater danger of portraying organizations in inappropriate terms which suggest an excess of unity, integration, coordination, and consensus. If one is nonspecific about boundaries in defining elements then it is easy—and careless—to assemble these ill-defined elements and talk about integrated organizations. It is not a trivial issue [to] explain how elements persevere over time. Weick (1974, pp. 363–64), for example, has argued that elements may appear or disappear and may merge or become separated in response to need-deprivations within the individual, group, and/or organization. This means that specification of elements is not a one-shot activity. Given the context of most organizations, elements both appear and disappear over time. For this reason a theory of how elements become loosely or tightly coupled may also have to take account of the fact that the nature and intensity of the coupling may itself serve to create or dissolve elements.

The question of what is available for coupling and decoupling within an organization is an eminently practical question for anyone wishing to have some leverage on a system.

Strength of Coupling

Obviously there is no shortage of meanings for the phrase loose coupling. Researchers need to be clear in their own thinking about whether the phenomenon they are studying is described by two words or three. A researcher can study "loose coupling" in educational organizations or "loosely coupled systems." The shorter phrase, "loose coupling," simply connotes things, "anythings," that may be tied together either weakly or infrequently or slowly or with minimal interdependence. Whether those things that are loosely coupled exist in a system is of minor importance. Most discussions in this paper concern loosely coupled systems rather than loose coupling since it wishes to clarify the concepts involved in the perseverance of sets of elements across time.

The idea of loose coupling is evoked when people have a variety of situations in mind. For example, when people describe loosely coupled systems they are often referring to (1) slack times—times when there is an excessive amount of resources relative to demands; (2) occasions when any one of several means will produce the same end; (3) richly connected networks in which influence is slow to spread and/or is weak while spreading; (4) a relative lack of coordination, slow coordination, or coordination that is dampened as it moves through a system; (5) a relative absence of regulations; (6) planned unresponsiveness; (7) actual causal independence; (8) poor observational capabilities on the part of a viewer; (9) infrequent inspection of activities within the system; (10) decentralization; (11) delegation of discretion; (12) the absence of linkages that should be present based on some theory—for example, in educational organizations the expected feedback linkage from outcome back to inputs is often nonexistent; (13) the observation that an organization's structure is not coterminous with its activity; (14) those occasions when no matter what you do things always come out the same—for instance, despite all kinds of changes in curriculum, materials, groupings, and so forth the outcomes in an educational situation remain the same; and (15) curricula or courses in educational organizations for which there are few prerequisites—the longer the string of prerequisites, the tighter the coupling.

Potential Functions and Dysfunctions of Loose Coupling

It is important to note that the concept of loose coupling need not be used normatively. People who are steeped in the conventional literature of organizations may regard loose coupling as a sin or something to be apologized for. This paper takes a neutral, if not mildly affectionate, stance toward the concept. Apart from whatever effect one might feel toward the idea of loose coupling, it does appear a priori that certain functions can be served by having a system in which the elements are loosely coupled. Below are listed seven potential functions that could be associated with loose coupling plus additional reasons why each advantage might also be a liability. The dialectic generated by each of these oppositions begins to suggest dependent variables that should be sensitive to variations in the tightness of coupling.

The basic argument of Glassman (1973) is that loose coupling allows some portions of an organization to persist. Loose coupling lowers the probability that the organization will have to—or be able to—respond to each little change in the environment that occurs. The mechanism of voting, for example, allows elected officials to remain in office for a full term even though their constituency at any moment may disapprove of particular actions. Some identity and separateness of the element "elected official" is preserved relative to a second element, "constituency," by the fact of loosely coupled accountability which is measured in two-, four-, or six-year terms. While loose coupling may foster perseverance, it is not selective in what is perpetuated. Thus archaic traditions as well as innovative improvisations may be perpetuated.

A second advantage of loose coupling is that it may provide a sensitive sensing mechanism. This possibility is suggested by Fritz Heider's perceptual theory of things and medium. Heider (1959) argues that perception is most accurate when a medium senses a thing and the medium contains many independent elements that can be externally constrained. When elements in a medium become either fewer in number and/or more internally contained and/or more interdependent, their ability to represent some remote thing is decreased. Thus sand is a better medium to display wind currents than are rocks, the reason being that sand has more elements, more independence among the elements, and the elements are subject to a greater amount of external constraint than is the case for rocks. Using Heider's formulation metaphorically, it could be argued that loosely coupled systems preserve many independent sensing elements and therefore "know" their environments better than is true for more tightly coupled systems which have fewer externally constrained, independent elements. Balanced against this improvement in sensing is the possibility that the system would become increasingly vulnerable to producing faddish responses and interpretations. If the environment is known better, then this could induce more frequent changes in activities done in response to this "superior intelligence."

A third function is that a loosely coupled system may be a good system for localized adaptation. If all of the elements in a large system are loosely coupled to one another, then any one element can adjust to and modify a local unique contingency without affecting the whole system. These local adaptations can be swift, relatively economical, and substantial. By definition, the antithesis of localized adaptation is standardization, and to the extent that standardization can be shown to be desirable, a loosely coupled system might exhibit fewer of these presumed benefits. For example, the localized adaptation characteristic of loosely coupled systems may result in a lessening of educational democracy.

Fourth, in loosely coupled systems where the identity, uniqueness, and separateness of elements is preserved, the system potentially can retain a greater number of mutations and novel solutions than would be the case with a tightly coupled system. A loosely coupled system could preserve more "cultural insurance" to be drawn upon in times of radical change than in the case for more tightly coupled systems. Loosely coupled systems may be elegant solutions to the problem that adaptation can preclude adaptability. When a specific system fits into an ecological niche and does so with great success, this adaptation can be costly. It can be costly because resources which are useless in a current environment might deteriorate or disappear even though they could be crucial in a modified environment. It is conceivable that loosely coupled systems preserve more diversity in responding than do tightly coupled systems, and therefore can adapt to a considerably wider range of changes in the environment than would be true for tightly coupled systems. To appreciate the possible problems associated with this abundance of mutations, reconsider the dynamic outlined in the preceding discussion of localized adaptation. If a local set of elements can adapt to local idiosyncrasies without involving the whole system, then this same loose coupling could also forestall the spread of advantageous mutations that exist somewhere in the system. While the system may contain novel solutions for new problems of adaptation, the very structure that allows these mutations to flourish may prevent their diffusion.

Fifth, if there is a breakdown in one portion of a loosely coupled system then this breakdown is sealed off and does not affect other portions of the organization. Previously we had noted that loosely coupled systems are an exquisite mechanism to adapt swiftly to local novelties and unique problems. Now we are carrying the analysis one step further, and arguing that when any element misfires or decays or deteriorates, the spread of this deterioration is checked in a loosely coupled system. While this point is reminiscent of earlier functions, the emphasis here is on the localization of trouble rather than the localization of adaptation. But even this potential benefit may be problematic. A loosely coupled system can isolate its trouble spots and prevent the trouble from spreading, but it should be difficult for the loosely coupled system to repair the defective element. If weak influences pass from the defective portions of the functioning portions, then the influence back from these functioning portions will also be weak and probably too little, too late.

Sixth, since some of the most important elements in educational organizations are teachers, classrooms, principals, and so forth, it may be consequential that in a loosely coupled system there is more room available for self-determination by the actors. If it is argued that a sense of efficacy is crucial for human beings, then a sense of efficacy might be greater in a loosely coupled system with autonomous units than it would be in a tightly coupled system where discretion is limited. A further comment can be made about self-determination to provide an example of the kind of imagery that is invoked by the concept of loose coupling.

It is possible that much of the teacher's sense of—and actual—control comes from the fact that diverse interested parties expect the teacher to link their intentions with teaching actions. Such linking of diverse intentions with actual work probably involves considerable negotiation. A parent complains about a teacher's action and the teacher merely points out to the parent how the actions are really correspondent with the parent's desires for the education of his or her children. Since most actions have ambiguous consequences, it should always be possible to justify the action as fitting the intentions of those who complain. Salancik (1975) goes even farther and suggests the intriguing possibility that when the consequences of an action are ambiguous, the stated intentions of the action serve as surrogates for the consequences. Since it is not known whether reading a certain book is good or bad for a child, the fact that it is intended to be good for the child itself becomes justification for having the child read it. The potential trade-off implicit in this function of loose coupling is fascinating. There is an increase in autonomy in the sense that resistance is heightened, but this heightened resistance occurs at the price of shortening the chain of consequences that will flow from each autonomous actor's efforts. Each teacher will have to negotiate separately with the same complaining parent.

Seventh, a loosely coupled system should be relatively inexpensive to run because it takes time and money to coordinate people. As much of what happens and should happen inside educational organizations seems to be defined and validated outside the organization, schools are in the business of building and maintaining categories, a business that requires coordination only on a few specific issues—for instance, assignment of teachers. This reduction in the necessity for coordination results in fewer conflicts, fewer inconsistencies among activities, fewer discrepancies between categories and activity. Thus, loosely coupled systems seem to hold the costs of coordination to a minimum. Despite this being an inexpensive system, loose coupling is also a nonrational system of fund allocation and, therefore, unspecifiable, unmodifiable, and incapable of being used as means of change.

When these several sets of functions and dysfunctions are examined, they begin to throw several research issues into relief. For example, oppositions proposed in each of the preceding seven points suggest the importance of contextual theories. A predicted outcome or its opposite should emerge depending on how and in what the loosely coupled system is embedded. The preceding oppositions also suggest a fairly self-contained research program. Suppose a researcher starts with the first point made, as loose coupling increases the system should contain a greater number of anachronistic practices. Loosely coupled systems should be conspicuous for their cultural lags. Initially, one would like to know whether that is plausible or not. But then one would want to examine in more fine-grained detail whether those anachronistic practices that are retained hinder the system or impose structure and absorb uncertainty, thereby producing certain economies in responding. Similar embellishment and elaboration is possible for each function with the result that rich networks of propositions become visible. What is especially attractive about these networks is that there is little precedent for them in the organizational literature. Despite this, these propositions contain a great deal of face validity when they are used as filters to look at educational organizations. When compared, for example, with the bureaucratic template mentioned in the introduction, the template associated with loosely coupled systems seems to take the observer into more interesting territory and prods him or her to ask more interesting questions.

Methodology and Loose Coupling

An initial warning to researchers: the empirical observation of unpredictability is insufficient evidence for concluding that the elements in a system are loosely coupled. Buried in that caveat are a host of methodological intricacies. While there is ample reason to believe that loosely coupled systems can be seen and examined, it is also possible that the appearance of loose coupling will be nothing more than a testimonial to bad methodology. In psychology, for example, it has been argued that the chronic failure to predict behavior from attitudes is due to measurement error and not to the unrelatedness of these two events. Attitudes are said to be loosely coupled with behavior but it may be that this conclusion is an artifact produced because attitudes assessed by time-independent and context-independent measures are being used to predict behaviors that are time and context dependent. If both attitudes and behaviors were assessed with equivalent measures, then tight coupling might be the rule.

Any research agenda must be concerned with fleshing out the imagery of loose coupling—a task requiring a considerable amount of conceptual work to solve a few specific and rather tricky methodological problems before one can investigate loose coupling.

By definition, if one goes into an organization and watches which parts affect which other parts, he or she will see the tightly coupled parts and the parts that vary the most. Those parts which vary slightly, infrequently, and aperiodically will be less visible. Notice, for example, that interaction data—who speaks to whom about what—are unlikely to reveal loose couplings. These are the most visible and obvious couplings and by the arguments developed in this paper perhaps some of the least crucial to understand what is going on in the organization.

An implied theme in this paper is that people tend to overrationalize their activities and to attribute greater meaning, predictability, and coupling among them than in fact they have. If members tend to overrationalize their activity then their descriptions will not suggest which portions of that activity are loosely and tightly coupled. One might, in fact, even use the presence of apparent overrationalization as a potential clue that myth making, uncertainty, and loose coupling have been spotted.

J.G. March has argued that loose coupling can be spotted and examined only if one uses methodology that highlights and preserves rich detail about context. The necessity for a contextual methodology seems to arise, interestingly enough, from inside organization theory. The implied model involves cognitive limits on rationality and man as a single channel information processor. The basic methodological point is that if one wishes to observe loose coupling, then he has to see both what is and is not being done. The general idea is that time spent on one activity is time spent away from a second activity. A contextually sensitive methodology would record both the fact that some people are in one place generating events and the fact that these same people are thereby absent from some other place. The rule of thumb would be that a tight coupling in one part of the system can occur only if there is loose coupling in another part of the system. The problem that finite attention creates for a researcher is that if some outcome is observed for the organization, then it will not be obvious whether the outcome is due to activity in the tightly coupled sector or to inactivity in the loosely coupled sector. That is a provocative problem of interpretation. But the researcher should be forewarned that there are probably a finite number of tight couplings that can occur at any moment, that tight couplings in one place imply loose couplings elsewhere, and that it may be the pattern of couplings that produces the observed outcomes. Untangling such intricate issues may well require that new tools be developed for contextual understanding and that investigators be willing to substitute nonteleological thinking for teleological thinking (Steinbeck 1941, chapt. 14).

Another contextually sensitive method is the use of comparative studies. It is the presumption of this methodology that taken-for-granted understandings—one possible "invisible" source of coupling in an otherwise loosely coupled system—are embedded in and contribute to a context. Thus, to see the effects of variations in these understandings one compares contexts that differ in conspicuous and meaningful ways.

Another methodological trap may await the person who tries to study loose coupling. Suppose one provides evidence that a particular goal is loosely coupled to a particular action. He or she says, in effect, the person wanted to do this but in fact actually did that, thus, the action and the intention are loosely coupled. Now the problem for the researcher is that he or she may simply have focused on the wrong goal. There may be other goals which fit that particular action better. Perhaps if the researcher were aware of them, then the action and intention would appear to be tightly coupled. Any kind of intention-action, plan-behavior, or means-end depiction of loose coupling may be vulnerable to this sort of problem and an exhaustive listing of goals rather than parsimony should be the rule.

Two other methodological points should be noted. First, there are no good descriptions of the kinds of couplings that can occur among the several elements in educational organizations. Thus, a major initial research question is simply, What does a map of the couplings and elements within an educational organization look like? Second, there appear to be some fairly rich probes that might be used to uncover the nature of coupling within educational organizations. Conceivably, crucial couplings within schools involve the handling of disciplinary issues and social control, the question of how a teacher gets a book for the classroom, and the question of what kinds of innovations need to get clearance by whom. These relatively innocuous questions may be powerful means to learn which portions of a system are tightly and loosely coupled. Obviously these probes would be sampled if there was a full description of possible elements that can be coupled and possible kinds and strengths of couplings. These specific probes suggest in addition, however, that what holds an educational organization together may be a small number of tight couplings in out-of-the-way places.

Illustrative Questions for a Research Agenda

Patterns of Loose and Tight Coupling: Certification versus Inspection

Suppose one assumes that education is an intrinsically uninspected and unevaluated activity. If education is intrinsically uninspected and unevaluated then how can one establish that it is occurring? One answer is to define clearly who can and who cannot do it and to whom. In an educational organization this is the activity of certification. It is around the issues of certification and of specifying who the pupils are that tight coupling would be predicted to occur when technology and outcome are unclear.

If one argues that certification is the question "Who does the work?" and inspection is the question "How well is the work done?," then there can be either loose or tight control over either certification or inspection. Notice that setting the problem up this way suggests the importance of discovering the distribution of tight and loosely coupled systems within any organization. Up to now the phrase loosely coupled systems has been used to capture the fact that events in an organization seem to be temporally related rather than logically related (Cohen and March 1974). Now that view is being enriched by arguing that any organization must deal with issues of certification (who does the work) and inspection (how well is the work done). It is further being suggested that in the case of educational organizations there is loose control on the work—the work is intrinsically uninspected and unevaluated or if it is evaluated it is done so infrequently and in a perfunctory manner—but that under these conditions it becomes crucial for the organization to have tight control over who does the work and on whom. This immediately suggests the importance of comparative research in which the other three combinations are examined, the question being, How do these alternative forms grow, adapt, manage their rhetoric, and handle their clientele? Thus it would be important to find organizations in which the controls over certification and inspection are both loose, organizations where there is loose control over certification but tight control over inspection, and organizations in which there is tight control both over inspection and over certification. Such comparative research might be conducted among different kinds of educational organizations within a single country (military, private, religious schooling in the United States), between educational and noneducational organizations within the same country (for example, schools versus hospitals versus military versus business organizations), or between countries looking at solutions to the problem of education given different degrees of centralization. As suggested earlier, it may not be the existence or nonexistence of loose coupling that is a crucial determinant of organizational functioning over time but rather the patterning of loose and tight couplings. Comparative studies should answer the question of distribution.

If, as noted earlier, members within an organization (and researchers) will see and talk clearly about only those regions that are tightly coupled, then this suggests that members of educational organizations should be most explicit and certain when they are discussing issues related to certification for definition and regulation of teachers, pupils, topics, space, and resources. These are presumed to be the crucial issues that are tightly controlled. Increasing vagueness of description should occur when issues of substantive instruction—inspection—are discussed. Thus, those people who primarily manage the instructional business will be most vague in describing what they do, those people who primarily manage the certification rituals will be most explicit. This pattern is predicted not on the basis of the activities themselves—certification is easier to describe than inspection—but rather on the basis of the expectation that tightly coupled subsystems are more crucial to the survival of the system and therefore have received more linguistic work in the past and more agreement than is true for loosely coupled elements.

Core Technology and Organizational Form

A common tactic to understand complex organizations is to explore the possibility that the nature of the task being performed determines the shapes of the organizational structure. This straightforward tactic raises some interesting puzzles about educational organizations. There are suggestions in the literature that education is a diffuse task, the technology is uncertain.

This first question suggests two alternatives: If the task is diffuse then would not any organizational form whatsoever be equally appropriate or should this directly compel a diffuse form of organizational structure? These two alternatives are not identical. The first suggests that if the task is diffuse then any one of a variety of quite specific organizational forms could be imposed on the organization and no differences would be observed. The thrust of the second argument is that there is one and only one organizational form that would fit well when there is a diffuse task, namely, a diffuse organizational form (for instance, an organized anarchy).

The second question asks if the task in an educational organization is diffuse then why do all educational organizations look the way they do, and why do they all look the same? If there is no clear task around which the shape of the organization can be formed then why is it that most educational organizations do have a form and why is it that most of these forms look identical? One possible answer is that the tasks of educational organizations do not constrain the form of the organization but rather this constraint is imposed by the ritual of certification and/or the agreements that are made in and by the environment. If any of these nontask possibilities are genuine alternative explanations, then the general literature on organizations has been insensitive to them.

One is therefore forced to ask the question, Is it the case within educational organizations that the technology is unclear? So far it has been argued that loose coupling in educational organizations is partly the result of uncertain technology. If uncertain technology does not generate loose coupling then researchers must look elsewhere for the origin of these bonds.

Making Sense in and of Loosely Coupled Worlds

What kinds of information do loosely coupled systems provide members, around which they can organize meanings; that is, what can one use in order to make sense of such fleeting structures? (By definition loosely coupled events are modestly predictable at best.) There is a rather barren structure that can be observed, reported on, and retrospected in order to make any sense. Given the ambiguity of loosely coupled structures, this suggests that there may be increased pressure on members to construct or negotiate some kind of social reality they can live with. Therefore, under conditions of loose coupling one should see considerable effort devoted to constructing social reality, a great amount of face work and linguistic work, numerous myths (Mitroff and Kilmann 1975), and in general one should find a considerable amount of effort being devoted to punctuating this loosely coupled world and connecting it in some way in which it can be made sensible. Loosely coupled worlds do not look as if they would provide an individual many resources for sense making—with such little assistance in this task, a predominant activity should involve constructing social realities. Tightly coupled portions of a system should not exhibit nearly this preoccupation with linguistic work and the social construction of reality.

Coupling as a Dependent Variable

As a general rule, any research agenda on loose coupling should devote equal attention to loose coupling as a dependent and independent variable. Most suggestions have treated loose coupling as an independent variable. Less attention has been directed toward loose coupling as a dependent variable with the one exception of the earlier argument that one can afford loose coupling in either certification or inspection but not in both and, therefore, if one can locate a tight coupling for one of these two activities then he can predict as a dependent variable loose coupling for the other one.

Some investigators, however, should view loose coupling consistently as a dependent variable. The prototypic question would be, given prior conditions such as competition for scarce resources, logic built into a task, team teaching, conflict, striving for professionalism, presence of a central ministry of education, tenure, and so forth, what kind of coupling (loose or tight) among what kinds of elements occurs? If an organization faces a scarcity of resources, its pattern of couplings should differ from when it faces an expansion of resources (for instance, scarcity leads to stockpiling [which] leads to decoupling). Part of the question here is, What kinds of changes in the environment are the variables of tight and loose coupling sensitive to? In response to what kinds of activities or what kinds of contexts is coupling seen to change, and what kinds of environments or situations, when they change, seem to have no effect whatsoever on couplings within an organization? Answers to these questions, which are of vital importance in predicting the outcomes of any intervention, are most likely to occur if coupling is treated as a dependent variable and the question is, Under what conditions will the couplings that emerge be tight or loose?

Assembling Loosely Connected Events

Suppose one assumes that there is nothing in the world except loosely coupled events. This assumption is close to Simon's stable subassemblies and empty world hypothesis and to the idea of cognitive limits on rationality. The imagery is that of numerous clusters of events that are tightly coupled within and loosely coupled between. These larger loosely coupled units would be what researchers usually call organizations. Notice that organizations formed this way are rather unusual kinds of organizations because they are neither tightly connected, nor explicitly bounded, but they are stable. The research question then becomes, How does it happen that loosely coupled events which remain loosely coupled are institutionally held together in one organization which retains a few controls over central activities? Stated differently, how does it happen that someone can take a series of loosely coupled events, assemble them into an organization of loosely coupled systems, and the events remain both loosely coupled but the organization itself survives? It is common to observe that large organizations have loosely connected sectors. The questions are, What makes this possible? How does it happen? What the structure in school systems seems to consist of is categories (for example, teacher, pupil, reading) which are linked by understanding and legitimated exogenously (that is, by the world outside the organization). As John Meyer (1975) puts it, "the system works because everyone knows everyone else knows roughly what is to go on.... Educational organizations are holding companies containing shares of stock in uninspected activities and subunits which are largely given their meaning, reality, and value in the wider social market." Note the potential fragility of this fabric of legitimacy.

It remains to be seen under what conditions loosely coupled systems are fragile structures because they are shored up by consensual anticipations, retrospections, and understanding that can dissolve and under what conditions they are resilient structures because they contain mutations, localized adaptation, and fewer costs of coordination.

Separate Intending and Acting Components

Intention and action are often loosely coupled within a single individual. Salancik (1975) has suggested some conditions under which dispositions within a single individual may be loosely coupled. These include such suggestions as follows: (1) If intentions are not clear and unambiguous, then the use of them to select actions which will fulfill the intentions will be imperfect. (2) If the consequences of action are not known, then the use of intention to select action will be imperfect. (3) If the means by which an intention is transformed into an action are not known or in conflict, then the coupling of action to intention will be imperfect. (4) If intentions are not known to a person at the time of selecting an action, then the relationships between action and intention will be imperfect. This may be more common than expected because this possibility is not allowed by so-called rational models of man. People often have to recall their intentions after they act or reconstruct these intentions, or invent them. (5) If there exists a set of multiple intentions which can determine a set of similar multiple actions, then the ability to detect a relationship between any one intention and any one action is likely to be imperfect. To illustrate, if there is an intention A which implies selecting action X and Y, and there is also an intention B which implies selecting actions X and Y, then it is possible that under both presence and absence of intention A, action X will be selected. Given these circumstances, an observer will falsely conclude that this relationship is indeterminant.

The preceding list has the potential limitation for organizational inquiry in that it consists of events within a single person. This limitation is not serious if the ideas are used as metaphors or if each event is lodged in a different person. For example, one could lodge intention with one person and action with some other person. With this separation, then all of the above conditions may produce loose coupling between these actors but additional conditions also come into play given this geographical separation of intention from action. For example, the simple additional requirement that the intentions must be communicated to the second actor and in such a way that they control his actions will increase the potential for error and loose coupling. Thus any discussion of separate locations for intention and action within an organization virtually requires that the investigator specify the additional conditions under which the intending component can control the acting component. Aside from the problems of communication and control when intention and action are separated, there are at least two additional conditions that could produce loose coupling.

1. If there are several diverse intending components all of whom are dependent on the same actor for implementing action, then the relationship between any one intention and any one action will be imperfect. The teacher in the classroom may well be the prototype of this condition.

2. The process outlined in the preceding item can become even more complicated, and the linkages between intention and action even looser, if the single acting component has intentions of its own.

Intention and action are often split within organizations. This paper suggests that if one were to map the pattern of intention and action components within the organization these would coincide with loosely coupled systems identified by other means. Furthermore, the preceding propositions begin to suggest conditions under which the same components might be at one moment tightly coupled and at the next moment loosely coupled.

Conclusion: A Statement of Priorities

More time should be spent examining the possibility that educational organizations are most usefully viewed as loosely coupled systems. The concept of organization as loosely coupled systems can have a substantial effect on existing perspectives about organizations. To probe further into the plausibility of that assertion, it is suggested that the following research priorities constitute a reasonable approach to the examination of loosely coupled systems.

1. Develop Conceptual Tools Capable of Preserving Loosely Coupled Systems

It is clear that more conceptual work has to be done before other lines of inquiry on this topic are launched. Much of the blandness in organizational theory these days can be traced to investigators applying impoverished images to organizational settings. If researchers immediately start stalking the elusive loosely coupled system with imperfect language and concepts, they will perpetuate the blandness of organizational theory. To see the importance of and necessity for this conceptual activity the reader should reexamine the fifteen different connotations of the phrase "loose coupling" that are uncovered in this paper. They provide fifteen alternative explanations for any researcher who claims that some outcome is due to loose coupling.

2. Explicate What Elements Are Available in Educational Organizations for Coupling

This activity has high priority because it is essential to know the practical domain within which the coupling phenomena occur. Since there is the further complication that elements may appear or disappear as a function of context and time, this type of inventory is essential at an early stage of inquiry. An indirect benefit of making this a high-priority activity is that it will stem the counterproductive suspicion that "the number of elements in educational organizations is infinite." The reasonable reply to that comment is that if one is precise in defining and drawing boundaries around elements, then the number of elements will be less than imagined. Furthermore, the researcher can reduce the number of relevant elements if he has some theoretical ideas in mind. These theoretical ideas should be one of the outcomes of initial activity devoted to language and concept development (Priority 1).

3. Develop Contextual Methodology

Given favorable outcomes from the preceding two steps, researchers should then be eager to look at complex issues such as patterns of tight and loose coupling keeping in mind that loose coupling creates major problems for the researcher because he is trained and equipped to decipher predictable, tightly coupled worlds. To "see" loosely coupled worlds, unconventional methodologies need to be developed and conventional methodologies that are underexploited need to be given more attention. Among the existing tools that should be refined to study loose coupling are comparative studies and longitudinal studies. Among the new tools that should be "invented" because of their potential relevance to loosely coupled systems are nonteleological thinking (Steinbeck 1941), concurrence methodology (Bateson 1972, pp. 180-201), and Hegelian, Kantian, and Singerian inquiring systems (Mitroff 1974). While these latter methodologies are unconventional within social science, so too is it unconventional to urge that we treat unpredictability (loose coupling) as our topic of interest rather than a nuisance.

4. Promote the Collection of Thorough, Concrete Descriptions of the Coupling Patterns in Actual Educational Organizations

No descriptive studies have been available to show what couplings in what patterns and with what strengths existed in current educational organizations. This oversight should be remedied as soon as possible.

Adequate descriptions should be of great interest to the practitioner who wants to know how his influence attempts will spread and with what intensity. Adequate description should also show practitioners how their organizations may be more sensible and adaptive than they suspect. Thorough descriptions of coupling should show checks and balances, localized controls, stabilizing mechanisms, and subtle feedback loops that keep the organization stable and that would promote its decay if they were tampered with.

The benefits for the researcher of full descriptions are that they would suggest which locations and which questions about loose coupling are most likely to explain sizeable portions of the variance in organizational outcomes. For example, on the basis of good descriptive work, it might be found that both tightly and loosely coupled systems "know" their environments with equal accuracy, in which case the earlier line of theorizing about "thing and medium" would be given a lower priority.

5. Specify the Nature of Core Technology in Educational Organizations

A surprisingly large number of the ideas presented in this paper assume that the typical coupling mechanisms of authority of office and logic of the task do not operate in educational organizations. Inquiry into loosely coupled systems was triggered partly by efforts to discover what does accomplish the coupling in school systems. Before the investigation of loose coupling goes too far, it should be established that authority and task are not prominent coupling mechanisms in schools. The assertions that they are not prominent seem to issue from a combination of informal observation, implausibility, wishful thinking, looking at the wrong things, and rather vague definitions of core technology and reward structures within education. If these two coupling mechanisms were defined clearly, studied carefully, and found to be weak and/or nonexistent in schools, then there would be a powerful justification for proceeding vigorously to study loosely coupled systems. Given the absence of work that definitively discounts these coupling mechanisms in education and given the fact that these two mechanisms have accounted for much of the observed couplings in other kinds of organizations, it seems crucial to look for them in educational organizations in the interest of parsimony.

It should be emphasized that if it is found that substantial coupling within educational organizations is due to authority of office and logic of the task, this does not negate the agenda that is sketched out in this paper. Instead, such discoveries would (1) make it even more crucial to look for patterns of coupling to explain outcomes, (2) focus attention on tight and loose couplings within task and authority induced couplings, (3) alert researchers to keep close watch for any coupling mechanisms other than these two, and (4) direct comparative research toward settings in which these two coupling mechanisms vary in strength and form.

6. Probe Empirically the Ratio of Functions to Dysfunctions Associated with Loose Coupling

Although the word "function" has had a checkered history, it is used here without apology—and without the surplus meanings and ideology that have become attached to it. Earlier, several potential benefits of loose coupling were described and these descriptions were balanced by additional suggestions of potential liabilities. If one adopts an evolutionary epistemology, then over time one expects that entities develop a more exquisite fit with their ecological niches. Given that assumption, one then argues that if loosely coupled systems exist and if they have existed for some time, then they bestow some net advantage to their inhabitants and/or their constituencies. It is not obvious, however, what these advantages are. A set of studies showing how schools benefit and suffer given their structure as loosely coupled systems should do much to improve the quality of thinking devoted to organizational analysis.

7. Discover How Inhabitants Make Sense Out of Loosely Coupled Worlds

Scientists are going to have some big problems when their topic of inquiry becomes low probability couplings, but just as scientists have special problems comprehending loosely coupled worlds so too must the inhabitants of these worlds. It would seem that quite early in a research program on loose coupling, examination of this question should be started since it has direct relevance to those practitioners who must thread their way through such "invisible" worlds and must concern their sense making and stories in such a way that they don't bump into each other while doing so.

References

Bateson, M.C. *Our Own Metaphor*. New York: Alfred A. Knopf, 1972.

Cohen, M.D., and J.G. March. *Leadership and Ambiguity: The American College President*. New York: McGraw-Hill, 1974.

Glassman, R.B. "Persistence and Loose Coupling in Living Systems." *Behavioral Science* 18 (1973): 83-98.

Heider, F. "Thing and Medium." *Psychological Issues* 1: 3 (1959): 1-34.

March, J.G., and J.P. Olsen. "Choice Situations in Loosely Coupled Worlds." Unpublished manuscript. Stanford University, 1975.

Meyer, J.W. and B. Rowan. "Notes on the Structure of Educational Organizations." In *Studies on Environment and Organization*, edited by M. Meyer et al. San Francisco: Jossey-Bass, 1978.

Mitroff, I.I. *The Subjective Side of Science*. New York: Elsevier, 1974.

Mitroff, I.I., and R.H. Kilmann. "On Organizational Stories: An Approach to the Design and Analysis of Organizations Through Myths and Stories." Unpublished manuscript. University of Pittsburgh, 1975.

Salancik, G.R. "Notes on Loose Coupling: Linking Intentions to Actions." Unpublished manuscript. University of Illinois, Urbana-Champaign, 1975.

Simon, H.A. "The Architecture of Complexity." *Proceedings of the American Philosophical Society* 106 (1969): 467-82.

Steinbeck, J. *The Log from the Sea of Cortez*. New York: Viking, 1941.
Stephens, J.M. *The Process of Schooling*. New York: Holt, Rinehart & Winston, 1967.
Weick, K. E. "Middle Range Theories of Social Systems." *Behavioral Science* 19 (1974): 357–67.

3

Organizational Characteristics of Colleges and Universities

J. Victor Baldridge

Organizations vary in a number of important ways: they have different kinds of clients; they employ workers with varying skills; they work with various types of technologies; they develop divergent styles of structure, coordination, and governance; and they have differing relationships to their external environments. To be sure, there are some common elements in the ways that colleges and universities, hospitals, prisons, business firms, and government bureaus are operated. No two organizations are really the same, however, and any adequate theory of decision making and governance must take their differences into account.

This chapter deals with the organizational characteristics of colleges and universities and with how these characteristics shape their decision processes. The basic argument can be summed up simply. Colleges and universities are unique kinds of professional organizations, differing in major characteristics from industrial organizations, government bureaus, and business firms. These critical differences force us to develop new images of organizational decision making; a "political" model will be offered to supplement the more common "bureaucratic" and "collegial" models.

Adapted, with permission, from "Organizational Characteristics of Colleges and Universities," in *Policy Making and Effective Leadership*, ed. J. Victor Baldridge et al. (San Francisco: Jossey-Bass, 1980).

Some Basic Characteristics

Colleges and universities are complex organizations. They have goals, hierarchical systems and structures, officials that carry out specified duties, decision-making processes for setting institutional policy, and routine bureaucratic administration for handling day-to-day work. Although colleges and universities share many characteristics with other complex bureaucracies, in this section we will explore some critical differences that make it necessary to construct revised theories of decision making if we are to analyze academic governance.

Goal ambiguity is common in academic organizations. Most organizations know what they are doing. Business firms seek to make a profit, government agencies perform tasks specified by law, hospitals try to cure sick people, and prisons attempt to incarcerate and rehabilitate. Since they know where they are going, they can build decision structures to get them there. By contrast, colleges and universities have vague, ambiguous goals, and they must build decision structures that grapple with uncertainty and conflict over those goals.

What are the goals of a university? That is a difficult question, for the list of possibilities is long and each has a strong claim: teaching, research, service to the local community, administration of scientific installations, housing for students and faculty, support of the arts, solving social problems. In their book *Leadership and Ambiguity,* Michael Cohen and James March comment: "Almost any educated person could deliver a lecture entitled 'The Goals of the University.' Almost no one will listen to the lecture voluntarily. For the most part, such lectures and their companion essays are well-intentioned exercises in social rhetoric, with little operational content. Efforts to generate normative statements of the goals of the university tend to produce goals that are either meaningless or dubious" (1974, p.195).

"Goal ambiguity" is one of the chief characteristics of academic organizations. Not only do they often try to be all things to all people but they rarely have a single mission. Because their preferences are unclear, they also find it hard to decline additional goals. Edward Gross and Paul Grambsch (1968, 1974) analyzed the goals of faculty and administrators in a large number of American universities. The result was remarkable in that both administrators and faculty marked as important almost every one of forty-seven goals listed by Gross and Grambsch. To be sure, they ranked some higher than others—academic freedom being one near the top. But the point is, people seem to feel the university should be doing almost everything. Under these circumstances, it is difficult to see how it can do anything.

Not only are academic goals unclear, they are also highly *contested*. As long as goals are left ambiguous and abstract, people agree; as soon as they are concretely specified and put into operation, disagreement arises. This link between clarity and conflict may help explain the prevalence of meaningless rhetoric in academic speeches and policy statements. If you talk in general terms about academic virtues—the scholarly counterparts of motherhood and apple pie—everybody nods wisely. If you talk specifically about how these virtues are to be translated into operational policy, conflict erupts. The choice seems difficult: rhetoric brings agreement; serious discussion creates conflict.

Academic organizations are client-serving institutions. Like public school systems, hospitals, and welfare agencies, colleges and universities are "people-processing" institutions. Society feeds clients with specific needs into the institution and the institution acts upon them and then returns them to the larger society. This is an extremely important fact, for the clients demand and often obtain a significant amount of influence over the decision-making processes of the institution. Even powerless clients such as small schoolchildren usually have protectors such as parents who demand a voice in the operation of the organization. This client-serving character of academic organizations raises another issue: what kinds of technology and personnel does the organization need to do its multifaceted job.

Problematic technologies. Because they serve clients with disparate, complicated needs, client-serving organizations often have problematic technologies. An organization that manufactures steel develops a specific technology that can be segmented and made routine. Unskilled, semiskilled, and white-collar workers can be used without a heavy reliance upon professional expertise. But it is difficult to construct a simple technology for dealing with minds, bodies, and spirits. Serving clients is difficult to accomplish, to evaluate, and to show short-term successes. Considering the entire person is a holistic task that cannot be easily separated into small, routine, technical segments. If, at times, colleges and universities do not know *what* they are doing, they furthermore often do not know *how* to do it. A holistic, unclear, and nonroutine technology demands a highly professional staff.

High professionalism dominates the academic task. What does a client-oriented organization usually do when its goals are unclear and contested, and its technology is nonroutine? Usually, it solves this problem by hiring expertly trained professionals. Hospitals employ doctors and nurses, social welfare agencies employ social workers, public schools employ teachers, and colleges and universities employ faculty members. These highly trained professional groups deal with the complex, nonroutine problems of clients using a broad repertoire of the skills necessary for the task. Instead of permitting the routine subdividing of the task, assembly-line style, professional work tends to require that a range of skills be encapsulated in a single professional employee.

Sociologists have suggested a number of important facts about professional employees, whether they work in hospitals, schools, law firms, or universities: (1) Professionals demand *work autonomy* and freedom from supervision; they base their work on skill and expertise and demand to be left alone to apply them. (2) Professionals have *divided loyalties;* they have "cosmopolitan" tendencies, and their loyalty to peers in their discipline around the nation sometimes conflicts with their "local" tendencies to be good employees for their organization. (3) There are strong tensions between *professional values* and *bureaucratic expectations* in an organization; these can intensify conflict between professional employees and organizational managers. And (4) professionals demand peer evaluation of their work; they feel only colleagues can judge their performance, and they reject the evaluations of noncolleague managers, even if those managers are technically "superior" in the hierarchy.

All of these characteristics undercut the traditional bureaucracy, rejecting its hierarchy, control structure, and management procedures. As a consequence, we can expect a distinct management style in a professional organization.

Colleges and universities tend to have "fragmented" professional staffs. In some organizations, there is one dominant professional group—for example, doctors in hospitals. In other organizations the professional staff is fragmented into subspecialities, with no one of them dominating—the faculty in a university provides a clear case. Burton Clark comments on fragmented academic professionalism:

The internal controls of the medical profession are strong and are substituted for those of the organization. But in the college or university this situation does not obtain; there are twelve, twenty-five, or fifty clusters of experts. The experts are prone to identify with their own disciplines, and the "academic profession" over-all comes off a poor second. We have wheels within wheels, many professions within a profession. No one of the disciplines on a campus is likely to dominate the others.... The campus is not a closely knit group of professionals, it is decentralized, loose, and flabby. The principle is this: where professional influence is high and there is one dominant professional group, the organization will be integrated by the imposition of professional standards. Where professional influence is high and there are a number of professional groups, the organization will be split by professionalism. The university and the large college are fractured by expertness, not unified by it [1961, pp. 37–51].

The governance processes in colleges and universities are highly influenced by the presence of these diverse professional staffs. In fact, this is one of the dominant features of academic organizations and justifies viewing the faculty as critical to the decision-making process—as we have done throughout our research for the Stanford Project on Academic Governance.

Colleges and universities are becoming more environmentally vulnerable. All complex organizations are vulnerable to outside pressure; there is simply no completely "independent" or "autonomous" organization. But they vary a great deal on how much the outside world controls them, with some institutions having considerably more freedom of action than others. The degree of autonomy that an organization has in regard to its environment is one of the critical determinants of how it will be managed.

In a free market economy, for example, business firms and industry have a substantial degree of autonomy. Although they are regulated by countless government agencies, they essentially are free agents responsive only to market demands. At the other extreme, there are a number of organizations that are virtually "captured" by their environments. Professionals in many government agencies such as public school districts feel the constant scrutiny of the entire community.

Colleges and universities are somewhere in the middle of this continuum from "independent" to "captured." In many respects they enjoy substantial insulation from the environment. Recently, however, powerful external forces have been applied to them. Particularly in the 1970s and 1980s have the conflicting wishes, demands, and threats of dozens of interest groups been made known to the administrations and faculties of academic organizations.

What impact does this kind of environmental pressure have on the governance of colleges and universities? When they are well-insulated from the pressures of the outside environment, then professional values, norms, and word definitions dominate the character of the organization. On the other hand, when high external pressure is brought to bear on those colleges and universities, the operating autonomy of the academic professionals is significantly reduced; faculties and administrators lose control over the curriculum, the institution's goals, and the daily operation of the college. Under these circumstances, the professionals within the organization are frequently reduced to the role of hired employees doing the bidding of bureaucratic managers.

Although colleges and universities are not entirely captured by their environments, they are steadily being penetrated by outside forces. As this vulnerability grows, the institutions change significantly in their management patterns. This is a major difference between academic organizations and traditional industrial bureaucracies that are relatively free from environmental constraints.

A Summary Image: "Organized Anarchy"

To summarize, academic organizations have several unique organizational characteristics. They have unclear and contested *goal* structures; almost anything can be justified, but almost anything can be attacked as illegitimate. They serve *clients* who demand input into the decision-making process. They have a *problematic technology,* for in order to serve clients the technology must be holistic and nonroutine. As a result, academic organizations are important instances of *professionalized organizations* where professionals serving the clients demand a large measure of control over the institution's decision processes. Finally, academic organizations are becoming more and more *vulnerable to their environments.*

What image captures the spirit of such a complex organizational system? Surely the standard term "bureaucracy" misses the point. Bureaucracy implies rigidity and stability; academic organizations seem more fluid, changing, and confused. Bureaucracy implies clear lines of authority and strict hierarchical command; academic organizations have autonomy-demanding professionals and the lines of authority often become blurred and confused. Bureaucracy suggests cohesive organization and unified goals; academic organizations are splintered and fragmented around an ambiguous, changing, and contested set of objectives. In sum, although the imagery of bureaucracy adequately describes certain aspects of colleges and universities—business administration, plant management, capital outlay, and auxiliary services, for example—at the heart of the academic enterprise, in their policymaking and professional teaching/research tasks, academic institutions do not resemble bureaucracies.

What useful shorthand terminology can be used to exemplify academic organizations? Cohen and March, in their book *Leadership and Ambiguity,* have suggested the term *organized anarchy.* They see a confused world with very little organizational coordination and central goal making: "In a university anarchy each individual in the university is seen as making autonomous decisions. Teachers decide if, when, and what to teach. Students decide if, when, and what to learn. Legislators and donors decide if, when, and what to support. Neither coordination ... nor control are practiced. Resources are allocated by whatever process emerges but without explicit reference to some superordinate goal. The 'decisions' of the system are a consequence produced by the system but intended by no one and decisively controlled by no one" (pp. 33-34).

To summarize Cohen and March, the image of organized anarchy differs radically from the well-organized bureaucracy. It is an organization in which people talk past each other, in which generous resources allow people to go in different directions without coordination, in which leaders are relatively weak and decisions are arrived at through the noncoordinated actions of individuals. Since goals are ambiguous, nobody is quite sure where the organization is going or how it will get there. The situation is fluid. Decisions are often by-products of activity that is unintended and unplanned.

In such fluid circumstances, presidents and other institutional leaders serve primarily as catalysts. They do not so much lead the institution as they channel its activities in subtle ways. They do not command, they negotiate. They do not plan comprehensively, they try to nudge problems together with preexisting solutions. They are not heroic leaders, they are facilitators of an ongoing process.

Decisions are not so much "made" as they "happen"—they are events in which problems, choices, and decision makers happen to coalesce to form temporary solutions. In a sense, then, a decision situation is a "garbage can" into which problems, decision makers, and preconceived solutions are poured and jostled around until a solution emerges that at least temporarily satisfies the organization's needs. Cohen and March suggest that university decision processes are "sets of procedures through which organizational participants arrive at an interpretation of what they are doing and what they have done while they are doing it. From this point of view, an organization is a collection of choices looking for problems, issues and feelings looking for decision situations in which they might be aired, solutions looking for issues for which they might be the answer, and decision makers looking for work" (1974, p. 81).

In many ways, the organized anarchy image is an exceptionally strong and persuasive concept. It breaks through much traditional formality that surrounds discussions of decision making. The imagery of organized anarchy helps capture the spirit of the confused organizational dynamics in academic institutions: unclear goals, unclear technologies, and environmental vulnerability.

To some people, the term *organized anarchy* may seem overly colorful, suggesting more confusion, disarray, and conflict than is really present. This may be a legitimate criticism. The term may also carry negative connotations to those who are not aware that it applies to specific organizational characteristics rather than an overall view of the entire campus community. Nevertheless, the term helps to expand our conceptions, dislodge the bureaucracy image, and suggest a looser, more fluid kind of organization. These virtues persuade us to adopt a modified version of the organized image to summarize some of the unique organizational characteristics of colleges and universities: (1) unclear goals, (2) client service, (3) unclear technology, (4) professional staffing, and (5) environmental vulnerability. In the next section we will try to answer a new question: What do decision and governance processes look like in an organized anarchy?

Governance of Organized Anarchies

People tend to reduce the confusing complexity of their world to simple symbols. Administrators, organization theorists, students or professors—almost everyone who has looked at academic governance—have developed one summarizing image after another to capture the essence of this complex process. We look at the bewildering detail of this process and summarize it as "collegial," or as "political" or "professional," "participatory" or "oligarchical." These images dominate our thinking, organize the way we see the world, and determine how we will go about analyzing the process. Our metaphors and images are not innocent, for the way we view the world and summarize it with models helps determine the way we act. If we believe the system is political, then we form coalitions and exert pressure on decision makers accordingly. If we think the situation is collegial, then we try to persuade people and appeal to reason. If we suspect the system is bureaucratic, then we employ legalistic formalities to gain our ends.

In one sense, the search for an all-encompassing model is simplistic, for no one model can delineate the intricacies of decision processes in complex organizations such as universities and colleges. In another sense, there is a pleasant parsimony about having a single model that summarizes a complicated world for us. This is not bad except when we allow our models to blind us to important features of the organization. For example, earlier we insisted that the term *bureaucracy* was inadequate by itself. That does not mean that bureaucracy *alone* is not an adequate term to describe everything that is happening.

In the past few years, as research on higher education has increased, images describing academic governance have also proliferated. Three models have received widespread attention, more or less dominating the thinking of people who study academic governance. We will examine briefly each of these models in turn: (1) bureaucratic, (2) collegial, and (3) political. Each has strong points, and together they can be used to examine slightly different aspects of the governance process.

Bureaucracy and the "Rational" Theory of Decision Making

One of the most influential descriptions of complex organizations was Max Weber's monumental work on bureaucracies. Weber identified the characteristics of bureaucracies that separated them from other, less formal work organizations. In skeleton form, he suggested that bureaucracies are networks of social groups dedicated to limited goals and organized for maximum efficiency. Moreover, the regulation of the system is based on the principle of "legal-rationality," as contrasted with informal regulation based on friendship, loyalty to family, or personal allegiance to a charismatic leader. The structure is hierarchical and is tied together by formal chains of command and systems of communication. Weber's description included such characteristics as tenure, appointment to office, and competency as the basis of promotion. Most of his ideas are well known and need little elaboration.

Several authors claim that university governance may be more fully understood by applying this bureaucratic paradigm. For example, Herbert Stroup (1966) points out some characteristics of colleges and universities that fit Weber's original discussion of the nature of bureaucracy. Stroup's conclusions about colleges include the following:

—Competence is the criterion used for appointment.

—Officials are appointed, not elected.

—Salaries are fixed and paid directly by the organization rather than determined in "free-fee" style.

—Rank is recognized and respected.

—The career tends to be exclusive; little other work is done.

—The style of life is centered around the organization.

—Security is present in a tenure system.

—Personal and organizational property are separated.

Stroup is undoubtedly correct in saying that Weber's paradigm can be applied to universities, and most observers are well aware of the bureaucratic factors involved in university administration. Among the more prominent of these are the following:

State charter. The university is a complex organization chartered by the state, and in this respect it is like most other bureaucracies. This seemingly innocent fact has major consequences, especially as states increasingly exercise control.

Formal hierarchy. The university has a formal hierarchy, with offices and a set of bylaws that specify the relations between those offices.

Professors, instructors, and research assistants are members of this bureaucratic hierarchy in the same sense as are deans, chancellors, and presidents.

Communication channels. There are formal channels of communication that must be respected, as many a student or young professor finds out to his dismay.

Authority relations. There are definite bureaucratic authority relations, with some officials exercising authority over others. In a university, authority relations are often blurred, ambiguous, and shifting, but they nonetheless exist.

Rules and regulations. There are formal policies and rules that govern much of the institution's work. Library regulations, budgetary guidelines, and procedures of the university senate are all part of the system of regulations and procedures that hold the university together and control its work.

People processing. Bureaucratic elements are most vividly apparent to students in the "people-processing" aspects of record keeping—registration, graduation requirements, and a thousand other routine, day-to-day activities that are designed to help the modern university handle its masses of students. Students often complain that these requirements and procedures result in impersonality and callousness, but they are necessary if the university is to cope with its overwhelming influx of students.

Decision processes. Decision-making processes are most often bureaucratic when routine decisions are at stake and are being made by officials who have been given the responsibility by the formal administrative structure. Admissions actions are formally delegated to the dean of admissions; procedures for graduation are routinely administered by other designated officials; research policies of the university are supervised by officials specified in the rules of the university; financial activities are usually handled in a bureaucratic manner by the finance office.

In many ways, however, the bureaucratic paradigm falls short of explaining university governance, especially if one is primarily concerned with decision-making processes. First, the bureaucratic model tells us much about "authority"—legitimate, formalized power—but not much about power based on nonlegitimate threats, mass movements, expertise, and appeals to emotion and sentiment. The Weberian paradigm is weak when it attempts to deal with these nonformal types of power and influence. Second, the bureaucratic paradigm explains much about the formal *structure* but little about the dynamic *processes* of the institution in action. Third, the bureaucratic paradigm deals with the formal structure at one particular time, but it does not explain changes over time. Finally, the bureaucratic model does not deal extensively with the crucial task of policy formulation. The paradigm explains how policies may be carried out most efficiently after they are set, but it says little about the process by which policy is established in the first place. It does not deal with political issues, such as the efforts of groups within the university to force policy decisions favoring their special interests. In these ways, then, the bureaucratic paradigm falls far short of explaining policymaking in the university.

The University as a Collegium

Many writers have consciously rejected the bureaucratic image of the university and instead have declared the university a "collegium," or "community of scholars." This is found to be a rather ambiguous concept when closely examined. In fact, there seem to be at least three different themes running through the literature based on this concept.

One theme is that *academic decision making should be like the hierarchical processes in other bureaucracies*; instead, there should be full participation of the members of the academic community—especially the faculty—in its management. Only a few small liberal arts colleges exist as actual examples of such "roundtable" democratic institutions, but the concept persists nonetheless. Under it the "community of scholars" administers its own affairs, with bureaucratic officials having little influence (see Goodman 1962).

John Millett, one of the foremost proponents of this model, has succinctly stated this view: "I do not believe that the concept of hierarchy is a realistic representation of the interpersonal relationships which exist within a college or university. Nor do I believe that a structure of hierarchy is a desirable prescription for the organization of a college or university. . . . I would argue that there is another concept of organization that is just as valuable a tool of analysis and perhaps even more useful as a generalized observation of group and interpersonal behavior. This is the concept of community. The concept of community presupposes an organization in which functions are differentiated and in which specialization must be brought together, or the coordination, if you will, is achieved not through a structure of superordination and subordination of persons and groups but through a *dynamic of consensus*" (1962, pp. 234–35).

A second theme concerns *the "professional" authority of faculty*. Talcott Parsons (1947) was one of the first to call attention to the difference between the "official competence" derived from one's office in the bureaucracy and "technical competence" derived from one's ability to perform a given task. Parsons concentrated on the technical competence of the physician, but others have extended this logic to other professionals who hold authority on the basis of what they know and can do, rather than on the basis of their official positions. The scientist in industry, the military advisor, the expert in government, the physician in the hospital, and the professor in the university are all examples of professionals whose influence depends on their knowledge rather than on their formal positions.

The argument for collegial organization is strongly supported by the literature on professionalism, for it emphasizes the professional's ability to make his own decisions and his need for freedom from organizational restraints. Proponents of this argument hold, therefore, that a collegium is the most reasonable method of organizing the university. Parsons, for example, notes that when professionals are organized in a bureaucracy "there are strong tendencies for them to develop a different sort of structure from that characteristic of the administrative hierarchy . . . of bureaucracy. Instead of a rigid hierarchy of status and authority there tends to be what is roughly, in formal status, a company of equals . . ." (1947, p. 60).

A third theme carries with it *a utopian operational prescription.* Supporters of this thesis argue that contemporary society is increasingly discontented with the impersonalization of life exemplified by the multiversity with its thousands of students and huge bureaucracy. The student revolts of the 1960s and 1970s, and perhaps even the widespread apathy of the 1980s, have been symptoms of a deeply felt alienation between the average student and the massive educational establishment. This discontent and anxiety are well summed up in the now-famous sign worn by a Berkeley student: "I am a human being—do not fold, spindle, or mutilate."

In response to this impersonal, bureaucratized educational system, many critics are calling for a return to the "academic community," with all of that concept's accompanying images of personal attention, humane education, and "relevant confrontation with life." Paul Goodman's work in *The Community of Scholars* (1962) appeals to many seeking to reform the university, citing the need for more personal interaction between faculty and students, for more "relevant" courses, and for educational innovations to bring the student into existential dialogue with the subject matter of his discipline. The number of articles on this subject, in both the mass media and the professional journals, is astonishingly large. Indeed, this version of the collegial, academic community is now widely advocated as one answer to the impersonality and meaninglessness of today's large multiversity. Thus conceived, the idea of the collegium and the academic community is more of a revolutionary ideology and a utopian projection than a description of the real shape of governance at any university.

How can we evaluate these three themes running through the collegial model? The calls for the professor's professional freedom, for consensus and democratic consultation, and for more humane education are all supported by legitimate and appealing arguments. Few would deny that our universities would more truly be centers of learning if we could somehow implement these objectives. However, there is a misleading simplicity about these otherwise persuasive arguments because they gloss over many of the realities of a complex university. Several of these weaknesses of the collegial model should be mentioned.

The collegial literature often confuses descriptive and normative enterprises. Are the writers saying that the university *is* a collegium or that it *ought* to be a collegium? Frequently, the discussions of collegium are more a lament for paradise lost than a description of present reality. Indeed, the collegial idea of roundtable decision making does not accurately reflect the actual process in most institutions, as our data in later chapters will clearly show. To be sure, at the department level there are many examples of collegial decision making, but at higher levels it can be found only in some aspects of the committee system. Of course, the proponents of the collegial model may be proposing this as a desirable goal or reform strategy rather than a present reality that helps us to understand the actual working of universities.

The collegial model also fails to deal adequately with the problem of *conflict*. When Millett emphasizes the "dynamic of consensus," he neglects the prolonged battles that precede consensus and the fact that the consensus actually represents the prevalence of one group over another. Collegial proponents are correct in declaring that simple bureaucratic rule making is not the essence of decision making, but in making this point they take the equally indefensible position that major decisions are reached primarily by consensus. Neither extreme is correct, for decisions are rarely made by either bureaucratic fiat or simple consensus. What is needed is a model that can include consensus factors and bureaucratic processes and that can also grapple with power plays, conflict, and the rough-and-tumble politics of many academic institutions.

The Political Model

In *Power and Conflict in the University* (1971), Baldridge proposed a "political systems" model of university governance. Although the major models of governance—collegial and bureaucratic—offer genuine insights, we believe that their analyses can be strengthened by insights from this political model.

The political model assumes that complex organizations can be studied as miniature political systems, with interest-group dynamics and conflicts similar to those in city, state, and other political situations. The political model has several stages, all of which center around the university's policy-forming processes. Policy formation was selected as the central focal point because major policies commit the organization to definite goals, set the strategies for reaching those goals, and in general determine the long-range destiny of the organization. Policy decisions are critical decisions, those that have a major impact on the organization's future. In any practical situation it may be difficult to separate the routine from the critical, for issues that seem minor at one point may later be of considerable importance, or vice versa. In general, however, policy decisions are those that bind the organization to important courses of action.

Since politics are so important, people throughout the organization try to influence their formulation in order to see that their own special interests are protected and furthered. Policymaking becomes a vital focus of special interest group activity that permeates the university. Just as the political scientist often selects legislative acts in congress as the focus for his analysis of the state's political processes, organization theorists may select policy decisions as the key for studying organizational conflict and change. With policy formation as its key issue, the political model then makes a series of assumptions about the political process.

One assumption is that *inactivity prevails.* To say that policymaking is a political process is not to say that everybody is involved. Quite the contrary. For most people most of the time, the policymaking process is an uninteresting, unrewarding activity, so they allow administrators to run the show. This is characteristic of political processes not only in colleges but also in the larger society. Voters do not vote, people do not attend city council meetings, school boards usually do what they please, and by and large the decisions of the society are made by small groups of elites.

A second assumption is that of *fluid participation.* Even when people are active they move in and out of the decision-making process. Individuals usually do not spend very much time on any given issue; decisions, therefore, are usually made by those who persist. This normally means that small groups of political elites govern most major decisions because only they invest the necessary time in the process.

A third assumption is that colleges and universities, like most other social organizations, are *fragmented into interest groups* with different goals and values. These groups normally live in a state of armed coexistence. When resources are plentiful and the environment congenial, these interest groups engage in only minimal conflict. They mobilize and fight to influence decisions, however, when resources are tight, outside pressure groups attack, or other internal groups try to take over their goals.

A fourth assumption is that *conflict is normal.* In a fragmented, dynamic social system, conflict is natural and not necessarily a symptom of breakdown in the academic community. In fact, conflict is a significant factor in promoting healthy organizational change.

A fifth assumption is that *authority is limited.* In universities, the formal authority prescribed in a bureaucratic system is severely limited by the political pressure that groups can exert. Decisions are not simply bureaucratic orders, but are often negotiated compromises between competing groups. Officials are not free simply to issue a decision; instead they must jockey between interest groups hoping to build viable positions between powerful blocks.

A sixth assumption is that *external interest groups are important.* Academic decision making does not occur in a campus-bound vacuum. External interest groups exert a great deal of influence over the policymaking process. And external pressures and formal control by outside agencies—especially in public institutions—are powerful shapers of internal governance processes.

Often the bureaucratic image of organizational structure is accompanied by a decision approach that can be called the "rational" strategy. It assumes not only that the structure is hierarchical and well-organized but also that decisions are made through clear-cut, predetermined steps. This traditional decision theory for bureaucracies starts with a basic premise: Mr. X (the dean, president, or whoever) must make a decision and, from conflicting advice, must therefore form a judgment. This formalistic theory suggests that a definite, rational approach will lead to the optimal decision. Once the problem is recognized (difficult in itself), then a number of steps are proposed: (1) setting goals to overcome the problem, (2) selecting alternatives to reach the goals, (3) assessing the consequences of various alternatives, (4) choosing the best alternatives, and (5) implementing the decision.

The rational model appeals to most of us who like to interpret our actions as essentially goal-directed and rational. Realistically, however, we should realize that the rational model is more an ideal than an actual description of how people act. In fact, in the confused organizational setting of the university, political constraints can seriously undermine attempts to arrive at rational decisions. A political interpretation suggests that this theory must be rethought in the light of actual decision processes if it is to amount to more than a formalistic, impractical scheme.

The first new question posed by the political model is *why* a given decision is made at all. The formalists have already indicated that "recognition of the problem" is one element in the process, but too little attention has been paid to the activities that bring a particular issue to the forefront. Why is *this* decision being considered at *this* particular time? The political model insists that interest groups, powerful individuals, and bureaucratic processes are critical in drawing attention to some decisions rather than to others. A study of "attention cues" by which issues are called to a community's attention is a vital part of any analysis.

Second, a question must be raised about the right of any person or group to make the decisions. Previously the "who" question was seldom raised, chiefly because the decision literature was developed for hierarchical organizations in which the focus of authority could be easily defined. In a more loosely coordinated system, however, we must ask a prior question: Why is Dean Smith making the decision instead of Dean Jones, or why is the university senate dealing with the problem instead of the central administration? Establishing the right of authority over a decision is a political question, subject to conflict, power manipulation, and struggles between interest groups. Thus the political model always asks tough questions: Who has the right to make the decision? What are the conflict-ridden processes by which the decision was located at this point rather than at another? The crucial point is that often the issue of *who* makes the decision has already limited, structured, and preformed *how* it will be made.

The third new issue raised by a political interpretation concerns the development of complex decision networks. As a result of the fragmentation of the university, decision making is rarely located in one official; instead it is dependent upon the advice and authority of numerous people. Again the importance of the committee system is evident. It is necessary to understand that the committee network is the legitimate reflection of the need for professional influence to intermingle with bureaucratic influence. The decision process, then, is taken out of the hands of individuals (although there are still many who are powerful) and placed into a network that allows a cumulative buildup of expertise and advice. When the very life of the organization clusters around expertise, decision making is likely to be diffuse, segmentalized, and decentralized. A complex network of committees, councils, and advisory bodies grows to handle the task of assembling the expertise necessary for reasonable decisions. Decision making by the individual bureaucrat is replaced with decision making by committee, council, and cabinet. Centralized decision making is replaced with diffuse decision making. The process becomes a far-flung network for gathering expertise from every corner of the organization and translating it into policy.

The fourth new question raised by the political approach concerns the choice of alternative solutions to the problem at hand. The rational decision theory suggests that all possible options are open within easy reach of the decision maker. A realistic appraisal of decision dynamics in most organizations, however, suggests that by no means are all options open. The political dynamics of interest groups, the force of external power blocs, and the opposition of powerful professional constituencies may leave only a handful of viable options. The range of alternatives is sharply limited; the realistic choices are narrow. Just as important, the time and energy available for seeking new solutions most likely is extremely short. Although all possible solutions *should* be identified under the rational model, administrators in the real world have little time to grope for solutions before deadlines are upon them.

These comments may be summed up by proposing a "political process" model of decision making. The political model suggests the following. First, powerful political forces—interest groups, bureaucratic officials, influential individuals, organizational subunits—cause a given issue to emerge from the limbo of ongoing problems and certain "attention cues" force the political community to consider the problem. Second, there is a struggle over locating the decision with a particular person or group, for the location of the right to make the decision often determines the outcome. Third, decisions are usually "preformed" to a great extent by the time one person or group is given the legitimacy to make the decision; not all options are open and the choices have been severely limited by the previous conflicts. Fourth, such political struggles are more likely to occur in reference to "critical" decisions than to "routine" decisions. Fifth, a complex decision network is developed to gather the necessary information and supply the critical expertise. Sixth, during the process of making the decision political controversy is likely to continue and compromises, deals, and plain head-cracking are often necessary to get any decision made. Finally, the controversy is not likely to end easily. In fact, it is difficult even to know when a decision *is* made, for the political processes have a habit of unmaking, confusing, and muddling whatever agreements are hammered out.

This may be a better way of grappling with the complexity that surrounds decision processes within a loosely coordinated, fragmented political system. The formal decision models seem to have been asking very limited questions about the decision process, and more insight can be gained by asking a new set of political questions. Thus the decision model that emerges from the university's political dynamics is more open, more dependent on conflict and political action. It is not so systematic or formalistic as most decision theory, but it is probably closer to the truth. Decision making, then, is not an isolated technique but another critical process that must be integrated into a larger political image.

Stages in the Political Process

If the decision process is really as fluid and complex as we suggest, then a more complex analytic framework is needed than the "rational" theory affords. As Baldridge described it in *Power and Conflict in the University* (1971), the political model offers an analytical scheme for describing and mapping the political events around individual organizational decisions.

The sociologist examining academic policymaking wants to know how the social structure of the college or university influences the decision processes, how political pressures are brought to bear on decision makers, how decisions are forged out of the conflict, and how formulated policies are implemented. Thus, the political model has five points of analysis.

Social Structure. Academic organizations are splintered into groups with basically different lifestyles and political interests. Those differences often lead to conflict, for what is in the best interest of one group may damage another. It is important to examine this social setting, with its fragmented groups, divergent goal aspirations, and conflicting claims on decision makers. Academic organizations have particularly pluralistic social systems because groups both inside and out are pushing in dissimilar directions according to their own special interests. One need only glance at the various outside "publics" of a college or university to see how diverse are the elements of its external social context; a glance inward reveals an internal social structure composed of similarly fragmented interest groups. Many of the current conflicts on campus have their roots in the complexity of this academic social structure and the complex goals and values held by these divergent groups.

Interest Articulation. Attempts at political intervention comes from external groups, faculty, student, staff, and administration. In this political tangle the articulation of interests is a fundamental process. A group must somehow effectively influence favorable action by decision-making bodies. How does a powerful group exert pressure, what threats or promises can it make, and how does it translate its desires into political capital?

The Legislative Stage. University legislative bodies respond to pressures on them and attempt to transform the conflict into politically feasible policy. Committees meet, commissions report, negotiators bargain, and powerful people haggle over the eventual policy. In the process, negotiations are undertaken, compromises are forged, and rewards are divided. Not only must we identify the different types of interest groups involved and the methods they use to bring pressure to bear but we must also clarify the translation process by which all of these pressures are negotiated into formal policy.

Formulation of Policy. All articulated interests have now gone through conflict and compromise stages, and the final legislative action is taken. The resulting policy is the official climax to the conflict, and it represents an authoritative, binding decision to commit the organization to one set of possible alternative actions, one set of goals and values.

Execution of Policy. The battle is now officially over and the resulting policy is turned over to the bureaucrats for its routine execution. This may oversimplify things, but it is remarkable the way yesterday's vicious confrontation may become today's boring bureaucratic chore. This may not be the end of the conflict, for the losers may take up arms again for a new round of "interest articulation." Too, execution of the new policy may generate new tensions, with new vested interests instigating a renewed cycle of political conflict.

In summary, the broad outline of the academic organization's political system looks like this: there is a complex social structure that generates multiple pressures, there are many sources and forms of power and pressure that impinge on decision makers, there is a legislative stage that translates these pressures into policy, and there is a policy execution phase that generates feedback and potentially new conflict.

This approach forces us to place several factors under close scrutiny. First, and primarily, we should examine the mechanics of goal setting and the conflict over values rather than the question of efficiency in achieving goals. Second, we should analyze change processes and the adaptation of the organization to its changing internal and external environment; political dynamics are constantly shifting, pressuring the university in many directions and forcing change throughout the academic system. Third, we should closely analyze conflict and conflict resolution, a crucial component of a political study. Fourth, we should explore the role that interest groups play in pressuring decision makers to formulate certain policy. Finally, we should give considerable attention to legislative and decision-making phases—the processes by which pressures and power are translated into policy. Taken together, these emphases are the bare outline for a political analysis of governance.

Implications for Academic Leadership

What implications does all this have for leadership in colleges and universities? The organizational characteristics are critical for determining the styles of management and leadership that work best in a unique setting. Let us examine the three models of academic governance and their implications for leadership.

Under the bureaucratic model the leader is seen as the hero who stands at the top of a complex pyramid of power. The hero's job is to assess the problems, consider alternatives, and make rational choices. Much of the organization's power is held by the hero, and great expectations are raised because people trust him to solve problems and fend off threats from the environment. The imagery of the authoritarian hero is deeply ingrained in the mentality of most nations and the philosophy of most organization theorists.

We expect leaders to be technically knowledgeable of their organizations and uniquely skilled at solving its problems. Often proposed as tools for accomplishing the latter are such "scientific management" methods as Planning, Programming, Budgeting Systems (PPBS) and Management by Objectives. Generally, schools of management, business, and educational administration teach such courses to develop the technical skills that the hero-planner will need for leading the organization.

Although the hero is deeply imbedded in our culture's concepts of leadership, the hero's place in organizations such as colleges and universities is not at all as all-powerful as many assume it to be. Power is more diffuse, lodged with the professional experts and fragmented into many departments and subdivisions. Under these circumstances, high expectations of leadership performance are often disappointed—the leader had neither the power nor the information to consistently make heroic decisions. Moreover, the scientific management procedures prescribed for organizational leaders quickly break down under conditions of goal ambiguity, professional dominance, and environmental vulnerability— the organizational characteristics of colleges and universities. They break down because they are founded on several basic assumptions: (1) that goals are clear; (2) that the organization is a "closed" system insulated from environmental penetration; and (3) that planners have the power to execute their decisions. These assumptions seem unrealistic in the confused and fluid world of university management.

Leadership in the collegial model contrasts strongly with the hero-bureaucrat image. The collegial leader is at most a "first among equals" in an academic organization supposedly run by professional experts. Essentially, this is management according to what John Millett calls the "dynamic of consensus in a community of scholars." The basic idea of the collegial leader is less to command than to listen, less to lead than to gather expert judgments, less to manage than to facilitate, less to order than to persuade and negotiate.

Obviously, the skills needed by a collegial leader differ from the scientific management principles employed by the hero. Instead of technical problem-solving skills, the collegial leader needs both professional expertise to insure high esteem among his colleagues and interpersonal abilities for developing the professional consensus needed to carry out organizational goals. Whereas the hero is always expected to make the decisions and take responsibility for them, the collegial leader is not so much a star standing alone as the developer of consensus among the professionals who must share the burden of the decision. In the university, therefore, expectations are more modest, more realistic, and more widely shared among the organization's members. Clearly, negotiation and compromise rather than authoritarian dictates are the strategies most employed by the collegial leader.

Under the political model, the leader is a mediator, a negotiator, a person who jockeys between power blocs trying to establish viable courses of action for the institution. Such was not always the case. But unlike the autocratic president of the past who ruled with an iron hand, the contemporary academic president must play a more political role, pulling together coalitions to fight for desired changes. The academic monarch of yesteryear has almost vanished, but in his place is not the academic "hero-bureaucrat," as many suggest, but the academic "statesman." Robert Dahl paints an amusing picture of the political maneuvers of Mayor Richard Lee of New Haven, and the same description applies to the new academic political leaders: "The mayor was not at the peak of a pyramid but rather at the center of intersecting circles. He rarely pressed, appealed, reasoned, promised, insisted, demanded, even threatened, but he most needed support and acquiescence from other leaders who simply could not be commanded. Because the mayor could not command, he had to bargain" (1961, p. 204).

The political interpretation of leadership can be pressed even further, for the governance of the university more and more comes to look like a "cabinet" form of administration. The key figure today is not the president, the solitary giant, but the political leader surrounded by his staff, the prime minister who gathers the information and expertise to construct policy. It is the "staff," the network of key administrators who actually make most of the critical decisions. The university has become much too complicated to be ruled by any one person, regardless of stature. Cadres of vice-presidents, research men, budget officials, public relations men, and experts of various stripes combine with the leader to reach collective decisions. Expertise becomes more important than ever, and leadership increasingly amounts to the ability to assemble, persuade, and facilitate the activities of knowledgeable experts.

References

Baldridge, J. Victor. *Power and Conflict in the University.* New York: John Wiley, 1971.

Clark, B.R. "The Role of Faculty in College Administration." In *Studies of College Faculty*, edited by L. Wilson and others. Boulder, Colo.: Western Interstate Commission for Higher Education, 1961.

Cohen, M.D., and J.G. March. *Leadership and Ambiguity: The American College President.* New York: McGraw-Hill, 1974.

Dahl, R. *Who Governs?* New Haven: Yale University Press, 1961.

Goodman, P. *The Community of Scholars.* New York: Random House, 1962.

Gross, E., and P.V. Grambsch. *University Goals and Academic Power.* Washington, D.C.: American Council on Education, 1968.

Millett, J. *The Academic Community.* New York: McGraw-Hill, 1962.

Parsons, T. "Introduction." In *The Theory of Social and Economic Organization*, edited by M. Weber. New York: Free Press, 1947.

Stroup, H. *Bureaucracy in Higher Education.* New York: Free Press, 1966.

4

The Structure of Educational Organizations

John Meyer and Brian Rowan

Large-scale educational organizations have become dominant forms in almost all countries (Coombs 1968). That is, not only has *formal* education become dominant, but this education is organized in large bureaucracies managed by political systems; no longer is it simply a matter of exchange between families and local educational organizations.

This circumstance is not surprising. Many other social activities have come under political and bureaucratic control in modern societies. It is customary to suppose that, as the scale of these activities expands, higher levels of coordination and control are required and that bureaucratic controls emerge to structure these activities efficiently. This view does not fit educational organization, however. There is a great deal of evidence that educational organizations (at least in the United States) *lack* close internal

Revised version of a paper presented at the annual meetings of the American Sociological Association (ASA), San Francisco, August 1975. The work reported here was conducted in the Environment for Teaching Program of the Stanford Center for Research and Development in Teaching, under a grant from the National Institute of Education (NIE), grant number NE-C-00-3-0062. Views expressed here do not reflect NIE positions. Many colleagues in the Environment for Teaching Program, the NIE, the Organizations Training Program at Stanford, and the ASA work group on organizations and environments, offered helpful comments. In particular, detailed substantive suggestions and comments were provided by Albert Bergesen, Charles Bidwell, Terry Deal, John Freeman, Paul Hirsch, James March, Barbara Payne, Jeffrey Pfeffer, Phillip Runkel, and W. Richard Scott, and Betty Smith provided much editorial assistance.

Reprinted, by permission, from *Environments and Organizations*, ed. Marshall W. Meyer and Associates (San Francisco: Jossey-Bass, 1978), pp. 78–109.

coordination, especially of the content and methods of what is presumably their main activity—instruction. Instruction tends to be removed from the control of the organizational structure, in both its bureaucratic and its collegial aspects. This property of educational organizations, among others, has led March and Olsen (1976) and Weick (1976) to apply the term "loosely coupled" to educational organizations. By this they mean that *structure is disconnected from technical (work) activity, and activity is disconnected from its effects.*

In this chapter, we offer an explanation of the rise of large-scale educational bureaucracies that consistently leave instructional activities and outcomes uncontrolled and uninspected. We argue that educational bureaucracies emerge as personnel-certifying agencies in modern societies. They use standard types of curricular topics and teachers to produce standardized types of graduates, who are then allocated to places in the economic and stratification system on the basis of their certified educational background. In such matters as controlling who belongs in a particular *ritual classification*—for example, who is a certified mathematics teacher, a fifth-grader, an English major—educational organizations are very tightly, not loosely, organized. As large-scale educational organizations develop, they take on a great deal of control over the ritual classifications of the curriculum, students, and teachers. The reason for this is that the standardized categories of teachers, students, and curricular topics give meaning and definition to the internal activities of the school. These elements are *institutionalized* in the legal and normative rules of the wider society. In fact, the ritual classifications are the basic components of the theory (or ideology) of education used by modern societies, and schools gain enormous resources by conforming to them, incorporating them, and controlling them (Meyer and Rowan 1977).

Schools less often control their instructional activities or outputs, despite periodic shifts towards "accountability." They avoid this kind of control for two reasons. First, close supervision of instructional activity and outputs can uncover inconsistencies and inefficiencies and can create more uncertainty than mere abstract, and unenforced, demands for conformity to bureaucratic rules. Second, in the United States, centralized governmental and professional controls are weak. Schools depend heavily on local funding and support. Maintaining only nominal central control over instructional outputs and activities maintains societal consensus about the abstract ritual classifications by making local variations in the content and effectiveness of instructional practices invisible. This also allows instructional practices, although prescribed by rules institutionalized at highly generalized levels, to become adapted to unique local circumstances.

In the American situation, attempts to tightly link the prescriptions of the central theory of education to the activities of instruction would create conflict and inconsistency and discredit and devalue the meaning of ritual classifications in society. Educators (and their social environments) therefore decouple their ritual structure from instructional activities and outcomes, and they resort to a "logic of confidence": higher levels of the system organize on the *assumption* that what is going on at lower levels makes sense and conforms to rules but avoid inspecting it to discover or assume responsibility for inconsistencies and ineffectiveness. In this fashion, educational organizations work more smoothly than is commonly supposed, obtain high levels of external support from divergent community and state sources, and maximize the meaning and prestige of the ritual categories of people they employ and produce.

Our argument hinges on the assertion that education is highly institutionalized in modern society. Its categories of students and graduates and its ritual classification of production procedures—types of teachers, topics, and schools—are all derived from highly institutionalized rules and beliefs. Educational organizations derive power and resources when such rules are institutionalized in society, and they are thus inclined to incorporate and remain in close conformity with such categorical rules.

In this chapter we (1) describe the prevailing pattern of control in educational organizations, (2) consider the inadequacies of conventional explanations of this pattern, (3) formulate an alternative interpretation, and (4) consider some research implications and issues in organization theory that arise from the discussion.

Patterns of Control in Educational Organizations

The literature on educational organizations manifests a peculiar contradiction. On the one hand, there are depictions of the educational system as highly coordinated and controlled—to the point of restricting local innovation (for instance, Holt 1964; Rogers 1968). On the other hand, conventional sociological discussions hold that actual educational work—instruction—occurs in the isolation of the self-contained classroom, removed from educational coordination and control. In this view, local innovations fail not because of the rigidity of the system, but because the system lacks internal linkage (Lortie 1973; Deal et al. 1976). Both of these views contain an element of truth. Instructional activities—the *work* of the organization—are coordinated quite casually in most American educational institutions. But the ritual classifications and categories that organize and give meaning to education are tightly controlled. Our first concern is to describe this situation in more detail.

Loose Coupling of Structure and Activities. Consider some of the ways in which educational organizations lack coordination and control over the technical activity within them—a situation called loose coupling by March and Olsen (1976) and Weick (1976).

Evaluation. Educational work takes place in the isolation of the classroom, removed from organizational controls of a substantive kind (see, for instance, Bidwell 1965; Dreeben 1973; and Lortie 1973). Neither teaching nor its output in student socialization is subject to serious organizational evaluation and inspection (Dornbusch and Scott 1975). The weak formal inspection of instruction is evident in a 1972 survey of San Francisco Bay Area elementary schools conducted by the Environment for Teaching Program (Cohen et al. 1976). Survey data were obtained from 34 district superintendents, 188 principals of schools within these districts, and 231 teachers in 16 of the schools. The schools were selected by stratified random sampling from the population of elementary schools in the eight counties adjoining San Francisco Bay. The data show that the inspection of instructional activity is delegated to the local school and takes place infrequently. For example, only one of the thirty-four superintendents interviewed reported that the district office evaluates teachers directly. Nor does it appear that principals and peers have the opportunity to inspect and discuss teachers' work: Of the principals surveyed, 85 percent reported that they and their teachers do not work together on a daily basis. Further, there is little evidence of interaction among teachers: A majority of the principals report that there are no day-to-day working relations among teachers within the same grade level, and 83 percent report no daily work relations among teachers of different grades. Teachers reaffirm this view of segmented teaching. Two-thirds report that their teaching is observed by other teachers infrequently (once a month or less), and half report a similar infrequency of observation by their principals.

Direct inspection of the teaching task is, of course, only one means of organizational control. Organizations can also exert control by inspecting outputs (Ouchi and Maguire 1975). Schools, for example, could determine which teachers have students that score well on standardized tests. But a striking fact about American education at all levels is that student achievement data are rarely used to evaluate the performance of teachers or schools. For example, in 1972 only one of the thirty-four superintendents in the Environment for Teaching survey reported using standardized achievement data to evaluate district schools. Many reasons have been given for this failure to employ output controls—among them, the unavailability and low reliability of the measures. These reasons are made less plausible by the fact that such measures are routinely used to assess and determine the life chances of students.

Curriculum and Technology. Another critical ingredient of organizational control—a teaching technology or even a detailed instructional program of socially agreed-on efficacy—is largely missing in schools. Routine technologies with high consensual standards of efficacy are thought, in organization theory, to create great pressures for effective control (Perrow 1970). But in schools there are few detailed standards of instructional content or procedure. For example, 93 percent of the principals interviewed in the Environment for Teaching survey report having only general or informal curriculum guidelines, as opposed to detailed policies. Such diffuse standards are even more the case with teaching methods. Only 4 percent of the principals report that they are extremely influential in determining the instructional methods used by teachers.

There is similar lack of coordination and control over technical interdependencies. Schools appear to minimize problems of coordination that might arise from instructional practices. For example, it may seem necessary for sixth-graders to have mastered fifth-grade work, but in fact students are often processed from grade to grade with little regard for how much they have learned. In this way, schools minimize sequential interdependencies inherent in their instructional core, and teachers adapt informally to student variability. Schools also minimize the interdependence among instructional programs. Webster (1976) reports that specialized program administrators seldom interact or discuss the activities of other programs.

Authority. It also seems that educational administrators have little direct authority over instructional work. While administrators have a generalized responsibility to plan and coordinate the content and methods of instruction, their authority to carry out these activities is in fact evanescent. As an illustration, only 12 percent of the San Francisco Bay Area principals say they have real decision power over the methods teachers use. On issues other than instruction, however, principals assume real decision rights: Of those surveyed, 82 percent claim to decide about scheduling, 75 percent about pupil assignment. And 88 percent claim to decide (alone or with district consultation) about hiring.

These data and examples suggest that educational organizations only marginally control their central instructional function—especially when it is remembered that the data concern elementary schools, which are the types of schools ordinarily thought to have the highest levels of control, as organizations, over the content and methods of instruction. But an important caveat is needed: This discussion is limited to American schooling. In contrast, schools observed in Britain show much more internal coordination. Evaluation and control are exerted under the authority of the headmaster, whose role in the school and in British society is substantial and is rooted in established tradition. Similarly, some continental systems also vest substantive power and authority in central ministries. Our description of the loose control of instruction, as well as our subsequent explanation, will therefore need to take into account particular features of American society and education.

The Tight Control of Ritual Classifications. The description just given has highlighted the structural looseness (Bidwell 1965) of educational organizations. But, although the evidence seems to show loose controls in the area of instruction, there is some evidence of tight organizational controls in such areas as the credentialing and hiring of teachers, the assignment of students to classes and teachers, and scheduling. This suggests that within schools certain areas of organizational structure are more tightly controlled than others. In contrast to instructional activities, there seem to be centralized and enforced agreements about exactly what *teachers, students,* and *topics of instruction* constitute a particular *school.* Also, in the allocation of space, funds, and materials schools exercise considerable control. Teachers in different, isolated classrooms seem to teach similar topics, and students learn many of the same things. One of the main emphasis in our discussion will be to explain how educational organizations, with few controls over their central activities, achieve adequate coordination, and how they persist so stably.

The tight control educational organizations maintain over the ritual or formal classification systems is central to our understanding of change as an institution. To a considerable extent, educational organizations function to maintain the *societally agreed-on rites defined in societal myths (or institutional rules) of education.* Education rests on and obtains enormous resources from central institutional rules about what valid education is. These rules define the ritual categories of teacher, student, curricular topic, and type of school. When these categories are properly assembled, education is understood to occur. But for the rites to occur in a legitimate way some general exigencies of the physical and social world require practical management. All participants assembled for their ritual performances must be properly qualified and categorized. Consider the procedures for controlling the properties of ritually defined actors, for assembling the legimate curricular topics, and for assembling these into an accredited school.

Teacher Classifications. There are elaborate rules for classifying teachers. There are elementary school teachers, high school teachers, and college teachers—each type with its own specifications, credentials, and categories of specialists. Each type has a legitimate domain outside of which instruction would be deemed inappropriate—for example, elementary teachers do not teach college physics. Each type also possesses appropriate credentials, which are defined and controlled in an elaborate way (see Woellner 1972 for specific descriptions). Educational organizations, then, have detailed, definitive specifications delineating which individuals may teach in which types of classes and schools.

Further, particular educational organizations maintain lists of teachers, with their formal assignments to topics, space, students, and funds. These teachers are defined by name, recorded background and training, and types of credentials. Schools are very tightly coupled organizations in defining who their teachers are and what properties these teachers have. Yet there is almost no formal control exercised to ensure that each teacher enacts the substance of the typological category in daily activity. That is, documents of what teachers *do* are either nonexistent or vacuous, while documents that *define persons as teachers* are elaborately controlled.

Student Classifications. Similarly, elaborate sets of formal rules define types of students. Students are sharply distinguished by level or grade, by programs or units completed, by subject area specialization, and even by special abilities (for instance, educationally handicapped). Student classifications are tightly controlled, and schools can define exactly which students are fifth-graders, chemistry majors, or enrollees. Adding a new type of student (for instance, economics majors or emotionally handicapped students) is an explicit and important organizational decision. But, while the documents and rules relevant to the classification of students are explicit and carefully maintained, little formal organization ensures that students are being treated (or acting in a manner) appropriate to their type (for instance, see Hobbs 1975). It is very clear whether a given school has an economics major or not, but there may be no one in the organization who keeps track of exactly what economics majors study or learn.

Further, there are rules governing the students' entrance into and movement through the system. Residence, age, previous education, or ethnic background often govern entrance into a particular school, grade, or program. Changes from any ritual category—for instance, to sixth-grader or to college student—require close coordination ensuring the propriety of the ritual transition. However, although there is great clarity in formal assignment or transition, few formal organizational mechanisms ensure that these assignments are enacted substantively—for instance, that twelfth-graders are actually doing twelfth-grade work or that third-graders who are being promoted have actually met some standards.

Topic Classifications. Definitive sets of topics are organized in schools and assigned to teachers, students, space, and funds. Each school has a formalized set of curricular topics. An elementary school, for instance, may cover the standard elementary curriculum from kindergarten through the sixth grade. A high school may offer instruction in history and business but not in Latin. There is a definitive agreement, built into the school's formal structure, about what topics the school is and is not offering instruction in at any given time. These topics are carefully documented, as are the particular teachers who manage them and the particular students who receive (or have received) instruction in them. But there is extraordinarily little formal control to define exactly what any given topic means or to ensure that specific topics are taught in the same way. Business courses, for example, can vary greatly from teacher to teacher. Similarly, what actually constitutes sixth-grade mathematics can show remarkable variation from classroom to classroom. Yet, despite the vacuity in specified content, elaborate rules make sure that each elementary school has something called *a sixth-grade,* and that this sixth-grade contains instruction in something called *sixth-grade mathematics.*

School Classifications. Finally, students, teachers, and topics are assembled into formal units by an elaborate and precise set of rules. Such units are then assigned to funds, space, and materials. The expected location of each teacher and student is recorded in detail as are the topics they will cover, and missing teachers or students are promptly recorded.

The assembly of teachers, students, and topics into classrooms creates the larger institutional classification called *school,* and although little attention may be focused on what actually goes on in these units, detailed records are kept by districts, local and state boards of education, and accrediting agencies that certify their existence as valid schools of a particular class (for instance, elementary schools or colleges). So, for example, elaborate lists of state "high schools" are kept, even though one may stress college-level work while another provides only very rudimentary instruction.

The internal and external emphasis on the formal categorical status of schools and their elements may seem at first to be a misdirected obsession. But in many ways the meaning of schooling in modern society seems to be captured by these definitions and categories. Without such general understandings, the educational system would not receive the massive social support that it does. Without such social classifications and understandings, parents and the state would not legitimately extend broad powers over children to random adult strangers. What sensible person would devote years and money to disorganized (and not demonstrably useful) study without the understanding that this is "college" or "economics"? These shared ideas of teacher, student, topic, and school—and some implicit assumptions about what will or will not go on—give schooling its social plausibility.

Conventional Explanations of the Organization of Schools

Educational organizations are formed to instruct and socialize. Their specific activity in these two areas, however, seems to be diffusely controlled, in good part outside formal organizational controls. On the other hand, the ritual classifications of schools are precisely specified, closely inspected, and tightly controlled. Our purpose here is to discuss explanations that are often used to account for this pattern of control in educational organizations. The conventional dynamic in these accounts begins with the question of what is wrong with schools and then goes on to a consideration of how it can be changed. Our problem, however, is to account for this situation, not to decry it. By way of clarification, we consider the following conventional accounts.

The Reform Perspective. Reformers abound in the world of education. They paint a picture of schools as archaic, as organizations not yet rationalized by proper output measures, evaluation systems and control structures, and therefore as systems that rely mainly on traditional types of authority among students, teachers, and school administrators. Reformers imagine that rationalized control and accounting measures can drive out less "modern" mechanisms of control once a few recalcitrant and reactionary groups are eliminated.

The difficulty with the reform view is its faith in the inevitable progression toward rationalization. This idea is not new. In many ways, it characterizes Horace Mann's ideas, and it certainly describes the perspective of the educational reformers of the late nineteenth century (for example, see Cubberly 1916). The "new" organizational forms advocated at that time were to bring measurement, evaluation, and organizational control to instruction (Tyack 1974). The guiding image was that of the factory, with its emphasis on organizationally controlled design and production. But a good case can be made that there is now less organizational control and evaluation of instruction than there was in the nineteenth century, before all the reforms (Tyack 1974).

One cannot keep on asserting that the educational system is archaic, a passive anachronism itching for reform, when it seems to systematically eliminate innovations that bring inspection, evaluation, coordination, and control over institutional activities (Callahan 1962). In any event, the view that education is weakly controlled because it lacks output measures is misdirected. Schools use elaborate tests to evaluate pupils and to shape the course of their present and future lives. But the same data are almost never aggregated and used to evaluate the performance of teachers, schools, or school systems. (Some data of this kind are made available for school and district evaluation in California, but only under the pressure of the state legislature, not the local school system.)

One other feature of the reform perspective deserves special note. Reformers tend to view American education as fragile, inept, disorganized, and on the edge of chaos and dissolution. Schools are seen to be a poor state of organizational "health" (Miles 1975). This is an astonishing description of a network of organizations that has grown rapidly for many decades, that obtains huge economic resources in a stable way year after year, that is protected from failure by laws that make its use compulsory, that is constantly shown by surveys to have the confidence and support of its constituency (Acland 1975), and that is known to have high levels of job satisfaction among its participants (Meyer et al. 1971). Reformers may wish educational organizations were on their last legs, but all the "crises" reformers have declared have subsided quickly, and the system has remained stable.

The Decentralist Stance. Another view has it that educational organizations are oligarchic structures, headed by educational administrators and the elites that control them. In this view, educators are entrenched bureaucrats, resisting local community control and evaluation and building up their status rights and immunities in the system. This system resists accountability, the argument goes, and should be decentralized to the local level where the lay public can be involved in educational decision making (for example, see Fantini and Gittell 1973; Rogers 1968).

This view does not easily come into accord with the following facts. First, the American educational system has enormous popular support. This is inconsistent with the view that the system is controlled by a resistent and entrenched bureaucracy, unless one argues that the entire populace is afflicted with false consciousness in the matter. Second, even if the bureaucrats who presumably control the educational system were uninterested in effective education and were only seeking self-aggrandizement, why would they not inspect and control teachers more carefully to make sure that they conform to elite or bureaucratic interests?

In fact, the main difficulty with the decentralist's position is that it ignores the fact that local control of education in America is not in conflict with the organizational structures we have described. We will later argue that the local community obtains important benefits from the present dearth of systematic inspection and evaluation and that accountability could only arise from more, not less, centralization of educational power.

The Professionalization of Teaching. It is possible to argue that educational instruction is not controlled by central administrators but rather by the teaching profession. In this view, schools are loosely coupled simply because they provide a setting in which professional teachers, thoroughly socialized to use the expert techniques of their discipline, ply their trade. Educational administrators merely form a sort of holding company to provide and maintain the facilities in which teachers work, in much the same way as hospital administrators service doctors.

This view is not seriously maintained in most quarters. Teachers themselves turn out not to believe this myth of professionalism. Dornbusch and Scott (1975) show that teachers report that their training has little to do with their ability to perform effectively (in sharp contrast to nurses, for example). And in the San Francisco Bay Area survey reported earlier (Cohen et al. 1976), of the elementary teachers interviewed, 77 percent agreed that the personality characteristics of the teacher were more important for success in teaching than any particular knowledge or professional skills a teacher might possess.

Moreover, the school is not organized to delegate all the responsibilities for instruction to teachers. Thus, a school is unlike a hospital, where doctors, not administrators, control task activities. In schools, there is a more generalized locus of responsibility for planning and coordinating instructional matters. Centralized policies about what teachers should teach, how they should teach, and what materials they should use to teach are often developed jointly by teachers, administrators, and sometimes parents.

Teachers, then, *appear* to be professionals because they have much discretion within a loosely coupled system. The myth of teacher professionalism is an interesting and important feature of the American educational system. It does not, however, provide an explanation for the structure of educational organizations.

Organization Theory. The most conventional idea in organizations research that could be used to explain the lack of central control over instructional activities is the idea of "goal displacement": the notion that organizations shift their control systems to focus on those outputs for which they are most accountable—in this case, the ritual classifications— and not on those which they were originally intended to maximize. This idea is, in large measure, true. But it does not go far enough. First, while both the school and the environment have evolved an elaborate scheme to control ritual classifications, the idea of goal displacement does not explain why a tacit agreement not to create an accounting scheme based on the "actual effectiveness" of these classifications evolved.

Second, in one sense goals may not be far displaced after all. We should not lose sight of the fact that a very high proportion of the resources schools receive *is* devoted to instructional activity. Teachers' salaries are a major expenditure item, as are instructional materials. Administrators and other district staff make up a very small proportion of the total employees of most school districts. The resources, in other words, continue to be focused on the instructional aspects of the system, even though achievement of instructional goals is not measured.

This fact suggests that educational organizations direct resources to their main goals but do not carefully control or evaluate the consequences of these allocations. It is as if society allocates large sums of money and large numbers of children to the schools and the schools in turn allocate these funds and children to a relatively uncontrolled and uninspected classroom. All of this seems to be done in a great act of ritual faith.

As we will see, this depiction is not inappropriate. Further, the parties involved may not be as foolish as they seem in conventional depictions of education. It is unfortunately true that most depictions of the educational system see its organizational administrators as somehow misdirected. The reformers see backwardness everywhere the magic of rationalization does not reach. The decentralists see self-aggrandizement. The myth of professionalism depicts administrators as factotums who submit to professional authority. And organization theorists see administrators who have lost sight of their original purposes. It may make sense, however, to consider another view of educational organization, one in which the participants are sensible people running a highly successful enterprise.

The Organization of Schooling: Another Interpretation

The explanation developed here begins with the context in which educational organizations are presently found. Modern education today takes place in large-scale, public bureaucracies. The rise of this kind of educational system is closely related to the worldwide trend of national development. The first step in our argument, therefore, is to relate national development to the organization of education.

The Growth of Corporate Schooling. From the preceding characterizations, we know that bureaucratic schooling has not arisen from a need to coordinate and standardize instruction, for this is precisely what modern American educational organizations do not do. Nor do these bureaucratic organizations merely fund and administer an exchange between educational professionals and families needing educational services. Educational bureaucracies present themselves not as units servicing education but as organizations that embody educational purposes in their collective structure. A theory of their emergence and dominance should explain why these bureaucracies assume jurisdiction over educational instruction.

The most plausible explanation is that modern schools produce education for *society,* not for individuals or families. In the nineteenth and twentieth centuries, national societies everywhere took over the function of defining and managing the socialization of their citizen personnel (Coombs 1968; Meyer and Rubinson 1975; Ramirez 1974). In national societies, education is both a right and a duty of citizenship (Bendix 1964). It also becomes an important way of gaining status and respect (for example, see Blau and Duncan 1967). For reasons that do not require elaborate discussion here, education becomes the central agency defining personnel—both citizen and elite—for the modern state and economy.

Since World War II, the trend toward corporate control of education has intensified. As nation-states have consolidated their control over a growing number of elements of social life, they have established educational systems to incorporate citizens into the political, economic, and status order of society. This incorporation is managed by a large public bureaucracy that uniformly extends its standardization and authority through all localities. Thus, educational organizations have come to be increasingly structured by centers of political authority (Meyer and Rubinson 1975).

Bailyn (1960), Field (1972), Katz (1968), and Tyack (1974) describe the steps of this process in pretwentieth-century American history. First local, and later national, elites became concerned with the social control of peripheral citizen groups—who need control precisely because they *are* citizens. At first, the rural New Englanders who escaped from the control of clergy and town community (Bailyn 1960), then the Irish immigrants (Field 1972; Katz 1958), and finally the great waves of nineteenth-century immigration (Tyack 1974) created the pressures to control, standardize, and coordinate the educational system. As these steps progressed, the impetus to organize schooling on a large scale—to certify and classify pupils, to certify teachers, to accredit schools, and to control formal curriculum—gained force.

The growth of corporate control of education has major implications for educational organizations. As citizen personnel are increasingly sorted and allocated to positions in the social structure on the basis of classified or certified educational properties, the ritual classifications of education—type of student, topic, teacher, or school—come to have substantial value in what might be called the societal identity "market." A workable identity market presupposes a standardized, trustworthy currency of social typifications that is free from local anomalies. Uniform categories of instruction are therefore developed, and there is a detailed elaboration of the standardized and certified properties comprising an educational identity.

The result of this social expansion of education is a basic change in social structure. Education comes to consist, not of a series of private arrangements between teachers and students, but rather of a set of standardized public credentials used to incorporate citizen personnel into society. Society and its stratification system come to be composed of a series of typifications having educational meaning—ordinary citizens are presumed to have basic literacy. Strata above ordinary citizens are composed of high school and college students. The upper levels contain credentialed professionals, such as doctors and lawyers.

Thus, as societies and nation-states use education to define their basic categories of personnel, a large-scale educational bureaucracy emerges to standardize and manage the production of these categories. The credentials that give individuals status and membership in the wider collectivity must come under collective control. Such collective control would not be necessary if instruction were conceived of as a merely private matter between individuals and teachers. But, as educational organizations emerge as the credentialing agency of modern society and as modern citizens see their educational and corporate identities linked—that is, as education becomes the theory of personnel in modern society—it is consequently standardized and controlled.

Society thus becomes "schooled" (Illich 1971). Education comes to be understood by corporate actors according to the *schooling rule:* Education is a certified teacher teaching a standardized curricular topic to a registered student in an accredited school. The nature of schooling is thus socially defined by reference to a set of standardized categories the legitimacy of which is publicly shared. As the categories and credentials of schooling gain importance in allocation and membership processes, the public comes to expect that they will be controlled and standardized. The large-scale public bureaucracy created to achieve this standardization is now normatively constrained by the expectations of the schooling rule. To a large degree, then, education is coordinated by shared social understanding that define the roles, topics, and contents of educational organizations.

The Organizational Management of Standardized Classifications. The political consolidation of society and the importance of education for the allocation of people to positions in the economic and stratification system explain the rise of large-scale educational bureaucracies. These processes also explain why educational organizations focus so tightly on the ritual classifications of education. Educational organizations are created to produce schooling for corporate society. They create standard types of graduates from standard categories of pupils using standard types of teachers and topics. As their purposes and structures are defined and institutionalized in the rules, norms, and ideologies of the wider society, the legitimacy of schools and their ability to mobilize resources depend on maintaining congruence between their structure and these socially shared categorical understandings of education (Dowling and Pfeffer 1975; Meyer and Rowan 1977; Parsons 1956).

Consider this matter from the viewpoint of any rational college president or school superintendent. The whole school will dissolve in conflict and illegitimacy if the internal and external understanding of its accredited status is in doubt; If it has too few Ph.D.'s or properly credentialed teachers on its faculty, it may face reputational, accreditational, or even legal problems. If it has one too many "economics" courses and one too few "history" courses (leave aside their actual content), similar disasters may occur as the school falls short of externally imposed accrediting standards. No matter what they have learned, graduates may have difficulty finding jobs. No matter what the school teaches, it may not be capable of recruiting funds or teachers. Thus, the creation of institutionalized rules defining and standardizing education creates a system in which schools come to be somewhat at the mercy of the ritual classifications. Failure to incorporate certified personnel or to organize instruction around the topics outlined in accreditation rules can bring conflict and illegitimacy.

At the same time, the creation of institutionalized rules provides educational organizations with enormous resources. First, the credentials, classifications, and categories of schooling constitute a language that facilitates exchange between school and society. Social agencies often provide local schools with "categorical funding" to support the instruction of culturally disadvantaged or educationally handicapped students or to support programs in bilingual or vocational education. Second, schools can exploit the system of credentials and classifications in order to gain prestige. They can carefully attend to the social evaluations of worth given to particular ritual classifications and can maximize their honorific worth by hiring prestigious faculty, by incorporating programs that are publicly defined as "innovative," or by upgrading their status from junior college to four-year college. Finally, the school relies on the ritual classifications to provide order. Social actors derive their identities from the socially defined categories of education and become committed to upholding these identities within the context of their school activities. To the degree that actors take on the obligation to be "alive to the system, to be properly oriented and aligned in it" (Goffman 1967), the whole educational system retains its plausibility.

In modern society, then, educational organizations have good reason to tightly control properties defined by the wider social order. By incorporating externally defined types of instruction, teachers, and students into their formal structure, schools avoid illegitimacy and discreditation. At the same time, they gain important benefits. In schools using socially agreed-on classifications, participants become committed to the organization. This is especially true when these classifications have high prestige (McCall and Simmons 1966). And, by labeling students or instructional programs so that they conform to institutionally supported programs, schools obtain financial resources. In short, the rewards for attending to external understandings are an increased ability to mobilize societal resources for organizational purposes.

The Avoidance of Evaluation and Inspection. We have explained why schools attend to ritual classifications, but we have not explained why they do not attend (as organizations) to instruction. There are two ways that instructional activities can be controlled in modern education bureaucracies. First, many of the properties of educational identities may be certified in terms of examinations. Second, many of the ritual classifications involve a reorganization of educational activity, and some school systems organize an inspection system to make sure these implications are carried through. Thus, two basic kinds of instructional controls are available to educational organizations—the certification of status by testing, and/or the inspection of instructional activity to ensure conformity to rules.

Our explanation of the loose control of instruction in United States school systems must in part focus on specific features of United States society, since most other societies have educational bureaucracies that employ one or both forms of instructional control. In many other nations, for example, assignment to a classification such as student, graduate, or teacher is determined by various tests, most often controlled by national ministries of education. Also, national inspectors are often employed to attempt to make sure that teachers and schools conform to national standards of practice, regardless of the educational outcome. Thus, in most societies the state, through a ministry of education, controls systems of inspection or examination that manage the ritual categories of education by controlling either output or instructional procedure (Ramirez 1974; Rubinson 1974).

In American society, tests are used in profusion. However, most of these tests are neither national nor organizational but, rather, are devices of the individual teacher. The results seldom leave the classroom and are rarely used to measure instructional output. In the United States, the most common national tests that attempt to standardize local output differences—the Scholastic Aptitude Test (SAT) and the Graduate Record Examination (GRE)—are creatures of private organization. Further, only the New York State Board of Regents examination approximates (and at that in a pale way) an attempt to standardize curriculum throughout a policial unit by using an examination system.

The apparent explanation for this lack of central control of instruction in American education is the decentralization of the system. Schools are in large part locally controlled and locally funded. While higher levels of authority in state and federal bureaucracies have made many attempts to impose evaluative standards on the educational system, the pressures of continued localism defeat them; category systems that delegate certification or evaluation rights to the schools themselves are retained. The reason for this is clear. A national evaluation system would define almost all the children in some communities as successes and almost all those in others as failures. This could work in a nationally controlled system, but it is much too dangerous in a system that depends on legitimating itself in and obtaining resources from local populations. Why, for instance, should the state of Mississippi join in a national credentialing system that might define a great proportion of its schools and graduates as failures? It is safer to adapt the substantive standards of what constitutes, say, a high school graduate to local circumstances and to specify in state laws only categories at some remove from substantive competence.

There is yet another way in which the institutional pattern of localism reduces organizational controls over instruction. In the United States, the legitimacy of local control in some measure deprofessionalizes school administrators at all levels (in contrast to European models). They do not carry with them the authority of the central, national, professional, and bureaucratic structures and the elaborate ideological backing such authority brings with it. American administrators must compromise and must further lose purely professional authority by acknowledging their compromised role. They do not have tenure, and their survival is dependent on laypersons in the community, not on professionals. Their educational authority of office is, therefore, lower than that of their European counterparts, especially in areas dealing with central educational matters such as instruction and curriculum. This situation is precisely analogous to the "red" versus "expert" conflict found in many organizations in communist societies, where organizational managers must often act contrary to their expert opinion in order to follow the party line. The profusion of local pressures in American society turns school administrators into "reds" as it were.

The Organizational Response:
Decoupling and the Logic of Confidence

Decoupling. American educational organizations are in business to maintain a "schooling rule" institutionalized in society. This rule specifies a series of ritual categories—teachers, students, topics, and schools—that define education. Elaborate organizational controls ensure that these categories have been incorporated into the organization. But the ritual categories themselves and the system of inspection and control are formulated to avoid inspecting the actual instructional activities and outcomes of schooling. That is, a school's formal structure (its ritual classifications) is "decoupled" from technical activities and outcomes.

External features of American education, especially the local and pluralistic basis of control, help to account for this pattern. But there are more elaborate internal processes involved as well. From the viewpoint of an administrator, maintaining the credibility of his or her school and the validity of its ritual classifications is crucial to the school's success. With the confidence of the state bureaucracy, the federal government, the community, the profession, the pupils and their families, and the teachers themselves, the legitimacy of the school as a social reality can be maintained. However, if these groups decide that a school's ritual classifications are a "fraud," everything comes apart.

There are several ways in which the decoupling of structures from activities and outcomes maintains the legitimacy of educational organizations. Consider some reasons why an American administrator would avoid closely inspecting the internal processes of the school.

First, the avoidance of close inspection, especially when accompanied by elaborate displays of confidence and trust, can increase the commitments of internal participants. The agreement of teachers to participate actively in the organized social reality of the ritual classifications of education is crucial, and an administator can trade off the matter of conformity to the details of instruction and achievement in order to obtain teachers' complicity and satisfaction. By agreeing that teachers have instructional competence and by visibly not inspecting instructional activities, an administrator shifts maximal social responsibility for upholding the rituals of instruction to the teachers. The myth of teacher professionalism and the autonomy associated with it, for example, function to increase the commitments of teachers.

A second reason for avoiding close inspection and evaluation arises from the fact that a good deal of the value of education has little to do with the efficiency of instructional activities. If education is viewed as a ceremonial enactment of the rituals of schooling, the quality of schooling can be seen to lie in its *costs:* spectacular buildings, expensive teachers in excessive number (a low student-teacher ratio), and elaborate and expensive topics (French for first-graders, or nuclear physics). To the state, the accrediting agencies, the community, and the participants themselves, costs of these kinds index the quality and meaning of a school. It therefore makes little sense to view a school as if it were producing instructional outcomes in an economic marketplace, since an economizing perspective would treat many of the critical features of a school as costly waste, as liabilities rather than assets. It is enormously damaging for a school to view the categories that validate it, as well as the cost of their upkeep and prestige, as liabilities. The ritual of schooling is evaluated according to a logic in which quality and costs are equivocal. Expenditures per student or the number of books in the library are among common indices of educational quality, even though maximizing these indices may require a studied inattention to an economizing logic. The wise administrator will call attention to the elaborate and expensive structure of ritual classifications his school has, not to the amount of learning achieved per dollar.

Third, decoupling protects the ritual classification scheme from uncertainties arising in the technical core. In education, it is quite common that rules of practice institutionalized at state and federal levels create technical uncertainty at the local level. State-mandated curricula may be too advanced for the students at hand. And innovative state and federal programs often need to be adapted to the specific circumstances unique to the local school. Measuring what pupils actually learn in these programs or what teachers are actually teaching introduces unnecessary uncertainty, increases coordinative costs and creates doubts about the effectiveness of the status structure of the school and the categorical rules that define appropriate education.

Fourth, decoupling allows schools to adapt to inconsistent and conflicting institutionalized rules. Schools, of necessity, are plural organizations adapted to plural environments (Udy 1971). This is especially true of American schools, with their welter of external pressure. One way to manage the uncertainty, conflict, and inconsistency created by this pluralistic situation is to buffer units from each other. Udy, in fact, sees this as a major explanation for the differentiation of modern organizations into specialized components. When differentiation is accompanied by isolation and autonomy of subunits rather than by interdependence and coordination, jurisdictional disputes among categories of professionals or incompatibilities among inconsistent programs are avoided. For example, in schools, the work of a large number of specialists—vocational educators, speech therapists, reading specialists—is organized separately and buffered from the usual classroom work.

Our point is this: By decoupling formal structures from activities, uncertainty about the effectiveness of the ritual categories is reduced. When the behavior of teachers and students is uninspected or located in isolated classrooms, the state, the community, and administrators are presented with little evidence of ineffectiveness, conflict, or inconsistency. And the teacher and student are free to work out the practicalities of their own unique relationship little disturbed by the larger social interpretation of which activity is appropriate to a given category. Further, in a pluralistic setting the number of ritual classifications institutionalized in the environment is large, and there are frequent additions and subtractions. By decoupling ritual subunits from one another, the school is able to incorporate potentially inconsistent ritual elements and to recruit support from a larger and more diverse set of constituencies.

By minimizing the resources devoted to coordination and control, the school furthers its ability to increase the ceremonial worth of its ritual categories. This strategy also cuts down the costs involved in implementing new categories and maximizes their chance of success. New programs or specialists need not be integrated into the structure; they merely need to be segmentally added to the organization. Further, new categories need not even imply a substantial reorganization of activity, as the activities of particular ritual actors and programs remain uninspected. The decoupling of the internal structure of education is therefore a successful strategy for maintaining support in a pluralistic environment.

The Logic of Confidence. The classifications of education, however, are not rules to be cynically manipulated. They are the sacred rituals that give meaning to the whole enterprise, both internally and externally. These categories are understood everywhere to *index* education. They are not understood to *be* education, but they are also not understood simply to be alienating bureaucratic constraints. So the decoupling that is characteristic of school systems must be carried out by all participants in the utmost good faith.

Interaction in school systems, therefore, is characterized both by the assumption of good faith and the actualities of decoupling. This is *the logic of confidence:* Parties bring to each other the taken-for-granted, good-faith assumption that the other is, in fact, carrying out his or her defined activity. The community and the board have confidence in the superintendent, who has confidence in the principal, who has confidence in the teachers. None of these people can say what the other does or produces, but the plausibility of their activity requires that they have confidence in each other.

The logic of confidence is what Goffman (1967) calls "face work"—the process of maintaining the other's face or identity and thus of maintaining the plausibility and legitimacy of the organization itself. Face work avoids embarrassing incidents and preserves the organization from the disruption of an implausible performance by any actor. Goffman (1967, pp. 12–18) discusses three dimensions of this face-saving procedure: *avoidance, discretion,* and *overlooking.* Decoupling promotes each of these dimensions. Avoidance is maximized when the various clusters of identities are buffered from each other, when the organization is segmentalized, and when interaction across units is minimized (as by the self-contained classroom). Discretion is maximized when inspection and control are minimized or when participants are cloaked with "professional" authority. Finally, participants often resort to overlooking embarrassing incidents or to labeling them as deviant, as characteristic of particular individuals, and therefore as nonthreatening to the integrity of the ritual classification scheme.

It must be stressed that face work and the logic of confidence are not merely personal orientations but are also institutional in character. For instance, a state creates a rule that something called "history" must be taught in high schools. This demand is not inspected or examined by organizational procedures but is controlled through confidence in teachers. Each teacher of history has been credentialed. There is an incredible sequence of confidences here, with faces being maintained up and down the line: The state has confidence in the district, the district in the school, and the school in the teacher. The teacher is deserving of confidence because an accrediting agency accredited the teacher's college. The accrediting agency did not, of course, inspect the instruction at the college but relied on the certification of its teachers, having confidence in the universities which the teachers attended. The accrediting agency also has confidence in the organization of the college—its administrators and departments. These people, in turn, had confidence in their teachers, which enabled them to label certain courses as *history* without inspecting them. The chain goes on and on. Nowhere (except in the concealed relation between teacher and pupil) is there any inspection. Each link is a matter of multiple exchanges of confidence.

The most visible aspect of the logic of confidence in the educational system is the myth of teacher professionalism. Even in higher education—where teachers typically have no professional training for teaching—the myth is maintained. It serves to legitimate the confidence the system places in its teachers and to provide an explanation of why this confidence is justified. This explains one of the most puzzling features of educational professionalism—why the professional status of teachers rises dramatically with the creation of an educational bureaucracy. It is conventional to assume that professionalism and bureaucracy are at odds, although the evidence rarely supports this view (Corwin 1970). In fact, even though the ideology supporting the creation of large American educational bureaucracies argued for close control, evaluation, and inspection of teachers, it seems clear that these bureaucracies greatly lowered the amount of such control (Tyack 1974). Prebureaucratic teachers were often under direct inspection and control of the community that hired them. The bureaucracy, justified on the grounds that it would assume responsibility for inspection and control of instruction, however, almost immediately began to inspect and control only the superficial and categorical aspects of teachers. To account for this lack of specific inspection and control of instruction, the myth of professionalism arose very early, despite the original intentions of the founders. Our argument—that professionalism serves the requirements of confidence and good faith—explains this growth: The myth of teacher professionalism helps to justify the confidence placed in teachers and to legitimate the buffering of uncertainty in the performance of pupils and teachers in educational organizations.

Overview of the Argument. With the growth of corporate society, especially the growth of nation-states, education comes into exchange with society. Schooling—the bureaucratic standardization of ritual classifications—emerges and becomes the dominant form of educational organization. Schools become organized in relation to these ritual categories in order to gain support and legitimacy. In America, the local and pluralistic control of schools causes these classifications to have little impact on the actual instructional activities of local schools. Thus the official classifications of education, although enforced in public respects, are decoupled from actual activity and can contain a good deal of internal inconsistency without harm. As a result, American schools in practice contain multiple realities, each organized with respect to different internal or exogenous pressures. These multiple realities conflict so little because they are buffered from each other by the logic of confidence that runs through the system.

In this fashion, educational organizations have enjoyed enormous success and have managed to satisfy an extraordinary range of external and internal constituents. The standardized categories of American society and its stratification system are maintained, while the practical desires of local community constituents and the wishes of teachers, who are highly satisfied with their jobs, are also catered to. As new constituents rise up and make new demands, these pressures can be accommodated within certain parts of the system with minimal impact on other parts. A great deal of adaptation and change can occur without disrupting actual activity. And, conversely, the activities of teachers and pupils can change a good deal, even though the abstract categories have remained constant.

Implications for Research and Theory

The arguments we have discussed have many implications for research on educational organizations. We see schools (and other organizations) as vitally—and in complex ways—affected by their institutional environments. Much more research is needed, carefully examining such institutional variations—among societies or among institutions within societies—and their organizational impact.

Propositions Comparing Societies. First, the formal structure of educational organizations tends to come into correspondence with environmental categories. These ritual categories, further, tend to be linked to the nation-state, implying that formal education structure ought to vary more between societies than within them. Second, educational content and instruction is organizationally most loosely coupled in societies with pluralistic systems of control, such as the United States, and is more tightly controlled in countries with centralized systems. Further, ambiguities and vacuities in the educational languages specifying the meaning and implications of the ritual elements of educational organization should be found to be greatest in pluralistic systems. Third, the more education is a national institution of central importance, the more loosely coupled its internal structure and the more control rests on the logics of confidence and of professionalization.

Propositions Comparing Education with Other Institutions. First, instructional work in institutionalized educational systems is less closely inspected or coordinated than similar work in other institutions such as businesses or armies. Second, educational structures are more responsive to even inconsistent environmental pressures than organizations in other institutional settings. In part, this is because they are buffered from their own internal technical work activity. This situation permits more internal and external constituent groups to perceive that they have power in education organizations than in other organizations.

Propositions Comparing Educational Organizations. First, the formal structure of educational organizations responds to environmental (or societal) categories. It varies less in response to variations in the actual characteristics of clienteles or of problems of instruction. Similarly, changes in environmental rules defining education produce more rapid formal structural changes than do changes in the content or methods of instruction. Second, educational organizations are internally coordinated and legitimated by their environmental categories, not primarily by their own technical activity or instructional output. Variations in their success at maintaining correspondence with environmental rules predict the success, survival, and stability of educational organizations more than do variations in their institutional effectiveness. Third, loosely coupled educational organizations structurally respond more effectively to environmental pressures and changes than do tightly coupled organizations. Instruction adapts more quickly in such organizations to the informal pressures of teachers and parents, while structures respond more quickly to environmental institutional categories.

Propositions Comparing Internal Components of Organization. First, in educational organizations, feedback concerning the work and output of teachers and schools tends to be eliminated, even if it happens to exist. Participants employ logic of confidence, and overlook observations of actual work and outcomes. Feedback on the categorical status of teachers, schools, students, and programs tends to be retained.

Second, educational organizations respond to external institutional pressures with programmatic or categorical change, minimizing the impact on instruction. They respond to variations in teacher or parent preference with activity change, but not necessarily with categorical change. Each part or level of the system responds relatively independently to its environment. Thus, the greatest part of organizationally planned innovation in instruction is never implemented, and the greatest part of instructional innovation is not organizationally planned.

Third, the loose coupling of instructional activity in educational organizations permits more internal and external constituent groups to perceive that they have power in this area than over other policy decisions.

Implications for Organization Theory. The arguments above have many implications for theory and research on organizations other than schools. Our arguments seem quite plausible in terms of the literature on school organizations, but some of them are sharply at odds with the theory of organizations (for a more detailed suggestion, see Meyer and Rowan 1977). Perhaps organization theory is imperfect. It seems unlikely that educational organizations are so extremely unusual. Indeed, a most fundamental observation in research on all sorts of organizations is that rules and behavior—the formal and the informal—are often dissociated or inconsistent. This is the same observation we have been making about schooling organizations, and it may be time to stop being surprised at it. The surprise arises not because the observations are novel but because researchers take too limited a view of formal organizations. They see formal structure as created to actually coordinate production in the case of market organizations and conformity in the case of political bureaucracy (see Thompson 1967; Scott 1975). And they are consequently surprised when formal structure and activity are loosely linked.

It is true that production requires some coordination, as political structure demands some conformity. But it is also true that the myth or social account of production and conformity is critical. Much of the value of what we purchase lies in intangibles. Much of the value of social control and order inheres in the faith that is generated. Put differently, organizations must have the *confidence* of their environments, not simply be in rational exchange with them. And those that have this confidence and legitimacy receive all sorts of social resources that provide for success and stability. That is, organizations must be legitimate, and they must contain legitimate accounts or explanations for their internal order and external products. *The formal structure of an organization is in good part a social myth and functions as a myth whatever its actual implementation.* In small part, it is a mythical account the organization attempts to institutionalize in society. In much greater part, the formal structure is taken over from the accounts already built into the environment. Incorporating the environmental myth of the organization's activities legitimates the organization both externally and internally (Dowling and Pfeffer 1975) and stabilizes it over and above the stability generated by its network of internal relations and production. Organizations integrate themselves by incorporating the wider institutional structures as their own.

Thus, if systematic safety problems are "discovered" by the environment, safety officers are invented: Their existence explains how the organization has "taken into account" safety problems. (Who actually deals with safety is another matter.) So also with pollution control, labor relations, public relations, advertising, affirmative action, or research and development. Some of these activities may, in a day-to-day sense, actually get done: Our point here is that incorporating them in the formal structure of the organization has the function of legitimating myths and that such myths may be created quite independently of the activities they index. All these units represent the formal incorporation by the organization of environmental definitions of activities that then become part of the firm's account. Incorporating them deflects criticism from internal coalitions. It also legitimates the organization externally: Banks lend money to *modern* firms. Role handles are provided: Other organizations have someone inside the firm "with whom they can deal." The legal system may require such forms of accountability. Firms often incorporate external values in a very explicit way by attaching to units and products "shadow prices" derived not from any production function but from market prices external to the firm.

The formal structure of an organization incorporates (and in some respects *is*) an environmental ideology or theory of the organization's activity. As the environmental ideology changes, so does the formal structure. No wonder the formal structure may be poorly adapted to the actual ongoing activity, which has to coordinate internal exigencies of its own.

A critical aspect of modern structure arises from the rationality of modern society and of organizations as myths. Formal organizational structures represent more than mere theories of activity: They must represent *rational, functional* theories. The structural account they present to society must give every appearance of rationality. Much of the irrationality of life in modern organizations arises because the organization itself must maintain a rational corporate persona: We must find planners and economists who will waste their time legitimating plans we have already made, accounts to justify our prices, and human relations professionals to deflect blame from our conflicts. Life in modern organizations is a constant interplay between the activities that we need to carry on and the organizational accounts we need to give.

This discussion generates several implications for organization theory. First, formal organizational structure reflects and incorporates prevailing environmental theories and categories, often without altering activity. These environmental rules constitute taken-for-granted understandings in the organization. Organizational actors are constantly in the business of managing categories abstracted directly from environmental theories.

Second, organizational structure has two faces: It conforms to environmental categories and categorical logics, and it classifies and controls activity. Organizational actors must take into account both what they are doing and the appearance of what they are doing.

Third, to accommodate both appearance and reality, organizational structure must always be partly decoupled from actual activity. Special managers may arise to adjudicate relationships between the categories of the formal structure and actual activities. Personnel officers classify persons and jobs into categories, registrars and admitting physicians institutionalize official diagnoses, accountants organize activity into budgets and budget categories, and so on. Linking the organization as a formal structure with the organization as a network of activities is a major task, and it tends to introduce inconsistencies and anomalies into both domains.

This view of organizations as constituted and coordinated at every point by taken-for-granted environmental understandings is considerably different from most prevailing views. Both "closed-systems" and "open-systems" views of organizations tend to see them as encountering the environment at their *boundaries.* We see the structure of an organization as derived from and legitimated by the environment. In this view, organizations begin to lose their status as internally interdependent systems and come to be seen as dramatic reflections of—dependent subunits within—the wider institutional environment.

References

Acland, H. "Parents Love Schools?" *Interchange* 6 (April 1975).

Bailyn, B. *Education in the Forming of American Society*. Chapel Hill: University of North Carolina Press, 1960.

Bendix, R. *Nationbuilding and Citizenship*. New York: John Wiley, 1964.

Bidwell, C. "The School as a Formal Organization." In *Handbook of Organizations*, edited by James G. March. Chicago: Rand McNally, 1965.

Blau, P.M., and O.D. Duncan. *The American Occupational Structure*. New York: John Wiley, 1967.

Callahan, R.E. *Education and the Cult of Efficiency*. Chicago: University of Chicago Press, 1962.

Cohen, E.G., T.E. Deal, J.W. Meyer, and W.R. Scott. "Organization and Instruction in Elementary Schools." Technical Report No. 50. Stanford, Calif.: Stanford Center for Research and Development in Teaching, 1976.

Coombs, P.H. *The World Educational Crisis*. New York: Oxford University Press, 1968.

Corwin, R.G. *Militant Professionalism*. New York: Appleton, 1970.

Cubberly, E.P. *Public School Administration*. Boston: Houghton Mifflin, 1916.

Deal, T.E., J.W. Meyer, and W.R. Scott. "Organizational Influences on Educational Innovation." In *Managing Change in Educational Organizations*, edited by J. Victor Baldridge and Terrence M. Deal. Berkeley: McCutchan, 1975.

Dornbusch, S., and W.R. Scott. *Evaluation and the Exercise of Authority*. San Francisco: Jossey-Bass, 1975.

Dowling, J., and J. Pfeffer. "Organizational Legitimacy: Social Values and Organizational Behavior." *Pacific Sociological Review* 18 (January 1975): 122-136.

Dreeben, R. "The School as a Workplace." In *Second Handbook of Research on Teaching*, edited by R.W. Travers. Chicago: Rand McNally, 1973.

Fantini, M. and M. Gitell. *Decentralization: Achieving Reform*. New York: Praeger, 1973.

Field, A. "Educational Reform and Manufacturing Development, Massachusetts 1837 to 1865." Ph.D. dissertation, University of California, Berkeley, 1972.

Goffman, E. *Interaction Ritual*. Garden City, N.Y.: Doubleday Anchor Books, 1967.

Hobbs, N. *Issues in the Classification of Children*. San Francisco: Jossey-Bass, 1975.

Holt, J.C. *How Children Fail*. New York: Pitman, 1964.

Illich, I. *Deschooling Society*. New York: Harper & Row, 1971.

Katz, M. *The Irony of Early School Reform*. Boston: Beacon Press, 1968.

Lortie, D. *Schoolteacher: A Sociological Study*. Chicago: University of Chicago Press, 1975.

March, J.G., and J.P. Olsen. *Ambiguity and Choice in Organizations.* Bergen, Norway: Universitets forlaget, 1976.

McCall, G.J., and J.L. Simmons. *Identities and Interactions.* New York: Free Press, 1966.

Meyer, J. W., E.G. Cohen, F.A. Brunetti, S.R. Molnar, and E.L. Salmons. "The Impact of the Open Space School Upon Teacher Influence and Autonomy: The Effects of an Organizational Innovation." Technical Report No. 21. Stanford, Calif.: Stanford Center for Research and Development in Teaching, 1971.

Meyer, J.W., and B. Rowan. "Institutionalized Organizations: Formal Structure as Myth and Ceremony." *American Journal of Sociology,* 1977.

Meyer, J.W., and R. Rubinson. "Education and Political Development." In *Review of Research in Education,* 1975.

Miles, M.B. "Planned Change and Organizational Health." In J. Victor Baldridge and Terrence E. Deal, *Managing Change in Educational Organizations.* Berkeley: McCutchan, 1975.

Ouchi, W. and M.A. Maguire. "Organizational Control: Two Functions." *Administrative Science Quarterly* 20 (December 1975): 559-69.

Parsons, T. "Suggestions for a Sociological Approach to the Theory of Organization." *Administrative Science Quarterly* 1 (June 1956): 63-85.

Perrow, C. *Organizational Analysis: A Sociological View.* Belmont, Calif.: Wadsworth, 1970.

Ramirez, F.O. "Societal Corporateness and Status Conferral." Ph.D. dissertation, Stanford University, 1974.

Rogers, D. *110 Livingston Street.* New York: Random House, 1968.

Rubinson, R. "The Political Construction of Education." Ph.D. dissertation, Stanford University, 1974.

Scott, W. Richard. "Organizational Structure." In *Annual Review of Sociology,* edited by A. Inkeles, vol. 1. Palo Alto, Calif.: Annual Reviews, 1975.

Thompson, J.D. *Organization in Action.* New York: McGraw-Hill, 1967.

Tyack, D.B. *The One Best System.* Cambridge: Harvard University Press, 1974.

Udy, S.N., Jr. *Work in Traditional and Modern Society.* Englewood Cliffs, N.J.: Prentice-Hall, 1971.

Webster, W. "Organizational Resistance to Statewide Educational Reform." Paper prepared for Conference on Schools as Loosely Coupled Systems. Palo Alto, Calif., November 1976.

Weick, K.E. "Educational Organizations as Loosely Coupled Systems." *Administrative Science Quarterly* 21(March 1976): 1-19.

Woellner, E.H. *Requirements for Certification.* Chicago: University of Chicago Press, 1972.

PART II

Complications of Rational Approaches to Change

A year without the public—or the educational profession—asking for major changes in education would be a modern miracle. Decade after decade, education has provided a visible and convenient target for society's worries and problems. When the Russians launch a satellite, math and science instruction in the public schools is questioned and revamped. Watergate produces a heightened concern about the place of ethics in law schools. The discovery of drug abuse in schools creates drug education; the increasing occurrence of pregnancies and venereal disease in teenagers results in sex education. Elementary and secondary schools, colleges and universities, will be held accountable for most things that go wrong, for whatever the public doesn't understand, or for any problem that no one seems able to control. The pressures for educational change and reform are fundamental facts of life. The nature of education encourages public—local, state, or federal—involvement; and the characteristics of educational organizations provide an interesting arena for various dramas to play out. Whatever the issue of the day or decade, schools, colleges, and universities can expect part of the action to take place within their organizational boundaries.

In recent years, much attention has centered on making educational organizations look and behave differently, and many reforms and programs have been proposed: differentiated staffing, diagnostic prescriptive instruction, goals and objectives, evaluation, accountability, management by objectives, lay participation, and strategic planning. These are just a few examples of changes and reforms that educational organizations have struggled with recently. In a social context where people have lost confidence in instruction and have gained faith in the efficacy of "rational" systems, there is a deep-seated belief that facts, systematic procedures, computers, and involving diverse constituencies in problem solving and planning will make things better.

89

Educational organizations have tried to implement such changes and reforms, but their track record has not been very impressive. In our 1975 edition we noted that most changes at that time, which were desired at the local level and encouraged by external resources, moved from initial hopes to disappointment. But many theorists or practitioners still felt that ample resources, improved change technologies, and a greater awareness of organizational features that promote or sustain changes would make it easier for schools, colleges, or universities to implement changes more successfully in the late 1970s and throughout the 1980s. In this part, we try to show how the cycle of hope to disappointment, which we documented in the case studies of the 1975 volume, has continued despite many of the improvements in the knowledge and technology of organizational change.

Changes that schools and universities consider and try are often planned locally or conceived by state or federal policymakers. As these changes are carried from planning board to reality, planners are typically surprised at the discrepancy between what was intended and what occurs. Either the change permits all constituencies to get what they want—a watered-down version of the original scheme—or the change pits various groups against each other—the original scheme is obliterated in no-holds barred warfare. In either case, the results are meager. After the initial flurry, the organization is left much as it was originally, unless the process produces some unintended effects that reform the setting in novel and unexpected ways. Both fall outside the scope of successive official conceptions of organizational change.

Rational ideas have dominated the change agenda for the last two decades. Organizations are encouraged to change as a solution to a well-defined problem, and they are led to anticipate a smooth transition as new ideas are implemented—as long as sufficient planning has been done. Organizations are held accountable for what is accomplished as a primary measure of whether or not the change has succeeded.

The first two articles suggest why different strategies to change educational organizations have encountered similar problems and have shared a comparable fate. In Chapter 5 Arthur Wise argues that educational change experiences difficulties because policymakers ignore the existing rationality in schools or universities in an attempt to make them "hyperrational." The ideas underlying educational reform are influenced by a prevailing ideology that values systematic procedures and empirical justifications of satisfactory performance. As these reforms are mandated in schools, they become unmanageable and counterproductive in the sense that they overburden the system and undermine the natural logic that binds schools together and binds them to their constituencies.

Farrar, DeSanctis, and Cohen turn our attention to how reform policies are viewed at the local level (Chapter 6). The rational assumptions embedded in policy are replaced by the imagery of a lawn party. Various people attend lawn parties for different reasons and with diverse expectations, but the beauty of a lawn party is that usually everyone gets what he or she wants. The metaphor is consistent with existing case studies, many of which the authors themselves present, and it helps to capture the essence of why changes unfold in predictable ways in educational organizations.

The first case study (Chapter 7), Kirst's analysis of a statewide effort to introduce planning, programming, and budgeting systems (PPBS) into California schools, documents how that pioneering effort encountered unexpected difficulties and was gradually undermined by politics and compromise. The second case study focuses on ten rural school districts that used federal money in a bold attempt to bring about "comprehensive change" in the fabric of elementary and secondary schools. But as these ten districts planned and implemented their experimental schools' changes, the expected benefits paled in comparison to hidden costs—conflict, administrative turnover, and scars in local communities that would take a long time to heal.

The main message from these cases is clear and consistent. Whether change is encouraged or required by state or federal policy, difficulties quickly arise that divert the effort from the initial target, and the usual result is a reaffirmed or only slightly revised status quo.

In the last article of this part Baldridge gives a critical assessment of one current example of the rational approach—the "strategic-planning" model. Surprisingly, he says, the strategic-planning mentality shows real promise for overcoming some of the difficulties of typical rationalistic long-range planning. This article, then, suggests a somewhat more optimistic view of change in educational organizations than do the other articles in this part.

There are many other ways to view the origins, processes, and outcomes of organizational change. The case studies hint at some of these. Wise, in his critique of hyperrationalization, and Farrar and others, in the introduction of an intriguing metaphor, encourage us to entertain some new perspectives. Pressures for change and the time and energy devoted to organizational change are not going to disappear in the near future. But it is essential that administrators broaden their perspectives to consider new ideas about why organizations change, what happens in the process, and the deeper—and less rational—needs that change may serve, either for the organization or for society. The articles in this part set the stage for the ideas presented in the following parts.

5

Why Educational Policies Often Fail: The Hyperrationalization Hypothesis

Arthur Wise

The Bureaucratic Rationalization of Schools

American schools are now being subjected to a variety of influences which either presuppose a very rational view of schooling or are designed to induce a further rationalization of schooling. State legislatures, demanding accountability in schooling, are imposing managerial accounting schemes adopted from industry. State boards of education, concerned with the diffuse goals of schooling, endeavor to reduce the goals of education to basic skills. State courts, concerned with the ineffectiveness of schooling, require that schools become "thorough and efficient" as mandated by their state constitutions. Congress, concerned about the lack of articulation between education and work, calls for career education. The executive branch, responding to concerns for equality, promulgates affirmative action procedures and goals. The federal courts, concerned with arbitrariness toward individuals, demand that schools observe due process. Unions, unsatisfied with the protections afforded by civil service and tenure provisions, seek additional procedural safeguards through collective bargaining. Educational researchers, unable to discover the

Reprinted, by permission of the publisher and the author, from *Journal of Curriculum Studies* 9: 1 (1977): 43-57. An expanded version of the argument appears in Arthur E. Wise, *Legislated Learning: The Bureaucratization of the American Classroom* (Berkeley: University of California Press, 1979).

effects which schools have, create models of efficient and effective schooling. In common, these influences are designed to make school more rational.

But schools are already bureaucratic and therefore "rational," as Max Weber put it long ago. Schools do have established procedures for handling their affairs. To the extent that more attention is given to procedures and to the extent that procedures are multiplied, schools become more proceduralized, more bureaucratized, more rationalized.

Rationalization, of course, has at least two meanings. In bureaucracies, rationalization is the purposeful organization of activities and goals; in fact, "rationalization" and "bureaucratization" are frequently used interchangeably. A second meaning of rationalization is to employ explanations that seem superficially reasonable and valid but actually are unrelated to the true explanation. Rationalization with both its positive and negative connotations seems to be operating in policy for schools.

That schools are bureaucratic and, therefore, rational seems evident. That external forces are operating to make schools even more rational seems also evident. *My conclusion is that the trend is so pronounced that it should be characterized as the hyperrationalization of education.*[1]

I attribute the hyperrationalization of schooling to policymakers outside the local school system who are endeavoring to influence the schools.[2] This essay is a preliminary effort to understand the motives of policymakers, to analyze the conception of education they hold, and to explain why their efforts at educational policymaking frequently fail. We will see how policymakers' efforts to reform school practices result from and in an excessively rational view of schooling and why this view of schooling fails to lead to real school reform. Some implications of the analysis for improved policymaking conclude the essay.

---

[1]Hyperrationalization is not an invented word. It appears in the *Random House Dictionary of the English Language* in a long list of "hyper" words which are not specifically defined. "Hyper," of course, means "excessive" or "over."

[2]There are legislative, executive, and judicial officials at the state, federal and local levels of government. They include state and local school board officials and state department of education officials but not local administrations or teachers.

Some Examples of Hyperrationalization

The phenomena to be described are efforts by policymakers to rationalize the means and ends of schooling. Since a rational view of the world is "natural," such efforts appear, on the surface, to be an appropriate way to change schools. Often they are appropriate; often they manifest a serious deficiency. That deficiency is the procession from rationale to action without adequate reason or evidence. What appears logical becomes the basis for action. However, what appears logical may or may not have a connection to reality. Where the connection to reality is absent, a policy intervention will fail.

Excessive Prescription

Policymakers have several means of influencing a school system. They may prescribe the inputs to the system, the process the system is to employ or the outcomes the system is to achieve. Traditionally, policymakers restricted themselves to prescribing inputs such as the minimum expenditure, the required number of days of school and the minimum qualification of teachers. Recently policymakers have begun to prescribe expected outcomes like reading level, functional literacy, and citizenship skills. Other legislated innovations such as individualized instruction, objectives-based education and class size are intended to prescribe the process of education. Usually these prescriptions are contained in separate pieces of legislation. Often an outcome prescription is made without considering whether it is attainable given resource (or input) constraints. Numerous logical and practical inconsistencies are the likely result of efforts to prescribe input, process, and outcome controls.

Procedural Complexity

Procedural complexity is often the result of efforts to respond to demands for sharing power. It results when those in power wish to appear to share authority without, in fact, surrendering authority. The response is a procedural rather than a substantive change. For example, the past decade has witnessed efforts to decentralize school systems, to provide for community participation, and to allow community control. But, prior to the advent of any of these reforms, school systems have procedures for arriving at decisions. Frequently, existing procedures are not removed to make way for the new procedures; the new procedures simply are added to the old. A rational system of decision making gives way to a hyperrational system as added procedures rather than redistributed authority becomes the response.

Inappropriate Solutions

Inappropriate solutions frequently are derived out of ignorance or an inability or unwillingness to deal with a problem. For example, a prevailing view is that schools exist to prepare a child to enter society. It is occasionally observed that schools are not adequately preparing students to enter society. This observation gives rise to the suggestion that schools should be better articulated with the needs of society. This suggestion leads to the creation of a program or a curriculum to further that articulation. If high school graduates cannot find jobs, create a career education program. If crime is on the rise, create a moral education program. Such programs are often inappropriate because the problems which they are designed to solve have their genesis in social structure rather than in individual behavior. The solution to the problem, in other words, may lie in reforming society or the school rather than in the creation of a specific program or curriculum. The logic that connects the problem to the solution is faulty.

First-Order Solution

A school problem is identified and the statement of the problem becomes the statement of the solution as a first-order analysis of the problem is made to yield the solution. Schools are not accountable, so create an accountability program. High school graduates are incompetent, so create a competency-based high school graduation program. Teachers are incompetent, so create a competency-based teacher education program. The creation of a program with the same name as the problem yields the appearance of coping with the problem. In fact, the problems referred to have solutions, if at all, at the very core of the education enterprise. Tinkering in superficial ways with the outcomes of schooling is very far from the real solution.

Wishful Thinking

When policymakers require by law that schools achieve a goal which in the past they have not achieved, they may be engaging in wishful thinking. Here policymakers behave as though their desires concerning what a school system should accomplish will, in fact, be accomplished if the policymakers simply decree it. The assumption appears to be that school officials are engaged in nonfeasance or malfeasance. For example, in 1965 the federal government enacted legislation designed to address the failure of schools to serve adequately the needs of some children, particularly poor children and children of certain racial minorities. School systems would receive federal funds to be spent on the education of poor children. The legislation required that school systems describe how those funds would be used to alter the education of poor children. The assumption was that change from preexisting educational practices could have beneficial educational consequences. School systems which presumably did not previously have the knowledge or will or wherewithal to affect such children would, with federal funds, discover the knowledge, gain the will, and have the wherewithal to solve the problem. Suffice it for now to say, these beneficial consequences have not quickly followed modest federal investment. One result, and a second example of wishful thinking, has been that state legislatures and state courts have been requiring by law specified levels of performance on the part of schoolpeople and schoolchildren. Competency-based graduation requirements and rulings for "thorough and efficient education" demand the schools to produce outcomes which they may not be able to achieve.

In apparent frustration and desperation, policymakers prescribe excessive controls, introduce complicated procedures, offer inappropriate solutions, devise simplistic solutions, and engage in wishful thinking. To buttress these interventions, policymakers often turn to educational and social science research. Yet research is seldom able to settle important policy issues. Despite this, policies often are rationalized by unverified or tentative research findings. Such inappropriate reliance on research may be going beyond science to scientism—yet another manifestation of hyperrationalization.

Rational Educational Management Systems

The hyperrational approach to schooling is best seen in the continual invention of rational educational management systems. Perhaps we should refer to the *reinvention* of the rational educational management system for, as we shall see when the jargon is stripped away, the systems are nearly identical. The period [from] 1910 to 1929 described by Raymond E. Callahan (1962) in *Education and the Cult of Efficiency* could be characterized by a few phrases like "efficiency," "educational cost accounting," and "scientific management." The years since then have seen an apparent sophistication in the application of industrial management practices to education. Now our vocabulary must include: (1) accountability, (2) planning, programming, budgeting systems (PPBS), (3) management by objectives (MBO), (4) operations analysis, (5) systems analysis, (6) program evaluation and review technique (PERT), (7) management information systems (MIS), (8) management science, (9) planning models, (10) cost-benefit analysis, (11) cost-effectiveness analysis, (12) economic analysis, and (13) systems engineering. Presumably these practices are ready for application; less ready for application but nonetheless applicable are: (1) operations research, (2) systems research, (3) simulation studies, and (4) productivity research. Since the period Callahan studied, public management practices have joined industrial management practices as perceived useful models for educational management.

While all of these techniques are purely management techniques which are perceived to be applicable to education, the ideology which has given rise to their use has also given rise to derivative approaches which are the adaptation of management science to education. These include (1) performance contracting, (2) educational vouchers, and (3) educational technology. Perhaps more important, however, the management ideology has focused concern upon the output of the educational system. That concern has manifested itself in two ways. First we have devised numerous systems for focusing attention upon outputs. These include: (1) competency-based education (CBE), (2) competency-based teacher education, (3) assessment systems (federal, state, and local), (4) program evaluation, (5) learner verification, (6) behavioral objectives, (7) mastery learning, (8) criterion-referenced testing, and (9) educational indicators. Second, we have devised rubrics for our minimum expectations for school output. We have sought to describe the nature of education which is designed to transform the output of the school system to the input of society. The term "functional literacy" best captures this transformation, but other dimensions of education are captured by (1) basic education, (2) basic skills, (3) career education, and (4) moral education. Consistent with the management ideology, research on education must now be concerned with school effectiveness and teacher effectiveness.

It is not self-evident that these terms represent the only or best ways to think about education. Let us consider the cumulative effect of a few of these schemes upon the role of the teacher in a hypothetical school district in a hypothetical state. (Actually, if all the accountability laws on the books in California were implemented, it could be substituted for the hypothetical state.) The simple accountability system holds the teacher "accountable" for achieving prespecified objectives but allows the teacher discretion to determine how these objectives are to be achieved. The derivative systems build from the simple system and, in their elaboration, eliminate the discretion of the teacher to determine how the prespecified objectives are to be attained.

Competency-based education is the simple accountability system viewed from the student's perspective. The competencies which a student is to demonstrate are prespecified so that the teacher knows what is to be accomplished. Since the school system knows what it expects of its students, it hires teachers who demonstrate in advance that they can teach in the manner necessary to ensure that the students gain the desired competencies. Hence the school system hires only graduates of CBTE (competency-based teacher certification) programs and/or persons certified as competent by CBTE procedures. It is assumed that research will have identified those competencies of teachers which enable them to develop the desired competencies in students. (This must be assumed because research has not thus far identified such competencies in teachers.) All teachers entering the system will demonstrate the appropriate competencies; all teachers presently in the system will receive in-service education. By this process the range of teacher behavior will be narrowed to the point at which the *method* of achieving student objectives will be prescribed. The operation of the general accountability system and its derivatives—CBE, CBTE, and CBTC—have determined what and how the teacher is to teach.

However, in the event that accountability, CBE, CBTE, and CBTC do not yield the desired result, alternative derivatives of general accountability theory provide redundant protection. "Learner verification," a less well known derivative of accountability theory, assesses the effectiveness of instructional materials. When this legislation is operative, a publisher will have to provide evidence that his materials have been tested with children and revised on the basis of this experience. An underlying assumption is that there is a best way to use the materials; the publisher must make the best way known through in-service education. Florida legislation, for example, requires that "such text revision . . . be interpreted as including specific revision of the materials themselves, revision of the teachers' materials and *revision of the teachers' skill through retraining*" (emphasis added). It the teacher's behavior (1) has not been sufficiently defined by the expected objectives; (2) has not been properly trained by CBTE; and (3) has not been properly selected by CBTC, then the residual variability in his or her behavior will be reduced by learner verification of the materials of instruction.

Should learner verification not complete the task, then a managerial derivative of accountability theory will. A planning, programming, and budgeting system is a mechanism by which the administration of the school system sets and tracks the accountability process. Given a set of objectives, the administration plans their implementation, programs the system, and budgets accordingly. Programming in this context can only mean programming the teacher.

Policymakers must be assuming a hyperrational view of the process of schooling with the school a closed, deterministic system. The relationship of the elements of the system are assumed to be known so that the manipulation of one element will have predictable consequences on the other elements. Said another way, given a set of educational objectives and a rational educational management system, the school is assumed to be under complete control.

The Motivations of Educational Policymakers

Efforts to rationalize schooling are not new. Callahan (1962) has well documented the excesses which were wrought in the name of "efficiency" in the early part of this century. Accompanying the early cult of efficiency was an emphasis on vocationalism. Rationalizing schooling has involved both the practice and the purposes of education. The new cult of efficiency, as H. Thomas James (1969) has dubbed it, is distinguished from the old by virtue of "rational planning models" having replaced "efficiency" and, it might be added, by "career education" having replaced "vocationalism."

Under our structure of government, policymakers have the duty to set the goals for schools and the conditions under which the goals are to be achieved. Not only do policymakers decide what the schools are to accomplish, but they also may insist that no laws be broken and that schools be run efficiently. Hyperrationalization is the unfortunate result of legitimate efforts by legislators and other policymakers to improve schools. Some problems arise chiefly because the technology for accomplishing school improvement by policy interventions is inadequate. Other problems arise from efforts to avoid difficult decisions. For example, policymakers are anxious to reduce costs in education as elsewhere. Because education is still a relatively high public priority, policymakers cannot simply maintain or reduce spending levels. Because they cannot legislate rising costs away, they must rationalize decisions to keep budgets from rising. This need gives rise to the demand for rational planning systems in the anticipation that the imposition of such systems will reveal ways to control costs. Evidence to date would suggest that rational planning systems are less effective means to control costs than the direct imposition of budget ceilings! Similarly, it has been shown that career education programs are a less effective means to reduce unemployment than the creation of jobs! Hyperrationalization then often results when policymakers do not want to make difficult decisions.

While policymakers, desirous of increasing the effectiveness and efficiency of schools, have created a demand for rational management models, a continuous supply has been forthcoming. While policymakers try to conceive of change as an industry, educational administrators and professors of educational administration try to conceive of educational management as industrial management. As new rational management models are invented in industry, educational administration, lacking an independent basis of expertise, adopts them. The existence of rational educational management models thus reinforces the propensity of policymakers to hyperrationalize education.

To create goals for education is to will that something occur. But goals, in the absence of a theory of how to achieve them, are mere wishful thinking. If there is no reason to believe that a goal is attainable—as perhaps evidenced by the fact that it has never been attained—then a rational planning model may not result in goal attainment. Rational planning models, as we shall see, do not contain adequate theories of education.

The Essence of Educational Policymaking

Educational policy is created by legislative enactment, executive decree, and judicial pronouncement. However created, its purpose is to affect the practice of change. Inevitably, then, an educational policy must be based upon some assumptions about educational practice. If these assumptions are correct, then the policy may have its intended consequence. If these assumptions are incorrect, then the policy will probably not have its intended consequences.

An educational policy contains two elements—an aim that the educational system is to achieve and a "theory of education" or set of hypotheses that explain how that aim is to be achieved. The aim may deal with the ends of education and may be drawn from religion, ethics, tradition, the law, or other normative sources. The schools must prepare students to read, to face the world of work, to accept their place in society, or to question the current social order. The aim may deal with the means of education and may be drawn from economic theory, the law, or other sources which prescribe how a society wishes to conduct its institutions. The schools must be efficient, treat all equally, provide due process, or secure order through force if necessary.

A theory of education may be drawn from common sense, professional lore, or social science. From common sense, we know that a large organization cannot function effectively unless it has highly developed bureaucratic procedures! From professional lore we know that a teacher cannot function as effectively in a large class as in a small! From social science we variously know that integration works or that it does not! If the theory of education or hypothesis is correct, then the policy may work. If the theory of education or hypothesis is incorrect, then the policy will probably not work. Needless to say, a policy may have unintended consequences. And a particular policy statement may or may not be explicit about its aims or its theory of education. But analyzing an educational policy in this way reveals that its educational theory component may be examined by the canons of science and scientific criticism.

Most educational policies of the 1960s and 1970s share a common set of assumptions about schooling:

1. While many goals for education are imaginable, society must find a limited set upon which agreement is possible. The emerging consensus appears to be that the purpose of schooling is to provide the child with the basic skills necessary for effective participation as a citizen and as a member of the work force. Establishing a limited goal for schools is thought to facilitate goal attainment.

2. This goal must be put in a form which will permit assessment of the extent to which the goal is attained. Most effort has been given to defining basic skills in reading and mathematics. Such definition is thought to facilitate goal attainment.

3. Tests are then devised to assess performance in reading and mathematics. When the scores are available they will be compared with other scores—district-wide, statewide, or nationwide. Such comparisons are thought to facilitate student, teacher, program, and school evaluation and improvement.

4. Some complexity is added by the realization that some children arrive at school less well prepared than others. For such children schools will variously either adjust expectations downwards or provide supplementary educational services.

5. Finally, education is to be conducted efficiently or in a cost-effective manner; the goal is to be attained at least cost. Planning, resource allocation, and test results are to be tracked by even more sophisticated evaluation and accounting systems.

Absent from this set of assumptions about education is reference to the process of education—to how educational practice affects the child. Thus educational policy is designed to alter the practice of education without an understanding of how education actually occurs. There are three possible explanations. First, policymakers wish to leave the process of education to the professionals. This seems unlikely since the kind of policymaking described is designed to force remediation in professional practice. Second, policymakers have not yet been furnished the tools for legislating about the educational process. This seems plausible since they do employ the tools that have been furnished by educational research. Witness the alacrity with which criterion-referenced testing has been adopted. Third, policymakers may believe that it is sufficient to cause something to occur by legislating that it should occur. At the very least this explanation is not inconsistent with the behavior of some policymakers.

The Limits of the Rational Model

To those who believe that reform of procedures will lead to reform of education, the rational model of schooling looks unquestionably correct. If only the schools will tighten up this or that procedure, good educational results will follow. If only the schools are given clear objectives to achieve, then the objectives will certainly be achieved. However, since such changes do not inevitably lead to the predicted result, perhaps there is something wrong with the rational model—the model which provides the basis for the predicted relationship between the change and the result. Perhaps the self-evident rational model does not, in fact, match the reality of schools.

The failure of schools to conform to the rational model may be seen in the failure thus far to create models which help explain the process of schooling empirically. The collection of elements which comprise schooling obviously and by definition interact with each other and affect one another. The history of disciplined inquiry in education is a search to describe, analyze, and predict the effects of these interactions. Research on teaching has been a search for the effects which teachers have; research on schools has been a search for the effects which schooling has. Yet, as we know so well by now, research on teacher effects and school effects has failed to explain much of the reality of schooling.

The 1966 *Equality of Educational Opportunity Report (EEOR)* epitomizes the use of the rational model in the search for school effects (see Coleman 1966). In abstracting reality, the study accepts the basic input-process-output paradigm that has become the basis for thinking about education. It assumes that aggregate achievement test score maximization is the goal of the schools. It assumes that resources are effectively deployed. It assumes that efficiency principles operate in schools. Yet all of these assumptions are likely violated in the way schools operate. The point here is not to undertake another critique of EEOR. Rather, it is to suggest that it rests on assumptions that may be violated by reality. If this disjuncture between the model and reality exists, then improvement in measurement, methodology, and research design will not yield great increases in the explanation of schooling. Moreover, efforts to increase explanation by means of experimental modifications of schooling would be beside the point; schooling as it now operates may defy the kind of logical assumptions which we are accustomed to make.

Further corroboration of the disjuncture between the rational model and school reality is to be found in the continual failure of the various rational management models. Accountability, PPBS, and the like have not had much effect upon the schools. On the one hand, the rational management models may have been poorly conceived and poorly executed and better conceptions and better executions may work. On the other hand, the operation of schools may be inconsistent with the assumptions of the rational management models. In this case, there is no reason to expect the rational management models to have an effect upon schools.

A model—like the rational model—leads us to make predictions. When these predictions generally fail, it is not reality but the model which is at fault.

To conclude from the *Equality of Educational Opportunity Report* that variations in inputs are unrelated to variations in output is to conclude only that a multiple regression analysis did not reveal relationships. Because schooling cannot be explained in this manner is not to imply that schooling cannot be explained. The acceptance of this implication would be tantamount either to the belief that schooling is random or to the rejection of science.

One Different Description of School Reality

Educational policymakers behave as though they believe that schools operate according to the rational model. That model postulates that schools operate by setting goals, implementing programs to achieve these goals, and evaluating the extent to which the goals are attained. The goal-oriented process is assumed to be effectuated through a bureaucratic distribution of formal authority and work responsibility. It is further assumed that the attainment of goals provides sufficient incentives to drive the system. Policies emanating from a belief in the rational model are designed to improve the operation of the goal-oriented process. Schemes which promise to increase accountability, efficiency, and effectiveness are imposed on the existing bureaucratic structure of the school in the anticipation that they will improve the school, conceived as a rational organization.

Despite the possibility that schools may not conform to the rational model, it remains the dominant framework in the discourse of educational policymakers, organizational theorists, and educational administrators. Interestingly, the rational model does not seem to have become the dominant framework for teachers' discourse on teaching, schooling, and education. This difference between teachers and others concerned with schools suggests several questions. Are there other frameworks for describing schools? Do these frameworks come closer to capturing school reality? Do the frameworks embraced by teachers help explain the failure of educational policies? One alternative source of frameworks is provided by the humanistically oriented reform literature.

A second alternative source of frameworks is provided by the ways in which teachers describe their work. One particularly useful formulation of how teachers see school reality is provided by Dan C. Lortie's (1975) analysis of interviews with teachers. The picture that he paints bears little resemblance to that imagined by those who believe in the rational model.

Those who believe in the rational model assume that the process of education rests on an underlying order. Lortie found that teachers may not share this "scientific" assumption:

A scientific approach, however, normally begins with the assumption that there is an underlying order in the phenomena under study. It is not clear that all or most teachers make that assumption about their world. Some see teaching outcomes as capricious and describe short-term results in almost mysterious terms. If that viewpoint is widespread, it is not surprising that teachers do not invest in searching for general principles to inform their work. If they suspect that classroom events are beyond comprehension, inquiry is futile [p. 212].

Not only does the rational model assume predictability in behavior, but it also simplifies reality:

Those trained in behavioral science are used to accepting short-run measurements as evidence of effectiveness; it would be easy to assume that these teachers do not want to confront the possibility of low impact on students. But one wonders: styles of thought which pervade science may not work for those who take personal responsibility for the development of children. Science moves ahead through deliberate and sophisticated simplifications of reality, but there is little to suggest that this is the approach of classroom teachers [pp. 146-47].

While the rational model abstracts and simplifies reality, a teacher will not; he or she is responsible for the whole child.

Lortie argues that a powerful force on the orientation of teachers is their observation over the years of their own teachers. Conceptions of education are formed before exposure to teacher training. The rational model implicitly adopts a view of change drawn from the behavioral sciences:

Teacher training is increasingly influenced by ideas drawn from behavioral science. Those trained in behavioral disciplines are inclined to conceptualize teaching in instrumental terms—to talk of "treatments" and "options" and to assess outcomes in terms of measurable and discrete objectives. One wonders how effectively such professors communicate with the many students who, it appears, see teaching as the "living out" of prior conceptions of good teaching. Students who conceive of teaching (consciously or not) as expressing qualities associated with revered models will be less attuned to the pragmatic and rationalistic conceptions of teaching found in behavioral science. The two groups—students and professors—may talk past one another [pp. 66-67].

The rational model of education is alien to the teachers' prior conceptions of education.

The rational model makes important assumptions about how the school operates. For example, it assumes that the goals of education are set politically, transmitted through the school district and school hierarchies, and then come to rest with the teacher for implementation. To what degree does this assumption accord with reality? To what extent do the formal goals of the school system guide the actions of teachers? According to Lortie:

If teacher pride were ordered in strict adherence to organizational, formal goals, we would expect to find heavy emphasis on results attained with entire classes; school systems present themselves as concerned with the learning of all students. It is provocative, therefore, that fewer than one-third (29 percent) of the Five Towns teachers mentioned generalized outcomes with entire classes, and that most of these did so in an off-hand manner. Such responses seemed to occur with teachers working in particular subjects and grades—the more tangible and visible the learning they were seeking to promote, the likelier they were to emphasize general gains with students. Examples are initial reading, physical education skills, typing, and skill subjects in home economics. A few elementary teachers linked pride to favorable outcomes on achievement tests, but they seemed hesitant to do so [p. 127].

Perhaps surprisingly, teachers do not naturally emphasize objective group results. Yet, the rational model assumes that the underlying objective of the teacher is to maximize aggregate achievement test scores. Advocates of the rational model will argue that accountability schemes are designed to focus the teacher's attention on output measures. And indeed, teaching for the test has occurred. However, whether the teacher has fundamentally altered his orientation is quite another matter. Until it can be understood why teachers do not now use tests as a gauge of successful teaching, policies which assume that teachers are trying to maximize test scores are not likely to improve education.

Formally stated goals will only affect students as they are mediated by teachers. Currently, teachers translate formal goals into personalized objectives:

Educational goals are often stated in global, even utopian terms ... [W]e observed that teachers "reduce" such goals into specific objectives they use in their daily work. This reduction apparently involves two conservative tendencies: relying on personal convictions and obtaining high satisfaction from outcomes that are less than universalistic. When teachers cannot use stated goals to guide their actions, organizational objectives give way to personal values; the personal values of teachers, as we saw ... are heavily influenced by past experience [p. 208].

Unless the underlying reward system is altered to modify the behavior of teachers, the process of goal redefinition will likely continue. In short, the picture of school reality, which emerges from interviews with teachers, stands in stark contrast to the school reality envisioned by the rational model. Other research methods may reveal yet other frameworks for understanding school reality.

The Disjuncture Between the Rational Model and School Reality

An important new concept—the idea that schools are "loosely coupled systems"—has entered the literature of organizational theory. The concept is meant to imply that the elements of the system of the school are not necessarily rationally or tightly related. Karl E. Weick (1976) has described loose coupling as conveying:

the image that coupled events are responsive, but that each event also preserves its own identity and some evidence of its physical or logical separateness. Thus, in the case of an educational organization, it may be the case that the counselor's office is loosely coupled to the principal's office. The image is that the principal and the counselor are somehow attached, but that each retains some identity and separateness and that their attachment may be circumscribed, infrequent, weak in its mutual affects, unimportant, and/or slow to respond. Each of those connotations would be conveyed if the qualifier loosely were attached to the word coupled. Loose coupling also carries connotations of impermanence, dissolvability, and tacitness all of which are potentially crucial properties of the "glue" that holds organizations together.

Glassman (1973) categorizes the degree of coupling between two systems on the basis of the activity of the variables which the two systems share. To the extent that two systems either have few variables in common or share weak variables, they are independent of each other. Applied to the educational situation, if the principal-vice-principal-superintendent is regarded as one system and the teacher-classroom-pupil-parent-curriculum as another system, then by Glassman's argument if we did not find many variables in the teacher's world to be shared in the world of a principal and/or if the variables in common were unimportant relative to the other variables, then the principal can be regarded as being loosely coupled with the teacher [pp. 1-19].

The idea of loose coupling provides another challenge to the rational model of the school. It also provides a way to describe the disjuncture between the rational model and school reality.

In fact, the concept of loosely coupled systems helps to make explicit at least four aspects of hyperrationalization. First, it explains why manipulating some elements in the system of the school may have no consequences for other elements. Second, it directs attention to the possibility that the educational policymaking system may be loosely coupled to the operating educational system. Third, it reveals that researchers have frequently assumed in advance that schools operate as rational organizations. Fourth, it suggests that hyperrationalization may be evidence that loose coupling exists. Loose coupling is thus a complementary concept to hyperrationalization.

Efforts to rationalize the processes or the goals of schools frequently do not have the anticipated effects. Two mechanisms which couple some nonschool organizations are technical core and authority of office. An automobile factory is coupled by its technical core as embodied in the assembly line. A military organization is coupled by the authority of office as embodied in the chain-of-command. The school may be coupled by neither of these and may, therefore, be loosely coupled. New policies which hold schools accountable for attaining specified goals may have no effect upon the *processes* of education. Without changes in the process, it is difficult to understand how new goals can be attained. A requirement that an individualized instruction plan be developed for every handicapped child will have no effect if it is not tied to budget and program decisions. If budget and program decisions continue to be made in the traditional way, the creation of individualized program plans is a paper exercise.

If educational policymakers are inclined to embrace the rational model of the school and teachers are inclined to embrace less rationalistic models of schooling, then the policymaking system may not be communicating with the operating system. The policymaking system shares few variables in common with the operating system. Indeed, the different actors in the education scene hold different ideologies and believe in different theories of education. Policymakers create policies which are consistent with the rational model and which would work if the rational model were a good representation of school reality. Practicing educators do not believe in the rational model and do not share its assumptions. The policies do not work because the rational model is incorrect. While policies may not work because practicing educators believe that they should not work, this seems unlikely given the unrealistic assumptions contained in rationalistic policies.

The idea of loose coupling alerts us to the possibility that we may learn more about schools if we do not assume in advance that they are rational. Traditionally, researchers have constructed rational models of schools in order to study them; researchers seem to have reached a limit in understanding school phenomena. Parenthetically, and ironically, the propensity of policymakers to view education rationally is reinforced whenever they turn to researchers for advice. Policymakers seeing that schools have been studied rationalistically believe that they can be made to conform to the researchers' model. In this fashion, research models prematurely become the basis for accountability and assessment schemes.

Weick has suggested that overrationalization (his term) may be evidence that loose coupling exists. When the couplings between elements receive excessive attention, it may be because they are loose. In this light, we can understand the monumental efforts occasionally undertaken by state superintendents of education to identify the goals of education. Arguably, because state superintendents lack influence over schools, they undertake ritual efforts to develop statements of goals for education. More recently, state legislatures, frustrated at the poor match between the competencies of high school graduates and the demands of society, have required the generation of lists of expected competencies for high school graduates. Efforts to rationalize in detail what the schools are to accomplish may reveal the loose coupling of the legislature and the school. Hyperrationalization is, then, the perceived antidote to loose coupling; that it does not work should not surprise us.

The Drive Towards Hyperrationalization

The drive towards extensive proceduralization and hyperrationalization is the result of the desire of those outside the traditional decision-making structure of the local school system to influence the schools. When an aggrieved group cannot secure a desired change via the traditional decision-making structure, it turns to other potential educational policymakers. When the schools seem unable or unwilling to teach the basic skills, there is a turning to the state legislature for a mandate for proficiency testing. When the schools are unwilling to desegregate, there is a turning to the federal courts. When the schools discriminate on the basis of sex, there is a turning to the federal government. When teachers cannot gain sufficient influence, there is a turning to collective bargaining. The response by these other educational policymakers is often to require new procedures. In turn, the response of the schools frequently is to accept these new procedures without altering the procedures which already exist. The result is the proliferation of procedures and the appearance of change. But because the existing procedures are not altered, progress has not occurred.

There is perhaps no more potent force for hyperrationalization than the increased use of the courts to alter (and thereby create) educational policy. It is in the nature of the judicial process to rationalize the subject matter with which it deals. Courts review legislation to ascertain whether a practice is consistent with constitutional or statutory law. However, certain features of the law render problematic the enunciation of court-created educational policy. First, a court's decision affects all schools within its jurisdiction. When it is the United States Supreme Court, the jurisdiction is the nation. Yet local circumstances vary. Second, a court decision is theoretically forever. Courts have great difficulty in reversing prior decisions. Yet circumstances do change. Third, courts do not have great flexibility in the application of policy. A ruling must be of general applicability. Yet local circumstances vary. The criticality of these features has been accentuated by the changing nature of court rulings.

The traditional function of the courts was to determine whether a particular case presented a finding that was unlawful or unconstitutional. The court, having found that a particular practice violated the law, would require that it be remedied. The finding of a violation and the demand for a remedy was as far as the court would go. More recently, the courts have, *in addition*, specified the criteria which the remedy would need to satisfy, thus constraining the range of remedies which the court would find acceptable. As the courts have continued to specify criteria, they have, in some cases, arrived at the point of prescribing the remedy. The problem is that the remedy may be wrong; or it may be superfluous in some circumstances; or it may be overrigid. Yet it blankets the jurisdiction and is difficult to reverse.

One effect of court action is to proceduralize actions which in the past have been accomplished by informal means. In fact, the court can dictate that its own procedures replace procedures which the local school has itself devised. In still other cases, a school may be led to have duplicative procedures. Often new procedures are mandated without full recognition of the functional consequences of the old procedures or of the dysfunctional consequences of the new procedures.

A dramatic example is provided by the District of Columbia schools which must assign teachers (and other educational resources) in consonance with a court order which requires that resources be distributed so that per-pupil expenditures do not vary by more than 5 percent. The procedures for assigning resources must also conform to educational requirements, union contracts, and various federal guidelines including the "comparability" requirement of Title I, ESEA, the latter being similar but not identical to the requirements of the court order. The effects of a school being subject to numerous policymaking bodies are apparent (see Baratz 1975).

A recent Supreme Court decision, *Goss v. Lopez* (1975), created "the right of a student not to be suspended for as much as a single day without notice and a due process hearing either before or promptly following the suspension." Thus every school in the nation must "give notice and a due process hearing" whenever a student is to be suspended. It is possible in the future that a school may have to "give notice and due process hearing" whenever a serious decision concerning a student is made. As the dissenting opinion in *Goss* said:

No one can foresee the ultimate frontiers of the new "thicket" the Court now enters. Today's ruling appears to sweep within the protected interest in education a multitude of discretionary decisions in the educational process. Teachers and other school authorities are required to make many decisions that may have serious consequences for the pupil. They must decide, for example, how to grade the student's work, whether a student passes or fails a course, whether he is to be promoted, whether he is required to take certain subjects, whether he may be excluded from inter-scholastic athletics or other extracurricular activities, whether he may be removed from one school and sent to another, whether he may be bused long distances when available schools are nearby and whether he should be placed in a "general," "vocational," or "college-preparatory" track.

The proceduralization of many discretionary school decisions constitutes the hyperrationalization of education.

The courts appear to be more avid consumers of research than the executive or legislative branches. The use of social science evidence has probably had more dramatic effects upon courts than has generally been recognized. Analysts have generally looked for explicit evidence that a court has based its decision upon scientific evidence introduced in the case. While evidence is frequently introduced, it often seems that the court reaches its decision on other grounds or that the court uses the evidence to reinforce its decision reached on other grounds. More important, however, is the prevailing ideology which surrounds an issue as it comes to the court. The courts seem to be influenced by the prevailing scientific opinion which surrounds the issue. That is, the assumptions which a judge knowingly or unknowingly brings to bear are colored by prevailing scientific opinion. When such opinion is incomplete, tentative, or wrong, efforts to base policy upon it may be inappropriate. A court's propensity to rationalize decisions on the basis of unvalidated knowledge may constitute hyperrationalization.

One result has been that the courts, perhaps encouraged by some expert's testimony, see demands on the schools which are beyond the capacity of educational science or technology. The New Jersey Supreme Court recently required "thorough and efficient" education which it defined as "that educational opportunity which is needed in the contemporary setting to equip a child for his role as a citizen, and as a competitor in the labour market" (*Robinson v. Cahill* 1973). Aside from the unsuperable value judgments required by the decree, we likely lack the technical capacity to achieve it, for its seems to demand results that we so far have not found a way to achieve for some children.

Towards More Effective Educational Policymaking

The concept of hyperrationalization helps to explain why educational policymaking frequently fails. As indicated at the outset, rationalization is synonymous with bureaucratization. Bureaucracies exist to rationalize the enterprises which they encompass. Educational bureaucracies have long served to rationalize the educational enterprise. Our thesis is that rationalization has reached the point at which further rationalization ceases to be functional. The forces of hyperrationalization are designed to remedy some group's perception of ineffectiveness, inefficiency, or unfairness in the schools. Yet there is a theoretical limit to the school's capacity to absorb new procedures without a fundamental redesign. The cumulative effect is burdensome to the point of unmanageability. Moreover, the rational model of the school is at best a partial representation of school reality. Schools have probably reaped the benefits of improvements that result from the application of the factory metaphor.

What are the implications of the hyperrationalization hypothesis for more effective educational policymaking? First, some may see the idea leading to the debureaucratization of schooling. I am inclined to reject this suggestion because school bureaucracy has evolved precisely to mediate the interests of the child and the state. Unless the state's interest in education is diminished—a prospect which seems most unlikely—bureaucracy seems essential. Second, some may see the humanistically oriented reform literature as an antidote to hyperrationalization. The humanization of schools by *policy initiatives* would require the development of concepts to link the reform movement and the policy process. So far the policy process has exhibited a greater affinity for the rationalistic rather than the humanistic conception of education.

Third, and most immediately, a distinction can be drawn between rationalization and hyperrationalization. The hypothesis should sensitize us to distinguish between proper and excessive rationalization of schooling. An affirmative answer to the following questions may mean that hyperrationalization is in evidence:

1. Does the policy introduce new procedures without altering or deleting old procedures?

2. Does the policy prescribe output without taking cognizance of existing input and process prescriptions?
3. Does the policy imply that a structural problem can be solved by the education of the individual?
4. Is the policy to be implemented without considering organizational and group dynamics?
5. Are tentative research findings being used to defend the policy?
6. Are solutions being proposed on the basis of superficial, incomplete, or incorrect analyses of the problem?
7. Are unattainable or never-before-attained goals being set?
8. Are uniform solutions being proposed for nonuniform situations? Evidence of hyperrationalization may suggest that the policy will not have its intended consequence.

Fourth, and most importantly, the idea of hyperrationalization underscores the need for a new paradigm for thinking about the schools. Educational policies fail because they are premised on the idea that the school is a rational organization—like a factory—which can be managed and improved by rational procedure. Indeed, much of the collective effort of policymakers, researchers, and administrators is aimed at making school reality conform to the rational model. We then bemoan the fact that the schools fail to conform to the model. It just may be that we need a new paradigm.

References

Baratz, J.C. *A Quest for Equal Educational Opportunity in a Major Urban School District: The Case.* Washington: Education Policy Research Institute of Educational Testing Service, 1975.

Callahan, R.E. *Education and the Cult of Efficiency.* Chicago: University of Chicago Press, 1962.

Coleman, J.A., et al. *Equality of Educational Opportunity.* Washington: U.S. Government Printing Office, 1966.

Goss v. Lopez, 419 U.S. 565 (1975).

James, H.T. *The New Cult of Efficiency and Education.* Pittsburgh: University of Pittsburgh Press, 1969.

Robinson v. Cahill, 62 N.J. 473, 303 A.2d 273 (1973).

Weick, K.E. "Educational Organizations as Loosely Coupled Systems." *Administrative Science Quarterly* 21: 3 (March 1976): 1-19.

6

The Lawn Party: The Evolution of Federal Programs in Local Settings

Eleanor Farrar, John DeSanctis, and David Cohen

For the past twenty years, the failure of federal education reforms to achieve their intended outcomes has been a persistent puzzle. Researchers have offered a variety of explanations for this failure, but most answers have had one thing in common: the view that implementation is the second stage of a two-stage process that begins with policy formulation. Implementation is seen as the process of carrying out policy. We believe that the outcomes of many federal attempts to upgrade local schools can be better understood if implementation is viewed as a process of policy evolution, in which local participation modifies and sometimes completely reformulates a program's federal blueprint. "Policy"—which is at the outset usually only a set of broad and often diverse intentions or dispositions—changes and develops as the federal program is harnessed to local needs and priorities. Implementation is not the carrying out of a formulated policy but part of its evolution. And in that evolution—in certain circumstances or with certain programs—a multitude of local dispositions and actions are more important than the dispositions and actions of federal agencies.

Reprinted from *Phi Delta Kappan* (November 1980): 167–71, by permission of Teachers College Press. The original version of this paper appeared in *Teachers College Record* 82: 1 (Fall 1980): 77–100.

Questions about implementation first came up in education research circles in reaction to the supposed failure of the Elementary and Secondary Education Act (ESEA) of 1965.[1] When sizable Title I grants to school districts appeared not to improve the achievement of disadvantaged youngsters, there were arguments over evaluation methodologies and politics. But it also seemed sensible to ask the next question: If students' test scores were not improving, was the money being spent as intended?

A series of federal audits and program reviews represented the first attempt to examine the local implementation of federal reforms. They concluded that there were two kinds of gross problems of implementation: first, federal money was being misspent; second, even when spent as intended, it yielded unimpressive results. In some cases no implementation of federal policy occurred because federal funds were indeed being used to supplant rather than supplement, or were spread too thin across all students to have any effect on target youth, or were spent on things quite unrelated to education. But why, in those cases where federal money was spent as intended, did the programs also fail to improve student achievement?

This question led to more elaborate efforts to evaluate program effectiveness. In the late sixties such federal efforts as Follow Through and Head Start Planned Variation were to experiment with different models of early childhood education to identify educational programs that "work." Evaluations of these efforts soon made it apparent that this was no easy task. Student outcomes suggested that many of these programs also did not work, and researchers began to suspect that perhaps the new models were not being used properly (Cohen 1975; Lukas 1975). Therefore, in a new generation of implementation studies, they tried to weigh fidelity to original plans in terms of detailed program components.

These studies were beset by problems such as rater unreliability and lack of instrument sensitivity to model changes over time. Site visits revealed that the models in practice were even more complex than they had seemed on paper. Site interpretations of the models varied from time to time and place to place; even the developers' ideas about the models changed over time, and it was not clear whose standard of implementation should prevail. The studies showed implementation to be a tangle of unresolved problems, of competing political values in the change process.

These early audits and implementation studies shared a view of implementation as a center-to-periphery process: programs initiated by

---

[1] For an account of the early evaluation of ESEA Title I implementation, see McLaughlin (1975) and Murphy (1971).

central (federal) officials were expected to be "carried out" at the periphery (school districts). From this perspective, the implementation of many compensatory education programs, such as Title I and Follow Through, was often foiled by the district. This conception of implementation fit with other views popular in research circles at the time. Social scientists recommended that federal officials use a more scientific approach to program development and monitor local programs more vigorously (see, for example, Guba 1968)—implying that implementation is simply the systematic translation into practice of carefully formulated policy.

In the face of continuing reports of program failure and growing skepticism about federal social intervention, researchers for the first time began to ask whether federal expectations were always reasonable.[2] That question, while still considering states and local districts as the installers of federally conceived plans, carried the seeds of quite a different view. These seeds began to germinate in the Rand Corporation's Change-Agent Study (1974-78),[3] which emphasized the importance of local contributions to implementation. This study provided the next stage in the history of research on implementation. Rand researchers saw motivation, commitment, and a sense of local ownership as important ingredients in program success. This meant that there must be bilateral adjustment— "mutual adaptation"—between federal intentions and local wishes (Rand Corporation 1974, vol. 1, p. 10). The study thus contained in embryonic form the idea of implementation as a continuous process of policy evolution. But it did not develop that notion. Paradoxically, while stressing the importance of local initiative, the Rand researchers still pictured implementation as the local installation of federal policy (Rand Corporation, vol. 4, pp. 3, 4).

These two views of implementation—as a linear (center-to-periphery) process or as a bilateral (mutually adaptive) process—have shaped most studies of federal education programs. In both views the federal program

---

[2]See, for example, Martha Derrick (1972) and Marshall Kaplan (1975). Organizational theorists had already questioned the role of rationality in decision making, among them Charles E. Lindblom, Herbert Simon, and Richard M. Cyert and James G. March. Jeffrey Pressman and Aaron Wildavsky (1973) applied such notions in an account of the problems of implementing an Economic Development Administration Program in Oakland. In education, the same ideas were used in Tyll van Geel's (1972) study; McLaughlin's (1975) study of Title I; and Jerome T. Murphy's (1974) analysis of ESEA Title IV.

[3]This is a study of twenty-nine planned change projects supported by four federal programs: ESEA Title III, ESEA Title VII, Vocational Education Part D Exemplary Programs, and Right to Read.

goals are the main criteria by which success is judged. With this perspective, evaluators have had to assume that federal programs are clearly specified. In reality, this is seldom the case. Giandomenico Majone and Aaron Wildavsky (1978) have pointed out that most policies and programs are not templates, but bundles of potentialities or predispositions waiting to be defined at the local level. Federal school-reform programs, for example, generally define a domain for action (such as education for the disadvantaged or vocational training), and within that domain they may establish priorities (such as teacher training or student achievement). But such definitions and priorities leave room for a variety of legitimate interpretations.

Local school districts get little guidance in making those interpretations because federal enforcement and compliance activities are generally weak. In reality, therefore, local education agencies have considerable autonomy to work their will on federal programs—with notable exceptions such as Title VI of the Civil Rights Act of 1964. No wonder, then, that studies based on a linear or a bilateral view of implementation have been hard put to explain the outcomes of federal education reforms.

We propose a perspective with more explanatory power: implementation is actually a complex and continuous process of policy evolution. This perspective springs in part from the phenomenological view of policy expressed by Majone and Wildavsky (1978), who argue that "attainment of a goal is a unitary process or procedure, not a double process of setting the goal and then devising an implementation plan." Majone and Wildavsky do not see implementation as an unanchored process of goal discovery, however. Rather, it is the development of the "capacities, potentialities, and other dispositional qualities of a policy idea." Thus the implementation of a policy idea will vary for two reasons: first, not all the policy's many potentialities will be recognized, and second, any given idea will be interpreted differently in different settings.

The perspective of implementation as policy evolution also has roots in sociological thought—especially the work of Daniel Lortie and Karl E. Weick. Lortie (1975) has argued that there is low interdependence among organizational units in schools, and Weick (1976) has suggested that school systems are "loosely coupled" and do not always function in a highly coordinated fashion. Both notions imply that school systems lack a unified response to an external stimulus such as a federal program. Rather, different local groups are likely to perceive and seek to use the program in different ways. The so-called implementation process is not simply one of federal and school district managers struggling to reconcile two views of a program, but one in which various local individuals and groups bargain among themselves as much as with external agencies—or perhaps simply do as they please.

Seen in this fashion, the translation of federal programs to local settings does not resemble a precision drill team marching in order toward a specific goal, nor even an orderly bilateral negotiation. Instead, it seems more like a large lawn party. The federal program is the stimulus, the occasion for the gathering. But the party is only a temporary convergence. The guests (local administrators, teachers, board members, and parents) have larger and more lasting concerns awaiting them at home. Moreover, these guests do not attend for the same reasons. Some have come for the food, some to hear the music, some to talk with friends, some from a sense of obligation; and some aren't sure why they've come. And they have different ideas about what they want the party to be and what they hope to gain by attending it. For some the party is an escape from dull routine, for others a chance to cultivate business prospects; and many guests have never consciously identified their wants. Nor does each guest recognize what the other guests want. Each is relatively free to make of the party whatever seems most appropriate.

Within limits, guests thus create their own party—ranging from lively entertainment to a decorous, sedate affair—by developing some of the party's original potentialities and discovering others. Since this creation occurs over time and across a range of participants whose reactions are sometimes interactive and sometimes not, the lawn party, like implementation, is evolution. Local forces (the guests) are at least as important as federal intention (the host) in determining the final form of federal policies and programs (the party)—and usually more so.

A good example is the test of education vouchers in Alum Rock, California, in the early seventies.[4] The U.S. Office of Economic Opportunity (OEO) sponsored the demonstration, hoping to discover whether competition for students would force schools to improve curricula and become more responsive to parents. But local participants had other priorities.

A major point of vouchers was to offer parents more options for their children. But Alum Rock parents did not seize the initiative. Instead, worried that children might not be able to attend their neighborhood schools, they negotiated a "squatters' rights" agreement whereby children

---

[4]See David K. Cohen and Eleanor Farrar (1977). For more detailed accounts of the implementation of education vouchers in Alum Rock, see the published reports of the Rand Corporation: Eliot Levison et al. (1975); Stephen S. Weiner and Konrad Kellen (1974); and Daniel Weiler (1974).

already enrolled could continue to attend a given school. Parents also saw
to it that every voucher school offered at least two alternative programs, so
that children would not be forced out of a neighborhood school by the
parents' distaste for an overly innovative or conservative program.

Alum Rock teachers for their part saw vouchers as a threat to job security.
Thus they obtained an agreement that, if they left voucher schools for
reasons associated with the demonstration, they would be given priority in
assignments to other schools, or OEO would cover their salaries while they
worked in the central office. This saved teachers from the threat of
punishment by consumer preference. But once the program was under way,
teachers began to realize that, along with some advantages and greater
choice, vouchers also brought problems: more students, more planning,
more meetings, more colleagues, more noise, more disruptions. They then
changed the market aspects of the voucher scheme by seeing to it that each
school was assigned an enrollment limit. This meant that less appealing
schools would get the overflow of students, reducing the chances of failure
all around.

Meanwhile, the superintendent used OEO funds to carry out his own
agenda, a decentralization program that transferred more power to the
principals. And these principals protected their new power from parental
encroachment by refusing to publish comparative data that might
encourage competition among schools.

From the federal perspective, then, Alum Rock is a story of program
plans and priorities foiled by unanticipated local obstacles that produced
major changes in the voucher design. But from the local view, vouchers
provided the opportunity to accomplish a variety of things. Principals
obtained more power, more money, and little competition, all of which
they wanted. Parents were guaranteed neighborhood schools and some
choice among programs, both of which they wanted. Teachers received the
resources and the freedom to innovate and to teach as they preferred, along
with job security. The superintendent made some progress in his efforts to
decentralize authority in the district, and the federal funds kept his school
system solvent.

Few of the Alum Rock participants paid attention to the voucher
blueprint or to OEO's formal assessments of its implementation. If they
measured success at all, it was not against central plans and priorities but
against their own differing needs and desires. These local needs and desires,
in fact, changed and shaped the federal initiative, much as guests shape a
lawn party.

The same thing occurs when a federal program is installed
simultaneously in several locations. Local needs and desires differ from
place to place, so that the federal initiative is shaped somewhat differently

by each locale. Since the federal intitiative is usually only a general statement of themes, what happens at the local level can be described as variations on those themes. Some variations are less discordant than others, but virtually none is a single composition with everyone playing from the same score.

Experience-Based Career Education (EBCE) is a case in point. Like many federal education reforms, EBCE saw rigid high schools and bored adolescents as education's biggest problems. It sought to create an alternative program that would be more flexible and more relevant to students' future needs. Two general concepts guided the development of model EBCE programs by four regional educational laboratories in the early seventies. First, the program was intended for all students—the college-bound as well as those planning to terminate schooling with a high school diploma. Second, EBCE sought to make education more relevant through a dual focus on academic skills and community-based exploration of potential careers.

Staff members at the four regional laboratories took these general concepts, interpreted them in light of regional needs and their professional backgrounds, and developed four somewhat different models. During the next four years, at a cost of more than $20 million, the program was implemented. Substantial evaluation efforts by the developers and by the Educational Testing Service concluded that the program was successful, both in teaching youths about work and in teaching the skills and social behavior deemed important for adulthood. Largely on that basis, EBCE was designated an exemplary vocational education program by the Joint Dissemination Review Panel and was made available for national dissemination with federal funding under the Vocational Education Act, Part D. By spring 1978 EBCE was operating in forty-two states under three-year Part D grants and in about one hundred districts with other funding. In record time it had become a national school and work program.

The implementation of EBCE was neither simply conceived nor simply executed; it was marked by negotiation, revision, and adaptation. Adaptation was rarely mutual, however. To meet local needs, school personnel did everything to the program models from fine-tuning to wholesale restructuring. In sites we visited, curriculum materials were revised or replaced, staff roles were redefined, program components were added or dropped, and student activities were redesigned. Model processes were also changed. Suggested sequences of project activities were altered to fit local practice, ready-made projects were revised to look like familiar classroom assignments, and much of the record keeping was reduced or eliminated altogether.

By comparison, schools and school systems made only minor

accommodations for the program. Students were given permission to be out of the building during school hours, and in some districts a bus or van made extra trips to carry EBCE students to and from community placements. Most schools set aside classrooms and sometimes office space for the program, and such support services as mailing, copying, and separate telephone lines were often provided. But the changes were not profound and often they were not new. Schools and school systems change much less than did the EBCE program design.

Teachers, of course, play a key role in determining the form of any education reform. Among EBCE teachers, we observed a diversity of views and interpretations of the innovation and a consequent diversity in programs. Some teachers saw EBCE as an opportunity to work closely with a few students. A West Coast science teacher, for example, became a half-time EBCE learning coordinator because this allowed him to work with small groups. "You get to know each student personally, get involved in their lives and their problems, and work things through with them," he explained. Not surprisingly, the EBCE program developed by this teacher and his colleagues heavily emphasized counseling.

Other teachers also showed a preference for small groups, but they turned their EBCE programs into academic tutoring sessions, playing down—and occasionally ignoring altogether—the career guidance and community exploration components. One teacher described his EBCE improvisation as "a one-room schoolhouse." He provided individual skills training for the full range of students, from those with learning disabilities to those who were academically talented. Meanwhile, teachers in a suburban EBCE program serving students with academic and behavioral problems set up a highly structured, individualized math and language skills program and postponed career exploration indefinitely. Although EBCE in this district gradually came to include some average and above-average students, the program itself remained largely unchanged.

Other EBCE programs reflected quite a different view; they emphasized career exploration and helped students find occupational placements, sometimes at the expense of the program's academic content. For example, an EBCE program director in a small Eastern city redesigned his job in order to spend much of his time in the community recruiting sites and maintaining relations with resource people. He paid little attention to his few classes. "The students are only in the EBCE center for social studies and some sciences," he told us, "so we don't spend that much time with them." This variation, besides slighting the academic component, caused other faculty members to resent the director's flaunted freedom and to resist the EBCE program whenever possible.

There also were teachers who totally ignored EBCE's stated goals, using the program instead as a vehicle for reaching non-EBCE ends. One counselor had long been committed to developing a minority studies program in his high school but had received little support from colleagues or administrators. When the school district's administrators selected his school for EBCE as part of a magnet school desegregation plan, he enlisted as a part-time learning coordinator and began to work out his minority studies program under EBCE auspices. "My objective is to get a core group of students who would come into EBCE and pursue . . . cultural projects," he told us. In this case, district administrators had interpreted EBCE in terms of certain legal needs, and this staff member created a further variation on what was already a local improvisation.

Meanwhile, teachers not directly involved with EBCE had welcoming, hostile, or mixed reactions to the innovation—reactions that also helped to shape local programs. Some teachers in academic disciplines resisted EBCE as an attempt to water down the curriculum or as a threat to job security. The entire English department at one school opposed EBCE on the ground that it did not challenge students sufficiently. In this urban district, hard hit by declining enrollments, the teachers also blamed EBCE for drawing students away from some elective courses. They obstructed the program in several ways, describing it as an inferior track, assigning unusually demanding makeup work for classes missed because of EBCE, and marking students absent for participating in officially sanctioned out-of-school activities. Not surprisingly, some students refrained from joining EBCE, others dropped out, and student recruitment and program maintenance became a problem for EBCE staff.

Other non-EBCE teachers simply regarded the program as a nuisance. In one large suburban school EBCE was set up as a school-within-a-school for low-achieving, disruptive students. As an alternative on-campus program it had considerable autonomy and few links to regular school life. Before the end of the first year, however, the social studies department, which shared a building with the EBCE program, complained to the principal that EBCE students were a source of disruption. The social studies teachers recommended that the program be moved to another building. EBCE staff members responded by persuading a widely respected teacher to join their program; they also persuaded the administration to designate EBCE as a regular school department. This helped legitimize the program for average and above-average students, who began to enroll. Thus the program survived, but it changed. Within four years the school-within-a-school serving a small subpopulation became an integrated department offering courses to all students.

If many non-EBCE staff members were hostile to the innovation, others welcomed it for providing a real service by meeting special student needs.

One special education teacher viewed EBCE mainly as an alternative for "youngsters with just-below-average IQs who cannot make it in the regular classroom." In this school EBCE developed into a highly individualized remedial program to serve high-risk students who were not being helped elsewhere.

Other teachers welcomed EBCE because they could use it as a dumping ground for students with academic or behavioral problems. The staff of one program, established to serve "difficult" students, tried to recruit a better cross section in the third year, hoping to provide role models for less able students and more manageable conditions for themselves. But they had little success. Counselors continued to refer their problem students to the program, and classroom teachers said, "If you're not taking the problem youngsters, what good are you?" This program changed little, continuing to focus on academic and conseling components while ambitious early plans—such as long-term community placements—never materialized.

The concerns of administrators and school board members differed from those of teachers. In one community we visited, administrators tried to use EBCE to attract white students to an all-black school. Fearing a court order, they promoted EBCE to white students for its individualization, its flexible crediting and scheduling, and its difference from other school programs— all themes that were emphatically played in this local improvisation.

In a New England town, by contrast, the school board approved adoption of EBCE to curtail dropouts (and because it brought the district more than $100,000 in federal and state grants). Here the program evolved into an effort to keep marginal students in school long enough to get their diplomas. Another district in a particularly conservative state was more concerned with students who remained in school. There the school board adopted an academically oriented program tailored for above-average students.

In one small suburban school system a bare majority of the board approved a middle-level administrators' proposal to start an EBCE program, allowing him only a tiny budget. The result was a one-dimensional version of EBCE: A lone teacher spent one-fourth of her time in classroom activities with a handful of students, and career development was virtually ignored. Even this tiny program did not survive when the district's financial situation worsened after eighteen months. Although one holdout board member spoke at length about how such a program might have helped his daughter, now floundering in college, the board voted to discontinue EBCE.

District administrators and school boards, like teachers, thus had varying views of EBCE. Some improvised on the innovation to solve nagging local problems ranging from desegregation to dropout rates; others, more concerned with average student populations and conventional agendas, adopted EBCE as a mainstream program instead of an alternative. In either case, the program evolved from a particular configuration of interpretations.

For building principals charged with keeping a school running smoothly and keeping track of students, EBCE was often a source of irritation. One rural school principal, for example, told us that he was annoyed when students wanted to quit EBCE because they considered their job placements menial. What bothered him was "the enormous hassle" of reabsorbing these students into the regular program midway through the semester.

Other principals had nothing against the innovation per se but saw it as just one more program and one more headache. One principal let his faculty know that he was no friend of the program. Some teachers followed his lead, discouraging students from joining, disparaging those who did participate, and obstructing the program in other ways. Naturally, the program became an enduring source of controversy in this district.

Some principals were truly committed to EBCE's stated goals. One assistant principal told us that he wanted to insure that "every student in the high school has the option" of experiencing EBCE. Others saw it as a way to get problem youngsters out of school, where they could not disrupt classes. In one district the assistant principals in the middle and high schools had been pushing for an alternative program for alienated students. Here EBCE was shaped to this purpose. Some principals recognized the public relations value of a community-oriented program; they welcomed the exposure EBCE afforded their schools—and, by extension, their own careers. Others were grateful for the increased budgets, which helped them meet other needs.

EBCE thus turned out to be many different programs, developed by diverse groups and individuals improvising on a set of central themes. Such local divergence stems from the fact that school districts lack a simple, single purpose, and school district organization allows wide variation in what goes on in individual schools and classrooms. Instead of encouraging consensus around formal goals, federal intervention in local school districts tends to aggravate differences as teachers, administrators, and specialists interpret the program in terms of varied work realities and role requirements. *The difference between federal hopes and local action is not simply or necessarily the result of federal mismanagement or local obstinacy; it is due to differing and often contradictory local perceptions of a program and its purpose.* From our perspective, then, implementation is a misnomer. It is wiser to think of local installation of federal programs as a continuing process of policymaking, during which various actors press their varied visions of policy.

EBCE is a particular kind of federal program, well suited to this interpretation. It was not mandated for a specific student population, nor was it intended to remedy a constitutionally defined inequity. Rather, it was made available to volunteering school districts by a combination of government and private agencies who had at their disposal no sticks and but a few carrots—some funds, but mostly recognition, free training, and free materials. The role of central authority is necessarily limited in such a program, and the influences at the periphery are consequently stronger. Thus "mutual adaptation" is more likely to occur among the elements at the periphery than between federal sponsor and local agency. But our interpretation of implementation as policy evolution is not limited to voluntary programs. The strong influence of local forces and the prevalence of mutual adaptation at the periphery seem typical of federal school programs. Even in categorical programs, where a strong federal role is possible in principle, there have been few instances in which federal directives authoritatively and uniformly steered local program development.

Our focus on program evolution in response to local diversity explains what was hard to explain in the inherited view: the persistent failure of local education agencies to do what is expected of them. In terms of evolution and organizational diversity, what once seemed irrational now seems natural and logical. But this raises new questions: How does one recognize good or successful implementation? Whose view of success should prevail?

Our answer is that there is no single, simple answer. A partial answer is to admit that there are varieties of success and that no single criterion can encompass them. Another but quite uncertain answer is to try to frame criteria for success in terms of processes, using such notions as problem solving to judge whether good things are happening. Yet another is to concede that no single intelligence can comprehend all the possible views of success, and to hope that helpful pictures will emerge out of diverse and divergent stories of implementation.

But if we can envision these and other solutions to the question of what constitutes successful implementation, it would be rash to imagine that we can pick the best one. For millenia human beings have examined their history, trying to assess the import of an action and the success of what was done. They have struggled to distinguish the important events and to identify what was important about them. They have tried to explain how men succeeded, how they failed, and why. These are the same issues that now bedevil students of federal program implementation. And there is no reason to believe that, in the study of federal program implementation, social scientists will solve these old and difficult problems.

References

Cohen, D.K. "The Value of Social Experiments." In *Planned Variation in Education: Should We Give Up or Try Harder?*, edited by A.M. Rivlin and P.M. Timpane. Washington, D.C.: Brookings Institution, 1975.

Cohen, D.K., and E. Farrar. "Power to the Parents? The Story of Education Vouchers." *The Public Interest* (Summer 1977): 72-98.

Derrick, M. *New Towns in-Town: Why a Federal Program Failed.* Washington, D.C.: Urban Institute, 1972.

Frieden, B., and M. Kaplan. *The Politics of Neglect: Urban Aid from Model Cities to Revenue Sharing.* Cambridge, Mass.: MIT Press, 1975.

Guba, E. "Development, Diffusion, and Evaluation." In *Knowledge Production and Utilization in Educational Administration*, edited by T.L. Eidell and J.M. Kitchell. Eugene, Ore.: Center for Advanced Studies of Educational Administration, University of Oregon, 1968.

Levinson, E., et al. "The Politics and Implementation of the Alum Rock Multiple Option System: The Second Year." *Analysis of the Education Voucher Demonstration, A Working Note.* Santa Monica, Calif.: Rand Corporation, May 1975.

Lortie, D.C. *School Teacher: A Sociological Study.* Chicago: University of Chicago Press, 1975.

Luckas, C. "Problems in Implementing Head Start Planned Variation Models." In *Planned Variation in Education: Should We Give Up or Try Harder?*, edited by A.M. Rivlin and P.M. Timpane. Washington, D.C.: Brookings Institution, 1975.

McLaughlin, M.W. *Evaluation and Reform.* Cambridge, Mass.: Ballinger, 1975.

Majone, G., and A. Wildavsky. "Implementation as Evolution: Exorcising the Ghosts in the Implementation Machine." *Russell Sage Discussion Papers*, no. 2. New York: Sage Foundation, 1978.

Murphy, J.T. "Title I of ESEA: The Politics of Implementing Federal Education Reform." *Harvard Educational Review* (February 1971): 35-63.

_____. *State Education Agencies and Discretionary Funds.* Lexington, Mass.: D.C. Heath & Co., 1974.

Pressman, J., and A. Wildavsky. *Implementation.* Berkeley: University of California Press, 1973.

Rand Corporation. *Federal Programs Supporting Educational Change.* 3 vols. Santa Monica, Calif.: Rand Corporation, April 1975.

van Geel, T. "Efficiency, Effectiveness, and Local School Systems: Will School Systems Adopt Planning, Programming, and Budgeting?" Doctoral dissertation, Harvard University, 1972.

Weick, K.E. "Educational Organizations as Loosely Coupled Systems." *Administrative Science Quarterly* (March 1976): 1-19.

Weiler, D. *A Public School Voucher Demonstration: The First Year at Alum Rock.* Santa Monica, Calif.: Rand Corporation, June 1974.

Weiner, S.S., and K. Kellen. "The Politics and Administration of the Voucher Demonstration in Alum Rock: The First Year, 1972-73." *Analysis of the Education Voucher Demonstration, A Working Note.* Santa Monica, Calif.: Rand Corporation, August 1974.

7

The Rise and Fall of PPBS in California

Michael Kirst

In August 1965, President Lyndon B. Johnson directed all the major civilian agencies of the federal government to install planning, programming, and budgeting systems [PPBS] along the general outlines of procedures used in the Defense Department. He also required each agency to establish a central program policy and planning staff to assist in installing the system and implementing its planning and analytical functions. In recent applications, PPBS has three major purposes: (1) the quantification of educational outputs, (2) the analysis of optimum resource combinations for attaining specified outputs (goals, objectives), and (3) a basis for multiyear funding.

Attempts to design this new planning and budgeting process quickly spread to many state and local units of government. Among the groups intrigued with PPBS was the California legislature. In October 1966, this body followed the recommendation of Speaker Jesse Unruh and established the Advisory Commission of School Budgeting and Accounting. This citizens' commission appeared to be the first step in state-mandated installation of PPBS in California's 1,056 school districts.

Seven years later, the California legislature made a 180-degree turn and abandoned PPBS. All that remains is an accounting system that provides some program information at a very high level of aggregation. Filed in the

Reprinted, by permission, from *Phi Delta Kappan*, no. 56 (April 1975): 535–38.

state archives are the elaborate PPBS manuals developed at a cost of several million dollars. State education department officials never use the word PPBS in public. Local school people have long forgotten the in-service training sessions on PPBS that were so prominently featured statewide in the late 1960s.

Why did PPBS almost become mandated state policy and then die so completely in 1972? The answer to this can tell us a lot about education politics and the conceptual problems of the current "accountability movement."

The Rise of PPBS

California's constitution empowers the State Board of Education [SBE] to establish budget categories for financial reporting by local school districts. Traditionally, the state superintendent of public instruction advised the SBE in budget planning matters. But State Superintendent Max Rafferty faced a state board and a legislature that disagreed strongly with his educational philosophy, major policies, and higher political ambitions.[1] Consequently, the Democratically controlled legislature created a series of citizen's advisory commissions that reported directly to the Democratically controlled SBE. In 1968 Rafferty confirmed the suspicions of his rivals (that he was not a non-partisan educational expert), by running as a Republican for the United States Senate against the ultimate winner, United States Senator Alan Cranston.

The eleven-member Commission on School District Budgeting and Accounting included representatives from a taxpayers' association, the business community, professors, school administrators, county government, school boards, and the accounting profession. The commission chairman adopted the broad mandate that the commission should reform all aspects of educational management, including procedures for setting educational goals. The legislature's charge to the commission, however, included only the terms "program budgeting and accounting system."

The commission's first order of business was to hire a management consulting firm to assist in experimentation with pilot districts and [to] draw up a detailed PPB manual for local use. The commission selected an accounting firm—Peat, Marwick, and Mitchell (PMM) from a group of six bidders.

Six pilot districts were selected to represent a cross section of the state. PMM set up a procedure for deriving educational goals and objectives,

---

[1]For an elaboration, see Berke and Kirst (1972, Chap. 3).

following the general concepts of the behavioral objectives adherents (see Mager 1968). As an example, PMM cited this objective:

By the end of the eighth grade, the student will read and pronounce with 90 percent accuracy ten lists of eighth-grade words selected from a basal reading text.

PMM's first progress reports indicated some disagreement between the consultants and pilot districts ("goals and objectives are not consistent with definitions provided in PMM manual"). Ten in-service meetings were held by the end of 1970, with a mixed reception. Some schoolmen objected to the PMM notion of goal setting as a prerequisite to establishing objectives that in turn provided the conceptual base for program budget categories.

In 1968, two hundred school districts applied for nine positions in the second group of pilot districts. The incentive was hardly financial, because the state offered $12,000—less than installation costs. As one school business officer remarked, his district believed PPBS was "the coming thing," so it was best to get on the bandwagon early. For example, Victor Veysey, Republican chairman of the Assembly Education Committee, remarked in 1970:

There's just this compelling cry from the people... an unsettling feeling of dissatisfaction with what they see in the schools. And PPBS is going to force them to sit down and do some things.

For the first time, the boards and the people in our communities will understand where their schools are going. [Los Angeles Times 1970].

Indeed, PPBS was only one of several legislatively initiated programs aimed in the same general direction. The legislature had established another commission to conduct education cost effectiveness experiments, and had passed a "Guaranteed Learning Achievement Act."

First Warning Signals

In November 1970, the SBE heard six hours of testimony on the PMM program structure, composed of six program levels. For instance, English would be broken down to speech, listening, spelling, handwriting, and so on. Given the momentum favoring PPBS, the amount of criticism was surprising. At similar hearings, the Advisory Commission on School Budgeting and Accounting heard procedural and technical suggestions from the major professional education interest groups. Only one group, the English Teachers of California, asked the SBE not to institute any PPBS system. They contended that the establishment of goals and objectives was impossible in their field. The AFT-affiliated California

Federation of Teachers, however, cautioned that PPBS could place the public schools in "an accounting straitjacket at the very time that educators say the education program needs drastic reform" (*Sacramento Bee* 1970). The State Board of Education, however, did not hear enough opposition to warrant a change of course and ordered the state department to rewrite the accounting manual by 1972.

The advisory commission held more public hearings on the conceptual approach of PPBS in 1971. These hearings focused on goals, objectives, and systematic analysis techniques to maximize effectiveness. At this point, determined and powerful opposition began to appear from three groups: the English teachers, the conservative United Republicans of California (UROC), and the legislature's Joint Committee on Education Goals and Evaluation chaired by John Vasconcellos, a liberal assembly man from San Jose. UROC envisioned PPBS as a centralized thought control system that would lead to behavioral modifications, with possible violations of personal freedom.

Today's educational planning can claim an unbroken ancestry running back to ancient times.... The Spartans, some 2,500 years ago, planned their education to fit their well-defined military, social, and economic objectives.... These early examples... show how educational planning has been resorted to in periods of great social and intellectual ferment to help change a society to fit new goals.[2]

Approval of a program accounting structure was portrayed by UROC as a shrewd strategy to implement acceptable, uncontroversial parts in order to pave the way for unacceptable education goal setting.

"Liberal" or "humanistic" opposition was led by a special Joint Legislative Committee on Educational Goals and Evaluation. There was an obvious overlapping of purposes between the joint committee and the PPBS commission. The former was opposed to any centralized planning "system" and favored goal setting with parent involvement at each school site. It supported a bottom-up goal-setting process from the school site and pictured PPBS as top-down central management. Moreover, the committee staff contended that the PPBS commission had gone beyond its original assignment and should not have concerned itself with educational goals. In short, the joint committee envisioned PPBS as a method for giving central school administrators the power to set goals instead of school-site community participation in goal setting. Chairman Vasconcellos was also troubled by the behavioral objectives orientation of PMM.

While opposition was building between 1970 and 1972, the commission

---

[2]UROC presentation to California State Board of Education, June 1972.

remained optimistic because of the positive attitude of the major professional education organizations. The California School Boards Association even helped pay for the printing of the commission's draft proposal and co-sponsored workshops around the state. The school administrator associations offered general support and made many suggestions for technical changes. The largest teacher organization, the NEA-affiliated California Teachers Association, favored the general concept of PPBS, but wanted to be sure the system was applicable to education and that teachers established the "working objectives."[3]

The Fall of PPBS

In May 1972, a crucial vote on statewide implementation was held by the State Board of Education. Contrary to most expectations, the PPBS draft failed. Five favorable votes were cast, and only two were opposed, but six votes are required for passage (an absolute majority of the ten-member board). There was one SBE vacancy and one member was absent. After the vacancy was filled in 1972, PPBS again failed by five to two, with one abstention. The two "no" votes were influenced by the conservative arguments. The abstainer, Tony Sierra, was a friend of Assemblyman Vasconcellos and came to agree with his viewpoint. One of the absent members supported PPB, but was injured in an auto accident.

In that same month, the legislature nailed the lid down on the PPBS coffin by passing ACR 98, a resolution to discontinue all efforts to

... encourage or establish the statewide implementation of an educational planning and evaluation guide for California school districts or any other form of a program planning and budgeting system whatsoever until such time as the legislature has ... taken any legislative action it deems appropriate, provided, however, that nothing in this resolution shall restrain local governing boards from their efforts to refine methods of accounting and budget reporting.

The resolution was passed with little discussion and there was no need for lobbying prior to the vote. In effect, support for PPBS had eroded from the right, left, and center. Assemblyman Robert Burke, an Orange County Republican, spoke strongly against PPBS. Burke is a UROC supporter and one of the most conservative members of the legislature. On the left, Vasconcellos played a key role in ACR 98's passage. But the bill carried the

---

[3] Data drawn from periodic summaries published by the Advisory Commission. I am indebted to Aaron Gunvitz and Van Alper for collecting much of this research.

name of Assemblyman John Dunlap, a moderate Democrat from Sacramento.

On July 1, 1972, the original PPBS commission was dissolved. Its successor recommended, and the state board approved, a limited program budget accounting format. It stops at the level of specifying elementary and secondary objectives, special projects, and so on. This is an improvement over function-object categories, but is a long way from the detailed program breakdowns (ceramics, aquatics, and life science) that PMM recommended. The legislature's opposition was viewed as so strong that SDE personnel have pulled back from any push in the cost-effectiveness or systems analysis areas. Ironically, other states have moved forward in this area while the initiator, California, has retreated.[4]

Why the Rise and Fall

The rise of PPBS in California schools was part of a national wave of interest in systematic analysis and improved management information. PPBS was implemented in the Department of Defense and in some other domestic areas (see Joint Economic Committee 1969). But the early enthusiasm was not based on a clear understanding of the peculiar problems in education. Indeed, the early presentations to California educators used the Defense Department's charts comparing air-lift versus sea-lift. Moreover, PPBS initially focused on the "motherhood" issues of efficiency and improved management in education. The early stress on output-oriented accounting could hardly provoke vociferous opposition. At the outset, PPBS was defined as a technical issue that could be handled by an accounting firm.

The advisory commission, with the legislature's initial support, chose to broaden its purview into such controversial issues as:

—What should be the goals and objectives of education?

—Who should set those goals and what process should be used?

—How can a program budget structure be linked to systematic analysis of the relationship between "inputs" and goals?

This broadening of focus mobilized opposition from forces on the left and right, which could not expect their favored goals to be chosen by the

---

[4]For a summary of state activity, see Education Commission of the States (1973). Some local districts in California still use elements of the PPBS system.

most powerful interest groups in California state education policy.[5] In a state as diverse as California, once an issue changes from a technical problem to a value conflict, political coalitions will mobilize.

PPBS also evoked competition among three perspectives on the nature of education: industrial, behavioristic, and biological.[6] The industrial metaphor springs from Frederick Taylor's scientific management movement. Education took place in the plant under the direction of a superintendent, with teachers engaged in a job of engineering inputs into outputs (Callahan 1962). This simplistic view has been refined and improved considerably by contemporary economists. The behavioristic metaphor emerged with efforts to construct a science of education. Its appeal lies in the assumption that educational and psychological research will reveal those capabilities that are essential to the performance of the activities which the school is responsible for cultivating. The school curriculum should give first priority to development of these scientifically identified capabilities. The third metaphor, the biological, is endorsed by the "humanistic" approach that stresses the concept that a teacher *follows* as well as leads the child in developing intellectual and emotional autonomy (see Combs 1972). Each of these three conceptions of education takes a different view of the nature and desirability of PPBS. In California, this disagreement led to disillusionment with the PPBS concept itself and a realization that there were more than technical issues involved.

Legislative moderates withdrew their support partly because proponents were unable to apply input-output, systems analysis, or production functions to education. One of the nation's foremost economics of education researchers, Jesse Burkhead (1973), has summarized his own research and the state of the art:

Apart from the data problem, which will continue to be serious, there are also some conceptual difficulties in the microeconomic analysis of education. In the estimation of production functions in the private sector, it is assumed that a factory manager, for example, has reasonably good knowledge of the marginal productivity of the factors that he utilizes and thus he is able to optimize factor combinations to maximize profit. But in elementary and secondary education there is no reason to assume that a school principal or district superintendent or board of education has knowledge of or interest in the marginal productivity of resource inputs. Even if these were known, it could not be assumed that it would be possible to secure least-cost combinations, given the institutional rigidities of mandates and conventional practice. Neither is there a reasonable substitute for the objective

---

[5]For an analysis of California interest group influence and organization, see Meltsner et al. (1973).
[6]I am indebted to William Furry, a Stanford graduate student, for this typology.

function of profit maximization. Thus the optimization rationale that underlies production functions in the private sector is inapplicable for elementary and secondary education [pp. 193–205].

Economist Henry Levin (1971) has expressed the view even more strongly:

... we have asserted that such studies [production functions] suffer from theoretical and econometric deficiencies that are so severe that their recommendations may spawn greater inefficiencies in the production of education.

Burkhead (1973) analyzed the PMM California budget manual and the use of it by Hillsborough, one of the pilot districts. His reaction [was]:

The striking characteristic about all of these PPB systems is their unbelievable complexity, the attention to the minutiae of budgetary classification, and their costliness—in terms of manhours, paid and unpaid, staff time, teacher time, community time [p. 201].

Hillsborough spent two years formulating goals through committees composed of school board members, administrators, teachers, parents, and some students. The committee for the primary mathematics program alone specified fifty-eight goals to be attained by the second grade. For example, Goal 50 is, "Analyze and solve story problems as presented in the GCMP math program with 80 percent accuracy." The primary social studies program for second grade specifies seven goals for civics and history, including the memorization of the Pledge of Allegiance. There is even one in economics: "By the end of the second grade, all students will be able to list the way foods are processed (packaged, stored, distributed, and marketed)."

Expenditure tabulations were developed for each program to yield costs per student, including overhead allocations. California legislators agreed with Burkhead's assessment that "this is systems analysis run riot, and it will inevitably bog down of its own weight." Moreover, the academics have overrefined the analytical techniques to the point where they cannot be operationalized by school administrators. Elegant journal articles on Monte Carlo techniques and Markov chains may provide promotions for professors but cannot be operationalized by school district budget officers. A less elaborate but perhaps more useful procedure would be for each large school district to retain some economists who can examine program issues that are susceptible to quantitative analysis. Better program budgeting formats have also been developed since the California experiment ended, and these are used in school districts in California and elsewhere (see

Knezevich 1973). Moreover, one of the outcomes of PPBS has been the efforts by many California districts to consider priorities among competing broad objectives.

The Incremental Step Forward

The current California accounting manual is the "disjointed incremental" step that political theorists would predict. An exceedingly large and diverse number of political actors was involved: activist citizens, public accountants, legislators, state department careerists, professional associations, the State Board of Education, and so on. The rather unusual political environment in California resulted in a Citizens' Advisory Commission as the vehicle for refining PPBS. This commission was not supported by any major political or institutional leader like the governor, a legislative committee chairman, or the state superintendent of schools. Unlike these public figures, the advisory commission had no constituency or reservoir of political resources that it could use to build a positive coalition. State Superintendent Wilson Riles adopted a wait-and-see attitude when he replaced Rafferty in 1970. Riles observed, "When I talk about goals and resources and evaluation, PPBS has to be a part of it. But I want to make sure all the bugs are shaken out first"(*Los Angeles Times* 1970).

Once the vocal opposition coalesced, the support for PPBS proved to be very shallow. It appears that legislators want public school accountability, but only if the particular accountability techniques used do not provoke organized opposition extending beyond professional educators. The California experience makes me suspect that accountability will be confined to technical issues and performance reporting. Much of the data will either obfuscate or avoid areas with significant value conflict. Consequently, parents and laymen will rarely become concerned or involved.

References

Berke, J.S., and M.W. Kirst. *Federal Aid to Education: Who Benefits, Who Governs?* Lexington, Mass.: D.C. Heath, 1972.

Burkhead, J. "Economics Against Education." *Teachers College Record* (December 1973).

Callahan, R. *Education and the Cult of Efficiency.* Chicago: University of Chicago, 1962.

Combs, A. *Educational Accountability: Beyond Behavioral Objectives.* Washington, D.C.: Association for Supervision and Curriculum Development, 1972.

Education Commission of the States. *Legislation and Achievements: Accountability, Assessment, and Testing.* Denver: ECS, 1973.

Joint Economic Committee. *The Analysis and Evaluation of Public Expenditures: The PPBS System.* Washington, D.C.: Government Printing Office, 1969.

Knezevich, S. *Program Budgeting.* Berkeley: McCutchan, 1973.

Levin, H.M. "Concepts of Economic Efficiency and Educational Process." Unpublished manuscript. Chicago: National Bureau of Economic Research, 1971.

Los Angeles Times. July 26, 1970.

Lumsdaine, A.M., and R. Glaser, eds. *Teaching Machines and Programmed Learning.* Washington, D.C.: National Education Association, 1960.

Mager, R. *Developing Attitude Toward Learning.* Palo Alto, Calif.: Fearon, 1968.

Meltsner, A., et al. *The Political Feasibility of School Finance Reform.* New York: Praeger, 1973.

Sacramento Bee. November 13, 1970.

8

Planned Change in Rural School Districts

Terrence Deal and Samuel Nutt

What happens when small rural school districts receive large federal grants to promote comprehensive changes? The Experimental Schools program was created by the U.S. Office of Education in 1970 to address a concern that previous efforts to change schools had not worked because of their piecemeal approach. By contrast, the Experimental Schools program encouraged comprehensive change in schools districts and, in some respects, eliminated many of the problems that frustrated earlier efforts. It provided ample monetary resources. It required that all aspects of districts—curriculum, instruction, time, space, facilities, governance, and citizen participation—be transformed simultaneously. It provided a year for communities to plan their own individual projects. Finally, it promised support for a locally controlled project tailored to the unique problems and needs of each district and community involved. In the minds of many

Adapted, with permission, from Terrence E. Deal and Samuel Nutt, *Promoting, Guiding, and Surviving Change in Educational Organizations* (Cambridge, Mass.: Abt Associates, 1979). This paper was prepared in connection with "The Longitudinal Study of Educational Change in Rural America," a research project conducted by Abt Associates, Inc., of Cambridge, Massachusetts, to contract No. 499-78-0034 with the National Institute of Education of the U.S. Department of Education. Both authors are affiliated with the Harvard Graduate School of Education.

policymakers and administrators, this approach provided all the necessary ingredients for capturing the elusive prize—major change in the American school system.

The announcement of a grants competition was sent initially to all school districts in the country. Responses to this first announcement produced a series of planning grants—all of which were awarded to large urban school districts. However, a later announcement was targeted solely to 7,500 small school districts in the country—those with enrollments of fewer than 2,500 students.

To many administrators working in these small school districts, the announcement was the answer to their prayers: substantial, long-term funding to create an ideal educational system. The only apparent string attached was that the changes be comprehensive, that is, to involve all important aspects of the district. But to create an ideal system, a major overhaul would be necessary anyway.

The announcement elicited letters of interest from 319 small districts. On the basis of initial screening, site visits, and geographical considerations, ten sites were selected to participate in the program. Six promptly received full five-year commitments. Four received conditional commitments for one year of planning activities, which were then followed by five years of additional funding. The ten sites were geographically dispersed (see Figure 8-1) and represented a cross-section of small school districts [See Deal and Nutt 1979 for details].

In addition to the federal dollars given directly to districts for planning and implementing comprehensive change, the Experimental Schools [ES] program commissioned a large-scale research study, the contract for which was awarded to Abt Associates, Inc., of Cambridge, Massachusetts. The purpose of the research was to document the experiences of each school district and to pinpoint factors across districts that facilitated or impeded progress toward comprehensive change. Trained anthropologists or sociologists were assigned as on-site observers to all ten districts and spent over three years observing events and gathering information. In addition, questionnaires were completed by teachers, administrators, on-site researchers, and others. The resulting case studies and longitudinal analysis document the impact of the ES program on local communities and on student achievement as well as highlight strategies that administrators used to address the problems of planning and implementing large-scale change projects in small rural communities.

The ideas and guidelines contained in this chapter were extracted from three principal sources: case studies of eight of the ten districts that participated in the Experimental Schools program (Burns 1979; Clinton

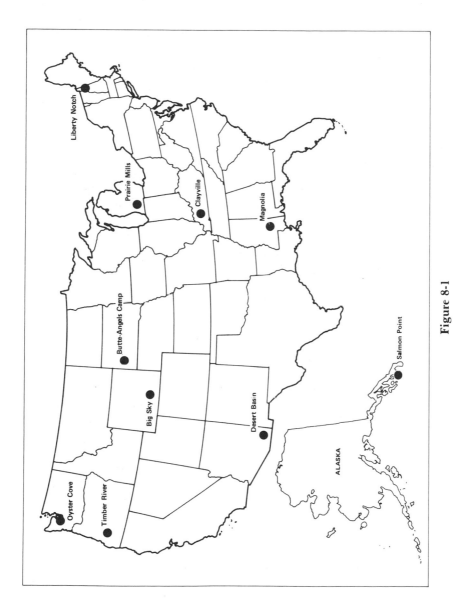

Figure 8-1

Geographical locations of the ten school districts participating in the rural ES program

1979; Colfer and Colfer 1979; Donnelly 1979; Firestone 1977; Hennigh 1979; Messerschmidt 1979; and Stannard 1979), a report analyzing questionnaire and interview responses from teachers and administrators across all ten sites (Rosenblum and Louis 1978), and a book containing chapter-length versions of five of the case studies and interpretations by several leading social scientists and practitioners (Herriott and Gross 1979).

As we read through the case studies and tried to extract common principles, an image of school organizations began to coalesce. Administrators were often surprised and caught off guard by events that arose as they planned and implemented their Experimental Schools projects. Strategies developed to make things better often made things worse. Effective strategies—where they existed—often evolved naturally as a result of random events rather than through conscious administrative design.

Planning and Implementing Change in Experimental Schools Districts: Surprises, Diplomacy, and Conflict

The stories of the ten school districts undertaking a mission of major change reflect the unique characteristics of the settings in which the dramas were played out. But, in three areas at least, the stories have a common ring, which may suggest what might be done differently as similar dramas are created in response to contemporary pressures for change.

First, administrators frequently were caught off guard when the script they had in mind seemed different from the lines that other actors delivered. Second, the anticipated joys of planning began to wane once the cast was assembled and everyone began to see that each had a different idea of what the play was supposed to be. As planning moved along, differences were buried in the eloquent lines of the script, and the director took an increasingly strong role in interpreting and determining what the main plot would be. Third, as the drama began to unfold, it was very clear that individual actors continued to hold very different ideas of the script, that they were determined to carry off their part as they saw it, that the director had no real power over either the actors' guild or the audience, that the patrons were not sure what they had commissioned or why, and that the drama that everyone had anticipated was quickly becoming either a comedy or a tragedy—no one was sure which. Finally, the squabbles and struggles began to take on a life of their own, resulting in the ten districts becoming stages on which actors, audience, sponsor, director, set manager, and others participated in a five-year skit.

Surprises in Planning and Implementing Change

The ten districts selected for participation in the ES program received federal funding for a somewhat amorphous yet awesome task—planning and implementing comprehensive change. Federal money was to be used to develop a plan and, over an extended period of time, to use the plan as a basis for making significant alterations in instruction, governance, community relationships, and other parts of the district and its schools.

The stages of the process of planning and implementing change in the ten ES districts are depicted in Figure 8-2, where it is apparent that, although planning activities were heavily emphasized in the initial year of the five-year effort, certain implementation activities were concurrently under way in many districts. In the next four years, the emphasis shifted to putting plans into action. Even so, some level of planning activity persisted throughout the life of each project. Two main points are illustrated in the figure: planning and implementation are distinct stages in a change process, yet they also overlap.

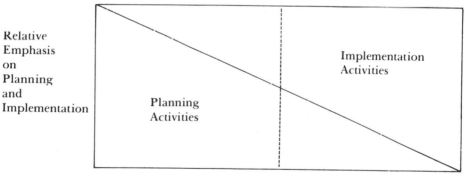

Planning Stage (1972–73)   Implementation Stage (1973–77)

Figure 8-2

Planning and implementing change in ES schools

Adapted from M. Miles, "Thinking About How to Do It: Alternative Models of Planning and Implementation of New Schools," Mimeographed (New York: Center for Policy Research, 1976).

During both stages, administrators were frequently caught off guard or surprised as events unfolded contrary to their expectations. In many cases, the discrepancy between expectations and actual events occurred either because administrators failed to accurately map the various constituencies and to anticipate their reactions, or because they failed to forecast important connections between the stages of change.

In Timber River, for example, the school district had been involved in a major improvement effort for five years prior to the announcement of the ES competition by the U.S. Office of Education. The superintendent saw the additional federal resources as a way of moving beyond mere improvement to a lighthouse school district. He and two of his district administrators drafted the initial letter of interest. That letter and subsequent negotiations secured an award of $1.2 million for the district. When the administration announced the award to the faculty at an orientation meeting opening the 1973 school year, expecting that it would be met with approval and enthusiasm, one faculty member stood up, pointed his finger at the superintendent, and shouted, "You dared to make such a decision without consulting the faculty?"[1]

In retrospect, this event makes sense. For five years administrators had pushed teachers to make needed changes in instructional approaches, changes that were strongly supported by the local community and made without significant internal or external conflict. In the course of the administrator's extended pressure on teachers, however, some implicit understandings had developed. In the year of the ES grant award, teachers were anticipating that they would have at least a year of rest, free of administrative pressure. The new grant was thus viewed as another potential intrusion by the administration.

An important lesson to be gleaned from this experience is that the history of a school district and the existing relationships among teachers, administrators, and parents or local residents—often subtle and implicit—can greatly influence how a new project is initially received. If administrators don't assess the history of understandings and relationships before initiating change, they may be caught off guard by the reaction.

In Clayville, for example, a consultant assumed that a workshop designed to attract teachers to diagnostic-prescriptive instruction would be well-received by teachers. To teachers, however, the event represented a political encroachment by the administration on their turf. (The consultant had been retained by the superintendent.) The consultant's

---

[1] See Hennigh (1979) for a more detailed description of this event. Throughout this chapter, we provide citations for quotes, ideas, illustrations, and events so that readers who wish can consult the specific case study.

optimism was based on an assumption that agreements that had been reached during the planning stage of the project would carry over as the plans were implemented. During the workshop, teachers began to complain about the ES project and then virtually ignored the consultant until he finally remarked, "I came here assuming that everyone was complying with the agreement we made last August. One thing I learned tonight is to make sure that I know what is going on before I made a damned fool of myself" (Clinton 1979).

Two faculty assumptions contributed to this event. The first was that administrators can encroach upon teachers' turf. In this case the consultant, clearly aligned with administrators, violated boundaries by attempting to influence how teachers teach. The second faulty assumption was that agreements reached during the planning stage remain mutually binding as proposed innovations begin to be implemented. In fact, agreements reached during planning are often vague and amorphous, so each group or constituency interprets agreements through the frame of its own interests. While vague agreements reduce or suppress conflict during planning, the conflicts surface during implementation when reactions to tangible events underscore the existing differences among various groups.

A contingent from Butte-Angels Camp was surprised by the treatment given them by representatives of ES/Washington when they negotiated their final contract. The group expected a routine meeting to clarify details and to fix the final dollar amount of the contract. Instead, they were subjected to abrasive questioning about minute details of their plan. One board member from Butte-Angels Camp was reduced to tears as a result of being grilled about some technical jargon buried in the plan. Following the session, the district superintendent and a counselor who had accompanied the group worked most of the night to revise the plan (Messerschmidt 1979).

Here again, failure to anticipate the divergent interests of constituencies resulted in a surprise. The group from Butte-Angels Camp naively anticipated that the federal government would abide by agreements announced early in the ES project when, in fact, there had been a unilateral shift at the federal level that redefined the relationship between the Experimental Schools program and local districts. The ES staff in Washington had established more stringent requirements for district plans and had abrogated previous constraints governing their influence over the development of the final plan. During the course of such a change effort, realignments between the levels are inevitable, and failure to assess the realignments accurately will product conflicts between the sponsoring agency and the local district.

A final example from Timber River illustrates how administrators can be thrown off balance by unanticipated changes in the relationship between the teachers and the local community. One of the major thrusts of the ES program in Timber River was to involve parents in the school, but issues began to develop around implicit agreements governing relations between the two groups. Problems between teachers and community aides or volunteers moved into wider community forums. Parent volunteers "leaked" confidential information to other residents, and some residents began to wonder, "If housewives can run the schools, should we pay teachers such high salaries?" In reaction, the teachers began to solidify territorial boundaries against the local community (Hennigh 1979).

As local residents began to intrude on the teachers' turf, conflicts developed between teachers and aides. In addition, representatives from the local community were now privy to internal information—"secrets"—and the sharing of this information with other residents began to undermine the implicit assumption that classrooms are immune to local community intrusions as long as things are running smoothly.

Each of these examples illustrates the kinds of surprises that administrators experienced in planning and implementing their ES projects. Most resulted from images of schools or of the change process that did not fit the realities of the situation. Existing alignments between constituencies, intrusions of one group on the territory of another, failure of administrators, teachers, or parents to meet obligations, abrogations of existing agreements, important differences among constituencies not addressed in the planning stage, and the conflict of interests that inevitably surface in implementation all produce important problems during the course of change. Anticipating these issues in advance may help administrators to minimize surprises and to avoid eliciting reactions that could undermine the effort.

Planning Change: Activities and Issues

Effective planning involves a relatively rational set of activities, although there is no prescribed sequence for those activities. In fact, in certain projects, some activities may even be omitted. But as organizations plan, the following activities are often observable:

—Determining needs.

—Identifying opportunities and obtaining resources.

—Deciding who the planners (representatives from various zones) will be and how they will be involved. Planning efforts can be highly participatory, involving not only administrators (choosers) but also those who will actually carry out the plans (implementers) or those who have some stake in the outcome (stakeholders). Or planning efforts can be centralized among choosers who merely solicit ideas from implementers and stakeholders.

—Selecting a planning process—adopting rational, systematic approaches or relying on more informal approaches ("muddling through").

—Learning of ideas, needs, and concerns from planners and communicating progress to other stakeholders.

—Selecting general directions and specific themes or strategies.

—Producing the plan—establishing its format and specifications.

—Communicating the plan to various constituencies (teachers, local community, and remote agencies who often are the "patrons" providing necessary resources).

—Negotiating and legitimizing the plan with various constituencies.

Around each of the planning activities, a number of issues and dilemmas arise. Who should be involved? How can a broad range of ideas be obtained without raising expectations that all ideas will be included? Should representatives from all groups have a role in determining general directions and selecting specific ideas from the "universe" of input received? How should events in the planning process be communicated to interested stakeholders to ensure their understanding and commitment and to minimize hearsay, gossip, and rumors? How can a coherent plan be produced by participants with diverse viewpoints in a limited amount of time? How can the plan be communicated to various constituencies to secure broad-based ownership and enthusiasm without encouraging either selective ownership over specific portions of the plan or unrealistic expectations? Who should be involved in the final negotiations with various constituencies—especially the funding agency? How can conflicts between competing interest groups be resolved?

How each of these issues and dilemmas was confronted or resolved played a major role in determining the relative success of the efforts to plan and implement changes in the ES districts.

Lessons from the Experimental Schools Districts

As the ten small school districts planned and implemented their projects, many of the general issues and dilemmas surrounding planning surfaced to frustrate and confound their efforts. Many were unanticipated surprises that made apparent a conflict of interests at the planning stage. For the most part, however, the conflicts were avoided or smoothed over during planning and did not surface in most districts until the implementation year.

Responding to the Announcement—An Administrative Initiative. The announcement of a grants competition from the Experimental Schools program reached local school districts in March 1972. In some respects, the announcement was a step in a different direction by the federal government, inviting a more intensive relationship with local communities and districts, but requiring local districts to write letters of interest that outlined their district's strengths and weaknesses and provided an idea of how a substantial influx of federal dollars might be used to support needed changes.

Response to the announcement was usually initiated and conducted by administrators, the primary initiative usually coming from the superintendent or district office administrator. In Oyster Cove, for example, the superintendent drafted the letter of interest by himself, and in Timber River, the superintendent and a cadre of district administrators prepared the letter of interest. In Magnolia, the letter of interest was drafted by a curriculum coordinator based on the district office, while in Desert Basin and Liberty Notch, the initiative came from a principal. In Clayville, the superintendent drafted the letter of interest with the assistance of consultants from a local university.

In drafting the letters, administrators were faced with several dilemmas. First, whose interests should predominate: those of the federal government, the local community, or teachers? For the most part, the letters tended to reflect the interests of the federal sponsors. "Ideas in good currency"—new knowledge, concepts, or practices produced by the academic community (either through the direct involvement of consultants or more indirectly through administrators' professional reading and course work) and used as underpinnings to gain the federal agency's approval—were generously sprinkled throughout the letters of interest.

Second, in which areas should weaknesses be identified: administrative, instructional, or local community? Generally, problems were identified in the instructional area—tired, undertrained teachers—or in the local community—apathetic residents and poorly performing students. In Timber River, the administrative team was touted as one of the district's primary strengths. In Oyster Cove, descriptions by administrators of weaknesses in other areas later created resentment on the part of teachers and community residents.

Third, how extensively should representatives from the local community or instructional constituencies be involved in drafting the letter of interest? Limitations of time and administrators' concerns about raising inappropriate issues and expectations made for limited involvement on the part of teachers, parents, and community members. The local community and teachers often were not informed until the awards of the planning grants were made. As already noted, the announcement of the grant award was greeted in Timber River with negative reactions from teachers. In Desert Basin and Prairie Mills the announcement of the award of Experimental Schools money was received with the same suspicion generally aroused in the community by any apparent federal intrusion into local affairs.

Generally, getting the ball rolling required the involvement of administrators with federal officials in a more intensive relationship. Early activities also granted ownership of the project to administrators—a legacy that often was difficult to overcome.

Project Leadership. One of the main issues to arise once planning grants were awarded was where to lodge the ES project within the administrative structure. The common strategy was to create a new staff position and to delegate responsibility for developing the ES plan to that staff member. The arrangement produced three sources of conflict. The first was uncertainty and ambiguity within the administrative structure itself, often between the superintendent and the project director. In Oyster Cove and Big Sky, for example, there was open conflict between the superintendent and the project director, as well as between the project director and principals, who were often confused about who was in charge of what.

Second, the new role of the project director created other conflicts. In some districts, outsiders were hired for the job, whose lack of knowledge of, and sensitivity to, local conditions produced conflicts between the project leaders and teachers or local residents. In Big Sky and Desert Basin, such conflicts were particularly evident.

But perhaps the most intense conflict around the issue of project leadership occurred between local districts and the federal government. Federal officials insisted that the superintendent exercise direct control over the project and often wanted a voice in the selection of the project coordinator as well. Local superintendents, on the other hand, wanted freedom to delegate responsibility to a director and to select whomever they wished for the position. Local compliance on this issue often increased the ambiguity of the director's role, and in both Liberty Notch and Magnolia, removing the locally preferred person from the position at federal insistence undercut the rapport that had earlier been established between administrators and the sponsoring agency.

Selecting a Planning Process. In addition to establishing a leadership structure, ES districts struggled to develop a planning process. The process was geneally overseen by a professional staff member—a director, evaluator, or documentarian—and a steering committee composed of representatives from several constituencies—teachers, administrators, students, parents, and other community members. The staff and steering committee provided direction for the project and channeled broad-based input from the planning process into the writing of the plan. In practice, however, this pattern commonly resulted in several problems. First, there were occasional jurisdictional conflicts between the steering committee and the school board. Second, it was hard to keep steering committees actively involved over the course of the entire planning year. Third, confusion often developed around the role of the project staff. The issue of project direction was particularly critical as the broad-based input was melded into the final plan.

Intermingling Constituencies to Obtain Ideas. Central to the Experimental Schools change effort was the idea that many participants in planning should be drawn from various groups—teachers, students, parents, and community members. Participation, an idea fashionable in academic communities, was consistently emphasized by ES/Washington. The underlying assumption was that, by intermingling representatives from different groups, proposed changes would reflect diverse interests— not just those of administrators—and would be easier to implement and sustain since central needs and interests were addressed and widely owned.

While the idea of participatory planning was appealing to the federal government, it proved difficult to operationalize in local districts. In Clayville, the superintendent of schools operated on the dictum, "One man's got to do it." His approach to community involvement was to use meetings to persuade teachers and the local community that his proposed changes were needed, rather than to solicit input and recommendations. To placate ES/Washington, the superintendent arranged for consultants to convene community meetings to "sell" citizens on the merits of the project. They also were the vehicle through which community groups were asked for recommendations. But only two recommendations became part of the final plan: providing a diagnostic center for problem children and planning more emphasis on raising achievement scores to the national norm. The superintendent was trying to develop the "best educational system in the state." His goal was consistent with community goals as long as "the football and basketball teams win, the band marches in perfect order, and the kids feel good when they come home from school." The superintendent perceptively stressed the prerogatives of administrators: as long as obligations are met and implicit agreements are honored, the community grants administrators discretion in determining how best to move ahead. The primary conflict in Clayville during the planning period was between the superintendent and ES/Washington, because the superintendent did not feel nearly as obligated as did the federal agency to involve the local community in planning the project (Clinton 1979).

In other districts, however, efforts during the planning year brought representatives from various constituencies together in a variety of settings. The involvement of teachers, parents, and citizens in planning seemed to follow basic patterns across districts: broad-based participation in large groups communicated specific interests and ideas, but did so without acknowledging contradictions and conflicts; screening groups composed of representatives from the various groups channeled diverse ideas into a common theme; writing teams (usually administrators or consultants) produced the plan; the even more select bodies negotiated the final plan with the federal agency. Across districts, the structure of the planning process resembled a funnel; ideas and interests from various groups were contributed and were channeled through a narrow "spout" controlled mainly by administrators.

As teachers, local residents, parents, and administrators (and occasionally students) intermingled in the process of planning change, the result was often ambiguity, confusion, and underlying tension and conflict. In Big Sky, for example, the advisory committee (composed of three representatives—two citizens and a teacher—from each of the district's five geographical areas) was selected late in the process. Although the committee was initially intended to be egalitarian, it soon came to be dominated by members from one of the geographical areas (Messerschmidt 1979).

In Butte-Angels Camp, teachers became confused and hostile over the mixed messages they were receiving: were their ideas being actively solicited by administrators, or were administrators merely trying to gain their acquiescence in supporting already existing ideas and projects? Widely attended meetings of parents and community residents resulted in an outpouring of general complaints about the school system and some very specific dissatisfactions with such things as the process used to select cheerleaders, or the controversy over the need for a student lounge in the high school. In these large assemblies where diverse interests were vociferously represented, each group experienced disappointment and frustration over the problems and ideas of others (Firestone 1979).

In Liberty Notch, confusion over whether the steering committee was an advisory or a decision-making body resulted in a sharp drop in participation. Each subgroup pushed for its own individual projects, and responsibility for planning the project ultimately shifted to an ad hoc committee dominated by administrators (Stannard 1979).

In Timber River, an eighteen-member coordinating committee was selected. Although the group was generally supportive of participation in the ES program, confusion arose over the group's role: was it to make decisions, inform the public, or merely serve as "window dressing"? (Hennigh 1979).

Despite confusion over the roles of teachers, community residents, and parents in the planning process, many districts were able to solicit input from different constituencies that represented their divergent interests. Administrators wanted general themes and a fit between local ideas and ideas in good currency such as personalized education or diagnostic-prescriptive instruction. Teachers wanted materials, in-service education, and resources to do a better job of what they were already doing. Some parents and community residents wanted greater emphasis on vocational education; others were concerned about achievement scores and academics; still others wanted a broadening of adult education and other services.

In most districts, elaborate structures were set up to solicit these divergent ideas. In Desert Basin, for example, twenty-two committees were formed with an average of six members each. Half the committees met only once, but some met as many as three times. Through a community survey, a list of diverse ideas for spending federal money was generated. It included such items as adult education, art, athletics, debate and public speaking, early childhood, environmental studies, extracurricular programs, middle school, music, reading improvement, summer school, writing, English, and language arts (Burns 1979).

In Oyster Cove, the faculty met and discussed and debated educational philosophies. The meeting did not produce many concrete ideas, but it kindled enthusiasm and bred expectations of what would be included in the plan. A large community meeting involved parents and residents in discussion of the shortcomings, past history, and the future of the district. Small groups formed at the meeting's end to list and prioritize what they wanted from the schools (Colfer and Colfer 1979).

In Big Sky, citizens presented a welter of ideas to the school board: vocational and on-the-job training, recreation, environmental and cultural programs, mental health and guidance programs, sex education, a school nurse, adult education, individualized instruction, improved programs for sports and athletics, mobile units for specialized training. In all, the planning efforts in Big Sky involved five hundred people in a total of seventy-six meetings (Messerschmidt 1979).

In Magnolia, planning took place in local schools. Principals were asked to appoint a committee, including a cross-section of community members, to develop a comprehensive plan for each school (Wacaster 1979).

In sum, broad-based participation in the planning stage produced predictable results: diverse ideas were generated, participants suggested ideas compatible with their respective needs and interests, and individuals developed high expectations that their ideas would be included in the final plan.

Selecting Ideas. Once ideas were obtained from teachers, parents, and residents, ES districts were faced with the task of selecting and condensing them into a central theme. In most districts, this task was carried out by a steering committee of representatives from various groups, with leadership provided by administrators.

In Desert Basin, the steering committee experienced difficulties in synthesizing diverse ideas. They developed a central theme in an intense and "emotionally fulfilling" session, and their consensus produced a euphoric optimism about their plan and its future:

So our steering committee, a farmer, his wife, two students, a machinist (very up-town, but still....), an electric co-op manager, and an auto parts store owner conceived a fantastic, unbelievable hope for our project.

Never, oh never, will anyone connected with the Rural Schools Project in [Desert Basin] ever doubt that democracy works! It's slow, it's halting, it's difficult, but people, just people, given the pot at the end of the rainbow can turn away and say: "Let's think about kids" [Burns 1979].

As with most themes, however, it meant very different things to individuals with different perspectives, most of whom did not participate in the "moment of creation." The theme was ultimately difficult to use as a criterion for sorting ideas for the final plan.

In Oyster Cove, a three-day community meeting ended with each group being responsible for sending a representative to convey the ideas generated by the group as a whole. The ideas of the three groups were not collated; rather, a steering committee later selected and organized the list of wants into three areas—basic, vocational, and environmental education (Colfer and Colfer 1979).

In Butte-Angels Camp, a theme of "personalized instruction" was established prior to soliciting ideas from the community. The theme was general and vague and was neither recognized nor understood system-wide. And when a group of administrators finally pulled together the ideas, many of the favorites of teachers and the community were eliminated (Messerschmidt 1979).

Delegating to the ES project staff or steering committee the task of selecting ideas generated through broad-based participation eliminated conflict from the larger arenas. In steering committees, conflicts among the diverse interests were often resolved by developing a vague theme as a criterion. But decisions about which ideas to include and which to eliminate were often made with an eye to what the federal government would buy. In Desert Basin, for example, at one point the project staff was telephoning ES representatives in Washington on a daily basis to test ideas emerging from the steering committee's deliberations (Burns 1979).

While the selection strategies used by most of the ES districts allowed decisions to be made, they raised some general issues that influenced later events; teachers and community people were frequently disappointed that their ideas were neither represented nor discernible as the plan developed. There was a decreased ownership of the plan and an increased suspicion about the original motive behind asking people to participate. The avoidance of conflict while sifting ideas created problems later.

Writing the Plan. As ideas moved into the writing stage, the "funneling" process edged out teachers and community residents. Writing the plan was usually done by a small group of administrators and/or consultants. In Timber River, the plan was written by an external consultant whose charge was to produce something that would conform as closely as possible to the expectations and ideas of the federal funders. What resulted was a document nearly unreadable to teachers and community residents. When teachers saw the plan, they could not see their individual proposals reflected and therefore saw their planning efforts as a "smoke screen." When the plan was presented to the steering committee, only two of the eighteen original members attended (Hennigh 1979).

In Butte-Angels Camp, the failure of the small group of administrators to include many of the proposals of teachers in the plan caused the teachers to believe their influence in the planning process had been minimal. Teachers' distrust of the administration increased, as did their cynicism, and led ultimately to their active resistance to the project (Firestone 1979).

In Desert Basin, intensive collaboration between administrators and the ES staff produced a plan reviewed favorably by Washington but received with suspicion and hostility by the local community. In general, administrators approached the task of producing the plan on the basis of three major criteria: meeting deadlines, pleasing the federal government, and avoiding potential conflicts among groups. This strategy excluded teachers, parents, and local residents and thus increased their sense of alienation (Burns 1979).

Negotiating the Plan. As plans were submitted to ES/Washington, the first major conflicts of the planning year erupted between administrators and the sponsoring agency. Conflicts arose from the federal concern with the fit of the plans to ideas in good currency—a timely general theme, comprehensive change, and citizen participation.

Negotiating the final plan with Washington was done largely by administrators or school board members of local districts; other participants were excluded from this late step of the planning process. Concerns or ideas of teachers or community members were deleted from the plan during negotiations between local representatives and federal officials. Since teachers and local residents were not privy to the details of the negotiations, it was easy for them to assume that their ideas had been sold out by administrators. Even where teachers and community members were part of the negotiating team, it was often difficult to convince people back home that pet ideas had been defended and advanced.

In other cases, federal demands that plans be rewritten shifted responsibilities from steering committees to other groups. In Liberty Notch, for example, responsibility shifted from the core group to principals of the various districts within the supervisory union. In Magnolia, as a result of pressure from ES/Washington, responsibility for rewriting the plan shifted to an external consultant.

Without opportunities to see the process by which decisions were made, participants developed further suspicions about their role in planning. For the most part, conflicts between local districts and the federal government were resolved in favor of federal preferences. ES/Washington held the trump card—resources needed by local communities.

The Legacy of the Planning Year. The planning effort, after serving a brief preliminary function as a "plum" for the community or a "plume" in the hat of the administration, shifted. In some communities the planning effort became a magnet for a series of unresolved issues within the community and school districts.

In Butte-Angels Camp, the planning year became an arena in which the long-standing conflict between teachers and administrators was played out. In Desert Basin and Big Sky, the planning grant created an arena in which the continuing concerns about federal intrusions were discussed and intensified. In Prairie Mills, the teachers became increasingly concerned about work conditions and ample compensation for their workloads beyond the normal teaching load.

In other districts, the planning effort became a catalyst for conflict. In Oyster Cove, the planning year saw a tax levy defeated and a superintendent fired. The main issues raised were student discipline, declining test scores, and finances, but underlying these issues was the ES project. In Desert Basin, an existing conflict between the administration (particularly the board and superintendent) and the community intensified over the issue of the federal grant. At the end of the planning year, the superintendent, a middle school principal, the project director, and the project documentarian resigned; the high school principal moved to another job, one school board member was recalled, and a tax override was voted down.

During the planning year, conflicts began to surface within all ten districts—even though these issues were seldom addressed explicitly in the planning process. Communities became concerned about the schools' performing important obligations when teachers seemed to spend more time planning than teaching. Teachers became increasingly concerned about potential administrative intrusions into their territory without ample compensation—in terms of salary increases or new resources. Within local communities, special interest groups began to wonder whether or not they were receiving their fair share of the federal dollars. In most districts, the planning process provided new visibility for existing issues and began to reveal potential realignments in the relationship among various constituencies.

Second, within the planning process itself, representatives of various groups intermingled to produce a unified plan for change. Putting these divergent interests together without a means of openly reconciling differences produced ambiguity and uncertainty. Such uncertainties and conflicting ideas in turn produced ambiguous themes, vague plans, purely token agreements, and unresolved conflicts.

In most cases, the planning effort generated expectations that representatives of various groups would participate as equals, and that the diverse needs and interests of their constituents would be reflected in the plan. As the planning effort progressed, however, administrators, consultants, and federal officials came to play an increasingly dominant role, excluding active participation by the teachers, parents, and local residents. Particularly at the end of the process, the planning effort was primarily a transaction between a district's administration and an agency of the federal government. Consequently, both in people's minds and in reality, the final plan represented an amalgamation of administrative desires and ideas in good currency prominent in the remote environment at that time. But the final planning documents were uniformly disappointing since it was difficult for virtually any group to find its interest and needs adequately represented. Even administrators often felt betrayed by ES/Washington.

Third, the planning effort ended with a number of unresolved conflicts, which were to a large extent the result of perceived failures of different groups to honor obligations and to live up to implicit agreements. To a lesser extent, these conflicts may have resulted from the intrusion of the ES program and the demands of the planning year—or the potential trespassing on the turf of various groups represented by the forthcoming implementation year.

Within the local community, there were unresolved conflicts between various factions: parents who hoped the Experimental Schools project would result in better education for their children allied themselves against taxpayers worried about the costs of continuing such activities; planners who had invested time and effort in producing the plan aligned against community residents who knew nothing about the ES project but rumors, hearsay, and gossip, and who had become concerned over the fact that teachers and administrators were spending time planning instead of leading and running the schools. Employees of federal agencies in local communities argued with locals who saw the federal "money" as a threat to community autonomy and control. Representatives from different geographical locations with a school district aligned against each other as they embraced radically different expectations for the ensuing year.

Within the administrative and governance structure, there were unresolved conflicts between board members and superintendents, superintendents and project directors, project directors and principals, and superintendents and principals. Between administrators and the community or teachers simmered the unresolved conflict over the elimination of many pet interests and projects. Also brewing was the possibility of an increased workload that would take teachers away from teaching and children. Some teachers even began to feel that administrators were enhancing professional reputations at their expense.

Tensions mounted among local communities, the administration, and the federal government over the unspoken issue of whose project the Experimental Schools funds would support. The initial expectations of "no-strings attached" resources to support local programs was shattered. Instead, traditional concerns about federal interference were reestablished and reinforced.

Finally, among the various constituencies there remained a climate of acute suspicion and distrust produced by the events of the planning year. The federal government was concerned about the misuse of funds. Teachers were suspicious of the motives of administrators in pursuing the Experimental Schools projects. Administrators were distrustful of teachers. And local citizens were suspicious and distrustful of all three groups.

Implementing Experimental Schools Projects: The Emergence of Open Conflict

As the Experimental Schools projects moved from planning to implementation, conflicts began to erupt in all the districts. Some of the conflict was to be expected, since implementation is a time of action when disagreements previously concealed by the ambiguous, abstract prose of a plan become obvious as concrete actions are taken. Flexible planning deadlines gave way to more rigid schedules of business as usual in districts and schools. Instructional materials and supplies were needed at the beginning of the school year to support new curricula and teaching approaches; workshops and other training activities were needed to help participants acquire needed skills; new personnel had to be hired and trained. The logical time for these crucial activities was the summer recess. But, unfortunately, the summer was filled with tasks—particularly negotiating and revising the final plans. Once the negotiations ended, plans were quickly undermined by the tasks left undone during the summer months. For many districts, the opening day of school and the inauguration of the ES project were marked by considerable confusion and conflict.

But not all of these conflicts can be attributed to the nature of implementation or untimely delays. Nor was the conflict caused entirely by suspicion, distrust, and misunderstandings carried over from the planning year. Many conflicts emerged later or lingered long after the difficulties posed by late funding or poor planning had been solved. These conflicts originated from several additional sources: characteristics of the innovative projects themselves, failures of various groups to observe constraints or fulfill obligations, or failures to clarify ambiguous roles and responsibilities.

Characteristics of Innovation that Induced Conflict

The main intent of the ES program was to produce comprehensive change. In each district, however, comprehensive change was divided into smaller innovative units or packages called components. Some plans included a large number of components—thirty-eight in Timber River, for example. Others, as in Big Sky, included only five. Some individual components were implemented with few problems, but others precipitated conflict both internally and between professionals and parents or local residents.

There are several distinctions between components that produced conflict and those that did not. (Rosenblum and Louis 1979). One distinction was how much the component differed from existing activities in the district. Components that conformed closely to ongoing practices and procedures caused few problems. In Big Sky, for example, a component brought a variety of cultural experiences—music, art, drama, and dance— to the community. Events were held in school buildings and open to both students and members of the local community. This activity was consonant with previous district practices. Students, community members, and staff often attended or participated in entertainment events in the school. Athletic events, school assemblies, or community or school-sponsored activities (such as "donkey" basketball) were a regular part of Big Sky's schools. The component altered the substance of the entertainment somewhat but meshed nicely with accustomed procedures. Consequently, the component caused no conflict either within the district or between the district and the local community (Messerschmidt 1979).

In contrast, Clayville's component, "diagnosis and prescription," called for a major departure from two fundamental characteristics of instruction: self-contained classrooms and small group instruction. The component required student learning problems to be diagnosed in special centers outside the classroom. Classroom teachers were then asked to follow the highly individualized methods prescribed in the diagnostic report. Attempts to implement this component produced sustained conflict in the district between the superintendent who was committed to the idea and teachers who opposed it (Clinton 1979).

One reason that compatible components produced little conflict may have been that districts could rely on previous experience to implement familiar practices. Necessary materials, supplies, and equipment were identified and easily located, teaching skills were familiar and easily transferred, organizational patterns that needed to be altered to support the component were known and easily changed. The Timber River district, for example, relied on its prior experience with overnight field trips in implementing a similar component, which established a resident school for marine biology on the Oregon coast. The district's pre-Experimental Schools experience served as a "pilot" program for many ES components, providing useful information and knowledge that was applied as the new components were implemented.

But previous experience did not always eliminate conflict. In the same district, a fifth-grade social studies program—*Man: A Course of Study* (or MACOS)—had been used successfully on an experimental basis in one elementary school for several years. The ES resources expanded this program—and a companion program for older students, *People and Technology*—to the other schools in the district. The district relied on its earlier experience to identify the necessary teacher skills, conduct the training, and provide the requisite equipment and materials. Because of the previous experiences, technical aspects were handled effectively and the program's expansion produced few problems. Conflict arose, however, when a group of parents found some of the materials of the course offensive and objected to the values that they felt the program espoused. In extensive public hearings, the program was reviewed and debated. Eventually it was eliminated from the district's curriculum (Hennigh 1979).

Even when administrators attend adequately to the technical aspects of implementation—clearly defining the innovation, properly motivating teachers, providing needed training and instructional materials, and installing mechanisms to feed back information and monitor the change—a particular component may foment conflict if it violates some aspect of an explicit or implicit set of obligations and constraints governing school/community relationships.

A second distinction between components that produced conflict and those that did not was the extent to which existing procedures were disrupted. "Add-on" components that did not displace current activities seldom created conflict, even when they represented major departures from traditional practices. The diagnosis and prescription component in Clayville, for example, displaced existing practices, and thus produced conflict. In Timber River, however, an equally radical change in the high school's business, vocational and marketing education curriculum did not. The district began a "storefront" business and restaurant in the community (open to students and the public) as an adjunct to the high school cafeteria. Both were student-operated and designed to provide students with direct work experience. Traditional textbook-based business and marketing courses were not displaced, however, since those courses were offered as electives or alternatives. As additions to the existing program, neither component created conflict during implementation (Clinton 1979).

Similarly, an environmental education component in the Oyster Cove district was added to the existing high school curriculum without creating conflict. This component capitalized on the nearby forests and beaches and a marine biology research center located in the community by engaging students in environmental projects outside the classroom. While this instructional strategy represented a major change for the district, it did not displace existing curricular offerings.

The critical influence of displacement on innovative practice is illustrated by the history of another of Oyster Cove's components, *Interim*. Small groups of high school students under faculty supervision took week-long excursions to urban areas, visiting other schools and colleges, attending museums, concerts, and plays, and talking with employers in various career areas. Such excursions were difficult to arrange in the local community, and this week-long interim program displaced a week of regular school for these students. Though effectively implemented and popular with students and teachers, the component produced conflict in the community. Some parents complained that students misbehaved during trips when "they were supposed to be in school," and these complaints doomed the effort: it was eliminated the following year. Displacing legitimate educational activities with experiences of questionable or unproven value played an important role in the early demise of an otherwise promising innovation (Colfer and Colfer 1979).

A third factor that distinguished components that produced conflict from those that did not was how closely the superintendent and other district administrators monitored implementation. When administrators did not look to see whether or not the component was actually in place, conflict seldom occurred. Some components needed little monitoring, because they were clearly defined, required no new skills or training to install, and were commonly understood and accepted as desirable and inexpensive for the district to continue. Carpeting the media center in Oyster Cove, adding playground equipment (a physical educational center) in Timber River, and purchasing new reading and math tests and materials in Prairie Mills and Oyster Cove are examples of innovations that required little monitoring. These innovations were widely acclaimed as improvements.

Other components did require systematic attention from administrators. They differed from existing practice, required new skills and training, and were not clearly defined, thoroughly understood, or accepted by teachers. When such innovations were not monitored by administrators, little conflict occurred—but neither were the components implemented effectively. In some instances, such components were never even attempted. In Timber River, for example, the district's plan called for a reorganization of the district's curricula into a series of five interdisciplinary "streams." The idea was originally proposed in the district's letter of interest and attracted ES/Washington's attention. It became a central aspect of the federal contract. But, after a year of attempting to clarify and operationalize the ideas, the district's administrators dropped the concept and ES/Washington stopped asking questions about its progress. Within a year, the idea of curricular streams—at one time the organizing principle of the entire ES project—had disappeared from the district's vocabulary. It simply required more monitoring than district administrators were prepared to provide.

Other components that required extensive monitoring were declared to be implemented even though only a portion of the changes described in the plan were observable in practice. Oyster Cove, for example, tried to convert its school libraries to media centers. The transformation consisted of two parts: the library was to be converted to a repository for nonprint media (for example, film strips, slides, records, three-dimensional models) in addition to print media, and students were to have access to these media directly, thereby using the media center for their individual projects. The librarian (now called a media specialist) was to participate jointly with teachers in planning individual and small group activities in the center as well as classroom use of a variety of media.

The first part of the innovation was implemented as planned. Nonprint media were ordered and became part of the library's inventory, the name was changed to the Media Center, and the librarian acquired a new title. But the second part of the innovation—its behavioral aspects—suffered a different fate. Students continued to use the media center for traditional class projects, such as preparing research reports utilizing only print media, and the media specialist continued to function as a custodian of the library collection instead of as a partner of teachers in planning curricula. Since the administrators either did not monitor the implementation effort or elected not to acknowledge that part, two projects never moved from the drawing board and no conflict occurred. But neither was an important aspect of the innovation carried into action (Colfer and Colfer 1979).

When administrators actually inspected project components to see whether desired changes were reflected in practice, or else confronted the gap between plans and reality, conflict ensued. In both Clayville and Butte-Angels Camp, for example, diagnostic-prescriptive instruction was a central part of the ES project. In both districts, superintendents challenged teachers' reports to their attempts to revamp the instruction practices in accordance with the innovation. Neither superintendent was willing to accept paperwork as evidence that the required changes in the roles of teachers had taken place. They looked; and in both cases their inspection and insistence on compliance produced conflict between themselves and teachers which lasted for a substantial period of time (Firestone 1977 and Clinton 1979).

Administrative monitoring and inspection was an unnegotiated intrusion into the territory of teachers. The intrusion provoked conflict because administrators failed to observe an implicit constraint in their relationship with teachers that was designed to protect teacher autonomy. Administrators are typically permitted to monitor and inspect teacher behavior and performance only under very carefully controlled conditions and at specified times—usually once or twice a year. District policies and/or labor contracts specify these conditions very precisely, including the format for providing feedback from such visits. Superintendents and other administrators who tried to monitor changes closely did not observe these constraints, and their intrusion provoked conflict. In many districts, administrators were clearly faced with a major dilemma. If they monitored and inspected the proposed changes, they risked provoking conflict. But if they did not monitor or inspect, they ran the risk that a component would be only partially implemented.

In sum, components that provoked conflict were those that proposed innovations that displaced and/or differed radically from current instructional practices or were inspected and monitored by the superintendent or other key administrators. In contrast, those that did not provoke conflict were either consistent with or did not displace existing practices or were not monitored by the superintendent or other district administrators.

Types of Conflict

Conflicts in school districts participating in the Experimental Schools program erupted when one group failed to carry out its obligations or observe constraints in relation to other groups. Parents' complaints in the Oyster Cove district about student misbehavior during Interim Week indicated that administrators failed to meet their obligation to control students. In the MACOS controversy in Timber River, administrators and teachers had not observed constraints governing what could not be included in the school curriculum.

But not all conflicts that occurred as districts implemented plans were between groups: conflict often erupted within groups. One common problem centered around the question of where to place the project administrator, director, or coordinator in the chain of command. In Prairie Mills, for example, the superintendent and the principals met as an administrative cabinet prior to the ES project. Principals operated in a traditional line relationship with the superintendent. When the ES project coordinator began making decisions that affected instruction in individual schools, the principals questioned his authority. Conflicts continued to arise until the superintendent reaffirmed the traditional chain of command and assigned the project coordinator a purely staff responsibility (Donnelly 1979).

Conflicts also arose between instructional personnel. In Butte-Angels Camp, for example, differences arose between elementary and secondary teachers as decisions were made about which components should be included in the final plan. Secondary teachers, wanting to emphasize the importance of subject matter, pushed to hire a math coordinator, while elementary teachers were more interested in developing a program focused on the learning needs of individual children. The conflict eventually was resolved by the superintendent in favor of the elementary teachers. His decision was based on support for a child-centered approach to instruction.

These examples indicate two important characteristics of conflict among administrators or instructional personnel. First, conflict usually arises as a result of ambiguity in roles and responsibilities—who is responsible for what? Does one owe allegiance to subject matter, to colleagues, or to individual students? Second, conflict often ends up in the laps of administrators, no matter where it originates. In each example above, it was the superintendent who acted to resolve the issues of the ambiguity in roles and responsibilities.

Strategies for Conflict Resolution

Three strategies for managing conflict are especially discernible in the ten case studies. Two strategies were used almost exclusively during planning—but also during implementation—to either avoid conflict (evasion) or to deny its existence (avoidance). A third strategy—used especially during implementation—emphasized the use of power or coercion as a means of resolving conflict. In power strategies, one party attempts to force or coerce others to do something they would not otherwise do. Often the strategies occurred sequentially. Conflict was first avoided or smoothed over, then suppressed through the application of power.

Evasion or diplomacy was not especially effective in dealing with conflicts that arose in the ES districts. When conflicts were avoided or denied, they were temporarily suppressed in one arena, only to appear later with renewed vigor in another. A good example occurred in Timber River. Administrators attempted to use diplomacy in dealing with the issue of mainstreaming handicapped students. Many teachers were strongly opposed to the mainstreaming and expressed this opposition during meetings with the superintendent and project director. The administrators, highly committed to implementing the idea, smoothed over the differences by suggesting that the special-education teacher could serve as a resource person to help the regular classroom teachers deal with any problems. But, several months later, the teachers association proposed and bargained hard for restrictions on the administration's authority to commit the district to experimental programs—including assigning handicapped students to regular classrooms—without prior teacher approval. Thus, the special-education issue, smoothed over in early meetings, reappeared in a more militant form on the collective bargaining table.

The use of power also had its negative consequences in the ES districts. Superintendents in both Clayville and Butte-Angels Camp attempted to force teachers to comply with diagnostic-prescriptive teaching. In doing so, the Butte-Angels Camp superintendent linked teacher evaluations and the reward of tenure and retention to teachers' compliance with new teaching approaches. The Clayville superintendent threatened to fire teachers who refused to attend workshops where consultants explained the procedure or suggested how to use the new teaching process in the classroom. In each case the teachers responded to threats by expanding the conflict into the local community and by using their political influence with the school board. Eventually the teachers were able to win over or elect enough members to the school board who supported their position and were able to force the superintendent's resignation.

A fourth strategy for resolving conflict, apparently the most effective, was that of active negotiations between the various interest groups. This strategy produced the fewest negative consequences. Ironically, however, negotiation was seldom employed. Rather, power strategies were used initially by administrators to force teachers to comply with project objectives. In response, teachers expanded the conflict into the community and used political influence with the school board to reduce the administrator's power. Only when administrative power and authority in the district had been reduced did administrators, particularly the superintendents, bargain with teachers. And generally it was a successor of the original superintendent who was willing to negotiate.

In Timber River, the superintendent and the central office administrative staff exerted a great deal of influence over the project during planning. Results of surveys of the staff indicated that teachers felt they had little influence over the contents of the plan. In fact, Timber River teachers' perceptions of their influence was the lowest of the ten ES districts. When the plan was funded and efforts began, the central office administrators took the position that the plan should be implemented as planned. The slogan was to "do as we agreed," and from the administrator's perspective, the agreements were faithfully recorded in the plan. The problem was that few teachers honored the agreements because they had had little influence in determining what they were.

The teachers, in effect, felt coerced by the superintendent and his staff and reacted with their own power strategy. A number of community members initiated a group called "Concerned Citizens for Education" in response to a phone call from one teacher who noted that: "Parents should be worried about what they [administrators] are doing to your children!" The superintendent became increasingly occupied with responding to demands and concerns of the community group. Over time, the group joined in a coalition with teachers to defeat several of the superintendent's key supporters on the school board and elected members who were more supportive of their interests. The turnover in board membership reduced the administrators' power and authority, making it necessary to rely more and more on bargaining and negotiating strategies to promote the intended changes.

In sum, a typical pattern of response by administrators to conflict can be discerned in the ten districts. As conflict surfaced during planning, administrators tried to smooth it over by avoiding conflict or by denying that it existed. Their rationale was often framed in terms of getting the plan done and meeting the deadlines imposed by ES/Washington. But, since underlying issues remained unresolved, conflicts predictably surfaced early as plans were put into action. The typical administrative response at this point was to resort to power couched in some variation of the "we must do as agreed" theme highlighted in Timber River. Teachers typically responded with a power strategy of their own, but since their power base lay outside the boundaries of the formal organization, conflict that began internally expanded beyond the formal organization boundaries. The effect of expansion outside was usually a reduction in the superintendent's power and authority; in some cases it led to the adoption of a bargaining/negotiation approach to resolving conflict.

This pattern of dealing with conflict left many casualties among administrators along the way. Superintendents became particularly vulnerable when conflict spread into the community and anti-administration school board members were elected. Only three administrators who signed the initial letter of interest remained after the final ES report was completed. In only two districts—Timber River and Prairie Mills—was the superintendent who had used power to resolve conflict during implementation the same superintendent who employed a negotiation strategy after the conflict expanded to include the community.

Summary

As districts planned and implemented their ES projects, existing relationships among various groups were set in flux. In the planning stage, emerging ambiguities, disagreements, and conflicts were avoided or smoothed over in the interests of producing a document that would secure federal resources. Primary attention was diverted from local needs and interests and emerging local conflicts among administrators, teachers, or community residents to focus mainly on what the "feds" would buy. The major conflicts of the planning period erupted over discrepancies between what local administrators had assumed and what ES/Washington actually wanted. With the federal agency holding the trump card during the delicate negotiations, many items that teachers and community residents had wanted were eliminated because, not being privy to the give and take of negotiations, it was easy for teachers and community residents to let "ownership" of the process shift substantially to administrators. Administrators were thus burdened with new obligations and constraints on their relationship with teachers or parents, which had further implications for the implementation of project goals.

As plans became operational, conflicts erupted among various groups or constituencies. Ambiguity over roles and relationships within groups— particularly between project staff members and nonmembers—created disagreements, hostility, and turf disputes. Aides and volunteers argued with teachers, teachers struggled with students, principals wrestled with project coordinators, and superintendents jousted with school boards or advisory committees.

Between groups and constituencies, relationships became particularly strained and disrupted. Teachers resisted attempts by administrators to change classroom instruction; local communities welcomed new services and opportunities, but resented changes in discipline, curriculum, and the instructional setting if they ran counter to conventional ideas of what school should be; administrators resisted intrusion on their authority by teachers, the local community, and especially the federal government.

Conflicts erupted around a number of issues. In the districts that implemented their ES projects most effectively, conflict was particularly high, either between administrators and teachers, within the local community, or both. Strategies to resolve conflicts were generally aimed at smoothing over or avoiding the control of issues, or using power to force one's values or interests on others. Negotiation or bargaining between groups was rare, but where such strategies were used, there was some evidence that new agreements were reached and that conditions improved.

References

Burns, A.F. *From Rural School Project to Rural School Problem: Wilcox, Arizona.* Cambridge Mass.: Abt Associates, May 1979.

Clinton, C.A. *Educational Change within a Political Arena: Shiloh County.* Cambridge, Mass.: Abt Associates, May 1979.

Colfer, A.M., and C.J. Pierce Colfer. *Life and Learning in an American Town: Quilcene, Washington.* Cambridge, Mass.: Abt Associates, May 1979.

Deal, T.E., and S.C. Nutt. *Promoting, Guiding, and Surviving Change in School Districts.* Cambridge, Mass.: Abt Associates, 1979.

Donnelly, W.L. *Continuity and Change in Rural Schooling: Constantine, Michigan.* Cambridge, Mass.: Abt Associates, May 1979.

Firestone, W.A. *Educational Conflict and Transformation: Butte-Angels Camp, South Dakota.* New York: Praeger Special Studies, 1977.

Hennigh, L. *Cooperation and Conflict in Long-Term Educational Change: South Umpqua, Oregon.* Cambridge, Mass.: Abt Associates, May 1979.

Herriott, R.E., and N. Gross, eds. *The Dynamics of Planned Educational Change: Case Studies and Analyses.* Berkeley: McCutchan, 1979.

Messerschmidt, D.A. *The Local-Federal Interface in Rural School Improvement: River District, Wyoming.* Cambridge, Mass.: Abt Associates, May 1979.

Miles, M., "Thinking About How to Do It: Alternative Models of Planning and Implementation of New Schools." Unpublished manuscript. New York: Center for Policy Research, 1976.

Rosenblum, S., and K.S. Louis. *A Measure of Change: The Process and Outcomes of Planned Change in Ten Rural School Districts.* Cambridge, Mass.: Abt Associates, May 1979.

Stannard, C.T. *Problems of Project Direction and Coordination: North County Supervisory Union, New Hampshire.* Cambridge, Mass.: Abt Associates, May 1979.

Wacaster, C.T. "Jackson County: Local Norms, Federal Initiatives and Administrator Performance." In *The Dynamics of Planned Educational Change: Case Studies and Analyses,* edited by Robert E. Herriott and Neal Gross. Berkeley: McCutchan, 1979.

9

Strategic Planning in Higher Education: Does the Emperor Have Any Clothes?

J. Victor Baldridge

About every six months a new fad sweeps through management circles in business, government, and education. Think back a few years and your mind will stumble on the carcasses of fads that were once lively issues, touted as the newest "scientific" way to manage an organization. Usually the fads had catchy acronyms:

PPBS—Planning, Programming, and Budgeting System
MBO—Management by Objectives
PERT—Project Evaluation and Review Technique
ZBB—Zero-Based Budgeting
Theory X and Theory Y
Theory Z
MIS—Management Information Systems

Remember when McNamara forced PPBS on the defense department, and Hitch introduced it to the University of California? Remember when Jimmy Carter announced zero-based budgeting for the federal bureaucracy, and then proceeded to ignore his own announcement? Remember when you went to all those seminars about PC (planned change) and HR (human relations)? The fads never stop. Composed of 10 percent new idea, 50 percent advertising hype, and 40 percent material you already knew, the fads come and go—usually fast.

Now this year's crop comes along, led by "strategic planning." The pages of conference programs are filled with sessions on "How to Use Strategic Planning," "Strategic Planning for Small Colleges," "Strategic

Planning for Large Systems," and so on. And the seminar business is booming, as shown by any edition of the *Chronicle of Higher Education* or by the advertising mail—measured in pounds—that crosses your desk. And the articles, like this one, proliferate in the journals, in the professional trade sheets, in the pop management magazines. Is strategic planning just another gimmick, destined to steal away into the night to join the ghosts of past tactics and management failures? Does, in fact, the emperor have any clothes?

Actually, for once the newest movement—strategic planning—seems to have some meat. In large part, strategic planning clearly directs the manager's attention to a whole new set of issues—environmental scanning, and intuitive as well as quantitative reasoning. Yes, strategic planning does seem to have some validity, does seem to offer some fresh insights, and does appear to be more than a passing fad.

In this article we will: (1) review the problems with traditional long-range planning, (2) outline the key focuses of strategic planning, and (3) offer an extension of the logic to what I call "jugular-vein decisions." Our comments are drawn from research—we issued questionnaires about management to seven hundred college presidents, and we conducted intensive case-study visits to eight campuses; the resulting information will be mentioned occasionally in this paper. (For a complete discussion, see Kemerer, Baldridge, and Green 1982.)

The Weakness of Traditional Long-Range Planning

Organizations have typically differed in how they have used long-range plans. In industry, corporate executives have been keenly interested in comparing the fit of day-to-day operations and profits with their projected long-range market and profit goals. Other organizations, of which higher education institutions are prime examples, have often given lip service to the idea of long-range planning and have, for the most part, let their master plans collect dust in some well-meaning administrator's office.

Master plans flourished in higher education during the 1950s. By the end of the 1960s almost every institution, system, and state government had some instrument or series of instruments that could be called a "master plan" (Glenny 1976). At that time, of course, these master plans were drawn to deal with rising enrollments and to ensure some orderliness in the expansion and growth of new programs and new campuses.

General Disillusionment with Planning

As education moved from the growth and expansion age of the 1960s to the increasingly troubled 1970s and 1980s, these master plans often failed to deal with the multiple complexities of the changing environment. In the course of our case-study interviews and our studies of college administration we invariably encountered evidence that long-range planning in higher education has not always been successful; frequently it has been ineffective.

Answers to our questions about planning activities on college campuses give us a fair idea of the disillusionment held by people who have participated in long-range planning. Planning practices are often dubbed "meaningless" and a "waste of time." People said things like "events are so unpredictable it is impossible to plan effectively," or "the process is so complicated and time-consuming we don't have the time to deal with the process." Other comments run something like this: "Yes, we do a lot of planning around here, and we even have a Master Plan for the college. We don't use it very much, and most of its predictions are wrong. But we have one in case the trustees ask."

Or like this: "Sure we have a Master Plan. It is essentially a cut-and-paste job. Every academic department wrote up a wish list and then we slapped them all together between two covers. It doesn't have much relationship to budget, and frankly, nobody pays much attention to it."

These themes seem to run through our interviews: (1) the process is so lengthy and complicated that planning loses its meaning; (2) the process becomes more important than the results; and (3) the plan does not make any sense to those who are actually doing the work because it is not linked to daily operations and to the budget. It would be naive to think that the planning process could not be made simple and less time-consuming. It is true, however, that often planners make the process more complicated than necessary for obtaining effective results. Models depicting elaborate stages and steps capture the fancy of theorists but become impractical for those trying to sensibly implement the process.

Specific Problems in Planning

The gap between the plan and the budget is a prevalent problem, common to both universities and industry (Hobbs and Heany 1977). This ineffectiveness in coupling planning to operational activities was illustrated in the reply of a university vice-president to our question, "How do you see the connection between what your office does and the long-range planning of the university?" After a rather significant pause for cogitation, the reply was, "The Board of Trustees is responsible for the long-range planning, we don't have anything to do with it. It is a completely separate thing." In our interviews with department chairpersons and faculty we found for the most part that these individuals had little or no input into long-range planning and, furthermore, saw little connection between what went on in their departments and the work done by the planning office or the board of trustees. The general attitude was "they do their job and we do ours."

The frequent turnover of top administrators in higher education constitutes another problem that affects institutional planning. Continuity in the planning process is disrupted by the arrival of new administrators. Since they bring with them their own frame of reference and sometimes appoint their own staffs, previous plans are relegated to the past as a new era is begun. The new era often includes the discarding of whatever might have been started by the previous administration. This is particularly true if institutional problems had been serious and the new administration was ushered in to resolve them. New administrators like to start a new regime. This proves very discouraging to those who have invested time and effort in previous planning attempts. Projects are halted and the planning process is stalled. If a college has had several presidents in a short time, which is not unusual, the faculty's attitude becomes "so here we go again." The *deja-vu* syndrome contributes to general lassitude toward institutional planning.

In one of our case-study situations, the president's task force on planning and budgeting had worked on a project for two years. Their stated purpose was to develop a process that would produce good planning and that would tie the planning to the budgeting of resources. A number of documents were developed, including a statement of the university's planning assumptions, the statement of the university's mission, and a step-by-step planning procedure. The process was pilot-tested on twenty departments of the institution. The task force worked hard to involve faculty representatives from various academic areas. But when the process was ready to be implemented there was a change in the presidency of the school. The process was halted, the project was discarded, and the planning system was not referred to again. Executive turnover is often the death of plans.

To summarize, these are some major stumbling blocks to effective planning:

1. Planning processes are complicated and time-consuming.
2. There is a gap between planners at the top administrative level and the planners on the operational level.
3. Frequent turnover of executives disrupts the planning process.
4. Budgets are poorly linked to plans.

The Key Failure of Planning: Mismatch with Administrative Behavior

Let us explore one last major criticism of traditional long-range planning. There is a fundamental problem: the behavior of administrators as described in planning models simply does not correspond with the way administrators actually work.

Planning models are very clear about how administrators *ought* to behave. A good administrator, goes the argument, should be oriented to long-range efforts and impacts, should set goals clearly and crisply, should organize efforts so that the goals are accomplished and evaluated, should avoid short-term crisis-oriented reactions, and should be highly "rational" in assessing the facts relevant to a decision. Long-term deliberative behavior is the ideal to which every administrator should aspire. Or at least that is the basic theory. (For examples of these emphases in the literature see Peterson 1981a; Cosand 1981; Fenske 1981.)

When compared to the theoretical ideal most administrators must be ineffective. They certainly do not describe their behavior the way the planners insist they should. In fact, interviews with administrators reveal a rather shocking ineptitude, at least when evaluated by the planners' ideals. Instead of long-term perspectives, they usually report that their lives are crisis-oriented; they move from one event to the next with little time for long-range planning.

Most importantly, these on-line administrators seem never to get their goals clear and can never line their objectives up neatly with their goals. And as soon as they get any clarity, the goals have a nasty habit of muddling up again. Instead of a crisp list of four or five primary goals, administrators seem to be wandering around in a bewildering maze of conflicting objectives, with a goal system that changes almost every day. In short, the real-world administrators seem to always commit a sin when they are compared with the planners' Bible—they have unclear, contested, and contradictory goals. Moreover, despite the concern about program evaluation over the last decade, the real-world administrators report that they rarely make decisions about program continuation based on rational evaluation. What little evaluation is done is usually highly political, focusing on the support a program can muster from various interest groups rather than on any "rational" evaluation of merit.

Last but not least among the sins listed in the administrator's true confessions is the cardinal transgression: even when the busy administrator finally makes a plan, rarely is it executed! People often do not follow the mandates of the plan, and staff turnover usually makes the plan out of date before it can be implemented. In short, the picture of real-world administration simply does not agree with the ideal world of the planners.

We have a problem here. Either the harassed administrators are demonstrating poor performance and should be pressured to become more organized and effective and follow the mandates of the planning, or the planning theorists are wrong, their theories are simply out of step with reality, and their abstract concepts need drastic revision.

Administrators would defend themselves by arguing that the real world does not neatly fit the theories of the planners. Planners would respond by saying, "Yes, we understand that things do not work like our theories suggest. However, you *ought* to try to work this way. If you did, administrative effectiveness would go up. Maybe we can change the real world and make it a better place."

Which is right, the administrator's *description* of the real world or the planner's goal of changing the behavior to a pattern that *ought* to make it better? We believe the theories should be adjusted to reality, not reality forced into a theoretical box.

We need a theory that addresses administrative practice rather than one that demands that a zebra change its stripes. If real-world administrative behavior is crisis-oriented, then we need a better theory of crisis management. If goals are complex, ambiguous, and contested, then we need a decision theory that handles goal complexity instead of demanding goal simplicity. If administrative time orientation is short-term instead of long-term, then we need a theory to improve short-term decisions so the long-term outcomes improve. If real-world administration is highly political as well as rational, then we need a theory for improving political skills. In other words, the theory should match reality, instead of forcing reality into the theory.

There have been a number of important steps in the literature of recent years. In particular, the attempt to understand the nonrational area of decision making has been substantially advanced by the research and writing of James G. March (see especially Cohen and March, *Leadership and Ambiguity*, 1976). At the same time, several important books have been written on the subject of political approaches to decision making, most notably the excellent book by Graham Allison (*The Essence of Decision*, 1974) and the work of J. Victor Baldridge (*Power and Conflict in the University*, 1970, and *Policy Making in Effective Leadership*, 1978). We will focus here on only one new approach of an alternative model of decision making that more realistically matches actual administrative behavior: that of *strategic planning*. This approach offers some promising alternatives to conventional long-range planning.

The Development of Strategic Planning in Higher Education

What is strategic planning? What are its intellectual origins? How is it different from traditional long-range planning? The central focus of strategic planning is developing a good fit between the organization's activities and the demands of the environment around it. Strategic planning looks at the big picture—the long-range destiny of the institution, the competition between this organization and others in the environment, the market for organizational products and services, the mix of internal resources to accomplish the organization's purpose. Strategic planning emphasizes flexibility and quick response to changes in the outside environment. Its basic perspective is external—looking at the environment around the organization—rather than internal—looking at the organization's structure. The goal of strategic planning is not so much to produce plans as it is to make critical decisions wisely. It is not so much interested in doing things right, it is more concerned with doing the right things. Effectiveness, not efficiency, is the goal of strategic planning.

Of course, good decision makers in complex organizations have always acted this way, long before anyone coined the term "strategic planning." In the last few years, however, writers in business schools and management centers have been trying to develop a more coherent theory and description of what the strategic management process looks like.

Strategic Planning in Higher Education

In his book entitled *Strategic Planning, Management, and Decision Making* (1982), Robert Cope reviews the development of the strategic-planning literature and examines its application to higher education in America. Cope comments on the intellectual roots of strategic planning:

The ideas and techniques of the strategic view are developing from a convergence of several disciplines and subdisciplines. The clearest connection is with schools of management from which policy, marketing, and effectiveness research is being adapted for use in higher education. Policy research is aimed at determining the nature of the activity in which the organization is to engage and what kind of organization it is to be. Marketing helps determine more directly what the organization's current and probable clients want. Effectiveness research seeks to determine what combination of organizational policies and need fulfillment results in success. The literature about policy, marketing, and effectiveness overlaps and converges in strategic planning. Nearly all of this literature has developed in the last fifteen years in the management schools and has been applied to higher education for only about three years.

An Illustration of Strategic Planning: A Military Analogy

In many ways, strategic planning is a state of mind rather than a planning technique. Perhaps a simple analogy will help explain this idea. Since the word "strategy" is often used as a military term, we will use a military analogy to demonstrate the key emphasis of strategic planning.

Let us assume that an army wanted to mount a major invasion, such as the American and British armies did in Normandy. What would they do about planning? Clearly, the first move would be to make a series of complicated plans about how the invasion should be conducted. We can easily imagine office buildings full of generals, admirals, and planning staffs drawing up attack plans, logistical requirements, and transportation needs. Undoubtedly people would be doing conventional long-range planning. They would lay out budgets and assemble the necessary armaments and men; they would analyze the need for new equipment and requisition its production; they would lay out maps of terrain, and they would specify how troops would move across it; they would set up a chain of command. In short, they would do many things we typically associate with traditional planning.

But what happens when the invasion is launched? Everyone knows that the original plans will almost certainly falter, that almost every parameter that went into the planning will change, and that the rapidly changing military environment will upset and unravel plans that were made in office buildings far from the front.

Now we switch to the mentality of strategic planning. The military unit going into battle undoubtedly will have a master plan. But its real success will rest on adequate response to changing conditions, on flexibility in meeting new demands, and on internal strength that allows rapid deployment. As every good military commander knows, no matter how carefully the plans have been made, the actual battle will take a different turn. If all the battle commander had were plans, he would be in a remarkably poor position.

Instead, knowing that real events will always turn out differently from the plans, a strong battle commander builds a *response capacity*. Troops are assembled with heavy elements of *redundancy* built in so extra strength is available for every move. Complex efforts are undertaken to scan the environment: intelligence networks are built to ferret out the enemy's movements; reconnaissance efforts are mounted to find out where the original plans go astray and by how much. Elaborate communications are structured so the commander can monitor the situation and rapidly deploy forces for new moves that were not in the old plans. Strategic reserves are held back so that fresh forces can be thrown when needed into the rapidly changing situations. And contingency plans are developed to provide alternatives when the original master plan does not work. In short, the battlefield requires a decidedly different mind set and a much different set of behaviors. The successful commander must be quick on his feet, must know when to adapt the original plans to the changing realities, must constantly scan the battlefield environment for the transformation, and must respond rapidly with critical decisions.

We are arguing that the leaders of American higher education must learn to think more like the battlefield commander than like the desk-top planner back at headquarters. Unfortunately, most planning models were designed for headquarters; the strategic-planning literature tries to reorient the discussion toward the battlefield.

Some people will argue that a battlefield analogy is inappropriate for higher education—in fact, people *have* argued this in seminars where we have discussed strategic planning. Nevertheless, we feel that this analogy clearly helps us establish the strategic perspective, the mental mind set, and the basic attitudes that are helpful in understanding the contrast between strategic planning and conventional long-range planning.

The Major Emphases of Strategic Planning

In this section we will try to draw out in more precise form the distinctions between conventional long-range planning and the emerging theory of strategic planning (see also Kotler and Murphy 1981).

Strategic Planning Focuses on the Organization's Destiny. In effect, strategic planning examines the "big" issues—the organization's purpose, its mission, its relationship to its environment, its share of the market, its interactions with other organizations. Strategic planning is not concerned with nuts-and-bolts issues, with routine allocation of resources, or with the details of operation. Strategic planning asks the basic questions of institutional health and survival. In fact, much of the early work in strategic planning focused on businesses that were either spectacular successes or spectacular failures! Both ends of the continuum were interesting because they showed how strategic planning was related to the institution's vitality and survivability.

Strategic Planning Is Usually the Task of Top Echelon Managers. Decisions about the institution's destiny, its role in society, and its competition with other organizations are major questions. Usually the only people with enough power and perspective to understand the whole situation are the top managers. Business literature, in particular, tends to view strategic planning as a task for top managers. Robert Cope (1982) challenges this view; he argues that educational institutions are more democratic, more professionalized, and more influenced by the voice of faculty and students. Consequently, he suggests that in higher education strategic planning should be not only the task of top managers but should have broad institutional participation. We agree with Cope's value judgments, and we also agree that people throughout the institution *ought* to be involved in the discussion of strategic ideas. We nevertheless feel that in the real world most major strategic decisions require the exercise of serious power and authority and invariably are controlled by top-echelon decision makers.

Time Orientations in Strategic Planning Are Short Range and Medium Range. The dogma of the conventional planner is that plans must extend far into the future. The reality of most on-line administrators is that such plans almost always fail because environmental conditions change too rapidly. It is not uncommon to find colleges and universities with documents called Five-Year or Ten-Year Plans; it *is* uncommon to find anybody frequently using such documents.

By contrast, strategic planning relies heavily on rapid assessment of the environment and on rapid decision making that grapples with short-term and medium-range issues. The emphasis is on doing the right thing today, so the organization will be better off in the long run. This does not mean that people using strategic-planning models ignore the future; it simply means that they tend to be more modest in their time frames and that they understand the long-term impacts of today's decisions.

Strategic Planning Is Extremely Sensitive to the Environment Around the Organization. Most key factors that determine the organization's long-range destiny are found in the outside environment. Higher education in the last decade has been brutally awakened to the significant role of environmental forces. Substantial demographic shifts in the student recruitment pools, coupled with a shakeup in governmental financial support, have made most administrators sensitive to environmental impacts.

Conventional long-range planning tended to rely on a "closed-system" model; strategic planning, however, is an "open systems" model. The key focus is on assessing the turbulent environment surrounding a college or university. Strategic planning examines issues like market segmentation, interorganizational competition, interaction with funding agencies, and matching the environment's needs with the organization's capabilities. The strategic planner knows the importance of developing a range of alternate scenarios and backup positions as contingencies for a changed environment. The strategic planner looks outward; the traditional planner seems to look more inward. This fundamental reorientation of perspective is probably the single most important contribution that the strategic-planning literature brings to higher education management.

Strategic Planning Is Fundamentally an Art Rather Than a Science.
Many people who stress traditional long-range planning argue that there is
a "management science" for the planning enterprise. Rationality,
quantitative analysis, and highly technical planning techniques are
among the long-range planner's package of skills.

By contrast, people who advocate strategic planning see it as an art
form—a subtle blend of facts, hunches, assessments, experiences, and trial-
and-error experiments. Both qualitative value judgments and quantitative
analyses are blended in a strategic planning effort. In particular, the
experiment judgments of professional faculty people are seen as important
inputs in a strategic planner's decision process. This is a much more subtle
and dynamic mixture of styles.

Stream of Decisions in the Strategic Process. The traditional long-range
planner sees a *plan* as the capstone of his efforts, a blueprint for the action
that is suppose to guide the organization. The strategic planner, in
contrast, sees the capstone effort as a *stream of decisions* that help move the
organization into the future. The long-range planner is usually concerned
about coming up with the *right* plan in view of the facts and figures and
crystallized goals. The strategic planner, on the other hand, is much more
interested in coming up with a *wise* decision that is the subtle blend of
qualitative and quantitative matters. Words like "wise" are almost
nonexistent in the lexicon of the long-range planner, but to the strategic
planner a word like "wise" is the heart of the matter. Good college
administrators, we believe, do not blanch at the thought of making wise
decisions.

A stream of critical decisions instead of a plan and a blueprint; an
emphasis on "wise" decisions instead of on "right" decisions; an
orientation to effectiveness rather than efficiency; an eye toward doing the
right thing instead of doing things right—these are subtle shifts in
meaning and perspective that characterize the strategic-planning approach
(see Table 9-1).

Mercy College: Strategic Planning at Work

Recent evidence suggests that small private liberal arts colleges will be
the institutions most threatened by enrollment difficulties, and the
Northeast will be the most vulnerable geographic area. Yet in spite of these
dire forecasts, one college contradicts the predictions, expanding its
enrollment and programs through aggressive action. Let us examine the
strategic decision Mercy College has made to pull off this coup.

Mercy College grew from an enrollment of 1,500 students in 1972 to over
9,500 students enrolled in day, evening, and weekend sessions in 1981. This

Table 9-1

Comparison of Strategic Planning and Conventional Planning*

Activity	Strategic Planning	Conventional Planning
Arena of Planning	Organization's Destiny Market	Wider Range of Issues, Nonroutine and Routine
Who Plans	Top-Level Officials	Planning Office
Time Orientation	Medium/Short Range	Long Range
System Perspective	External, Environmental	Internal, Organizational
Theoretical Perspective	Open System	Closed System
Decision Data	Both Quantitative and Qualitative	Quantitative
Decision Process	Complex Art Form	Exact Science
Outcome	Stream of Critical Decisions	Plan, Blueprint

*This chart is heavily dependent on ideas developed by Robert Cope (1982).

phenomenal growth in Mercy College in just a decade was due primarily to the changes in directorship, philosophy, and mission of the school as it converted from a small, all-female, Catholic school to an expanding, coeducational and nonsectarian institution. The philosophy and personal administrative style of the man who led Mercy College through this transitional period to its current status is of particular interest.

A Shift in Institutional Mission

Mercy College, whose main campus is located in Dobbs Ferry, Westchester County, New York, began as a Catholic junior college in 1950 under the auspices of the Sisters of Mercy. The original mission of the school was to train nuns to teach in grammar schools. In 1961 the institution became a four-year college that offered academic programs leading to the baccalaureate degree. As the number of nuns decreased in the Catholic church during the 1960s, the college began to admit an increasing number of lay women.

In 1969 the Sisters of Mercy decided to relinquish the college because it no longer served the mission for which it was founded. The college was turned over to a lay board and became nonsectarian and coeducational. Eligibility for participation in the state-funding programs for private institutions was a major impetus for the decision to change Mercy College to nonsectarian status. In 1972 Dr. Don Grunewald was appointed as the college's first permanent lay president, and under his leadership the institution grew and expanded.

Strategic Decision: "Take the Campus to the Students"

The first major strategic decision in developing the new mission was to drop all pretext of being a small residential college and shift to a service orientation for commuting students. According to Dr. Grunewald, the college "functions in the capacity of what a state university normally would do. SUNY, at Purchase, New York, for instance, is 'more elitist' than Mercy." There was a gradual emergence and expansion of summer, evening, and weekend sessions and of offerings in bilingual and adult education. The development of the college's branch campus in Yorktown Heights and the offering of courses at a variety of other sites in the metropolitan area were evidence of further growth. Today, there are extension centers in Peekskill, White Plains, Yonkers, and the Bronx. In addition, courses are offered at six correctional facilities. And, since 1975, the Brooklyn Center for Long Island University has offered graduate courses on the Mercy College campus.

Because academic offerings are available at all locations, the educational processes are more convenient and accessible to students from the New York Metropolitan area. Programs are offered in liberal arts and sciences and professional studies; the college grants the Bachelor of Arts, Bachelor of Science, Associate in Arts, and Associate in Science degrees. Also offered are career-oriented certificate programs in a variety of areas.

Mercy College draws students from Westchester County and the New York/New Jersey/Connecticut Metropolitan area. Eighty percent of the students live within four miles of the campus. There are approximately two hundred students from foreign countries, the largest group being from Nigeria; and the largest minority groups are blacks and Hispanics who constitute about 20 percent of the total student population. The average age of the student is around twenty-seven years, and there are approximately the same percentage of male and female students.

Monitoring the Environment

Dr. Grunewald's approach to planning is strategic—he constantly monitors the environment, and he calculates how Mercy College can respond to trends, changes, and needs. Aside from the once traditional but now accepted programs like the Weekend College, Mercy has also tried some novel approaches to meeting student needs, which, in Dr. Grunewald's estimation, "have worked." One approach is parallel scheduling. The same courses are given by the same faculty both in the morning and evening. Parallel scheduling is helpful to students who work shifts, which in that location is not unusual. If the shift changes, the student may switch from the morning to the evening class, or vice versa, without "going through any red tape."

Maintaining Flexibility

Mercy College rents all properties except the one main campus. This provides for more flexibility: if more spaces and facilities are needed, Mercy College rents them. If less space is needed, the college does not have "to sell or waste; just don't lease." By leasing, the college goes to where the market is. If one area is losing students and not doing well, another location for the campus is considered.

The same contingent and strategic thinking is applied to academic programs. A number of associate degree and certificate programs are offered at Mercy. Students, particularly adults, are recruited for these programs, and, once enrolled, are encouraged to continue for four years. Essentially a four-year college, Mercy College nonetheless makes provision for programs that do not lead to a bachelor's degree. Whenever feasible, associate-degree programs are offered in the same fields of study as in the four-year program. The college has currently applied to the state for Associate Degrees in Secretarial Science and Graphic Arts; these programs are first intended to attract students who will ultimately apply for the four-year program in the same areas.

Institutional Accomplishments

In 1972 when Dr. Grunewald became president, succeeding an acting lay president, the college had an enrollment of 1,500 students, approximately 70 percent of whom were women. Approximately two years earlier the college had become nonsectarian and coeducational. One-half of the department chairpersons and less than 55 percent of the faculty held doctorate degrees. The college owned one building, and classes were offered on the one campus. The library had holdings of 60,000 volumes, and the only career programs offered were teacher training and medical technology.

Today, the college has an enrollment of 9,400 students with an additional 800 students in a graduate program affiliated with Long Island University. All department chairpersons and 60 percent of full-time faculty have earned doctorate degrees. There are two campuses, four extension centers, and courses (mainly lower division and some remedial) offered at six correctional facilities. The main library houses a total collection of 280,000 volumes as well as extensive audio-visual materials.

Career programs include business administration, criminal justice, education, computer-information science, medical technology, nursing, public safety, and social work. The college will soon offer a program in veterinary technology management, a four-year program to educate individuals to function as assistants to veterinarians and to work in veterinary laboratories. This program is the first of its kind to be offered. The Weekend College draws interested students in business administration, criminal justice, behavioral science, and computer science. Continuing education programs were started a year ago.

Lessons to Be Learned

What can we learn from the Mercy College case study? Several points are important:

1. *Environmental monitoring* is a key administrative action, for it can help match the institution's service with the market's demands.
2. A key factor in this institution's growth and development is *administrative leadership.* An administrator who provides a strong, stable, and enthusiastic leadership enables the college to establish itself as an expanding and independent educational force in the community. Mercy College is committed to providing a variety of educational opportunities to both traditional and nontraditional students and, in keeping with this philosophy, has made no attempt to develop an "elitist" image so frequently pursued by private schools.
3. An *organizational climate,* in part fostered by the president, encourages flexibility and leads to a contingency-strategic way of thinking. Generating creative ideas for program development and new approaches to traditional practices in keeping with environmental changes and trends is congruent with today's concepts of strategic planning in organizations.
4. *Problem areas* need to be continually monitored at Mercy. The institution must maintain both quality as well as quantity if it is to remain viable and effective. Too, there is the issue of effective leadership, if and when administrative changes occur.

The Concept of Jugular-Vein Decisions

I will add one modification to the strategic-planning concept. Since strategic planning is primarily concerned with a stream of decisions, it is helpful to coin some terminology to identify those crucial decisions—I like the term "jugular-vein decisions."

During the research, we interviewed the provost of a large university who used the phrase "jugular-vein decision." He contrasted this type of decision to the activities of the master planners, the group that was trying to plan for his institution's future in five or ten years. He offered this comment:

I am more than happy to let my enemies run the long-range planning committees. They are off in the corner running their statistical projections, devising their "mission statements," and making up their master plans. In the meantime, I am doing the unimportant stuff—at least from their point of view. I am setting the budgets, selecting the key people, and funding key programs. I call these the jugular-vein decisions. In the long run I am positive that I will have more influence over this institution's future. The staff I select and the funding decisions I make will outmaneuver the grand planners with their schemes and statistics.

This provost was probably correct. The medium-range decisions about budget, staffing, and major problems will determine at least as much about the institution's destiny as the master plans. These jugular-vein decisions build the institution's infrastructure and its flexibility for responding to an uncertain future. In effect, this approach argues for an "uncertainty" principle in academic management. We obviously must have plans and we must have planners, but we must match those plans with built-in flexibility that will carry the institutions through when the planners are wrong.

Examples of Jugular-Vein Decisions

What are some examples of jugular-vein decisions? The following list contains some nominations:

1. *Implementing major budget changes.* Most budgeting is certainly not "zero based" in spite of all the promotion for this model in recent years. Instead, budgets are largely incremental extensions with minor adjustments from the previous year. However, when substantial budget changes can be made to emphasize new priorities, programs, or constituent demands, these changes become opportunities for important decisions.

2. *Selecting key faculty and administrators.* Nothing shapes an institution like the quality of its people. One president we interviewed stated it simply: "The most important thing I've done in the past six years has undoubtedly been the selection of the key deans. Nothing else even comes close in terms of the impact that these decisions have." This same president went on to argue: "I don't worry too much about the content of the master plans, as I get to select the people that implement them"—a notion that seems eminently sensible to us.

3. *Shaping the relationship to the outside environment.* A key strategic decision is the relationship between the organization and the outside world. Top administrators are like the Roman god Janus—they must constantly be looking outward at the world and inward at the organization. Several environmental questions constitute jugular-vein decisions: What are the basic demographics of population, migration, and age distribution? What is our client pool and how can we best tap it? What other organizations compete with us, and how do we interact with them? Who are the key funding agents and what is our relationship to them? What is the political context and how is it changing? Information gathering is essential to successful strategic decision making.

4. *Influencing key policies.* In every college or university a handful of basic institutional policies shapes the institution's destiny— admissions policies, collective-bargaining contracts, affirmative action mandates, promotion and tenure policy, and graduation requirements. Unfortunately, administrators often feel that shaping these policies is routine work, an activity frequently handed over to middle-level staff people. This is a substantial mistake because these policies are "preformed decisions" that will guide the institution for a long time. These preformed decisions are simply applied in most decision situations. Unless wisdom and effectiveness are built into these policies, they cannot handle the bulk of the decision making. Unfortunately, administrators do not often think the policy arena is important because it is rarely as exciting as crisis situations. Nevertheless, shaping important policies is a critical jugular-vein decision and should not be neglected.

5. *Building more effective organizational systems:* The organizational structure is usually well formed and rarely changes significantly. However, from time to time administrators have an opportunity to reshape the very structure of the organization. Examples of "system-building" jugular-vein decisions are adding another school, college, or division; eliminating major program sets; building a management-information system; shaking up the organizational hierarchy; or constructing a better linkage to outside organizations.

These decisions share common features: they are medium-range in their time span, they can usually be controlled at the local campus, they are within the span of influence of key administrators; if changed, factors would have important consequences. There are, of course, many other issues that might be considered jugular-vein decisions—the above list is not exhaustive.

Summary

To conclude, let us review our major arguments. First, we have suggested that traditional planning models are not likely to be as helpful as their proponents suggest—there are many flaws in the long-range planning perspective.

By contrast, the literature on strategic planning has a rather different set of emphases. Strategic planning focuses on the organization's destiny and ultimate mission, with particular reference to its place in the external environment. Constituency, market, and competing organizations are salient features of the strategic mentality. Usually, strategic planning is seen as a function of key executives rather than as an activity lodged in a staff planning-office. Strategic planning has several other features: its time perspective is medium- or short-range, it uses an open-system perspective instead of a closed-system perspective, and it utilizes both qualitative and quantitative information in a process that is more an art form than a science. Mercy College is an excellent case study of these strategies, and we have used the term "jugular-vein decision" to give us a label for the stream of decisions in strategic planning. The key objective of strategic planning is a stream of wise decisions rather than a plan or a blueprint bound in a volume to be forgotten.

References

Allison, G. *The Essence of Decision*. Boston: Little, Brown, 1971.

Baldridge, J. Victor. *Power and Conflict in the University*. New York: John Wiley, 1971.

Baldridge, J. Victor, D.V. Curtis, G. Ecker, and G.L. Riley. *Policy Making and Effective Leadership*. San Francisco: Jossey-Bass, 1978.

Cohen, M.D., and J.G. March. *Leadership and Ambiguity: The American College President*. New York: McGraw-Hill, 1974.

Cope, R.A. *Strategic Planning, Management and Decision Making*. AAHE/ERIC Higher Education Research Report No. 9. Washington, D.C.: American Association for Higher Education, 1981.

Cosand, J.P. "Developing an Institutional Master Plan." In *Improving Academic Management*, edited by P. Jedamus, M.W. Peterson and associates. San Francisco: Jossey-Bass, 1980.

Fenske, Robert. "Setting Institutional Goals and Objectives." In *Improving Academic Management*, edited by P. Jedamus, M.W. Peterson, and associates. San Francisco: Jossey-Bass, 1980.

Glenny, L.A., J.R. Shea, J.H. Ruyle, and K.H. Freschi. *Presidents Confront Reality*. San Francisco: Jossey-Bass, 1976.

Hobbs, J.M. and D.F. Heany. "Coupling Strategy to Operating Plans." *Harvard Business Review*, May-June, 1977: 119–126.

Kemerer, F.R., J. Victor Baldridge, and K.C. Green. *Strategies for Effective Enrollment Management.* Washington, D.C.: American Association of State Colleges and Universities, 1982.

Kotler, P., and P.E. Murphy. "Strategic Planning for Higher Education." *Journal for Higher Education,* Vol. 52, No. 5, 1981: 470–489.

Peterson, M.W. "Analyzing Alternative Approaches to Planning." In *Improving Academic Management,* edited by P. Jedamus, M.W. Peterson, and associates. San Francisco: Jossey-Bass, 1980.

PART III

Politics and the Environment

In our earlier book, *Managing Change in Educational Organizations*, we stressed that organizational change was often prompted by environmental demands and that the environmentally stimulated changes were usually implemented through a political dynamic. That emphasis on environmental stimulation and political dynamics continues in this volume.

Both organizational theorists and administrators are aware that environmental demands are a prime stimulus to change. Although the "change" literature of the past decades emphasized the powerful role of internal change agents and institutional planning for the destiny of educational organizations, it is increasingly clear that major organizational changes are usually a result of interaction with the environment. Think about these significant forces responsible for educational change:

—Demographic patterns that determined student flows over the last two decades, flows that went from boom to bust.

—Public funding patterns that determine the institutional life blood.

—Court decisions affecting integration, affirmative action, and education for the handicapped.

—Student-aid policies that significantly impact private schools and colleges.

—Curricular changes in science and engineering, forced upon education by military confrontation with the Soviets and by technological challenges by the Japanese.

In short, environmental dynamics are often the key to large-scale changes in educational organizations.

The political theme is also very prominent in this section. What do we mean by a "political" analysis of change? The political approach assumes that complex organizations can be studied as miniature political systems, with interest group dynamics and conflicts similar to those in city, state, and other political situations. The political model has several stages, all of which center around policy-forming processes. Policy formation is selected as the central focal point because major policies commit the organization to definite goals, set the strategies for reaching those goals, and in general determine the long-range destiny of the organization. Policy decisions are critical decisions, those that have a major impact on the organization's future. In any practical situation it may be difficult to separate the routine from the critical, for issues that seem minor at one point may later be of considerable importance, or vice versa. In general, however, policy decisions are those that bind the organization to important courses of action. The political model makes a series of assumptions about the political process.

One assumption is that *inactivity prevails*. To say that policymaking is a political process is not to say that everybody is involved. Quite the contrary. For most people most of the time, the policymaking process is an uninteresting, unrewarding activity, so they allow administrators to run the show.

A second assumption is that of *fluid participation*. Even when people are active they move in and out of the decision-making process. Individuals usually do not spend very much time on any given issue; decisions, therefore, are usually made by those who persist. This normally means that small groups of political elites govern most major decisions because only they invest the necessary time in the process.

A third assumption is that educational organizations, like most other social organizations, are *fragmented into interest groups* with different goals and values. These groups normally live in a state of armed coexistence. When resources are plentiful and the environment congenial, these interest groups engage in only minimal conflict. They mobilize and fight to influence decisions, however, when resources are tight, outside pressure groups attack, or other internal groups try to take over their goals.

A fourth assumption is that *conflict is normal*. In a fragmented, dynamic social system, conflict is natural and not necessarily a symptom of breakdown in the academic community. In fact, conflict is a significant factor in promoting healthy organizational change.

A fifth assumption is that *authority is limited*. In "loosely coupled" educational organizations the formal authority prescribed in a bureaucratic system is severely limited by the political pressure that groups can exert. Decisions are not simply bureaucratic orders, but are often negotiated compromises between competing groups. Officials are not free simply to issue a decision; instead they must jockey between interest groups hoping to build viable positions between powerful blocks.

A sixth assumption is that *external interest groups are important.* Educational decision making does not occur in a campus-bound vacuum. External interest groups exert a great deal of influence over the policymaking process. And external pressures and formal control by outside agencies—especially in public institutions—are powerful shapers of internal governance processes.

In Part II we discussed the limits of the "rational" approach to change. The rational decision theory suggests that all possible options are open within easy reach of the decision maker. A realistic appraisal of decision dynamics in most organizations, however, suggests that by no means are all options open. The political dynamics of interest groups, the force of external power blocs, and the opposition of powerful professional constituencies may leave only a handful of viable options. The range of alternatives is sharply limited; the realistic choices are narrow. Just as important, the time and energy available for seeking new solutions most likely is extremely short. Although all possible solutions *should* be identified under the rational model, administrators in the real world have little time to grope for solutions before deadlines are upon them.

These comments may be summed up by proposing a "political process" model of decision making. The political model suggests the following. First, powerful political forces—interest groups, bureaucratic officials, influential individuals, organizational subunits, environmental imperatives—cause a given issue to emerge from the limbo of ongoing problems and certain "attention cues" force the political community to consider the problem. Second, there is a struggle over locating the decision with a particular person or group, for the location of the right to make the decision often determines the outcome. Third, decisions are usually "preformed" to a great extent by the time one person or group is given the legitimacy to make the decision; not all options are open and the choices have been severely limited by the previous conflicts. Fourth, such political struggles are more likely to occur in reference to "critical" decisions than to "routine" decisions. Fifth, a complex decision network is developed to gather the necessary information and supply the critical expertise. Sixth, during the process of making the decision, political controversy is likely to continue and compromises, deals, and plain headcracking are often necessary to get any decision made. Finally, the controversy is not likely to end easily. In fact, it is difficult even to know when a decision *is* made, for the political processes have a habit of unmaking, confusing, and muddling whatever agreements are hammered out.

This may be a better way of grappling with the complexity that surrounds decision processes within a loosely coordinated, fragmented political system. The "rational" decision models seem to have been asking very limited questions about the decision process, and more insight can be gained by asking a new set of political questions. Thus the decision model that emerges is more open, more dependent on conflict and political action.

The articles in Part III develop the environmental and political themes. Rubin's study of retrenchment in a university (Chapter 10) starts with a strong environmental theme and shows how external imperatives work themselves out inside a loosely structured educational organization. The other articles in Part III have political overtones: they show the dynamics of interest groups in educational change. In Chapter 11 Baldridge outlines some "political rules" for a would-be change agent; Bennis explains in Chapter 12 how institutional change can be sabotaged if people do not carefully consider political issues; and Boyd shows in Chapter 13 the political dynamics surrounding curriculum innovation.

Taken together the four articles in this section demonstrate the important role the external environment plays in *stimulating* change and explain how political processes are central to *implementing* changes.

10

Retrenchment, Loose Structure, and Adaptability in the University

Irene Rubin

Problems of organizational retrenchment have become increasingly salient in the past few years as cities totter on the edge of bankruptcy and schools and universities struggle with recurrent deficits. The extent of the problem and the mechanics of organizational shrinkage have attracted much interest. Beyond the practical concerns, retrenchment poses some interesting theoretical questions.

Retrenchment provides a new set of circumstances in which to observe organizational behavior. As a result, scholars can compare organizational behavior under conditions of high and low resource levels. By carefully delineating and examining retrenchment phases, researchers will also improve their understanding of growth, since many of the effects of growth occur during retrenchment. Without examining retrenchment, theorists are liable to overstate the benefits of growth. Finally, a retrenchment perspective may emphasize different variables and processes than a growth perspective, because retrenchment may reveal aspects of the organization not apparent during growth.

I would like to thank Charles Bidwell, Michael Aiken, and Herbert Rubin for reading and critiquing earlier versions of this article.

Reprinted, by permission, from *Sociology of Education* 52 (October 1979): 211–22.

One of the questions which becomes more salient when viewed from a retrenchment perspective is whether there are any structural[1] aspects of organizations that increase their ability to adapt when resource levels decline. It is this question which is addressed here. The retrenchment experiences of five state universities are used to examine propositions relating structure to adaptability.[2] These propositions are derived from the literature and are modified in light of the case study data. The propositions explore only one dimension of structure, its looseness, and only one factor causing adaptation, reduction in resources. The goals of this article are two-fold: to lay some of the groundwork for a theory of relating structure to adaptability and to provoke further discussion and research.

The literature on organizational decline can be categorized in terms of three orienting models. The first is a homeostatic model, in which retrenchment triggers adaptive processes (Ansoff 1970; March and Cyert 1963). The second is a model of continuous decline. In this model, the organization becomes rigid as it grows and is unable to cope with retrenchment. Decline continues unchecked (Downs 1967; Merton 1940). The third model is a contingency model. It argues that the degree of flexibility in the organization at the time when the environment becomes threatening determines the survival capacity of the organization (Kaufman 1976).

Each of these theoretical positions describes some aspect of organizational behavior. Yet even a cursory examination of the first two suggests they are too simple: not all organizations successfully engage in self-corrective behavior; and not all large old organizations are rigid and moribund. The third avenue of enquiry seems to be the most profitable to both theoreticians and practitioners: that is, when or under what circumstances will an organization be able to adapt?

Though not yet fully developed in the literature, the contingency model of adaptability has been outlined by Herbert Kaufman in *Are Government*

---

[1] There is little consensus in the organizational literature on the meaning of "structure." It is used here to refer to such things as the characteristic division of labor, patterns of authority, and areas of dependence on the environment. While some elements of structure may be determined by the type of organization and the environment in which it is operating, structure represents outcomes of prior decisions and nondecisions, which bind or influence current decisions. It is both changeable and changing.

[2] This article is derived from a larger study on administrative response to university retrenchment. Only the theoretical framework is emphasized here. For more information on the study, and more details on the universities, see Rubin (1977).

Organizations Immortal? (1976).[3] Kaufman argues against the inevitability of sclerosis as organizations age. "Some organizations are rigid from the moment of establishment"; others "are flexible from the start or grow flexible over the years." [The crucial determinant of survival is the degree of flexibility in the organization at the time when the environment becomes turbulent and threatening.]

Kaufman's contingency theory depends on the undefined term, "flexibility." In order to explore the contingency notion, we will substitute the somewhat more manageable notion of "loose structure." "Loose structure" is only one way of conceptualizing flexibility, but it has the advantage that there is an existent theory linking it with adaptability during retrenchment. Simon (1962, 1973), Aldrich (1971), Weick (1976), and Glassman (1973) have all discussed the effect of loose structure on adaptability.[4] The two authors of particular concern here are Simon and Glassman.

Simon's conception of the relationship between loose structure and adaptability is developed through comparison to the human body. He describes the body as a series of loosely coupled subassemblies, such as circulation, digestion, and the like. The independence of the subsystems allows a change to take place in one of them without affecting all the other subsystems. Weak systems can be eliminated; new, better systems can be adopted, within the constraints posed by interrelations to other subsystems. If there are too many constraints, it is difficult to adopt a new subsystem that does the intended job better and also fits into the system.

The application of Simon's analogy to organizations during retrenchment is evident. When there are inadequate resources to change by continuous addition of new units, the functional independence of subunits should make it possible to continue improving the organization. New or

---

[3] There are a number of other structural contingency theories in existence which are much more fully developed than Herbert Kaufman's. These theories (such as James Thompson's, 1967) argue that certain structural patterns develop in an organization depending on the kind of environment they typically deal with. The question posed here is somewhat different: we ask what determines whether an organization will be able to adapt to a sudden specific negative change in the environment. Moreover, we are concerned here with the problem of maintaining adaptability within retrenchment rather than the more general problem of maintaining adaptability to all the elements in the environment. For these reasons, though Kaufman's work is less developed, it is more relevant to the study at hand.

[4] March has also written on loose structure, but not specifically as it relates to adaptability. Consequently, his writing has had less impact on the analysis than Simon's or Glassman's.

improved units can substitute for older, weaker ones with a minimum of constraints from other existing units. Size and resource demands can be reduced by elimination of weaker units without affecting the function of the remaining units.

To Simon's concepts, Glassman adds the idea that the function of looseness for adaptability is to provide buffering against overadaptation to short term changes. (This is also Aldrich's [1971] position.) Feedback loops to the environment must be good enough to tell the organism that a change has taken place, but internal networks must not respond to change so quickly and automatically that the organism is overadapted to a vanishing niche. Glassman's work suggests that a particular pattern of looseness and tightness in different areas of organizational functioning might be more adaptive.

Simon and Glassman point out key issues and useful approaches, but they do not agree on definitions. Neither they nor others have tested their theories with empirical data. What follows is an attempt to define key terms and extend the theoretical insights of Simon and Glassman, applying them to an organizational context.

Operationalizations and Propositions

The argument developed here rests on two key concepts, adaptability and loose structure. Adaptability is defined as the capacity of the organization to change in order to continue to achieve organizational goals when changes in the environment threaten the accomplishment of those goals. Adaptability can be viewed as the ability to accomplish four tasks:

1. To survey the environment and distinguish long-term and short-term change.
2. To determine and execute responses to perceived long-term threats to organizational goals while buffering out short-term pressures.
3. To evaluate units, eliminate, reduce or strengthen the weak ones and expand the strong ones; to add new units which will facilitate achievement of goals under new circumstances.
4. To monitor the success of changes made and alter or continue behavior accordingly.

Looseness is here defined (in Glassman's terms) as the likelihood that a change in "a" will rapidly produce a change in "b"; (low likelihood-high looseness). To make the analysis more concrete and more congruent with accepted ideas about organizational structure we specify three areas of looseness: between horizontal units, between vertical units, and between the organization and its environment.

For this analysis, loose horizontal linkage has three components. The first is the degree of functional integration between horizontal units. How dependent are the horizontal units on each other for the accomplishment of the organization task? If they are intricately dependent on each other, then a halt or disturbance in one area "a" will rapidly produce chaos or work stoppage elsewhere, "b." The second aspect of loose horizontal linkage is financial interdependence. Does the resource level of one unit depend on the activities of other units, or primarily on its own efforts? Again, a high level of interdependence means a change or interruption in one area will rapidly produce responses elsewhere. The third type of horizontal linkage is (organizationally relevant) informal ties between individuals in horizontal units. The greater the number of informal ties, the greater the likelihood and speed with which a change in one unit will effect a change in another unit.

The second area of looseness considered here is that in vertical relationships.[5] In a loose hierarchy, levels are relatively independent of each other. They each make decisions affecting their own level with a minimal amount of control from above. Not only are orders from above not carried out by those far below, but information from below may not be conveyed back up the hierarchy. There may be an absence of appropriate measures of performance as well as of surveillance techniques. The greater the independence of each hierarchical level, the less likely a change in "a" will produce a change in "b."

The third area of looseness considered here is looseness in feedback loops to and from the environment. The likelihood that a change in the organization will not rapidly produce a change in the environment, and that a change in the environment will not rapidly produce a change in the organization, is the degree of looseness in feedback loops.

Looseness is thus used here as a series of continua. While the degree of looseness in any area is theoretically free to vary independently of looseness elsewhere, in practice, there is liable to be a pattern of relationships between them. For example, tight horizontal interdependence is liable to require or generate tight vertical linkage in order to coordinate closely timed sequences of activities. A change in the degree of looseness in one area may bring about changes in looseness elsewhere.

In the body of this paper, three propositions relating the degree of looseness with adaptability will be discussed in light of case study data on

---

[5]Loose vertical linkage is not the same as decentralization. As many authors have pointed out, decentralization is normally compensated for with various control devices. If these devices fail, vertical looseness could result. An organization can be decentralized and not loose.

retrenching universities. The data are not intended to prove or disprove the propositions in any formal sense, but only to illustrate and modify them.

Data were collected in five state universities. The schools were chosen to provide enough similarity to each other so that the same instruments could be used. All the schools were located in the same state, to control for funding structures and state policies. All have been subject to a statewide retrenchment in higher education. Each school was considered to be a university in the sense that it had several graduate programs of at least the Master's level. Within this broad similarity, the schools were varied on the dimension of emphasis on research and teaching. The schools in the study therefore represent a broad spectrum of public universities. Despite (or because of) the selection criteria, there was not enough variability in the degree of looseness among the universities to explore cross-sectional differences in structure as they related to outcomes. The impact of structure on adaptability was determined by examining this relationship within each university, rather than comparing between universities.

The fieldwork was carried out over a year's time in order to cover the events of one fiscal year. One university was studied first to determine the feasibility of the project and pretest interview questions. The work then rotated among the remaining universities so that responses between universities to the same event could be compared. The same pattern of approach was used in each university: identify and talk with general informants, collect and examine documents, interview administrators, from the bottom of the organization up. This approach allowed for comparisons between quantitative and qualitative data, and between the responses of superiors and subordinates.

There were fifty formal interviews. In each university, five interviews were with department chairmen (the same five departments were used in each university), and five were with upper-level administrators. The latter included deans, business offices, vice presidents and their assistants, and in some instances, the president and his assistants. Interviews averaged one hour. Less structured interviews with general informants were used to reconstruct the recent administrative history of the universities.

Supplementing and complementing the interviews, many documents were used, including budgets, audits, annual reports, faculty load studies, newsletters, newspapers, internal memos, minutes of meetings, and reports. Insofar as possible, documents were gathered for a ten-year period, including five years of growth and five years of decline.

Analysis

The first proposition deals with the ability of an organization to avoid rigidity by adding, deleting, expanding, or contracting units. The self-corrective model of decline suggests the organization will be able to make such structural changes; the model of inevitable decline suggests the organization will be too rigid to make such changes. The contingency model offers a cautious "it depends." Relying on inspiration from Simon, the proposition argues that it depends on the degree of horizontal looseness. Since three types of horizontal looseness are used here, the simplifying assumption is made that they all work in the same way.

Proposition 1. Loose horizontal linkage (functional and financial independence, lack of informal ties) facilitates adaptation by allowing units to be added or subtracted, expanded or contracted, permitting a reduction in size or cost and redirection of efforts toward new goals. The reasoning behind the proposition is analogous to Simon's model of human evolution: if one unit has to be changed or eliminated, there should be a minimum of harm done to other units; consequently, other units should have no interest in sustaining units slated for reduction or elimination.

In discussing this proposition, the looseness characteristic of the universities in the beginning of the retrenchment period will be established, the successes and failures of the universities in cutting back units will be described, and the proposition will be modified as needed on the basis of the universities' experiences.

Beginning with the level of horizontal looseness, at the time retrenchment began all the universities in the study were loosely integrated. With respect to functional independence, each department could do its job whether or not other departments did theirs well. There was some interdependence based on subject matter, such as between mathematics and physics, but the interdependence was kept to a minimum by duplication of similar courses in different departments. Financial independence was also high. Departmental budgets were almost completely determined by each department's enrollment, within overall budget constraints. One department did not tend to support another department with lesser enrollment. The third area of horizontal looseness is organizationally relevant, informal ties; these too were quite loose. Chairmen seldom met together, except with the dean, in which case most of the communication was vertical rather than horizontal. Chairmen reported getting information more often from deans than from other chairmen, and some indicated that they distorted information they gave to other chairmen.[6]

Since the universities were characterized by a high degree of horizontal looseness, it should have been possible (according to proposition 1) to eliminate or reduce some units and expand or add other units in order to help the organization adapt. In actuality, none of the universities in the study was able to delete units during the period covered by the study (1971–1974). One was able with great difficulty to combine some units. Most were able marginally to shrink or expand selected units. The reports of their failures and partial successes are enlightening in terms of why the hypothesized benefits of loose structure were not achieved.

In one university, a combined committee of faculty and administrators was set up to establish criteria and evaluate units. They had technical difficulties combining criteria into a single score. They also met political opposition from units who were afraid the evaluation would lead to cuts. Finally, their work was extremely time consuming. It was five years before they were in a position to recommend reorganization and elimination of units. After the end of the study, they managed to eliminate a college and a department.

In other universities, similar attempts were made without any success. Faculty were unwilling to participate in determining criteria for elimination because they felt such cooperation would be interpreted as consent. Upper-level administrators, left to their own devices, picked various departments and colleges and announced they would be cut. In one case, a dean simply refused to cut the designated department. In another, the department organized its students, the employers of its graduates, and its dean to fight for its continued existence. This effort was successful in reversing the decision. In another instance, a college was to be eliminated.

---

[6]The degree of functional interdependence was not formally measured in the study because only five departments in one college were used in each university. A simple measure of this variable over time can be easily derived from college catalogues as the number of courses outside the major department a student can or must take for a major, summed across departments, divided by the number of departments. Financial interdependence was formally measured for departments in Arts and Science colleges in each university. If some departments were receiving in budget much more than they generated in revenue, while others received much less, financial interdependence was considered high (Gini coefficients were used to measure the sum of inequality across departments). Informal horizontal linkage was measured by the size of union membership, frequency of informal horizontal meetings, and reports from chairmen as to where they got various pieces of information. See Rubin (1977) for detailed data.

A study was done and it recommended overhaul and improvement instead of elimination; the college was reorganized, but not eliminated.

To summarize, efforts were made to eliminate departments and colleges, but the vertical authority structure was too weak to carry out its decisions without faculty consent and involvement. Where that cooperation was lacking, the attempt failed; even when there was cooperation, the establishment of criteria and the evaluation process were slow. But it was the inability of the authority structure to carry out cuts rather than the horizontal linkage which was the obstacle to adaptation.

The proposition implied that the horizontal units would not band together to prevent elimination of units (because they had no interest in doing so). This part of the proposition was generally borne out, but with limits. It turned out that having no stake in the success or failure of other units in accomplishing organizational tasks was not enough to keep units from interfering with the elimination of other units. In order to cooperate, horizontal units needed to feel that they would actually benefit from the elimination or reduction of other units. Horizontal units were most likely to try to interfere if they felt that the criteria being used to cut others could also be used against them. Several examples illustrate these limitations on the proposition.

In one university, there had been considerable faculty reduction, especially in the departments with declining enrollments. One faculty member proposed a policy that no one be hired in any department until those who were fired because of retrenchment were hired back. The effect of such a policy would have been to prevent reduction of units to build stronger units. The policy was voted on by arts and science faculty and was narrowly defeated. The narrowness of the vote indicated there was no clear consensus. Some faculty members wanted the dean to continue to have the ability to reallocate, but feared he would reallocate only on the basis of enrollment, not on the basis of quality. If the dean allocated on quality, their departments would gain by the reduction in other units; if he allocated on the basis of enrollment, some of their departments would also be threatened. The vote turned on (1) the belief that the dean would allocate one way or another and (2) the understanding that one's own department was liable to benefit or suffer depending on the criterion used. The decision on whether the dean should be allowed the discretion to reallocate depended on perceived self-interest, not on dependence on the success or failure of other horizontal units in performing organizational tasks.

A similar set of issues arose in a second university. The president was reorganizing the administration. He cut back on the administrative structure of the colleges, he cut out student services, and had begun to reorganize the departments. Faculty watched with an attitude of "if it happened to them, it won't happen to us." However, the chairmen eventually saw the reorganization as a threat to all of them; there were no selective criteria being used that could assure them they would not be next. Informal horizontal groupings arose to challenge presidential procedures, and the reorganization of departments was stopped.

To summarize, despite loose horizontal linkage, none of the universities in the study was totally successful in eliminating or reducing units. Vertical linkage was too loose to determine and carry out selective retrenchment. The units were able to muster vertical support when they could not muster horizontal support. Also, if the criteria for elimination or reduction of units were seen as threatening to the majority, they banded together, thwarting plans for change. Based on the case-study data, it seems that in order to take advantage of the adaptive potential of loose functional integration between horizontal units, there must be a relatively tightly coupled vertical hierarchy and a moderate degree of financial interdependence, so that one unit benefits from cutting another. The impact of vertical looseness on adaptability will be further examined in the discussion of proposition 2.

The second proposition deals with the ability of an organization to determine and execute responses to reduced resources without overadapting to short-term trends. The literature suggests that the degree of looseness in vertical hierarchy may be the crucial structural component of this portion of adaptability. There is little consensus in the literature on the effects of loose hierarchy: authors such as Glassman (1973) and Aldrich (1971) emphasize the need for looseness as a buffer against overadaptation to short-lived trends, while other authors such as Downs (1967), Tullock (1965), and Evans (1975) emphasize the need for tight vertical linkage in order to communicate organizational objectives, monitor outcomes, and order corrective action. The proposition here combines both these views by listing presumed advantages and disadvantages of loose vertical linkage.

Proposition 2. Loose vertical hierarchy has dual effects: it buffers the organization against short-term changes, but it also hampers attempts to determine and coordinate responses to stress.

At the beginning of the period of retrenchment, all the universities in the study were characterized by loose vertical linkage. In several cases deans had their own support staff to handle budgeting and personnel decisions at that level. Top-level administrators tended not to make detailed decisions binding on those several layers below. Within broad guidelines and resource constraints, budget and personnel decisions at each level tended to be decided either at that level for that level or in *consultation* with the *immediately higher* level only. There was little direct supervision or evaluation by upper-level administrators of faculty or department heads.

Information gathering about lower-level units was poorly developed at the upper reaches of administration.[7]

According to the second proposition, the universities could be expected to have had difficulty determining and coordinating responses to stress. In that event, the higher-level administrators did not have much difficulty figuring out what they wanted to do. Higher-level administrators at each university tried some or all the following:

1. Increase faculty loads (to reduce unit costs and prevent future budget cuts).
2. Control the allocation of new positions, rank and salary at entry, temporary or permanent contracts (control new growth).
3. Control promotion and tenure awards and salary increments (avoid overstaffing in areas which will later have to be cut back; avoid rigidity).
4. Create a pool of uncommitted resources (as a buffer against cuts and a way of repairing damage from overly hasty or unwise cuts, and a way of maintaining loyalty and administrative stability).
5. Delete or combine units (reduce unit costs, free up funds for reallocation).

As suggested under proposition 1, the administrators had a great deal of difficulty actually carrying out these tasks. Devising and implementing reallocation schema frequently took several years, and in one university several administrators responsible for such schema lost their support and were consequently fired. None of the universities had much success in freeing up funds by the elimination of units. They had somewhat more success in taking control of personnel decisions, but the battle was dramatic in some places. In one university, a union sprang up when a vice-president tried to change the criteria for tenure and actually forced the decision not to grant tenure to be reversed. The vice-president was fired within the year. In other universities the change was more gradual, with higher-level

---

[7]At the department level, this was done through a pretested checklist of possible departmental functions, followed up with interview questions on the scope of budgetary decisions and personnel decisions. Similar detailed questions were asked at the dean's and at the provost's level. In addition, an attempt was made to discover overall patterns of top-down resource allocation and budgeting procedures. Budgetary decisions included control of discretionary funds and latitude for making allocations, as indicated by rules of allocation that come down with the budget. Personnel decisions included rank and salary at entry for new personnel and promotion and tenure awards. One question in this set was "how often were departmental recommendations overturned?"

administrators taking more and more of a direct role in decision making. In none of the universities was it possible to determine and execute the tasks of retrenchment quickly and without turmoil. For all the universities in the study, during the whole retrenchment period, administrators accomplished an average of half the tasks they tried to do and had least success in the most important tasks of reallocation.

To summarize, although there was considerable variation between universities in the degree of vertical looseness, they were all on the high side of looseness. Although administrators seemed to have little difficulty deciding what to do in the abstract, the working out of detailed plans for reallocation seemed more problematic, and the execution of retrenchment tasks was extremely difficult, slow, and fraught with job insecurity. It took too long to seek lower-level approval, and sometimes it was impossible to obtain; yet if administrators went too far without the approval of horizontal units, lower-lever opposition formed and worked against them. The very slowness of response had the benefit of preventing too rapid change in adaptation to external pressures. Because the universities could not distinguish long- and short-term environmental fluctuations, this buffering effect was of crucial importance. The inability of the universities to successfully monitor the environment and determine short- and long-term changes will be discussed under proposition 3.

The third proposition deals with the characteristic relations of the organization with its environment. The proposition is a simple application of Aldrich's and Glassman's shared concerns that the linkage to the environment must be tight enough so that the organization can perceive change and evaluate its permanence, but not so tight that every change in the environment is automatically translated into consequences inside the organization.

Proposition 3. Loose feedback loops to the environment have several effects: they buffer against short-term changes, but prevent understanding of short- and longer-term trends and prevent self-corrective behavior.

The universities had generally loose feedback loops to the environment. The universities were dependent on the state legislature for resources. Even student tuition had to be appropriated by the legislature before the universities could budget the revenues. Despite this dependence, there was little direct contact between the universities and the legislature. The State Board of Higher Education mediated between the legislature and the universities. It was given the task of coordinating university budget reductions, but it had no independent power over the universities. The board was therefore dependent on the universities for the accomplishment of its task, despite its implied power as budget cutter. The result of this pattern of indirection and mediation was some peculiar university-environment relationships.

Because the board had no power over the universities, it adopted the tactic of secrecy to prevent the universities from developing strategies to bypass the intent to their allocation schemes. To prevent the universities from conforming in advance in their allocation criteria, and thereby evading cuts, the board changed the allocation criteria every year. The universities thus had great difficulty in finding out how prior cuts had been determined and had no way of finding out how future cuts would be calculated. The board's secrecy made it difficult for the universities to distinguish short- and long-term trends and to correct their own behavior.

The universities were unable to adapt to board pressures and thereby prevent cuts, so there was a strong temptation to bypass the board and interact directly with the legislature. Because such a lobbying effort would undercut the purpose of the state board, it tried to prevent the universities from acting in their own behalf. With its budgetary control, the board prevented the universities from spending money on publicity or lobbying. The board appointed members of its own staff to represent the universities. Since the staff members had no vested interest in the universities, they made indifferent lobbyists. The universities struggled along as best they could. One developed extensive lobbying efforts but disguised the costs in the budget. Others did what they could with telephone calls and visits to get information and publicize their needs. These efforts were haphazard, and legislative action, like board action, frequently took the universities by surprise.

Even if the universities had been able to monitor or control the legislature and the state board, the universities would still have had loose feedback loops in some areas. It was relatively easy to measure the effects of budget reductions and the effects or lack of effects of university actions on budget levels. But other effects besides fluctuations in budget levels went unmeasured. Actions were taken by upper-level administrators without the means or the knowledge to evaluate success or failure. Because consequences went unmeasured, self-corrective behavior was impossible. The lack of appropriate measures was due partly to the lack of a clear idea of long-term goals, and partly due to the difficulty of measuring the quality of education—a major organizational output.

Proposition 3 suggests that organizations with loose feedback loops to the environment, such as those just described, will have difficulty discriminating between long- and short-term environmental changes and will have difficulty engaging in self-corrective behavior. The universities in the study certainly had such difficulties. The proposition also suggests a countervailing benefit of loose feedback loops, namely that loose feedback loops would provide a buffering effect. The universities in the study did not seem to get this advantage, however.

The universities had trouble discriminating between long- and short-term environmental changes partly for simple lack of information, but more importantly because of the kinds of measures of success used by the state board and the universities. From the point of view of university administrators, the measure of success and failure was budgetary level; from the point of the board, it was some measure of efficiency. Universities concentrated on whatever they had to do or felt they had to do to sustain budget levels, regardless of long-term consequences. The long-term consequences were not even measured.

Some of the pressure from the state board was precisely aimed at preventing universities from taking short-term adaptations that would jeopardize the future, but many of their policies had the opposite effect. Their concern with efficiency led them to emphasize enrollments and unit costs. To keep unit costs down, administrators tried to allocate resources to high-enrollment departments and take them away from departments with declining enrollments. This way of allocating pays no attention to long-term needs for growth. It speaks only to current demands and subsidizes fads which may prove expensive, both to initiate and sustain. There is no logic to this kind of change except the hope of preventing immediate cuts by satisfying the state board.

As a further illustration of pursuit of the budget without regard to the future, in one university a president made an agreement with the board that would enable the university to hire new faculty, but with strings attached. The new faculty had to be hired in classes where large enrollment had resulted from budget cuts. The size of these classes was to be fixed. The type of contract offered to faculty was to be temporary (one year only). Thus, the chairmen could not decide where the academic need was greatest or build the department in any way. Nor could they increase class size in introductory classes in order to be able to afford smaller classes in other areas. Finally, neither the chairmen nor upper-level administrators had any say in whether the contracts were to be temporary or permanent. The university had given up considerable autonomy and flexibility for a very limited and temporary commitment of funds.

The universities as a group paid little attention to determination of what elements in the environment they should resist, hoping they could assuage the board and prevent future cuts. This did not turn out to be a realistic hope, as a better monitoring of the environment would have shown. The board had to allocate cuts, whether or not the universities conformed to implicit or explicit directives.

The inability of the universities to adapt to board demands and thereby prevent future cuts is well illustrated by one university which had been severely cut after an enrollment decline. The enrollment decline took place in 1971 and 1972. In 1973 the board did a unit cost study and found the university's costs to be high. In 1975 the board allocated cuts on the basis of that cost study and spread out the cut over a three-year period. Once the university realized that it had been cut because of the enrollment decline, it tried to increase enrollment. A new extension program was added, but even though enrollment increased, the budget did not. The university was in a worse position than before, having more students within the limited budget. The university was unable to improve its situation by learning from prior mistakes.

To summarize, feedback loops to the environment were loose. The universities were unable to distinguish long- and short-term trends and ignore short-term pressures. They were forced to concentrate on current environmental pressures, as well as they could understand them, in the hope of sustaining budget levels. No attention was paid to long-term consequences. The danger of overconforming to short-term trends was therefore great. The universities were unable to improve their situations through trial and error because the state board (1) had to allocate cuts and (2) kept secret the criteria for cuts and kept changing these criteria. Proposition 3 suggests that loose feedback loops can also provide a benefit during retrenchment because the long time lag before the outcome of decisions is known can prevent an overly rapid series of adaptations. This advantage was not realized because universities acted on anticipated responses when actual ones were not forthcoming. Not only was the advantage of delay lost, but it was possible to adapt to nonexistent pressures.

Summary and Conclusions

This article focuses on the structural components of adaptability during retrenchment in five case-study universities. It briefly outlines three theories of organizational decline and adaptability, choosing one, Herbert Kaufman's contingency model of adaptability, as a basis for further development and analysis. In the effort to apply Kaufman's insights, his term "organizational flexibility" was conceptualized as "loose structure." The works of Simon and Glassman on loose structure were combined, adapted to organizations, and organizationalized in order to arrive at propositions on how looseness might affect adaptability. These propositions were then examined in light of case study data. Based on this analysis, the article offers some possible (researchable) relationships between particular types of looseness and adaptability, and between particular patterns of loose structure and adaptability.

On examining the data, it is clear that the hypothesized benefits of loose structure did not generally occur. The impact of loose structure in any area of operation was dependent on the degree of looseness elsewhere in the organization. The effect of loose horizontal linkage depended on the degree of loose vertical linkage; the effect of loose feedback loops to the environment depended on the looseness in the vertical linkage. It also became apparent that loose horizontal coupling was in fact a cluster of interacting variables. The effect of loose functional linkage was dependent on the perception of actors of the type of financial integration between horizontal units (resource allocations). To complicate matters still further, the impact of tighter vertical linkage was tighter informal ties among horizontal units. Based on these results, it seems that a particular pattern of looseness and tightness is required to provide flexibility and adaptability.

From the study, it would appear that the following combination might help universities adapt during retrenchment: loose functional integration among horizontal units, with an allocation system that benefits some units on the demise of others, a moderate degree of vertical tightness and a moderately tight linkage with the environment. The moderately tight links to the environment will allow the universities to perceive and distinguish long- and short-term trends, while the moderately tightly coupled vertical hierarchy will enable administrators to conceive of appropriate responses but will not allow them to execute such responses too quickly. The loose functional linkage then allows for reallocation schema that can give outlet to creative ideas, reward excellence, or help the institution change direction.

In the light of these conclusions, we need to reflect back on how far we have come from the original biologically inspired models of Simon and Glassman. Simon's idea of looseness seemed to combine vertical and horizontal looseness in the notion of independent subassemblies, so the possibility that different kinds of looseness could vary separately was not provided for. Glassman provided for the possibility of varying degrees of looseness in different areas, but didn't specify the areas. In his model, everything is related to everything else, which while realistic, is difficult if not impossible to operationalize. In both biological models, there was no possibility that units might identify with each other and perceive that what was happening to one might happen to others, yet this possibility was important in the organizational setting. Neither of the biological models differentiated well between types of interdependence between horizontal units, yet the effect in organizations of different types of interdependence was not only opposite, but interactive; the effect of one depended on the effect of the other. Underlying the difficulty of translating the biological model for organizations is the possibility in organizations that horizontal units can band together informally to prevent hierarchically directed change. There is no analog to this process in the work of Simon or Glassman. In short, while the modified propositions still show the influence of Simon and Glassman, they have changed considerably from the original sources.

Finally, a few words are in order with respect to Kaufman's contingency model in comparison to the simpler alternative models of self-corrective improvement and inevitable decline. The retrenchment period began after a period of rapid growth in which all the state universities began to clash with each other and with other state agencies for resources. Given the overall resource limitations of the state something had to be cut back, and the universities were the choice. It was delegated to the state board to cut the universities' budget requests. Given the kind of secrecy and shifting of formulae that the board was engaged in, and the perceived necessity of making cutbacks, there was little possibility of the universities engaging in self-corrective behavior that would eliminate the need for retrenchment. To the extent that the university retrenchments tried to maintain budget levels in this ambiguous situation, they tended to overadapt to short-term trends. The universities slowed down their rates of growth and in many cases were unable to change through internal reallocations. An overall leveling [and] sinking to mediocrity occurred in some places, while in others, universities were frozen in badly adapted positions. To this point, the model of inevitable decline seems to describe what happened.

At this juncture, the contingency model becomes salient. The record suggests that the universities in the study found it very difficult to survey the environment, to evaluate their own units, [and] to devise reallocation schema that would encourage excellence and help achieve the universities' goals. According to the analysis presented here, the troubles encountered by these universities were not simply the working out of an inevitable process of decline. Rather, previous administrations and prior decisions had left the universities with a particular set of vertical, horizontal, and environmental linkages that were less than ideal for adaptation during retrenchment. Unless future research is able to show that the structure of the universities at the beginning of retrenchment was a necessary product of growth, the model of inevitable decline does not describe the case-study universities, even though they did not adapt very well.

References

Aldrich, H.E. "Organizational Boundaries and Interorganizational Conflict." *Human Relations* 24 (1971): 279–87.

Ansoff, I. "Toward a Strategic Theory of the Firm." In *Business Strategy*, edited by I. Ansoff. Baltimore: Penguin, 1970.

Downs, A. *Inside Bureaucracy*. Boston: Little Brown, 1967.

Evans, P.B. "Multiple Hierarchies and Organizational Control." *Administrative Science Quarterly* 20 (1975): 250–59.

Glassman, R. "Persistence and Loose Coupling in Living Systems." *Behavioral Science* 18 (1973): 83–98.

Kaufman, H. *Are Government Organizations Immortal?* Washington, D.C.: Brookings, 1976.

March, J.G., and R. Cyert. *A Behavioral Theory of the Firm*. Englewood Cliffs, N.J.: Prentice-Hall, 1963.

Merton, R. "Bureaucratic Structure and Personality." *Social Forces* 17 (1940): 560–68.

Rubin, I. "Financial Retrenchment and Organizational Change." Doctoral dissertation, University of Chicago, 1977.

Simon, H.A. "The Architecture of Complexity." *Proceedings of the American Philosophical Society* 106 (1962): 467–82.

————. "The Organization of Complex Systems." In *Hierarchy Theory: The Challenge of Complex Systems*, edited by Howard Pattee. New York: George Braziller, 1973.

Thompson, J. *Organizations in Action*. New York: McGraw-Hill, 1967.

Tullock, G. *The Politics of Bureaucracy*. Washington, D.C.: Public Affairs Press, 1965.

Weick, K. "Educational Organizations as Loosely Coupled Systems." *Administrative Science Quarterly* 21 (1976): 1-19.

11

Rules for a Machiavellian Change Agent: Transforming the Entrenched Professional Organization

J. Victor Baldridge

This is the age of the expert. The professional reigns supreme in many areas of life. Doctors heal our bodies. Teachers shape our children's minds. Lawyers handle our disputes. Professors create new generations of professionals. All are part of an intricate network of experts in modern society, and we have allowed them much power. They often control entry into positions of power; they certify who is educated and who is uneducated; they determine life and death on the sickbed; they turn the wheels of justice so that some win and some lose. Probably never before in the history of mankind have experts maintained such a stranglehold on the operation of society. The professionals are in many senses the gatekeepers to success, the wielders of power, and the deciders of right and wrong, truth and beauty. The claim to knowledge has become a claim to control.

The Problem: Entrenched Professionals

The dilemma has always been simple: Who guards the guardians? If modern society has relinquished all this power to professionals, it may have done so to its own peril. That professionals work more to benefit themselves than to serve their clients is a very real possibility. In many ways the professional groups have become an entrenched, privileged oligarchy

Reprinted from *Managing Change in Educational Organizations*, ed. J. Victor Baldridge and Terrence Deal (Berkeley: McCutchan, 1975). Copyright © McCutchan Publishing Corporation.

that enriches itself at the expense of clients, all the while cloaking self-interest under the slogan of "service to mankind." A physician's first loyalty may be to the Hippocratic oath, but at least part of his loyalty is dictated by his pocketbook. A teacher may be dedicated to the education of children, but strong teachers' unions have not always sought educational gains as they struggled for bigger paychecks. A university professor may first seek truth as he goes about the business of shaping the minds of the youth, but there is a nagging suspicion that he is more interested in free time and his own esoteric research than his students. A lawyer may be concerned primarily with justice for all men, but he can become wealthy in the process.

Not only are individual professionals suspect, but they unite in powerful organizations to protect the privileges they have gained. The American Medical Association wages a war against a responsible national system of medicine more to protect the financial interests of physicians than to protect the public against poor health service. Bar associations rarely disbar members, even in the face of flagrant violations of the legal ethic. Teachers' unions, despite proclaimed objectives related to the educational innovation and the welfare of children, seem more interested in money and benefiting the teacher. Associations of professors dedicated to the advancement of science are also very dedicated to the advancement of professors' financial and social status. In short, professional organizations reinforce the self-serving activities of individual professionals.

Finally, professionals control the organizations where they work. Hospitals are more responsive to the desires of doctors than patients; law firms are more sensitive to the needs of lawyers than clients; universities respond more to professors than students; schools are more in tune with teachers than pupils. In every case, the professionals have entrenched themselves behind strong organizational structures that enhance their status, reward them financially, and protect them from outside criticism. This is particularly true for older professionals, the aristocracy that controls power in the guild.

Storm clouds of criticism have, however, been gathering. Professors came under intense fire in the 1960s because of student revolts. Teachers are now feeling public hostility because of strikes that keep children on the street. Even the venerable and virtually untouched medical establishment is sensing tremors beneath it. Many of the moves to call the professions to account have come from outside pressure groups and legislatures. Outside pressure and legal moves can bring change in professional organizations, but equal attention should be given to change from within. Much of the power to change the professions still lies in the institutions or establishments where the work is done—hospitals, universities, schools, law firms, social work agencies. Levers of power are often lodged in the decision-making councils of these professional organizations. How can the levers of power within professional organizations be moved in order to change them? How can younger members of the professions get power to deal with oligarchies already established? How can the clients insist on more responsive organizations? These questions have political answers since they are essentially questions of power and its use within professional organizations. Let us assume the existence of some dedicated change agents who really want to change the professional organizations. How should they go about it? The first move is to be clear about the *goals* of change.

Vision: What Should be Changed

Over the last few years planning committees for professional conferences have expressed deep concern about problems of "organizational change." Over those same few years I have discovered that the professionals who run organizations are not really interested in changing them, and especially not the aristocracies who plan such conferences! My suspicions regarding professional conservatism have been reinforced by the way people at such meetings have responded to one simple question: What would you change about the organization to make it accomplish its purposes better? The results have always been astonishing.

Typical replies from teachers included: make classes smaller, assign more aides to classes, increase salaries for teachers, and handle discipline problems outside the classroom. A group of professors wanted better-quality students, better pay, more participation in decision making, and fewer restrictions on tenure. Social workers would reduce the amount of red tape, eliminate supervision by superiors, encourage more participation of social workers in decision making, and increase pay. A group of doctors suggested that there be fewer Medicare patients, more efficient collection of bills, protection against malpractice suits, and greater participation of doctors in making policy for the hospital. These lists are not only representative; they are also remarkably similar.

Most of the changes listed would benefit the professionals, not the clients. There were four areas of concern. Money was a primary issue, and professionals seem to want more of it. Decision participation was an issue, and professionals express an insatiable urge to control the institution. Decreasing the amount of evaluation is consistent with the desire to ease tenure requirements on the part of professors, cut down on supervision on the part of the social workers and the teachers, and protect against malpractice suits on the part of doctors. Finally, *making working conditions easier,* or lightening the load of the professionals and in general making their lives more pleasant, is another persistent theme.

The "General Motors" assumption seems to pervade: Eisenhower's Defense Secretary, Charles Wilson, once stated that, "What is good for General Motors is good for the country." Professionals often use similar logic: What is good for the professional has to be good for the client. If professionals' lives are pleasanter, the client will somehow benefit. The changes requested by professionals, however, are usually self-serving, small in scale, and have little impact on clients' needs. This judgment of professionals may be overly harsh, but the vision of organizational change desired by core professionals is too often restricted and egocentric.

What should that vision be? Clearly, any serious change agent must propose changes that directly benefit the client. This is the only goal that seems worth fighting for. Making life easier for the professional may make the professional happier, but it is no guarantee that the client will also benefit.

In order to serve the client better, any vision of change must take into account political realities. First, it must allow for the *structure* of the organization as well as the attitudes of the people involved. Altering structures without a corresponding change in attitudes will affect behavior only minimally; attitudes that change without accompanying structural change are quickly squelched by the system. Second, changes must be *politically feasible,* that is, they must be organized and implemented so that political support can be marshaled and professional leadership can be harnessed to help promote the changes.

If client service, structural as well as attitudinal changes, and political feasibility are goals, then what kinds of change efforts make sense? To answer that question requires a look at the *decision structure* of professional organizations. Unless we know how the organization operates, we cannot know how to change it.

Decision Processes in Professional Organizations

Professional organizations have a number of unique characteristics. Fundamentally, they are people-processing organizations, and, in order to handle that complex and delicate task, they usually have large staffs of highly trained professionals. Since people cannot be divided into segmentalized tasks in the same way that physical products can, professionals with a high level of expertise are needed to deal holistically with clients' needs. Thus it is that the first characteristic of professional organizations is that they are highly professionalized, client-serving systems.

Second, people-processing organizations have extremely ambiguous goals, and a list of legitimate activities for a university, a public school, or a social work agency would be extremely long. Because the goals are unclear, almost anything that serves the client is legitimate. On the other hand, the goals can be contested. Anything can be considered legitimate, but anything can also be questioned. Since the organizations themselves are not exactly clear about their functions, they are often racked with conflict over what they should or should not do. This is important for understanding change processes. If an organization does not know its specific objectives, then an individual with an idea and the energy can often bend the organization in his direction. Ambiguity and contest over goals pave the way for the skillful politician.

Finally, professional organizations are extremely vulnerable to outside pressures. Since the clients themselves—students, the physically or mentally ill, welfare recipients, law breakers—are relatively powerless, society generally demands accountability from the organizations. As a consequence, outsiders demand the right to influence internal decisions. The public's success varies considerably: in school systems outside voices are often influential; in hospitals or law firms the organization has generally listened with deaf ears.

What we see, then, is an unusual kind of organization that serves clients, has a highly professionalized staff, has unclear and contested goals, and is subject to much external pressure. It is fluid, complex, and changing. Sociologist James March has called it "organized anarchy." The decision-making process in an organized anarchy has some of the following characteristics:

Decision is by committee. Since expertise, not hierarchical office, is the organizing principle, then committees of experts decide many of the critical issues.

Fluid participation. Many of the decision makers are amateurs, engaged in pursuing their professions, not in making decisions. As a consequence, they wander in and out of the decision process, and power belongs to those who stay long enough to exercise it.

There is an issue carousel. Issues have a way of always coming around again. Decisions are not made forever, because pressure from outside groups, from clients, and from professionals pushes the same issues full circle. Decisions are not made as much as they are pinned down temporarily.

There is a "garbage can" process. The longer it takes to make a decision, the more issues get piled onto the original subject. People, hoping to accomplish several things at one time, burden simple decisions with countless subsidiary issues.

Conflict is common. Professional groups, clients, and outsiders support divergent interests in setting the ambiguous goals of professional organizations. As a consequence, conflict over goals is common as decision makers cope with the pressures from diverse interest groups.

How can we summarize? The image that captures the spirit of the decision process in professional organizations does not resemble a normal bureaucracy; nor does it look like the "community of peers" that is often considered the model of professional management. Three images capture the spirit of the process. First, the structure of the organization does resemble March's organized anarchy. Second, within organized anarchies the decision process looks like a political system because of competing groups and the high degree of conflict. Finally, the fluid, unsettled character of the decision process can be captured by using the term *decision flowing* instead of decision making. Decision making has a final ring to it; decision flowing sounds like a never-ending process that must continue in order to make outcomes really work.

Rules and Tactics for the Change-Oriented Machiavellian

The problem is clear: entrenched professionals are more interested in serving themselves than in serving their clients. The vision is compelling: the organization has to be changed so that the client's needs are in the forefront. The decision process is complex: an organized anarchy with the political decision process is an ugly monster to alter. What tactics will work for the reformer who might want to tackle the dragon? It would probably be important to remember the following rules of strategy.

Rule 1: Concentrate Your Efforts

A basic mistake made by people interested in changing the system is that they frequently squander their efforts by chasing too many rainbows. An effective political change agent, realizing that change is really difficult, concentrates efforts on only the important issues. Remember that most people do not care about most issues. If you care enough to concentrate, you have enormous power to win. The frustration caused by the resistance offered by an immovable system is usually the result of scattered and dispersed efforts. Remember, if "fluid participation" is the rule, then most people wander in and out of the issue. If you stick with one or two critical issues, you are more likely to win.

Rule 2: Know When to Fight

To concentrate is to choose a few issues, and a tactical genius knows which ones to choose. Most of the time it makes sense to support issues when you know you can win. If it is obvious that you will lose, wait. Remember, with the "issue carousel," the situation will probably return, allowing you time to master your resources for the next battle. There are exceptions to the "fight to win" rule. Sometimes it is wise to fight because the moral issue is great, or because it is possible to make future martyrs. We do not always fight to win today; sometimes we fight today so that we can win tomorrow. Most of the time, however, the rule is to choose issues with high payoff. The sophisticated and astute observer can usually tell the difference between a winner and a loser.

Rule 3: Learn the History

Every issue has roots deep in the past. The issue carousel has trotted it past several times before. Consequently, the wise tactician searches for the historical bases of an issue. When was it around before? Who took what position? Who won? Who lost? Knowing the history can reveal what coalitions fight together and what tactics prove useful—information that helps in planning strategy. Under most circumstances the person who is historically naive about the issue is a loser.

Rule 4: Build a Coalition

Never go it alone. Good politicians know that much of their job is not influencing decisions as much as it is building a political base for influencing decisions. This means that a dedicated cadre of change agents must be formed, a committed group that exchanges ideas and reinforces each other's efforts. In addition, a strong change group needs equally strong links to those in viable political coalitions.

Rule 5: Join External Constituencies

As we noted earlier, professional organizations usually have strong external constituents who apply pressure to the decision-making process. The wise strategist uses support from these external constituencies to influence the internal process. In building coalitions it is useful to associate with outside groups as well as inside groups, particularly since major decision makers themselves are often tied to outside groups. Insiders, with their limited view of the outsiders' role, naively overlook the political strategy of cultivating external allies. Welfare recipients and legislators can be strong forces in changing social welfare agencies; parents, alumni, and foundations can help change universities; community groups can be marshaled to transform public schools. The potential power of external constituencies must never be neglected.

Rule 6: Use Committees Effectively

Most major decisions in professional organizations are made by committees of experts who combine their specialized knowledge to solve organizational problems. Therefore, organizational politics often center around committee politics. Having influence on a committee is frequently equal to having influence over the decision.

How can a Machiavellian change agent best use a committee to effect organizational change? First, get on the right committee by simply asking for an appointment from an incumbent official. If the organization has a "committee on committees" it is wise either to know someone on it or to be on it yourself. Such rule-making appointive committees wield power in large professional organizations, and this can be exploited to the best advantage. In addition, after acquiring membership it is critical simply to *be there*. Remember, fluid participation is a characteristic of professional organizations, and the person who sticks with the committee is likely to have enormous impact. In a recent study, for example, Steve Weiner of Stanford University analyzed decision making in a San Francisco school board committee charged with proposing plans for racial integration. He concluded that expertise, social prestige, and personality characteristics were important in the early stages of the committee's work. In later stages, however, those who had the most staying power had the most influence. The first move, then, is to get on the committee, to be there with great regularity, and to stick it out even when others drop off.

The second rule of committee success is to do your homework. Expertise is vital in a professional organization. If you observe the earlier rule of concentrating your efforts, you have more time to accumulate the knowledge that will put you ahead of others. In addition, it is always useful to make part of your homework the job of being secretary or chairman of a group. The chairman can set the agenda and often has the power to call committee meetings, while the secretary controls the memory of the committee. Committees are blessed with short memories since most members do not recall or care what is recorded in the minutes. Controlling the memory of a committee means reiterating the issues that you consider important, a definite advantage for political bargaining. Doing your homework—whether it is gathering knowledge, learning the history, being the chairman, or doing the secretarial chores—puts you in a strategically advantageous position.

Finally, a major tactical procedure in committees is to "fill the garbage can." Since decision issues, like garbage cans, attract various irrelevant material, they can be used to the change agent's advantage. Dump new garbage into the can, and then compromise readily on the unimportant issues. Helping to load the garbage can leaves plenty to bargain over when the deadlines are close and allows you the chance to insist stubbornly about retaining key issues.

Rule 7: Use the Formal System

Professional organizations, like other bureaucracies, have complex formal systems to carry out their activities. Often naive change agents are not aware that they can achieve a desired outcome simply by asking the appropriate official for it. This requires savvy. It requires experience within the organization. It requires knowing where the levers are, and which ones to push.

Inexperienced change agents may fail to realize that most organization officials are eager to please. Success is difficult to judge in most professional organizations because the tasks are too ambiguous to be assessed. As a consequence, most officials depend upon "social validation" for judgments of success. That is, they are successful if people are pleased and think they have done a good job. The ambiguity of the task, the lack of hard evaluation criteria, and the psychological need of most administrators for approval gives tremendous advantage to partisans who want to get something done. Do not forget a basic tactic: ask for what you want and you will be surprised how many times you get it.

Rule 8: Follow Through to Push the Decision Flow

We have said that the concept of "decision making" is a delusion. Decisions are not really made; instead, they come unstruck, are reversed, get unmade during the execution, or lose their impact as powerful political groups fight them. In real life, decisions go round and round in circles, and the best one can hope for in the political battle is a temporary win.

As a consequence, the aware politician knows that he must follow important decisions even after they have supposedly been made. What do most people do after the committee has reached its decision? They evaporate. The person who traces the decision flow on through to execution, and who fights when issues are distorted, is the person who really has the power. The truly dedicated partisan who wants to see changes really work will be a tenacious watchdog, monitoring the steps of the decision, staying on the backs of administrators, and calling public attention to administrative lapses.

There are a few tricks to the trade of following through on decisions.
First, be sure to set deadlines in the process of making the decisions. Delay is
the enemy of change; deadlines are flags that help call attention to stalling.
Second, give the idea a sheltered start. If placed back into the regular
routine of the organization, a new change will usually be smothered by the
powerful old routines. As a consequence, the shrewd change planner builds
a shelter around the change in its infancy. This often means giving the
program a home under the wing of a strong, hospitable executive of the
organization. Only later, after the new idea has established roots, should it
be placed into the regular structure of the organization.

Several follow-through techniques involve people. It is always useful to
place your allies in the vanguard of the people responsible for executing the
decision. If people embodying your ideas are running the show, then the
change is more likely to succeed. In addition, the reward system is very
important. Do you want things to change? Then reward people whose
behavior helps promote the change. Rewards can be straightforward in the
form of money, or they can take the equally valuable form of prestige,
status, and public acclaim.

A Glance Backward When the Change is Completed

Let us assume the changes have really been made. The last piece of advice
is the hardest to swallow: be skeptical about your own changes. Few good
changes have eternal lives. A deep ego-investment can be made in a project
that does not work. Don Campbell, a psychologist, once commented that
the world would be better off if people could be dedicated to solving
problems rather than to promoting particular projects or changes. In this
sense, following through means evaluating, judging, and deciding
whether the performance lives up to the expectation. If it does not, you
must start all over. The problem is still there, but the solution did not quite
make it. Evaluating your own idea as objectively as possible and listening
carefully to the evaluations of others are valuable and necessary skills for
true change agents.

Any organization's vitality and creativity depend heavily on the constant
influx of new ideas. Even the bright, new change that you worked so hard to
establish will, in time, be dull and old. The last step, then, is the most
ruthless of all: kill your own project when it has outlived its usefulness.
This is where most change agents fall down. After building their ego-
investments they fight like stuffy bureaucrats to hang on to an idea long
since grown old. The cycle must continue, and the change agent must once
more struggle to infuse creativity and excitement into the professional
organization.

In modern technological societies the professions and their elite organizations are the centers of much social power. Unfortunately, the professionals have learned too well to serve themselves, not their clients. The vision, then, is to change the professional organizations so that they really focus on client needs. Although it seems nearly impossible to make changes in those organizations, it is not out of the question. What is needed for successful organizational revolution?

First, it is important to understand the nature of the decision system. Most professional organizations act like "organized anarchies" with high environmental input, unclear technologies, high professionalism, and fluid participation. This is a messy, politicized kind of decision structure, best characterized as a miniature political network. Second, if the decision structure is political, then a Machiavellian change agent must learn a few basic tactics: organize, work through committees, do your homework, and follow through the change process to the end.

The task is not easy, and failure may be more common than success. Often these tactics will not work; nor may any others. Nevertheless, if professional organizations are to be called back to their prime goal— serving clients—then the effort must be made. Most important, the vision must guide the tactics, not the other way round.

12

The Sociology of Institutions, or
Who Sank the Yellow Submarine?

Eleven Ways to Avoid Major Mistakes in Taking Over a University Campus and Making Great Changes

Warren Bennis

One cannot expect to know what is going to happen. One can only consider himself fortunate if he can discover what has happened.—Pierre du Pont

On December 19, 1966, I received a phone call from an assistant to [ex-] President Martin Meyerson at the State University of New York at Buffalo. The assistant began the conversation with almost sinful empathy: "I bet you don't know what's going on here at Buffalo, do you?" I allowed that I did not, and he proceeded to describe an academic New Jerusalem of unlimited money, a new $650-million campus, bold organizational ideas, a visionary president, a supportive chancellor and governor, the number of new faculty and administrators to be recruited, the romance of taking a mediocre upstate college and creating—well—the Berkeley of the East. Would I consider taking part in the effort? I was smitten by the verve, the *chutzpah*—and by the thought of having a hand in the transformation. S.U.N.Y. at Buffalo had been a relatively unnoticed local college founded by the thirteenth U.S. President, Millard Fillmore, "His Accidency." It had gained an uneven distinction between 1930 and 1962, the year it became part of the University of New York.

New York wanted to create a multiversity and in 1966 had lured Meyerson from Berkeley (where he was the acting chancellor) to make the dream materialize.

Reprinted, by permission, from *Psychology Today* 6:6 (November 1972): 112–120. Copyright Ziff-Davis Publishing Company.

Meyerson arrived with a monumental plan to redesign Buffalo's conventional academic structure. Within two months, the faculty senate had ratified the plan, which provided as follows:

1. The ninety existing departments would be restructured into seven new faculties, each with a provost as the chief academic and administrative officer. Each faculty would consist of the basic disciplines within the newly defined area, plus the relevant professional schools. (Meyerson wanted me to head the social science disciplines that included anthropology, psychology, and—to the chagrin of the Arts and Letters Provost—philosophy and history. My domain also would include the schools of management and social welfare.) The provosts would have ample resources and administrative leeway to create interdisciplinary programs and launch new education ventures.

2. The university would build thirty small colleges on a new campus. Each would house only four hundred students with up to six hundred day students as affiliates. Faculty and students would live and work together in the intimate atmosphere of these intellectual neighborhoods. Meyerson hoped the small college would offset the apathy and anomie that characterize enormous campuses. In addition, they would break the stranglehold that traditional departments traditionally leave on the university. Undergraduates would not get a watered-down version of what professors taught their graduate students; they would learn directly from their teachers in a communal setting.

3. Action-research centers and councils on international studies, urban studies, and higher educational studies would unite scholars and students from the entire university (and from the outside) for work on vital issues.

Esteem. Meyerson's overall concept impressed me. Several aspects of the plan were especially attractive: the decentralization of authority, the potential of the program (if you did not fit in with a department, you could always connect with a college, center, or council), and Meyerson's clear intent to raise the self-esteem of the university, and the self-esteem of the faculty and students, and the self-esteem of the Buffalo community. Meyerson assured me that, with the new campus, there would be enough money to build quality on top of the university's inevitable deadwood.

I was sold on the man and his conceptual vision. The timing seemed perfect, the new organizational design would go into effect on the same day my term of office was to begin. I arrived at Buffalo in the fall of 1967 and during 1967-68 I recruited nine new chairmen and two deans for the faculty, and changed about 90 percent of the leadership structure in the social sciences area. The faculty gained forty-five new full-time teachers. I spent almost three-fourths of my first year in recruiting.

Buffalo raided Harvard, Yale, and Princeton. Each new appointment increased enthusiasm, generated new ideas, and escalated the Meyerson optimism. The tiny, crowded campus barely contained the excitement. Intellectual communities formed and flourished.

Steam. The change was pervasive. Almost 75 percent of the present Buffalo faculty got their appointments under Meyerson.

The newcomers were eager recruits—committed to innovation and risk taking. The student body also was changing. By 1968, eight in ten of the entering freshmen were from the top 10 percent of their high school graduating classes, compared to only one in ten a decade before. Buffalo was regarded as one of the State University's radical campuses according to *Esquire* magazine (along with Stony Brook on Long Island). Meyerson's Berkeley-of-the-East approach may have had an appeal that he had not fully calculated. For one year, Buffalo was an academic Camelot. The provosts met around the president's conference table to work miracles. Occasionally I got signals that not everyone on campus took us quite as seriously as we took ourselves. One morning I found a Batman cape on my coatrack. The anonymous critic had a point: the atmosphere was a bit heavy with omnipotent fantasy.

Although construction had not started for the living quarters on the new campus, the six human-size colleges got underway at once. Almost immediately they provoked controversy. Rumors began to circulate that course cards for College A—the unit devoted to independent study and self-evaluation—were being sold, snatched up by students who did little or nothing and rewarded themselves with A's at the end of the semester. "Why do you think they call it 'College A'?" one cynical student asked. There were tales of credit for trips to Europe and the building of bird cages.

The master of College A regarded any impugning of its grading system as an antirevolutionary tactic. No one in the Meyerson administration, including myself, wanted to take a harsh public stand against this nonsense, particularly after College A and its master became the target of vicious community attack.

Status. There were other rumblings in paradise. The centers were not doing well. We learned that it was easier to break down barriers than to build bridges. For example, the Center for Higher Education did not generate new programs or attract faculty and students as planned. The Center for International Studies began to publish a newsletter—the only substantial sign of its new status. The Center for Urban Studies undertook a series of much-needed but thoroughly conventional projects in Buffalo's inner city.

In one form or another all the faculties had problems. Many departments raised questions about the new faculty structure. I felt that the many individual accomplishments, the promising new programs, [and] the appointment of a particularly good teacher or administrator did not add up to a significantly changed university. We were not consolidating our gains, and I feared that they might somehow slip away. These feelings were eventually confirmed. Camelot lasted barely a thousand days.

Setting. I took part in many of the crucial decisions that affected the progress of the Meyerson plan. And I now see, with all the unsettling clarity of hindsight, that we undermined many of our own best aspirations for the University. If I were asked today how to bring about change in a university setting, I would offer the following guidelines:

1. Recruit with scrupulous honesty. Most of the faculty who came to Buffalo shared the academic vision of its new president, Martin Meyerson.

Meyerson's gift as a recruiter was his ability to transmogrify all of the highly visible and terribly real drawbacks to Buffalo and make them reappear in the guise of exhilarating challenges. Those he attracted recruited others.

Sweetener. My personal recruiting at Buffalo depended on a falsely bright picture of the situation. It was not that I lied. But, consciously or not, I sweetened the package even when I was trying to be balanced and fair. Recruiting is a courtship ritual. The suitor displays his assets; the recruit, flattered by the attention and the promises, does not examine the assets closely. We were naive. The recruiting pitch at Buffalo depended on the future. We made little of the past and tended to deemphasize the present. Buffalo was the university of the future—of course, it would take time to catch up.

New arrivals had barely enrolled their kids in local schools before reality intruded. A labor union dispute delayed construction of the promised new facilities. Inflation nibbled away the buying power of the allocated construction funds at a rate of one and a half percent a month. It was easy to put up with the inconvenience of overcrowding when one was sure that the condition was temporary. But the dispute dragged on for months, and there was no room on the old campus. The situation might have been challenging if we had not led the new faculty to expect something magical. We had urged them to reveal their most creative, most imaginative educational thinking, then had assured them that their plans would receive generous support. In reality, money to staff new programs was difficult to come by. After one year, the state legislature began to pare the budget. Many new faculty members felt they had been conned. As recruiters, we had not pointed out our ultimate inability to control the legislatively determined budget. We had promised a new university when our funds could provide only an architect's model.

Shock. Inadvertently, we had cooked up the classic recipe for revolution as suggested by Aaron Wildavsky: "Promise a lot; deliver a little. Teach people to believe that they will be much better off, but let there be no dramatic improvement. Try a variety of small programs but marginal in impact and severely underfinanced. Avoid any attempted solution remotely comparable in size to the dimensions of the problem you are trying to solve.... "

The intensity of the disaffection felt by some of those I had brought to the university came to me as a shock. We had raised expectations as high as any in modern educational history. When our program met only a part of these expectations, the disillusionment that followed was predictable and widespread. The disparity between vision and reality became intolerable. No one had said a word during the seductive recruiting days about triplicate forms, resentful colleagues, and unheeded requests for help from administrative headquarters.

Support. Those who rose above the mundane annoyances provoked by university bureaucracy felt cheated in other ways. Recruits had joined our academic revolution because they shared our goal and wanted to participate. To keep such a cadre committed, an administration must keep them involved. But the warmth of our man-to-man recruiting interviews was not evident in later meetings with administrators. In fact, such meetings became fairly infrequent. The continuing evidence of personal support that might have overcome the unavoidable lack of concrete support was not forthcoming.

2. Guard against the crazies. Innovation is seductive. It attracts interesting people. It also attracts people who will take your ideas and distort them into something monstrous. *You* will then be identified with the monster and will have to devote precious energy to combating it. A change-oriented administrator should be damned sure about the persons he recruits, the persons who will be identified as his men or women.

A few of the persons who got administrative posts under the new administration were committed to change, but they were so irresponsible or antagonistic that they alienated more persons than they converted.

Sense. It is difficult to distinguish between agents of responsible change and those who rend all they touch. The most successful innovators often are marginal to the institution, almost in a geographical sense. They have contacts in other institutions, other areas. Their credentials are unorthodox. They are often terrible company men with little or no institutional loyalty. Change-oriented administrators must be able to distinguish the innovators, however eccentric they may be, from the crazies. An academic community can tolerate a high degree of eccentricity. But it will brutally reject an individual it suspects of masking mediocrity with a flashy commitment to innovation.

3. Build support among like-minded people, whether or not you recruited them. Change-oriented administrators are particularly prone to act as though the organization came into being the day they arrived. This is an illusion, an omnipotent fantasy. There are no clean slates in established organizations. A new president cannot play Noah and build the world anew with two hand-picked delegates from each academic discipline. Rhetoric about new starts is frightening to those who suspect that the new beginning is the end of their own careers. There can be no change without history, without continuity.

Stayers. What I think most of us in institutions really want—and what status, money, and power serve as currency for—is acceptance, affection, and esteem. Institutions are more amenable to change when they preserve the esteem of all members. Given economic sufficiency, persons stay in organizations and feel satisfied in them because they are respected and feel competent. They are much freer to identify with the adaptive process and much better equipped to tolerate the high level of ambiguity that accompanies change when these needs are heeded. Unfortunately, we did not attend to these needs at Buffalo. The academic code, not the administrative one, determines the appropriate behavior in the university. The president is a colleague, and he is expected to acknowledge his intellectual equals whatever their relative position on the administrative chart. Many old-guard professors took the administration's neglect as a personal snub. They were not asked for advice; they were not invited to social affairs. They suspected that we acted coolly toward them because we considered them to be second-rate academics who lacked intellectual chic and who could not cut it in Cambridge or New York. Ironically, some of the old-guard academic administrators who kept their positions were notoriously second rate. Meyerson extended the appointments of several such, perhaps hoping to avoid the appearance of a purge. Among the incumbents were a couple whose educational philosophy had rigidified sometime in the early 1950s. Instead of appeasing the old guard, these appointments added insult.

The old guard suspected that the new administration viewed them as an undifferentiated mass. They wondered why we kept the second-raters and overlooked a pool of potentially fine veteran candidates.

We succeeded in infusing new blood into Buffalo, but we failed to recirculate the old blood. We lost an opportunity to build loyalty among respected members of the veteran faculty. If veteran faculty members had been made to feel that they, too, had a future in the transformed university, they might have embraced the academic-reorganization plan with some enthusiasm. Instead the veteran faculty members were hurt, indignant, and—finally—angry.

4. Plan for change from a solid conceptual base—have a clear-cut understanding of how to change as well as what to change. Buffalo had a plan for change, but we lacked a clear concept of how change should proceed. A statement of goals is not a program.

The Buffalo reorganization lacked the coherence and forcefulness that would have guaranteed its success. The fault may have been that it was too abstract. Or perhaps it was too much a pastiche. A great many influences were evident: the late Paul Goodman and the community of colleges; the colleges and sense of academic tradition of Oxbridge; the unorthodoxy and informality of Black Mountain; the blurring of vocational-professional lives practiced at Antioch and Bennington; the collegiality of Santa Cruz; the college-master system of Yale. Each of these elements was both desirable and educationally fashionable, but the mix never jelled. No alchemy transformed the disparate parts into a living organism.

Students. We had no coherent mechanisms for change. Instead we relied on several partially realized administrative models. The burden of change fell upon the faculty senate, which emphasized the small-group model. Change depended on three things: (1) participation by the persons involved, (2) trust in the persons who advocate the change, and (3) clarity about the change itself. None of these conditions was fully present at Buffalo, and, as a result, the change was imperfectly realized.

Radical students utilized a revolutionary model. The students saw an opportunity for radical educational change in the Romantic tradition—the result was the College A controversy. The administration relied heavily on the model of successive limited comparisons, popularly known as muddling through. This is the model of most organizational decision making. It is a noncomprehensive, nontheoretical approach. Most administrators are forced to muddle through because the decisions they are called upon to make are simply too complex to treat comprehensively—even by committees. As a result, we neglected possible outcomes, overlooked alternative solutions, and could not predict the ultimate impact of the resulting policy on values.

Sensitivity. Ultimately the reorganization failed to concentrate its energies on the model that would have satisfied the ambitions of all parts of the university: an incremental reform model. Revolution inevitably produces reaction. All power to the French people one day, and to Thermidor the next. If change is to be permanent, it must be gradual. The incremental reform model depends on a rotating nucleus of persons who continuously read the data provided by the organization and the society around it for clues that it is time to adapt. These persons are not faddists, but they are hypersensitive to an idea whose hour has come. In a university such persons know when an idea is antithetical to the values of an academic institution and when it extends the definition of a university and makes it more viable. One cannot structure these critical nuclei, but an organization cannot guarantee continuous self-renewal without them. At Buffalo a few departments and programs developed these nuclei. Most did not.

5. Do not settle for rhetorical change. We accomplished the change at Buffalo by fiat. The faculty senate announced that the president's plan had been ratified. (This was a good beginning, but only that. Ratification occurred only two months after Meyerson arrived and almost one year before the plan was implemented. The senate was not exactly representative and the plans were barely understood. It was basically a paper plan with virtually no commitment except to a vague and poetic vision.) Significant change does not take place that way. An organization has two structures: one on paper and another one, deep, that is a complex set of intramural relationships. A good administrator creates a good fit between the two. We allowed ourselves to be swept along by our rhetoric and neglected the much more demanding business of building new constituencies and maintaining established ones.

6. Do not allow those who are opposed to change to appropriate such basic issues as academic standards. I became Meyerson's academic vice-president in August of 1968. Members of the old guard soon began to accuse me of being soft on standards. I had refused to disavow some of the more fluent abuses of self-evaluation in the new colleges, and I had failed publicly to chastise faculty who subverted traditional academic practices as part of the radical revolution (although I did so unofficially).

Silence. The problem of academic standards soon became a political issue. Privately we avowed our commitment to standards; publicly we were silent. The approach was notably unsuccessful. We did not want to undermine the fledgling colleges or violate the rights of radical faculty members. After "fascist," "McCarthyite" is the dirtiest word you can use on a liberal campus, and none of us was eager to hear it. We allowed the least change-oriented faculty members to make the issue of standards their own. They persuaded a great majority of moderate faculty members that administration was committed to change-for-change's sake, whatever the price in academic excellence. We made a mistake that no successful revolutionary ever makes: we did not make sure that respectable people were unafraid of what was about to happen.

7. Know the territory. A peculiar balance exists between the city of Buffalo and its one major university. Buffalo is not a university town like Princeton or Ann Arbor. The university is not powerful enough to impose its style and values on the city. Philadelphia and Los Angeles have several powerful universities that divide the city's attention and diffuse its rancor. Buffalo has a single target for its noisy anti-intellectuals. Two years ago some powerful forces in the town tried to close the university. I do not know of another campus in the country that has had to function with such constant unsympathetic pressure from the surrounding community. (The period I had in mind was the year of Kent State. From all I have heard about Meyerson's successor, he has worked hard at reviving a more sympathetic and supportive reaction to the campus.)

Meyerson barely had arrived in Buffalo whan a group called "Mothers Against Meyerson" (MAM) began to petition for his removal. Their argument was that he was a Jew (a charge erroneously made against Meyerson's predecessor by an earlier group, "Mothers Against Furnas") and that the campus harbored such dangerous criminal types as critic Leslie Fiedler.

Buffalo blamed the disruptions of 1970 on the "permissiveness" of the new administration. I got mail recommending that Curtis LeMay succeed Meyerson as university president. The local ex-marine who nominated LeMay believed that only the general's exotic blend of authoritarianism and right-wing values could undo the harm that we had perpetrated.

We never mastered the politics of local chauvinism. At the same time that the national press was romancing the university, one of the two local dailies was libeling her unmercifully. We devoted too little energy and imagination to public relations.

8. Appreciate environmental factors. Like any other human activity, change proceeds more smoothly in optimal environmental conditions. Buffalo's chief environmental problem was not its miserable weather. (Buffalo has two seasons—winter and the 4th of July. Residents recognize summer as three weeks of bad ice skating.) The problem at Buffalo was (and still is) overcrowding. The faculty we recruited expected to move their books into futuristic offices like those promised by the architect's model of the new campus. Instead, they moved in on top of the faculty already there. The university assembled some prefab annexes for the overflow. Barbara Solomon, writing on the paranoia at Buffalo, noted that we pursued the life of the mind in quarters so ugly as to seem calculated. (Her article, "Life in the Yellow Submarine," appeared in a 1968 issue of *Harper's*. It pictures S.U.N.Y.-Buffalo at the crest of the Meyerson dream, zany, careening, spectacularly lush, as played by the Marx Brothers in a World War II movie set of sallow, wooden barracks.)

The new university campus barely had begun to rise by the time we reached the originally proposed completion date of 1972. The university had to lease an interim campus near the new campus site. Eleven academic departments moved out to this temporary facility in the spring of 1971. The leased buildings had been designed for commercial and light industry use. The fifteen-minute bus trip is a drag for students and the isolation of the interim campus is contrary to the whole spirit of the Meyerson plan.

We neglected to protect new programs from external forces. College A began an experimental program in community action that was housed off-campus because of space priorities. College A is located directly across from a parochial grammar school and a diocesan center for retarded children. Every time a Scarsdale Maoist wrote "fuck" on the wall or a braless coed player her guitar in the storefront window, the residents of the neighborhood understandably reacted. Students of College A were determined to interact with their neighbors; mothers of the schoolchildren were equally determined not to interact. They picketed. The whole business snowballed, increasing the community's normally high level of outrage against the university.

9. Avoid future shock. Buffalo aspired to be the university of the year 2000. The future limited the campus just as the past limits the neurotic. The future insinuated itself into every attempt to deal with current issues and distorted our perception of the present. The unfinished new campus became an albatross, reminding everyone of the limited progress that was being made toward limitless goals. We put so much stock in the vision of future greatness that our disillusionment was inevitable. The problem with planning for the future is that there are no objective criteria against which to measure alternative solutions. There is not yet a contemporary reality against which to test. As a result the planner generates future shock along with valid ideas, and there is no surefire way to separate the two.

10. Allow time to consolidate gains. The average tenure of an American university president is now 4.4 years and decreasing. It is impossible to transform a university in so short a time. Only a year after Meyerson assumed the Buffalo presidency, rumors began to circulate that he was leaving. Supporters of the new administration feared abandonment. Social critic David Bazelon commented to me, "In every other university I've been to, the faculty hated the administration. Here they worry about desertion." The changes proposed by Meyerson depended on continued presidential support for their success. The campus had, in effect, undergone major surgery and did not have sufficient time to heal before a series of altogether different demands, including a semester of unrest, a new president, and a major recession, were made on it.

When Meyerson finally did resign in late January 1970, it was as though someone had prematurely pulled out the stitches.

The last guideline I offer to the would-be university reformer is so basic that it might well come first:

11. Remember that change is most successful when those who are affected are involved in the planning. This is a platitude of planning theory, and it is as true as it is trite. Nothing makes persons as resistant to new ideas or approaches as the feeling that change is being imposed upon them. The members of a university are unusually sensitive to individual prerogatives and to the administration's utter dependence on their support. Buffalo's academic plan was not generated popularly. Students and faculty did not contribute to its formulation. People resist change, even of a kind they basically agree with, if they are not significantly involved in the planning. A clumsier, slower, but more egalitarian approach to changing the university would have resulted in more permanent reform.

Surprise. The problems surrounding innovation and change in an entrenched bureaucracy are not peculiar to universities. Every modern bureaucracy—university, government, or corporation—is essentially alike and responds similarly to challenge and to crisis, with much the same explicit or implicit codes, punctilios and mystiques.

Bureaucracy is the inevitable—and therefore necessary—form for governing large and complex organizations. Essentially we must find bureaucratic means to stimulate the pursuit of truth—that is, the true nature of the organization's problems—in a spirit of free inquiry, and under democratic methods. This calls for those virtues our universities and colleges have proved so capable of inspiring in others: an examined life, a spirit of inquiry and genuine experimentation, a life based on discovering new realities, of taking risks, suffering occasional defeats, and not fearing the surprise of the future.

The model for truly innovative and creative organizations in an era of enormous change becomes nothing less than the scientific spirit. The model for science becomes the model for all.

Assault. Now, four years after the dream was born, the campus mood is dismal. Many of the visionaries are gone—those left must live with the wreckage. The spirit of change has been stamped out.

Meyerson has officially disappeared. The state considers his administration to have been the reign of an educational antipope. There is rarely mention of him or his works.

Last year the American Council on Education released its current evaluation of the nation's graduate programs. Buffalo had improved dramatically in the ACE ratings. The university proudly held a news conference at which campus officials announced that the upgrading of graduate education at Buffalo took place under the late-President Furnas.

What saddens me is a suspicion that this gross assault would have been successful if we had been more effective. Meyerson wanted to transform the university, but the current administration resembles that of Meyerson's predecessor, Clifford Furnas. By all appearances, our efforts changed nothing.

Epilogue

I wrote the above several months after I resigned from Buffalo—an outsider, though still living in Buffalo, supported by a grant from the Twentieth Century Fund. Outsiders and expatriates adopt a more critical perspective, I suppose, than those who remain.

Perhaps this article is not "objective" truth but "exiled" truth, not especially appropriate for those presently at Buffalo. Still and all, I would hope that some external validation of their former plight will help sustain their vitality.

At the same time, I hope that this critique of the Buffalo attempts at change will provide a template of action—for myself and my new Cincinnati administration, for faculty and students as well—that will conform more closely to a humane and democratic effort at university reform. We begin with more total community support and involvement than is enjoyed by any other urban university.

13

The Politics of Curriculum Change and Stability

William Lowe Boyd

The business of trying to change or reform the public schools of America has become just that: from a hobby for "do-gooders" and a vocation for muckraking journalists, the pursuit of educational innovation and reform has emerged as a big business involving a broad array of public and private foundations and R&D organizations. Yet, after more than two decades of systematic efforts at reform—from the new curriculum materials of the 1960s to more recent federally sponsored innovation projects—recent research (for example, Goodlad et al. 1979; Berman and McLaughlin 1976) has revealed that, contrary to numerous claims, little really has changed. We thus are left with the problem of understanding the paradox of how there could be so little change when there seemed to be so much evidence of momentous change.

The most succinct explanation is that . . . all too often innovative policies which were *enacted* were at best only partially *implemented*. As we shall see, this fact has profound implications for curriculum policymaking, innovation strategies, and the "business" of reform. But the vitally important distinction between policymaking and policy implementation

This is a revised and much abridged version of a paper commissioned by the Curriculim Development Task Force of the National Institute of Education, U.S. Department of Health, Education, and Welfare. The original paper appears in the *Review of Educational Research* 42:4 (Fall 1978) and has been reprinted in Gary Sykes and John Schaffarzick, eds., *Value Conflicts and Curriculum Issues: Lessons from Research and Experience.* Berkeley: McCutchan, 1979.

does not tell the whole story. Inherent in the educational policymaking process itself are contradictory pressures which restrain educational change. Indeed, policymakers are confronted with the dilemma of the schools being asked to simultaneously preserve and change society. And whether they attempt to preserve or reshape society, curriculum policymakers are inescapably involved in a political act, for their positions will have some bearing upon "who gets what, when, and how" now and in the future.[1]

Currently, the accelerated pace of social change has exacerbated the tension between pressures for societal maintenance and for societal change, and, with the upsurge of ethnic and minority consciousness and the pursuit of equality, curriculum policymaking has been dramatically politicized. In this context, we clearly need a better understanding of the character of curriculum policymaking and the circumstances under which the curriculum changes or remains constant.

Social Change and Incremental and Nonincremental Curriculum Policymaking

If there is one proposition about curriculum politics that is clear, it is that the school curriculum becomes an issue in communities and societies that are undergoing significant change (Iannaccone 1967; Coleman 1965). Such change calls into question the adequacy or appropriateness of existing curricula. For example, as Kirst and Walker (1971) note, national political tensions, generally arising from one or another kind of change, inevitably seem to make themselves felt in curriculum policy debates. Yet, if the most notable and spectacular curriculum politics are associated with crisis and the problems of managing change, Kirst and Walker suggest that curriculum policymaking usually proceeds quietly and *incrementally*, with value conflicts "resolved through low profile politics." In other words, curriculum policymaking, rather than being characterized by dramatic crisis policymaking or by the often prescribed but seldom realized model of *rational* decision making, generally is characterized by the modest and mundane strategy of *disjointed incrementalism*, such as acceptance of the broad outlines of the existing situation with only marginal changes contemplated and [with] serial analysis and piecemeal alterations rather than a single comprehensive attack on the policy problem (Braybrooke and Lindblom 1963).

---

[1] The quotation is Lasswell's (1936) succinct statement of the focus of political science.

However, this aspect of Kirst and Walker's (1971) analysis becomes confusing when they later say that:

Crises occur at such short intervals in the history of American education— immigration, the great Red scare, war, depression, war again, Sputnik, racial violence, war again—*that crisis policymaking is normal and normal policymaking exceptional* [p. 498, emphasis added].

This observation is striking and insightful, but where does it leave us in terms of understanding the curriculum policymaking process?

The conventional, informed view of educational policymaking— curricular or otherwise—is that it is characterized by incrementalism, perhaps even more so than policymaking in most other organizations and institutions (Elboim-Dror 1970). The strong tendency toward incremental-ism in educational policymaking can be seen to have a number of sources. Many analysts have called attention to the fact that education's dependence upon, and vulnerability to, its societal environment causes the public schools to have to serve multiple and sometimes conflicting goals. New goals are acquired even while the established goals are retained. Expectations for the role of the schools seem to expand continuously. The school is asked to be an engine for progress and reform, but at the same time is always expected to maintain society. Thus, by a process of accretion, goals proliferate and increasingly compete with one another for scarce resources. The result is an ever more cumbersome context and structure for decision making, making incremental policymaking increasingly likely.

Yet, *nonincremental* or innovative curriculum policies nevertheless emerge with surprising frequency. Kirst and Walker imply that innovative policies have emerged frequently because they have been elicited by the surprisingly frequent crises our nation has experienced. In turn, this suggests that the *key* curriculum politics we need to understand are those surrounding crisis policymaking, for the curriculum policy decisions made then presumably will be only incrementally modified until the next crisis.

However, this is a troublesome conclusion. As Elboim-Dror (1970) notes, the incrementalism of educational policymaking

might be satisfactory for an organization that only tries to adjust itself to a stable and slowly changing environment, but it does not suit a rapidly changing and demanding environment pressing for innovation and change from within. If education is to meet successfully its many demanding tasks and missions, it will have to find new and more dynamic decision strategies [p. 247].

And so it has: *education in fact has found such a strategy,* and this strategy, which has been called the "professionalization of reform," has contributed substantially to the increased complexity and politicization of curriculum policymaking. But, at the same time that the "professionalization of reform" fosters nonincremental policymaking, a number of significant restraints upon policy innovation impede and transform innovative policy initiatives. Thus, to understand contemporary curriculum politics one must look beyond crisis policymaking, for a focus upon it alone is incomplete and misleading.

The Professionalization of Reform

Significantly, the nationally sponsored curriculum reform movement was underway *before* the Sputnik crisis lent a sense of urgency to the venture. Indeed, it is characteristic of the evolving policymaking process that many innovative policies have emerged under *noncrisis* conditions. Contrary to the theory of incrementalism, Moynihan (1973) suggests that some innovative policies arise through the recognition that existing policies are failing, that "marginal changes, 'tireless tinkering,' will no longer do." This kind of recognition may also be tied, Moynihan proposes, to the "institutionalization" in and about the federal government of the use of social scientists as professional policy advisors. However, given the extreme modesty of the analytical and predictive capabilities of contemporary social scientists, in the face of the awesome complexities of social policy problems, the most intriguing explanation Moynihan (1969, pp. 21–37) offers for the increasing emergence of innovative policies in noncrisis situations is what he calls "the professionalization of reform."

Moynihan (1969) argues that whereas in the past efforts to reform societal institutions generally arose due to discontent and pressures which had built up in the public external to the institutions, by mid century the process of reform had acquired a degree of institutionalization and expertise such that it began to take on the characteristics of an enterprise with "a self-starting capacity of its own." "Increasingly, efforts to change the American social system for the better arose from initiatives undertaken by persons whose profession was to do just that" (Moynihan 1969, p. 23). Moynihan (1969) says that this development first became evident when President Kennedy's election

brought to Washington as office-holders, or consultants, or just friends, a striking echelon of persons whose profession might justifiably be described as knowing what ails societies and whose art is to get treatment underway before the patient is especially aware of anything noteworthy taking place [p. 23].

Thus, with the professionalization of reform came a cadre of full-time social critics and advocates for change, devoted to *raising* or *creating issues* and sometimes, according to Moynihan, succeeding in creating *crises* as well, as in the case of the urban unrest brought on (aggravated?) by the strategy of maximum feasible participation of the poor in federally sponsored reform programs. While a more complete, and charitable, interpretation of the professionalization of reform would acknowledge that professionals positioned in national organizations and agencies have an important responsibility to attend to, and anticipate, national needs—and may have accomplished much good (as well as some ill) in so doing—it nevertheless is hard to deny that the generally liberal-activist ideology of these professionals, in combination with their self-interest in career advancement and the maintenance and enhancement needs of their organizations, must influence their policy recommendations. Indeed, as Moynihan (1973) notes, speaking of the various councils of advisors serving the President, they "tend to measure their success by the number of things they get started" (p. 546).

The "professionalization of reform" helps us to understand the growth and nature of the national network concerned with the business of curriculum reform as well as its penchant for policy innovations, many of which become controversial. Thus, just as Moynihan (1969) proposes that "the war on poverty was not declared at the behest of the poor; it was declared in their interest by persons confident of their own judgment in such matters" (p. 25), so too, Hottois and Milner (1975) find evidence that the initiative for introducing sex education in most instances came from educators, *contrary* to educators' claims that such instruction was being added to the curriculum in response to public demands. In turn, the origin of the whole national movement came from a professional sex education "establishment," which was convinced that such instruction was needed, and which actively propagated the idea and showed local educators how to "finesse" the public relations problems involved in introducing it. For example, just as Moynihan spoke of "getting the treatment underway before the patient is especially aware," Hottois and Milner (1975) note that:

Some proponents argued that since sex education occurred in classrooms in most schools prior to the existence of any formal program, it was educationally sound, completely honest, and politically astute to claim that the programs were not really new. Thus, the proper strategy was to emphasize that sex education was really being expanded and improved rather than initiated [p. 40].

While the introduction of sex education frequently may have constituted a particularly blatant example of the professionalization of curriculum reform, there are other interesting and provocative examples worth noting. For instance, it is unlikely that public school educators often began teaching the scientific theory of evolution due to popular demand for it. In fact, just the opposite frequently has been the case, with the only visible public opinion on the matter running strongly *against* the teaching of the theory, due to fundamental religious objections to it. Of course, as Nelkin (1976) notes, most scientists scarcely would think that the question of whether to teach evolution is a matter to be decided on religious or democratic grounds. From their point of view, evolution is a scientifically validated theory and its inclusion in biology courses is both imperative and a matter only to be decided on the basis of scientific evidence and expertise. Just as the professionals generally have taken the lead in adding evolution to the curriculum, it also is likely that they usually have taken the initiative in introducing the new social studies, including the controversial *Man: A Course of Study* (MACOS) (Nelkin, 1976).

In short, the professionalization of reform has introduced an extraordinary, dynamic, and controversial new force into the social and educational policymaking process. Convinced of their expertise and prerogatives, armed with "solutions looking for problems," supported by federal and foundation funding, and stimulated by the discovery, as a result of the civil rights movement, of whole new classes of disadvantaged students and forms of discrimination (such as non-English-speaking students, handicapped students, sex discrimination), the professional reformers energetically pursue their visions of equal educational opportunity and a better and more just society. A key means of this pursuit, and one of the most important aspects of this development, clearly is the "litigation explosion." Although not confined to educational affairs, this phenomenon has been extraordinarily salient and influential in these affairs, frequently and heavily affecting the nature of the public school curriculum (compare van Geel 1976).

While it is likely that much good has come out of these efforts, the discussion so far should be sufficient to suggest why from some points of view the professionalization of reform is a mixed blessing. Not only has it increased the pace of disturbing changes, but, with the assistance of the law, it increasingly has imposed the cosmopolitan and secular values of the professional reformers upon the people of "middle America."

Constraints upon Policy Innovation

On the other side of the coin are the various constraints upon policy innovation which inhibit change or *even the consideration* of certain kinds of alternatives. The importance of these constraints is such that they require a search well beyond the dramatic domain of crisis policymaking in our quest for a complete understanding of curriculum politics.

Viewed as a group, all of the constraints upon policy innovation can be seen to be related to the maintenance needs of society, communities, organizations, and individuals. While the literature on the subject tends to focus on either the institutional level or on the individual level, in reality, individuals make choices with regard to innovations in the context of the structure of incentives created by the institutions within which they find themselves. Thus, "professional reformers" housed in action/innovation-oriented organizations maximize their advancement by being innovative. But within the perverse structure of incentives in the quasi-monopolistic, nonprofit bureaucracy of the public schools, the costs of innovation for administrators and teachers often, or even generally, appear to outweigh the benefits (Michaelsen 1977). Yet, public schools do adopt innovations. However, as Pincus (1974) suggests, "private firms are more likely to adopt innovations that promote economic efficiency, whereas [public] schools are more likely to adopt innovations that promote bureaucratic and social stability" (p. 119).

Nondecision Making

Some of the most potent of these constraints upon policy innovation emanate from the fascinating realm of *nondecision making*. In an oft-cited article, Bachrach and Baratz (1962) argue that there are two faces of power—one manifest in actual political disputes and their resolution, and the other expressed covertly through the ability of powerful interests to control the agenda of decision making and prevent the discussion of "unsafe" or "undesirable" issues. The suppression of possible issues or alternatives can result from them actually being vetoed in *nonpublic* deliberations or, even more effectively, by the creation by powerful interests (past and present) of a "mobilization of bias" in terms of widespread and pervasive values and beliefs—throughout an organization, community, region, or society—which delimits what it is safe to do and what should not be done.

Nondecision making and the mobilization of bias, by keeping potential issues and alternatives from being discussed or, in some cases, even recognized, are formidable barriers to change. The strength of local, regional, and ethnocultural mobilizations of bias mandate that professional reformers often have to work hard at "consciousness raising" to get their reform proposals taken seriously. For example, as Tyler (1974) notes in reviewing the educational issues attacked by the federal government during the 1960s, such as segregation and the problems of the disadvantaged: " ... in most cases, they were not even recognized as problems on the local level until the Congressional debates and the availability of federal funds brought them to local attention" (p. 185). In matters such as the segregation issue, it took years of effort to get the initial federal action started.

A graphic example of the problems associated with the mobilization of bias—in terms of the WASPish myth of the culturally homogeneous, unitary community and its educational corollary that all students should be treated alike—is found in the frequent "invisibility" of culturally different students (Waserstein 1975). A similar kind of problem has often existed in regard to the various classes of students with special physical, emotional, or learning problems, whose needs sometimes are ignored or who sometimes are misclassified and then effectively consigned to oblivion. Budoff (1975), for example, describes the extraordinary efforts that were required by a coalition of concerned citizens and child advocates to get the Boston Public Schools to treat these kinds of students properly. A conclusion which emerges time and again from accounts such as this is that, because of the combination of cultural blinders and insufficient educational resources, special classes of students, whose needs are expensive and troublesome to meet, are likely to remain neglected in many school systems unless the systems are compelled, by some legal means, to behave otherwise. Thus, a substantial part of the litigation explosion in education has been necessitated by this cold reality.

The Zone of Tolerance, Vulnerability, and Conflict Avoidance

Within the boundaries set by the mobilization of bias in a given community, and the predominant community values and expectations concerning the public schools, there exists a "zone of tolerance" within which local educators are free to exercise professional leadership. When educators exceed the boundaries of the zone of tolerance (which may be broad or narrow and clearly or poorly defined) they come into conflict with values dear to the particular community and face the likelihood of controversy and opposition. However, educators are strongly inclined to avoid conflict and hence are cautious about testing the boundaries of the zone of tolerance. Thus, this cautiousness inhibits innovation in the curriculum as well as in other aspects of the educational enterprise.

Conflict avoidance tends to be a salient orientation in the minds of school administrators because it is a leading theme in the ideology of their profession, because it is reinforced through the nature of the typical recruitment and socialization process they go through, and because of their frequently keen sense of political vulnerability (Boyd 1976). This sense of vulnerability, along with the paucity of incentives for risk taking within the nonprofit, quasi-monopolistic structure of the public schools, tends to make school administrators and teachers reluctant to incur the psychic costs and risks of innovation and possible controversy.

Research indicates that the latitude or discretion granted to local educators varies primarily according to the *type of community* and, even within communities, according to the *type of issue or policy question* that is faced (Boyd 1976). For instance, speaking in broad generalities, rural school districts and districts located in the "sun belt" of the United States tend to have relatively conservative constituencies. These conservative constituencies are more sensitive and restrictive about the content of courses, such as social studies, literature, and biology, which touch core cultural values; but in all but the most cosmopolitan districts, educators have less freedom of action in these kinds of courses than in the more abstract and value-free subjects such as mathematics. At the same time, however, the method of teaching abstract skills such as mathematics and reading is sometimes a matter of public controversy, especially in conservative communities.

Noninstruction

There is evidence that community socioeconomic status may influence the content and mode of instruction of politically and culturally sensitive courses. In a study of high school civic education in three Boston suburban communities—one upper-middle class, one lower-middle class, and one working class—Litt (1963) found differences among political themes in civics texts, attitudes of community leaders concerning the proper orientation of the community school's civic education program, and in the effects of the civics courses on student political attitudes. Significantly, the differences in political themes emphasized were nearly identical with the preferences of the community leaders.

In an interesting article which relates to Litt's research, Zeigler and Peak (1970) have discussed the political significance of *unrealistic* civic education, that is, instruction which de-emphasizes or neglects the central role of conflict and its resolution in the political process. They contend that such apolitical civic education is common, cite considerable research to support this contention, and argue that unrealistic civic education fosters a conservative orientation in the public which contributes to the maintenance of the status quo. Building on the notion of nondecision making, they propose that high school civic education is unrealistic due to *noninstruction*, that is, "not because of what is said, but more because of what is *not* said" (p. 126). However, contrary to Litt's findings, they suspect that the cause of unrealistic civic education is less the result of the influence of community elites than it is of the *conservative* characteristics of the recruitment and socialization processes of the education professions.

The Politics of Controversy and Nonpublication

Teachers have long recognized that educators can get into a great deal of trouble by teaching controversial matters. But even when educators have substantial public support and are willing to take the "heat" which may be generated by venturing into sensitive areas, those who are offended, even if only a small minority, sometimes can exploit the situation to gain their ends through a "politics of controversy." In other words, as Block and van Geel (1975) put it, " . . . if one can merely make the program 'controversial' there is a good chance both politicians and bureaucrats will back off from it."

The politics of controversy has perhaps its greatest impact on education by causing textbook publishers to go to great lengths to try to avoid inclusion of potentially controversial material in their publications. With very large investments at stake in the production of new textbooks, most publishers feel they cannot take the risks of controversy.

The effects of *overt* censorship and *prior* censorship, or *nonpublication*, on the curriculum might not be quite so bad if teachers and school systems commonly produced their own basic or supplementary curriculum materials. Sadly, as Kirst and Walker (1971) have noted, the vast majority of teachers and systems are almost entirely dependent upon the available published materials. The consequence is that although most curriculum decisions ultimately are made at the local school district level, the choices usually are restricted to the available alternatives prepared, and generally precensored by external groups.

To make matters worse, the problems of censorship and nonpublication are exacerbated by the understandable inclination of publishers to design their products to fare well in the large market controlled by the state textbook adoption agencies. The problems here are aggravated to start with by the fact that most of the twenty-some adoption states are located in the south, which tends to be more conservative than the rest of the country. Moreover, both Texas and California, the two largest adoption states, have engaged in textbook censorship which, because publishers find it less costly to issue a single, nationwide edition, has affected the content of texts distributed nationally.

Given the numerous disincentives to innovation and risk taking faced by publishers, it appears that only the federal government can command or bring into play the resources—dollars, authority, prestige—to overcome these barriers and launch and legitimate curriculum and innovations that local educators and textbook publishers by themselves would be unable or unwilling to attempt. In other words, without federally supported curriculum development efforts it is quite likely that most published curriculum materials would only evolve incrementally and conservatively because of the market conditions publishers face. One example of this can be found in the fact that few biology textbooks *even mentioned* evolution until the publication in 1963 of the Biological Science Curriculum Study (BSCS), which was supported by the National Science Foundation.

Noncompliance and Nonimplementation

Unhappily for reformers it turns out that it is one thing to get innovative schemes accepted and launched and quite another to get them implemented successfully. Though this might seem obvious, it really was not until the generally meager results of the "Great Society" and "War on Poverty" reform efforts of the 1960s prompted a close examination of what was actually going on at the sites of innovative projects that the full and extraordinary significance of the implementation problem became clear.

One of the best documented examples we have of the complex politics of implementation is found in studies of Title I of ESEA (for example, Murphy 1971; Hughes and Hughes 1972). As van Geel (1976) has noted, if all the statutory requirements, regulations, and guidelines of Title I had been fully enforced, it would have resulted in a virtual revolution in educational programming at the local level. But, a host of political and organizational problems blunted the intent of Title I.

Of course, depending upon one's point of view and the issue at hand, the *looseness* in the federal system that enables evasion and non-compliance may be a good thing. One of the goals of our founding fathers, of course, was to build into our governmental structure "checks and balances" that would prevent the abuse of centralized authority and promote the need for persuasion, cooperation, and compromise. The structured necessity for this kind of dialogue, though it may prolong the agony of change on one level, on another level ameliorates possible destructive tensions and facilitates meeting the simultaneous need to maintain society while changing it. The difficulty for educational reformers, however, is that they sometimes wonder if they are succeeding in changing schooling at all, for the problem of the looseness of the federal system is exacerbated by the peculiar "loose coupling" of ends, means, and authority in the educational system. This state of affairs makes enforcement, supervision, and evaluation of educational programs, whether traditional or innovative, quite difficult and obscures accountability for educational outcomes.

But the failures of public schooling, and efforts to reform it in the 1960s, increasingly have led to calls for accountability. However, there are a host of technical and political problems inherent in all educational accountability schemes so far devised. Indeed, the magnitude of these problems is such that it ironically is proving quite difficult to implement the very schemes designed in part to circumvent the implementation problem.

Perhaps the most disturbing of a great many disturbing revelations to educational reformers in the past decades has been the discovery of the extent to which nonimplementation of educational innovations occurs even when local school district authorities and teachers seem favorably disposed toward them. In other words, beyond active and conscious noncompliance, there is the equally important problem of how to successfully and fully translate innovative ideas into practice among nominally compliant educators who, nevertheless, normally have few tangible incentives for innovative behavior. As the authors of *Behind the Classroom Door* concluded, on the basis of observations in 158 classrooms in 67 schools:

> ... some of the highly recommended and publicized innovations of the past decade or so were dimly conceived and, at best, partially implemented in the schools claiming them. The novel features seemed to be blunted in the effort to twist the innovation into familiar conceptual frames or established patterns of schooling [Goodlad et al. 1970, p. 72].

These conclusions have been substantiated by the large, systematic study of federally supported innovation programs conducted by the Rand Corporation. The Rand researchers found that nonimplementation was common and that the most that could be hoped for was a process of *mutual adaptation* in which both the practices in a given school and the innovative project being attempted were modified by one another (Berman and McLaughlin 1976).

Conclusion

Having briefly surveyed the ethereal world of the "professional reformers" and the subterranean world of "nondecision making" and its cousins, we are now in a better position to assess the extent to which curriculum policymaking is characterized by incrementalism—or, alternatively, the extent to which "crisis policymaking is normal and normal policymaking exceptional." Although analysts typically have concluded that educational policymaking is preponderantly incremental, there is a very real sense in which the ambivalence that Kirst and Walker (1971) display on the subject is justified. When one examines the nature of curriculum policymaking closely there is a paradoxical appearance of incremental and nonincremental policymaking going on simultaneously. Beyond the frequency with which nonincremental policymaking occurs due to closely spaced national crises, the "professionalization of reform" and the growth of the business sector concerned with this enterprise have greatly increased the incidence of innovative policymaking. But the paradoxical simultaneity of incremental and nonincremental policy-making also is the result of the complexity of policymaking within our federal system. Thus, we often have both kinds of policymaking going on simultaneously, with local policymakers usually maintaining the status

quo or slowly deciding to adopt innovative curriculum ideas developed
and advocated at higher levels.

Yet, since many of the curriculum policy decisions at higher levels come
down in the form of mandates, the local policymakers—and ultimately the
teaching personnel delivering the educational services—also are occupied
with deciding the extent to which, and the speed with which, they will
comply with these mandates. Thus, the impact of nonincremental
policymaking, whether due to the stimulation of crises or the efforts of
professional reformers, is heavily tempered by the numerous constraints
upon policy innovation. Indeed, nonincremental policy thrusts are far
more than increasingly modified by the snares and hazards of the
implementation process. This process amounts to a continuation of the
policymaking process through the politics of administration.

In sum, the puzzling simultaneity of incrementalism and nonincre-
mentalism in the policymaking process can be seen as two sides of the same
coin. On one side is the complex apparatus of organizations and agencies
involved with curriculum policymaking at the national level, a set of
machines lubricated by professionals attentive to potential crises and
devoted to heroic visions, nonincremental reform, and their own career
advancement. On the other side is the labyrinthine, "loosely coupled"
system by which education is governed at the subnational levels and
ultimately delivered at the local level. The extraordinary complexity and
massive inertia of this loosely linked system easily can transform heroic
ventures into pedestrian projects. Thus, along with the high human and
monetary costs of curriculum change, these characteristics—in part
reflecting societal, organizational, and individual maintenance needs—
insure that real change will take place slowly.[2]

Moreover, it is essential to note that recent far-reaching changes in the
structure of authority over curriculum policymaking seem likely to
increase the probability of incremental, rather than nonincremental,
policymaking. In his comprehensive treatment of this subject, van Geel
(1976) calls attention to the increased involvement in policymaking of the
court, state and federal agencies, and teachers' unions. He concludes that
the curriculum policymaking system is now more complex, legalized,
centralized and bureaucratized and includes more veto points. These
characteristics, plus their tendency to become more pronounced and to
reinforce one another, seem likely to make nonincremental curriculum
policymaking increasingly difficult. While we can expect the professional

---

[2]For insightful discussions amplifying these problems in curriculum change, see
Cuban (1976) and McKinney and Westbury (1975).

reformers to continue their valiant efforts on behalf of innovative policymaking, they increasingly may become entrapped in the very machinery they helped to create.

It is hard to escape the conclusion that the business of reform has grown and proceeded according to a principle of "top-down," externally imposed innovation that is sadly out of tune with the realities involved in changing American public education. If the public were not now demanding results it might be possible for the professional reformers to continue "business as usual," assisted, as LaNoue (1971) has noted, by an "educational research establishment, with its built-in incentive to discover failure which justifies ever more research" (p. 305). But the public is now far less tolerant of this sort of thing, though this is what the public may continue to get, like it or not. However, if we are really serious about reforming public education, it appears that we must strike at the heart of the problem, namely, the perverse structure of incentives that discourages innovation and provides few rewards for excellence within the nonprofit, monopolistic milieu of the public schools (compare Michaelsen 1977). Assured of a captive clientele—at least insofar as the birth rate permits—and utilizing a "lockstep" reward system based upon seniority rather than merit, the public schools scarcely provide a climate conducive to risk taking, experimentation, and responsiveness to consumers. Indeed, it is remarkable that many public schools perform as well as they do, considering their basic reward structure.[3]

The most promising way out of this insulated morass appears to be some variant of the voucher plan with adequate safeguards against racial, ethnic, and socioeconomic discrimination. A voucher scheme would not only introduce competition for students and a consequent strong incentive to satisfy consumers, but it would free schools of the necessity of trying to be "all things to all men." Social and political realities are inclined to compel the public schools to offer a "neutral" program which accords with the perceived preferences of "average" citizens. But along with these pressures for a "common denominator" approach, the public schools also must engage in activities which at least symbolize responsiveness to the wishes of powerful special interest groups. The result is that the public schools are forced to pursue multiple and sometimes conflicting goals, with the

---

[3]Research is needed on what might be called the "secondary" reward structure of public schools, the extent to which the circumstances under which quasi-intrinsic motivations, flowing, for example, from school or community traditions, skilled leadership, or the "professionalism" of educators, produce a level of faculty performance beyond what might be expected simply from the basic "lockstep" reward structure.

consequence that their effectiveness is dulled and no one is entirely satisfied. A voucher plan would enable schools and people to sort themselves out according to their philosophical and pedagogical preferences and the result would be reasonably focused institutions capable of pursuing consistent educational programs.

It is a great tribute, however, to the almost blind belief in the unmitigated virtues of the public schools—as well as to the power of the vested interests which have developed among employee groups in the perpetuation of the public system as it stands—that the voucher plan has not yet been tried on even an experimental basis. The organized resistance to the idea has been so formidable that even the much touted Alum Rock demonstration was so diluted as to scarcely approximate the essential principles of the notion (Michaelsen 1978). The issues raised by the voucher idea, of course, are complex and this complexity in fact is one of the obstacles to gaining support for the idea (van Geel 1978). But the policy question we are left with, then, is, "If some variant of the voucher plan cannot be made digestible in the present environment, what can be done about the incentive system of public education that might facilitate reform?" This is indeed a troublesome question, but it is one that seems inescapable.[4]

References

Bachrach, P., and M.S. Baratz. "Two Faces of Power." *American Political Science Review* 56 (1962): 947-52.

Berman, P., and M.W. McLaughlin. "Implementation of Educational Innovation." *The Educational Forum* 40 (1976): 345-70.

Block, A., and T. van Geel. "State of Arizona Curriculum Law." In *Authority to Control the School Curriculum: An Assessment of Rights in Conflict*, edited by T. van Geel with the assistance of A. Block. A study completed under a grant from the National Institute of Education, 1975, ERIC Document No. ED 125070.

Boyd, W.L. "The Public, the Professionals, and Educational Policymaking: Who Governs?" *Teachers College Record* 77 (1976): 568-70.

Braybrooke, D., and C.E. Lindblom. *A Strategy of Decision*. New York: Free Press, 1963.

Budoff, M. "Engendering Change in Special Education Practices." *Harvard Educational Review* 45 (1975): 507-26.

---

[4]On the theoretical and practical problems confronting voucher plans, see Cohen and Farrar (1977), Michaelsen (1978), and van Geel (1978). For a provocative proposal for reform that is related to the voucher idea, see Garms, Guthrie, and Pierce (1978). For a voucher-related "new public school compromise" that for some reason leaves the "lockstep" reward structure in place, see Swanson (1977).

Cohen, D.K., and E. Farrar. "Power to the Parents? The Story of Education Vouchers." *The Public Interest,* no. 48 (Summer 1977): 72-97.

Coleman, J.S., ed. *Education and Political Development.* Princeton, N.J.: Princeton University Press, 1965.

Cuban, L. "Determinants of Curriculum Change and Stability, 1870-1970." Paper prepared for N.I.E. Curriculum Development Task Force. Arlington, Va., October 15, 1976.

Elboim-Dror, R. "Some Characteristics of the Education Policy Formation System." *Policy Sciences* 1 (1970): 231-53.

Garms, W.I., J.W. Guthrie, and L.C. Pierce. *School Finance: The Economics and Politics of Public Education.* Englewood Cliffs, N.J.: Prentice-Hall, 1978.

Goodlad, J.I., et. al. *Behind the Classroom Door.* Columbus, Ohio: Charles Jones, 1970.

Hottois, J., and N.A. Milner. *The Sex Education Controversy.* Lexington, Mass.: D.C. Heath & Co., 1975.

Hughes, J.F., and A.O. Hughes. *Equal Education.* Bloomington, Indiana: Indiana University Press, 1972.

Iannaccone, L. *Politics in Education.* New York: Center for Applied Research in Education, 1967.

Kirst, M.W., and D.F. Walker. "An Analysis of Curriculum Policymaking." *Review of Educational Research* 41:5 (1971): 479-509.

LaNoue, G.R. "The Politics of Education." *Teachers College Record* 73:2 (1971): 304-19.

Lasswell, H.D. *Politics: Who Gets What, When and How?* New York: McGraw-Hill, 1936.

Litt, E. "Civic Education, Community Norms, and Political Indoctrination." *American Sociological Review* 28 (1963): 69-75.

McKinney, W.L., and I. Westbury. "Stability and Change: The Public Schools of Gary, Indiana, 1940-70." In *Case Studies in Curriculum Change,* edited by W.A. Reid and D.F. Walker, pp. 1-53. London: Routledge and Kegan Paul, 1975.

Michaelsen, J.B. "Revision, Bureaucracy, and School Reform: A Critique of Katz." *School Review* 85 (1977): 229-46.

_____. "Financing Life Long Learning: The Case Against Institutional Grants." *School Review* 86 (May 1978).

Moynihan, D.P. *Maximum Feasible Misunderstanding.* New York: Free Press, 1969.

_____. *The Politics of a Guaranteed Income.* New York: Random House, 1973.

Murphy, J.T. "Title I of ESEA: The Politics of Implementing Federal Education Reform." *Harvard Educational Review* 41 (1971): 35-63.

Nelkin, D. "The Science-Textbook Controversies." *Scientific American* 234: 4 (1976): 33-39.

Pincus, J. "Incentives for Innovation in the Public Schools." *Review of Educational Research* 44 (1974): 113-44.

Swanson, A.D. "Equality, Integration, and Metropolitanism: New Public School

Compromise." *Educational Administration Quarterly* 13 (Winter 1977): 1–15.

Tyler, R.W. "The Federal Role in Education." *The Public Interest*, no. 34 (Winter 1974): 154–87.

van Geel, T. *Authority to Control the School Program.* Lexington, Mass.: D.C. Heath & Co., 1976.

──────. "Parental Preferences and the Politics of Spending Public Educational Funds." *Teachers College Record* 79 (1978): 339–63.

Waserstein, A. "Organizing for Bilingual Education: One Community's Experience." *Inequality in Education*, no. 19 (February 1975): 23–30.

Zeigler, L.H., and W. Peak. "The Political Functions of the Educational System." *Sociology of Education* (Spring 1970): 115–42.

PART IV
Process Descriptions of Change

Out of sheer ingratitude, man will pay you a dirty trick, just to prove that men are still men and not the keys of a piano . . . And even if you could prove that a man is only a piano key, he would still do something out of sheer perversity— he would create destruction and chaos—just to gain his point. . . . And if all of this could in turn be analyzed and prevented by predicting that it would occur, then man would deliberately go mad to prove his point.

—Dostoevsky

Organizations, like individuals, seem almost determined to derail efforts to bring collective efforts under rational control. At the heart of this perversity are processes that may be understandable if we suspend the view that they must follow the law of reason. Rationality has limits, and those who probe behind the curtain try to examine organizational processes unencumbered by the dictate that they should make "sense."

Since the early twentieth century, educational and other social science researchers have borrowed the techniques and methods of the physical scientists, hoping to achieve a comparable degree of precision and control in their research. Frederick Jackson Taylor introduced scientific management to business and brought to business management the same concerns of rationality found in the natural sciences.

By the late 1950s modern analytic approaches to management began to take hold in American business. Modern managers, with facts, figures, and analytical techniques, became masters. With the facts and figures, the modern manager advocated a rational model of choice, designed to help managers make better decisions by systematizing the process and eliminating irrational forces and sentiments.

Robert McNamara, as secretary of defense during the Vietnam War, relied heavily on rational analysis to manage the war. McNamara and his statistics and ratios became a symbol of hope in a conflict that seemed to drag on endlessly without a clean-cut victory in sight. But confidence in McNamara and his methods began to wane as stories from the battlefield described a more complex and less optimistic reality than the equations had depicted. What had worked well at Ford seemed incapable of improving our position in Southeast Asia. At some level, the experience in Vietnam brought many Americans closer to understanding the limits of rationality.

It is, of course, important to define problems, develop a range of possible solutions, and systematically select the best alternative according to its merits and costs. But it is equally important to recognize the limitations of the process and to understand how problem solving, planning, decision making, and other activities actually take place in most organizations, most of the time.

Herbert Simon and James G. March were among the first theorists to note the constraints of rational choice. Human beings and human organizations do not have the time or expertise to find optional solutions. Instead, searching for an answer to a problem ends when a satisfactory solution is found. The introduction of the idea of bounded rationality opened the field to explorations into organizational processes unfettered by earlier assumptions. Rather than investigating how things should be and treating deviations as error or slothfulness, researchers began to treat as interesting the ways decisions and choices are really made in organizations. Henry Mintzberg's studies of how managers spend their time, Charles Lindbloom's explication of the science of "muddling through," and James March's studies of decision making are examples of the emerging knowledge in the field that question the presumption that organizations are governed by rational logic. Instead, these studies see organizational processes as controlled by chance and serendipity—somewhat predictable but very difficult to manage.

The five articles in this section shed light in various ways on the theme that "men are still men and not the keys of a piano." In Chapter 14 Olsen describes the reorganization of academic departments in a university. The rational model of reorganization argues that a realignment in an organization should produce more efficient and effective decision-making processes and clearer lines of authority. With a great deal of care and detail, Olsen shows us how the reorganization collected or attracted emotionally charged issues in the university. Since these emotional issues were not being directly dealt with by the organization, the collective fears and anxieties of various groups were dumped into the events around reorganization—decision making became a receptacle for an organization's "garbage." Olsen also shows how the larger environment legitimizes and sanctions a focus on certain issues in an organization at a particular time.

Weiner's case study of the desegregation of San Francisco public schools, described in Chapter 15, is an interesting example of the old cliche of being at the right place at the right time. The rational decision-making model argues the wisdom of putting all the known, and ideally knowable, facts into a computer. From this data base, the computer can help consolidate the most appropriate solution to a problem, in this case how to desegregate a large urban school district. Instead of rational decision makers following rational patterns and plans, Weiner reports that a group largely composed of white, middle- and upper-middle-class women with the time, money, and energy to devote to the problem—a group labeled "Round the Clock"—ultimately decided the major parameters of desegregating the schools. The Round the Clock group knew and understood the political forces and dynamics of the city and were willing to pay attention to the various constituencies. The assistant superintendent and the other rational decision makers are portrayed as insensitive to the political forces, and even if they could have, the rational managers would not have satisfied the numerous ethnic groups in the city. Public institutions like schools are seen as organized anarchies, because anyone can play—a function of time, energy, and competing demands. Participation is not controlled by formal dictates or rules. The head of an organization may block certain players from an arena, but at a cost of time and energy, and these resources are always in short supply. In a public institution it is hard to throw citizens out of the game; participants are managed only occasionally by attempting to divert their time and attention somewhere else. Weiner's case study is a perfect example of fluid participation and the impact that fluidity has on opportunities for choice in organized anarchies.

Davis and Stackhouse present in Chapter 17 five case studies of change in elementary schools. Following the line of reasoning of the process view of an organized anarchy, they show how, in two schools, important changes occurred not because of need or plan but through a serendipitous interplay of events or motives such as career aspirations, architectural design, demographic changes, and educational values. Davis and Stackhouse go on to document how changes often play an important symbolic role by "appearing" to respond to a problem or pressure without being tightly linked to other organizational processes or closely inspected to determine the degree of implementation or success or failure.

In School C, for example, Davis and Stackhouse show how the district office demanded that teachers in that school and in other schools in the district concern themselves with the moral education of each child. Each week teachers were to examine each child on such abstract concepts as power, wealth, and rectitude. School C responded to the district's demand by introducing the program but not by evaluating it or checking in any other way to see if it were properly implemented. This example suggests that perhaps the only judicious response to an unreasonable request is a symbolic gesture.

Most of us in education remember the optimistic pageantry that launched the National Institute of Education on its vigorous mission to reform educational R & D. And, unless memories have been dimmed by disappointment, we recall the rapid set of events that seemed to propel the agency in a different—if not downward—direction. In Chapter 16 Sproull, Wolf, and Weiner rely on their case study of NIE to show how the nebulous and ambiguous task of educational R & D contributed to the institute's problems. Under such conditions, trying to bring the R & D enterprise together in a well-planned, coordinated, and consistent direction creates indefensible expectations and fractionalizes the many diverse and loosely linked constituencies whose confidence and support is essential for successful research.

From the case study, the authors outline a series of questions that managers should ask in creating a new agency, or in reforming an old one. These questions direct attention to the idiosyncratic play of people and events in organizations, to the limits of managerial control, and to the importance of symbols in maintaining internal cohesion and external support.

Cohen and March go even further than do Sproull, Weiner, and Wolf in addressing the question: How do leaders lead in an organized anarchy? Their answer in Chapter 18 is: not easily and definitely not through conventional strategies of leadership or control. Their depiction of organizations of higher education and their guidelines for what leaders can do challenge many management trends while reinforcing older ideas of intuition and virtue.

They believe it is better to find "good" goals than to make good decisions and that we should relearn the art of playfulness. When we are sensibly foolish, Cohen and March argue, we temporarily suspend the rules of consistency, purpose, and rationality, allowing our intuitive, imaginative, creative side to emerge. As educational leaders we need to play and to enjoy our jobs and ourselves; and in so doing we may, ironically, do our jobs more efficiently and effectively.

The process view of organizations emphasizes the continuous flow of people, events, choices, and time in a kaleidoscope image of change and activity. The direction of the flow is difficult to control; it is, however, possible to influence—but not usually through the rational strategies that administrators often employ.

14

Reorganization as a Garbage Can

Johan Olsen

Introduction

Organization implies intention. Although we recognize that any particular organization is also a collection of history and a relatively complex set of activities, relations, and symbols, we ordinarily interpret organizations as social instruments. They are intended to facilitate the accomplishment of objectives. They are intended to exhibit elements of efficiency and effectiveness.

Reorganization similarly suggests intention. Reorganizations have been proposed, implemented, and understood mainly as solutions to problems. Organizations are changed deliberately in order to achieve greater efficiency, more human satisfaction, or some new type of substantive policy (Mosher 1967). The idea is a familiar one (March and Olsen 1976, Chap. 1): Problems arise; analysis suggests that the problem lies in the organization; a reorganization is adopted; the problem is solved (or sometimes not if the analysis is faulty). An organizational decision can sometimes be viewed as a result of a process in which decision makers, or some winning coalition, solve their problems or resolve their conflicts. A similar interpretation of reorganization may often capture important elements of the phenomenon.

Often, however, reorganization is a garbage can. It is a choice opportunity that collects an assortment of loosely connected problems, solutions, and participants. The collection may include a variety of substantive concerns; different participants may graft onto a reorganization decision solution to almost any current problem. Thus,

Reprinted, by permission, from James G. March and Johan Olsen, *Ambiguity and Choice in Organizations* (Bergen, Norway: Universitetsforlaget, 1976), pp. 314–36.

reorganizations have become simultaneous vehicles for discussing efficiency of communication, firing managers, concealing unfortunate budgetary comparisons, and changing the standard operating procedures. Reorganization is a choice opportunity that provides relatively open access for problems of almost any type.

Because it is a choice opportunity with relatively free access for problems and solutions, discussions of reorganization are likely to attract not only any number of independent practical problems but also a disproportionate number of symbolic issues. As a result, a reorganization sometimes may be most adequately described as a process through which an organization arrives at an interpretation of what it has become or what it has been doing, what it is becoming or what it is doing, what it is going to become or what it is going to be doing. Such a perspective emphasizes the expressive, symbolic, and image-exercising aspects of a reorganization. It underlines the need for examining reorganizations as occasions for discovering or accepting new organizational values, or occasions for confirming and giving reassurance about old ones.

In this chapter we consider the interplay of practical problems and image exercising in the reorganization garbage can. The base is a case study of a major reorganization in a Norwegian university. The study combined the examination of archival materials, interviews, and a general questionnaire. It is reported in greater detail elsewhere (Olsen 1968, 1971).

The institute directorship of the university has been described as the last stronghold of feudalism in Europe (see, for example, Consolazio 1961). As late as 1963–64 the department chairman of a Norwegian university was an autocrat, in the sense that he had all *formal* authority and responsibility in his hands. In the middle of the 1960s a major reorganization took place in some departments. The "classical" (German) model with small, one professor-ruled institutes, without any administrative staff was abandoned. The role of the full professor and chairman was dramatically changed. The idea was to construct large departments, governed through a system of collective decision making. A council, a board, and a chairman were to be elected. Nontenured faculty, technical and administrative staff, and students were for the first time formally allowed to take part in departmental governance. At the same time, the role of a department secretary was introduced as an attempt to strengthen the office organization. This new departmental organization became known as the "physics model," and has played a major role in Norwegian discussions of university governance over recent years.

The new departmental organization was developed for the Department of Physics at the University of Oslo.[1] The present study began as an attempt to understand why the reorganization took place, and why it came first in the physics department. As the study developed, it exposed several counterintuitive features to this "victory for democracy." Instead of being a bloody battle around the last stronghold of feudalism, the reorganization took place without many people attending to it, and with very little conflict. As a matter of fact, the autocrats themselves (full professors and administrative leaders) were the most active in changing the system. Although those without any formal power seldom showed much interest, they ended up with substantially increased representation in the new decision-making units.

While in retrospect celebrated as a crusade for democracy and participation, the reorganization did not begin as an issue of power and influence. On the contrary, it started as an attempt to solve a classic practical problem for the department leaders. They wanted to be relieved from routine work. As time went by, reorganization became a "garbage can," a meeting place for participants, solutions, and problems. Many of the issues ultimately related to the choice were distant from the day-to-day life of the Department of Physics. They became elements of the definition of reorganization as the reorganization accumulated extensive symbolic meaning.

The exercising of issues, problems, solutions, and images cannot easily be understood as attempts to affect the immediate, substantive (material) outcome of the choice at stake. The symbolic-expressive exercises seemed to be ways of testing and changing conceptions of the "ideal" department. They were related to the character, the mission, the goals, and the beliefs that different participants wished to have dominate a university department. Partly these exercises need to be understood in terms of their potential impact in other choice arenas. Physics was the arena, but not the only object.

The process is an extended garbage can. As a result, we analyze it by considering the streams of problems, solutions, and participants. We look at how different groups defined the situation in 1963–64: what problems they brought, what had caused the problems, and how the problems could be solved. Further, the patterns of activation are described: how some

---

[1] The first part of the process went on in both the Department of Physics and the Department of Chemistry. Later some other departments introduced a version of the new organizational arrangement. In order not to overload this version with too many details, the story is focused upon the physics department, which also was driving the process.

groups took strong initiatives and became heavily involved; how others more or less ignored the reorganization. We then turn to the solutions chosen by the organization. The process is divided into two phases. The first was primarily focused on making the organizations more "rational and efficient" and on reducing the costs of participation for leaders. In the second phase the demands for participation among nonleaders became more important, and the new representation system was developed.

The First Phase

The first phase of the reorganization discussion covers the period from May 1963 to April 1964. During this period the choice opportunity (reorganization) collected an assortment of problems, solutions, and a little participation energy. It was a minor set of issues for most people, a moderate concern for a few, a major concern for almost no one.

Problems, Solutions, and Participants

At the beginning, and through the first phase, most potential participants had completely empty models of the situation. They did not formulate their points of view. They were unconcerned and uninvolved. This was true for a majority of the faculty, the students, the research assistants, and the technical-administrative staff. The chief body of university governance (the Collegium) did not involve itself. The faculty in other departments [seemed] to have barely noticed what was going on. Relative to all the other claims on their attention, reorganization of the Department of Physics was insignificant and distant.

Amidst this extensive sense of irrelevance, there were two groups who saw reorganization initially as an opportunity for exercising (and perhaps solving) some problems. The groups defined the problems somewhat differently. The first group was a group of full professors who were, or recently had been, department chairman. Their problems were the pragmatic concerns of academic lower management:

1. The administrative burdens had become too heavy for the department leaders because of the growth in the department.
2. The growth had also made the "section" unfit as an administrative unit.[2] Too many people were involved. The section was difficult to handle and very time-consuming.

---

[2]The section is a unit discussing teaching affairs but not research matters. Its formal status most places is as a school—not a department unit, but the heterogeneity of its way of functioning was (and is) very great across the university. The Collegium is the highest governing unit of the university.

3. The department had a strong need for making joint decisions. Projects had become very expensive. When one group got money, all the others were affected. Thus, the department needed an organizational structure that could establish priorities.
4. The department had grown unevenly. There were only a few new full professorships or associate professorships, but many assistant professorships. Several of the latter had become highly qualified professionally. It was difficult to give any professional rationale why they should not participate in department governance.[3]
5. There existed a large discrepancy between the way the department actually was run and its formal constitution. It was of some importance to legalize and formalize the changes which had already taken place. The department for a decade had had a council which had no formal standing, but which was accepted as binding internally. The section (in which all participated) had been very active. Nobody had tried to limit the discussions and decisions to pure teaching matters. The chairmanship had rotated among the senior professors.
6. One of the secretaries had assumed considerable informal responsibility. It seemed necessary, in order to keep her in the department, to find a position which better reflected the work she was actually doing. The administrative leaders of the department considered it very important to keep this secretary in the department.

The second group of participants were the administrators on the school and university level. They clearly perceived the existing department structure of the university as "inefficient." They wanted to make the system less costly to run, and they wanted to reduce the "chaos." They saw the Department of Physics as only one instance of some general problems. They believed:

1. The general growth in the activity of the university had made existing channels of communication and control inadequate.
2. The large number of small departments governed by professors with little interest in administration and little information about the increasingly complex web of laws and rules produced a stream of questions from the departments to the school and university

---

[3] It is impossible to say *how* important this argument was in the beginning (1963–1964). In the written material it seems to be of little importance. There may be two reasons. First, that it simply was not important. Second, that it was not stressed for tactical reasons. Full professors in other departments, for instance, were perceived as relatively negative to increased participation of junior faculty.

administration. It also produced some incorrect handling of issues, which the administration had to correct.

3. As the university was asking for more and more money, it was important to develop better documentation for the budget proposals. (Wetlesen 1967, pp. 52–53.)

The early ideas about reorganization grew out of these simple concerns for solving ordinary problems. Both groups (though for somewhat different reasons) saw a need for eliminating the sections, consolidating the structure into a smaller number of larger units, strengthening the position of the secretary, and introducing a more formalized decision-making system. For the department chairman this provided a justification for enlarging the job of the secretary (and thus retaining her), getting rid of the sections, and providing a formal justification of the existing departmental council. For the university administrators the proposed reorganization introduced a useful arm of the administration (the secretary) into the department and reduced the span of control. On both sides, the values that were emphasized explicitly were those of administrative efficiency and the improvement of professional quality.

These proposals for solutions, in combination with the ambiguity of the issues of efficiency and the ease of access to the reorganization garbage can, stimulated two other groups of participants. The first were the defenders of the classical institute. Their thinking was made explicit in letters from the Head of Theoretical Physics, a subdepartment of the Department of Physics. The basic argument was that nothing had happened which made changes in the organization structure necessary.

1. Professional authority was still seen as the only basis for department government. The way full professors were appointed was the guarantee that they were the best-qualified people. Using a voting procedure was unfitting to decision making within academe. Such a procedure would be working against the authority and responsibility of having a university chair. It would be natural for the full professor (chairman) to consult his colleagues before he made decisions, but *whom* he should consult, *when*, and *about what*, were the decision and responsibility of the professor.

2. The need for professional, administrative help was also denied. The general development of a stronger university administration was perceived as a burden, not as a help to the professor. What he primarily needed was more help in typing his manuscripts, and the like.

3. The recent changes in curricula toward a course system, with credit connected to each course (and not as earlier with exams only after two

or more semesters), had weakened the students' ability to think independently, had made the university more school-like, and had given each professor less control over his subject. The new reorganizations were viewed as unfortunate extensions of these tendencies.

4. As long as all parts of a department were not gathered in one building, a joint decision-making system and administration would be costly and inefficient.

The organizational solution suggested was to keep an arrangement with smaller departments with full authority and responsibility over a limited area for each full professor. The demand for more coordination was met with a strong demand for autonomy. Each institute should be allowed to arrange its own affairs as it wanted. This would both increase the professional quality and be more efficient. A modified version was to accept that the professors had to be relieved of routine work, but to deny the importance of coordination of different subdepartments. Each subdepartment should make all the important decisions and be governed by the full professor in the field.

The second group of new participants in the discussion of reorganization were the leaders of the university association of junior faculty, representing junior faculty throughout the university. While the chairman of the association was an assistant professor in physics, those most concerned with the rights, power, and status of junior faculty on the department level in this period mainly came from other departments, where these issues in general were perceived as more important and more problematic than in the physics department. The activity of junior faculty in the Department of Physics was rather modest. The reorganization of their department became a garbage can with respect to the rights, power, and status issues. However, these concerns were clearly not created by the activities in the physics department.

Three months before the events in the Department of Physics (February 1963), representatives from the junior faculty discussed the relative emphasis they should put on demanding participation at the department, school, and collegium level. The participants realized that both the actual arrangements and the wishes for participation at the department level varied across the schools. The minutes from the meeting in the association state that the discussants talked little about *how* (if at all) the nontenured personnel should go about to increase its influence in the sections and in the departments. One possible solution mentioned was that the department was to be organized by establishing a board for the chairman which would be under some control from the section. A committee was appointed to work on the issue.

The events in the physics department provided an opportunity for discussing participation rights. Leaders of the association of junior faculty protested that the new arrangements gave the junior faculty less influence and were less democratic than the existing arrangements. At the same time, the existing organization and its distribution of formal authority in general were attacked. The protesting letter stated: "It is not seldom that decisions with great importance for the nontenured faculty members' work are made without being submitted to organs where this group has a real possibility to influence the decision." The department chairman should not be allowed (the letter said) to decide if junior faculty members should participate. It was emphasized that junior faculty should be involved in the decision-making process as early as possible in all important decisions (that is, budgets, allocation of resources, and personnel policy). The demand concerning stronger influence for the junior faculty was related both to the well-being of this group and to professional quality.[4] It was argued that the new organizational arrangement would work against these values. The group suggested that the Collegium appoint a committee to analyze the situation in the different schools and propose a new administrative arrangement for the university as a whole.

Thus at the outset, the discussion involved problems ranging from the highly specific and localized problem of reclassifying a valued secretary, to issues of general university policy with respect to administrative coordination and faculty governance. Only a few people were involved; this was only one of several arenas for them. For most of them the problems of the Department of Physics, per se, were incidental to the relevance of those problems for the symbolic battles for administrative efficiency, participatory democracy, and professional competence.

The Flow of Events and Activity

Table 14-1 shows the time line of the more important events in the reorganization process. The plans for reorganization were initiated by the upper levels in the organization. They came from some full professors who had had administrative responsibilities, and from some full-time administrators. The committee proposing the new department rules was appointed by the dean, a former chairman of the Department of Physics who also took an active part in its work. It consisted of four full professors,

---

[4]In 1968 only 9.4 percent of our respondents in a university-wide survey (N = 752) agreed completely to a statement saying that many decisions of great importance and interest for the non-tenured faculty were (today) made without any consultation of any representatives of the non-tenured faculty.

Table 14-1

Time line of events

Dates	Events
May 15, 1963	The Council of the School of the Sciences discusses the proposition of reorganization of the departments from the Administrative Board of the School and decides to support it.
May 22, 1963	The association of nontenured faculty at the university sends a letter to the Collegium demanding that the question of the participation of nontenured faculty at the department level has to be considered. The Collegium postpones the decision.
November 2, 1963	The Administrative Board of the School of the Sciences asks the Departments of Physics and Chemistry to make an outline for an administrative arrangement for the two departments built on the decision in the Council of the School. The committee is asked to work quickly.
December 21, 1963	After some consultation, two meetings are arranged. The committee proposed a department council (in addition to the chairman, board, and administrative staff). This proposal is discussed informally in the two departments.
January 3, 1964	The committee proposal is ready.
February 24, 1964	The Administrative Board of the School accepts the proposal (with some smaller changes). The Council of the School does not discuss it.
February 27, 1964	A letter is sent from the assistant university director (earlier secretary of the school and a signer of the initial proposal from the administrative board about reorganization) to the school, saying that since the school has already decided to try out the new arrangement, it is better that the Collegium accepts this formally.
March 3, 1964	The school asks the Collegium to accept the arrangement.
March 13, 1964	The Collegium accepts the arrangement temporarily for one year.
March 21, 1964	In a letter to the Collegium the leader of the subdepartment for theoretical physics says that he will not take part in the new arrangement.
November 29, 1965	The Department of Physics in a letter to the school proposes a permanent arrangement which accepts the reorganization made, but (a) introduces a stronger representation of the

nontenured faculty members, (b) states that all the members of the council and the board should be elected, (c) introduces permanent committees for teaching policy and personnel policy, and finally, (d) eliminates the subdepartments. All the research areas should be represented in the council and the tenured faculty members should not necessarily any longer be in a majority.

December 14, 1965   Collegium accepts this arrangement for one year.

---

one junior faculty, and the secretary who later became department secretary of the physics department.

Other groups either reacted, trying to delay the decisions and win time, or they ignored the choice. The junior faculty association and the defender of the "classical institute" model both (but on very different premises) tried to get the decision postponed. However, not even the decision in the Collegium (June 19, 1963) to postpone the decision had any significant effect on the process. When it was discovered that in spite of the decision in the Collegium the school had continued working out the plans for the new department organization, the highest governing body of the university did not try to force its will (February 27, 1964). The Council of the School of the Sciences did not even discuss the final proposal.

Junior faculty were represented in all units handling the decision. They never dissented, even when the participation issue did not become important. We observed an increasing interest in the participation question but solutions and strategies were still very unclear. The reorganization initiative worked as a "spark," leading the junior faculty to take points of view they did not express earlier. The letter on behalf of the association of junior faculty (June 19, 1963) attempted to make the participation question a university-wide decision, but the events in the Department of Physics took place so rapidly that all problems were "solved" on the department level. In the Department of Physics junior faculty took less interest in the participation issue.

The strongest defender of the "classical institute" model also tried to stop or postpone the decision. When he did not succeed, he simply declared that he did not intend to participate in the new arrangement with "his subdepartment." Nobody tried to force him. The decision in the School of the Sciences was made unanimous with the exception of a paragraph on uniting small departments into larger ones. Here two voted against. In general the faculty in other departments remained passive. The students, assistants, and the technical and administrative staff never became activated.

It should be added that the *absolute* level of activity was low. In terms of the number of meetings held, the number of people involved, and the degree of writing, the level of activity was much lower than one might expect in an apparently important decision. The process was characterized by a very limited search for alternative organization models. There was very little data or argumentation. No studies were made. The reports from the administrative board and the departmental committee were extremely short papers. Few participants tried to clarify the consistency in their values and beliefs. Few attempts were made to build coalitions against the proposal.

The Solution in the First Phase

The Administrative Board of the School stated as its task the development of an administrative arrangement adapted to the large size of the departments, which, as much as possible, would relieve the scientists of administrative burdens if they were willing to delegate responsibility and authority over routine functions. The administrative unit which should be the point of departure for the future organization of the departments had to be the large departments like pharmacy, physics, chemistry, and mathematics. These units were to be "administered as any other large firm" by (a) a board, (b) an administrative director (chairman), and (c) a strong office organization, the department secretariat. The latter was perceived as the most important element in relieving the professors of administrative responsibilities and burdens and providing close contact to the administration at the school and university level. The administrative board proposed to dissolve the sections as administrative units and to dissolve the positions of section chairman and secretary. It was proposed to merge smaller departments into larger units as soon as "the external conditions made this appropriate."

The new department board would "be responsible for the great lines in the department's policies, internally and externally." It would consist of all the leaders of the subdepartments, and a number (to be specified later) of the professors, associate professors, assistant professors and students. It is not clear from the document whether administrative and technical personnel would be represented. The chairman would be elected from among the full professors or associate professors for a one-year term. He would decide whether decisions had general interest and therefore should be presented for the board. The subdepartments would be kept, but only as working units, not administrative units.

The committee from the Departments of Physics and Chemistry, which was appointed to work out the new rules in more detail, proposed one important change: the introduction of a council.[5] The council was supposed to work out the long-range policies, but at the same time the committee stated that they wanted to try out these arrangements before the division of labor between council, board, chairman, and secretary was decided. The stated dilemma was to find a balance between, on the one hand, keeping the number of participants so low that the units could work and, on the other hand, letting all interests in the department have access to the governing organs. The interests of the leaders of the subdepartments were especially taken care of: The chairman was not allowed to make decisions in any important issues without discussing it with them. Discussing the committee proposal and whether the students would be represented in the board of the departments, the conclusion in the administrative board was that "It was agreed that such representation was not appropriate in an executive unit as this."

The new council consisted of the following: (a) All leaders of subdepartments, all full professors and associate professors, (b) the department leaders for teaching affairs, (c) two representatives from the junior faculty (besides those otherwise included), (d) one representative from the technical staff, [and] (e) the chairman of the (department) student body.

In the board all subdepartments would be represented and, in general, all interests in the departments would be taken care of. The members were: (a) the department chairman, (b) one full professor or associate professor from all the subdepartments not having the chairman, (c) one junior faculty member, and (d) one of the department leaders for teaching affairs (who should participate only in pure teaching matters). The chairman would be elected from among the full professors or associate professors by the council, and the department secretary should function as secretary both in the council and the board.

The discussion of reorganization exercised two broad kinds of concerns: On the one hand, there were the concerns with the everyday organization of the Department of Physics. How should things be done in the department? On the other hand, there were the concerns with the major symbolic issues of efficiency, professional quality, and participation. Whose definition of the issues before the university would be accepted and what precedents would be set? As might be expected in such a situation, discussion and decision tended to become relatively independent.

----

[5]The reasons for this change were not made clear. However, the new proposal was closer to the existing organizational arrangements. Also the change could be viewed as a concession to the claim that the proposal from the administrative board would decrease the level of participation for junior faculty.

Very little was written during the process, and the written documents by and large were of modest relevance for the situation in the physics department. The size aspect, emphasized in the administrative board, was completely irrelevant. Even if theoretical physics were separated, both departments were larger than the new norm proposed. The new council did not operate very differently from the section, and the real governance of the departments [was] still dominated by consultation among a few leaders. The felt need for a new bureaucrat was very real, but it should be remembered that one of the secretaries was already doing this job. In order to understand the process observed we have to look for potential relevance of this process for events *outside* the immediate arena.

The department leaders, being concerned with their own load of routine matters, tried to secure a better position, in terms of status and salary, for the person already working as secretary.[6] To get a new position, the image of the department held by the governmental bureau had to be changed. They had to believe that the new department organization would be more efficient.[7] By and large this could be done through formalizing the system as it was operating already.

Neither was the university administration primarily concerned with changing the physics department. The reorganization provided an opportunity to create a formal position (department secretary) which might be useful as an incentive in future bargaining with other departments. At the same time the administration through the reorganization got a definition of the "ideal" department, which could be used as a model for other (smaller, nonbureaucratized) departments in the future. For the university administration the reorganization became a garbage can into which they dropped the problems they had in their relations with these other departments. These issues were closely related to the long-run problem of the administration: reducing the amount of administrative chaos and building more "efficient" routines.

The reorganization also became a choice opportunity into which the

---

[6]There may also be some more subtle effects. Demands for being relieved from administrative burdens reminded everybody that the most important activity in the organization was research, and that the administrative leaders, while using most of their time on administration, still perceived themselves as scientists.

[7]In the Norwegian system the creation of a new type of position like department secretaries first has to be accepted by the governmental bureau. The central value of this bureau clearly was "efficiency," and the modern firm was viewed as being the most efficient type of organization. Thus, the argumentation has to be understood as an attempt to get a new position by affecting the image of a "university department" held by the "0 and M" people.

leader of theoretical physics could throw the problems he perceived relating to the general development of the Department of Physics, (such as a trend toward a more "school-like" institution and the changes in the role of the full professor). The defender of the classical institute model did not succeed in having his definition of the situation accepted. The new constitution represented a break with important elements in his model. But he claimed his price: It was accepted that he (and thus others like him)[8] could withdraw from the new arrangement. The passivity of the professors in some other departments has (at least partly) to be understood on the basis of this understanding that no full professor should be forced into the new arrangement.

The leaders of the junior faculty in the university at large tried to have the problem of junior faculty participation related to the choice. They perceived it as easier to have a formal representation of junior faculty accepted in the Department of Physics than in most other places. In this way it would be important to provide a model which could be used in future bargaining in other departments. However, the garbage can moved too fast in the first period. The participation issue never became central. For the first time, junior faculty, students, and the technical/administrative staff became formally represented in department government; but compared to the arrangements that had operated informally, they gained little in the physics department.

During this first phase the different participants by and large stressed the same general (and nonoperational) values, but they had different opinions about what was going on, and about the effects of the possible alternatives. The choice process became a dumping place for problems and issues which were primarily related to definitions, problems, and images outside the Department of Physics. Several groups did not attempt to change anything in the physics department, but found the process of reorganization fitted for exercising their general problems. There was no conflict, leadership by the full professors with administrative responsibilities, a steady expansion of participation rights, and a continuation of informal professional authority exercised by physicists of recognized professional stature. Although the symbolism of participation became a frequent theme, there was almost no overt conflict in which the lines of cleavage divided senior and junior faculty.

---

[8]The reorganization provided an opportunity for exercising the principle of nonintervention on issues where one full professor had strong opinions. At this point in the process full professors in other departments who were ambivalent to the new plans or against them, probably stayed inactive because they believed they would not be forced to introduce the new arrangements in their own departments.

The Second Phase

The Flow of Events and Activities

The new rules (November 1965) of the Department of Physics stated as the two most important principles: (1) to introduce a stronger representation of the junior faculty; (2) all seats should now be filled through elections, to eliminate all ex-officio memberships in the council and the board. The new rules deemphasized hierarchical groups as the basis for representation, and focused on the research groups. Senior people were given 50 percent of the seats in the council. If, however, a junior faculty member was elected as representative of a research group, he should count within these 50 percent. Thus, the senior faculty for the first time could become a minority in the council. In 1968 the council had eleven professors/associate professors, eight assistant professors, one student, and one representative from the technical administrative staff.

Another important change was the introduction of standing committees, first for teaching and personnel policies, then for research. Formally, these had only a recommending role vis-a-vis the council. Informally, it was agreed to give them the real decision-making power. In none of these committees did the rules automatically give the senior faculty a majority. At the same time the new committees weakened the position of the subdepartments. The committee for research policy was recruited from the different research projects active in the department. Thus, representation became dependent on the activities going on, not [on] the hierarchical positions of the different participants.

The importance of the subdepartments was deemphasized in many different ways. The department chairman in general praised the new organizational arrangement because it made possible the formulation of better priorities from a joint organizational point of view (rather than being based on the special interests of the subdepartments). The dean of the School of the Sciences stated very strongly that:

"The subdepartments are subordinated to the department. The authority and responsibility of the single professor or subdepartment leader is limited to activity within the constraints the department sets for his activity."

These changes represented another step away from the "classical institute" model. In 1968 the attack was made even more explicit. The dean, in particular, was attacking the one-professor dominated department. The large, "democratic" department was described as superior both in relieving the scientist of administrative burdens, getting a better overview and coordination of the whole organization (which certainly was in opposition to the principle of "non-intervention"), "educating" people, and providing well-being in the organization.[9]

While there is a relationship between increased activity by junior faculty and changes giving them stronger formal participation, it is much more difficult to find any connection between demands from assistants, students, and technical-administrative staff and the fact that these groups received a stronger representation. In the physics department the participation problem never became a strong issue among students, assistants, and technical-administrative staff. Moreover, in the second phase, the university administration, and other groups external to the department, have been less involved. The university administration first tried to "sell" the physics model to other departments. Their desire for larger departments was met, but not through the uniting of smaller departments. A general growth process in the university increased the size of many departments. Several of these growing departments wanted secretaries. The administration did not have to campaign in order to sell the idea. Soon the demand was larger than the supply of such positions. External events then made the participation and governance issues more central and reorganization became a choice opportunity in several departments. The university administration and the leaders of the association of junior faculty could meet again over the same issues of the rights, power, and status of junior faculty. The most visible of these meetings took place in departments in the humanities and the social sciences. Here students and sometimes junior faculty activism seemed to threaten the values of efficiency (thus attracting the university administration). The general interest in the symbols of participation, power, and status was higher, and at the same time these issues were to a lesser degree than in physics solved in informal ways (attracting the students and junior faculty leaders). Furthermore, in 1967 the University of Oslo appointed a committee with the mandate to give a recommendation about the general organization of the university. This committee attracted much of the time and attention of faculty interested in the issues of participation and organization. Thus the

---

[9]The trend toward stronger emphasis on the participation-aspect has continued since 1968. In the Department of Physics the difference between senior and junior faculty in department governance has been eliminated, and both the students and the technical-administrative staff have stronger representation. In 1970 the department council had thirty representatives, seventeen faculty members, five from the technical-administrative staff and eight students. In the fall term a junior faculty member was elected chairman (the senior faculty argued that some of the junior faculty "had to take their term"). The department has also introduced an open assembly as an advisory body in all department affairs.

attractiveness of the relatively quiet physics arena dropped dramatically. While the outside participants faced each other in new arenas, the most active participants in physics were some of the traditional leaders (full professors with administrative responsibilities), and the key issues have not been hierarchical but professional.

There was no dramatic break with "feudalism." The process observed has been one of continuous, incremental increases in the formal rights of new groups. The reorganization worked as a spark for this issue by first getting acceptance for the representation in department governance of faculty fully qualified professionally, but without chances of getting full professorships for budgetary reasons. Then the issue became participation for other reasons than professional qualification. The general drift of the process has been away from the "classical" institute model, but this drift is a long process—starting before the reorganization became a choice opportunity in the Department of Physics, and still under way. In the period observed it resulted in the elimination of most differences in formal authority between senior and junior faculty. With a minor exception all decisions were unanimous. The reorganization has not been a process where different alternatives have clashed; there never was a major confrontation with traditional leaders on one side and nonleaders on the other.

The Context of Events

In order to understand the development of reorganization in the Department of Physics and the way in which the expansion of participation rights to junior faculty in the department took place without seriously posing the issue of hierarchical conflict, we need to attend to the other things of potential relevance that were going on before and during the process of reorganization. The fact that the new organizational arrangement was made temporary, made it necessary to return to it each year. It became a choice opportunity and "garbage can" open during a period [when] a lot of things relevant for the physics department took place. Reorganization took place in a specific economic and professional context.

In Norway, as in most other industrialized countries, the decade from 1958–1968 was an exciting one for people in physics. A stream of students and money flowed into the field. The Norwegian situation is summarized in Table 14-2. We attend to the growth in new positions since most other resources in the Norwegian university system are closely related to the number of positions.

While the physics department as late as 1958 was very small—employing only 29 persons, in 1968 the number was 115 (in addition to this there were

Table 14-2

The growth in different categories of faculty and in technical-administrative staff in the Department of Physics, University of Oslo 1950-1970

Position	Year																				
	1950	'51	'52	'53	'54	'55	'56	'57	'58	'59	'60	'61	'62	'63	'64	'65	'66	'67	'68	'69	'70
Professor	3	3	3	3	3	3	3	3	3	3	5	7	7	7	7	7	7	8	8	8	8
Associate professor	2	2	2	2	2	2	2	2	2	2	2	2	5	6	6	6	6	6	6	11	11
Assistant professor	6	6	6	6	6	6	6	6	9	18	23	31	33	36	37	39	41	42	42	42	43
University scholars and assistants*	5	5	6	5	5	5	4	4	4	9	12	17	22	27	29	29	29	23	26	27	28
Faculty (total)	16	16	17	16	16	16	15	15	18	32	42	57	67	76	79	81	77	79	82	88	89
Technical-administrative staff	5	5	6	6	6	8	9	10	11	17	18	22	25	27	27	29	35	36	44	45	45
TOTAL	21	21	23	22	22	24	24	25	29	49	60	79	92	103	106	110	112	115	126	133	134

*Scholars and assistants paid through research councils and other grants excluded.

several fellows and assistants paid through outside sources, especially research councils). Although the number was still increasing, the growth had clearly started to level off by 1968. In 1967–68 the budget was 12–13 million Norwegian kroner (approximately 2.3 million dollars) per year. Close to 100 percent was public money. While some parts of the budget clearly were "bounded" (for example, in salaries which the department could not affect), the department was allocating resources that interested most of the employees. The extension of participation rights came, not when the department was static, not when it was growing very rapidly, but about the time growth leveled off.

Physics was the first academic discipline in Norway which had to make decisions connected to the question of survival of whole subfields. During the period studied it became clear that a small country like Norway could not develop all branches of physics. Much of the discussion and decision making became focused upon whether, and where, a particular field of physics should exist in Norway. Should Norway participate in large international projects? How large a percent of the total grants should be used outside the country? (Riste and Spangen 1968; The Central Committee of Norwegian Research 1968.)

Attitudes on these major choices were not likely to follow hierarchical status lines. On the contrary, they must have worked toward uniting different status groups within each field. Full professors, junior faculty, students, and technical-administrative staff within each project all had a common interest in getting equipment or fighting the proposals. We assume that different types of conflicts compete for the attention of decision makers (Schattschneider 1960). Hence, the emphasis on nonhierarchical conflicts has made it more difficult for hierarchical issues, like the participation issue, to get much attention. If this is true, the technology of the field, making teamwork necessary and producing a common interest in certain types of (expensive) equipment, can be expected to produce a tendency toward making nonleaders less interested in demanding formal participation and leaders less interested in resisting such demands. The groups demanding formal participation would primarily be those which were not established already and thus were not represented by a full professor, the fields in which the full professors were not viewed as very competent in defending the field, and fields that may gain by extending participation to junior faculty.

The lines of cleavages produced by the technology also became very relevant to the distribution of other resources, for instance new positions. After the leveling-off period had started, each project had to compete with each other in order to expand. These trends are consistent with the fact that after 1965 it became clear that representation would be based on the research activities going on. Under such circumstances potential participants will perceive the right to participate important in the discussion *between groups,* but may have problems finding people willing to represent the groups (viewing participation as a duty within the group). This expectation has been supported by the development in the Department of Physics. After the representation of the research groups had been solved through the reorganization, we find a tendency toward increasing difficulties in finding people willing to represent the groups and in general to take leadership.

The description of the context of the choice so far helps us understand why the issue of the representation of the hierarchical groups did not produce a high level of activation and conflict. Why then, was the question of participation attended to at all if it was not related to demands for a redistribution of the resources and burdens allocated through the department? We have suggested one reason why leaders might have pressed the participation issue: They expected help with the burden of administration and with the issues dividing the fields. In a similar fashion, we can observe that junior faculty may have become somewhat more interested in participation during the latter part of this period because of changes in their position. During the latter part of the decade of the 1960s, both the alternatives to formal participation and the prospects for assuming leadership roles in the future were shifting for junior members of the physics department.

Consider some alternatives to formal participation. We find considerable consensus on the view that the Department of Physics, long before the reorganization started, had allowed nonleader groups to participate informally. Until 1958 the size of the department was very moderate, making informal participation much easier. The rapid growth in the next five to six years clearly reduced the chances of informal influence.

Exit was also easy. The expansion and the "richness" in the period 1958–1963, where the faculty positions increased from eighteen to seventy-six, made it easy for most potential academic entrepreneurs to get the new positions they wanted [for] their fields. The problem in these years was to find people to hire. The policy was to hire only new graduates, and up to 60 percent of the graduates were recruited for university positions some years (Lindbekk 1967, p. 220). The tendency toward greater interest in participation came when it became clear that the growth had stagnated. The possibility of staying in the department[10] and compensating

---

[10]The possibility of leaving the university has not been viewed as very attractive by the faculty in physics. Most basic research takes place in the university context. The communication between scientists inside and outside the university has been modest, and the mobility between top positions inside and outside academe has been near nonexistent (Riste and Spangen 1968; Skoie, 1969).

nonparticipation in department governance through being financed from outside had been present, but this alternative had clearly been of declining importance since 1965 (Olsen 1971, table 5 and note 24). Most important, the Research Council for Scientific and Industrial Research [in] 1970 had withdrawn its support [of] nuclear physics and high energy physics. We should expect increasing size, low mobility, decreasing richness, and the reduction in outside sources to increase the interest in formal participation to the degree [that] such participation was viewed attractive.

Finally, we look upon the prospects for future leadership, assuming that a potential participant may view gaining participation through his group, and through leaving his group in the future, as competing alternatives.

In 1957 the ratio between, on the one hand, full professorships/associate professorships and, on the other, assistant professorships was 5:6 (.83). The heavy inflow of students, however, changed this ratio very strongly. The number of assistant professors with the highest teaching load (lektor) increased from two in 1957 to twenty-nine in 1965. During the first half of the 1960s the ratio of full professors/associate professors to assistant professors was .3. The prospects for getting leadership through the usual channels (scientific merit) decreased in the beginning of the 1960s. The prospects became even worse because the department had recruited only among new graduates, producing a cohort problem of a whole age-group reaching the level of professional qualification for full professorships at the same time. This happened around 1965. The department was not able to get new top positions, and the people filling the full professorships were still relatively young. In situations where participation in the government of the department is viewed as attractive, we should expect these tendencies to generate a demand for influence and participation.

In general we could expect these tendencies to produce an increasing interest in formal participation. Clearly, the organization has been distributing rewards attractive for both leaders and nonleaders. However, we suggest that the technology in the field has made hierarchical conflicts, with strong demands for participation from nonleaders and strong resistance against these demands from leaders, less likely. The ways in which the main rewards could be divided have not followed the hierarchical lines. On the contrary, they have followed the subdisciplines and made it more difficult for hierarchical conflicts to attract attention. The emphasis on the research groups reflects this tendency. Junior faculty will increase demands for participation but *not* as representatives of the class of junior faculty. There is no evidence indicating that the priorities of the department became changed after junior faculty, the technical-administrative staff, and the students were given participation rights.

So far this interpretation has been built upon the assumption that the technology of the field and the equipment used produced decisions where the potential outcomes had to be divided *across* more than *along* hierarchical groups. This view may now be expanded: Even where the technology of the field is not reflected in any material structure, the subdisciplines will strongly affect the ways decision outcomes can be divided and thus provide the most likely lines of cleavages and conflicts. Also, the impact of professional authority, the social inertia following a long training and socialization period, and so on will modify the effects and the importance of any change of organizational blueprints.

Some data on the differences between the departments that accepted the new organizational arrangements and those who keep the classical model support such an interpretation. In a university-wide survey (1968) there were no differences in attitudes toward formal participation in the two types of departments. Neither did the faculty in the "new" departments feel more influential or more satisfied than their colleagues in other departments (Olsen 1971, tables 21–23). All the fellows and assistants in the reorganized chemistry department, with *one* exception, answered that the leader of the subdepartment [made] the most important decisions. The same answer was given by 50 percent of the other nontenured faculty. Only 26 percent of the total faculty viewed the department council (which in the new "constitution" was made the highest governing body of the department) as the place where the most important decisions were made (Olsen 1968, p. 114). In the physics department one-third of the fellows and assistants perceived the leader of the subdepartment as the single most important decision-making unit. That was more than four years after the subdepartments had been formally abolished.

Finally, it should be obvious to anyone who has lived through the period of the 1960s in higher education that a part of the symbolic importance of participation rights came from considerations far beyond the confines of the University of Oslo and the Department of Physics. The external critique of university governance found the reorganization garbage can attractive here, as it did in many universities around the world.

First, the criticism [was] raised through several publications of the Organization for Economic Co-Operation and Development (OECD). Here the European institute organization dominated by one professor was attacked as outdated. The American department organization was described as more efficient, more able to innovate, and more able to make decisions and state priorities (see, for example, Ben-David 1968). The argumentation, for instance, of the dean closely followed these lines. Second, the criticism [was] raised through the international wave of students' demand for participation, both in Norway and more strongly in other countries. These demands by the students were closely related to central values as democracy and equality in the Norwegian community. In the physics department the values of being "progressive," "democratic," "egalitarian," and so forth could easily be accepted and the "problems" related to them "solved." A major argument of this study is that these values could be applauded, and the symbolic-expressive rewards collected, with very little effect upon the basic priorities of the department.[11] This is not to deny the importance of the symbolic commitment that was reflected. It was real. We have simply rediscovered the ancient observation that it is easier to be virtuous when there is some incentive.

Conclusion

The reorganization arrived as a choice opportunity at a point in time when an overwhelming majority in the physics department did not view organizational arrangements as problematic. Reorganization was stimulated by full professors who were administrative leaders, together with full-time administrators at the school and university level. In the first period they could move the process at a rapid pace. They did not have to search for or create a solution. The Department of Physics had become large, the office organization had been strengthened, and informal participation had been increased. The "solution" suggested by those taking the initiative was to acknowledge these changes, making them an ideal for arranging other departments. The two groups of administrators had different reasons for doing it, and they perceived different consequences following their initiative.

A key to the understanding of the process is the fact that physics was the first department at University of Oslo to open the question of reorganization as a choice opportunity. For some time this was the only garbage can available for such general issues as participation, power, and university governance. Because of this, it attracted participants who had little direct interest in the physics department. Physics was the only arena available for expressing their concerns. Major features of the process, such as the drop in outside participants during the second phase of the process, is related to the increase in the number of available garbage cans. In this period several departments considered the reorganization question as a choice opportunity. A university-wide committee on reorganization also became attractive for participants interested in the issues of participation

---

[11]In a study of the technical university in Copenhagen, Christensen (1971) shows that the senior and junior faculty have the same preferences concerning what the university should do and not do across a wide range of options.

and governance. The relative attractiveness of reorganization in the physics department as a garbage can clearly declined.

The new position of department secretary was a means for coping with a management and cost problem. Management costs were an issue throughout the period studied. They still are. The big department was celebrated at the same time as the leader of theoretical physics was allowed to break away (and reduce the size of the Department of Physics). The university administration had its desire for larger departments fulfilled. However, this took place through a general growth process, not through the uniting of smaller departments. As a consequence of the growth, the traditional opposition against "bureaucrats" in the departments disappeared from most parts of the university (Olsen 1968). There was no need for convincing departments of the advantages of having department secretaries.

While we find aspects of problem solving, problems were "solved" in unexpected ways. Furthermore, the reorganization initiative in both unintended and unexpected ways activated new groups. The leaders of the Association of Junior Faculty arrived too late to have their problems connected decisively to the reorganization garbage can. The reorganization of physics, however, became a catalyst for a debate where important differences in the situation of junior faculty across different departments were clarified. Especially, it became evident that status, power, and participation issues were less salient in the Department of Physics than in many other departments. When new choice opportunities arrived, these issues and these participants shifted their attention away from physics.

A debate was started also inside the Department of Physics. Since the new organizational arrangements were announced as preliminary, the garbage can was kept open for several years. The context of the department changed. In particular, as alternatives for junior faculty declined, they became more interested in participation. The change from rapid growth to leveling off also changed the senior faculty's focus of attention from problems of efficiency to problems of stating priorities. This shift was not related to a change in the dominant coalition of the department. The process was managed by the same leaders during the whole period. The most important aspect of the process was, however, that both senior and junior faculty came to the conclusion that the dominant cleavage in interests divided different research groups, not different status groups. This recognition produced a decision-making system with representation based on the research groups.

The reorganization process in physics also helped encourage the highest governing body of the university (the Collegium) to attend to these issues. The immediate impact of this body was insignificant, except for the (important) fact that they made the new arrangements tentative and therefore kept the garbage can open. But in the Collegium, as elsewhere in the university, a process of interpretation was started. It culminated in the establishment of a general reorganization committee, which in the next turn provided an area for the senior faculty in physics to interpret what had taken part in the physics department.

While our data indicate that the rewriting of the constitution had only moderate effects upon the everyday life of the Department of Physics, the results were presented publicly in terms of a victory for increased participation and "democracy." This interpretation has to be related to the definitions of problems and solutions presented from outside, especially the OECD discussion and the general student movement. Thus, in keeping with ancient tradition, the interpretations construed the past in terms of the virtues of the present.

References

Ben-David, J. *Fundamental Research and the Universities.* Paris: OECD, 1968.

The Central Committee for Norwegian Research. "Grunnforskning i fysikk i Norge," *Hovedkomiteen for norsk forskning.* Oslo: Melding nr. 3, 1968.

Christensen, Soren. *Institut og laboratorieorganisation pa Danmarks Tekniske Hojskole.* Mimeographed. Copenhagen, 1971.

Consolazio, W.V. "Dilemma of Academic Biology in Europe." *Science* 1961.

Lindbekk, Tore. *Mobilitets- og stillingsstrukturer tre akademiske profesjoner, 1910-63.* Oslo: Universitetsforlaget, 1967.

March, J.G., and J.P. Olsen. *Ambiguity and Choice in Organizations.* Bergen, Norway: Universitetsforlaget, 1976.

Mosher, Frederick, ed. "Government Reorganizations, Cases and Commentary." Indianapolis: The Inter-University Case Program, 1967.

Olsen, J.P. "Universitetet—En organisasjon i endring," Mimeographed. Oslo, 1968.

————. "Reorganization of Formal Authority in a Norwegian University." Mimeographed. Bergen, Norway, 1971.

Riste, T., and E. Spangen. *Norsk fysikk. Omfang, struktur og vekst.* Oslo: Universitetsforlaget, 1968.

Schattschneider, E.E. *The Semi-Sovereign People.* New York: Holt, Rinehart and Winston, 1960.

Skoie, Hans. "The Problems of a Small Scientific Commmunity: The Norwegian Case." *Minerva* 7: 3 (Spring 1969).

Wetlesen, T. Schou. "Universitetsbudsjettering." Mineographed. Oslo, 1967.

15

Participation, Deadlines, and Choice

Stephen Weiner

Introduction

Organizational life within urban school districts in the United States is currently characterized by a heavy flow of problems and insistent demands that problems be resolved. In response to these conditions, conventional administrative theory tends to emphasize the identification of clear and consistent organizational goals and the creation of long-range plans as major ingredients in the remedy for the managerial woes of urban school districts. Above all, we are often informed, "management by crisis" must be avoided.

Yet, attempts to establish goals for urban school districts inevitably arrive at one of two destinations. On the one hand, goals may be highly abstract and vague and, thus, yield no guidance for implementation. On the other hand, goals may turn out to be specific but yet be ripped asunder and made inoperable by contending factions within the organization's political process. Similarly, efforts in such districts to create long-term plans either are never initiated or, if begun, are likely to be ignored. If goal setting and long-range planning are impossible within some organizations, then the presence of crises may be an unavoidable aspect of decision making.

Urban school districts exhibit the basic characteristics of organized anarchy—vague and inconsistent goals, unclear technology, and fluid

Reprinted, by permission, from James G. March and Johan P. Olsen, *Ambiguity and Choice in Organizations* (Bergen, Norway: Universitetsforlaget, 1976), pp. 225–49.

participation. Therefore, we will view decisions in such a context as a result of the confluence of four streams: choice opportunities, solutions, problems, and participant energies (Cohen, March, and Olsen 1972). In particular, our aim is to detect how these streams interact under crisis or deadline conditions.

A keener understanding of organizational response to deadlines should prove useful not only in providing retrospective explanations of the nature of decisions reached under deadline conditions, but also in providing guidance to individuals who are interested in the creative use of deadlines to affect participation in organizational choices and, hopefully, to affect decisions themselves.

There can be no question that life in a school district prone to crisis is likely to erode seriously the energy of even the most dedicated leader. However, it may also be true that leadership within such organizations is possible. The very existence of crises, and their accompanying deadlines, can create useful opportunities to move an organization in a direction deemed desirable by its leaders.

The existing theory of organized anarchies does not require that decisions be reached or problems solved by a specified time. By implication, the theory holds that such requirements are neither generated within the organization nor imposed by the organization's environment. The organization simply works on decisions until they are made.

However, when one observes the actual operation of organizations, it becomes evident that organizational environments are not always indifferent as to whether organizations reach a given decision or resolve certain problems. Environmental impatience, at least sometimes, results in deadlines being imposed upon the organization. Such deadlines serve as a cue to direct attention to those choices and problems subject to a deadline and divert attention away from choices and problems unaffected by deadlines.

Where an organization's goals are ambiguous, the nature of its processes in transforming inputs into outputs are unclear, and the probable reactions of its environment to a given decision are difficult to anticipate, it becomes difficult to determine which choices are "important" and which are "unimportant." In such organizational settings deadlines for decisions may provide a convenient substitute set of signals that enable decision makers to select current choice opportunities and problems that "deserve" immediate attention.

Like the choice opportunities to which they are applied, deadlines may be ambiguous for two reasons:

1. Deadlines may be ambiguous with regard to the problems that must be considered in connection with a given choice.

2. Deadlines may be ambiguous with regard to the date of the deadline. The effectiveness of deadlines as a cue for attracting the attention of organizational participants is drastically reduced by uncertainties associated with the date of the deadline or the firmness of the date.

To be maximally effective as an attention cue the deadline must not only be certain, it must also be coercive. That is, compliance with a deadline is based upon incentives or sanctions involved in the deadline situation. The incentive may be a grant of resources and the sanctions may include denial of resources, public harassment for failure to comply, or the threat of imposing a decision in which the affected organization has not been consulted.

Deadlines are not an unusual feature of organizational life. Some deadlines are imposed by elements of the organization's environment; others may be created within the organization. Some deadlines are familiar and the organization's response to them may become quite routine. Other deadlines may be unanticipated by most, if not all, of the participants in a given organization. In this chapter we are concerned with the effects of deadlines that are both nonroutine and are imposed externally.

The Case Study

We wish to inquire into the impact of a deadline upon participation rate and the flow of problems and solutions in an organizational decision-making situation. The inquiry is conducted within the context of the decision-making process within the San Francisco Unified School District concerning racial desegregation of the city's elementary schools. The history of this decision-making process permits us to examine the flow of problems, solutions, and participant energy both before and after a deadline was imposed on the choice process.

The Organizational Setting

The San Francisco Unified School District was founded more than one hundred years ago. It is currently responsible for the schooling of more than eighty thousand children, between kindergarten and the twelfth grade, within the city of San Francisco.

The highest policymaking body within the district is the board of education. At the time of the study described in this chapter, the board was composed of seven members appointed by the mayor of San Francisco.[1]

---

[1] In November 1971 the voters in San Francisco approved an amendment to the city Charter creating an elective school board. The new board was elected in June 1972 and took office in August 1972.

The superintendent of schools is the chief executive officer of the district and is hired by the board of education. Three associate superintendents (business, administration, and instruction) report to the Superintendent. In turn, eight assistant superintendents report to one of the associate superintendents. The twelve individuals who occupy the positions of superintendent, associate superintendent, and assistant superintendent comprise the "top" decision-making group within the district's administrative hierarchy.

The district is a highly labor-intensive enterprise. During the 1971-72 fiscal year personnel costs represented approximately 85 percent of the organization's $116 million operating budget.

In recent years the ethnic composition of the district's student body has been undergoing a significant change.

Table 15-1

Ethnic composition of San Francisco public school enrollment

	1966 Percent	1970* Percent	1971* Percent	Change 1966–71 Percent
Black	26.3	28.3	30.0	+ 3.7
Spanish surname	12.1	13.3	13.8	+ 1.7
Chinese	13.6	14.9	13.9	+ 0.3
Filipino	2.2	4.1	5.9	+ 3.7
Japanese	1.7	1.8	1.8	+ 0.1
Korean	0.1	0.3	0.3	+ 0.2
American Indian	0.2	0.3	0.3	+ 0.1
Other nonwhite	1.3	1.9	2.2	+ 0.9
Other white	42.4	35.1	31.9	-10.5
Total enrollment	91,359	87,363	80,896	-11.4

*1970 statistics reflect enrollment before city-wide desegregation of elementary schools. 1971 statistics reflect enrollment after city-wide desegregation of elementary schools.

During the five-year period between 1966 and 1971 the single most dramatic change in student enrollment was the decline of white enrollment from 42.4 percent to 31.9 percent. The declining proportion of enrollment represented by whites and the shrinking total enrollment means that the number of white students in the district, which stood at 38,774 in 1966, had declined to 25,805 in 1971 for an overall reduction of 33 percent in white enrollment in only five years.

As we shall see, the "flight" of white students from the San Francisco public schools, both through enrollment of children in private and parochial schools and the movement of families with school age children out of the city, proved to be a factor which influenced the nature of the desegregation plan which was ultimately adopted.

Changes in the ethnic composition of the district's administrative and teaching staff have failed to keep pace with changes in student enrollment. As of 1971, approximately 80 percent of the administrative and teaching staff [were] white, 10 percent [were] black, and the other 10 percent were drawn from other minority groups.

Conflict Over Desegregation

Throughout the decade of the 1960s desegregation of the district's student body represented the most controversial issue confronting the organization.

Although the district maintained no official policy requiring segregation of the races, the nature of residential patterns within the city meant that black students were largely concentrated in the Western Addition, Hunters Point, and Ocean View–Merced Heights–Ingleside areas; Latin or Spanish surname students largely attended schools in the Mission district and Chinese students were to be found primarily in schools serving the Chinatown area.

In 1961 several civil rights groups initiated demands that the district conduct a count of the students of various racial and ethnic groups in the schools so that the precise extent of segregation could be determined. In addition, these groups, including the National Association for the Advancement of Colored People (NAACP), asked that a citizens committee be established by the board of education to consider steps that might be taken to desegregate the schools. These suggestions were largely ignored by the board and the superintendent, Dr. Harold Spears.

Under growing pressure the board finally released a racial census of the schools in 1965. In 1966 the board asked the Stanford Research Institute to examine alternative means of desegregating the schools.

Stanford Research Institute completed its work in 1967 and suggested twelve alternative desegregation plans. Among the alternatives were plans that provided for the "cross-town bussing" of white students in western San Francisco into black ghetto areas in eastern San Francisco. Stanford Research Institute also released the results of a survey of the San Francisco teaching staff that showed 51 percent of the teachers favoring retention of the neighborhood school system regardless of that system's implications for racial balance. Only 17 percent of the teachers favored bussing as a means of relieving racial imbalance.

In 1967 and 1968 civil rights advocates succeeded in persuading the mayor of San Francisco, John Shelley, to appoint several new members [to] the board of education who favored racial desegregation. During this period Dr. Spears retired and the board appointed Dr. Robert Jenkins, an educator well known for his previous efforts on behalf of school integration in other districts.

Early in 1968 Dr. Jenkins submitted recommendations on desegregation which were based, in part, on the Stanford Research Institute's proposals. Jenkins advocated the desegregation of some schools along with a simultaneous increase in resources and special programs for integrated schools, a concept he termed "education equality-quality."

These proposals were submitted to a series of public forums in the district in early 1968. These forums were the most heavily attended meetings in the history of the district with attendance exceeding 1,000 in several cases. The meetings produced a tumultuous outpouring of sentiment opposed to any plan involving cross-town bussing. Chastened by the public opposition, the board and Jenkins decided to create a citizens committee in the hope that a more acceptable plan could be devised.

During a year of deliberation the resulting citizens committee decided to propose a modified plan to create two elementary school "complexes" in the northwest portion of the city. The complex plan involved the enlargement of neighborhood school attendance areas and the initiation of localized bussing to integrate the schools in two subareas of the city, the Richmond and the Park-South. Only 20 percent of the city's elementary school students were to be involved. In order to make the plan more attractive, the expenditure of additional money on the affected schools was also proposed. Neither the all-white Sunset district, the center of opposition of bussing, nor the poorest ghetto area, Hunters Point, were involved.

The board of education withstood an onslaught of antibussing sentiment and authorized the initiation of the Richmond Complex for September 1971. However, the gradual approach to integration angered the NAACP and, in the summer of 1970, that organization filed suit in the United States District Court asking for the immediate desegregation of all 102 elementary schools in San Francisco.

The Judge's Warning and District Response

In September 1970 United States District Judge Stanley Weigel announced that the NAACP had submitted sufficient evidence to persuade him that the district had committed official acts that helped to maintain the segregation of black children in the elementary schools of the city. However, he added that unresolved cases then before the United States Supreme Court raised questions as to whether bussing was a permissible tool available to the courts to remedy school segregation. Weigel concluded that he would issue no order on behalf of desegregation until the Supreme

Court acted on the pending cases. He added a warning that if the Supreme Court authorized the use of bussing he would require the desegregation of all elementary schools in San Francisco by September 1971. Weigel urged the district to commence planning at once so that such an order could be implemented.

The district failed to respond to the judge's request for an immediate beginning of desegregation planning. Four factors contributed to this lack of response.

First, although the district's steps toward desegregation had won the plaudits of some, they had also brought the wrath of many. Planning for additional desegregation held little promise of increasing public support for the schools.

Second, the district had initiated the Richmond Complex in the same month that Judge Weigel had issued his warning. The energies of the small corps of district staff that was both supportive of integration and skilled in the processes necessary to implement it were already fully absorbed in the complex and the daily problems inherent in its first weeks of operation. Similarly, the energy of citizens who had worked for integration were devoted to the complex.

Third, the district, which in past years had benefited from healthy annual increases in property tax revenue, now found that increases in costs were outrunning increases in revenue. For the first time since the depression, the district faced a very tight budget. Money could not be easily diverted into desegregation planning, especially since the fiscal year had already begun.

Fourth, Superintendent Robert Jenkins had resigned in the summer of 1970 and had been replaced by Dr. Thomas A. Shaheen. Shaheen had been in office for less than sixty days when Weigel made his announcement. Although personally committed to desegregation, Shaheen was busy with the myriad tasks inherent in assuming leadership in a large and complex organization.

In December 1970 civil rights groups began to direct their attention to the district's lack of response to Weigel's warning. At a December board meeting representatives of thirteen civil rights groups demanded the immediate creation of a new citizens committee to plan district-wide desegregation. The board directed Shaheen to prepare recommendations for action in January.

Unknown to the integration advocates the district's business office had begun to respond to at least one requirement for desegregation planning. The district did not have any data that linked the residence of students to their ethnic group. Nor did the district have the experience within their data processing office to exploit their computer facilities in a desegregation planning process. Anxious to use desegregation planning as a means to strengthen their capability to collect and analyze diverse types of data for a variety of planning purposes, the district hired a computer and planning consultant, David Bradwell. But the response of the business office was an exception. Elsewhere in the district the judge's statement had failed to produce new activity.

The superintendent's reply to the board's December directive was constrained by three important factors. The district's Human Relations Office, created in 1963 as a concession to integration demands, did not have a reputation as an aggressive advocate for desegregation. There was considerable doubt that this existing entity could be used to mount a city-wide integration plan. The only alternative was the creation of a new office. At the same time, experience in the Richmond Complex had demonstrated the need to involve central office staff, school site staff and citizens in the planning effort. There was no simple blueprint indicating how this might be accomplished. Finally, as already noted, the district had little slack in the budget and the money for planning efforts had to be taken from the carefully husbanded undistributed reserve fund.

In late December, after informal consultation with the board, Shaheen decided to appoint Donald Johnson, planning officer for the Richmond Complex, as director of desegregation, a new position. Throughout the balance of the fiscal year Johnson's only full-time staff support was one secretary. Aside from office expenses, all of the other money in Johnson's new budget went to defray expenses in the separate data processing office where new student files had to be created and new computer programs written, and to pay for Bradwell's services.

Shaheen also recommended the creation of three committees to work with Johnson. The first, the Staff Committee, was appointed by the various divisions of the central office.

Examination of the minutes of the Staff Committee's meetings reveals that this committee fully expected to be the key architect of the desegregation plan. Such an expectation was consistent with past practice in the district where major policy recommendations were brought to the board as a result of consultation in the central office with little or no input from school site administrators, teachers, parents, or community groups.

Although each member of the Staff Committee was ostensibly appointed to work on desegregation on a full-time basis, in fact each staff member was not relieved of his other duties. Partly because of the press of other duties, the Staff Committee proved to be a group that merely met periodically to hear reports from the data processing office and Bradwell. Due to its inactivity it had no discernible impact on the outcome of the planning process.

The second group, the Certificated Staff Committee, was composed of teachers and school site administrators. Money was provided to pay for substitutes for these individuals only on one afternoon per week.

Members of the Certificated Staff Committee were not well known to one another before appointment to this group. They were selected from different schools in the district. The geographical separation of the members and the lack of preexisting ties among the membership led to an absence of informal consultation between their regularly scheduled meetings. After an initial spurt of weekly meetings, the Certificated Staff Committee met less and less frequently until shortly before the deadline. This committee proved to be even more peripheral to the planning process than did the Staff Committee.

The lack of effective participation from the Certificated Staff Committee may have been due in part to a policy adopted by the Citizens Advisory Committee. The Citizens Advisory Committee (CAC) invited members of the Certificated Staff Committee to become active on CAC committees. Thus, the handful of Certificated Staff members with time and energy to expend were diverted into CAC meetings and had correspondingly less time for meetings of the Certificated Staff.

The third group, the Citizens Advisory Committee, became the prime instrument in the decision-making process. Composed of sixty-seven citizens appointed by members of the board of education, the CAC began its formal meetings later than either of the other two committees. A further delay occurred when the CAC voted during its second meeting to dissolve itself on the grounds that its ethnic composition did not reflect the ethnic composition of the district's student enrollment in that whites were "overrepresented" on the committee.

In mid March of 1971 the CAC was able to elect officers and to establish subcommittees.

Deadline and Response

On April 28, 1971, Judge Weigel ordered both the district and the NAACP to prepare separate plans for the desegregation of elementary school students in San Francisco. The judge's order came one week after the United States Supreme Court had approved bussing as one means to remedy official acts of discrimination against children from racial minority groups. The judge set June 10, 1971, as the deadline for submission of both plans.[2]

In his order the judge also required that the plans to be submitted to him must also outline steps to relieve segregation in the school staffs. However, the judge declined to set forth a numerical formula that would define desegregation of the schools.

Thus, as often is the case in governmental organizations, the district was directed to "do something" about segregation in the absence of any clear definition of what would constitute a satisfactory solution. The ambiguous order from the judge left a good deal of flexibility to the district's internal decision-making processes both in terms of defining the problems to be considered and in constructing a solution to those problems.

Prior to the judicially imposed deadline the response of the district and its three committees had been largely one of delay and indecision. The one exception to this characterization was the initial data collection efforts of the data processing office.

The response to the deadline included substantial changes in the flow of participation, the generation of solutions and the flow of problems.

---

[2] Johan Olsen (1972) has pointed out that Judge Weigel was a unique participant in the planning process inasmuch as he was able to substantially affect the decision merely by issuing written orders. The judge did not have to attend any meetings during the choice process nor did he have to expend substantial energy as did other participants who affected the final outcome.

The judge's influential position depended upon the acceptance of his authority by the other participants. With the exception of Chinatown residents, none of the groups opposed to bussing even suggested that the judge's order be disobeyed.

Acceptance of the judge's order was dependent upon socialization of the citizenry into the American system of law. Residents of Chinatown, many of them recent immigrants from Hong Kong, did not accept the judge's authority and openly demanded that Weigel simply be ignored.

The order came as a welcome relief to long-time advocates of school desegregation in San Francisco. After a decade of controversy, these advocates finally had the strong shield of the federal judiciary behind which they could plan a city-wide integration plan.

It is interesting to note that the judge himself became a victim of the deadline he set. When the district and NAACP plans were submitted to the Court in June 1971 the judge admitted that he was overwhelmed by the details and complexity of the plans. However, the judge did not have the time to carefully review each plan in detail because of the self-imposed necessity to implement the plans in September.

Flow of Participation

The imposition of the deadline caused an immediate increase in the amount of time that an active participant in decision making had to expend on the choice process.

One measure of the increase in time expenditure is the fact that between February 16, 1971, the date of the first meeting of the Citizens Advisory Committee, and April 28, 1971, the date that the deadline was set, there were twenty-five meetings of the full committee or its subcommittees. In the predeadline period the Citizens Committee and its subcommittees thus averaged a meeting every third day. Between April 28 and June 2, the day that the Citizens Committee completed work on the plan, there was a total of forty-five committee or subcommittee meetings, for an average of more than one meeting per day.

A major feature of participant reaction to the deadline was that the participation rate of a small group increased dramatically, whereas the participation rate of most members either remained stable or declined.

Table 15-2

**Rates of participation by CAC members (Hours/month)
before and after imposition of the deadline**

| | Participants | | | | |
Month	Less than 20 hrs./mo.	20–40 hrs./mo.	40–60 hrs./mo.	60–80 hrs./mo.	More than 80 hrs./mo.
March (predeadline)	64	0	2	1	0
April (predeadline)	57	3	1	5	1
May (postdeadline)	52	5	1	2	7

The data in Table 15-2 indicates that one effect of the deadline was to widen the gap in participation rates between the highly active minority and the largely passive majority within the Citizens Advisory Committee.

As noted earlier, the Citizens Committee had voluntarily disbanded in February so that the board of education might appoint additional minority members to eliminate overrepresentation by whites on the committee. The imposition of the deadline, however, foreclosed full participation in the decision making by those who were unable because of work or other commitments to expand their rate of participation. Thus, the deadline led to a domination of the decision-making process by middle- and upper-class white women, who had available time during the day because they were not employed and could arrange care for their children, and by other participants whose employers permitted them to devote daytime hours to the decision-making process.[3] Table 15-3 compares the ethnic composition of the Citizens Advisory Committee, the thirty-nine CAC members present when the final plan was adopted on June 1, 1971, and the ethnic composition of the most active twelve members of the committee, as judged by a sample of committee members and measured by meeting attendance data:

Table 15-3

Ethnic composition of the Citizens Committee and the most active twelve members of the committee

| | Percentage | | |
	Full committee	June 1 vote	Active members
White	37.0	51.2	66.7
Black	25.5	17.9	0.0
Chinese	10.5	12.8	8.3
Latin	13.5	5.2	16.6
Japanese	3.0	5.2	0.0
Filipino	6.0	5.2	8.3
Korean	1.5	2.6	0.0
Samoan	1.5	0.0	0.0
American Indian	1.5	0.0	0.0
	100.0	100.1	99.9

Interviews with members of the committee, representing a cross-section of activity levels, indicate that the expansion of energy expenditures was governed by the time available to the individual participant (and hence the nature of competing demands upon the participant's time); whether the individual participant possessed knowledge necessary to participate in the complex mapping process inherent in desegregation planning; and by the participant's attitude toward desegregation and bussing.

---

[3] Interviews with the white women who dominated the planning process indicate that their participation was motivated not only by a desire to participate in decisions that affected the future school assignment of their own children and by an ideological commitment to civil rights but also by a desire to exercise untapped organizational skills. For many of these women, participation in school district affairs became an outlet for existing personal competencies that ranged beyond the skills required of a homemaker and wife.

Interviews with black members of the committee who were not active participants revealed that their lack of participation was due primarily to competing demands for their time. Black CAC members were in sympathy with the objective of desegregating the schools, including bussing. Some black members who were not active declared that it was not necessary for them to participate because the CAC "was in good (white integrationist) hands." Some black interviewees also expressed a measure of discomfort at participating because members of CAC had a detailed grasp of desegregation planning, and thus were far more knowledgeable or because the blacks were not familiar with parliamentary procedure.

On the other hand, interviews with Latin members of the committee who were not active participants indicated that their lack of participation was due both to competing demands for their time as well as a basic hostility to the idea of bussing children to desegregate the schools.

Several Latin interviewees said that they sensed that the CAC was dominated by advocates of bussing and that the needs of Latin children, especially the need for bilingual instruction, would not be addressed by the CAC.[4] Thus, inactivity by Latins on the CAC was due, in part, to a desire to deprive the probussing CAC of the "legitimacy" it might have gained had Latins participated more vigorously.[5] Similarly, the two inactive Chinese members of the CAC were individuals who actively participated in antibussing protests.

The theory of organized anarchies predicts that participation will be affected by the time requirements of a particular choice opportunity and by the relative attractiveness of other choice opportunities for individual participants. However, the theory does not call attention to the impact upon participation rates that arises from individual attitudes concerning the legitimacy of the decision that may emerge from the choice process.

Interviews with members of the board, the superintendent, associate superintendents, assistant superintendents, and members of CAC, and

---

[4] In fact, CAC had established an active bilingual subcommittee that made strong recommendations for the expansion of the school district's bilingual program, including added services for Latin students. Of the total Latin delegation of nine members on CAC only two Puerto Rican women were active. Both of these women supported desegregation.

[5] Dahl (1964) discusses this legitimacy aspect at some length. However, while a participant may express his negative feelings by leaving the choice, he may also remain and use the choice as an opportunity for expressing his negative feelings. That is, he may know that he cannot affect the immediate, substantive outcome, but assume that, through expressive behavior, he may affect the conditions under which future choices will be made (Olsen 1972).

examination of internal memoranda written by top district officials during the period [from] September 1970 [to] June 1971 indicate that none of the district's top officials devoted any significant amount of time to directing or influencing the planning for desegregation during this period.

Based upon the organization's experience of the prior ten years it was obvious that the nature of the final plan for district-wide desegregation of fifty thousand elementary school children would have a profound impact upon the future of the district. How do we account for the lack of attention by top decision makers to this supremely important decision-making process?

We speculate that three elements contributed to this surprising inattention to desegregation.

First, as already noted, desegregation was a policy question fraught with complexity and in which the possibility of adverse public reaction existed at every step. It was not an arena into which a prudent district official would voluntarily cast himself.

Second, although the judge's warning was clear, the final issuance of a desegregation order was contingent upon future decisions of the Supreme Court. Those decisions were not rendered until the latter part of April 1971. Until that time it was entirely possible that energy devoted to district-wide desegregation planning could be obviated by a stroke of the Supreme Court's pen.

Third, and we believe this reason is central, the district was beset by a veritable nightmare of other crises and catastrophes between September 1970 and June 1971. No sketch of these events can adequately portray the turmoil they caused. Here, however, are the major troubles and decisions which the district faced between September 1970 and June 1971:

1. In September 1970 teachers and parents boycotted the Sir Francis Drake school in Hunters Point because the school was in an acute state of disrepair. The boycott lasted ten days and ended after the superintendent agreed that a male, black principal would be hired at the school.

2. In October over 600 teachers appeared at a meeting of the board of education to protest the district's alleged failure to implement "quality" educational programs in the Richmond Complex. This protest followed a petition, signed by 1,700 teachers and administrators, which condemned "large class sizes" and other ills in the schools.

3. In October students and teachers boycotted classes at Woodrow Wilson High School after a Samoan student had been shot at the predominantly black school.

4. In November the district's bond issue designed to finance the rebuilding of schools in Hunters Point was defeated by the voters.
5. An antibussing group initiated a school boycott in the Richmond Complex in November.
6. In December the major Latin-American organization in the city, the Mission Coalition, sued the district for "short-changing" thirteen schools in the Mission District.
7. In the same month two hundred angry teachers walked out of a board meeting after the board had refused to promise to rehire sixty-four of the teachers for the next semester.
8. In December the board was informed that it would have to cancel plans to build either the Diamond Heights High School or Cabrillo Elementary School unless it could appropriate an additional $1.5 million for construction. These schools had been part of a 1964 bond issue and it had taken six years to get the projects out to bid. In the interim construction costs had inflated tremendously.
9. In January 1971 one hundred members of the Elementary School Administrators Association attended a meeting to discuss affiliation with the Teamsters Union. This meeting was held in the aftermath of debate over state legislation to deprive San Francisco school administrators of tenure in their jobs. San Francisco is the only school district in California that provides tenure for school administrators.
10. In January the board learned they faced a $6.7 million deficit in their budget for the next fiscal year. This constituted the most severe financial crisis since the Depression.
11. In the same month hundreds of students picketed and boycotted at several schools to protest the transfer of popular administrators due to the operation of the tenure system.
12. In February the superintendent presented a plan to decentralize the district into three administrative areas. The board refused to adopt the plan.
13. In February the Black Student Union began a protest at Balboa High School. Investigators reported no toilet paper, towels, or soap in the boy's restrooms; absence of hot water in the girl's showers; leakage of water from the showers on to cafeteria tables; and replacement of windows with plywood. Rehabilitation costs were estimated at $3.8 million.
14. In the same month State Supreme Court Justice Mosk charged that 40 percent of the Chinese-speaking students in San Francisco weren't receiving instruction in the English language in San Francisco schools.
15. In March the superintendent proposed the demotion of more than

half of the school administrators in the district. The board voted to demote only white administrators, exempting racial minorities from the plan.

16. In March the American Federation of Teachers began a strike affecting all schools in the city. The local chapter of the California Teachers Association later joined in the strike. The walkout extended into April.

17. In April the superintendent presented his budget. Due to the lack of new revenue the budget proposed that 340 teaching positions be left vacant as a result of attrition and urged the elimination of 120 "relief" teachers currently employed so that other teachers could have a preparation period during the school day. As a result of the strike settlement a 5 percent increase in school taxes was proposed.

18. In the same month a leading structural engineer reported that a major earthquake would lead to disaster in the schools. An associate superintendent announced that he would recommend immediate closing of five of sixty-three unsafe schools.

19. In late April Federal Judge Weigel ruled that the district had less than fifty days to submit a plan for the complete desegregation of 102 elementary schools.

20. In May school administrators sued to retain their jobs and state hearings on the demotions were begun.

21. In late May a petition drive was opened to replace the appointed school board with an elected body.

Thus, before the imposition of the deadline board members and top administrative officials were occupied with a heavy flow of other problems and choices. And, as noted above, before the imposition of the deadline some uncertainty existed as to the necessity for devising a city-wide desegregation plan.

Once the deadline was established the flow of competing problems persisted. In addition, a top administrative official who wished to inject himself into the desegregation planning process would have found himself in the midst of a complex and time-consuming decision-making process that was already the subject of attention by highly active members of the CAC who had developed a sense of ownership concerning the desegregation planning process.[6]

---

[6] Administrative participation may have also been discouraged by the fact that CAC members had been appointed by the board. "Undue interference" with the citizens by top administrators might have led to citizen complaints to individual board members. Generally speaking, however, members of CAC expressed disappointment that they saw so little of the top administrators during the planning process.

The experience in San Francisco of federal consultants on desegregation is instructive in terms of the difficulty of gaining entrance to the decision-making process under deadline conditions. In response to the San Francisco superintendent's request to the United States Office of Education for assistance with desegregation, USOE dispatched a team [of] consultants in late May 1971. These consultants attempted to become involved in the planning process but were ignored by the local school staff and the CAC. Apparently, the federal consultants failed to gain entrance because of the shortness of the time deadline and the time commitments of the existing participants did not permit diversion of energy to brief the consultants on prior developments. In addition, the past experience of the federal consultants in the South disposed them to advocate a desegregation plan that required the bussing of children across the city. Such an approach was deemed unacceptable by the active CAC members. The experience of the federal consultants was a duplicate of the fate met by a consultant from the California Department of Education who had been dispatched to San Francisco earlier in May.

Generation of Solutions

Imposition of the deadline led to the generation of more than two dozen different plans to desegregate the schools. These plans were generated in May 1971 by a self-selected group of participants termed the "Round the Clock" group. This group was present during the day and evening at the school district headquarters during May. Although some members of the district staff were a part of this group, the majority of members were drawn from the Citizens Committee. Again, the active citizens who dominated this process were largely drawn from the ranks of white women on the full committee. Several of these women brought long experience in the politics of desegregation planning to their task in May. In addition, their intensive participation in the Round the Clock group sharpened their knowledge of the distribution of various ethnic groups throughout the city and afforded them detailed knowledge of the subtle differences among the many plans then being suggested. The overwhelming competence of these women in the planning process discouraged participation by others, particularly from minority groups, who felt themselves at a severe relative disadvantage in their knowledge of the complexities of planning for desegregation.

Unlike the professional planners on the district staff who were immobilized by lack of data and formal criteria for a plan, the white women were able to devise zonal maps for desegregation based upon their impressionistic grasp of ethnic composition and attitudes toward bussing in various San Francisco neighborhoods.

The generation of alternative plans was guided by only one formal criterion for desegregation adopted by the Citizens Committee five days after the deadline was imposed. This standard, originally suggested by the State Department of Education, defined a school as desegregated if the proportion of any ethnic group within that school was within 15 percent of the proportion of that ethnic group within the school enrollment of the entire district.[7] This criterion for planning was adopted before its full implications for a student assignment plan were understood. Adoption of the state guideline was later to be regretted by some members of the committee because it foreclosed the possibility of adopting a plan that might have been met with greater acceptance among vocal opponents of bussing in the Chinatown area.

In addition to the state guidelines the other major premises that shaped the planning process resulted from the "lessons" of the recent history of desegregation conflict as perceived by the active white women on CAC.

The first lesson was that a citizens committee was an effective device for formulating desegregation plans. Belief in the effectiveness of using citizens committees was based largely on the success of the earlier citizens committee in promoting "school complexes."

The second lesson was that a desegregation plan that appeared to require cross-town bussing would prove to be politically unacceptable and would only stimulate additional white flight from the schools. This lesson was accepted by most of the active white women on the CAC as a result of their experience at the 1968 public forums. As noted earlier, thousands of San Franciscans attended these emotional rallies of resistance to cross-town bussing. Several individuals had been subjected to physical harassment and assault at these meetings and the result was the intimidation of integration advocates at the forums. Thereafter, integrationists in San Francisco were convinced that advocacy of cross-town bussing could only aggravate racial tensions and defeat any form of desegregation.

As a result of the 15 percent guidelines and avoidance of cross-town bussing, the final "Horseshoe" plan adopted by the committee on June 1, 1971, emphasized the creation of seven zones in the city in an effort to minimize cross-town bussing and to give the public the impression that the integration plan was merely enlarging the boundaries of neighborhood school attendance areas. In addition, the Horseshoe plan made only token

---

[7] This state "guideline" was devised for use in school districts with two ethnic groups—white and black. It proved to be poorly suited to the multi-ethnic character of school enrollment in San Francisco. For example, using this guideline, a San Francisco elementary school with 40 percent black enrollment was considered desegregated while a school with 40 percent Chinese enrollment was considered to be segregated.

alternations in the two complex areas that had already been established. Protection of the complexes was a product both of strong representation on the committee by residents of the complexes and a persistent lobbying campaign by parents and staff members within the complexes. Thus, the Horseshoe plan strongly reflected the lessons of experience learned by desegregation advocates in the prior ten years.

Bradwell, the state and federal consultants, and several members of the district's professional staff advanced an alternative plan that would have subdivided the city into only three zones. The alternative, called "Tri-Star," violated the "lessons of experience" by appearing to require longer bus rides and by requiring the mixture of children from the centers of opposition to bussing, the Sunset and Chinatown, with students from the black ghetto in Hunters Point. The professional planners urged adoption of Tri-Star because it assured more thorough racial and socio-economic integration of the schools while permitting better utilization of the schools' physical capacities. Until the end of the planning process the professionals refused to accede to the arguments raised by white members of the Round the Clock group that the Tri-Star plan involved unacceptable political risks. The Citizens Committee turned the Tri-Star plan aside and adopted Horseshoe instead.[8]

The dispute over "Horseshoe" and "Tri-Star" is but one example of the conflict that existed between the "professionals" and the "citizens." We now turn to that conflict and its relation to the process of generating solutions.

In the latter part of 1970 and the early months of 1971 David Bradwell, members of the district's data processing staff, and desegregation consultants from the California Department of Education ("the professionals") proposed and pursued a rational model for decision making concerning desegregation in San Francisco.

These planners proposed the following sequence of steps:

1. all relevant data bearing upon desegregation to be collected,
2. clear, consistent, operational criteria for a "best" plan be established,
3. that all feasible alternatives for a plan be examined,
4. finally, that a choice among the alternatives be guided by the state criteria.

---

[8]The Citizens Committee approved the Horseshoe Plan on the evening of June 1, 1971. It was submitted to an all-night meeting of the Board of Education on June 3. Faced with a court deadline only one week away, the board members had little choice but to accept the recommendation of the Citizens Committee they had appointed. The Horseshoe Plan, in a slightly revised form, was deemed acceptable by Judge Weigel and was implemented in September 1971.

The professionals were frustrated and angered by the CAC's failure to cooperate in the implementation of the rational model. Part of the failure to implement the rational model is attributable to a lack of data.[9] But, more fundamentally, the rational model proved to be inconsistent with the nature of the decision-making process that the professionals sought to affect.

The rational model required a stable definition of the choice to be resolved. But the decision-making process produced a fluctuating number of problems associated with the choice. Participants in the CAC brought the issues of bilingual instruction, new techniques of innovative education, secondary school desegregation, and integration with suburban school districts to the choice process. The instability of the definition of the choice to be resolved is further elaborated in our subsequent discussion of problem flow.

The rational model also required clear and consistent criteria; but the process did not provide them. CAC members [were] unwilling to state criteria for plan selection unless and until the implications of those criteria for specific neighborhoods became clear. The complex nature of the process of drawing zonal boundaries in a desegregation plan meant those implications were far from obvious. In the one instance where the CAC adopted a clear criterion, the 15 percent rule, the committee later found that this criterion interfered with their ability to draw a plan that would have helped reduce opposition to bussing expressed by representatives of Chinatown. Representatives of other school communities, such as the West Portal area, who served on CAC were unwilling to consent to abstract criteria until the details of a plan adhering to those criteria were established.

In addition, some of the criteria considered crucial by some white participants would have created tension in the CAC had they been publicly announced. White members of CAC did not feel they were in a position to publicly announce their desire that the desegregation plan not embrace cross-town bussing or involve other features that would spur white flight from the schools. Such sentiments might have been viewed as "antiblack" by black members of CAC. The whites who were concerned about white backlash also considered themselves to be friends of the black community and did not wish to be the target for black criticism.

---

[9] The district lacked data concerning the residence and ethnicity of its student body; data on utilization of its classrooms; data on the socio-economic status of its students; data on migration patterns of families with school age children within the city; and information on feasible bus routes within the district. The professionals insisted that this data was required before decisions could be reached.

Finally, the rational model required the derivation of a solution from the criteria. Contrary to the expectations of the professionals, solutions existed before the criteria and data were available. In particular, white women on the CAC produced a number of plans before either criteria or extensive data were available.

Frustrated by a decision-making process that they viewed as irrational and parochial, the professionals sought at the last moment, in late May, to advance the Tri-Star plan. This plan, although it met technical criteria important to the planners, also opened the possibility for extensive cross-town bussing. Tri-Star was defeated in the final vote taken by the committee. Each of the outside consultants ultimately came to view the CAC process with both bewilderment and bitterness.[10]

The Flow of Problems

The theory of organized anarchy views the stream of problems entering or leaving an organization as a flow that is independent of the other streams of choices, solutions, and energy. Thus, the flow of problems, seen as "disembodied" problems, move in a fashion that is unaffected by the movement of people.

The theory holds, further, that problems move autonomously among choice opportunities in a search for a choice process in which the problems can be resolved.

Analysis of the case study suggests several modifications of the theory. Problem movement can be seen as intertwined with the movement of people. That is, problems are carried to and from choice opportunities by participants. However, within the context of a given choice, a problem may be exercised or activated by participants other than its original carrier. Problems may move of their volition but they are also subject to ejection from a choice opportunity. Under deadline conditions the movement of a problem away from a choice opportunity may occur in one of two ways:

1. The problem leaves with its carrier. As noted earlier, the time requirements of participating in a decision under deadline constraints may become substantially greater than the time requirement under nondeadline conditions. If a specific problem

---

[10] Undoubtedly the presence of a deadline exacerbated this situation. Given a much longer planning period the professionals might have been able to present detailed plans prepared in conformance to a number of different criteria. This elaboration of various alternatives might also have reduced the relative advantage (over other CAC members) enjoyed by the Round the Clock group inasmuch as members of this group were able to devise plans without the assistance of the professionals.

carrier cannot meet these higher time demands, then he may choose to withdraw entirely from the choice process. Unless other participants share his concern with a given problem, then the problem will depart with its carrier.

2. The problem departs followed by its carrier. Under deadline conditions a participant who is busy elsewhere may not choose to withdraw entirely but to participate in a given choice on a part-time basis—he or she is present part of the time and absent part of the time. The possibility then arises that a problem of concern to the part-time participant is activated when its carrier is absent. In such instances other participants may decide to exclude the problem from further consideration because none of those present are willing to expend energy in resolving it. Its carrier will subsequently discover exclusion of his or her problem and, therefore, may withdraw entirely from the choice because it is no longer dealing with a problem of interest to the participant. Alternatively, a problem may be excluded by some formal decision (for example, through voting), or given such low priority that the carrier leaves the choice.

The foregoing view of the interaction between problems and participation relies on an assumption that participants may be attracted to a choice both by desires to complete choices and by desires to raise and solve problems. This contrasts with the assumption used in the theory wherein participants are only attracted to a choice because of a desire to complete a choice.

These aspects of the theory may be illustrated by specific reference to the San Francisco study. The flow of problems with respect to the choice opportunity is characterized in Table 15-4.

Eight of the above problems were still intertwined with the desegregation planning process when the deadline was set by Judge Weigel. Consideration of five of the problems—socioeconomic integration, integration with suburban schools, school innovations, desegregating secondary schools, and forecasting future enrollment—ceased shortly after the deadline was imposed. The first four problems had been brought to the choice opportunity by individuals who were expending only small amounts of energy on desegregation planning. In the fifth case, forecasting student enrollment, Bradwell's energy was absorbed elsewhere during the month of May.

Three of the eight problems, bilingual education, minority hiring, and setting bussing guidelines, had all been brought to the choice opportunity by individuals who expended a great deal of energy after the deadline was set.

Table 15.4

Flow of problems with respect to the desegregation choice opportunity

Problem	Problem carrier	Date at which problem became intertwined or disengaged from desegregation
Socioeconomic integration of schools	Superintendent Shaheen	February 1971
Administrative decentralization of district	Superintendent Shaheen	Plan proposed in February. Killed by the school board in the same month.
Integration with suburban school districts	One member of the school board and one member of the Citizens Committee	February 1971
Including school "innovations" in desegregation plan	Several members of the Citizens Committee	March and April
Strengthening bilingual programs in the district	Chinese and Latin members of the Citizens Committee	March
Desegregating secondary schools	Citizens Committee	April
Forecasting student migration and future enrollment	David Bradwell	December 1970
Developing bussing policy and setting up bussing office	Member of CAC and Desegregation Office	April
Setting guidelines for minority hiring	Minority members of CAC	April

Thus, the nature of the problems considered as part of the final desegregation plan appears to have been more dependent upon the energy expended on them by interested participants rather than on any rational definition of the problems that "should" have been considered in the planning process.

Summary of Theoretical Implications

The theory of organized anarchies suggests a choice opportunity is a passive receptacle for solutions, problems, and participant energy; that a choice has permeable boundaries such that solutions, problems, and participants may move into and away from the choice at their own volition; and that a choice will benefit from the energy of participants not already absorbed by other choices.

The San Francisco study [demonstrates] flows of problems, solutions, and energy, when the choice is subject to a deadline, that varies from the theoretical predictions. Problems and solutions, on the one hand, and participants, on the other hand, are intertwined. Problems and solutions are carried by participants. Deadline conditions erect a barrier (due to time requirements and the relative competence of active participants in the deadline choice) around the choice that resists the entrance of new problems and participants. Deadline conditions cause a dramatic increase in the energy that must be devoted to the choice by active participants. Participants are forced to either withdraw from other obligations to stay "on top" of the deadline choice or become partially or totally inactive in the deadline choice. Thus, for active deadline participants, time contributed to the choice is not freely given but is largely coerced. As a result of the partial or total withdrawal of some participants, some problems will be ejected from the choice.

This altered view of the behavior within a choice process under deadline may be seen as the consequence of three effects: A garbage ejection effect, an energy conservation effect, and a competence multiplier.

A choice opportunity, before a deadline is imposed, can be viewed as a garbage can into which various kinds of problems and solutions are dumped as they are generated. The choice opportunity behaves as a passive receptacle. However, once a deadline is imposed certain problems and solutions are ejected from the garbage can.

It appears that the *garbage ejection process* is initiated as the result of a comparison by participants between the amount of energy that would be required to solve all the problems they have accepted and the amount of energy it then appears they will be able to apply to the choice opportunity before the deadline. If such a comparison leads to a conclusion by participants that they have accepted more problems than they can handle, then the participants actively undertake to eject some of the problems they had previously accepted. Thus, energy deficit calculations appear to be essential elements of the garbage ejection process under deadline conditions.

Under deadline conditions, where problem "overload" exists, choice opportunities change from a passive mode of receiving problems into an active mode of excluding some problems from consideration, thus setting the excluded problems adrift either to be considered elsewhere in the organization or to flow out of the organization entirely.

The garbage ejection process proceeds in a manner that *conserves energy*. It retains those problems that have attracted participants who are willing and able to spend substantial energy on the choice opportunity. In the case study none of the "garbage" ejected from the decision-making process was associated with participants who evinced high participation rates. Each of the problems ejected from the garbage can under deadline conditions had received lip service but no substantial energy expenditure by a participant.

Thus, it would appear that the garbage ejection process functions in a fashion independent of any rational definition of the problems that must be resolved by the choice, but rather in a way that conserves high energy expenditures on the choice. Participants in the choice process are content to allow certain problems to remain after a deadline is imposed if such problems can "pay their own way" through attracting participants with time to spend on them.

Before the imposition of the deadline, modest variations appear in the energy contributions of participants. These modest variations in participation rates are associated with differences in levels of competence, with those participants having competency in current problems and solutions tending to be somewhat more active than other participants.

The effect of the deadline is not only to eject some "garbage" from the garbage can but also to concentrate attention upon the problems that remain for consideration. Those participants who are able to expand their participation rates do so and dramatic differences quickly appear between those who are most actively involved and the balance of [the] participants.

The tendency for the most active participants to spend greater energy on the choice is reinforced by two things. The first is the fact that they are relatively free of other obligations and thus are able to spend large amounts of time on decision making. The second is the fact that as high participation rates continue the most active members become a relatively small group possessing a near monopoly position concerning the competencies required in decision making.

The joint operation of these factors constitutes a positive feedback loop where activity causes greater competence, and greater competence leads to increased activity. The total effect of this feedback process quickly cumulates along both dimensions of activity and competence, leading to what we describe as the *competence multiplier*.

Thus, one effect associated with the sharply increased participation rates by some participants in the choice is that the most active participants gain a much higher share of the competence and experience necessary to deal with the remaining problems. As they become substantially more competent it becomes more difficult for other potential participants to gain access to the decision-making process.

Conclusion

Our study of decision making on desegregation within the San Francisco Unified School District illustrates several key respects in which traditional models of organizational decisions fail to describe accurately the processes within an organized anarchy: Operational criteria for a "good" decision either do not exist or are not widely shared among participants in the decision-making process. Data essential to even a rudimentary understanding of the impact of various decision alternatives is often missing or garbled. The definition of the problems to be solved within the context of the decision is not stable; problems flow to the choice opportunity and flow away from it largely in response to concerns that are being generated within and without the organization, as a function of the relative attractiveness of other choices, and as a function of the time constraints imposed upon a given choice. Deadline conditions lead to the emergence of several distinctive alternations in the flow of problems and participation: garbage ejection, energy conservation, and the multiplication of competence.

What tactical advice to participants in organized anarchies can be distilled from these observations? We believe that these major rules for administrative leadership present themselves:[11]

1. Distract the opposition. Participants within an organization have limited attention and energy. Therefore, rational actors should seek to assign their opponents on a given issue to work on competing issues. If other issues are not under debate, then create some as an alternative object for the energy of your enemies.
2. Be selective in your ambitions. A participant in an organized anarchy must be modest in the number of decisions he seeks to mold at any given time. There are limitations on the energy of your opponents, but there are limitations on the time of your allies as well.

---

[11] For a related set of rules for college presidents see Cohen and March (1974, chap. 9).

3. Impose deadlines judiciously. The legitimacy of decisions, and thus their prospects for implementation, depend upon perceptions that "all sides" have been heard and represented in the decision-making process. Therefore, committees and task forces should ordinarily contain both allies and opponents. But the ability of committee members actually to participate in a given decision depends upon the time each individual must spend on alternative choices and time requirements of the choice you wish to shape. Impose an unexpected and short deadline when your allies on a given committee have time available and your opponents are hard pressed elsewhere. Extend and relax deadlines when your allies are busy elsewhere and your opponents have the luxury of concentrating on the choice that is vital for you. When you are unable to impose deadlines, seek the cooperation of others (courts, the press, pressure groups) in creating them. Thus, from your perspective, some decisions may be "better" if they can benefit from more planning, others will be better if they are deprived of planning time.

4. Use your friends in the environment as a resource. In low technology organizations, outsiders may possess as much expertise as insiders. This means that advisory committees composed, either in part or in total, of outsiders can be used to expand the ranks of your allies within the decision-making process. In an organized anarchy that is overloaded with problems, the significance of formal position for the outcome of decisions is depressed and the significance of time availability is accentuated. If your friends on the outside have time available, use it.

If our description of the process of decision in an organized anarchy is correct, such rules may have some modest validity. Certainly, the course of events leading to the desegregation procedure in the San Francisco schools suggests that organizational leadership involves the careful management of scarce attention and energy as much as it does the exercise of decision skills.

References

Cohen, M.D., J.G. March, and J.P. Olsen. "A Garbage Can Model of Organizational Choice." *Administrative Science Quarterly* 17: 1 (March 1972): 1-25.

Cohen, M.D., and J.G. March. *Leadership and Ambiguity: The American College President.* New York: McGraw-Hill, Carnegie Commission on the Future of Higher Education, 1974.

Dahl, R.A. *Who Governs?* New Haven, Conn.: Yale University Press, 1964.
Olsen, J.P. "Voting, 'Sounding Out,' and the Governance of Modern Organizations." *Acta Sociologica* 15: 3 (1972).

16

Observations on Organizing an Anarchy

Lee Sproull, Stephen Weiner, and David Wolf

Introduction

Between 1970 and 1975 the National Institute of Education [NIE] evolved as an idea, was created as a new federal agency, and came close to extinction. We have viewed this short history as one episode in the continuing federal effort to support education R&D, as a case study in the development of a new organization, and as a means for increasing our understanding of many organizations in the public sector. Our ... description of NIE ... has three components:

1. A consideration of the political processes involved in the birth of a public agency and an examination of the flow of events in NIE's environment. NIE was not the result of an immaculate conception; its creation served some concrete political, bureaucratic, and personal objectives only loosely related to education research. It was caught in a context that had some importance for it, but over which it had almost no control.
2. A detailed exposition of the pattern of bureaucratic development and action in the agency. NIE had to hire people, spend money, establish procedures, prepare budgets, make reports, and get organized.
3. A description of the development of belief about the agency. NIE was an ambiguous stimulus. Over time people inside and outside the agency developed opinions about it and conflicting impressions of what was happening there.

Reprinted, by permission, from Lee S. Sproull, Stephen S. Weiner, and David Wolf, *Organizing an Anarchy* (Chicago: University of Chicago Press, 1978), pp. 217-27.

Many of our speculations about public sector organizations are implicit in the case study analysis. We do not attempt to review all of them here. Rather, we try to identify some themes having broad significance for understanding the implementation of public policy through bureaucratic mechanisms. They are organized as comments on two broad sets of issues: (1) What can be expected from federal efforts in education R&D? and (2) What should managers keep in mind when creating and organizing a new agency?

What Can Be Expected from Federal Efforts in Education R&D?

There are only a few readily available tools for the redirection of the federal education R&D effort.[1] Preeminent among them are shifts in budget levels, reorganization of the bureaucracy, installation of new leadership, and declaration of new goals. In the past decade the federal government has run through this repertoire of responses to the "failure" of education R&D. The primary result has been the growth of disillusionment. Every suggestion for reform in federal sponsorship can be quickly countered by citing recent evidence that such a reform does not work. Reorganizations do not work; new leadership has little, if any, effect; new goals have insignificant impact; and vastly increased funds can not be won from the Congress unless and until evidence is produced that reorganizations, new leadership, and fresh goals do, in fact, work.

The record of the past decade—the reorganizations within OE, the creation of NCERD, the creation of NIE, and the changes in NIE—leads us to suspect that there are no dramatic differences in short-term effectiveness among different organizational structures, different leaders, or different official goals. Memories are too long and the proclaimed failure of every excuse for hope is too recent. A rapid cycling through the entire repertoire of "reforms" has bred frustration and threatens persistence in the very slow, inherently uneven, and difficult-to-manage federal education R&D enterprise.

NIE's original conception is as deeply implicated in any failures as is its subsequent implementation. The axiomatic beliefs...in both the

---

[1] Although our study provides no evidence on this point, we suspect that the tools for redirection of other low-technology federal programs in the social sector are similarly limited. Community mental health and manpower training and development, for example, share some of the characteristics of the R&D enterprise: ambiguous goals, fluid participation, and an unclear technology. One major difference may be that these programs are easier to justify on the grounds that they are "helping people."

likelihood of tangible progress resulting trom education R&D and the possibility of a strong, centralized management of the R&D process underlie this cycle of reform and despair. Simply stated, the basic tenets of "progress" and "R&D management" are inconsistent with the realities of schooling and research in the United States. The inconsistencies arise from two basic factors. First, education research does not closely resemble its alleged analogues in the natural sciences. Second, education research must be managed with a sensitivity to the decentralized aspects of American schooling.[2]

Changes attributable to education research are rarely achieved through a tangible product or device. Education research often plays the comparatively modest role of recording events, identifying problems, weeding out factors of lowest relevance, and illuminating alternative solutions to limited problems. The theoretical basis for curriculum design is much weaker than the theoretical basis for missile design. There is only a distant relationship between translating physical science research into the practical work of engineers and translating education research into school practices. Further, education R&D has no impact on many important causes of educational difficulties, such as malnutrition in children and racial discrimination.

There are severe limits on the diffusion of educational innovations even when new procedures and devices have produced encouraging results in small-scale studies. The highly decentralized nature of American education means that disseminating information about new practices and providing

---

[2]The analyses concerning the weak scientific base of and diffuse political support for education R&D are not new. Similar points were raised by former OE research officials at the Brademas hearings in 1971. They were largely ignored there, however. Chief among those who critically assessed the pro-NIE assumptions in 1971 were Hendrik Gideonse, former director of program planning and evaluation for NCERD; James Gallagher, former deputy assistant secretary for planning, research and evaluation in OE; and Robert Dentler, then director of the OE-supported Center for Urban Education in New York City. The conclusion of much of this testimony was that the solution lay in the massive expansion of federal education R&D budgets. For example, Gideonse urged annual expenditures in the range of $2-3 billion. Although we concur in the analysis, our conclusions differ. A similar analysis was presented by a panel of consultants convened by NIE in 1975 to advise it on funding policies for the regional laboratories and R&D centers (Campbell et al. 1975, pp. 5-8). The conclusions of this group also seemed to be founded on the axiomatic beliefs: they included a recommendation for an immediate budget increase of 100 percent and a more directive role for NIE staff in managing the R&D process. Again, we found ourselves in agreement with much of the analysis but not with the conclusions.

technical assistance to help implement them is a massive task in a school district with many schools, much less in the nation as a whole. Equally important, pressures against any particular reform can come from one or more of the large number of potential veto groups that exist within the community of teachers, administrators, parents, and taxpayers. School administrators learn to prefer the known shortcomings of present practice to the political dangers of attempting the new and unknown.

The conventional argument for federal direction of education R&D is that because state and local school districts cannot fully "capture" the benefits of education R&D (other localities or regions will benefit from research they did not support), these levels of school governance will underinvest in such research. For this reason, education R&D is an appropriate activity for the federal government to support. However, this argument is reasonable only to the extent that the agenda of desirable research topics at the federal level overlaps those at state and local levels. Certainly, everyone wishes to have surer methods of teaching reading, for example. But there is much less agreement across localities on the desirability of learning more about vouchers, ethnic studies, or sex education curricula. Even with regard to widely approved research topics, such as reading, there are local variations in particular emphasis—for example, regional interests in teaching bilingual children to read. There are also factional splits in the research community as to which basic strategies for teaching reading hold the best prospects for further investment. These variations in the incidence of educational problems, splits over basic educational values, and disagreements over research approaches give rise to political pressures upon any agency that supports education research.

The crucial political question at the federal level is that of constituencies. It is most unlikely that an R&D program operating under a consistent overall strategy, even if such a strategy could be conceptualized, could satisfy the requirements of divergent constituents. Further, the optimism about building a political constituency for R&D assumes the infusion of substantial new money to attract participants into the coalition. Yet one condition for winning new money is to have the coalition already formed. Education research is supported primarily by federal funds, and the record indicates that new federal funds can be obtained only in the context of a broad increase of funding for education programs, as was the case in 1965. Therefore, without a change in federal views toward education, and a corresponding shift in national budgetary priorities, the prospects are dim for either a new coalition or substantial new money for education R&D.

The foregoing factors help explain the fragmentation, duplication, modest size, and marginal impact upon practice that characterizes, and will continue to characterize, American research and development in education. In summary, education R&D will not yield insights or products that will continuously improve American schools. It is questionable whether an enterprise as diverse, value laden, and technologically underdeveloped as education R&D can be managed at the level of the prespecification of results or the coordination of diverse efforts. And, in terms of public priorities, it has not been demonstrated that education R&D deserves constant growth or that the R&D enterprise would benefit from unceasing expansion.

In place of the beliefs in rational management and tangible progress, we assert the following:

1. Education is important, but not supremely important as compared with other governmental endeavors.
2. Innovations can improve education, but probably not dramatically.
3. Research and development can aid in creating sensible innovations, but they are not always a major factor in such stimulation.
4. It is possible to achieve some sense of direction in a growing R&D enterprise, but in weak technology fields such as education, it does not require much growth to swamp any capacity for managing the system.
5. Education research serves competing values and varied audiences. It cannot be conducted within a single conceptual framework, or according to a single long-range plan.
6. Education research and development is worthy of investment but not necessarily at levels dramatically different from the present.

Education R&D is not a panacea. But it need not be abandoned. Research and development do help to discover problems; they help in formulating useful ways to view problems; they sometimes suggest ameliorative steps. These are not heroic contributions. But as long as education R&D does not espouse heroic goals, it can honestly seek modest returns in exchange for a modest investment.

Research and development inevitably involve the risk of failure. It is vital to recognize that failure is not always the result of incompetence. Nor is failure always attributable to lack of leadership, lack of money, or the structure of the organization. Education research has made a small amount of progress. It is capable of some progress in the future. But at the moment the enterprise desperately needs a period of stability. A vastly disproportionate amount of energy has been invested in crusades to change leadership, funding, and structure. But the value of such changes is small even under optimum conditions and vanishes entirely when such reforms are implemented in the naive belief that they will achieve quick substantive results. Within the institute the inclination to reorganize, to seek vastly expanded resources, or to seek a comprehensive conceptual framework should be resisted. Outside the institute, the inclination to charge wholesale incompetence or to put the agency to death should be resisted. What is required now is internal persistence, external monitoring at a low level of intensity, and a sympathetic ear to the results the institute may gather.

The education R&D enterprise can best accommodate conflicting political pressure if the advocates of different research problems and different research strategies can turn to one or more of a series of federal, state, and local agencies that are prepared to support education research. In turn, each of these agencies should sponsor efforts in a variety of directions without being consumed with guilt at their failure to achieve a single, overarching plan for using research to improve education. Although these diverse efforts will undoubtedly continue to find most of their financial support coming from federal dollars, we hope that state agencies and local institutions can be persuaded to use a small fraction of their own budgets to support research in education as well.

The pursuit of modesty, diversity, and stability fails to set the heart beating faster. But, in this case, it may serve to sustain life and lead to productivity.

What Should Policymakers and Managers Keep in Mind When Creating and Organizing a New Agency?

Those who decry the lack of planning in government might well have been encouraged by the early history of the National Institute of Education. Although the planning period was not perfect, there was a genuine commitment to formulating organizational goals and structure before the agency was created. The determination to analyze alternatives and to plan carefully before acting also characterized the early days of the agency's existence. Yet the planning, even though performed by able analysts, was of little use once the institute began to accumulate experience. Indeed, we have suggested that the commitment to planning was itself the cause of significant mischief.

The conventional model of planning relies upon assessing the experiences of other people in other places to produce "learning." Hence, in the NIE case, planners could look to NSF, NIH, and NASA experiences to "learn" what to do; the OE experiences to learn what not to do. But this kind of learning (and hence the planning based on it) is necessarily thin.[3] The planners know little of the myriad people, procedures, processes, constraints, opportunities, and accidents producing the artifacts they study. This ignorance is even more striking in de novo planning—in which few useful analogies exist, even thin ones.

This point is of general importance. As a practical matter, a new bureaucracy must act. The press of events simply cannot be resisted while plans and analyses are constructed. But more important, a new agency must act in order to learn—to understand its strengths, limitations, and context. There is little a new agency can learn until it has experiences that can be subjected to its own processes of interpretation. Action precedes understanding.[4]

But action is no guarantee of understanding. First, the answer to the question, "What happened?" is often arguable. And, second, even given a single, stable interpretation of what happened, it is often difficult to discern why it happened. In this latter respect, managers often mistakenly view events and their "causes" as being closely coupled. As the history of NIE illustrates, there are many instances in which planning is only loosely connected to action, decisions are only distantly linked to problems, reputation is not correlated with activity, and belief is disconnected from policy.[5]

Nevertheless, to a significant degree the construction of a new bureaucracy is an intellectual problem that requires trying to make sense out of events as they occur. It is not a passive problem like putting together a jigsaw puzzle on the dining room table. Rather, it is an active problem in which the table moves, the pieces change shape, and, not infrequently, the lights go out. We have no recipe or cookbook to offer those confronted by the dilemmas of constructing a new bureaucracy. But we can suggest some

---

[3]We use this word as Geertz (1973) uses it.

[4]In social psychology, Weick (1969) has argued that a variety of experiences enhances learning and leads to goal discovery. He suggests, "Chaotic action is preferable to orderly inaction" (p. 107). A different perspective, that of computer programming, also points to the value of action. Anyone who has ever written a computer program knows that you have to try to run it before you can debug it.

[5]We do not mean to imply that loose connections produce nothing but difficulties; loosely connected systems have advantages as well as disadvantages. Weick (1976) suggests seven positive attributes of loosely coupled systems, including the ability to persist, locally adapt, and seal off mistakes.

questions managers may find helpful in making sense of an institution's formative stages.[6]

1. What Are the Political Terms of Creation?

Managers can incorrectly attribute historical inevitability and significance to a new organization. They often interpret the act of creation as a sign that important people are interested in the organization and consider it significant. Intimations of future resources and expressions of confidence are taken to be redeemable pledges. But it is often the case that a significant part of the coalition that creates a new agency loses interest once the symbolism of creation is exhausted. The initial patrons of the new bureaucracy wander away or are assigned elsewhere.

The creation of a new agency is no sure testament to its importance. Nor is it a sign that people agree on its goals. Enthusiastic expressions of high expectations may well mask either the absence of any operational definition of agency goals or the presence of serious conflict over them. A new bureaucracy can imagine itself to be a well-protected tiger cub even as monsoon [rains soak its fur]. Who has a deep and lasting stake in the success of this organization? What rewards do they seek for their support? Who wrote the "minority reports" opposing the creation? On what basis could opponents and skeptics be persuaded to be friends? These are questions that the managers of new organizations must place at the top of their list for exploration in the early days.

2. What Are Limitations of the Models of "Success" and "Failure" Embedded within the New Agency's Historical Context?

The models of success or failure are inevitably oversimplified and thin. Therefore the manager can usefully inquire into the substantive and stylistic cues that generated them. What "reforms" have been tried in the past? Do these reforms tend to come and go in a cyclical fashion? If so, where are we on the cycle? What bureaucratic and political constraints have impeded previous attempts at success? Not only are the models oversimplified, but they are not necessarily shared in a consistent fashion by everyone important to the fate of the new agency. Managers should assume everyone has some model of the agency but should not assume those models bear any relationship to the one held by the manager.

---

[6]Each of these questions is predicated on the assumption of an environment that is either neutral or hostile. If the environment is benign, the agency will probably prosper (that is, budgets will increase) no matter what the manager does or thinks.

3. Given My Inheritance, What Can I Aspire to Improve?

Managers are often determined to create a new organization of unique style and productivity. They pursue perfection, not marginal improvement. The pursuit of perfection presents at least two risks. First, it impedes action and therefore learning from the consequences of action. Early in an agency's life it can afford to experiment with organizing and managing its work. Its environment and staff are usually willing to tolerate initial experimentation (or chaos). But if managers eschew any action in order to plan for the perfect action, they lose the opportunity to experiment and therefore to learn from their own early experiences. Over time, the demands for a coherent explanation of the agency's work will inevitably grow more insistent; toleration for experimentation will decline.

Second, without major improvements in its underlying technology (not only "hardware," but also people and procedures), it is unlikely that a new organization can be dramatically more productive than its predecessors. NASA could not have placed a man on the moon in 1969 without benefit of the technology that matured during and after World War II. Yet most new agencies do not fall heir to a legacy of new technology. (It is unlikely, for example, that Amtrak will significantly exceed the performance of the private railroad management that preceded it.) Nor do they have access to a substantially different work force or system of procedures than did their predecessors. Even though it may be desirable to alter some standard operating procedures inherited from the past, a requisite for these modest changes is to have the vast bulk of other standard procedures in place and operating smoothly. No organization can simultaneously establish entirely new patterns in organizational hierarchy; job descriptions; methods of recruiting, hiring, and promoting; techniques of budget preparation and planning; means of letting and monitoring contracts; and sweeping changes in its relationships with its environment without courting disaster. The stability of some established procedures is the foundation for changing others. And, in this regard, the skills, experience, and intuition of established bureaucrats are invaluable allies in the change process.

Change is often desirable; sometimes it is possible; but no "new" organization starts with a clean slate. Pursuing perfection impedes learning and incremental change.

4. How Can I Intervene in the External Generation of Demands and Evaluations?

A new bureaucracy must cope with a larger bureaucratic and political community that may have little enthusiasm for the organization's creation or its continued good health but that will inevitably make demands on the new organization. In some instances, those who create demands can be persuaded to insist that the new agency do what the agency managers privately wish. Thus, the managers of a new agency may have a chance to educate their superiors and colleagues about how to make the agency respond. Of equal importance, managers should consider means to affect the impressions that will rapidly form about the adequacy of the new agency. What people think about an organization is not simply the concern of gossip-column readers. It forms the basis of how people act toward it. Hence, influencing people's beliefs about a new organization can also affect their actions with respect to it. In effect, we suggest that leaders of organized anarchies must depend not so much on their power to compel as on their ability to conjure. We use the term "symbolic leadership" to denote the ability to affect the beliefs about or perceptions of the new organization in the eyes of others.[7]

Two factors contribute to the possibility for symbolic leadership: ambiguity of organization goals or expectations and ambiguity of experience. Constituencies experience some uncertainty about what they want. Lobbyists are as interested in taking credit for what has happened as they are in determining what will happen. Elected officials are generally interested in demonstrating that "progress" is being made while having an incomplete set of a priori notions on what constitutes progress. Thus the initial, ambiguous charter for the new organization is subject to some definition by management.

Furthermore, the outputs of a bureaucracy are complex, subtle, and often hard to detect or evaluate. Those who evaluate a new organization are sometimes willing to equate the testimonials of good performance proffered by management with the testimonials that should be expected. (Those who have never seen a game of tennis can be persuaded that one scores points by putting a large rubber ball through elevated hoops.) To the extent that a new bureaucracy can be defined by its leadership as a new game, creativity in defining rules for winning and losing is possible.

There are some simple procedures to affect the indexes for evaluation. One is to assemble a group of commentators who will be prone to rate the new bureaucracy a success rather than a failure and to disseminate their findings widely. Another is to declare intentions to reach goals that have already been attained and, subsequently, to discover one's success.

One possible objection to these tactics is that such behavior is simply charlatanism. To be sure, there is the spirit of sleight of hand in our

---

[7]Edelman (1972) provides an extensive discussion of symbolic leadership.

counsel. But there is also the recognition that interpretations of organizational performance are often a matter of superficial impression and social contagion. Therefore, leaders have the obligation to intervene in the development of interpretations and in their contagion in relevant social networks.

5. What Can We Be Proud Of?

Confusion, conflict, exhaustion, and missed opportunities inevitably accompany new organizations. For some, these elements are essential ingredients of their charm. A new agency can accept large doses of these difficulties and still thrive. What it cannot suffer for long is an active sense of demoralization. Adequate standard operating procedures are a good antidote for demoralization. But equally, if not more, important is an excuse for pride. It is easy for top management, caught up in the heady and portentous activities of the new agency, to forget that subordinates may have little sense of the significance of their actions. Managers must be sure that subordinates can complete the sentence, "What we are proud of around here is . . . "[8]

Even the problems of new agencies can be turned to advantage. If there is confusion, the new agency can be proud that it is open to new ideas. If there is conflict, the new agency can be proud that, in the democratic tradition, competing voices are heard and respected. If there is redundant effort, the new agency can be proud of its "fail-safe" procedures. If there is exhaustion, the new agency can be proud of the dedication of its staff. Just as managers should create positive interpretations for external consumption, they should promote inspiring messages for internal purposes as well.

6. What Are the Disadvantages of Bureaucratic Growth?

Managers usually respond to incentives for organizational growth. Such incentives arise from both the selfless and the selfish motivations of leaders. On the one hand, increased quality of service to the public is often associated in the manager's mind with an expanding budget and staff. On the other hand, a simple and widely used index of a manager's success, and hence career potential, is the number of dollars and employees under his or her direction. But there are disadvantages as well as advantages to agency growth. In political terms, growth implies giving up obscurity and the

---

[8]Selznick (1957) describes this process as the "elaboration of socially integrating myths . . . efforts to state, in the language of uplift and idealism, what is distinctive about the aims and methods of the enterprise" (p. 151).

autonomy that accompanies it. . . . A single department within a large organization can often conduct its affairs without being subject to searching examination from those outside the organization. However, if that department is transformed into a separate organization, it attracts a higher level of attention and scrutiny. In terms of internal organization, rapid growth can break the tenuous ties of understanding and common concern that can develop in a small group. For both these reasons, the assumed link between increase in size and increase in achievement should be challenged continually and mercilessly.

7. Is It Time for a Turnover in Management?

Every manager harbors the suspicion that he or she is invaluable. It is difficult for any individual, let alone a "manager," to believe he or she cannot intervene to improve a course of events. Yet it may occasionally be that the most helpful intervention is an exit. When a new agency is in trouble the easiest means of easing external pressure is to remove top management. If for no other reason than the need for fresh symbolism, the managers of new bureaucracies are well advised to think of themselves as expendable and to keep their resumes up to date.[9]

General answers to these seven questions are not available. Answers depend upon a particular organization's context, strengths, and weaknesses. Moreover, even the existence of these questions is not reassuring on a crucial point: How can they be raised within an

---

[9] It is difficult for any manager to recognize or accept failure, especially when a new enterprise has been undertaken with high hopes. However, in the event of involuntary departure, there are constructive purposes that disappointed managers can serve. These purposes are often best served by public protest rather than quiet submission. A graphic description of the political, programmatic, and organizational constraints and uncertainties that promoted failure provides some leverage for the next set of managers. The resignation in protest often causes at least a momentary relaxation of external pressure upon the new bureaucracy, thus providing the new managers with some flexibility. Further, the resignation in protest, by declaring the existence of a crisis, provides a sense that new leadership has only one direction to go—toward improvement—and thus lays the basis for a favorable evaluation of the new managers. This course of action is unlikely to be pursued by individuals who hope to be employed in the same context in the future. Thus, managers who pursue Washington-based careers often leave federal posts quietly for fear of spoiling their future chances for high-level appointment. For further discussion of the trade-offs in various forms of resignation see Hirschman (1970) and Weisband and Franck (1975).

organization in a timely and forceful manner? A number of devices might be considered to foster such institutional self-examination. Retreats to conference centers, employment of outside consultants, and arrangement for internal dissenters all come to mind.[10] All these techniques are worthy of serious consideration, but it is not likely that they or any other simple techniques will insure the serious examination of these questions, for three reasons.

First, raising and debating questions of fundamental importance is time-consuming. And time is in short supply in a new organization. Dealing with day-to-day problems involves less ambiguity and leads to a more immediate sense of efficacy than does challenging the fundamental assumptions of top managers and their key external sponsors.

Second, new bureaucracies encourage the display of some attitudes and styles within the agency and suppress others. (For example, in the early days of NIE, it was appropriate to engage in intellectual debate over the goals of education, but it would have been inappropriate to bring up questions of political expediency. In the early days of the Office of Economic Opportunity, agreement with the notion of grass-roots community organization was obligatory.) Employees who fail to demonstrate the prevailing attitude and style are often perceived as having their primary loyalty elsewhere and hence are ignored or distrusted.

Third, new agencies attract personnel who are efficacious, ambitious, and optimistic. Those who choose managers for new agencies look for "winners," or people with a "good track record." The new manager who has been previously successful is likely to bring to the new organization both general feelings of personal efficacy and specific beliefs about useful techniques and procedures for handling particular problems. Past failures are perceived to be the result of incompetence in the previous generation of managers; the newcomers are convinced that they will not fall into similar traps. Not only top management but other agency personnel as well tend to be optimists.[11] They tend to believe that the existence of a problem implies the existence of a solution. They tend not to take a Tolstoyan view of bureaucratic history. Hence, they would find it difficult to consider questions such as those we raise above.

Only severe and sustained bureaucratic disappointment is likely to engender an interest in our questions. Ironically, of course, by that time it may be too late.

---

[10] See George (1972) for an exposition of multiple advocacy in foreign policy. A similar argument can be made for domestic policy.

[11] Downs (1967) suggests that the new bureau attracts "zealots" or "advocates." We believe that zealots are simply a special class of optimists—optimists with an ideology.

Conclusion

Creating organizations is an extraordinarily complex and delicate endeavor.[12] Chance occurrences and uncontrollable factors will always play a large role in the success—or failure—of any new organization. Even if the organization must overcome seemingly impossible difficulties, it may do so and succeed. That is reason for being optimistic. On the other hand, even though the organization's success may seem assured, it may fail. That is reason for tempering optimism with an understanding that success may not occur.[13]

One should not necessarily conclude that individual policymakers and managers are likely to have little positive influence upon the fate of organizations. It is the case, however, that their primary impact is likely to be upon how people feel about the agency, not upon conventional organization outcomes.

Because new organizations are usually created with optimism and ambitious expectations, disappointment is common, even in the "successful" agency. Disappointment should not lead to disillusionment, however. It should lead instead to the realization that organizations are not perfect instruments of human intention. They are, however, a means for discovering better intentions.

---

[12] We would like to [emphasize] three points [for the study of organizations that are new or can be characterized by ambiguous goals, unclear technology, and fluid participation. . . .] (1) Beware of arbitrary distinctions between "organization" and "environment" that tend to obscure the ways each influences the other. We found it useful to realize that internal decision processes are more permeable to the environment than past work may have indicated. (2) Cognitive images of the organization that develop in the minds of participants and observers can have a profound influence on organization action. (See Sproull and Weiner 1976 for a more extended discussion of the function of cognitive images in creating new organizations.) Understanding what people believe and how those beliefs develop is an important task for students of organizations. (3) Conventional assumptions about tightly connected systems are not necessarily useful in understanding certain kinds of organizations. These points suggest reassessing the appropriateness of conventional methods of cross-organization questionnaire analysis. They require careful attention to what people are doing and to what else is going on at the same time. They demand that the investigator look for complicating factors, not simplifying ones, in every explanation of organization action. And they suggest that the researcher treat informant responses as projective tests as much as objective data.

[13] See March (1975) for a discussion of optimism without hope in education organizations.

References

Campbell, R., et al. "R&D Funding Policies of the National Institute of Education: Review and Recommendations." Washington, D.C.: National Institute of Education, draft report. Unpublished 1975.

Downs, A. *Inside Bureaucracy.* Boston: Little, Brown, 1967.

Edelman, M. *The Symbolic Uses of Politics.* Urbana: University of Illinois Press, 1972.

Geertz, C. *The Interpretation of Cultures.* New York: Basic Books, 1973.

George, A. "The Case for Multiple Advocacy in Foreign Policy." *American Political Science Review* 66: 3 (1972): 751–85.

Hirschman, A. *Exit, Voice, and Loyalty: Responses to Decline in Firms, Organizations, and States.* Cambridge: Harvard University Press, 1970.

March, J. "Education and the Pursuit of Optimism." *Texas Tech Journal of Education* 2: 1 (1975); 5–17.

Selznick, P. *Leadership in Administration.* New York: Harper & Row, 1957.

Sproull, L., and S. Weiner, "Easier 'Seen' than Done: The Function of Cognitive Images in Creating a New Organization." Paper presented at annual AERA convention, San Francisco, 1976.

Weick, K. *The Social Psychology of Organizing.* Reading, Mass.: Addison-Wesley, 1969.

———. "Educational Organizations as Loosely Coupled Systems." *Administrative Science Quarterly* 21: 2 (1976): 1–19.

Weisband, E., and T.M. Franck. *Resignation in Protest: Political and Ethical Choices Between Loyalty to Team and Loyalty to Conscience in American Public Life.* New York: Grossman/Viking, 1975.

17

Anomalies in Elementary Schools: Illustrations of the Garbage Can and Institutional Models Applied to School Organizations

Margaret Davis and E. Anne Stackhouse

Introduction

In this paper we shall attempt to illustrate the nature of some of the complex processes which produce or accompany programmatic change in elementary schools. Conventional organizations theories generally attempt to explain variations in instructional activity among schools as direct responses to either environmental or technological factors. However,

This is a jointly authored paper. Authors are listed in alphabetical order. The research reported herein was conducted at the Stanford Center for Research and Development in Teaching and was supported by a grant from the School Capacity for Problem-Solving Group of the National Institute of Education (U.S. Department of Health, Education, and Welfare) under Contract No. NE-C-00-3-0062. The opinions expressed do not necessarily reflect the position, policy, or endorsement of the NIE.

The authors wish to thank John W. Meyer and W. Richard Scott for their helpful comments on an earlier draft of this paper, and to gratefully acknowledge assistance given by Terrence E. Deal and Brian Rowan.

Reprinted, by permission, from *The Structure of Educational Systems: Explorations in the Theory of Loosely Coupled Organizations*, ed. Margaret R. Davis, Terrence E. Deal, John W. Meyer, Brian Rowan, W. Richard Scott, and E. Anne Stackhouse (Stanford: Stanford Center for Research and Development in Teaching, 1977).

there are many unique programs in schools and many instances of irregular responses by school staffs to new programs originating outside of a school, which are not satisfactorily explained by theories with this perspective. We shall call these singular programs and uncommon responses "anomalies."

Anomalies are often dealt with as if they were entirely idiosyncratic—treated as part of the unexplained or residual variance in these analyses. However, anomalies can be found in almost every elementary school, and their very prevalence makes them deserving of closer inspection. We suggest that the formulations of recent "loose coupling" theorists provide guides for introducing some degree of order into many of these situations.

Theoretical Background

Conventional approaches to the study of schools as organizations have generally attempted to explain innovative programs and activities in schools as rational adaptive responses to environmental demands or structural or technological imperatives (see, for example, Katz 1964; Griffiths 1967; Dreeben 1971; Baldridge 1971; Bredo and Bredo 1975; Baldridge and Burnham 1973). Yet recent literature on complex organizations includes repeated notations to the effect that the formal structure of a school—that is, its formally designated system of roles, relationships, policies, and procedures—and the nature of the environment of the school are of limited utility in explaining actual activities of organizational participants (see, for example, Bidwell 1965; Cohen, Deal, Meyer, and Scott 1979).

The literature that focuses on the implementation of innovative programs in schools abounds with descriptions of unsuccessful attempts to institute changes and reforms in either instructional or structural facets of schools. (For a summary of this literature, see Baldridge and Deal 1975.) Furthermore, there are many reports of idiosyncratic instructional programs in schools, which appear to be direct responses to neither educational needs nor external demands, and there is also much programmatic variance among schools, which is not explained by conventional lines of reasoning. This lack of correspondence between structure and activity has led writers to describe schools as loosely coupled systems. (See, for example, Cohen and March 1974; Corwin 1976; March and Olsen 1976; Meyer and Rowan 1976; Weick 1976.) Two theoretical approaches that explain these observations seem particularly relevant to the examination of what we have called anomalies; these are the "organized anarchy" and the "institutional" approaches.

Organized Anarchies

An organized anarchy is defined as an organization that has ill-defined, inconsistent, or constantly changing goals; an unclear technology; or fluid participation by members (Cohen and March 1974). Such a system is a "series of loose connections among a large number of changing elements" (Sproull, Weiner, and Wolf 1977, pp. iii-4). In an organized anarchy, theorists of this tradition point out, any decision or activity is likely to be the product of a particular juxtaposition or interaction of a very large number of factors. For example, a particular educational decision may be influenced by such diverse factors as the personal background and career aspirations of the principal or others involved, by legal or financial constraints, by state or district requirements, and by the demands or desires of teachers, parents, community members and students. Furthermore, the mixture of variables that interact to determine outcomes in a particular school will change over time. As these theorists stress, the amount of time and attention that organizational participants pay to different factors vary considerably from one occasion to another.

Institutionalized Organizations

The "institutional" approach to loose coupling stresses the importance of formal organization structure, even though this structure may not bear much resemblance to actual activity within the organization (Meyer and Rowan 1976). Theorists in this tradition point out that it is essential for an organization to incorporate "environmental myths" into its formal structure. They claim that quite apart from any possible effect on the efficiency and effectiveness of the organization, this incorporation maximizes survival. (The term "environmental myth" is used here to describe a widely held belief or definition of reality that guides activity; however, no judgment is implied as to the validity of such a belief.) For example, if there is a widespread societal belief that it is important for schoolchildren to have regular psychological testing, then it is important for schools to acknowledge this sentiment by formally establishing the position of a school psychologist, instituting regular procedures for testing, and so on. Failure to respond in this manner may jeopardize the school's claim to legitimacy and public support.

Furthermore, these theorists point out that many formal requirements arise from pressures external to the school and may be incompatible with the views or aims of principals or teachers. As a result, schools may attempt to shield or buffer their internal activities from such requirements. One common buffering device, for example, is the lack of evaluation or inspection of the implementation of formal policies or programs (see Davis and Stackhouse 1977). By making the appropriate formal response, a school can maintain an appropriate public image; by not insisting on implementation of formal requirements, the organization can protect its internal activities from inappropriate or disruptive external demands. According to this approach, it is the formal incorporation of responses to an environmental myth, and not changes in activity corresponding to the change in structure, which is vital for the school.

Methods

Large-scale studies of school organizations (for example, Cohen, Deal, Meyer, and Scott 1976) do not provide the kind of data that would permit examination of these issues. Therefore, we undertook a small pilot study in which we interviewed the principals of seven San Francisco Bay Area elementary schools. During these interviews, we tried to determine (1) the formal process involved in the establishment of new programs and activities, (2) the actual history of existing programs, and (3) the actual procedures for evaluating and inspecting instructional programs. In addition to our interviews of principals, we were able to visit classrooms and talk with teachers in some of the schools we visited.

We have not, of course, attempted to report descriptions of all of the anomalies we encountered. Rather, we present the examples which seem most interesting and are most easily described....(Note that even the "custodial function" of the school was not safe from innovation; in one school the students were let out at noon on Wednesdays and kept longer during the rest of the week so that the principal could institute a regular in-service training program for his staff.)

Description and Analysis of Selected Cases

Schools as Organized Anarchies

In this section, we present illustrations of the processes described by the organized anarchy theorists, and we discuss examples from three schools in which a complex mixture of factors interacted to produce a new program. In each of these cases the primary impetus for change arose *within* the school. For example, in Schools A and B, the career paths of the principals affected both the nature of their roles as change agents within their schools and the progress of the innovations they introduced. In School C, the educational philosophies of the teachers, an architectural "accident," and an increase in student enrollments combined to produce a quite unique educational program.

Principal Career Paths. This first account is a comparison of two schools in adjoining school districts. In each school, the principal had been personally instrumental in developing special methods of instruction for use in elementary schools. One program dealt with handwriting instruction, the other with mathematics and reading. Each of these principals reported that his special method of instruction was used in every classroom of his school. (We did not, however, visit classrooms in these schools to determine the actual degree of implementation of these programs.)

One interesting difference between the two schools was that while Principal A had spread the news of his special method throughout the school district and claimed that many other district schools were employing it, Principal B had kept a "low profile." Principal B had, in fact, copyrighted his special program and sought to avoid its dissemination throughout the district, even though he thought his program was extremely successful.

As the organized anarchy theorists point out, the career paths of individuals may affect the nature of the decisions made by the organizations in which they participate. One very important difference between these two principals, which seems to have affected the progress of their innovations, was the nature of their career paths. Principal A had a joint appointment as vice-superintendent of instruction for the district. He had worked in the district office full time before becoming principal of this school and clearly had a strong desire to improve instructional practices throughout the district. It is thus not too surprising to learn that his methods for handwriting instruction were disseminated through all schools in the district.

By contrast, Principal B had once been a teacher and seemed to identify with teachers rather than with the district office. He spoke sympathetically of the "ridiculous" impositions made by district office red tape on teachers. He was apprehensive of recent state legislation that mandates collective bargaining between teachers and the district office and defines the principal as a member of the administrative "team" for these negotiations. He felt this would destroy the good rapport that existed between himself and his staff and had decided to take an early retirement. After retirement from the school, he planned to work full time teaching his copyrighted methods of reading and mathematics to disadvantaged students, and he had already received some government grants for this purpose. No wonder then that this principal was anxious to keep his special methods confined to his own school.

In both these cases, the career orientation of the principal affected decisions that shaped the curricular programs of his school. Each principal apparently had different motivations for developing and implementing an innovative instructional program. Further, we found that the path of dissemination of each individual's special method was directly tied to his career history and plans.

Open-Space Activities Center. In School C, a wide variety of factors within the school combined to produce a novel program. What started out as a mismatch between the staff and the physical layout of the school ended up as an unique instructional program. A new school had been constructed with an open-space design because, as the principal candidly explained, it was the cheapest option available. No other schools in the district were open-space schools, and at the time neither the teachers nor the principal had any particular desire to have anything other than a traditional school with self-contained classrooms. When the school was first constructed, the movable walls were arranged so that two clusters of six classrooms each opened onto one of two open areas, which served initially as large hallways. The twelve teachers assigned to the school thus had one classroom each, an arrangement which resembled the traditional classroom design.

Problems developed a year or so later when the student population of the new school grew much faster than anticipated. The district assigned two new teachers to handle the overcrowding. There were obviously no classrooms for the new teachers. Further, such measures as rearranging the walls and assigning two teachers to team teach in one room were apparently not acceptable solutions to the rather traditional teaching staff. After much staff and principal discussion, a novel solution was devised. The two hallways onto which the classroom clusters opened would each be used as multigrade "activities centers"—one for grades one to three, the other for grades four to six. A teacher would be assigned full time to each center, thus absorbing the two new staff members. These resource teachers would take some children from the other classes at various times of day and conduct special activities with them. Thus, overcrowding would be relieved and existing teaching arrangements (and the walls) would remain undisturbed. It apparently took some time before all teachers could decide exactly *how* to employ the centers; and the two special teachers assigned to them had to work hard to keep the centers fully utilized.

There is a sequel to this story. Apparently the novel activities centers aroused much enthusiasm among neighborhood parents, and it seems that they and the school staff were proud of this unique feature of School C. Accordingly, when funds became available for the construction of a second building, the principal requested that a large activities center be incorporated in the plans. He requested and received funds for a resource teacher to run it. The situation in this school has remained the same over recent years. Each teacher has his or her individual classroom; the walls between classrooms remain in place except for special events like folk dancing lessons or movie showings. The resource teacher in charge of the activities center spends a large amount of time trying to keep the center in full use. In fact, a school-wide pastime among teachers and parents is to suggest center projects. Even students are encouraged to submit ideas.

This example illustrates an idiosyncratic program arising not from a rational decision to create such a program but rather through the combination of a complex set of factors: the physical layout of School C (in itself the result of a relative shortage of building funds); the adaptation of traditional teachers to the open-space architecture; and the threat posed to the arrangements of classrooms and teachers by the addition of two new staff members. This case also illustrates the process described by some organized anarchy theorists (see Cohen, March, and Olsen 1972) of preference being discovered *after* an action is taken—rather than the rational reverse process. The innovative centers were perpetuated even after the initial reasons for their creation had been eliminated due to the pride and interest the centers aroused in the school and community.

Schools as Institutionalized Organizations

We shall now present accounts of the progress of three innovations where the central impetus for change within the school was external to the school itself and originated from a source of legitimacy and (directly or indirectly) funding for the school. These accounts illustrate some of the processes described by the institutional theorists who, it may be recalled, stress the importance of incorporating "myths" about education into the formal structure of schools while insulating actual activity from formal requirements.

Quite often a school will implement a new program that has been proposed by some source external to the school, such as the school district, the school board, the state, or some parent or community group. Presumably, in some cases such innovations will be heartily welcomed by the school staff. However, there are also cases when the new programs are costly or otherwise difficult to implement. In the latter situation, the institutional theorists propose that a school will try to buffer its internal core of technical activity from the impact of these external demands by noninspection and nonevaluation of the innovation. At the same time, they suggest, the school's legitimacy remains intact if the innovation is incorporated into formal policies and procedures and the appropriate ceremonies of implementation are maintained. The following example illustrates this process at work.

Values Program. In School D, a certain district "values program" had been instituted. The principal we interviewed spoke of it with reverence, stressing that it ranked in importance on the level of the mathematics and reading programs. The program required that each teacher evaluate every child once a week on a set of "values"; for example, power, wealth, enlightenment, rectitude, and others (which, interestingly, the principal could not remember). District support for this program was evidently such that any school that refused to adopt it might seem guilty of lack of concern over moral education. It is not surprising then that Principal D spoke highly of its value, that the school had officially adopted it, and appropriate forms had been distributed to all classroom teachers.

The problem was, of course, that the ranking of all children every week was a tedious chore—and presumably somewhat arbitrary as it would seem to be exceedingly difficult to apply consistent standards across all students on judging progress on such abstractions as "rectitude" and "power." Both the myth and legitimacy of the school were kept intact by the simple process of lack of inspection or evaluation of the program. Thus, Principal D made no note of which teachers complied and which did not; he never furnished any reports to the district office, which, conveniently, did not ask for them. In effect, no one actually knew which teachers, if any, actually carried out the program. But, to reiterate, the principal's public position (expressed emphatically to the interviewer) was that this was an extremely important program, which everyone took very seriously.

A Triple Program. Our second example of this buffering process focuses on an innovation with a somewhat different external origin. The California school system is fairly highly penetrated by parent groups. Because the community legitimates and provides resources for public schools, parent activism frequently initiates the incorporation of new programs. Indeed, sometimes a school must demonstrate active parental involvement in order to get special state fundings (for example, Early Childhood Education—a California State Department of Education program). As mentioned earlier, such externally created innovations can cause difficulties if, for instance, teachers do not like them or if they are difficult or costly to implement. We have already discussed one way in which existing arrangements can be buffered from externally imposed innovations—that is, by failing to inspect or evaluate the new programs.

The situation is complicated, however, when there are strong but diverse pressures from within the same community and the school finds itself faced with conflicting demands. In School E, for example, different factions within the community demanded quite different instructional approaches. Furthermore, the principal himself was an ardent supporter of an open-classroom system of education that clashed with the desires of one group of parents who wanted the school to institute rigid discipline and a back-to-basics approach.

School E's solution was to institute three completely separate educational programs. There was a conservative, back-to-basics program; a more moderate team-teaching program; and an open-education program. Parents were able to choose the program they preferred for their children; teachers were never assigned to a program against their wishes. There was a separate parent advisory committee for each group. Competition among the three groups was avoided by discouraging any attempts at comparison, such as comparing test scores. In fact, there was a schoolwide philosophy—forcefully stated by the principal and the teachers with whom we spoke—holding test scores to be meaningless, thus discounting any differences that came to light.

Clearly, this triple-program solution has resulted in a wider base of support for School E than would be obtained by the uniform adoption of any single program. The three groups are buffered from one another by a careful lack of comparison, facilitated by the philosophy that rejects the validity of standardized testing as a measure of success. If this were not the case, then any program performing especially poorly would lead to the unhappy situation where the school would either be accused by advocates of competing programs of wasting money on poor educational practices or, if the school were to drop the low-performance program, by loss of support from those in the community who wanted it.

As it happens, this school is maintaining a seemingly precarious position. Although the principal and teachers downgrade the importance of test scores, many parents do not. Even parents who have chosen the open-education program for their children often show concern about their children's standing on standardized achievement tests. It may be that in the long run comparisons among the three programs will be unavoidable.

A Multicultural Program. A somewhat different example of a school's response to community pressure was provided by School F, which had been recently and abruptly integrated due to the closing of a neighboring all-black school. Principal F explained that there had been many conflicts with the black parents when the transition first took place. His response had been to form a "multicultural" program in the school by adding a black parent to the enrichment team (a group of volunteers available to teachers as resource persons). This enrichment team is not a policymaking group; in fact, it may have little or no impact on the instructional program of the school, since it functions entirely as a resource group available at the discretion of the teachers. The important point is that regardless of its actual impact Principal F, by taking such a step, was able to avert trouble and establish the school's legitimacy in the eyes of the new parent population.

To summarize, in each of the three cases we have just described, the formal structure of the school has been changed in response to some external demand (or "environmental myth"); yet in each case the actual instructional activities within the school have been insulated from the full impact of the innovation: (1) The values program was formally instituted—but, by failing to inspect or evaluate it, existing activities were protected from its full impact. (2) By incorporating a triple-instructional program, a school was able to accommodate conflicting community demands; by avoiding comparisons among the three segments and by having separate parent advisory committees for each, it was able to buffer the programs from one another. (3) By making a black parent an official member of a school's enrichment team, a potentially disruptive segment of the parental population was placated; but, as this team was used only at the discretion of teachers, conflicts with teachers who were opposed to this innovation were minimized.

Conclusions

In this paper we have presented several accounts of anomalies that we encountered in California elementary schools. We have termed our examples "anomalies" because they are situations not readily explained by conventional organization theory.

We have tried to show the utility of recent loose coupling approaches to the study of organizations in explaining these anomalous situations. The first two cases, we feel, illustrate particularly well the "organized anarchy" approach; they show how multiple factors—career paths and aspirations of individual principals, architectural design of the school, discovery of preferences after action has occurred, and so on—can interact both to create new programs and to affect their progress over time. The last three accounts are especially illustrative of the ideas proposed by the "institutional" approach; they show how a school can incorporate external demands into its formal structure in order to maintain its legitimacy in the eyes of the community, while at the same time shielding its internal activities from the full impact of formal requirements.

Although we divided our examples into two groups for purposes of presentation, we want to stress that the two theoretical approaches are not mutually exclusive. For instance, the triple program, presented as an illustration of the institutional argument, shows an organized anarchy in action. Rather complex interacting factors produced the present instructional program: among them, conflicting community demands and the principal's personal preferences. Moreover, it seems likely that a third factor—that is, parents' concern for their children's test scores—may ultimately render untenable the school's present policy of insulating the three programs from one another.

As another example, the open-space activities center, which we have presented as an illustration of organized anarchy processes, also provides a good instance of the buffering process described by the institutional theorists: the creation of the new activities center was, in the first place, an attempt to insulate the existing teaching technology from the impact of an increase in staff.

Our choice of these two branches of loose coupling theory also represents somewhat of an oversimplification. For example, the multiple program in School E is also a good illustration of the process described by Weick (1976), wherein an organization with a loosely coupled structure can simultaneously reflect diverse elements of the environment of the organization.

In summary, we believe that each of the two loose coupling approaches to the study of organizations has value in ordering seemingly random and idiosyncratic features of schools. When one analyzes apparently anomalous aspects of school organizations from either the organized anarchy or institutional perspective, one finds that these idiosyncrasies often represent patterned variations in the activities of schools.

References

Baldridge, J. Victor. *Power and Conflict in the University.* New York: John Wiley & Sons, 1971.

Baldridge, J. Victor, and R. Burnham. *The Adoption of Innovations: The Effect of Organizational Size, Differentiation and Environment.* SCRDT Research and Development Memorandum No. 108, Stanford University, Stanford, California, 1973.

Baldridge, J. V., and T.E. Deal. *Managing Change in Educational Organizations.* Berkeley: McCutchan, 1975.

Bidwell, C.E. "The School as a Formal Organization." In *Handbook of Organizations,* edited by James G. March. Chicago: Rand McNally, 1965.

Bredo, A.E., and E.R. Bredo. *A Case Study of Educational Innovation in a Junior High School.* SCRDT Research and Development Memorandum No. 132, Stanford University, Stanford, California, 1975.

Cohen, E., T. Deal, J. Meyer, and W. Richard Scott. "Technology and Teaming in the Elementary School." *Sociology of Education* 52 (January 1979).

Cohen, M.D., and J.G. March. *Leadership and Ambiguity*. New York: McGraw-Hill, 1974.

Cohen, M.D., J.G. March, and J.P. Olsen. "A Garbage Can Model of Organizational Choice." *Administrative Science Quarterly* 7 (September 1972).

Corwin, R. "Organizations as Loosely Coupled Systems: Evolution of a Perspective." Paper presented at the Conference on Schools as Loosely Coupled Organizations, Stanford, California, November 1976.

Davis, M.R., and E. Anne Stackhouse. "The Importance of Formal Appearances: The Implementation of Programs for the Evaluation of Elementary Schools and Teachers." Paper presented at the 1977 meetings of the Pacific Sociological Association, Stanford University, Stanford, California, 1977.

Dreeben, R. "American Schooling: Patterns and Processes of Stability and Change." In *Stability and Social Change*, edited by Bernard Barker and Alex Inkeles. Boston: Little, Brown, 1971.

Griffiths, D.E. "System Theory and School Districts." In *Readings in the Sociology of Education*, edited by Patricia Cayo Sexton. Englewood Cliffs, N.J.: Prentice-Hall, 1967.

Katz, F.E. "The School as a Formal Organization." *Harvard Educational Review* 32 (1964): 428-55.

March, J.G., and J.P. Olsen. *Ambiguity and Choice in Organizations*. Bergen, Norway: Universitetsforlaget, 1976.

Meyer, J.W., and Brian Rowan. "Institutionalized Organizations." Unpublished paper, Stanford University, Stanford, California, 1976.

Sproull, L., S. Weiner, and D. Wolf. *Organizing an Anarchy: Belief, Bureaucracy, and Politics in a New Federal Agency*. Chicago: University of Chicago Press, 1977.

Weick, K.E. "Educational Organizations as Loosely Coupled Systems." *Administrative Science Quarterly* 21 (March 1976).

18

Leadership in an Organized Anarchy

Michael Cohen and James March

The Ambiguities of Anarchy

The college president faces four fundamental ambiguities. The first is the ambiguity of *purpose*. In what terms can action be justified? What are the goals of the organization? The second is the ambiguity of *power*. How powerful is the president? What can he accomplish? The third is the ambiguity of *experience*. What is to be learned from the events of the presidency? How does the president make inferences about this experience? The fourth is the ambiguity of *success*. When is a president successful? How does he assess his pleasures?

These ambiguities are fundamental to college presidents because they strike at the heart of the usual interpretations of leadership. When purpose is ambiguous, ordinary theories of decision making and intelligence become problematic. When power is ambiguous, ordinary theories of social order and control become problematic. When experience is ambiguous, ordinary theories of learning and adaptation become problematic. When success is ambiguous, ordinary theories of motivation and personal pleasure become problematic.

The Ambiguity of Purpose

Almost any education person can deliver a lecture entitled "The Goals of the University." Almost no one will listen to the lecture voluntarily. For the

Reprinted, by permission, from *Leadership and Ambiguity* (New York: McGraw-Hill, 1974), pp. 195–229. Copyright © by the Carnegie Foundation for the Advancement of Teaching.

most part, such lectures and their companion essays are well-intentioned exercises in social rhetoric, with little operational content.

Efforts to generate normative statements of the goals of a university tend to produce goals that are either meaningless or dubious. They fail one or more of the following reasonable tests. First, is the goal clear? Can one define some specific procedure for measuring the degree of goal achievement? Second, is it problematic? Is there some possibility that the organization will accomplish the goal? Is there some chance that it will fail? Third, is it accepted? Do most significant groups in the university agree on the goal statement? For the most part, the level of generality that facilitates acceptance destroys the problematic nature or clarity of the goal. The level of specificity that permits measurement destroys acceptance.

Recent discussions of educational audits, of cost-benefit analysis in education, and of accountability and evaluation in higher education have not been spectacularly successful in resolving this normative ambiguity, even in those cases where such techniques have been accepted as relatively fruitful. In our judgment, the major contributions (and they are important ones) of operational analysis in higher education to date have been to expose the inconsistencies of current policies and to make marginal improvements in those domains in which clear objectives are widely shared.

Similarly, efforts to infer the "real" objectives of a university by observing university behavior tend to be unsuccessful. They fail one or more of the following reasonable tests. First, is the goal uniquely consistent with behavior? Does the imputed goal produce the observed behavior and is it the only goal that does? Second, is it stable? Does the goal imputed from past behavior reliably predict future behavior? Although it is often possible to devise a statement of the goals of a university by some form of revealed preference test of past actions, such goal statements have poor predictive power.

The difficulties in imputing goals from behavior are not unique to universities. Experience with the complications is shared by revealed preference theorists in economics and psychology, radical critics of society, and functionalist students of social institutions. The search for a consistent explanation of human social behavior through a model of rational intent and an imputation of intent from action has had some successes. But there is no sign that the university is one of the successes, or very likely to become one.

Efforts to specify a set of consciously shared, consistent objectives within a university or to infer such a set of objectives from the activities or actions of the university have regularly revealed signs of inconsistency. To expose inconsistencies is not to resolve them, however. There are only modest signs that universities or other organized anarchies respond to a revelation of ambiguity of purpose by reducing the ambiguity. These are organizational systems without clear objectives; and the processes by which their objectives are established and legitimized are not extraordinarily sensitive to inconsistency. In fact, for many purposes the ambiguity of purpose is produced by our insistence on treating purpose as a necessary property of a good university. The strains arise from trying to impose a model of action as flowing from intent on organizations that act in another way.

College presidents live within a normative context that presumes purpose and within an organizational context that denies it. They serve on commissions to define and redefine the objectives of higher education. They organize convocations to examine the goals of the college. They write introductory statements to the college catalog. They accept the presumption that intelligent leadership presupposes the rational pursuit of goals. Simultaneously, they are aware that the process of choice in the college depends little on statements of shared direction. They recognize the flow of actions as an ecology of games (Long 1958), each with its own rules. They accept the observation that the world is not like the model.

The Ambiguity of Power

Power is a simple idea, pervasive in its appeal to observers of social events. Like *intelligence* or *motivation* or *utility*, however, it tends to be misleadingly simple and prone to tautology. A person has power if he gets things done; if he has power, he can get things done.

As students of social power have long observed, such a view of power has limited usefulness.[1] Two of the things the simple view produces are an endless and largely fruitless search for the person who has "the real power" in the university, and an equally futile pursuit of the organizational locale "where the decision is *really* made." So profound is the acceptance of the power model that students of organizations who suggest the model is wrong are sometimes viewed as part of the plot to conceal "the real power" and "the true locus of decision." In that particular logic the reality of the simple power model is demonstrated by its inadequacy.

As a shorthand casual expression for variations in the potential of different positions in the organization, *power* has some utility. The college president has more potential for moving the college than most people, probably more potential than any one other person. Nevertheless,

---

[1] For anyone who wishes to enter the literature, see by way of introduction Raymond Wolfinger (1971*a*, 1971*b*) and Frederick W. Frey (1971).

presidents discover that they have less power than is believed, that their power to accomplish things depends heavily on what they want to accomplish, that the use of formal authority is limited by other formal authority, that the acceptance of authority is not automatic, that the necessary details of organizational life confuse power (which is somewhat different from diffusing it), and that their colleagues seem to delight in complaining simultaneously about presidential weakness and presidential willfulness.

The ambiguity of power, like the ambiguity of purpose, is focused on the president. Presidents share in and contribute to the confusion. They enjoy the perquisites and prestige of the office. They enjoy its excitement, at least when things go well. They announce important events. They appear at important symbolic functions. They report to the people. They accept and thrive on their own importance. It would be remarkable if they did not. Presidents even occasionally recite that "the buck stops here" with a finality that suggests the cliché is an observation about power and authority rather than a proclamation of administrative style and ideology.

At the same time, presidents solicit an understanding of the limits to their control. They regret the tendency of students, legislators, and community leaders to assume that a president has the power to do whatever he chooses simply because he is president. They plead the countervailing power of other groups in the college or the notable complexities of causality in large organizations.

The combination is likely to lead to popular impressions of strong presidents during good times and weak presidents during bad times. Persons who are primarily exposed to the symbolic presidency (for example, outsiders) will tend to exaggerate the power of the president. Those people who have tried to accomplish something in the institution with presidential support (for example, educational reformers) will tend to underestimate presidential power or presidential will.

The confusion disturbs the president, but it also serves him. Ambiguity of power leads to a parallel ambiguity of responsibility. The allocation of credit and blame for the events of organizational life becomes—as it often does in political and social systems—a matter for argument. The "facts" of responsibility are badly confounded by the confusions of anarchy; and the conventional myth of hierarchical executive responsibility is undermined by the countermyth of the nonhierarchical nature of colleges and universities. Presidents negotiate with their audiences on the interpretations of their power. As a result, during the recent years of campus troubles, many college presidents sought to emphasize the limitations of presidential control. During the more glorious days of conspicuous success, they solicited a recognition of their responsibility for events.

The process does not involve presidents alone, of course. The social validation of responsibility involves all the participants: faculty, trustees, students, parents, community leaders, government. Presidents seek to write their histories in the use of power as part of a chorus of history writers, each with his own reasons for preferring a somewhat different interpretation of "Who has the Power?"

The Ambiguity of Experience

College presidents attempt to learn from their experience. They observe the consequences of actions and infer the structure of the world from those observations. They use the resulting inferences in attempts to improve their future actions.

Consider the following very simple learning paradigm:

1. At a certain point in time a president is presented with a set of well-defined, discrete action alternatives.
2. At any point in time he has a certain probability of choosing any particular alternative (and a certainty of choosing one of them).
3. The president observes the outcome that apparently follows his choice and assesses the outcome in terms of his goals.
4. If the outcome is consistent with his goals, the president increases his probability of choosing that alternative in the future; if not, he decreases the probability.

Although actual presidential learning certainly involves more complicated inferences, such a paradigm captures much of the ordinary adaptation of an intelligent man to the information gained from experience.

The process produces considerable learning. The subjective experience is one of adapting from experience and improving behavior on the basis of feedback. If the world with which the president is dealing is relatively simple and relatively stable, and if his experience is relatively frequent, he can expect to improve over time (assuming he has some appropriate criterion for testing the consistency of outcomes with goals). As we have suggested earlier, however, the world in which the president lives has two conspicuous properties that make experience ambiguous even where goals are clear. First, the world is relatively complex. Outcomes depend heavily on factors other than the president's action. These factors are uncontrolled and, in large part, unobserved. Second, relative to the rate at which the president gathers experimental data, the world changes rapidly. These properties produce considerable potential for false learning.

We can illustrate the phenomenon by taking a familiar instance of learning in the realm of personnel policies. Suppose that a manager reviews his subordinates annually and considers what to do with those who are doing poorly. He has two choices: he can replace an employee whose performance is low, or he can keep him in the job and try to work with him to obtain improvement. He chooses which employees to replace and which to keep in the job on the basis of his judgment about their capacities to respond to different treatments. Now suppose that, in fact, there are no differences among the employees. Observed variations in performance are due entirely to random fluctuations. What would the manager "learn" in such a situation?

He would learn how smart he was. He would discover that his judgments about whom to keep and whom to replace were quite good. Replacements will generally perform better than the men they replaced; those men who are kept in the job will generally improve in their performance. If for some reason he starts out being relatively "humane" and refuses to replace anyone, he will discover that the best managerial strategy is to work to improve existing employees. If he starts out with a heavy hand and replaces everyone, he will learn that being tough is a good idea. If he replaces some and works with others, he will learn that the essence of personnel management is judgment about the worker.

Although we know that in this hypothetical situation it makes no difference what a manager does, he will experience some subjective learning that is direct and compelling. He will come to believe that he understands the situation and has mastered it. If we were to suggest to the manager that he might be a victim of superstitious learning, he would find it difficult to believe. Everything in his environment tells him that he understands the world, even though his understanding is spurious.

It is not necessary to assume that the world is strictly random to produce substantially the same effect. Whenever the rate of experience is modest relative to the complexity of the phenomena and the rate of change in the phenomena, the interpretation made of experience will tend to be more persuasive subjectively than it should be. In such a world, experience is not a good teacher. Although the outcomes stemming from the various learned strategies in the personnel management example will be no worse because of a belief in the reality of the learning, the degree of confidence a manager comes to have in his theory of the world is erroneously high.

College presidents probably have greater confidence in their interpretations of college life, college administration, and their general environment than is warranted. The inferences they have made from experience are likely to be wrong. Their confidence in their learning is likely to have been reinforced by the social support they receive from the people around them and by social expectations about the presidential role. As a result, they tend to be unaware of the extent to which the ambiguities they feel with respect to purpose and power are matched by similar ambiguities with respect to the meaning of the ordinary events of presidential life.

The Ambiguity of Success

Administrative success is generally recognized in one of two ways. First, by promotion: An administrator knows that he has been successful by virtue of a promotion to a better job. He assesses his success on the current job by the opportunities he has or expects to have to leave it. Second, by widely accepted, operational measures of organizational output: a business executive values his own performance in terms of a profit-and-loss statement of his operations.

Problems with these indicators of success are generic to high-level administrative positions. Offers of promotion become less likely as the job improves and the administrator's age advances. The criteria by which success is judged become less precise in measurement, less stable over time, and less widely shared. The administrator discovers that a wide assortment of factors outside his control are capable of overwhelming the impact of any actions he may take.

In the case of the college president all three problems are accentuated. As we have seen earlier, few college presidents are promoted out of the presidency. There are job offers, and most presidents ultimately accept one; but the best opportunities the typical president can get are not usually as good, and can lead to administrative semiretirement. The criteria of success in academic administration are sometimes moderately clear (for example, growth, quiet on campus, improvement in the quality of students and faculty), but the relatively precise measures of college health tend neither to be stable over time nor to be critically sensitive to presidential action. For example, during the post–World War II years in American colleges, it was conventional to value growth and to attribute growth to the creative activities of administrative leaders. In the retrospective skepticism about the uncritical acceptance of a growth ethic, we have begun to reinterpret a simple history that attributed college growth to the conscious prior decision of a wise (or stupid) president or board. The rapid expansion of higher education, the postwar complex of student and faculty relations and attitudes, and the massive extension of governmental subsidies to the research activities of colleges and universities were not the simple consequences of decisions by Clark Kerr or John Hanna. Nor, retrospectively, does it seem plausible to attribute major control over those events to college administrators.

An argument can be made, of course, that the college president should be accustomed to the ambiguity of success. His new position is not, in this respect, so strikingly different from the positions he has held previously.

His probable perspective is different, however. Success has not previously been subjectively ambiguous to him. He has been a success. He has been promoted relatively rapidly. He and his associates are inclined to attribute his past successes to a combination of administrative savoir-faire, interpersonal style, and political sagacity. He has experienced those successes as the lawful consequence of his actions. Honest modesty on the part of a president does not conceal a certain awareness of his own ability. A president comes to his office having learned that he is successful and that he enjoys success.

The momentum of promotion will not sustain him in the presidency. Although, as we have seen, a fair number of presidents anticipate moving from their present job to another, better presidency, the prospects are not nearly as good as the hopes. The ambiguities of purpose, power, and experience conspire to render success and failure equally obscure. The validation of success is unreliable. Not only can a president not assure himself that he will be able to lead the college in the directions in which others might believe, he also has no assurance that the same criteria will be applied tomorrow. What happens today will tend to be rationalized tomorrow as what was desired. What happens today will have some relation to what was desired yesterday. Outcomes do flow in part from goals. But goals flow from outcomes as well, and both goals and outcomes also move independently.

The result is that the president is a bit like the driver of a skidding automobile. The marginal judgments he makes, his skill, and his luck may possibly make some difference to the survival prospects for his riders. As a result, his responsibilities are heavy. But whether he is convicted of manslaughter or receives a medal for heroism is largely outside his control.

One basic response to the ambiguities of success is to find pleasure in the process of presidential life. A reasonable man will seek reminders of his relevance and success. Where those reminders are hard to find in terms of socially validated outcomes unambiguously due to one's actions, they may be sought in the interactions of organizational life. George Reedy (1970) made a similar observation about a different presidency: "Those who seek to lighten the burdens of the presidency by easing the workload do no occupant of that office a favor. The 'workload'—especially the ceremonial workload—are the only events of a president's day which make life endurable."

Leader Response to Anarchy

The ambiguities that college presidents face describe the life of any formal leader of any organized anarchy. The metaphors of leadership and our traditions of personalizing history (even the minor histories of collegiate institutions) confuse the issues of leadership by ignoring the basic ambiguity of leadership life. We require a plausible basic perspective for the leader of a loosely coupled, ambiguous organization.

Such a perspective begins with humility. It is probably a mistake for a college president to imagine that what he does in office affects significantly either the long-run position of the institution or his reputation as a president. So long as he does not violate some rather obvious restrictions on his behavior, his reputation and his term of office are more likely to be affected by broad social events or by the unpredictable vicissitudes of official responsibility than by his actions. Although the college library or administration building will doubtless record his presidency by appropriate portraiture or plaque, few presidents achieve even a modest claim to attention twenty years after their departure from the presidency; and those who are remembered best are probably most distinguished by their good fortune in coming to office during a period of collegiate good times and growth, or their bad fortune in being there when the floods came.

In this respect the president's life does not differ markedly from that of most of us. A leadership role, however, is distinguished by the numerous temptations to self-importance that it provides. Presidents easily come to believe that they can continue in office forever if they are only clever or perceptive or responsive enough. They easily come to exaggerate the significance of their daily actions for the college as well as for themselves. They easily come to see each day as an opportunity to build support in their constituencies for the next "election."

It is an old story. Human action is frequently corrupted by an exaggeration of its consequences. Parents are intimidated by an exaggerated belief in their importance to the process of childrearing. Teachers are intimidated by an exaggerated belief in their importance to the process of learning. Lovers are intimidated by an exaggerated belief in their importance to the process of loving. Counselors are intimidated by an exaggerated belief in their importance to the process of self-discovery.

The major consequence of a heroic conception of the consequences of action is a distrust of judgment. When college presidents imagine that their actions have great consequences for the world, they are inclined to fear an error. When they fear an error, they are inclined to seek social support for their judgment, to confuse voting with virtue and bureaucratic rules with equity. Such a conception of the importance of their every choice makes presidents vulnerable to the same deficiencies of performance that afflict the parents of first children and inexperienced teachers, lovers, or counselors.

A lesser, but important, result of a heroic conception of the consequences of action is the abandonment of pleasure. By acceding to his own importance, the college president is driven to sobriety of manner. For reasons we have detailed earlier, he has difficulty in establishing the correctness of his actions by exhibiting their consequences. He is left with the necessity of communicating moral intent through facial intensity. At the same time, he experiences the substantial gap between his aspirations and his possibilities. Both by the requirements of their public face and by their own intolerant expectations, college presidents often find the public enjoyment of their job denied to them.

The ambiguities of leadership in an organized anarchy require a leadership posture that is somewhat different from that implicit in most discussions of the college presidency. In particular, we believe that a college president is, on the whole, better advised to think of himself as trying to do good than as trying to satisfy a political or bureaucratic audience; better advised to define his role in terms of the modest part he can play in making the college slightly better in the long run than in terms of satisfying current residents or solving current problems. He requires an enthusiasm for a Tolstoyan view of history and for the freedom of individual action that such a view entails. Since the world is absurd, the president's primary responsibility is to virtue.

Presidents occupy a minor part in the lives of a small number of people. They have some power, but little magic. They can act with a fair degree of confidence that if they make a mistake, it will not matter much. They can be allowed the heresy of believing that pleasure is consistent with virtue.

The Elementary Tactics of Administrative Action

The tactics of administrative action in an organized anarchy are somewhat different from the tactics of action in a situation characterized by clearer goals, better specified technology, and more persistent participation. Nevertheless, we can examine how a leader with a purpose can operate within an organization that is without one.

Necessarily, any presentation of practical strategies suggests a minor Machiavellianism with attendant complications and concerns. There is an argument that strategies based upon knowledge contribute to administrative manipulation. There is a fear that practical strategies may be misused for evil ends. There is a feeling that the effectiveness of the strategies may be undermined by their public recitation.

We are aware of these concerns, but not persuaded by them. First, we do not believe that any major new cleverness that would conspicuously alter the prevailing limits on our ability to change the course of history will be discovered. The idea that there are some spectacularly effective strategies waiting to be discovered by some modern Machiavelli seems implausible. Second, we believe that the problem of evil is little eased by know-nothingness. The concern about malevolent manipulation is a real one (as well as a cliché), but it often becomes a simple defense of the status quo. We hope that good people interested in accomplishing things will find a list of tactics marginally helpful. Third, we can see nothing in the recitation of strategic recommendations that changes systematically the relative positions of members of the organization. If the strategies are effective, it is because the analysis of organization is correct. The features of the organization that are involved are not likely to change quickly. As a result, we would not anticipate that public discussion of the strategies would change their effectiveness much or distinctly change the relative positions of those (for example, students, presidents) who presumably stand to profit from the advice if it is useful.

As we will indicate later in this chapter, a conception of leadership that merely assumes that the college president should act to accomplish what he wants to accomplish is too narrow. A major part of his responsibility is to lead the organization to a changing and more complex view of itself by treating goals as only partly knowable. Nevertheless, the problems of inducing a college to do what one wants it to do are clearly worthy of attention. If presidents and others are to function effectively within the college, they need to recognize the ways in which the character of the college as a system for exercising problems, making decisions, and certifying status conditions their attempts to influence the outcome of any decision.

We can identify five major properties of decision making in organized anarchies that are of substantial importance to the tactics of accomplishing things in colleges and universities:

1. Most issues most of the time have *low salience* for most people. The decisions to be made within the organization secure only partial and erratic attention from participants in the organization. A major share of the attention devoted to a particular issue is tied less to the content of the issue than to its symbolic significance for individual and group esteem.

2. The total system has *high inertia*. Anything that requires a coordinated effort of the organization in order to start is unlikely to be started. Anything that requires a coordinated effort of the organization in order to be stopped is unlikely to be stopped.

3. Any decision can become a *garbage can* for almost any problem. The issues discussed in the context of any particular decision depend less on the decision or problems involved than on the timing of their joint arrivals and the existence of alternative arenas for exercising problems.
4. The processes of choice are easily subject to *overload*. When the load on the system builds up relative to its capabilities for exercising and resolving problems, the decision outcomes in the organization tend to become increasingly separated from the formal process of decision.
5. The organization has a *weak information base*. Information about past events or past decisions is often not retained. When retained, it is often difficult to retrieve. Information about current activities is scant.

These properties are conspicuous and ubiquitous. They represent some important ways in which all organizations sometimes, and an organization like a university often, present opportunities for tactical action that in a modest way strengthen the hand of the participant who attends to them. We suggest eight basic tactical rules for use by those who seek to influence the course of decisions in universities or colleges.

Rule 1: Spend Time. The kinds of decision-making situations and organizations we have described suffer from a shortage of decision-making energy. Energy is a scarce resource. If one is in a position to devote time to the decision-making activities within the organization, he has a considerable claim on the system. Most organizations develop ways of absorbing the decision-making energy provided by sharply deviant participants; but within moderate boundaries, a person who is willing to spend time finds himself in a strong position for at least three significant reasons:

—By providing a scarce resource (energy), he lays the basis for a claim. If he is willing to spend time, he can expect more tolerant consideration of the problems he considers important. One of the most common organizational responses to a proposal from a participant is the request that he head a committee to do something about it. This behavior is an acknowledgment both of the energy-poor situation and of the price the organization pays for participation. That price is often that the organization must allow the participant some significant control over the definition of problems to be considered relevant.[2]

---

[2]For a discussion of this point in the context of public school decision making, see Stephen Weiner (1972).

—By spending time on the homework for a decision, he becomes a major information source in an information-poor world. At the limit, the information provided need have no particular evidential validity. Consider, for example, the common assertions in college decision-making processes about what some constituency (such as board of trustees, legislature, student body, ethnic group) is "thinking." The assertions are rarely based on defensible evidence, but they tend to become organizational facts by virtue of the shortage of serious information. More generally, reality for a decision is specified by those willing to spend the time required to collect the small amounts of information available, to review the factual assertions of others, and to disseminate their findings.

—By investing more of his time in organizational concerns, he increases his chance of being present when something important to him is considered. A participant who wishes to pursue other matters (such as study, research, family, the problems of the outside world) reduces the number of occasions for decision making which he can afford to attend. A participant who can spend time can be involved in more arenas. Since it is often difficult to anticipate when and where a particular issue will be involved (and thus to limit one's attention to key times and domains), the simple frequency of availability is relatively important.

Rule 2: Persist. It is a mistake to assume that if a particular proposal has been rejected by an organization today, it will be rejected tomorrow. Different sets of people and concerns will be reflected each time a problem is considered or a proposal discussed. We noted earlier the ways in which the flow of participants leads to a flow of organizational concerns.[3] The specific combination of sentiments and people that is associated with a specific choice opportunity is partly fortuitous, and Fortune may be more considerate another day.

For the same reason, it is a mistake to assume that today's victory will be implemented automatically tomorrow. The distinction between decision making and decision implementation is usually a false one. Decisions are not "made" once and for all. Rather they happen as a result of a series of episodes involving different people in different settings, and they may be unmade or modified by subsequent episodes. The participant who spends much time celebrating his victory ordinarily can expect to find the victory short-lived. The loser who spends his time weeping rather than reintroducing his ideas will persistently have something to weep about. The loser who persists in a variety of contexts is frequently rewarded.

Rule 3: Exchange Status for Substance. As we have indicated, the specific substantive issues in a college, or similar organization, typically have low

---

[3] For a discussion of the same phenomenon in a business setting, see R.M. Cyert and J.G. March (1963).

salience for participants. A quite typical situation is one in which significant numbers of participants and groups of participants care less about the specific substantive outcome than they do about the implications of that outcome for their own sense of self-esteem and the social recognition of their importance. Such an ordering of things is neither surprising nor normatively unattractive. It would be a strange world indeed if the mostly minor issues of university governance, for example, became more important to most people than personal and group esteem.

A college president, too, is likely to become substantially concerned with the formal acknowledgment of office. Since it is awkward for him to establish definitively that he is substantively important, the president tends to join other participants in seeking symbolic confirmation of his significance.

The esteem trap is understandable but unfortunate. College presidents who can forgo at least some of the pleasures of self-importance in order to trade status for substance are in a strong position. Since leaders receive credit for many things over which they have little control and to which they contribute little, they should find it possible to accomplish some of the things they want by allowing others to savor the victories, enjoy the pleasures of involvement, and receive the profits of public importance.

Rule 4: Facilitate Opposition Participation. The high inertia of organizations and the heavy dependence of organizational events on processes outside of the control of the organization make organizational power ambiguous. Presidents sense their lack of control despite their position of authority, status, and concern. Most people who participate in university decision making sense a disappointment with the limited control their position provides.

Persons outside the formal ranks of authority tend to see authority as providing more control. Their aspirations for change tend to be substantially greater than the aspirations for change held by persons with formal authority. One obvious solution is to facilitate participation in decision making. Genuine authoritative participation will reduce the aspirations of oppositional leaders. In an organization characterized by high inertia and low salience it is unwise to allow beliefs about the feasibility of planned action to outrun reality. From this point of view, public accountability, participant observation, and other techniques for extending the range of legitimate participation in the decision-making processes of the organization are essential means of keeping the aspirations of occasional actors within bounds. Since most people most of the time do not participate much, their aspirations for what can be done have a tendency to drift away from reality. On the whole, the direct involvement of dissident groups in the decision-making process is a more effective depressant of exaggerated aspirations than is a lecture by the president.

Rule 5: Overload the System. As we have suggested, the style of decision making changes when the load exceeds the capabilities of the system. Since we are talking about energy-poor organizations, accomplishing overload is not hard. In practical terms, this means having a large repertoire of projects for organizational action; it means making substantial claims on resources for the analysis of problems, discussion of issues, and political negotiation.

Within an organized anarchy it is a mistake to become absolutely committed to any one project. There are innumerable ways in which the processes we have described will confound the cleverest behavior with respect to any single proposal, however imaginative or subjectively important. What such processes cannot do is cope with large numbers of projects. Someone with the habit of producing many proposals, without absolute commitment to any one, may lose any one of them (and it is hard to predict a priori which one), but cannot be stopped on everything.

The tactic is not unlike the recommendation in some treatments of bargaining that one should introduce new dimensions of bargains in order to facilitate more favorable trades. (See, for example, Iklé 1964 and Walton and McKersie 1965.) It is grounded in the observation that the press of proposals so loads the organization that a large number of actions are taken without attending to problems. Where decisions are made through oversight or flight, considerable control over the course of decision making lies in the hands of two groups: the initiators of the proposals, who get their way in oversight, and the full-time administrator, who is left to make the decision in cases of flight. The college president with a program is in the enviable position of being both a proposal initiator and a full-time administrator. Overload is almost certainly helpful to his program. Other groups within a college or university are probably also advantaged by overload if they have a positive program for action, but their advantage is less certain. In particular, groups in opposition to the administration that are unable to participate full time (either directly or through representatives) may wish to be selective in the use of overload as a tactic.

Rule 6. Provide Garbage Cans. One of the complications in accomplishing something in a garbage can decision-making process is the tendency for any particular project to become intertwined with a variety of other issues simply because those issues exist at the time the project is before the organization. A proposal for curricular reform becomes an arena for a concern for social justice. A proposal for construction of a building becomes an arena for concerns about environmental quality. A proposal for bicycle paths becomes an arena for discussion of sexual inequality.

It is pointless to try to react to such problems by attempting to enforce rules of relevance. Such rules are, in any event, highly arbitrary. Even if they were not, it would still be difficult to persuade a person that his problem (however important) could not be discussed because it is not relevant to the current agenda. The appropriate tactical response is to provide garbage cans into which wide varieties of problems can be dumped. The more conspicuous the can, the more garbage it will attract away from other projects.

The prime procedure for making a garbage can attractive is to give it precedence and conspicuousness. On a grand scale, discussions of overall organizational objectives or overall organizational long-term plans are classic first-quality cans. They are general enough to accommodate anything. They are socially defined as being important. They attract enough different kinds of issues to reinforce their importance. An activist will push for discussions of grand plans (in part) in order to draw the garbage away from the concrete day-to-day arenas of his concrete objectives.

On a smaller scale, the first item on a meeting agenda is an obvious garbage can. It receives much of the status allocation concerns that are a part of meetings. It is possible that any item on an agenda will attract an assortment of things currently concerning individuals in the group; but the first item is more vulnerable than others. As a result, projects of serious substantive concern should normally be placed somewhat later, after the important matters of individual and group esteem have been settled, most of the individual performances have been completed, and most of the enthusiasm for abstract argument has waned.

The garbage can tactic has long-term effects that may be important. Although in the short run the major consequence is to remove problems from the arena of short-term concrete proposals, the separation of problem discussion from decision making means that general organizational attitudes develop outside the context of immediate decisions. The exercise of problems and the discussion of plans contribute to a building of the climate within which the organization will operate in the future. A president who uses the garbage can tactic should be aware of the ways in which currently irrelevant conversations produce future ideological constraints. The same tactic also provides a (partly misleading) device for the training and selection of future leaders of the organization. Those who perform well in garbage can debates are not necessarily good leaders, though they may frequently be identified as potential leaders. Finally, the tactic offers a practical buffer for the organization from the instabilities introduced by the entry and exit of problems that drift from one organization to another. In recent years universities have become an arena for an assortment of problems that might have found expression in other social institutions. Universities and colleges were available and accessible to people with the concerns. Although the resulting strain on university processes was considerable, the full impact was cushioned by the tendency of such problems to move to decision-irrelevant garbage cans, to be held there until they could move on to another arena in another institution.

Rule 7: Manage Unobtrusively. If you put a man in a boat and tell him to plot a course, he can take one of three views of his task. He can float with the currents and winds, letting them take him wherever they wish; he can select a destination and try to use full power to go directly to it regardless of the current or winds; or he can select a destination and use his rudder and sails to let the currents and wind eventually take him where he wants to go. On the whole, we think conscious university leadership is properly seen in the third light.

A central tactic in high-inertia systems is to use high-leverage minor actions to produce major effects—to let the system go where it wants to go with only the minor interventions that make it go where it should. From a tactical point of view, the main objection to central direction and control is that it requires an impossible amount of attention and energy. The kinds of organizations with which we have been concerned are unable to be driven where we want them to go without making considerable use of the "natural" organizational processes. The appropriate tactics of management are unobtrusive and indirect.

Unobtrusive management uses interventions of greater impact than visibility. Such actions generally have two key attributes: (1) They affect many parts of the system slightly rather than a few parts in a major way. The effect on any one part of the system is small enough so that either no one really notices or no one finds it sensible to organize significantly against the intervention. (2) Once activated, they stay activated without further organizational attention. Their deactivation requires positive organizational action.

Given all the enthusiasm for elaborating a variety of models of organizations that bemoan bureaucracy and the conventional managerial tools associated with bureaucratic life, it is somewhat surprising to realize that the major instruments of unobtrusive management are bureaucratic. Consider the simple act of committing the organization by signing a piece of paper. By the formal statutes of many organizations, some people within the organization are conceded authority to sign pieces of paper. College presidents tend, in our judgment, to be timid about exercising such authority. By signing a piece of paper the president is able to reverse the burden of organizing the decision-making processes in the system. Many people have commented on the difficulty of organizing the various groups and offices in a college or university in order to do something. What has been less frequently noted is that the same problems of organization face anyone who wants to overturn an action. For example, the official charter of an institution usually has some kind of regulation that permits a desired action, as well as some kind of regulation that might be interpreted as prohibiting it. The president who solicits general organizational approval for action is more likely to obtain it if the burdens of overcoming organizational inertia are on his opposition. He reverses the burden of organization by taking the action.

Major bureaucratic interventions lie in the ordinary systems of accounting and managerial controls. Such devices are often condemned in academic circles as both dreary and inhibiting. Their beauty lies in the way in which they extend throughout the system and in the high degree of arbitrariness they exhibit. For example, students of business have observed that many important aspects of business life are driven by accounting rules. What are costs? What are profits? How are costs and profits allocated among activities and subunits? Answers to such questions are far from arbitrary. But they have enough elements of arbitrariness that no reasonable business manager would ignore the potential contribution of accounting rules to profitability. The flow of investments, the utilization of labor, and the structure of organization all respond to the organization of accounts.

The same thing is true in a college or university, although the process works in a somewhat different way because the convenient single index of business accounting, profit, is denied the university executive. Universities and colleges have official facts (accounting facts) with respect to student activities, faculty activities, and space utilization. In recent years such accounting facts have increased in importance as colleges and universities struggled first with the baby boom and now with fiscal adversity. These official facts enter into reports and filter into decisions made throughout the system. As a typical simple example, consider the impact of changing the accounting for faculty teaching load from number of courses to student credit hours taught. Or, consider the impact of separating in accounting reports the teaching of language (number of students, cost of faculty) from the teaching of literature in that language at a typical American university. Or, consider the impact of making each major subunit in a university purchase services (for example, duplication services, computer services, library services) at prices somewhat different from the current largely arbitrary prices. Or, consider the consequences of allowing transfer of funds from one major budget line to another within a subunit at various possible discount rates depending on the lines and the point in the budget year. Or, consider the effect of having students pay as part of their fees an amount determined by the department offering the instruction, with the amount thus paid returning to the department.

Rule 8: Interpret History. In an organization in which most issues have low salience, and information about events in the system is poorly maintained, definitions of what is happening and what has happened become important tactical instruments. If people in the organization cared more about what happened (or is happening), the constraints on the tactic would be great. Histories would be challenged and carefully monitored. If people in the organization accepted more openly the idea that much of the decision-making process is a status-certifying rather than a choice-making system, there would be less dependence on historical interpretation. The actual situation, however, provides a tactically optimal situation. On the one hand, the genuine interest in keeping a good record of what happened (in substantive rather than status terms) is minimal. On the other hand, the belief in the relevance of history, or the legitimacy of history as a basis for current action, is fairly strong.

Minutes should be written long enough after the event as to legitimize the reality of forgetfulness. They should be written in such a way as to lay the basis for subsequent independent action—in the name of the collective action. In general, participants in the organization should be assisted in their desire to have unambiguous actions taken today derived from the ambiguous decisions of yesterday with a minimum of pain to their images of organizational rationality and a minimum of claims on their time. The model of consistency is maintained by a creative resolution of uncertainty about the past.

Presidents and Tactics

As we observed at the outset, practical tactics, if they are genuine, will inevitably be viewed as somewhat cynical. We will, however, record our own sentiments that the cynicism lies in the eye of the beholder. Our sympathies and enthusiasm are mostly for the invisible members of an organized anarchy who make such tactics possible. We refer, of course, to the majority of participants in colleges and universities who have the good sense to see that what can be achieved through tactical manipulation of the university is only occasionally worth their time and effort. The validity of the tactics is a tribute to their reluctance to clutter the important elements of life with organizational matters. The tactics are available for anyone who wants to use them. Most of us most of the time have more interesting things to do.

But presidents, as full-time actors generally occupying the best job of their lives, are less likely to have more interesting things to do. In addition, these tactics, with their low visibility and their emphasis on the trading of credit and recognition for accomplishment, will not serve the interests of a president out to glorify himself or increase his chances to be one of the very few who move up to a second and "better" presidency. Instead, they provide an opportunity chiefly for those who have some conception of what might make their institution better, more interesting, more complex, or more educational, and are satisfied to end their tenures believing that they helped to steer their institutions slightly closer to those remote destinations.

The Technology of Foolishness

The tactics for moving an organization when objectives are clear represent important parts of the repertoire of an organizational leader.[5] Standard prescriptions properly honor intention, choice, and action; and college presidents often have things they want to accomplish. Nevertheless, a college president may sometimes want to confront the realities of ambiguity more directly and reconsider the standard dicta of leadership. He may want to examine particularly the place of purpose in intelligent behavior and the role of foolishness in leadership.

Choice and Rationality

The concept of choice as a focus for interpreting and guiding human behavior has rarely had an easy time in the realm of ideas. It is beset by theological disputations over free will, by the dilemmas of absurdism, by the doubts of psychological behaviorism, and by the claims of historical, economic, social, and demographic determinism. Nevertheless, the idea that humans make choices has proved robust enough to become a matter of faith in important segments of contemporary Western civilization. It is a faith that is professed by virtually all theories of social policymaking.

The major tenets of this faith run something like this:

Human beings make choices. Choices are properly made by evaluating alternatives in terms of goals and on the basis of information currently available. The

---

[5]These ideas have been the basis for extended conversation with a number of friends. We want to acknowledge particularly the help of Lance Bennett, Patricia Nelson Bennett, Michael Butler, Søren Christensen, Michel Crozier, Claude Faucheux, James R. Glenn, Jr., Gudmund Hernes, Helga Hernes, Jean Carter Lave, Harold J. Leavitt, Henry M. Levin, Leslie Lincoln, André Massart, John Miller, Johan Olsen, Richard C. Snyder, Alexander Szalai, Eugene J. Webb, and Gail Whitacre.

alternative that is most attractive in terms of goals is chosen. By using the technology of choice, we can improve the quality of the search for alternatives, the quality of information, and the quality of the analysis used to evaluate alternatives. Although actual choice may fall short of this ideal in various ways, it is an attractive model of how choices should be made by individuals, organizations, and social systems.

These articles of faith have been built upon and have stimulated some scripture. It is the scripture of the theories of decision making. The scripture is partly a codification of received doctrine and partly a source for that doctrine. As a result, our cultural ideas of intelligence and our theories of choice display a substantial resemblance. In particular, they share three conspicuous interrelated ideas:

The first idea is the *preexistence of purpose*. We find it natural to base an interpretation of human-choice behavior on a presumption of human purpose. We have, in fact, invented one of the most elaborate terminologies in the professional literature: "values," "needs," "wants," "goods," "tastes," "preferences," "utility," "objectives," "goals," "aspirations," "drives." All of these reflect a strong tendency to believe that a useful interpretation of human behavior involves defining a set of objectives that (1) are prior attributes of the system and (2) make the observed behavior in some sense intelligent vis-à-vis those objectives.

Whether we are talking about individuals or about organizations, purpose is an obvious presumption of the discussion. An organization is often defined in terms of its purpose. It is seen by some as the largest collectivity directed by a purpose. Action within an organization is justified or criticized in terms of purpose. Individuals explain their own behavior, as well as the behavior of others, in terms of a set of value premises that are presumed to be antecedent to the behavior. Normative theories of choice begin with an assumption of a preexistent preference ordering defined over the possible outcomes of a choice.

The second idea is the *necessity of consistency*. We have come to recognize consistency both as an important property of human behavior and as a prerequisite for normative models of choice. Dissonance theory, balance theory, theories of congruency in attitudes, statuses, and performances have all served to remind us of the possibilities for interpreting human behavior in terms of the consistency requirements of a limited-capacity, information-processing system.

At the same time, consistency is a cultural and theoretical virtue. Action should be consistent with belief. Actions taken by different parts of an organization should be consistent with each other. Individual and organizational activities are seen as connected with each other in terms of their consequences for some consistent set of purposes. In an organization the basic pattern of consistency is the hierarchy with its obligations of coordination and control. In the individual, the structural manifestation is a set of values that generates a consistent preference ordering.

The third idea is the *primacy of rationality*. By rationality we mean a procedure for deciding what is correct behavior by relating consequences systematically to objectives. By placing primary emphasis on rational techniques, we have implicitly rejected—or seriously impaired—two other procedures for choice: (1) the processes of intuition, through which people do things without fully understanding why, and (2) the processes of tradition and faith, through which people do things because that is the way they are done.

Both within the theory and within the culture we insist on the ethic of rationality. We justify individual and organizational action in terms of an analysis of means and ends. Impulse, intuition, faith, and tradition are outside that system and viewed as antithetical to it. Faith may be seen as a possible source of values. Intuition may be seen as a possible source of ideas about alternatives. But the analysis and justification of action lie within the context of reason.

These ideas are obviously deeply embedded in the culture. Their roots extend into ideas that have conditioned much of modern Western history and interpretations of that history. Their general acceptance is probably highly correlated with the permeation of rationalism and individualism into the style of thinking within the culture. The ideas are even more obviously embedded in modern theories of choice. It is fundamental to those theories that thinking should precede action; that action should serve a purpose; that purpose should be defined in terms of a consistent set of preexistent goals; and that choice should be based on a consistent theory of the relation between action and its consequences.

Every tool of management decision making that is currently a part of management science, operations research, or decision-making theory assumes the prior existence of a set of consistent goals. Almost the entire structure of microeconomic theory builds on the assumption that there exists a well-defined, stable, and consistent preference ordering. Most theories of individual or organizational choice accept the idea that goals exist and that (in some sense) an individual or organization acts on those goals, choosing from among some alternatives on the basis of available information. Discussions of educational policy, with their emphasis on goal setting, evaluation, and accountability, are in this tradition.

From the perspective of all of man's history, the ideas of purpose, consistency, and rationality are relatively new. Much of the technology currently available to implement them is extremely new. Over the past few centuries, and conspicuously over the past few decades, we have substantially improved man's capability for acting purposively, consistently, and rationally. We have substantially increased his propensity to think of himself as doing so. It is an impressive victory, won—where it has been won—by a happy combination of timing, performance, ideology, and persistence. It is a battle yet to be concluded, or even engaged, in many cultures of the world; but within most of the Western world individuals and organizations see themselves as making choices.

The Problem of Goals

The tools of intelligence as they are fashioned in modern theories of choice are necessary to any reasonable behavior in contemporary society. It is inconceivable that we would fail to continue their development, refinement, and extension. As might be expected, however, a theory and ideology of choice built on the ideas outlined above is deficient in some obvious, elementary ways, most conspicuously in the treatment of human goals.

Goals are thrust upon the intelligent man. We ask that he act in the name of goals. We ask that he keep his goals consistent. We ask that his actions be oriented to his goals. We ask that a social system amalgamate individual goals into a collective goal. But we do not concern ourselves with the origin of goals. Theories of individual, organizational, and social choice assume actors with preexistent values.

Since it is obvious that goals change over time and that the character of those changes affects both the richness of personal and social development and the outcome of choice behavior, a theory of choice must somehow justify ignoring the phenomena. Although it is unreasonable to ask a theory of choice to solve all the problems of man and his development, it is reasonable to ask how such conspicuous elements as the fluidity and ambiguity of objectives can plausibly be ignored in a theory that is offered as a guide to human choice behavior.

There are three classic justifications. The first is that goal development and choice are independent processes, conceptually and behaviorally. The second is that the model of choice is never satisfied in fact and that deviations from the model accommodate the problems of introducing change. The third is that the idea of changing goals is so intractable in a normative theory of choice that nothing can be said about it. Since we are unpersuaded of the first and second justifications, our optimism with respect to the third is somewhat greater than that of most of our fellows.

The argument that goal development and choice are independent behaviorally seems clearly false. It seems to us obvious that a description that assumes that goals come first and action comes later is frequently radically wrong. Human choice behavior is at least as much a process for discovering goals as for acting on them. Although it is true enough that goals and decisions are "conceptually" distinct, that is simply a statement of the theory, not a defense of it. They are conceptually distinct if we choose to make them so.

The argument that the model is incomplete is more persuasive. There do appear to be some critical "holes" in the system of intelligence as described by standard theories of choice. Incomplete information, incomplete goal consistency, and a variety of external processes facilitate goal development. What is somewhat disconcerting about the argument, however, is that it makes the efficacy of the concepts of intelligent choice dependent on their inadequacy. As we become more competent in the techniques of the model and more committed to it, the "holes" become smaller. As the model becomes more accepted, our obligation to modify it increases.

The final argument seems to us sensible as a general principle, but misleading here. Why are we more reluctant to ask how human beings might find "good" goals than we are to ask how they might make "good" decisions? The second question appears to be a more technical problem. The first seems more pretentious. It claims to say something about alternative virtues. The appearance of pretense, however, stems directly from the prevailing theory of choice and the ideology associated with it.

In fact, the conscious introduction of goal discovery for consideration in theories of human choice is not unknown to modern man. For example, we have two kinds of theories of choice behavior in human beings. One is a theory of children. The other is a theory of adults. In the theory of children, we emphasize choices as leading to experiences that develop the child's scope, his complexity, his awareness of the world. As parents, teachers, or psychologists, we try to lead the child to do things that are inconsistent with his present goals because we know (or believe) that he can develop into an interesting person only by coming to appreciate aspects of experience that he initially rejects.

In the theory of adults, we emphasize choices as a consequence of our intentions. As adults, educational decision makers, or economists, we try to take actions that (within the limits of scarce resources) come as close as possible to achieving our goals. We try to find improved ways of making decisions consistent with our perceptions of what is valuable in the world.

The asymmetry in these models is conspicuous. Adults have constructed a model world in which adults know what is good for themselves, but children do not. It is hard to react positively to the conceit. The asymmetry has, in fact, stimulated a large number of ideologies and reforms designed to allow children the same moral prerogative granted to adults—the right to imagine that they know what they want. The efforts have cut deeply into traditional childrearing, traditional educational policies, traditional politics, and traditional consumer economics.

In our judgment, the asymmetry between models of choice for adults and for children is awkward; but the solution we have adopted is precisely wrong-headed. Instead of trying to adapt the model of adults to children, we might better adapt the model of children to adults. For many purposes, our model of children is better. Of course, children know what they want. Everyone does. The critical question is whether they are encouraged to develop more interesting "wants." Values change. People become more interesting as those values and the interconnections made among them change.

One of the most obvious things in the world turns out to be hard for us to accommodate in our theory of choice: A child of two will almost always have a less interesting set of values (indeed, a *worse* set of values) than a child of twelve. The same is true of adults. Values develop through experience. Although one of the main natural arenas for the modification of human values is the arena of choice, our theories of adult and organizational decision making ignore the phenomenon entirely.

Introducing ambiguity and fluidity to the interpretation of individual, organizational, and societal goals obviously has implications for behavioral theories of decision making. We have tried to identify and respond to some of those difficulties in the previous chapters. The main point here, however, is not to consider how we might describe the behavior of systems that are discovering goals as they act. Rather it is to examine how we might improve the quality of that behavior, how we might aid the development of interesting goals.

We know how to advise a society, an organization, or an individual if we are first given a consistent set of preferences. Under some conditions, we can suggest how to make decisions if the preferences are consistent only up to the point of specifying a series of independent constraints on the choice. But what about a normative theory of goal-finding behavior? What do we say when our client tells us that he is not sure his present set of values is the set of values in terms of which he wants to act?

It is a question familiar to many aspects of ordinary life. It is a question that friends, associates, students, college presidents, business managers, voters, and children ask at least as frequently as they ask how they should act within a set of consistent and stable values.

Within the context of normative theory of choice as it exists, the answer we give is: First determine the values, then act. The advice is frequently useful. Moreover, we have developed ways in which we can use conventional techniques for decision analysis to help discover value

premises and to expose value inconsistencies. These techniques involve
testing the decision implications of some successive approximations to a
set of preferences. The object is to find a consistent set of preferences with
implications that are acceptable to the person or organization making the
decisions. Variations on such techniques are used routinely in operations
research, as well as in personal counseling and analysis.

The utility of such techniques, however, apparently depends on the
assumption that a primary problem is the amalgamation or excavation of
preexistent values. The metaphors—"finding oneself," "goal clarification," "self-discovery," "social welfare function," "revealed preference"—
are metaphors of search. If our value premises are to be "constructed"
rather than "discovered," our standard procedures may be useful; but we
have no a priori reason for assuming they will.

Perhaps we should explore a somewhat different approach to the
normative question of how we ought to behave when our value premises
are not yet (and never will be) fully determined. Suppose we treat action as a
way of creating interesting goals at the same time as we treat goals as a way
of justifying action. It is an intuitively plausible and simple idea, but one
that is not immediately within the domain of standard normative theories
of intelligent choice.

Interesting people and interesting organizations construct complicated
theories of themselves. To do this, they need to supplement the technology
of reason with a technology of foolishness. Individuals and organizations
sometimes need ways of doing things for which they have no good reason.
They need to act before they think.

Sensible Foolishness

To use intelligent choice as a planned occasion for discovering new
goals, we require some idea of sensible foolishness. Which of the many
foolish things that we might do now will lead to attractive value
consequences? The question is almost inconceivable. Not only does it ask
us to predict the value consequences of action, it asks us to evaluate them.
In what terms can we talk about "good" changes in goals?

In effect, we are asked either to specify a set of supergoals in terms of
which alternative goals are evaluated, or to choose among alternatives *now*
in terms of the unknown set of values we will have at some future time (or
the distribution over time of that unknown set of future values). The former
alternative moves us back to the original situation of a fixed set of values—
now called "supergoals"—and hardly seems an important step in the
direction of inventing procedures for discovering new goals. The latter
alternative seems fundamental enough, but it violates severely our sense of
temporal order. To say that we make decisions now in terms of goals that

will be knowable only later is nonsensical—as long as we accept the basic framework of the theory of choice and its presumptions of preexistent goals.

As we challenge the dogma of preexistent goals, we will be forced to reexamine some of our most precious prejudices: the strictures against imitation, coercion, and rationalization. Each of those honorable prohibitions depends on the view of man and human choice imposed on us by conventional theories of choice.

Imitation is not necessarily a sign of moral weakness. It is a prediction. It is a prediction that if we duplicate the behavior or attitudes of someone else, not only will we fare well in terms of current goals but the chances of our discovering attractive new goals for ourselves are relatively high. If imitation is to be normatively attractive, we need a better theory of who should be imitated. Such a theory seems to be eminently feasible. For example, what are the conditions for effectiveness of a rule that one should imitate another person whose values are close to one's own? How do the chances of discovering interesting goals through imitation change as the number of people exhibiting the behavior to be imitated increases? In the case of the college president we might ask what the goal discovery consequences are of imitating the choices of those at institutions more prestigious than one's own, and whether there are other more desirable patterns of imitation.

Coercion is not necessarily an assault on individual autonomy. It can be a device for stimulating individuality. We recognize this when we talk about education or about parents and children. What has been difficult with coercion is the possibility for perversion, not its obvious capability for stimulating change. We need a theory of the circumstances under which entry into a coercive relationship produces behavior that leads to the discovery of interesting goals. We are all familiar with the tactic. College presidents use it in imposing deadlines, entering contracts, making commitments. What are the conditions for its effective use? In particular, what are the conditions for goal-fostering coercion in social systems?

Rationalization is not necessarily a way of evading morality. It can be a test for the feasibility of a goal change. When deciding among alternative actions for which we have no good reason, it may be sensible to develop some definition of how "near" to intelligence alternative "unintelligent" actions lie. Effective rationalization permits this kind of incremental approach to changes in values. To use it effectively, however, we require a better idea of the metrics that might be possible in measuring value distances. At the same time, rationalization is the major procedure for integrating newly discovered goals into an existing structure of values. It provides the organization of complexity without which complexity itself becomes indistinguishable from randomness.

The dangers in imitation, coercion, and rationalization are too familiar to elaborate. We should, indeed, be able to develop better techniques. Whatever those techniques may be, however, they will almost certainly undermine the superstructure of biases erected on purpose, consistency, and rationality. They will involve some way of thinking about action now as occurring in terms of a set of future values different from those that the actor currently holds.

Play and Foolishness

A second requirement for a technology of foolishness is some set of guidelines for breaking out. Even if we know which of several foolish things we want to do, we still need a mechanism for allowing us to do it. How do we escape the logic of our reason?

Here we are closer to understanding what we need. It is playfulness. Playfulness is the deliberate, temporary relaxation of rules in order to explore the possibilities of alternative rules. When we are playful, we challenge the necessity of consistency. In effect, we announce—in advance—our rejection of the usual objections to behavior that does not fit the standard model of intelligence.

Playfulness allows experimentation at the same time that it acknowledges reason. It accepts an obligation that at some point either the playful behavior will be stopped or it will be integrated into the structure of intelligence in some way that makes sense. The suspension of the rules is temporary.

The idea of play may suggest three things that are, in our minds, quite erroneous in the present context. First, play may be seen as a kind of "holiday" for reason, a release of the emotional tensions of virtue. Although it is possible that play performs some such function, that is not the function with which we are concerned. Second, play may be seen as part of some mystical balance of spiritual principles: fire and water, hot and cold, weak and strong. The intention here is much narrower than a general mystique of balance. Third, play may be seen as an antithesis of intelligence, so that the emphasis on the importance of play becomes a support for simple self-indulgence. Our present intent is to propose play as an instrument of intelligence, not a substitute.

Playfulness is a natural outgrowth of our standard view of reason. A strict insistence on purpose, consistency, and rationality limits our ability to find new purposes. Play relaxes that insistence to allow us to act "unintelligently" or "irrationally" or "foolishly" to explore alternative ideas of purposes and alternative concepts of behavioral consistency. And it does this while maintaining our basic commitment to intelligence.

Although play and reason are in this way functional complements, they are often behavioral competitors. They are alternative styles and alternative orientations to the same situation. There is no guarantee that the styles will be equally well developed, that all individuals, organizations, or societies will be equally adept in both styles; or that all cultures will be sufficiently encouraging to both.

Our design problem is . . . to specify the combination, for we most of the time use an alternation of strategies rather than persevering in either one. It is a difficult problem. The optimization problem looks extremely complex on the face of it, and the learning situations that will produce alternation in behavior appear to be somewhat less common than those that produce perseverance.

Consider, for example, the difficulty of sustaining playfulness as a style within contemporary American society. Individuals who are good at consistent rationality are rewarded early and heavily. We define consistent rationality as intelligence, and the educational rewards of society are associated strongly with it. Social norms press in the same direction, particularly for men. "Changing one's mind" is viewed as feminine and undesirable. Politicians and other leaders will go to enormous lengths to avoid admitting an inconsistency. Many demands of modern organizational life reinforce the same rational abilities and preferences for a style of unchanging purposes.

The result is that many of the most influential and best-educated citizens have experienced a powerful overlearning with respect to rationality. They are exceptionally good at maintaining consistent pictures of themselves, of relating action to purposes. They are exceptionally poor at a playful attitude toward their own beliefs, toward the logic of consistency, or toward the way they see things as being connected in the world. The dictates of manliness, forcefulness, independence, and intelligence are intolerant of playful urges if they arise. The playful urges that arise are weak ones, scarcely discernible in the behavior of most businessmen, mayors, or college presidents.

The picture is probably overdrawn, but we believe that the implications are not. Reason and intelligence have had the unnecessary consequence of inhibiting the development of purpose into more complicated forms of consistency. To move away from that position, we need to find some ways of helping individuals and organizations to experiment with doing things for which they have no good reason, to be playful with their conceptions of themselves. We suggest five things as a small beginning:

First, we can treat *goals as hypotheses*. Conventional theories of decision making allow us to entertain doubts about almost everything except the thing about which we frequently have the greatest doubt—our objectives. Suppose we define the decision-making process as a time for the sequential testing of hypotheses about goals. If we can experiment with alternative goals, we stand some chance of discovering complicated and interesting combinations of good values that none of us previously imagined.

Second, we can treat *intuition as real*. We do not know what intuition is or even if it is any one thing. Perhaps it is simply an excuse for doing something we cannot justify in terms of present values or for refusing to follow the logic of our own beliefs. Perhaps it is an inexplicable way of consulting that part of our intelligence and knowledge of the world that is not organized in a way anticipated by standard theories of choice. In either case, intuition permits us to see some possible actions that are outside our present scheme for justifying behavior.

Third, we can treat *hypocrisy as a transition*. Hypocrisy is an inconsistency between expressed values and behavior. Negative attitudes about hypocrisy stem mainly from a general onus against inconsistency and from a sentiment against combining the pleasures of vice with the appearance of virtue. It seems to us that a bad man with good intentions may be a man experimenting with the possibility of becoming good. Somehow it seems more sensible to encourage the experimentation than to insult it.

Fourth, we can treat *memory as an enemy*. The rules of consistency and rationality require a technology of memory. For most purposes, good memories make good choices. But the ability to forget or overlook is also useful. If you do not know what you did yesterday or what other people in the organization are doing today, you can act within the system of reason and still do things that are foolish.

Fifth, we can treat *experience as a theory*. Learning can be viewed as a series of conclusions based on concepts of action and consequences that we have invented. Experience can be changed retrospectively. By changing our interpretive concepts now, we modify what we learned earlier. Thus we expose the possibility of experimenting with alternative histories. The usual strictures against "self-deception" in experience need occasionally to be tempered with an awareness of the extent to which all experience is an interpretation subject to conscious revision. Personal histories and national histories need to be rewritten continuously as a base for the retrospective learning of new self-conceptions.

If we knew more about the normative theory of acting before thinking, we could say more intelligent things about the functions of management and leadership when organizations or societies do not know what they are doing. Consider, for example, the following general implications.

First, we need to reexamine the functions of management decision making. One of the primary ways in which the goals of an organization are developed is by interpreting the decisions it makes, and one feature of good managerial decisions is that they lead to the development of more interesting value premises for the organization. As a result, decisions should not be seen as flowing directly or strictly from a preexistent set of objectives. College presidents who make decisions might well view that function somewhat less as a process of deduction or a process of political negotiation, and somewhat more as a process of gently upsetting preconceptions of what the organization is doing.

Second, we need a modified view of planning. Planning can often be more effective as an interpretation of past decisions than as a program for future ones. It can be used as a part of the efforts of the organization to develop a new consistent theory of itself that incorporates the mix of recent actions into a moderately comprehensive structure of goals. Procedures for interpreting the meaning of most past events are familiar to the memoirs of retired generals, prime ministers, business leaders, and movie stars. They suffer from the company they keep. In an organization that wants to continue to develop new objectives, a manager needs to be tolerant of the idea that he will discover the meaning of yesterday's action in the experiences and interpretations of today.

Third, we need to reconsider evaluation. As nearly as we can determine, there is nothing in a formal theory of evaluation that requires that criteria be specified in advance. In particular, the evaluation of social experiments need not be in terms of the degree to which they have fulfilled our prior expectations. Rather we can examine what they did in terms of what we now believe to be important. The prior specification of criteria and the prior specification of evaluational procedures that depend on such criteria are common presumptions in contemporary social policymaking. They are presumptions that inhibit the serendipitous discovery of new criteria. Experience should be used explicitly as an occasion for evaluating our values as well as our actions.

Fourth, we need a reconsideration of social accountability. Individual preferences and social action need to be consistent in some way. But the process of pursuing consistency is one in which both the preferences and the actions change over time. Imagination in social policy formation involves systematically adapting to and influencing preference. It would be unfortunate if our theories of social action encouraged leaders to ignore their responsibilities for anticipating public preferences through action and for providing social experiences that modify individual expectations.

Fifth, we need to accept playfulness in social organizations. The design of organizations should attend to the problems of maintaining both playfulness and reason as aspects of intelligent choice. Since much of the literature on social design is concerned with strengthening the rationality of decision making, managers are likely to overlook the importance of play.

This is partly a matter of making the individuals within an organization more playful by encouraging the attitudes and skills of inconsistency. It is also a matter of making organizational structure and organizational procedures more playful. Organizations can be playful even when the participants in them are not. The managerial devices for maintaining consistency can be varied. We encourage organizational play by insisting on some temporary relief from control, coordination, and communication.

Presidents and Foolishness

Contemporary theories of decision making and the technology of reason have considerably strengthened our capabilities for effective social action. The conversion of the simple ideas of choice into an extensive technology is a major achievement. It is, however, an achievement that has reinforced some biases in the underlying models of choice in individuals and groups. In particular, it has reinforced the uncritical acceptance of a static interpretation of human goals.

There is a little magic in the world, and foolishness in people and organizations is one of the many things that fail to produce miracles. Under certain conditions, it is one of several ways in which some of the problems of our current theories of intelligence can be overcome. It may be a good way, for it preserves the virtues of consistency while stimulating change. If we had a good technology of foolishness, it might (in combination with the technology of reason) help in a small way to develop the unusual combinations of attitudes and behaviors that describe the interesting people, interesting organizations, and interesting societies of the world. The contribution of a college president may often be measured by his capability for sustaining that creative interaction of foolishness and rationality.

References

Cyert, R.M., and J.G. March. *A Behaviorial Theory of the Firm*. Englewood Cliffs, N.J.: Prentice-Hall, 1963.

Frey, F.W. "Comment: On Issues and Nonissues in the Study of Power." *American Political Science Review* 65 (1971): 1081–1101.

Iklé, F.C. *How Nations Negotiate*. New York: Harper & Row, 1964.

Long, N.A. "The Local Community as an Ecology of Games." *American Journal of Sociology* 44 (1958): 251–61.

Reedy, G.E. *The Twilight of the Presidency*. New York: World Publishing, 1970.

Walton, R.E., and Robert B. McKersie, eds. *Behavioral Theory of Labor Negotiations*. New York: McGraw-Hill, 1965.

Weiner, S.S. "Educational Decisions in an Organized Anarchy." Doctoral dissertation, Stanford University, Stanford, Calif., 1972.

Wolfinger, R. "Nondecisions and the Study of Local Politics." *American Political Science Review* 65 (1971): 1063–80.

————. "Rejoiner to Frey's 'Comments'," *American Political Science Review* 65 (1971): 1102–04.

PART V

Drama and Culture: The Symbolic Aspects of Change

Theories of organizational process question the common expectation that individuals or organizations will consistently perform rationally. Decisions are rarely made on the basis of clear-cut preferences or well-formed criteria. Instead, decisions evolve from a complicated mix of people, solutions, problems, and opportunities. Change, as theories of process see it, happens serendipitously—mostly the result of uncontrollable forces. As a planned activity, change attracts energy and attention. But the link between process and planned outcomes is marginal at best. Inside organizations, change serves as a magnet or a sponge to absorb conflict or excess energy, or it becomes an arena to negotiate or renegotiate power relationships, ideologies, or informal understandings.

The "symbolic" school of thought, like the process theories, relaxes assumptions of direct cause-and-effect relationships and a lockstep path of organizational activities. The symbolic perspective concentrates on the beliefs of participants and the faith of external constituencies. Planning, decision making, and change become rituals, ceremonies, and signals that communicate or express myths and values to the world inside and outside an organization. Organizations are social theatres, and, on the stage, social dramas are enacted, appreciated, and reveal the psyche of people to themselves, as in the Balinese cockfight (Geertz 1972). Thus, change becomes a pageant—an elaborate organizational ceremony that reconciles contradictions, mediates conflict, renegotiates deep-seated agreements, alters expectations, and helps maintain the faith and confidence of important constituencies.

Change is not expected to merely produce results; a key function is to create or reestablish illusions. And such illusions or myths enable a society and its institutions to exist. "Rob the average man of his life illusion and you rob him of his happiness at the same stroke" is the classic line from Ibsen's *Wild Duck*. The symbolic view applies this insight to larger social units: rob a people of their illusions or myths and you destroy the social fabric that bonds them together. As a social drama, change is a ritual that can restore confidence in institutions when faith begins to wane. But, if organizations promise results rather than more abstract ideas of reform, change can backfire. This is precisely what has happened in recent efforts aimed at making educational organizations more rational and accountable. Rather than recreating important illusions, changes have sometimes eroded faith and confidence.

The idea of organizational activities as symbolic events is not confined to theory. Many studies provide empirical support for the proposition that what activities *express* is as important to organizations as what they *accomplish*. For example, PERT (Performance Evaluation and Review Techniques) charts, management meetings, and control strategies conveyed an image of accountability and rationality that kept Congress and outside agencies from interfering in the day-to-day operations of the development of the Polaris Missile. (Sapolsky 1972). Evaluations of social programs serve as a ritual; they maintain the faith in our ability to control social problems and to improve peoples' lives (Floden and Weiner 1978). Administrative agencies such as the FBI are created at least partly to symbolize that such inequities as crime can be controlled (Edelman 1977). Reorganizations are important in shoring up our belief in government agencies (Sproull et al. 1978). Long-range planning makes only a limited difference in a school district but is vital in providing outlets for energy, reducing conflict, getting people to participate, and in renegotiating shared educational myths (Edelfson, Johnson, and Stromquist 1977). Large-scale intervention projects in schools produce only limited measurable change, but they do increase satisfaction, establish shared beliefs, and restore confidence and support among key constituencies (Deal and Huguenin 1978; Deal and Ross 1977; Deal, Gunner, and Wiske, 1979).

The dramaturgical perspective also focuses its attention on how organizations *appear* and on what they *say*. Faith and confidence is critical to organizational effectiveness. Myths, rituals, ceremonies, shared values and beliefs are central to the creation and maintenance of a believable fiction—or mythology. And the illusion is at least as important as the results. Illusions, in fact, help create results and provide explanations in their absence. In a loosely coupled organization where goals are elusive and procedures are unclear, faith and belief play an important role.

The articles in this part consider change in educational organizations as drama. The first four articles are conceptual. Burton Clark discusses in Chapter 19 the growth of "organization sagas" in three distinctive colleges. Clark argues that establishing a college depends heavily on symbols, values, and ideals—all part of the "saga." Meyer, Scott, and Deal compare institutional and technical approaches to organization and raise a number of important questions about changing schools and school districts. They argue that in technical environments, with clear goals and well-understood technologies, the formal structure faces the technical core and turns its back on the environment in an attempt to ward off "irrational" influences. Educational organizations, which operate in strong' environmental networks and with unclear goals and undeveloped technologies, do the opposite. Structures do not control the instructional technical core. Instead, when the formal structure of schools or districts reflect prevailing myths and expectations, then external communities are willing to provide support. The very characteristics that many reformers have tried to change—poorly managed instruction, diffuse goals, and loose controls— are seen as strengths that enable schools to survive in a difficult and ambiguous environment. The failure of such innovations to take hold is no surprise. For schools or districts to survive, they must either conform to social myths and local expectations or work to transform them. The Meyer, Scott, and Deal article provides explanations for earlier problems of change and outlines some guidelines for the future.

The Cohen and Rosenberg article extends the argument of the previous chapter by showing in more detail the role change plays in educational organizations. Considering the Bowles and Gintis economic analysis of educational change and reform, the article highlights the predominant functionalist approach to change—that schools are instrumental creations chartered to produce results. Relying on a historical perspective, Cohen and Rosenberg develop an alternative idea that schools as organizations are created to embody social values and ideals. Following the Bowles and Gintis article, they argue that structures and activities in schools are important for what they express, signal, or convey. Metaphors of play and theatre are juxtaposed against prevailing ideas of schools as factories. As theatre, schools provide dramatic expressions of deep-seated, intangible values. By reminding society of itself—its core values and beliefs—these expressions provide the symbolic images that hold a culture together. Testing and ability grouping are singled out as events that symbolize the values of science, economic progress, modernity, and merit. To a society still close to an agrarian past, these values were held in high esteem. In this historical moment, schools provided a stage on which these values could be dramatized and reaffirmed.

Chapters 22 and 23 in this section apply the dramaturgical approach to two contemporary problems: teacher evaluation in staff reduction and strategies for making cutbacks in response to declining enrollments and shrinking resources.

Johnson, a parent and former teacher, began her study of teacher evaluation convinced that personnel decisions should be based on competency rather than seniority. As she studied four New England school districts more closely, she began to see some undesirable and unintended consequences of using evaluations to make decisions about teacher transfers or dismissal. Rating teachers can unravel the loose fabric that holds schools together. Principal authority and autonomy will fall victim to greater district involvement, coordination, and standardization of evaluation procedures. Principals will be unable to treat teachers individually, anxiety about evaluation will increase, and the role of evaluation in instructional improvement will be overshadowed by its formal role in career decisions. Teacher-principal relationships will become more strained and formalized as will relationships between district offices and teacher unions. In short, the difficulties of defining and measuring teaching (or learning) and the delicate informal ties that hold schools together make rational approaches to teacher dismissal less desirable than those relying mainly on seniority.

Deal and Wiske extend Johnson's concerns to cover all decisions about cutbacks during the difficult times now confronting most educational organizations. Three approaches emerge from the authors' review of literature on termination. The authors compare rational and political approaches with a symbolic approach drawn from the dramaturgical perspective. Their analysis moves in the direction of outlining the administrative implications for change that this school of thought would suggest.

Chapter 24, by Tyack, Kirst, and Hansot, relies again on history to highlight the development of change activities in American schools. The authors follow the reform waves, beginning with the common school ideology of the nineteenth century and tracing, up to the 1980s, the waves that followed this ideology. The Progressive Era brought in the educator as expert and centralized educational decisions in the many professional administrators whose conceptions of proper education overshadowed those of parents and laymen. The movement expanded to embrace ideas of science and testing—the rationalization of schools thus began. The 1960s and 1970s were a time when the wisdom of professionals was questioned and schools were subjected to a large number of efforts to change governance patterns, programs, and other prevailing patterns of structure or behavior. In the 1980s, however, the climate of change has shifted from reform to decline. The article sees the 1980s as a time to revive the earlier common-school ideology of the nineteenth century, which saw public schools as a public good. By renegotiating the common-school myth and focusing on schools as the primary instrument for realizing democracy, the authors see an opportunity in the 1980s to revitalize American education. A theme runs across these four articles. Schools are more like temples or theatres than factories. In local communities, schools serve an important symbolic role, and to restore the faith, we need to renegotiate and revitalize the original missions that schools were organized to promote and celebrate.

References

Deal, T., Gunner, and M. Wiske. "Linking Knowledge to Schools: The Process of Change in Six Sites." *Case Studies in Program Improvement.* Consortium Report Series, Andover, Mass.: The Network, Inc., 1979.

Deal, T., and K. Huguenin. "Removing the Clouds from Sunshine School." In *Alternative Schools: Ideologies, Realities, Guidelines,* ed. T. Deal and R.R. Nolan. Chicago: Nelson-Hall, 1978.

Deal, T., and F. Ross. "The Impact of an OD Intervention on the Structure of a Small School District." Unpublished manuscript. Stanford University, April 1977.

Edelfson, C., R. Johnson, and N. Stromquist. "Summary and Policy Recommendations." *Participatory Planning in a School District,* NIE Grant, June 1977.

Edelmann, M. *The Symbolic Uses of Politics.* Urbana, Ill.: University of Illinois Press, 1977.

Folden, R., and S. Weiner. "Rationality to Ritual: Multiple Roles of Evaluation in Governmental Process." *Policy Sciences* 9: 1 (1978): 9–18.

Geertz, C. "Deep Play: Notes on the Balinese Cockfight." *Daedalus* (Winter 1972).

Sapalsky, H. *The Polaris System Development.* Cambridge, Mass.: Harvard University Press, 1972.

Sproull, L., S. Weiner, and D. Wolf. *Organizing an Anarchy.* Chicago: University of Chicago Press, 1978.

19

The Organizational Saga in Higher Education

Burton Clark

Saga, originally referring to a medieval Icelandic or Norse account of achievements and events in the history of a person or group, has come to mean a narrative of heroic exploits, of a unique development that has deeply stirred the emotions of participants and descendants. Thus, a saga is not simply a story but a story that at some time has had a particular base of believers. The term often refers also to the actual history itself, thereby including a stream of events, the participants, and the written or spoken interpretation. The element of belief is crucial, for, without the credible story, the events and persons become history; with the development of belief, a particular bit of history becomes a definition full of pride and identity for the group.

Introduction

An organizational saga is a collective understanding of unique accomplishment in a formally established group. The group's definition of the accomplishment, intrinsically historical but embellished through retelling and rewriting, links stages of organizational development. The participants have added affect, an emotional loading, which places their conception between the coolness of rational purpose and the warmth of

Reprinted from *Administrative Science Quarterly* 17:2 (June 1972): 178-84. *Author's note:* Revised version of paper presented at the 65th Annual Meeting of the American Sociological Association, September 1970, Washington, D.C. I wish to thank Wendell Bell, Maren L. Carden, Kai Erikson, and Stanley Udy for discussion and comment. Parts of an early draft of this paper have been used to connect organizational belief to problems of governance in colleges and universities (Clark 1971).

sentiment found in religion and magic. An organizational saga presents some rational explanation of how certain means led to certain ends, but it also includes affect that turns a formal place into a beloved institution, to which participants may be passionately devoted. Encountering such devotion, the observer may become unsure of his own analytical detachment as he tests the overtones of the institutional spirit or spirit of place.

The study of organizational sagas highlights nonstructural and nonrational dimensions of organizational life and achievement. Macro-organizational theory has concentrated on the role of structure and technology in organizational effectiveness (Gross 1964; Litterer 1965; March 1965; Thompson 1967; Price 1968; Perrow 1970). A needed corrective is more research on the cultural and expressive aspects of organizations, particularly on the role of belief and sentiment at broad levels of organization. The human relations approach in organizational analysis, centered largely on group interaction, showed some awareness of the role of organization symbols (Whyte 1948, chap. 23), but this conceptual lead has not been taken as a serious basis for research. Also, in the literature on organizations and purposive communities, "ideology" refers to unified and shared belief (Selznick 1949; Bendix 1956; Price 1968, pp. 104–110; Carden 1969); but the concept of ideology has lost denotative power, having been stretched by varying uses. For the phenomenon discussed in this paper, "saga" seems to provide the appropriate denotation. With a general emphasis on normative bonds, organizational saga refers to a unified set of publicly expressed beliefs about the formal group that (a) is rooted in history, (b) claims unique accomplishment, and (c) is held with sentiment by the group.

To develop the concept in this paper, extreme cases and exaggerations of the ideal type are used, but the concept will be close to reality and widely applicable when the phenomenon is examined in weak as well as strong expression. In many organizations, even some highly utilitarian ones, some segment of their personnel probably develops in time at least a weak saga. Those who have persisted together for some years in one place will have had, at minimum, a thin stream of shared experience, which they elaborate into a plausible account of group uniqueness. Whether developed primarily by management or by employees, the story helps rationalize for the individual his commitment of time and energy for years, perhaps for a lifetime, to a particular enterprise. Even when weak, the belief can compensate in part for the loss of meaning in much modern work, giving some drama and some cultural identity to one's otherwise entirely instrumental efforts. At the other end of the continuum, a saga engages one so intensely as to make his immediate place overwhelmingly valuable. It can even produce a striking distortion, with the organization becoming the only reality, the outside world becoming illusion. Generally the almost complete capture of affect and perception is associated with only a few utopian communities, fanatical political factions, and religious sects. But some formal rationalized organizations, as, for example, [in] business and education, can also become utopian, fanatical, or sectarian.

Organizational sagas vary in durability. They can arise quickly in relatively unstructured social settings, as in professional sports organizations that operate in the volatile context of contact with large spectator audiences through the mass media. A professional baseball or football team may create a rags-to-riches legend in a few months' time that excites millions of people. But such a saga is also very fragile as an ongoing definition of the organization. The story can be removed quickly from the collective understanding of the present and future, for successful performance is often unstable, and the events that set the direction of belief can be readily reversed, with the great winners quickly becoming habitual losers. In such cases, there seems to be an unstable structural connection between the organization and the base of believers. The base of belief is not anchored within the organization nor in personal ties between insiders and outsiders, but is mediated by mass media, away from the control of the organization. Such sagas continue only as the organization keeps repeating its earlier success and also keeps the detached followers from straying to other sources of excitement and identification.

In contrast, organizational sagas show high durability when built slowly in structured social contexts, for example, the educational system—specifically, for the purposes of this paper, three liberal arts colleges in the United States. In the many small private colleges, the story of special performance emerges not in a few months but over a decade or two. When the saga is firmly developed, it is embodied in many components of the organization, affecting the definition and performance of the organization and finding protection in the webbing of the institutional parts. It is not volatile and can be relegated to the past only by years of attenuation or organizational decline.

Since the concept of organizational saga was developed from research on Reed, Antioch, and Swarthmore, three distinctive and highly regarded colleges (Clark 1970), material and categories from their developmental histories are used to illustrate the development of a saga, and its positive effects on organizational participation and effectiveness are then considered.[1]

---

[1]For some discussion of the risks and tensions associated with organizational sagas, particularly that of success in one period leading to later rigidity and stagnation, see Clark (1970, pp. 258-61). Hale (1970) gives an illuminating discussion of various effects of a persistent saga in a theological seminary.

Development of Saga

Two stages can be distinguished in the development of an organizational saga: initiation and fulfillment. Initiation takes place under varying conditions and occurs within a relatively short period of time; fulfillment is related to features of the organization that are enduring and more predictable.

Initiation

Strong sagas do not develop in passive organizations tuned to adaptive servicing of demand or to the fulfilling of roles dictated by higher authorities (Clark 1956, 1960). The saga is initially a strong purpose, conceived and enunciated by a single man or a small cadre (Selznick 1957) whose first task is to find a setting that is open, or can be opened, to a special effort. The most obvious setting is the autonomous new organization, where there is no established structure, no rigid custom, especially if a deliberate effort has been made to establish initial autonomy and bordering outsiders are preoccupied. There a leader may also have the advantage of building from the top down, appointing lieutenants and picking up recruits in accord with his ideas.

Reed College is strongly characterized by a saga, and its story of hard-won excellence and nonconformity began as strong purpose in a new organization. Its first president, William T. Foster, a thirty-year-old, high-minded reformer, from the sophisticated East of Harvard and Bowdoin went to the untutored Northwest, to an unbuilt campus in suburban Portland in 1910, precisely because he did not want to be limited by established institutions, all of which were, to his mind, corrupt in practice. The projected college in Oregon was clear ground, intellectually as well as physically, and he could there assemble the people and devise the practices that would finally give the United States an academically pure college, a Balliol for America.

The second setting for initiation is the established organization in a crisis of decay. Those in charge, after years of attempting incremental adjustments (Lindblom 1959), realize finally that they must either give up established ways or have the organization fail. Preferring that it survive, they may relinquish the leadership to one proposing a plan that promises revival and later strength, or they may even accept a man of utopian intent. Deep crisis in the established organization thus creates some of the conditions of a new organization. It suspends past practice, forces some bordering groups to stand back or even to turn their backs on failure of the organization, and it tends to catch the attention of the reformer looking for an opportunity.

Antioch College is a dramatic example of such a setting. Started in the 1860s, its first sixty years were characterized by little money, weak staff, few students, and obscurity. Conditions worsened in the 1910s under the inflation and other strains of World War I. In 1919 a charismatic utopian reformer, Arthur E. Morgan, decided it was more advantageous to take over an old college with buildings and a charter than to start a new one. First as trustee and then as president, he began in the early 1920s an institutional renovation that overturned everything. As president he found it easy to push aside old, weak organizational structures and usages. He elaborated a plan of general education involving an unusual combination of work, study, and community participation, and he set about to devise the implementing tool. Crisis and charisma made possible a radical transformation out of which came a second Antioch, a college soon characterized by a sense of exciting history, unique practice, and exceptional performance.

The third context for initiation is the established organization that is not in crisis, not collapsing from long decline, yet ready for evolutionary change. This is the most difficult situation to predict, having to do with degree of rigidity. In both ideology and structure, institutionalized colleges vary in openness to change. In those under church control, for example, the colleges of the most liberal Protestant denominations have been more hospitable than Catholic colleges, at least until recently, to educational experimentation. A college with a tradition of presidential power is more open to change than one where the trustees and the professors exert control over the president. Particularly promising is the college with a self-defined need for educational leadership. This is the opening for which some reformers watch, the sound place that has some ambition to increase its academic stature, as, for example, Swarthmore College.

Swarthmore began in the 1860s and had become, by 1920, a secure and stable college, prudently managed by Quaker trustees and administrators and solidly based on traditional support from nearby Quaker families in Pennsylvania, New Jersey, and Maryland. Such an organization would not usually be thought promising for reform, but Frank Aydelotte, who became its president in 1920, judged it ready for change. Magnetic in personality, highly placed within the elite circle of former Rhodes scholars, personally liked by important foundation officials, and recommended as a scholarly leader, he was offered other college presidencies, but he chose Swarthmore as a place open to change through a combination of financial health, liberal Quaker ethos, and some institutional ambition. His judgment proved correct, although the tolerance for his changes in the 1920s and 1930s was narrow at times. He began the gradual introduction of a modified Oxford honors program and related changes, which resulted in noteworthy achievements that supporters were to identify later as "the Swarthmore saga" (Swarthmore College Faculty 1941).

Fulfillment

Although the conditions of initiation of a saga vary, the means of fulfillment are more predictable. There are many ways in which a unified sense of a special history is expressed; for example, even a patch of sidewalk or a coffee room may evoke emotion among the believers, but one can delimit the components at the center of the development of a saga. These may center, in colleges, on the personnel, the program, the external social base, the student subculture, and the imagery of the saga.

Personnel. In a college, the key group of believers is the senior faculty. When they are hostile to a new idea, its attenuation is likely; when they are passive, its success is weak; and when they are devoted to it, a saga is probable. A single leader, a college president, can initiate the change, but the organizational idea will not be expanded over the years and expressed in performance unless ranking and powerful members of the faculty become committed to it and remain committed even after the initiator is gone. In committing themselves deeply, taking some credit for the change and seeking to ensure its perpetuation, they routinize the charisma of the leader in collegial authority. The faculty cadre of believers helps to effect the legend, then to protect it against later leaders and other new participants who, less pure in belief, might turn the organization in some other direction.

Such faculty cadres were well developed at Reed by 1925, after the time of its first two presidents; at Antioch, by the early 1930s, after Morgan, disappointed with his followers, left for the board of directors of the new TVA; and at Swarthmore, by the 1930s, and particularly by 1940, after Aydelotte's twenty years of persistent effort. In all three colleges, after the departure of the change agent(s), the senior faculty with the succeeding president, a man appropriate for consolidation, undertook the full working out of the experiment. The faculty believers also replaced themselves through socialization and selective recruitment and retention in the 1940s and 1950s. Meanwhile, new potential innovators had sometimes to be stopped. In such instances, the faculty was able to exert influence to shield the distinctive effort from erosion or deflection. At Reed, for example, major clashes between president and faculty in the late 1930s and the early 1950s were precipitated by a new change-oriented president, coming in from the outside, disagreeing with a faculty proud of what had been done, attached deeply to what the college had become, and determined to maintain what was for them the distinctive Reed style. From the standpoint of constructing a regional and national model of purity and severity in undergraduate education, the Reed faculty did on those occasions act to create while acting to conserve.

Program. For a college to transform purpose into a credible story of unique accomplishment, there must be visible practices with which claims of distinctiveness can be supported; that is, unusual courses, noteworthy requirements, or special methods of teaching. On the basis of seemingly unique practices, the program becomes a set of communal symbols and rituals, invested with meaning. Not reporting grades to the students becomes a symbol, as at Reed, that the college cares about learning for learning's sake; thus mere technique becomes part of a saga.

In all the three colleges, the program was seen as distinctive by both insiders and outsiders. At Swarthmore it was the special seminars and other practices of the honors program, capped by written and oral examination by teams of visiting outsiders in the last days of the senior year. At Antioch it was the work-study cycle, the special set of general education requirements, community government, and community involvement. At Reed it was the required freshman lecture-and-seminar courses, the junior qualifying examination, and the thesis in the senior year. Such practices became central to a belief that things had been done so differently, and so much against the mainstream, and often against imposing odds, that the group had generated a saga.

Social Base. The saga also becomes fixed in the minds of outside believers devoted to the organization, usually the alumni. The alumni are the best located to hold beliefs enduringly pure, since they can be as strongly identified with a special organizational history as the older faculty and administrators and yet do not have to face directly the new problems generated by a changing environment or students. Their thoughts can remain centered on the past, rooted in the days when, as students, they participated intimately in the unique ways and accomplishments of the campus.

Liberal alumni, as those of Reed, Antioch, and Swarthmore here, seek to conserve what they believe to be a unique liberal institution and to protect it from the conservative forces of society that might change it—that is, to make it like other colleges. At Reed, for example, dropouts as well as graduates were struck by the intellectual excellence of their small college, convinced that college life there had been unlike college life anywhere else, and they were ready to conserve the practices that seemed to sustain that excellence. Here, too, conserving acts can be seen for a time as contributing to an innovation, protecting the full working out of a distinctive effort.

Student Subculture. The student body is the third group of believers, not overwhelmingly important but still a necessary support for the saga. To become and remain a saga, a change must be supported by the student subculture over decades, and the ideology of the subculture must integrate with the central ideas of the believing administrators and faculty. When the students define themselves as personally responsible for upholding the image of the college, then a design or plan has become an organizational saga.

At Antioch, Reed, and Swarthmore, the student subcultures were powerful mechanisms for carrying a developing saga from one generation to another. Reed students, almost from the beginning and extending at least to the early 1960s, were great believers in the uniqueness of their college, constantly on the alert for any action that would alter it, ever fearful that administration or faculty might succumb to pressures that would make Reed just like other colleges. Students at Antioch and Swarthmore also offered unstinting support for the ideology of their institution. All three student bodies steadily and dependably transferred the ideology from one generation to another. Often socializing deeply, they helped to produce the graduate who never quite rid himself of the wish to go back to the campus.

Imagery of Saga. Upheld by faculty, alumni, and students, expressed in teaching practices, the saga is even more widely expressed as a generalized tradition in statues and ceremonies, written histories and current catalogues, even in an "air about the place" felt by participants and some outsiders. The more unique the history and the more forceful the claim to a place in history, the more intensely cultivated the ways of sharing memory and symbolizing the institution. The saga is a strong self-fulfilling belief; working through institutional self-image and public image, it is indeed a switchman (Weber 1946), helping to determine the tracks along which action is pushed by men's self-defined interests. The early belief of one stage brings about the actions that warrant a stronger version of the same belief in a later period. As the account develops, believers come to sense its many constituent symbols as inextricably bound together, and the part takes its meaning from the whole. For example, at Antioch a deep attachment developed in the 1930s and 1940s to Morgan's philosophy of the whole man and to its expression in a unique combination of work, study, community participation, and many practices thought to embody freedom and nonconformity. Some of the faculty of those years who remained in the 1940s and 1950s had many memories and impressions that seemed to form a symbolic whole: personnel counselors, folk dancing in Red Square, Morgan's towering physique, the battles of community government, the pacifism of the late 1930s, the frequent dash of students to off-campus jobs, the dedicated deans who personified central values. Public image also grew strong and sharp, directing liberals and radicals to the college and conservatives to other places. The symbolic expressions themselves were a strong perpetuating force.

Conclusion

An organizational saga is a powerful means of unity in the formal place. It makes links across internal divisions and organizational boundaries as internal and external groups share their common belief. With deep emotional commitment, believers define themselves by their organizational affiliation, and, in their bond to other believers, they share an intense sense of the unique. In an organization defined by a strong saga, there is a feeling that there is the small world of the lucky few and the large routine one of the rest of the world. Such an emotional bond turns the membership into a community, even a cult.

An organizational saga is thus a valuable resource, created over a number of years out of the social components of the formal enterprise. As participants become ideologues, their common definition becomes a foundation for trust and for extreme loyalty. Such bonds give the organization a competitive edge in recruiting and maintaining personnel and help it to avoid the vicious circle in which some actual or anticipated erosion of organizational strength leads to the loss of some personnel, which leads to further decline and loss. Loyalty causes individuals to stay with a system, to save and improve it rather than to leave to serve their self-interest elsewhere (Hirschman 1970). The genesis and persistence of loyalty is a key organizational and analytical problem. Enduring loyalty follows from a collective belief of participants that their organization is distinctive. Such a belief comes from a credible story of uncommon effort, achievement, and form.

Pride in the organized group and pride in one's identity as taken from the group are personal returns that are uncommon in modern social involvement. The development of sagas is one way in which men in organizations increase such returns, reducing their sense of isolation and increasing their personal pride and pleasure in organizational life. Studying the evocative narratives and devotional ties of formal systems leads to a better understanding of the fundamental capacities of organizations to enhance or diminish the lives of participants. The organization possessing a saga is a place in which participants, for a time at least, happily accept their bond.

References

Bendix, R. *Work and Authority in Industry*. New York: John Wiley, 1956.

Carden, M.L. *Oneida: Utopian Community to Modern Corporation*. Baltimore, Md.: Johns Hopkins Press, 1969.

Clark, B.R. *Adult Education in Transition: A Study of Institutional Insecurity*. Berkeley : University of California Press, 1956.

_____. *The Open Door College: A Case Study*. New York: McGraw-Hill, 1960.

_____. *The Distinctive College: Antioch, Reed, and Swarthmore*. Chicago: Aldine, 1970.

_____. "Belief and Loyalty in College Organization." *Journal of Higher Education* 42: 6 (1971): 499-515.

Gross, B.M. *The Managing of Organizations*, 2 vols. New York: Free Press, 1964.

Hale, J.R. "The Making and Testing of an Organizational Saga: A Case-Study of the Lutheran Theological Seminary at Gettysburg, Pennsylvania, with Special Reference to the Problem of Merger, 1959-1969." Unpublished dissertation, Columbia University, 1970.

Hirschman, A.O. *Exit, Voice, and Loyalty*. Cambridge: Harvard University Press, 1970.

Lindblom, C.E. "The Science of 'Muddling Through.'" *Public Administration Review* 19 (1959): 79-88.

Litterer, J.A. *The Analysis of Organizations*. New York: John Wiley, 1965.

March, J.G., ed. *Handbook of Organizations*. Chicago: Rand McNally, 1965.

Perrow, C. *Organizational Analysis*. Belmont, Calif.: Wadsworth, 1970.

Price, J.L. *Organizational Effectiveness: An Inventory of Propositions*. Homewood, Ill.: Richard D. Irwin, 1968.

Selznick, P. *TVA and the Grass Roots*. Berkeley: University of California Press, 1949.

_____. *Leadership in Administration*. New York: Harper & Row, 1957.

Swarthmore College Faculty. *An Adventure in Education: Swarthmore College under Frank Aydelotte*. New York: Macmillan, 1941.

Thompson, J.D. *Organizations in Action*. New York: McGraw-Hill, 1967.

Weber, M. *From Max Weber: Essays in Sociology*. Translated and edited by H.H. Gerth and C. Wright Mills. New York: Oxford University Press, 1946.

Whyte, W.F. *Human Relations in the Restaurant Industry*. New York: McGraw-Hill, 1948.

20

Functions and Fantasies: Understanding Schools in Capitalist America

David Cohen and Bella Rosenberg

Schooling in Capitalist America (Bowles and Gintis 1976) will make waves in the history of education, but it is only incidentally concerned with history. Rather, it is an effort to locate schooling in the social and economic context of capitalist society. The authors seek to offer a comprehensive account of the role schools have served in the American economic structure; they advance a critique of efforts to change or reform schools; and they suggest an alternative vision of how school reform should work.

On the first point, Bowles and Gintis argue that United States schools' chief role has been to "reproduce" inequality in the larger society—to pass along differences arising in the social relations of production. In this the schools legitimate, reflect, and transmit inequality; they socialize students to inequality and the beliefs required to support it. But they neither cause inequality nor do they relieve it.

On the second point, the authors argue that most school reform efforts have failed. In some cases the book says that reforms materialized but were wrong because they sought to reinforce the capitalist order; in others the reforms failed to materialize because they sought the opposite—more liberation or equality. Furthermore, those few efforts that succeeded in liberalizing or equalizing some aspects of schooling were failures: mere

Mr. Cohen is grateful for comments and arguments on the subject offered during the course of several years by Joseph Featherstone and Eleanor Farrar.

Reprinted, by permission, from *History of Education Quarterly* 17:2 (Summer 1977): 113–37.

cosmetics to keep the contradictory face of capitalism from appearing too ugly. School reform, in their view, either fails because it succeeds in doing the economy's bidding or fails because it doesn't succeed in doing the opposite. Either type of failure succeeds, because it meets the needs of capitalism.

On the third point, the book holds that reform can at least have the hope of success if it represents steps in a larger program of revolutionary transformation. Making schools more open, for example, can work if it is part of a program to make society more democratic. Making schools more equal can work if it is part of an effort to extend political democracy to the economy and the work-place. But taken alone, simply as solutions to school problems, such reforms will fail. School reform can only succeed if it is more than reform of schools.

As this summary suggests, the history of education in its own right has no real role in this book. Implicitly, at least, the book tells us that the history of education has been misplaced, just as liberal school reform has been misplaced. Both aspire to an existence independent of those economic forces and factors which are said actually to determine the character of social and cultural life. In the place of history of education as a discipline which pieces together pictures of the schools' past, Bowles and Gintis offer a conception of ordered structural economic and social change in which education was implicated. In the traditional history of education we apprehend the educational past through a collection of fragmentary views and visions, bound together chiefly by a focus on the social organization of academic life and its content. In the view of this book, however, we should apprehend the educational past as one pattern in a deeper and more comprehensive system of change. We cannot, Bowles and Gintis imply, grasp the schools' role in this system if we persist in looking only at schools.

Of course this was not a main point in the book, but it is worth noting here. The implicit notion is that history of education should not be cut off from a connection to social relations more broadly conceived. It is also worth noting the plain implication that it would be unfair to discuss the book as though there were historical parts of it that could be excised and evaluated alone. They will be, no doubt—given the academic division of labor—but the authors would doubtless feel that the sum of such evaluations may not entirely reach the whole of their book. It seems only right to respond to the book on its own terms, as a sweeping vision of the role which education plays in the American social and economic structure and as an effort to weld our grasp of the past to a vision of the future.

But if fair is fair, time is short. There is no way the book's entire sweep can be fully dealt with here. Instead we will content ourselves with discussing one of the book's central assumptions in a way which may raise useful questions about the broader structure of the argument.

The assumption we have in mind is commonplace enough—namely that schools can best be understood in terms of the social functions they perform. This is a habit of mind particularly familiar to social scientists. They tell us, for example, that schools exist because a socialization function once served by families and churches fell into disuse; formal organizations had to be created to take up the slack. As a result schools teach morals, manners, and minding your elders, as well as reading—that is, even the curriculum is shaped by the schools' social function. The functions of schooling thus identified run a broad gamut, including the legitimation of established political ideas (the political-socialization function), the creation of skills and knowledge needed in an advanced industrial society (the economic growth and human capital formation functions), and minding hapless herds of children who otherwise would annoy adults during working hours (the child-care and noise-control functions).

We will discuss this set of ideas in several ways. First, we will explore some of the functionalist notions apparent in *Schooling in Capitalist America,* and will raise questions both about their logic and their value as a form of historical explanation. In general we are doubtful about functionalism, not only as displayed in Bowles's and Gintis's book but in much contemporary social analysis. Second, we will discuss a few alternative ways of understanding social and historical phenomena. We are particularly interested in exploring their expressive aspects. Our argument is that while it is often useful to "explain" phenomena in terms of causes, effects, or functions, it is equally useful to apprehend them as moral, political, or aesthetic expressions. For in explaining we often reduce, and in reducing we lose much of the meaning and significance of social life.

Finally, through all this we will of course explore the historical argument and evidence presented in *Schooling in Capitalist America.* However, this is not a review of the book but an essay examining one key aspect of its explanatory apparatus. Our treatment of the book's historical sections is therefore partial and spotty. Nonetheless, we could hardly proceed without reference to how the functionalist explanatory structure and the historical evidence engaged one another.

Functional Analysis

The notion of social functions provides a useful and sometimes analytically powerful way of thinking about schools and other institutions. We regularly observe commonalities in the ways an institution behaves, or in the ways it is treated by those whose lives it touches. Equally regularly these observations make us wonder if there are "purposes" which the institutions serve. We observe that college basketball players who make the varsity teams are much more likely than their nonvarsity compatriots to have played basketball in high school. We go on to wonder if in fact the "function" of high school basketball has become one of preparing and screening students for college ball. That is an interesting and perhaps useful question about high school sports. Or we may observe that students' academic rank upon high school graduation is moderately related to their parents' economic and social rank, and that this was roughly equally true at high school entry as well. We wonder if one function of high school is to perpetuate inequality. Again, an interesting and perhaps useful question.

While Bowles and Gintis have nothing to say about basketball, their book is an example par excellence of functionalist thinking in social science. In one sense there is nothing unusual in this, for social science is quite thoroughly marinated—not to say nearly drowned—in functionalist ideas. One can barely find a sociological, political, economic, or psychological analysis of schooling which does not seek to comprehend the subject matter in the terms suggested above. But in another sense this book is different, for the analysis is explicit and comprehensive to an unusual degree. Only a few other scholars (one thinks of Talcott Parsons) have tried to present such a sweeping functionalist vision of anything. In fact, Bowles's and Gintis's book strikes us as a case of flamboyant functionalism: much like flamboyant Gothic architecture, it displays the style and its strengths and problems more clearly because of the extreme and somewhat ornate quality of the work. Problems we might never have noticed in more ordinary social science become clear, for familiar ideas and assumptions stand out in higher relief, or are massed in a density we cannot fail to observe.

This is particularly evident in examining a notion closely associated with functionalist thinking—namely, the existence of a rational structure of purpose, or *telos*, in society. We go from observing that college varsity players are more likely to have played in high school to saying that a "function" of high school ball is to screen and prepare for college ball. We thus imply (at least) that this is a *purpose* of high school basketball. We ordinarily do not pause somewhere in between and say simply that high school ball screens and prepares for college ball—whatever its "purpose." The statement about function carries an imputation of rational order and, at some level, intent. The other simply posits an association or observes what may be a causal relationship without ascribing any deeper social rationality or purpose. This is done on the assumption that there may be no deeper purpose, or that if there is a purpose it may be at odds with the results, or that there are competing purposes whose relative importance and results are terribly difficult to sort out.

This seems harmless enough in the case of basketball, but the example of academic rank upon high school graduation is more potent. We can observe that academic rank upon graduation is related to parents' economic and social rank, and that it is related in roughly the same degree as it was at high school entry. We then infer that high schools apparently do not either increase or decrease inequality. So far so good. But can we go on to say that this shows that high schools' *function* is to preserve inequality? The last statement takes several great leaps beyond the first, proceeding from an observed regularity in social organization to a statement about some deeper purpose which this regularity serves.

This sort of high jumping is common enough in social science, but *Schooling in Capitalist America* carries it to Olympic Games proportions. Not only does the book seek to demonstrate, for example, that evidence on inequality in educational achievement reveals the inegalitarian purposes of schools, but it also seeks to demonstrate that these results of schooling occur because of broader social aims. In this book's analytical scheme, the schools are assigned specific social purposes within a larger hierarchy of social purposes. Schools are said to preserve inequality because the function of schools in capitalist America is to reproduce the unequal social relation of production (Bowles and Gintis 1976, pp. 9-11). Evidence on patterns of student inequality is related to evidence on the purposes of schooling, as culled from data on the class composition of school boards or the statements of board members and other prominent figures. Both are thought to reveal the larger social purposes motivating the education enterprise. Schooling is explained in terms of a complex system of rational ends-means relationships, where the ends—the maintenance and growth of capitalism—are not always readily apparent and often masquerade as their opposite.

There are some deep problems with such approaches to social and historical analysis. The most easily detected is the difficulty of adequately linking evidence about social phenomena to evidence about underlying social purposes. One reason for this is that such underlying purposes are virtually immune to falsification. Much as in the case of psychoanalytic explanations for behavior, there is no evidence which can refute them. But while this may be true in a formal sense, functionalist scholars often ignore the logic and take much trouble trying to produce convincing evidence.

Bowles and Gintis take this trouble, but have a hard time with the evidence. One result is frequent outbreaks of ambivalence. For example, the authors set out ambitiously in their section on the origins of public education, asserting that

...the U.S. educational system works to justify economic inequality and to produce a labor force whose capacities, credentials, and consciousness are dictated in substantial measure by the requirements of profitable employment in the capitalist economy...an essential structural characteristic of U.S. education is what we have called the correspondence between the social organization of schooling and that of work [Bowles and Gintis 1976, p. 151].

But later, having examined the decidedly recalcitrant evidence, they strike a different note:

...no very simple or mechanistic relationship between economic structure and educational development is likely to fit the available historical evidence.... political factors have intervened between economic structures and educational outcomes in complex and sometimes, apparently, contradictory ways [Bowles and Gintis 1976, p. 179].

Further on, however, at a greater distance from the unruly evidence, they seem to take back the qualification:

Major periods of educational change are responses to alternatives in the structure of economic life associated with the processes of capital accumulation. The common school movement of the nineteenth century, we have seen, developed to complement a burgeoning factory system increasingly rendering the family inadequate to the task of reproducing the capitalist division of labor [Bowles and Gintis 1976, p. 199].

Their ambivalence waxes and wanes, depending upon whether the evidence or the overarching framework of economic ends and social means is coming into view. But in any case, the historical evidence doesn't really play a central role. Bowles and Gintis periodically admit that it is sketchy, but this does not at all disturb their analysis or their larger conceptions about the functions of schooling.

In a sense this is not surprising, for as we noted functionalist ideas of this sort are not primarily matters of evidence. The ideas themselves are grand theories to whose level empirical social science could not rise even if it so wished. Social science, after all, describes relations among social events and analyzes possible causal connections among them. But the data are deeply ambiguous in most causal arguments. This is due partly to the fact that in explaining any persistent association among several phenomena, such as the fairly stable relationship between parents' status and students' academic rank at the beginning and end of high school, equally plausible alternative meanings are possible. One can argue, for example, that high schools maintain inequality because the association is not reduced over time. But one can also argue that they increase equality by preventing inequalities in the broader society from becoming even larger. High schools might be pictured, on the one hand, as stemming the normal tendency for inequality to widen—as might well happen among people of unequal social inheritance were there no school at all. Or, by contrast, high schools can be portrayed as maintaining the inequities which they inherit. Evidence to resolve such differences is rarely available. In this case, for example, we can hardly produce data on the effects of no schooling on inequality because schooling is too widespread.

This example points up one problem of using relational statements about social phenomena to make inferences about underlying and unseen social purposes: the inferences depend much more on beliefs about the purposes than on evidence about the relations among social phenomena. This problem is not eased by trying to use evidence which seems to bear more directly on society's purposes, such as announcements and declarations by contemporaries about the purposes of public action. Bowles and Gintis, for example, present statements by Horace Mann that extol the economic value of education. Schools, Mann wrote, would produce more educated, obedient, and productive workers. The authors say that this shows that men of wealth and power who embraced the coming capitalist order used schools to reproduce the social relations of production.[1] But Mann argued with equal passion and at greater length that schools were important to produce a citizenry educated and independent enough for self-government and liberty in a democratic society. He wrote, in fact, that schools would "counteract this tendency to the domination of capital and the servility of labor" (Mann 1891). This latter statement hardly reflects an unabashed capitalist, let alone one who promoted schools to fuel the industrial inferno.

What do we make of these differences? Do we place more weight on Mann's embrace of capitalism and the coming industrial system, or on his belief that education would prevent the excesses and miseries of that system? Do we pay more attention to his advocacy of schools to restore a past economic and social order, or to his notion that they would usher in a

---

[1]See Bowles and Gintis (1976, pp. 166-67). It should also be noted that some early capitalists argued against the extension of schooling on the grounds that it would overeducate workers beyond usefulness. (See, for example, Wyllie, 1954). Moreover, there is evidence that the skills required for Massachusetts factories during this period decreased. Following Bowles's and Gintis's argument, increased schooling seems dysfunctional and its support by capitalists irrational (see Field 1976).

new one?[2] Or do we simply dismiss Mann's economic argument? After all, some interpreters have argued plausibly that Mann's use of economic arguments in his Fifth Report was a political strategy which he found distasteful but necessary to enlist support for education (Vinovskis 1970). In this view Mann is portrayed as being quite ambivalent about the role of economics in public education. How are we to know which purpose was *really* Mann's? Or what the balance of his motivations were? Or how they were connected to society's purpose, if such a thing can be imagined?

Thus, just as there are competing interpretations for most evidence about relations among social phenomena—and quite distinct inferences about implied social purposes—there are similarly competing explanations for any evidence on the announced purposes of individuals or groups. In matters of complex social causation, there is simply no such thing as direct evidence on society's underlying purpose. The notion of underlying purpose is a construct which organizes evidence drawn from appearances, conflicting motivations, and contemporary confusions—all to make attributions about an underlying reality whose very existence is a conundrum. How can one know if "American Capitalism" arranged public education to carry out its intention to "reproduce the social relations of production"? The gauzy fabric of inferences required in such statements is torn at every turn by competing interpretations and giant inferential stretches. Of course many social scientists persistently write about society's inner purposes and underlying aims. But the best one can say about social science evidence in such ventures is that it may bear a more or less pleasing decorative relation to the ideas. Evidence certainly cannot confirm either the existence or the effects of inner social purposes.

A Historical Alternative

Functional analysis is not the only way of thinking about the causal meaning of social phenomena. One of the common explanations for institutional arrangements is "that's the way they always were." Historical explanation, to put this notion in slightly more dignified terms, is an

---

[2] Horace Mann, railroad and factory enthusiast that he was, was also intensely ambivalent about the new order. Indeed, many of his schooling arguments were offered in the hopes of preserving an essentially Jeffersonian society. (See, for example, Messerli 1972.) It is also interesting to note that Mann managed to "preserve the legal and economic foundations of the society in which he had been raised"; as Bowles and Gintis claim (1976, p. 173), capitalism as we know it would have been forestalled. (See, for example, Horwitz 1977; Handlin and Handlin 1969.)

important alternative to functional analysis. For example, when Bowles and Gintis try to explain the origins and spread of public education in the United States they follow many other recent scholars in trying to relate these phenomena to the economic and social functions they imagine schooling served: raising workers' skills due to the "needs" of industrialism, or promoting obedience in the labor force due to the "needs" of capitalism. In both cases the extension of schooling is portrayed in terms of some larger web of rational social purposes. But these events might also be seen partly as outgrowths of the old and abiding American enthusiasm for education, an enthusiasm evident in the informal educational activities of families, churches, and voluntary associations in rural and small-town America, as well as in the enlightenment ideas of urban cosmopolites and the reformist dreams of Protestant do-gooders horrified at the unwashed masses pouring into their cities. Americans undertook public education in part because education had always been an American passion (see, for example, Graham 1974). And when America became a political democracy, dependent upon an informed citizenry, passion became faith.

History in this sense is hardly a complete explanation for the spread of public schooling, but our point has less to do with how complete it is than with how different it is. Functionalist accounts subsume events, institutions, and human action to overriding social purposes. These larger forces are imagined to inhere in and perhaps to cause social events and human action. But history, in the sense we have used it here, calls attention to the role which many unique and particular circumstances can have in social structure and human action. The emphasis is on the ways in which the gradual accretion of culture, tradition, and social organization can influence what happens. In the first case, one's attention is turned on the ways in which society's deepest aims are worked out in events; in the second, one's attention is drawn to the ways in which individual action and communal traditions build deep habits over time and provoke or limit change. In the first case, one notices the expected and the necessary; in the second, one attends to the interplay of individuality, continuity, and surprise.

This argument between functionalist and historical approaches to analysis of the past has, of course, been quite thoroughly worked over by historians, philosophers, and other interested bystanders for the last century. This will doubtless continue, for having lost the sense that overarching purposes can be found in the heavens, many historians and social analysts seem bound to reincarnate them in the social world, finding order in "necessary" social functions, in "inevitable" movements of history, or in "inner" needs, drives, and structures.

Expressive Aspects of Social Phenomena

Different as the two views summarized just above are in certain respects, there is one important way in which they are remarkably similar. It is that the most interesting questions in either account are causal: Why do events happen, and what effects do they have? In both historical and functional analysis, explaining the effects and causes of historical phenomena is the way we try to grasp their meaning. There is an alternative, though. We might take the past as a series of texts, to be read much as we read prose and poetry. The meaning, in this view, lies in what the texts express, not in their function or what they were caused by.[3]

We might, for example, think of the past in the metaphoric terms of theatre. Social action might be grasped in terms of the expressive qualities—feelings, values, and form—"broadcast" to an audience. In the historic struggles over Progressivism, for example, the schools might be seen as a great social proscenium, a stage on which terrific struggles over the content and character of the culture were played out. The creation or adoption of a progressive curriculum was in some respects a declaration about culture, childhood, and society. These wars were of course serious; powerful forces were arranged in the struggles, they could be won or lost, and the consequences were often far from trivial. But in some measure the materials in the struggles were also theatrical—they were manifestations and expressions important in their own right. This is equally true of cultural wars over discipline and open education presently being waged in the school-theatre. Discipline is said by its proponents to be important for what it is thought to cause—character or achievement. But it is also valued for what it displays—order, regularity, and authority—and valued as well for what that display expresses about the culture. Such social expressions are like theatre, for both engage our attention with the values, feelings, and ideas they express, and with the various formal structures used to shape and achieve that expression. These cultural conflicts over school can be seen in the same way as we see a play. To understand a play we need not understand what caused the play—though it helps a great deal to understand its context. But given that understanding we focus on what is expressed in the play and what it means. The play's significance—like the significance of many social phenomena—lies partly in the act, in its content, and formal qualities.

These rough metaphors suggest a helpful way of thinking about social analysis. They assume that in some important respects human action and

---

[3] For a valuable treatment of urban life from this perspective, see McDermott (1974). See also the essays by Geortz and Fernandez (1972).

social organization can be usefully understood in terms of their expressive qualities. They assume that the meaning of social phenomena, like the meaning of aesthetic phenomena, lies partly in the ideas, values, and feelings conveyed, and in the formal terms of conveyance. And they also assume that these meanings can be apprehended in their own right without reference to their causes or social functions. Thus, institutions, social movements, speeches, buildings—even the arrangement of chairs in a classroom—express attitudes, states of mind, and feelings. These can be read, heard, seen, and felt—just as we do with art.

Consider, for example, the heavy, dark, and severe exteriors of those three-story brick city schools built in the late nineteenth century. They speak much about the quality of what was to go on inside. Or take, on the inside, the screwed-down rows of desks and chairs, all facing the single desk and chair raised up front. This deliberate and formal structure of human space speaks volumes about the organizational values of these institutions. And Americans presently make contrary social declarations as they rework the interior space of schools: putting chairs and desks in halls; creating flexible clusters of working space within larger, open, and undefined areas, facing chairs inward on children's small places rather than serried up in long ranks facing the leader. Like prose and poetry, like architecture or stage design, these things have motives. They have effects and may even have functions. But they also have content and form which stand in their own right. We can "read" these uses of space in comprehending schools, just as we read the use of space in Romanesque churches to help comprehend the culture and society in which they were built.

These metaphoric connections of artistic and social phenomena are not made because we believe that in some literal sense schools are theatres, or that the declamations of public men and women about schools are poetry. Neither, unhappily, is usually the case. Rather, we connect the two because we are so unused to apprehending in social phenomena those qualities which we readily appreciate in artistic creations—namely, expressive values. Or rather, regularly apprehending those values in social phenomena as part of our everyday social life, we are not in the habit of using those perceptions in social analysis. Perhaps these examples from the arts may help to wrench eyes away from social causes and functions and focus them on expressive values.

A few more extended examples may also help. In the middle and late nineteenth century most states passed laws making school attendance compulsory—laws whose enactment was accompanied by considerable debate and fanfare. For some the laws seemed the best instrument to insure equality, by compelling all children to learn together in common schools; for others they seemed a way of curbing delinquency by providing instruments whereby "disobedient and wayward" children could be brought to heel and their manners and morals repaired; to still others the laws seemed a way of assuring education in a society which needed more of it in order to meet the challenge of industrialism and technology.

These stories about the laws were all told at the time of their passage. Later, other stories appear. Bowles and Gintis, looking back on both Horace Mann's work and the expansion of public schools in which such laws figure, make this assessment:

> ...he [Mann] embraced the capitalist order and sought through social amelioration and structural change to adjust the social institutions and people of Massachusetts to its needs. At the same time Mann's reforms had the intent (and most likely the effect as well) of forestalling the development of class consciousness among the working people of the state and preserving the legal and economic foundations of the society.... It was truly an innovative solution to the problem of the conservative adaption [sic] to change. It was soon to be duplicated around the country [Bowles and Gintis 1976, p. 173].

Thus, the meaning of these laws has been seen in terms of one or another causal scheme: preventing delinquency, promoting economic growth, pursuing obedience, or producing social relations in schools which reproduced those of factories. But one perplexing thing about these laws—like many aspects of official action in education—is that they seemed utterly without any of the intended effects. Enactment of the statutes appears to have been quite uncorrelated with any increase in school enrollments, let alone declines in delinquency or anything else. Bowles and Gintis note this, but pass over any discussion of its meaning. A functionalist account might fairly note exceptions, but in the case of compulsory attendance laws dysfunction seems to have been built in, for the laws typically were accompanied by inadequate mechanisms for enforcement. Penalties were provided, but appropriations for truant officers were either minuscule or nonexistent. How could the penalties be applied, lacking means of implementation?

One answer is that the laws were not simply rational instrumentalities of policy. For if legislation is an instrumental mechanism to achieve social ends, it is also an expression of attitudes, values, and states of mind. The compulsory school laws might be seen in this second way—a declaration about a class of persons who seemed to threaten social order in the cities. The laws could even be seen as a declaration of war, but like some wars of the very old-fashioned European sort, this declaration was observed more in the fanfare than in the fighting. For while the objects of the law stirred great concern, this hatred and fear seems to have inspired the same sort of unenforceable legislation as resulted from former Governor Rockefeller's legislative crusade against drug users and sellers in New York a few years ago. Both sets of laws were immensely popular, not because of the punishing effects they produced (there were few), but because of the feelings they expressed, especially the severity of retribution they declared. Like Sunday oratory, the laws were there less for what they produced than for what they promised and preached.

Thus, if we think about the school attendance laws in terms of some "need" society had to domesticate youth or as a "function" of increasing productivity, they seem a puzzling and inexplicable failure—a social function that didn't. By contrast, if we think about the laws as a declaration of faith, as a form of political theatre, they make a certain sense. Of course, one wants to know if policy achieves its announced aims. But since there is more to policy than announced aims, restricting the inquiry to instrumental success or failure can unnaturally constrain comprehension. It would be like discussing the import of the *Orestia* in terms of its effects on Greek morality.

Like theatre, then, laws can usefully be understood in terms of the values and states of mind they convey and the form in which they are presented, as well as in terms of the aims they achieve. Like plays, laws can be understood in terms of how they shape moral and emotional expression for an audience, not just in terms of their functional impact on a "target population." Like plays, laws can be seen as an encounter between an organized presentation of meaning and an audience. Legislation involves expressive and communicative encounters between those who shape and articulate meaning in the culture and those who listen and respond. These features may be as important as the law's instrumental role in implementing policy. But whatever their relative importance, understanding their meaning requires attention to the expressive as well as the instrumental features of public life.

Other examples may seem less likely. Standardized testing, for example, has rarely struck anyone as a policy which failed. Advocates and critics alike seem to agree that testing has a real function and that it works. They quarrel chiefly over whether it should. Perhaps a policy of this sort is less amenable to interpretation in expressive terms than the compulsory school statutes. Perhaps policies that seem to "work" are more functional and less expressive than laws which don't.

Certainly there has been general agreement about the function of testing since it was introduced on a large scale just after the first World War. Scientific identification of students' ability would permit their assignment to appropriate classes and curricula and would facilitate the process of channeling them toward suitable work. The underlying notion was that knowledge, skills, and intellectual ability were the precious stuff of individual success and economic advance in the modern world. The ranking of occupations was rapidly coming to correspond to the ranking of intellect, it was thought; schools could fit students into this new order and improve the correspondence of brains and work by ability testing and tracking. Students would learn more; they would learn more appropriate things; and they would be more productive as a result.

In a very compressed form, this story about tests was told by both advocates and critics. The former celebrated the increased efficiency and effectiveness of testing and tracking. The latter agreed that their effects were as declared, but they deplored them. Bowles and Gintis are numbered among the critics, and they portray testing as follows:

> ... the capitulation of the schools to business values and concepts of efficiency led to the increased use of "intelligence" and scholastic-achievement testing as an ostensibly unbiased means of measuring the product of schooling and classifying students.[4]

In fact, however, they argue that a central aim of testing was: " ... to justify tracing by race, ethnic origin, and class background" (Bowles and Gintis 1976, p. 198). In Bowles's and Gintis's view, testing had an overriding social function. They write that " ... a school system geared toward ... domesticating a labor force for the rising corporate order might readily embrace standardization and testing ... " (p. 200).

There is no doubt that testing was a centerpiece in efforts to modernize the schools and thereby to bring America into the modern industrial age. But did testing play a major role in "domesticating a labor force for the corporate order," or was it an expression—a sort of organizational epic—of what modernity was supposed to be? Bowles and Gintis note in a small aside that the streaming of students substantially predated the introduction of testing (p. 191). While they make nothing of this, it suggests that if "domestication" was the name of the game, everything may have been already quite solidly in place. If differentiation and its attendant discriminatory effects were already in full bloom, one wonders why such claims for the function of testing?

The book does not follow this thought, but it holds elsewhere that schools do little either to mitigate or compound inequality. Testing may thus sanction what is given in the larger economic system, but itself neither creates nor reduces inequality. As the authors say:

---

[4]See Bowles and Gintis (1976, p. 195). One of this paper's authors once even shared this view (see Cohen and Lazerson 1972).

...the educational system does not add to or subtract from the overall degree of inequality or repressive personal development. Rather, it is best understood as an institution which serves to perpetuate the social relationships of economic life...schools foster legitimate inequality through the ostensibly meritocratic manner by which they reward and promote students and allocate them to distinct positions in the occupational hierarchy [p. 11].

In a curious way, this comes close to a quite different slant on testing. The authors seem to be saying that in certain respects testing was a ritual that was unrelated to the net amount of inequality. This idea is especially intriguing because of the evidence that testing never performed its announced functions very well. For example, there is a great deal of evidence that ability groups based on test scores don't seem to improve students' learning. This practice doesn't even much simplify instruction by reducing variability in student ability, for the test variance within ability-grouped classes is typically only a bit less than the overall test variance in that grade. Similarly, there is a good deal of evidence that ideas about the importance of cognitive skills to work and economic success—ideas which played such a key role in the testing movement—were vastly exaggerated. The cognitive abilities measured in those tests seem little related to productivity, success on the job, and the like. In short, this and other evidence suggests that testing didn't perform the social functions it was supposed to perform. It didn't even seem to be much of a help to teachers in figuring out what to do with their classes: in fact, there is a good bit of evidence that while teachers nearly everywhere gave tests they also often ignored them (see, for example, "Educational News and Editorial Comment" 1927).

Thus, tests have all sorts of effects, many of them quite pernicious. Students are sorted and grouped, sometimes into classes which give them advantages in the competition for more schooling and sometimes into classes which stigmatize them in various ways and/or deprive them of a decent education. But the tests don't seem to serve the functions— economic, social, occupational, and instructional—which both critics and advocates supposed. If this is true, what then are we to make of the "function" of testing? Bowles and Gintis are familiar with the evidence and they deal with it by presenting a different notion of function: testing was a meritocratic ritual, they agree, but not just any old ceremony. Its function was to "legitimate" the existing order and thus "perpetuate the relationships of economic life." Testing was a ritual with a rationale, a ceremony with a function.

Now it is certainly true that the sponsors of testing fervently hoped it would legitimate distinctions among students. But it did not always work so neatly—though this is less well known. For example, early in this century Columbia University was casting about for a way to weed out the undesirable eastern European Jews who were rapidly sullying its ivory tower. Not only did these Jews make up close to the majority of the graduating class of New York City high schools at that time—despite some IQ test results that showed them to be feeble-minded—but they also threatened to make up a majority of Columbia's students. In 1919 Columbia turned to using as part of its admission procedure an IQ test devised by R.L. Thorndike, a psychologist on its own faculty. The test was expected to restore a proper student body and provide a legitimate basis for preserving higher education for the genteel. But much to Columbia's chagrin, it did not work: for a short time the test, coupled with discriminatory application forms, did lead to a decline in the percentage of Jews eligible for admission. But they were replaced by equally undesirable Catholics, especially Italians (Wechsler 1974 and 1977).

This is not to say that the hopes of testing sponsors were always thwarted; they were not. But it does raise questions about the extent to which testing was functional—did it actually "legitimate" and "perpetuate the social relationships of economic life"? This is really an empirical question, one to which Bowles and Gintis assert an affirmative answer—as have the champions and critics of testing since it began. But to our knowledge, no one has ever produced much evidence on the point. This is not surprising, for the evidence would be quite hard to come by. Suppose we wish to make a convincing case that testing and tracking did in fact legitimate the social relations of production in schools, and thus perpetuated the existing capitalist order. Can one simply cite the motives of testing advocates, the money of their sponsors, and then note that capitalist America still stands, untouched by revolution?

We think not. For apart from the fact that the absence of revolution may be explained by any number of things quite distinct from the "legitimation function" of testing, in order to make a plausible argument that testing actually played this role one should present some evidence on how it worked—rather than just evidence on how it was intended to work. This would require empirical, among other things, research on the states of mind of members of society, resulting in evidence which linked their willing acceptance of different levels of status and power to their belief that their different places in the order were just and deserved because of their performance on tests taken long since in school. To our knowledge no one has ever undertaken an effort to show that testing and tracking play such a role in the attitudes of America's victors and victims.

It may well be that tests have played this role. Our skepticism is confined only to the notion that we know they have. In fact all we know is: (1) that some advocates of testing hoped—and some critics believed—that this would be the case; and (2) here we all still are, before the revolution. But we don't know much about the connection between these things, or the role of tests in it. This point seems especially worth noting in view of the fact that the established order seemed to be keeping itself quite securely in place before tests ever made their appearance.

Thus, there is a serious lack of evidence on both functional accounts of testing. First, testing seems not to have performed the instructional, academic, and occupational functions it was supposed to, nor is there evidence that testing is functional in the sense that the abilities it measures are critical to the abilities required on jobs. Second, there is no evidence that tests actually have performed an important legitimating function in American capitalism, sanctifying the social order given by economic power. The absence of support for these functionalist arguments does not necessarily mean they are wrong—more evidence might be turned up. Nor does it mean that tests do not have all sorts of effects in schools—they do, and many of them are unhappy. But it does suggest some serious reservations about analyses which attempt to explain these effects as results of the social function testing is intended to play. And it suggests the usefulness of exploring other angles on testing.

Bowles's and Gintis's view of testing as a ritual strikes us as a particularly fruitful alternative. But rituals need not be reduced to functions. We are inclined to interpret testing as a ritual which took on central significance in American beliefs about the role of science, knowledge, and modernization. These beliefs were widely displayed around the turn of the century, but they were particularly important in schools. It was in schools, after all, that knowledge—that most precious alloy in the modern industrial skeleton— would be welded onto workers. Thus schools were to be the chief instruments for becoming modern. These beliefs, which amounted to a faith, were displayed in any number of ways at the time—including studies of the money value of schooling, an avalanche of high school vocational courses, and the rapid replacement of apprenticeship by schooling in any number of professional fields. There was virtually a religious commitment to the idea that formal schooling held the key to success in an increasingly technological civilization. Schools were the magic matter of modernity, and the faithful flocked.

The ritual role which testing played in this faith was simple enough, for tests captured three essential elements in ideas about modernization. First, the tests were scientific: as such they provided a seemingly authoritative measure of students' skills and abilities. Second, there was merit: assigning students within schools on the basis of this authoritative information would be fair—to each according to his or her ability and need. And, finally, there was progress: the combination of tests and ability groups would allow schools to connect their "products" to society's "economic needs." Thus, if knowledge made the world go round with an increasingly efficient hum, tests would help schools play their role—providing the world with skilled workers in a scientific, meritocratic, and progressive fashion.

Our view, then, is that testing became a pervasive phenomenon because of these beliefs, but not because the beliefs were true. Indeed, the fact that the beliefs seemed to be rather weakly founded, combined with the persistent popularity of testing, strikes us as added evidence that testing was in large measure an expressive phenomenon. But this view has distinct limits. For in arguing that testing can be understood as an expressive ritual central to beliefs about the role of science and knowledge in modernization, we have made only part of a case. We have tried to show that testing didn't effectively fulfill the various functions it was supposed to; we have said that in understanding testing, therefore, functionalist interpretations remain unsupported; and finally we have briefly made some assertions about testing as a ritual within a broader system of social beliefs about knowledge and science. Explaining our case requires at least some expansion of these last assertions, and we think it would be useful to focus both on the development of this ritual and on its expressive properties.

On the first point, we think testing should be considered as part of a larger social invention which established a new set of ritual forms in schooling. For if standardized testing was genuinely new in 1910, this novelty occurred in the context of something much older—a larger and long-standing search for fair and rational ways to interpret the inner organization of schools. A variety of methods had already been proposed or tried. Much earlier, sorting on the basis of phrenological differences or "humors" threatened to capture educators' imaginations (it certainly did Horace Mann's), and many other ideas were tried in the ensuing decades. By 1915 efforts had long been underway to organize students within elementary schools on the basis of ability, achievement, or what was then called "progress." This search had become increasingly pressing, for the schools had growing herds of students, and in the cities great piles of "academically retarded" youths were heaping up in the grades, caught like unwilling warriors on the barbed-wire fences of age-grading, uniform evaluations of progress by grade, and year-end promotion. Worse yet, popular writers were saying that the schools had no orderly way of dealing with these problems.

This was not entirely fair, for schools had invented ways to solve these troubles. But there were many ways and each raised questions. Many tried to organize just on the basis of age, but the trouble there was the enormous variability of "class progress" within age grades. Others tried to differentiate students instead on the basis of class progress—but often they couldn't figure out what measure of it to use. For what, after all, was the right criterion of class progress in a country that used so many different books, and whose teachers made up so many different test questions? And then there was the matter of timing. Should differentiation—and thus promotion—occur every month, or every few months, or every year? And how should schools decide this? On the basis of teachers' judgments? Students' work on classroom tests written up by teachers? Or just on how far students got in their lessons?

. These were terrific puzzles, puzzles not so much of what to do but of why, and what to call it. Standardized achievement tests and differential class assignment based on tests seemed to provide virtually an instant solution. It was a striking social invention. In its purely technical form, of course, the invention had been quite different—namely, Binet's ingenious device to determine whether children had serious learning disabilities. But the real invention for American schools was not the test—that was only a condition. The invention was using it in schools to identify and order what already was happening in a troubled and only half-understood way. *Testing and ability grouping named what was occurring, gave it a particular order, and did so in a seemingly authoritative way.* Schools would be organized now on the basis of science, merit, and progress. The struggle to find order and authority for school organization was over; testing and tracking brought schools into harmony with modernity. Like Pirandello's six characters, the schools had found an author.

Neither the differentiated organization of schools nor the use of evaluative instruments to accomplish the differentiation were new. Both had been used widely for decades. What was new was the notion of a single method to replace what struck contemporaries as an undisciplined variety of approaches, and the notion that this method was authoritative. Not only was the method one system, but it was based on science, merit, and economic progress. There was no earthly practical reason school could not have gone on forever, testing and differentiating students in the same old ways. What the tests and groups solved was not so much a practical problem of organization, but rather a theoretical or metaphysical problem concerning the meaning and authority of whatever organization was used. Teacher-made tests and school-organized groups had only the authority of the school professionals who created them. Needless to say, this was minimal. With the new psychometric instruments, both the schools and the professionals took on a much greater authority, one based not in education but in those principles of science and merit believed to underly modernity itself. Americans had a new way of ordering their notions about schooling, and a powerful way of connecting these ideas to a vision of society's nature and purpose.

Testing and grouping, then, became a crucial focus for the great saga about science, knowledge, and modernity which first engaged Americans on a grand scale around the turn of the century. It was, to be sure, a saga which overflowed with wishes and projections—about the authority of science, about the social importance of merit, and about the role of formal learning in economic growth and individual social mobility. But it was a saga filled with the crucial beliefs of the modern West. And in scientific ability testing the schools had found one device—the only one they ever did find, in fact—which seemed to connect directly the schools' daily work to this saga. For testing and tracking meant that at one strike the boring, frustrating, and ordinary features of school life—assigning students to classes, promoting or retarding them, deciding their curriculum—were suffused with a fundamental social significance. That is why we say that the problem testing solved was not essentially one of organization, but of the mythology or metaphysics of organization. Testing became a vehicle for expressing ideas and attitudes about what modern life ought to be—and for exhibiting the schools' harmony with those ideals. The invention lay more in the realm of myth and ideas than in the realm of organization.

It was as if the bowels of the schools—troubled, rumbling, and disordered—had suddenly been transformed into shiny stainless steel machinery, working in perfect symmetry and polished smoothness. No wonder it was so enthusiastically promoted, for testing was a sort of contemporary heraldry. Tests were the visible incarnation of a new order, and they received loving attention from school people all over America. Education journals in the 1920s and 1930s were full of announcements and celebrations. The story of its adoption in Detroit was published here; the celebration of how well it worked in Peoria was published there; stories of how many districts had adopted it were recited; and the tributes from teachers and administrators heaped up in professional journals and the proceedings of annual meetings. There was little careful scrutiny and little contradictory opinion: just a torrent of worshipful testimony.

Of course, it was not long before contradictory evidence and complaints began to accumulate. Beginning in the 1930s and growing through the 1940s and 1950s, studies showed that testing and tracking didn't seem to perform their functions. But some evidence of the power of the beliefs underlying this ritual of school organization is suggested by the fact that these were the very decades in which testing and tracking became virtually universal in American schools. Empirical evidence, after all, has never been the sustaining power of either myth or ritual. What upholds such things is the sense that the underlying order which they name and celebrate is both solid and legitimate. And here we find one more suggestive bit of evidence on the expressive character of testing and tracking: for while these practices did finally come into question, it was not because of the long-accumulated studies which showed that they were not working as advertised. Rather, the testing and tracking ritual came into question when, for a variety of reasons entirely unrelated to the ritual, Americans' faith in the underlying mythology—in the redeeming power of science, formal learning, and modernity—was first severely jolted. Testing and tracking came into question in the [1960s, which was a decade] marked by extraordinary visions of the destructive power of things modern and American: visions of massive technological and scientific warfare on innocent peasants; visions of the democratic American state become devious and oppressive, its effectiveness enhanced by electronic technology; visions of modern industry and technology out of control, wreaking havoc on the countryside; and visions of angry poor and minority youth for whom stories about the power of knowledge and the economic fruits of schooling had become a frustrating trick—a great promise which the very institutions of hope seemed incapable of redeeming.

These messages began trickling into the media in the past decade or so, and it was the first inkling Americans had, on a popular scale, that modernity might be their undoing. Certainly it was a very different story than the one told about...World War II, in which this country's staggering death-dealing potential and its industrial capacity seemed forces for international salvation and human uplift. It was in this more recent climate of doubt about the underlying mythology of modernity that questions about testing—questions researchers had asked, unheard, for decades—first found something of an audience. By now the issue is something of a *cause célèbre*, the protests and questions supported by the same foundations and social elites that originally supported the tests. The fate of testing and tracking rituals, then, seems to have been tied to the fate of large mythic ideas about science, merit, and modernity.

One might, of course, say that this ritual had a function—that myth and ritual are central needs in all societies, and that in the modern West old religious myths and rituals are replaced with new scientific and technical ones. One might thus suggest that testing and tracking meet deep social "needs" or serve essential religious functions. But while these notions are interesting—suggesting as they do some persistent inner order in the human condition despite great changes of circumstance—we are not sure exactly what they add to our understanding of testing and tracking in America. The question of this inner order is hardly a small one, but it is possible to appreciate the meaning and character of this ritual without solving the puzzle of its connection to deeper social functions.

Thus, the display of tests in schools can be understood as eloquent organizational testimony to the modernity of the enterprise. It was an announcement that education was scientifically up to date, that it was in touch with all that was new and valuable. Testing and grouping was in some sense a celebration of meaning, a social creation which displayed connections between the ordinary materials of everyday life and the deeper order and meaning of things. Such things seem common enough in all known cultures, but we need not fall into the linguistic apparatus of social functions to understand these expressive phenomena. We need only note that the prominent display of these rituals in schools, like the prominent display of sacred figures and texts in other holy places, gave evidence that the institution was securely connected to those deeper sacred forces on which everything in the modern West is founded—science, economic progress, and merit. Their display was a visible, tactile declaration of faith. Such devotion deserves to be appreciated in its own terms.

Conclusion

This essay began by focusing on the functionalist assumptions underlying the Bowles and Gintis book. We questioned the logic of these assumptions, went on to question their usefulness in the history of education, and then spent most of the essay exploring the expressive content of social phenomena.

Concerning the history of education, the book's great value is that it invites us to a broader view. This is an old theme—that schools and education are best understood in a larger social and economic context. But Bowles and Gintis give it a particularly sharp twist, namely that American schools should be understood in terms of their functions in life under capitalism. They summarize this in the notion that schools have "reproduced the social relations of production." As one might expect in any grade functionalist analysis, the authors were content mostly to illustrate this notion with a bit of historical material. They had no intention of writing a history of education, but did intend to suggest by analysis and example how it ought to be written. Unfortunately, their functionalist framework makes it difficult for them even to suggest the complex, capricious, and contradictory relations between the American economic order and education. For anything which didn't fit the functionalist frame was either ignored, mentioned but unexplained, or presented as a "contradiction." Thus, while the authors' effort to see the history of American education in economic and class perspective is on an important track, the way they construed this task was unfortunately narrow. The book presents an important invitation to a broader history of education, but it was engraved with too simple a picture.

Concerning functionalist analysis, we have focused attention on its limits as a way of understanding social phenomena. We approached this in two ways. First, we explored some of the logical difficulties in making functionalist inferences from social or historical evidence; such analysis often tends toward a reductionism which obscures much of the richness, variety, and perversity of social life. This is probably as dangerous to the health of historical writing as it evidently has already been to sociology. A curiosity about the "functions" of social arrangements is an important element in social studies of any sort, but so is a healthy skepticism about the inferential giant steps to which this curiosity often leads.

Most of our attention to the problems of functionalism, however, has been given to exploring an alternative approach. The meaning of social phenomena, we think, can often be discerned as much in their expressive qualities as in their causes or functions. The meaning of tracking and testing may partly be found in their ritual celebration of modernity. The compulsory school laws may be as meaningful as expressive declarations, not just as instruments for accomplishing policy goals. In these and other examples we tried to suggest that historians can read social arrangements as we do a text, or as we experience a play. To understand some social meanings we need a sensitive eye and a critical ear—an awareness of the expressive content of things.

In conclusion, it may be useful to note several ideas which underlie this analysis. A first point concerns our argument that the expressive aspects of schooling deserve particular attention. This is no accident, for we think schools have been an especially rich focus for expressive meaning in modern America. More than factories, fields, and office buildings, schools are sacred places in this society. Education, after all, is in many respects the nearest thing we have to a faith. And this faith has long been closely linked to science, which is the nearest thing we have to genuine authority, to contact with the underlying order of things. Thus schools are places in which important cultural ideals find a focus and form, or in which great wars over the culture's content are fought.

So it is no accident that the longest, hardest, and most wrenching battles in the recent movement for black civil rights occurred around schools, rather than lunch counters, public parks, or voting booths—even though the latter were surely the most important in purely instrumental terms. Nor do we think it an accident that so much of the mythology of becoming American has centered on the role of education. Despite massive evidence from everyday life about all the other ways in which people became Americans and "made it," only schools became the focus of this durable mythology. Nor has it been an accident that so many American movements for social reform—from preventing delinquency in the 1840s, to improving immigrant families in the 1890s, to ending poverty in the 1960s, and preserving ethnicity in the 1970s—have focused on schooling.

Partly this is due to our notion that education has great potency, a nearly magical transforming power. But this combines with other circumstances to enhance the school's role as a social theatre—a place in which great stories can be told and great dramas acted out. After all, what other forums are everywhere, open to everyone, and invested with virtually sacred significance? It is no wonder that arguments over curriculum content and building styles can assume the terrific significance they often do—for they are also arguments over the content of the culture and styles of social life. There are precious few significant public arenas in which such arguments can be made with meaning, in which feelings can be given form in a way that counts, in which declarations can be made on common ground.

But understanding social life in expressive terms does not mean ignoring its effects. If testing and tracking had expressive features, these features had consequences. They affected the lives of students in school and later on, they helped create a problematic culture of education, and they contributed to a notion of education's social role which strikes us as objectionable in many ways.

The question, then, is not whether effects exist, but to what they should be attributed. The effects of testing presently engraved in America's schools and culture, for example, are not so much the result of well-oiled relations between rational social means and ends as they are the effects of a great illusion about the power of science and formal learning. The social structure of schools with which we presently struggle—tests and tracts included—can be understood as the inheritance of an old saga about the authority of science just as well as it can be seen as the result of successful capitalist efforts to "reproduce the social relations of production." Schools did sometimes seek to remodel themselves on what they thought the social relations of production were, but the result was more a sad charade than a necessary social function. It occurred because school people and nearly everyone else believed a story about science, knowledge, and economic progress—not because the logic of capitalism required it. As even Bowles and Gintis point out, schools were not essential to the economic functions of capitalism.

Our argument, then, is that in understanding the expressive features of schooling we are not engaged in the social equivalent of critical formalism. Schools are not poems, bereft of origins, contexts, and consequences. The rituals we construct around tests, the feelings formally organized in legislation, the dreams manifest in meritocratic ability groups all have consequences. But they were consequences as much of expressive as of purposive action. The institutions and culture of schools today are in many respects simply the cold and hardened organizational results of myths and rituals believed and celebrated several generations ago.

This strikes us as particularly worth understanding, for pictures of the past are not unconnected to present ideas about change. Social science, which presents ordered and purposive hierarchies of functions, not only leaves much unexplained but offers an unnaturally narrow and rationalistic reading of society and how it works. And this leads to naively reasonable notions about how present reforms should proceed. The institutions we have inherited, however, are the result of more than orderly means-ends relationships. Pictures of the past organized around such orderly ideas are not only constricted, but misleading, for they imply that change can be carried out if only we have a precise notion of our goals and fit the appropriate means to them. Bowles and Gintis make such assumptions in their closing arguments about school reform, but in this they offer only a left-wing version of rationalistic notions which currently pervade the so-called policy sciences. In our view history and social science should ask whether such rationalism is rational. For what presently seems rational policy—such as tying states' school aid to local districts' test scores—could appeal only because of mythic notions about tests and "accountability." The same thing is true of instruments for implementing policy: program evaluation, for example, seems rationally tailored to the achievement of federal policy goals; but it also might be understood in expressive terms, as a ritual of scientific government. History and social analysis steeped in naive rationalism seem likely to blind us to the power of current myths and rituals. And that will surely mislead and frustrate efforts at action.

It is precisely because of the limits on these rational formulations that it seems important to look in other directions. By stressing dramatic and ritual aspects in the history of schooling we have tried to suggest that schools have been a central focus for expressive action. Schools, we have argued, therefore incarnate great stories about life in the modern world. The stories and rituals which surrounded testing, for example, did not exist merely in our minds. Being told and believed the stories took on institutional form, and then had all manner of effects—many weighing heavily on us for generations thereafter. Instead of thinking of schools as our factories, then, we also might view them as theatres and temples. We might then puzzle less over their apparent failures to perform social functions, to achieve announced goals, or to respond to rational reform.

References

Bowles, S., and H. Gintis. *Schooling in Capitalist America: Educational Reform and the Contradictions of Economic Life.* New York: Basic Books, 1976.

Field, A.J. "Educational Expansion in Mid-Nineteenth Century Massachusetts: Human-Capital Formation or Structural Reinforcement?" *Harvard Educational Review* 46 (November 1976): 544-45.

"Educational News and Editorial Comment." *School Review* 35 (1927): 733-35.

Graham, P. Albjerg. *Community and Class in American Education, 1865-1918.* New York: John Wiley, 1974.

Geortz, C., and J. Fernandez. "Myth, Symbol and Culture." *Daedelus* (Winter 1972).

Handlin, O., and M. Flug Handlin. *Commonwealth, A Study of the Role of Government in the American Economy: Massachusetts 1974-1861,* rev. ed. Cambridge: Harvard University Press, 1969.

Horwitz, M.J. *The Transformation of American Law 1780-1860.* Cambridge: Harvard University Press, 1977.

McDermott, J.J. "Space, Time, and Touch: Philosophical Dimensions of Urban Consciousness." *Soundings* (Fall 1974): 253-74.

Mann, H. *Life and Works of Horace Mann,* quoted in Rush Welter, *Popular Education and Democratic Thought in America.* New York: Columbia University Press, 1965.

Messerli, J. *Horace Mann: A Biography.* New York: Alfred Knopf, 1972.

Vinovskis, M. "Horace Mann on the Economic Productivity of Education." *New England Quarterly* 43 (1970): 550-71.

Wechsler, H.S. "The Selective Function of American College Admissions Policies, 1870-1970." Doctoral dissertation, Columbia University, 1974.

———. *The Qualified Student, A History of Selective Admission in America.* New York: John Wiley, 1977.

Wyllie, Irvin G., *The Self-Made Man in America: The Myth of Rags to Riches.* New Brunswick, N.J.: Free Press, 1954.

21

Research on School and District Organization

John Meyer, W. Richard Scott, and Terrence Deal

Increasingly, social researchers have looked at schools from the vantage point of the current theory of organizations, which emphasizes how organizations succeed by finding effective structures to link their technologies with environmental demands and resources. From this viewpoint, schools are peculiarly ineffective organizations: schools do not control their technologies very well, and they do not even possess technologies of known efficacy. In fact, schools control the activities most closely related to their central educational purposes in only the weakest ways: teaching goes on behind the closed doors of the isolated classroom. Indirect "professional" controls are weak, and the ability of school organizations to buffer themselves from their environments is very limited—schools are highly penetrated organizations.

Thus the standard social science picture of schools is painted: schools are weak and ineffective organizations with little capacity to produce useful technical effects or to defend themselves from the environment. To a few, the schools are essentially fraudulent organizations; to many others, they are classic examples of organizational ineptitude.

This is an astonishing picture of social structures that, as formal organizations, have been spectacularly successful. Huge amounts of money

Reprinted, by permission, from *The Structure of Educational Systems: Explorations in the Theory of Loosely Coupled Organizations,* ed. Margaret R. Davis, Terrence E. Deal, John W. Meyer, Brian Rowan, W. Richard Scott, and E. Anne Stackhouse (Stanford: Stanford Center for Research and Development in Teaching, 1977). Funded by a grant from the National Institute of Education, contract #NE-C-CO-3-0062.

are consistently spent year after year to fund the extant set of schools; personnel and programs are maintained stably. Further, certain school organizations maintain themselves with great success: they fail infrequently. Perhaps one-twelfth of the small businesses in the United States fail every year, but when a single school organization closes down unexpectedly for a few weeks we are all so astonished that newspaper accounts appear far and wide. Similarly, accounts of school-bond elections that fail are spread as if they foreshadowed a coming doom (or reforms), but little notice is taken that schools are funded in a much more stable way from year to year than many other kinds of organizations. Finally, there is much public discussion—mostly by educators—of the failures of the schools, but few notice that levels of constituent satisfaction, as reported from surveys of parents and community members, are very high.

The weakness of schools lies not in the fragility of educational organization but in the models often applied from organization theory. Contemporary theories emphasize organizational structures built around the coordination of technical production and exchange. Schools, which in our view represent organizations formed around quite different issues, look weak and inept from such a perspective. In this paper, we sketch out an institutional model of organizations that better describes educational organizations. (See also Meyer and Rowan 1975, 1977.) We then go on to review some of the features of educational organization, which this alternative model explains. In doing this, we present some empirical data from our own research—data that conform closely to images of educational organization found in other empirical studies.

Theory: Institutional and Technical Sources of Organizational Structure

Formal organizational structures arise through two main processes. First, complex technologies and social environments with complex exchanges such as markets foster the development of rationalized bureaucratic organizational structures to efficiently coordinate technical work (see Thompson 1967; Scott 1976). Second, institutional structures emerge in society and define various roles and programs as rational and legitimate. These structures encourage the development of specific bureaucratic organizations that incorporate these elements and conform to these rules (Meyer and Rowan 1977). The emergence of the factory predominantly reflects a process of the first type, while the emergence of the school, we argue, reflects primarily a process of the second type (Meyer and Rowan 1975).

The history of schools has been misunderstood as reflecting the emergence of educational organizations that coordinate the technical work of education—and schools have been frequently criticized for their failure to manage this work efficiently. From our point of view, this criticism is misplaced: educational organizations are formed to bring the process of education under a socially standardized set of institutional categories, not necessarily to rationalize the "production processes" involved in carrying on this work.

What difference does it make whether the processes creating modern educational organizations are technical or institutional? In our view, it makes a crucial difference: organizations formed in connection with technical flows closely control and manage these flows. Their structures act to regulate these flows, to buffer them from uncertainty, and thus to insulate them in some measure from external forces. Such organizations, in other words, are under pressure to become relatively closed systems, sealing off their technical cores from environmental factors (Thompson 1967). Techniques such as coding, stockpiling, leveling, anticipating, and rationing help to buffer the technical processes from external uncertainties. The intent is to decouple technical work from environmental conditions so that it can be more tightly managed by the organization.

By contrast, institutionalized organizations closely integrate their own structural arrangements with the frameworks established by the larger institutional structures. In doing so, they tend to buffer their structures from the actual technical work activities performed within the organizations. Using such techniques as certification, delegation, secrecy, and ritual, these organizations attempt to decouple their technical work from the organizational structure so that it can be more closely aligned with the institutional framework.

Thus the technical organization faces in toward its technical core and turns its back on the environment; the institutional organization turns its back on its technical core in order to concentrate on conforming to its institutional environment. More concretely, in order to survive, a factory must develop a well-understood production process that can produce desired products at a competitive price and then must insure that the system has an adequate supply of raw materials, trained personnel, market outlets, a reasonable tax situation, and so forth. However, the crucial thing a school needs to do to survive is to conform to institutional rules—including community understandings—defining teacher categories and credentials, pupil selection and definition, proper topics of instruction, and appropriate facilities. It is less essential that a school make sure that teaching and learning activities are efficiently coordinated or even that they are in close conformity with institutional rules.

Six propositions, depicted graphically in Figure 21-1, summarize the theory:

1. Organizations evolving in environments with complex technologies create structures that coordinate and control technical work.
2. Organizations with complex technologies buffer their technical activities from the environment.
3. Organizations with efficient coordinative structures tend to succeed in environments with complex technologies.
4. Organizations evolving in environments with elaborated institutional rules create structures that conform with those rules.
5. Organizations in institutional environments buffer their organizational structures from their technical activities.
6. Organizations with structures that conform to institutional rules tend to succeed in environments with elaborated institutional structures.

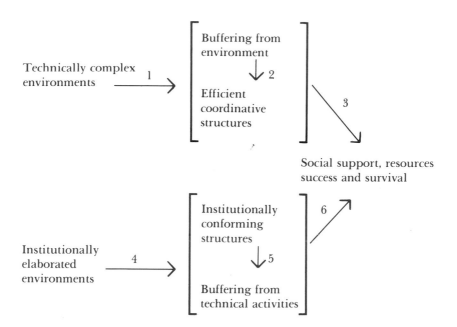

Figure 21-1
Institutional and technical theories of organization structure

Schools appear to exist in environments that are highly elaborated in their institutional structures but relatively poorly developed in their technical systems. The absence of clearly understood and efficacious technical processes for obtaining desired outcomes has been noted by others (compare March and Olsen 1976; Weick 1976). This combination of circumstances can explain many of the current features of educational organizations—their sensitivity to environmental pressures, their inclination to avoid evaluation of instructional programs or outputs (Dornbusch and Scott 1975), their failure to implement adopted programs (Baldridge and Deal 1975), and so on. For in many respects conformity to wider institutional rules is inconsistent with detailed control over technical work activity. Such control reveals inconsistencies and conflicts between institutional rules, raises questions about the effectiveness of the programs, esposes vague and vacuous goals and procedures, and makes explicit the difficulties and problems of implementation. Under such circumstances tight coupling of the organizational structure with the technical activities can only lower the legitimacy and threaten the resources of the organization.

Explanations and Predictions Offered by an Institutional Model of Educational Organizations

Our institutional model is built around two main ideas. First, school organizational structures reflect environmental institutional rules of education. Second, these organizational structures are decoupled from the technical work of education and many of its vagaries and problems. In maintaining the socially standardized categories of the educational system (the same structure that builds social support and legitimacy), the schools delegate the technical work and uncertainty of education beyond the purview of the organizational structures. We now turn to a description of the ways educational organizations fit this model and to how the model can explain some of their distinctive features.

Educational Organization as a Reflection of Institutional Rules

We first consider the ways educational organizations are structurally formed not to coordinate their own technical work but to conform to rules institutionalized in their environments. We also consider some of the consequences this has for educational organizations.

Structural Conformity. In one sense, the point is obvious: school organizations go to the greatest lengths not to accomplish instructional ends but to maintain their legitimate status as schools. They seek *accreditation*, which depends on structural conformity, and they react in panic when accreditation is threatened. School organizations hire teachers with proper *credentials* (which is nearly independent of teaching effectiveness). The teachers are assigned to carefully defined *students*, who are classified in *grades*, which are given standardized meanings all around the country (but there is enormous educational heterogeneity in any given grade). The teachers apply a *curriculum* to the student, which is given definition at district and state levels, but which is rather homogeneous across the country (but there is little inspection to see that this curriculum is actually taught or learned). Instruction occurs in buildings and classroom spaces that conform to state laws.

This apparatus is managed by *principals* and *superintendents*, whose roles are also defined (and sometimes credentialled) by the wider environment. Similarly, schools and districts have in their organizational structure functionaries mandated or funded by state and federal programs (not internal coordinative exigencies). Thus, as the state creates and credentials reading specialists and provides incentives for the discovery of handicapped readers, the schools elaborate these positions in their structures. There is little evidence of effective implementation, since many parents might object to the segregation of their children from age-mates, but the programs exist. Schools even create counterprograms—as when radicals object to the formal organizational stigmatization of pupils created by one set of programs and demand the installation of another set of formal programs to make sure that the hypothetically segregated handicapped students are effectively "mainstreamed."

At the district level, many parts of the organizational structure are similarly mandated, or made advantageous, by features of the institutional environment. All sorts of special state and federal fundings create the need for special functionaries.

The more important point here is that school organizations structurally conform to environmental rules that define what education is, and further that they obtain substantial advantages by doing so. Schools conforming to official and unofficial standards of propriety obtain routine funding and high levels of public support. Schools in any way questioned in terms of their legitimacy or accreditational status have drastically reduced survival prospects, whatever the evidence of their instructional effectiveness.

Consider a hypothetical study, for instance, that compared two small samples of schools selected in 1950. Sample One is simply a random sample of the routinely organized and accredited elementary schools in the country. Sample Two is made up of those structurally experimental elementary schools understood by sophisticated observers and researchers to be most effective in instruction or socialization. Now suppose we return in 1977—which sample of schools will show the greatest survival value? Obviously, the standard set, not the effective set. The standard set will have gone on, unquestioned, for year after year. The experimental set will have experienced waves of conflict and questioning—finally, their leaders will have retreated to research and ideology as professors of education.

Formal Organizational Responsiveness. An institutional model suggests that schools maintain high levels of interpenetration with their environments, not as a part of their organizational weakness but as a source of their strength. Empirically, this is a well-known property of American schools. Schools are constantly creating and renewing the organizational elements that link them with the surrounding community in their attempts to retain high levels of legitimacy and support.

Similar links connect the school system to the specialized constituency of educational authorities. Patterns of consultation develop. Most important, fashionable innovations are formally adopted. It is common to decry the traditionalism of American educational organizations, but it is important to note the extraordinarily fast rate at which innovations of various kinds are incorporated (and disappear). Our own survey of San Francisco Bay Area schools and districts shows enormous numbers of currently fashionable innovative programs in the schools—team teaching, individualized instruction, and so on (Cohen et al. 1976, 1977). A set of organizations more constrained by the need to coordinate a core technology would obviously be more restricted in its capacity to adopt current trends in innovation.

Client and Member Satisfaction. Our argument suggests that schools live and die according to their conformity to environmental rules rather than to particular output demands. A school is a school if everyone is satisfied that it is a school; it is not a school if no one is satisfied that it is a school, regardless of its success in instruction or socialization. This leads to the supposition that schools attend carefully to their reputations and to the generalized satisfaction of their relevant constituencies.

Two aspects are involved here. First, schools need to keep their environmental constituencies happy, and the evidence suggests that they do. Any number of parent and community surveys (for instance, see Acland 1975) show high levels of satisfaction with the schools—much higher than levels of satisfaction with most other public and private organizations. Second, the schools need to keep their own members happy. If there is no objective or "market" definition of success, the consensus of those most involved is obviously most crucial. For this reason, school organizations are most sensitive to dissidence and dissatisfaction, which they attempt to moderate, co-opt, and conceal. By and large they succeed. Table 21-1 reports some data from our own survey of a sample of Bay Area elementary schools, with information from teachers, principals, and superintendents (Cohen et al. 1976, 1977). Panel A reports data on teachers', principals', and superintendents' satisfaction with their jobs, their organizations, and their effectiveness. The data show—as do the results of many similar studies—rather high levels of satisfaction among the participants in the system.

The same findings are found in studies of students; by and large they describe themselves as quite satisfied with their schools and their work. Many studies—commonly ignored—show these simple results. In our own S.F. Bay Area survey, a sample of third graders in a number of classrooms reported great satisfaction with schools (Cohen et al. 1976, chap. 8). Similar data at the high school level have been collected by Dornbusch and others at Stanford, and suggest that even students who are academic failures and frequently truant tend to define their schools as very satisfactory. The schools succeed in maintaining support even among those who are labeled "failures" by them.

Institutional Homogeneity Among Schools and Districts. Many observers have noted the surprising homogeneity of the American school systems, despite the absence of organizational mechanics forcing consistency. A more abstract way of showing how the structure of school organizations reflects institutional considerations is to show that the understandings shared in schools reflect, in fact, consensus at this level. Table 21-2 shows data from our S.F. Bay Area sample, in which we asked 30 district superintendents, 103 school principals, and 469 teachers the extent to which explicit school-wide policies exist in each of a series of substantive areas in their organizations. Table 21-2 presents the simple marginal tabulations of their answers.

Several results deserve notice. First, there is surprising overall agreement between the three role groups in describing the presence of formal rule structures. Superintendents, as we would expect, perceive the presence of more organizational structure, and teachers see a little less. But the parties substantially agree on the kind of organization they are in and on the roles of the various groups within it.

Second, the three groups agree that some issues are the foci of organizational policy while others are not. There are usually explicit school or district policies on specially classifying students with learning disabilities, but there are very rarely general policies on teaching methods. We will return to this observation later.

Table 21-1

Superintendent, principal, and teacher answers to questions on
job satisfaction, conflict, and interaction and evaluation:
San Francisco Bay Area study

Questions	Responses (in percent)		
	Superintendent n = 30	Principal n = 103	Teacher n = 46
A. Reported Satisfaction			
very or extremely satisfied with job	80	86	88
very or extremely satisfied with school	—	76	79
very or extremely satisfied with teachers	85	81	—
very or extremely satisfied with principal(s)	94	—	66
reporting better-than-average teacher satisfaction	61	76	—
reporting above-average community satisfaction	62	70	—
reporting active community support	89	98	—
B. Reported Conflict:			
reporting little or no conflict among teachers	—	70	69
reporting little or no teacher-principal conflict	—	86	64
reporting little or no school–district conflict	79	68	—
C. Reported Evaluation and Work Interaction:			
reporting frequent reading-teacher evaluation	—	49	20
reporting district evaluation of schools more than once a year	11	14	—
reporting principal is well in-formed about their instruction	—	—	36
reporting faculty meetings at least weekly	—	15	—
reporting frequent principal advice on teaching	—	29	2

Table 21-2

**Percentage of superintendent, principals, and teachers reporting
the presence of school-wide policies in a number of areas**

Question: To what extent are there explicit schoolwide policies in each of the
following areas? We are interested in the existence of policies, *not* in
how they are implemented.

Areas	Responses*		
	Supt.	Principal	Teacher
Type of curricular materials to be used			
Little or no policy	16	24	11
General guidelines only	47	65	75
Detailed explicit policy	33	11	13
Instructional methods or techniques teachers use			
Little or no policy	47	58	39
General guidelines only	49	41	52
Detailed explicit policy	—	1	8
Rules for student conduct on school grounds			
Little or no policy	11	2	3
General guidelines only	33	48	52
Detailed explicit policy	52	51	42
Written reports of student progress or grades			
Little or no policy	3	6	5
General guidelines only	14	22	44
Detailed explicit policy	79	72	50
Identifying students with learning disabilities			
Little or no policy	—	2	(not asked)
General guidelines only	17	26	—
Detailed explicit policy	79	72	—
Dealing with chronic student absence			
Little or no policy	6	14	19
General guidelines only	38	46	52
Detailed explicit policy	52	40	28

Ensuring that needy students have adequate food and clothing			
Little or no policy	18	31	24
General guidelines only	43	37	46
Detailed explicit policy	35	31	29
Criteria to be used in evaluating student learning			
Little or no policy	25	12	13
General guidelines only	33	48	61
Detailed explicit policy	37	41	25
Student conduct in classroom			
Little or no policy	25	18	17
General guidelines only	24	57	70
Detailed explicit policy	22	20	12
N =	30	103	469

*Percentages have been rounded off

Table 21-2 suggests a system in which there is a great deal of overall agreement on the nature of schools and districts and on the roles of teacher, principal, and superintendent within them. We believe that this is correct. But there are two very different processes by which such consensus could arise. One is organizational: schools face similar technical problems and environmental constraints and work out similar policies to deal with them. Agreements evolve within each district and school around issues and are weaker between schools and districts.

The other process is institutional: agreements on the nature of the schooling system and the roles within it are worked out at quite general collective levels (through political processes, the emergence of educational language, and so on). Each school and district—each teacher, principal, and district officer—acquires an understanding, not from relating to others within the same unit but from the general educational culture. While an organizational theory would suggest especially high levels of agreement within each school and district, an institutional theory would predict system-wide agreement but no special consensus within each organizational unit.

Table 21-3 shows the story. On each of the policy questions reported in Table 21-3, we show the correlations between a superintendent's answers and the (aggregated) answers of the principals in that superintendent's districts. We also show the correlations between the answers of principals and those of their (aggregated) teachers. We finally report analyses of variance, which show the proportion of variance in principal answers that

Table 21-3

Correlations between superintendents and principals and between teachers and principals; proportions of variance in principal reports

A. Correlations between superintendents and principals and between teachers and principals in reporting the presence of schoolwide policies.

B. Proportions of variance accounted for in principal reports of the presence of policy by which district they are in. And proportions of variance accounted for in teacher reports of policy by which school they are in.

Question: To what extent are there explicit schoolwide policies in each of the following areas?

Areas	A. Correlations		B. Analyses of Variance	
	Principal–Super-intendent (n = 97)	Principal–Teachers (n = 28)	Principal Reports Eta-Squared*	Teacher Reports Eta-Squared**
Curricular materials	.11	.29	.35	.27
Instructional methods	.12	–.06	.24	.28
Student conduct on school grounds	–.04	–.21	.27	.32
Reports of student progress	.23	.23	.38	.21
Identifying learning disabilities	–.16	(not available)	.22	(not available)
Dealing with chronic absence	.09	.24	.42	.30
Ensuring needy students have food	.01	–.24	.29	.27
Criteria for evaluating learning	–.05	.02	.23	.34
Student conduct in class-room	.09	.00	.28	.23

*Percent of variance between districts. N = 106, 26
(chance value about .28)

**Percent of variance between schools. N = 469, 28
(chance value about .14)

are accounted for by the district they are in, and which show the proportion of variance in teachers' answers to be accounted for by the school they are in.

The findings are dramatic. Superintendents and principals in the same district show no special inclination to report the same organizational policies. Principals show no special agreement in describing school policies with the teachers in their own schools. And the analyses of variance show that very low proportions of the variance in principal answers are in any way related to the district they are in. The same observation holds for teacher data.

Table 21-3 reflects many other findings that have appeared in our research (Cohen et al. 1976, chap. 6; see the parallel findings of Gross and Herriott 1965). Findings such as these reflect very negatively on a conventional organizational interpretation, which would have role performers in the organizational network of the school system working out relationships with those they deal with. The phenomena we observe in Tables 21-2 and 21-3 can be described much more accurately from an institutional perspective. The participants in the educational system have a system-wide vision of the appropriate structure and roles, and they interact with each other in terms of these general roles. The high level of agreement in the system (as reflected in data such as those in Table 21-2) arises because these participants are describing a coherent general world. Each school and district is a more or less accidental reflection of this world; the parties within any given organizational unit share only the most limited set of special organizationally worked out rules and roles. Most of their world, and most of their interpretations of their world, is institutionally prefabricated.

Of course, an alternative interpretation might be that schools and districts are rent with conflict—that the lack of consensus peculiar to each school and district shown in Table 21-3 indicates not institutional or system-wide consensus but organizational conflict. Nothing in our data supports this view (see Table 21-1). Principals and teachers report low levels of conflict among teachers (70 percent of the principals and 69 percent of the teachers say there is little or none). Eighty-six percent of the principals and 64 percent of the teachers report little or no conflict between teacher and principal. And 79 percent of the superintendents and 68 percent of the principals report little or no conflict between school and district.

Summary

An institutional theory of educational organization offers explanations of the structural conformity and overall homogeneity of the system and of its overall focus on organizational responsiveness to internal and external constituents. The system maintains its coherence and legitimacy by conforming to an agreed upon set of institutional rules, by maintaining high levels of interpenetration with its environment, and by maintaining high levels of member satisfaction.

Educational Work as Decoupled within Schools

We turn now to the second main aspect of an institutional theory of educational organization: the decoupling of educational work from the formal structure as the latter maintains its linkages with environmental and institutional rules.

The Organizational Deemphasis on Instruction. The data in Table 21-2 show a striking substantive result: two of the areas in which respondents report the existence of the lowest levels of organizational policy are the "type of curricular materials to be used" and the "instructional methods or techniques teachers use." In other words, schools develop few policies in the areas of greatest significance for their central goals and purposes. These areas are delegated beyond the responsibility of the organization. Other studies have reported the same distinctive feature of schools (for example, Bidwell 1965; Lortie 1973).

Some interpret this absence of policy control over instruction as reflecting the absence or perversion of instructional goals among educators (for example, "goal displacement"), while others see it as a form of technological weakness to be repaired by soon-to-arrive reforms (which were also anticipated by Horace Mann). It makes more sense to see instructional goals as central for school personnel, but the actual direct control over instruction introduces enough arbitrariness and uncertainty into organizational life to cause all sorts of difficulties in enacting the standardized categories institutionally required of schooling. These uncertainties can be stabilized by rendering them invisible—they can be assigned to the trusted care of a particular teacher who operates backstage, behind closed doors.

Absence of Organization-Level Consensus. We have already discussed the data in Table 21-3, which show very low levels of distinctive consensus in describing school policies between superintendents, principals, and teachers in the same organization. These data in themselves show the decoupling characteristic of educational organizations. Participants, perhaps precisely because they live in the same institutional world, show little organizational consensus. As we noted above, many other data show the same patterns—participants in given educational organizations show little agreement in describing their organizations.

Absence of Instruction-Related Control and Interaction. The weaknesses of the systems of evaluation and of the control over instruction and its outcomes have been extensively discussed elsewhere (for example, Dornbusch and Scott 1975). Teachers are as infrequently observed or evaluated as principals are (see Table 21-1). Few school systems utilize pupil achievement data to evaluate the outcomes being produced by their schools and teachers.

In most interpretations, this situation arises from the structural and technical weaknesses of schooling organizations. In our argument, the situation arises out of the institutional strength of the schools—from their ability to lock themselves into place in a series of society-wide agreements, which legitimate education if it is conducted according to institutional rules and which immunize education from the uncertainties involved in actual educational work.

Disimplementation. The educational system is well known for its propensity to adopt, but not to implement, instructional innovations (see, for example, the case studies in Baldridge and Deal 1975). This tendency has been seen as an indication of organizational weakness and incompetence. From an institutional point of view, however, it can be seen as part of the process by which the system retains its strength. As innovations arise and become legitimated in the environment, they are organizationally incorporated. Those that have little impact on instruction can be built into the organizational structure as segmented programs— specialized counseling programs are examples. Data collected by Rowan (1977) show that such special structures have enormous staying power in district organizations, apparently in part because they are supported by the rules of the state. But innovations that threaten to make the hidden instructional core of the school more public and coordinated bring enormous potential costs to school organizations—the costs of coordination, of managing instability and unpredictability, of conflict, of revealed failure and delegitimation, and so on. They must be incorporated to bring legitimacy, but the incorporation need not be accompanied by effective implementation. Thus innovations are adopted, but they rarely filter down through the organization to effective implementation: this situation is part of the basic structure of the enterprise. It is particularly the case that structural changes that alter and integrate technical work relations are especially unlikely to survive (Rowan 1977).

It should be noted, however, that the picture of educational instruction sometimes drawn as a consequence of this situation—of a set of highly traditional classrooms resisting penetration by enlightened outsiders—is quite wrong. An enormous amount of innovation in classrooms routinely goes on as individual teachers use new techniques and new materials. Little of this is systematically organized at the district or school level, however; it proceeds more like a random diffusion process as new devices sweep through the educational world and die out. In our own S.F. Bay Area research, we have found a great deal of variation from classroom to classroom and a great many variations on traditional classroom structure, but these are, in all our analyses, little predicted by organizational features of the school or district (Deal et al. 1975; Cohen et al. 1979). Classrooms are sufficiently decoupled from school and district formal structures, and a good deal of innovation is possible; but it is unlikely to be structured by the school or district organization.

Conclusion

We have developed an organizational model that defines schooling organizations as strong and stable reflections of highly institutionalized rules in society. These organizations retain their strength by remaining closely linked with standardized institutional rules and at the same time becoming relatively decoupled from the technical work of instruction. We are not in a position to evaluate the adequacy of these kinds of organizations, but their obvious defects are accompanied by considerable virtues. They do indeed maintain high levels of support for the educational enterprise. And they do immunize, to some extent, the uncertain work and unpredictable consequences of the actual teaching enterprise. Teaching work is delegated on a "good faith" and uninspected basis to teachers. By and large they do the best they can, one supposes. There is certainly no reason to believe that some process that brought the whole enterprise under mechanistic organizational control—even if the mechanisms involved were effective ones—would in the long run be beneficial.

The main purpose of this paper, however, is to model educational organizational structure and to see its features as resulting from definite structural features rather than from mistakes and incompetence. The institutionally integrated but technically decoupled educational organization is a stable and successful organizational form. It is unlikely that a few "reforms" will drive it away.

References

Acland, H. "Parents Love Schools?" *Interchange* 6 (April 1975).
Baldridge, J. Victor, and T.E. Deal, eds. *Managing Change in Educational Organizations.* Berkeley: McCutchan, 1975.
Bidwell, C. "The School as a Formal Organization." In *Handbook of Organizations*, edited by J.G. March. Chicago: Rand McNally, 1965.

Cohen. E.G., T.E. Deal, J.W. Meyer, and W. Richard Scott. *Organization and Instruction in Elementary Schools*. Technical Report No. 50. Stanford: Stanford Center for Research & Development in Teaching, 1976.

Cohen, E.G., T.E. Deal, J.W. Meyer, and W. Richard Scott. "Technology and Teaming in the Elementary School." *Sociology of Education* 52 (January 1979).

Deal, T.E., J.W. Meyer, and W. Richard Scott. "Organizational Influences on Educational Innovation." In *Managing Change in Educational Organizations*, edited by J.V. Baldridge and T.E. Deal. Berkeley: McCutchan, 1975.

Dornbusch, S.M., and W. Richard Scott. *Evaluation and the Exercise of Authority*. San Francisco: Jossey-Bass, 1975.

Gross, N., and R.E. Herriott. *Staff Leadership in Public Schools: A Sociological Inquiry*. New York: John Wiley, 1965.

Lortie, D.C., "Observations on Teaching as Work." In *Second Handbook of Research on Teaching*, edited by R.M.W. Travers. Chicago: Rand McNally, 1973.

March, J.G., and J.P. Olsen. *Ambiguity and Choice in Organizations*. Bergen, Norway: Universitetsforlaget, 1976.

Meyer, J.W., and B. Rowan. "Notes on the Structure of Educational Organizations." In *Studies on Environments and Organizations*, edited by M. Meyer et al. San Francisco: Jossey-Bass, 1977.

Meyer, J.W., and B. Rowan. "Institutionalized Organizations: Formal Structure as Myth and Ceremony." *American Journal of Sociology* (September 1977).

Rowan, B. "Bureaucratization in the Institutional Environment: The Case of California School Districts, 1930-1970." Annual Meetings of the Pacific Sociological Association, Sacramento, Calif., April 1977.

Scott, W. Richard. "Organizational Structure." *Annual Review of Sociology* 1 (1975).

Thompson, J.D. *Organizations in Action*. New York: McGraw-Hill, 1967.

Weick, K.E. "Educational Organizations as Loosely Coupled Systems." *Administrative Science Quarterly* 21 (March 1976): 1-19.

22

Performance-Based Staff Layoffs in the Public Schools: Implementation and Outcomes

Susan Moore Johnson

As children of the baby boom filled school after new school during the 1950s and 1960s, administrators faced seemingly relentless demands for more space, programs, and staff. The credentials and expertise of hastily recruited teachers received only passing notice. One teacher recalls, "I was hired because I was alive." Contract renewal was virtually automatic for the teacher who reported to work and avoided charges of moral turpitude.

National public school enrollments peaked in 1971–1972 and began a sudden, accelerating decline projected to continue through 1984 (National Center for Education Statistics 1977, p. 15). At first, reduced student numbers promised the opportunity for program improvement as more space and faculty time became available. Class sizes and pupil-teacher ratios declined noticeably. As inflation decreased the purchasing power of the school dollar, however, local budgets could no longer provide the same level of services. Diseconomies of scale made it impossible to reduce budgets proportionate to enrollment declines. Meanwhile, public opposition to the property tax that financed the schools grew, forcing school systems to review their personnel costs—typically 80 percent of the total budget—and to consider reduction-in-force as the primary response to fewer students.[1]

---

[1] The larger issues of resource allocation—whether school costs might be reduced in other ways—is an important one that is beyond the scope of this study.

[2] The two school districts are Framingham, Mass., and Sherborn, Mass. See Johnson 1978, p. 6.

Uneven patterns of enrollment declines meant that school systems in the same region faced dramatically different staffing demands. One Massachusetts school system, which hired seventy-five new teachers in 1971, reduced its staff by twenty-four positions five years later. Another system projected the loss of one-third of its enrollment by 1980, losing 500 students per year, while a neighboring system continued to grow.[2] One administraor remarked, "During the sixties, we were chasing warm bodies. Now we're telling good teachers to walk the streets."

In considering how reduction-in-force decisions might be made, educators turned first to industry. Since the 1960s, when state laws first provided collective bargaining rights to public school teachers, union organizing efforts, contract negotiations, and grievance procedures in public education have been cut from the patterns provided by private industry. However, while industry relies largely on seniority to determine the order of layoffs during a reduction-in-force, many educators contend that this particular industrial pattern will not fit the shape of educational concerns. Experience in teaching may not be synonymous with competence, and the criterion of seniority may not produce a diverse and flexible staff that demonstrates a range of teaching skills. It does not guarantee that schools can retain their best teachers.

While many educators advocate performance over seniority as the criterion for teacher layoffs, they express skepticism that it is possible in practice. In fact, a few states, including New York and California, prohibit such practices. The skeptics maintain that even if state laws were to permit performance-based layoffs, unions would staunchly oppose them. Further, they argue that arbitrators and the courts would probably reverse performance-based job decisions because they are regarded as subjective and unverifiable. Implicit in such arguments is the conviction that, given the choice, local administrators would keep their best teachers.

I began this study sharing that conviction. As an educator, parent, and citizen, I was dismayed by seniority policies that suggested administrative cowardice and incompetence. In reviewing the contracts of school systems throughout Massachusetts, I was surprised to find many that included performance criteria in their reduction-in-staff provisions and few that relied on seniority alone. I set out, therefore, to demonstrate that performance-based reduction-in-staff was possible.

I selected four comparable suburban school systems that had performance criteria in the reduction-in-staff provisions of their collective bargaining agreements and interviewed central office administrators, school principals, evaluation committee heads, and teacher association officers about their policies and practices. Collective bargaining agreements, evaluation instruments, minutes of evaluation committee meetings, and central office memoranda were examined.

It was my expectation that the experiences of these four systems would demonstrate that a school district confronted with staff cuts could be resolute and keep its best teachers, whatever their seniority. I assumed that a layoff policy based on performance would stimulate healthy competition among teachers and would yield a staff superior to one determined by the cutoff line on a seniority list. I anticipated that these four systems might provide models of success for other districts soon to face the problems of reduction-in-force.

While the findings of this study demonstrate that performance-based layoffs are indeed possible, they also illustrate that the existence of such policies does not guarantee automatic implementation. Local institutional factors including school committee and administrative leadership, community attitudes, and past practices in staff evaluations seem to determine whether the policies are successfully instituted. Furthermore, the interviews with principals indicate that such practices cannot be implemented without a price. From the principal's perspective, performance-based layoff practices have unintended consequences at the school site. The requirements for equitable procedures throughout the district compromise the autonomy of the local school; alter the role of the principal as protector, provider, and instructional leader; jeopardize the cooperative and collegial relations among staff; and diminish the effectiveness of teacher supervision. These unintended consequences of performance-based layoff practices call into question their educational worth.

While no authoritative projections on the number of anticipated teacher layoffs exist, reductions are generally expected to increase as enrollment declines proceed to the secondary level, where teaching positions are more narrowly defined and staffing patterns are consequently more rigid. Whereas large districts with flexible staffing patterns may avoid extensive layoffs and satisfy necessary reductions largely by attrition, smaller districts and those with substantial enrollment declines will probably find that attrition does not meet reduction requirements.

Even if the number of teachers affected by performance-based layoffs is small in any one school or district, as it was in the districts included in this study, the character of staff relations may be dramatically changed by instituting these practices. Moreover, with a surplus of teachers and a shortage of teaching positions, administrators may be inclined to use merit appraisals in making other staffing decisions.

This exploratory study provides a view of the initial effects of performance-based layoff practices in four similar districts. The findings of the study may well require modification and elaboration as empirical data become available from districts that vary in size and character, but the issues raised by this study warrant consideration by educators in a variety of settings.

Common Policies: Different Practices

The four school systems selected for this study—Alden, Boland, Camford, and Devon[3]—are all moderately sized suburban school districts that have experienced substantial enrollment declines.[4] All four districts have reduced their total number of teaching positions, although staff reductions have affected only nontenured teachers in Devon and Camford.

The teachers' contracts of these four systems include similar reduction-in-force provisions.[5] Each provides that seniority will determine the order of layoffs only if measures of performance and qualifications do not discriminate sufficiently among the staff members. The Camford contract requires only that differences in performance be demonstrated, while the contract language of Alden, Boland, and Devon requires that those differences be "significant" or "substantial." The language of collective bargaining agreements is typically the result of long and hard negotiations. When a school district administration has negotiated the right to reduce its staff by performance, one might expect that it would exercise that right. However, the following brief accounts of actual evaluation and layoff practices indicate that there are wide differences in the applications of these provisions.

The Alden school administration anticipated severe student declines and projected staff reductions of 23.8 percent by 1978-1979, resulting from the closing of one elementary school and the curtailment of underenrolled programs. When these projected staff cuts were first announced it was unclear how they would be made. The contract stated simply that the school committee would "retain those teachers whom it deems most qualified."

---

[3] The districts have been assigned fictitious names.

[4] Alden, with 3,112 students, is the smallest of the four systems, followed by Camford with 6,372, and Boland and Devon with 7,185 students each. Since 1973-74 Devon has lost 19 percent of its enrollment, Boland is down by 18 percent, Alden by 17 percent, and Camford by 13.5 percent.

[5] The Alden contract states: "Unless, within the discipline, there is a significant difference in the teachers' performance as evidenced by evaluations from up to the previous five years, length of service . . . shall prevail." The Boland contract reads that "seniority . . . shall govern provided that teacher qualifications and performance are substantially equal." In Camford, "professional training, competency, proved performance, as well as the needs of the System, shall be reviewed. If the above factors are equal, the most junior teacher(s) within their discipline shall be laid off first." The Devon contract provides that seniority will prevail "unless the Committee determines that there is a significant difference in the teachers' performances as evidenced by evaluations during the previous five years."

On the initiative of the Alden Teachers Association, procedures for layoffs were negotiated and finalized in February 1978. These procedures are unusual in that they require all reduction-in-force decisions to be based solely on written evaluations.[6] While this requirement guarantees some objectivity and accountability, it places great demands on the writing skills of evaluators and great faith in the judgment of the director of personnel, who reads them and recommends layoff decisions.

The Alden director of personnel outlined a procedure to be used by evaluators in writing evaluations and conducted workshops to train principals in preparing complete, fair, and legally defensible documents. After all evaluations had been submitted, he began his assessment with the least senior teacher and read the five most recent years of evaluations for all teachers in vulnerable disciplines. He scored each evaluation on a scale of one to five and computed an average score for each teacher. All teachers subsequently laid off had composite scores below 2.8.

Of the 23.8 staff reductions, sixteen ultimately affected nontenured teachers and seven affected tenured teachers, one of whom had twenty-two years seniority in the system. Seniority was a deciding factor in only one of the teacher layoffs, when the director of personnel determined that the evaluations did not reveal a "significant difference" in the performances of a group of art teachers. Of the seven layoffs of tenured teachers, only two have been contested through grievance procedures.

The size of the Boland School District, thirteen schools in all, has provided flexibility during a period of staff reductions. Although twenty-five certified positions were dropped for 1978–79, attrition prevented layoffs from affecting more than a few tenured teachers. Although there is general agreement among administrators and the Boland Education Association officers that performance will be the primary factor in determining the order of staff reductions, the layoffs that have been made do not unequivocally establish such a precedent.

In 1977 two industrial arts teachers were laid off from a fully tenured department. The final decisions in this case were made on the basis of seniority when the Boland director of personnel could not determine a substantial difference in competence among the teachers. Principals involved in that decision report that the teachers were "quite exceptional"

---

[6]The Alden evaluative instrument includes no checklist or scale. There are only blank spaces in which each teacher is evaluated according to eight criteria. These include: organizing and planning for instruction, pedagogy, attention to individual pupil needs, extent of student involvement in learning, evaluation of student progress, contributions to the general life of the school, interpersonal relationships, and professional development.

and "equal in ability." Therefore, they concluded, it was appropriate to allow seniority to determine who would be laid off.

A second layoff decision in 1978 provides similarly inconclusive evidence. The home economics department, which was entirely tenured, was to be reduced by .6 of a position. The least senior teacher, with nine years of experience, had been appointed department head. Several teachers, including the department head, were not included in the pool from which the layoffs were made because of their superior performance ratings. When it became apparent that there could be no final decision based on clear performance distinctions, the three least senior teachers from the pool were required to accept 80 percent teaching schedules.

Boland administrators contend that the prominence of seniority in these two decisions was "happenstance" and that subsequent decisions will be largely determined by competence. Because the administration has in the past used evaluations to dismiss tenured teachers and to withhold salary increments for unsatisfactory performance, the expectation seems warranted.

There have been as yet no layoffs of tenured staff in Camford. The contracts of two nontenured teachers, both the least senior in their departments, were not renewed for 1978–79 because of staff cutbacks. Because regular evaluations were available for all nontenured staff, it would have been possible for the administration to rely on performance records in making those decisions. That they did not is revealing.

Unlike Alden and Boland, where the annual evaluation of tenured teachers has been a standard practice for many years, tenured teachers in Camford are not formally evaluated. There is nothing in the contract that provides for the evaluation of either tenured teachers or administrators; nor is there a standard instrument for evaluating tenured staff. One principal noted, "There are as many forms of evaluation as there are schools." Another explained that the K–12 directors have established individually preferred methods of evaluating staff: "Some have developed their own criteria, some require self-evaluations, and some teachers evaluate the supervisors."

On December 6, 1977, the superintendent of Camford schools wrote to his administrative staff requesting that they conduct evaluations of tenured staff. Few complied. One junior high principal chose to limit the number of teachers evaluated to ten in order to complete the job "thoroughly and properly." An elementary principal who did not complete any written evaluations explained that there was no standard instrument available and that "it didn't seem too pressing." Clearly, until Camford conducts system-wide evaluations of all staff, no performance-based layoffs of tenured staff will be legally defensible.

Devon cut fifty-seven positions between 1977 and 1978 and anticipated twenty to thirty additional reductions in 1979. Layoffs have not yet affected tenured teachers. All layoffs of nontenured teachers have been determined by seniority, and there is general agreement that seniority will prevail in tenured layoffs as well.

Like Camford, Devon's evaluation practices are uneven. School committee policy requires that all nontenured teachers be evaluated three times each year, and that tenured teachers be rated every third year. Some administrators meet these standards, but many do not. One principal explained that he has not had the time to conduct the evaluations, and there is no monitoring by central office to assure that he comply. Furthermore, a variety of evaluation instruments and approaches is used throughout the districts.

The pursuit of a standard evaluation process has been further complicated by the pilot experiment at the elementary level of an evaluative instrument and process. Volunteers for the pilot were assured that the experimental evaluations would not be included in their permanent files and that they would not be evaluated for another three years. These teachers may well teach six years without having had any written evaluations included in their records, making it impossible to consult the contractually specified five years of evaluations in the event of a performance-based reduction-in-force.

Several Devon principals contend that they would fight seniority layoffs in order to save an outstanding teacher. Two speculated that they could use written evaluations to document the excellence of one teacher over the shortcomings of another. However, the absence of system-wide evaluations would confine their efforts to rating the faculty of only one school and therefore make such decisions subject to grievance by the Association.

Although there are common policies for reduction in staff written into the collective bargaining agreements of the four school districts, different practices are being implemented. Performance will likely play a prominent role in the layoff decisions in Alden and Boland while seniority will probably determine layoffs in Camford and Devon.

The Determinants of Practice

Teacher unions and associations are most often blamed for the prevalence of seniority layoff practices. However, no administrator or teacher association officer interviewed for this study reported poor relations between labor and management. All were characterized positively—"good," "cooperative," "accommodative," or "excellent."

The teacher organizations of these four school systems have never pushed for straight seniority language in their contracts. The president of the Alden Teacher Association believes that the administration has the right to "get rid of someone who is not good—as long as our judgments agree." The Camford Teacher Association president explains that the CTA has never fought for straight seniority because they recognize that such a provision would be unfair to young, competent teachers.

In 1976 the Devon Teacher Association membership failed to ratify a contract because of disputes over reduction-in-force language similar to that in the Camford contract.[7] They opposed the provision not because they favored seniority, but because they lacked confidence in the system's evaluation procedures. During ratification sessions, teachers shared stories of inequitable evaluation procedures. One teacher claimed that he had not been observed in ten years, yet evaluations had been submitted about his work. The teachers feared decisions that might be made on political grounds or on the basis of incomplete evaluations. The language was subsequently renegotiated to provide that seniority would prevail "unless the Committee determines that there is a significant difference in the teachers' performances as evidenced by evaluations during the previous five years." Because such evaluations were not available, both parties understood the language to imply seniority practices.

Conventional wisdom holds that the more adverse the labor-management relationship, the more fervently teachers pursue seniority. Because all school districts included in this study had cooperative relationships, this opinion cannot be assessed. It is clear, however, that teacher organizations are not invariably opposed to performance-based layoffs. The experiences of Camford and Devon suggest that cooperation between the teacher association and the administration may lead to an avoidance of conflict and consequent administrative reluctance to impose standard evaluation procedures.

The second supposed deterrent to instituting performance-based layoffs is legal review. Arbitrators and judges, it is said, will overturn job decisions based on subjective judgments of competence. Because layoff decisions for tenured staff have only begun to reach the courts, there is no certainty that performance-based layoffs will be upheld. Decisions in related areas, however, suggest that while the courts will insist on procedural protections, they will not interfere with decisions on substantive grounds.

---

[7] It provided that the committee consider "professional training, evaluations, and the needs of the system" in determining layoffs. Seniority would be the determining factor if teachers were judged to be equal according to these criteria.

Past decisions to dismiss tenured teachers for cause, to withhold salary increases for unsatisfactory performance, and to lay off nontenured staff indicate that the judgments of school boards will be upheld if they conform to the collective bargaining agreement and provide due process to affected teachers. Holley and Feild (1977), in a review of court cases involving performance evaluations in education, concluded that "judges are reluctant to give more weight to their own personal judgment than they are to the professional judgments of experts in a given discipline, especially when these judgments are given in a setting which is procedurally fair and equitable" (p. 447). Similarly, Rosenberger and Plimton, in their review of teacher-dismissal cases, found that the courts regularly upheld the school system's performance evaluations in such areas as knowledge of subject matter, teaching methods, effect on pupils, and personal attitudes (Rosenberger and Plimton 1975, p. 472). Like the courts, arbitrators customarily refrain from interfering with the prerogative of school committees to base job decisions on performance judgments.[8]

It is clear, however, that while arbitrators and judges grant considerable professional latitude to school administrators, they insist that procedures for making layoff decisions be equitable. In addition to compliance with the contractual provisions for observing and evaluating teachers, the requirements of procedural fairness may include the use of a standard evaluation instrument, reports evaluating the full extent of a teacher's job, judgments based on observable data, and the opportunity for teachers to correct their performances before adverse job decisions are made.

These procedural standards present unusual demands for a school district that does not tightly coordinate evaluation practices and that endorses a variety of procedures in its schools. Until recently, it was unnecessary for school systems to conduct rigorous staff evaluations that conformed to these requirements for uniformity and equity. Dismissal cases were largely based on the documentation of an individual teacher's incompetence or insubordination rather than on comparative evaluations of all teachers. During two decades of teacher shortages, principals attended more to the pressing needs for increased space and staffs than to rigorous evaluation procedures.

Administrators in Alden and Boland are well informed about their legal right to conduct performance-based layoffs as well as their legal obligation to guarantee equitable procedures. In the past, Alden has successfully withheld salary increments for unsatisfactory performance and has

---

[8]Arbitration decisions from 1970 to 1977, summarized in Stone 1977, include no cases in which the performance assessment of a school committee was reversed for substantive reasons. Some were reversed on procedural grounds.

dismissed tenured teachers—five were removed for incapacity in 1976. Similarly, the Boland director of personnel has expressed confidence in the school district's legal right to use performance ratings in making job decisions. In May 1978 nine teachers were notified that salary increments would be withheld for unsatisfactory performance. The decisions were not challenged. In each of two prior years, a grievance went to arbitration challenging the right of the school committee to withhold salary increases of teachers at the maximum salary level for reasons of performance. The school committee was upheld in each of these decisions. While the right of a school board to base job decisions on performance is not likely to be overturned, the legal demands for equitable procedures require unprecedented rigor and standardization in teacher evaluation practices.

Implementation studies have demonstrated that we should not be surprised when federal policies are not always implemented at the local level. That implementation practices vary widely from district to district and that they are amended to fit the particular needs of the local institution have been well documented. (See, for example, Murphy 1971; McLaughlin 1976; Pressman and Wildavsky 1973; Williams and Elmore 1976.) The findings of the present study indicate that contracts, though negotiated locally, offer no more assurance of implementation than policies negotiated in Washington. Contract negotiations are conducted, in part, before a public audience, and the agreements reached may be designed for public approval. The policies may bear little resemblance to actual practices because they do not fit the priorities held by the school committee, the district superintendent, and the traditions set by past practices.

Not all the contract provisions have the full backing of the school committees, the communities they represent, or the superintendents. In fact, the Alden and Boland school committees were reported by all those interviewed to be unified in their determination to lay off teachers by competence, while the committees of Camford and Devon were reported to be divided in their support for performance-based layoffs. Such differences may reflect community values. While the populations of Alden and Boland are largely professional, Camford and Devon both have substantial numbers of municipal and industrial workers who might be expected to support traditional seniority practices.

In Devon, for example, the superintendent reported that three of the nine members of the school committee favored seniority layoffs, while six others supported competency-based layoffs. Two principals contended that the school committee's support for performance criteria was a public posture assumed to pacify taxpayers expecting policies of teacher accountability. However, one principal predicted that the school committee would not defend performance assessment if they were challenged in any way. He suggested that while it may be politically expedient to negotiate performance-based reduction-in-force policies, it may well become politically necessary to rely on the clearcut simplicity of seniority.

There are also important differences among the superintendents' attitudes toward perfomance-based layoff practices. The superintendents of Alden and Boland were said to be unswerving in their determination to implement performance-based layoffs. Those of Camford and Devon were reported to be less committed, more ambivalent. The superintendent of Devon stated that while he preferred performance criteria over seniority, Devon had yet "to test the quality of the evaluation system." The superintendent of Camford notes that performance-based layoffs will not be easy: "It leads to intraprofessional uneasiness."

It is worth noting that the superintendents in both Camford and Devon have worked in their systems for many years and have themselves acquired considerable seniority. By contrast, in Alden and Boland, the superintendents are relative newcomers, free from longstanding commitments to traditional practices and to senior staff members.

Alden and Boland are atypical of most school districts in that they have long monitored the performance of tenured teachers and penalized those whose work was unsatisfactory. Both systems have evaluated tenured teachers annually, withheld increments for unsatisfactory performance, and dismissed teachers for cause. These past practices now provide the foundation for the standardized evaluations required by performance-based layoff policies. By contrast, the tenured teachers of Camford and Devon have neither been regularly evaluated nor disciplined for poor performance. Consequently the introduction of standard evaluation practices in Camford and Devon during a period of staff reductions would be both administratively difficult and disruptive.

Therefore, while interference by teacher organizations, arbitrators, and the courts cannot account for the reliance on seniority rather than on performance in Camford and Devon, certain interrelated institutional factors—past evaluation practices, and community, school committee, and administrative leadership—seem to determine the actual layoff practices. Some who are familiar with implementation studies will consider it more notable that practices in Alden and Boland conformed to the negotiated policy than that those of Camford and Devon varied from it. Such a conclusion implies either that school districts are usually mismanaged or that the practices required to institute performance-based layoffs are contrary to the way schools work and therefore must encounter considerable resistance in their implementation.

Unintended Consequences: The Principal's Perspective

Performance-based layoffs introduce requirements for standardizing, regulating, and rating that create new strains at the school and district levels. While industries may be tightly controlled, schools are notably lacking in coordination, predictable outcomes, and centralized control of instructional matters. In their survey of San Francisco Bay Area elementary schools, Stanford researchers found that agreement between principals and superintendents in describing typical district organizational and educational policies is "quite limited." Also, "the particular level of agreement distinctive to principals in the very same district, in describing district rules or educational policies, is *very low*. Moreover, the more influential district offices do not exercise their influence through regular bureaucratic channels and do not impose greater uniformity on their schools" (Meyer, Scott, Cole, and Intili 1978, p. 257). Critics of education assume that this lack of agreement and control indicates incompetence and irresponsible management—that any properly run organization would operate in a more centralized, organized, and predictable fashion. However, recent theoretical analyses of schools and school districts as "loosely coupled systems" (Deal and Cellotti 1975; Meyer, Scott, Cole, and Intili 1978; Weick 1976) suggest that the absence of tight linkages, or "couplings," among the parts of the school organization may be functional in ensuring the flexibility necessary for the task of education.

The characteristically loose administrative control of the teaching activities in schools may be functional in certain respects, but it does not adapt well to the rigor imposed by central offices in implementing performance-based layoffs. Teachers must be evaluated competitively and rating procedures must be standardized across schools. Building and department administrators must coordinate their evaluations to assure reliable ratings, substituting the collective interests of the school district for the particular concerns of their individual schools.

The principals interviewed for this study expressed different concerns than did their central office counterparts. While system-wide administrators spoke of uniformity, control, and compliance, principals talked about flexibility, autonomy, and diversity. In many respects, the objectives of central office administrators were seen to interfere with the objectives of building principals. The principals' story catalogs the unintended consequences of instituting performance-based layoffs. It suggests that there is something in the nature of teaching and evaluation, in the roles of principal and teacher, and in the traditional organization of the school district that accounts for the reluctance, ambivalence, and resistance of building principals to embrace the task of competitively assessing teachers' work—a responsibility that is thought to be routinely accepted by supervisors in business.

The principals interviewed from the four school districts were those recommended by central office administrators[9] as being particularly interested in, or well informed about, the issues of evaluation and reduction-in-force. They were not representative of principals in the system but rather were regarded as exemplary. The fifteen principals interviewed are all former teachers, having three to seventeen years experience before assuming administrative positions. Most (64 percent) taught in the same districts where they are now administrators. Several principals have remained in the same buildings where they taught, assuming supervisory responsibility over teachers who were once their peers.

Principals often perceive themselves as instructional leaders and regard managerial responsibilities as annoyances that interfere with their real work. As one Camford principal described her role: "I am supportive, a helper, a catalyst. I give the teachers what they need to do their job well." Similarly, an Alden principal considered it her responsibility to be "the instructional leader of the school." She sought to maintain close involvement with the classroom teachers, building trust and "supporting good teaching with resources, money, and ideas."

The principals interviewed did not talk like cool-hearted managers, dissatisfied with the efficiency or productivity of their staff. They were convinced that teachers work hard and show considerable intelligence, imagination, caring, and stamina. They spoke of building trust among the teachers, recognizing differences among children, and encouraging spontaneity and diversity in the program.

Principals traditionally have had considerable autonomy to run their schools. In exchange for the freedom granted them by the central office, principals are expected to keep their schools running smoothly. It is the principal who assures student discipline, responds to parental complaints, oversees evaluations of special-education students, schedules teaching assignments, supervises fire drills, and monitors the collection of milk money. As many have noted, however, principals do not have extensive powers. (See, for example, Lortie 1975, p. 196.) The principal must rely on the loyalty and good will of his teachers when they are urged to attend yet another evening PTA meeting, prepare the holiday assemblies, or

---

[9]In all school districts except Alden, I interviewed both elementary and secondary principals. In Alden, where staff layoffs had been substantial at the elementary level, I interviewed all elementary principals.

administer burdensome system-wide tests. One Devon principal characterized her position: "A principal can't be strictly management and run a good school. I need the teachers' help and advice. I can't make decisions in a vacuum. I have to maintain a certain level of trust if I expect the school to function well." Therefore, because principals see a large part of their role as facilitating effective instruction, and because they must rely on the cooperation of their teachers to run the schools well, they have typically fostered collegial relationships with their staffs.

These relationships may be strained during periods of teacher observation and evaluation. In his ethnographic study of the role of the principal, Wolcott (1973) observed that the act of evaluation "conflicted blatantly with the ideal of democratic administration in which most principals preferred to present themselves among their teacher colleagues as a first among equals" (p. 194).

In Alden, where staff layoffs have affected all elementary schools, principals spoke emphatically about the effects of these layoffs on administrator-staff relationships. One said, "The time of collegiality of principal and teachers is gone." Another principal complained that his relationship with teachers had become difficult, that they had become more aggressive in challenging his observations or in making themselves known. There are "hard dealings over single words" in the written evaluations, and disputes over what constitute strengths and weaknesses. "The relationship changes subtly, but it changes."

The Alden experience suggests that maintaining an intermediary position between teaching and management will be difficult for the principal who evaluates teachers for layoffs. Alden principals found that they could no longer provide protection or even reassurance for their staff as they anticipated layoffs. One principal called in a very competent teacher who was "devastated by the unbearable amount of tension." He assured her, "Over my dead body, you'll go out. Don't you know where you stand?" Later, in recounting this incident to the director of personnel, he was told that if he offered reassurance to any teachers he would be open to charges of unfairness.

The principal's inclination to reassure, protect, and defend his or her teachers continues to be strong, particularly if those teachers have been hired by the principal. The superintendent of schools in Devon explained how principals resist rating their staff. "They say, 'Everybody's good to excellent,' or 'I was told to get super staff members. I did it. Why do you now expect me to knock some of those people?'" A Devon elementary principal who regards himself as a "tough supervisor" nevertheless assured his teachers that he would protect them. "I know my people are good. And every other principal knows the same thing. They would do the same and protect their people."

Principals in all systems expressed concern about the effects of performance-based layoffs on the morale of teachers. The one Boland secondary principal who argued that staff reductions would not affect teacher morale—"good teachers are above that"—was the exception. One Alden principal reported that he had never seen morale as bad: "This tension will, in the long run, be counterproductive to the teaching and learning process."

Improving the quality of instruction through teacher supervision is regarded by central office administrators as a primary responsibility of principals and department heads. However, some principals and department heads neglect to observe classes, either because of laziness, embarrassment, uncertainty, intimidation, or because they choose not to violate norms protecting the teacher's privacy in the classroom (Lortie 1975, p. 169). This is not unusual (Meyer and Rowan 1978, p. 81).

Teachers unaccustomed to being regularly observed often find that the presence of a principal in the classroom itself provokes considerable anxiety, even when constructive advice is the aim. One newly appointed Devon principal found that all twenty-eight teachers in his new school had received similarly positive evaluations. When he explained to the staff his procedures for observing and evaluating them, they were visibly upset. His secretary finally explained, "They're very upset because you're in the classroom."

All the principals in this study reported that, while some of their peers neglected teacher evaluations, they observed classes regularly. Several characterized themselves as teachers of teachers. One Alden principal noted that "a teacher thinks of kids as 'good,' 'better,' and 'best,' and assumes that everyone is capable of improvement." She suggested that principals regard teachers in the same way and find it difficult to give up on one who might improve.

However, improvement may not be easily achieved when the tension routinely aroused by observation and supervision intensifies as job decisions come to depend on the results of the evaluation process. School policies almost uniformly list two conflicting purposes of evaluation. In Boland, for example, they are: (1) to be used by the teacher as a means of self-evaluation of strengths and weaknesses for self-improvement; (2) to provide an objective and comprehensive record for evaluation of teaching effectiveness which can be used as *one* of the criteria when reappointment and/or the withholding of increment is being considered.

The assistant superintendent of Devon schools explains the objectives of evaluation in two separate memoranda; the difference between them is revealing. In addressing the nontenured elementary staff in October 1977, he emphasized the self-improvement aspects of evaluation:

I have prepared this memo to help you better understand the purpose for evaluation in the Devon Public schools. First, our major goal is to assist each teacher with the improvement of instruction. As such, it is a means by which you and your principal can get together and share ideas to improve upon the teaching-learning cycle. Second, it is a process used to help you take a look at what you are doing so that you might ask yourself, "Is there a better way to teach this material?" Third, it is an opportunity for you to receive feedback about your performance in the total school setting.

In a memorandum written to elementary principals in July 1977, the same assistant superintendent stressed the other face of evaluation: "Teacher evaluation is in actuality a process of research, and as such requires the collection of data and the sorting of that data to form a conclusion."

But since reduction-in-force has been introduced in Alden, the emphasis in the evaluative process has shifted from the first purpose to the second. One principal characterized his evaluation role as changing from "coach to umpire." He believes that he is perceived less to be helping a teacher improve than to be judging whether a teacher is "out or safe."

Once principals could treat teachers as individuals with particular personal needs and learning styles. They are now under pressure from central office administrators to deal with all staff uniformly and to make all the criticisms very explicit. Judgments that once were spoken must now be committed to writing. A Camford principal observed that in times of growth: "Evaluations could be indirect and hard judgments could be couched in nice words. The philosophy was one of amelioration. Now, no matter how nice and supportive you are, you will be seen as the one who has to make the decisions. You can't simply think about how to help everyone. You have to think, 'Who is it that I can do without?'"

Reporting all strengths and weaknesses rather than selected ones further interferes with the objective of instructional improvement. Three years ago in Alden, principals could comment freely on whatever criteria seemed appropriate. Some criteria received more attention than others, and any balance preferred by the principal was acceptable. Now all criteria must receive comment on each evaluation. While some factors may not seem important now for supervision, they may prove important five years from now for job decisions. One Boland principal resisted directions from central office administrators to make him a "tougher" evaluator because of his philosophy of how people change. "Everybody builds on strengths. I should identify those strengths and then help the teachers to build on them. I don't think they can correct weaknesses."

This shifting purpose of the written evaluation troubled administrators at all levels. The Devon superintendent recognized that layoffs require "a different kind of concept of evaluation.... Now you intend to use evaluations that have traditionally been used for personal improvement to fire someone." An Alden principal expressed similar thoughts: "We always talk about evaluation for growth, and this works when there aren't big stakes. However, when it comes to the evaluation document, this is not a growth experience, definitely not. When you come down to sorting out the goods, the greats, the wells, and the quite wells, it's a very different story."

New requirements for uniform procedures and reliable ratings threaten conventional patterns of organization within the school district. Traditionally, the building principal could exercise considerable discretion in shaping the unique character of a school. Variation from building to building was acceptable as long as it was not extreme and the parent community was not dissatisfied. The central office exercised few controls and the principal acted as an advocate within the larger system for his or her students, staff, and programs.

Recently, there are increasing efforts to coordinate programs and policies among schools. This is due, in part, to the procedural requirements for mandated programs such as special education. It may also be a response to demands for public accountability during a period of falling test scores and tight finances. But coordination is also essential for the successful implementation of a performance-based reduction-in-staff program.

The importance of coordinating evaluation procedures becomes clear when we consider how written evaluations might be used comparatively within a district. If no system-wide comparisons of ratings were required, rater reliability would not be a concern. As one principal explained, "If the evaluator inflates all scores, no one suffers. If the evaluator is tough on everybody, that is okay. But when the scores of different evaluators are compared, then there is trouble."

Some principals were skeptical that evaluation could ever be fair, given the "priorities and ticks" of the individual principals. One Boland principal had seen exclusively laudatory written evaluations submitted by principals and department heads concerning teachers he was convinced were capable of improvement. He knew of department heads who never observed classes and yet submitted written evaluations. One Devon principal who strongly advocated performance-based layoffs changed his mind when he considered how his evaluations might be compared with those of other principals. He explained facetiously:

I am building-oriented and I am pigheaded. I did the work to recruit the staff for my building and I know what my building needs and I don't want to leave it up to someone else to decide who will be here. And I know that guy at the other school on the other side of town. I've heard that he is an easy marker. I know that someone on my staff that would get a C from me would probably get a B from him. And so I mark all of my people higher because I don't want to lose my people while his stay on. I want to steer my own ship.

Despite such declarations of independence, the additional threat of layoffs of principals provides central office administrators with a new level of control. Just as teachers are becoming more responsive to principals' expectations, principals are conforming more to system-wide policies. Where once principals selected who would teach in their buildings, transfer practices now determine the composition of the staff. Alden teachers have been reminded often that they work for the town of Alden rather than for the particular school. The extensive teacher transfers made in the spring of 1978 emphasized that fact. Subsequently, the principals in Alden were all moved to different buildings. The espoused reason was to revitalize the system in which the least-senior principal had served eight years in the same building. The Alden director of personnel notes that this change will also provide another set of staff evaluations, thus assuring more equity in layoff decisions.

In Boland and Alden, the formal evaluations written by central office administrators for principals and department heads are used to redirect the attention of school principals to system-wide needs. Boland's personnel director believes that this practice is forcing principals to adhere to the requirements for standardized procedures. Boland's superintendent wrote in one evaluation that the principal sometimes had "difficulty seeing how [his school] fit in the overall picture of the school system." When this same principal defends the quality of his staff, he is told, "If you have so many good people, maybe you should send some of them to other schools."

In Camford and Devon the situation is somewhat different. Several principals said the Devon central office has long supported the autonomy of individual schools and principals. One recalled, "When we were hired as principals, we were told that we were the queens and kings in our own buildings. We would call the shots." Recently, however, there is more talk of "centralized authority, articulation and coordination of everything both vertically and horizontally, more budgetary austerity, and much more teacher accountability." One principal saw this trend as a "grave mistake.... The superintendent's responsibility is to make it possible for the principals to run the schools. They have no business running the buildings themselves."

In Camford, as in Devon, the principals are thought to be "strongly attached to the identity of the individual school." Although teachers on leave are now notified that they cannot expect to return to their original buildings, such efforts to put system-wide interests above local school interests are still rare. Principals and department heads are not formally evaluated by the central office, and there are few efforts to coordinate their practices. This, the Camford Teachers' Association president contends, reflects the superintendent's unspoken preference for educational diversity over standardization.

School administrators' resistance to performance-based layoffs cannot be ascribed to professional cowardice or ineptitude. While there may be chickenhearted bunglers in their ranks, the principals interviewed seemed quite able to take hard stands and administer complex programs. They [seemed] to have anticipated that strict procedural controls cannot be imposed on schools without a price. In the case of performance-based layoffs, that price may include a change in the principal's role from advocate to adversary; a deterioration of teacher-principal cooperation; diminished teacher commitment; increased distrust and dissembling in supervision; and a loss of identity, autonomy, and flexibility for the local school.

The theoretical view of schools as loosely coupled systems is supported by the evidence from these four school districts. For example, the Camford School Committee required that teachers be evaluated, the superintendent recommended it with ambivalence, and many principals simply disregarded the task. Devon administrators disagreed about whether the primary purpose of teacher evaluation should be professional improvement or job decisions. Boland principals refused to rank order teachers although it was in the interests of central-office personnel practices to do so.

There are, as Deal and Cellotti note, organizational advantages to loosely coupled systems. They can readily adapt to changing conditions, free the administration from the "duties of overseer," lessen the "strain of negotiation and compromise," reduce the time and money costs of coordination, and provide individuals the autonomy to "go their own way" (Deal and Cellotti, 1975, pp. 17–19). The introduction of strict procedural controls in Alden and Boland limited these freedoms, pursuing the benefits of accountability and coordination at the expense of school site autonomy and flexibility. Principals could no longer adopt different evaluative procedures as their supervisory needs changed; evaluators would be required to spend considerable time observing classes and writing detailed evaluations; and evaluators would be required to coordinate their ratings and practices across schools.

The decision makers in these four districts may not have formulated the advantages and disadvantages of implementing performance-based layoffs before electing one policy over another. Devon's acceptance of seniority as the deciding criterion was not a purposeful effort to preserve collegiality. Alden's commitment to keep its best teachers was not expected to jeopardize the principal's traditional role. However, after the first year of tenured-staff reductions in Alden, the personnel director acknowledged that "the process has a tremendously negative impact on the staff and supervision." Nevertheless, he concluded, "There is no alternative in a contracting industry."

For those assessing the practices of local school systems, there remains the complicated problem of distinguishing flexible policies from laissez-faire neglect and well-coordinated practices from ill-advised constraint. The administrators who expressed ambivalence about performance-based layoffs did not endorse straight seniority. Most, in fact, adamantly opposed it. These principals supported the school system's efforts to dismiss incompetent teachers, and in several instances they decried the politics of a school system that seemed to make dismissals impossible. However, the principals' concerns about the unintended consequences of performance-based layoffs suggest that it might be wise to reach some compromise between the performance and seniority criteria.

One solution would be to group all teachers into one of three or four clusters on the basis of performance. Within a cluster, which would presumably include teachers of comparable competence, seniority rather than performance would determine the order of layoffs. Administrators would not be forced to make minute and perhaps invalid distinctions among teacher's performances, and teachers whose performance was satisfactory would not be unnecessarily preoccupied with the issue of job security. Providing some certainty for a large part of the staff might well ease some of the organizational strain of implementing performance-based layoffs, while guaranteeing that outstanding teachers would be retained. Support for this approach can be drawn from research on the assessment of teacher effectiveness and from the testimony of principals in this study.

Underlying a performance-based layoff system is the assumption that teacher effectiveness can be defined, observed, and measured. However, after eighty years of research, there is virtually no consensus among either educational psychologists or practitioners about what constitutes effective teaching. Researchers have tried to discover the personal prerequisites of teaching success, such as teaching experience, training, and grades— characteristics now generally acknowledged to be "pedagogically weak variables" (McNeil and Popham 1973).

Researchers scrutinizing the classroom behaviors of teachers have focused on such things as personal warmth, enthusiasm, and indirectness (Gage 1972, pp. 34–49). Thus far, however, research has not yielded a composite description of the effective teacher, but only recommendations for particular behaviors. Rosenshine and Furst observe that "a complete list of educational 'shoulds' can only be guessed at . . . research in this area has barely begun" (Rosenshine and Furst 1973, p. 162).

Efforts to correlate measures of student achievement with particular teaching styles and practices have also been inconclusive.[10] While there may be "no more obvious truth than that a teacher is effective to the extent that he causes pupils to learn what they are supposed to learn" (Dunkin and Biddle 1974, p. 14), the assessment of schooling outcomes is complicated by ideological issues. Should students be trained to succeed on tests, socialized to function in an industrial society, or motivated to love learning? McNeil and Popham (1973) note: "The teacher may be labeled ineffective not because his pupils failed to achieve, but because the achievement was in directions that were not valued by the rater" (p. 229).

Despite the similarity of the evaluation forms from district to district, there are important and telling differences in the performance criteria they list reflecting the lack of consensus about what is required for good teaching. For example, the Boland evaluation form includes the item, "teacher consistently assists pupils in appraising their own work"; no comparable item appears on the evaluation forms of the other three districts. The Devon instrument alone includes the item, "displays a contagious enthusiasm for teaching," while the Camford form asks whether the teacher "provides guidance in pupils' personal problems," a service that is not evaluated in the other districts.

A review of the four evaluation forms also reveals the measurement problems inherent in assessing teacher effectiveness. The Alden form does not include a scale, but instead requires evaluators to provide their own language for each criterion. The three other districts use scales ranging from "needs improvement" to "outstanding" or "superior." The Boland scale includes three grades, while Devon provides four and Camford has five. All allow for additional comments. No instrument advises the evaluators how to distinguish among the various levels of performance. The lack of consensus among researchers and the diversity of evaluative instruments are predictable, given the range of views about what schooling is and ought to be. One might, however, anticipate consistent standards in the assessments made by an individual evaluator. Yet in response to the question, "Could you rank order the teachers in your building?" most principals responded that rank ordering was both impossible and ill-advised. One Boland principal who confidently asserted that he could rank

---

[10]Fifty studies of the relationship between teacher behaviors and student achievement are reviewed in Rosenshine 1971.

order his staff, later chuckled and suggested that his rankings would probably differ from Monday to Friday. Another said that he could rank order his staff, but that he couldn't justify it with "hard evidence." A Devon principal said that the "intuitive dimensions" in evaluation would make it impossible to defend the hierarchy he created. If asked why number one was ranked above number two, he might say, "He cares more about the students." However, when asked why number two was ranked above number three, he might offer a different reason based on a different criterion, such as "He works more effectively with other teachers. To someone from the outside, it would seem to be based on caprice." He went on to explain: "The truth of it all is that you evaluate different teachers differently. For some, you are giving particular consideration to their age. For others, you are looking at how they function on a team, because they work on a team. For another, you concentrate on teaching style because that is the most outstanding factor. All the time you are looking at the need in the building for a variety of teaching styles and values."

Principals generally did find it easy to identify both the superior and the incompetent teachers. One Camford principal's comments are typical of the others': "I think that I could rank order the teachers in my building, but I wouldn't have much confidence in the process. It is easy to identify the weak ones and the superstars. But there is a large gray area in the middle that probably couldn't be ranked. I have more confidence in a cluster system that would require me to place a teacher with others, but not to rank them."

An Alden principal also spoke of his staff in three clusters, characterizing those in the first group as "noticeably outstanding." Those in the second group he called "good solid teachers who stay, give, do everything that has to be done." Those in the third group are clearly less effective, both in the classroom and in the larger school.

Because school systems are now just beginning to lay off tenured teachers, it is not clear how narrowly a system such as Alden's will define and pursue a "significant difference" in performance. Most principals in the four districts reported that there remain a few teachers whose performance is poor. Yet in all systems of this study that number falls far short of the projected staff cuts. Soon staff reductions will affect teachers who are judged to be quite competent. At that point, one might legitimately challenge whether the goal of retaining superior teachers warrants the discontent, distrust, and dissent that may be fueled by the process of performance-based layoffs, particularly when the distinctions among those teachers become slight and uncertain.

The Boland personnel director outlined the following scenario as the "best hope for performance-based layoffs": "Ten teachers are eligible for a reduction-in-force. The first seven are clearly not vulnerable because of their outstanding performance. They would be set aside. From among the last three who had similar evaluations, the reduction-in-force would be determined by seniority." This plan may offer the most reasonable and realistic resolution.

It seems worthwhile to speculate briefly about the long-range effects of performance-based layoffs on community-school relations, labor-management dealings, and the informal social and work organization of the schools. Performance-based layoffs are in part a response to the public cry for accountability, but layoffs may soon affect competent teachers—those whom parents are satisfied with and perhaps beholden to. What will be the consequences of performance-based layoff practices? Parents may be drawn into the fray of disruptive and divisive layoff controversies. Performance-based layoffs may undermine community confidence in the schools as respected teachers lose their jobs. Performance-based layoff practices may alter day-to-day assumptions about the appropriate role of the public in school business.

It is also important to consider how the continued pursuit of performance-based layoffs will affect labor-management relations within a school district. The teachers' association leadership and central office administration in each district in this study maintained flexible working relationships, informally averting controversies and resolving grievances, without resort to ritualized combat. As management exercises its right to retain teachers on the basis of competence, the unions shift slightly to more impersonal exchanges, uncompromising stances, and formal defenses. Labor-management relations, prized for their accommodative nature, may be profoundly altered.

Finally, and perhaps most troubling, are the potential long-term effects of performance-based layoffs on the informal organization of schools. The requirements for uniform procedures were shown, even in the short run, to alter the role of the principal, undermine staff morale, and threaten the autonomy of the teacher, principal, and local school. Little is understood about what holds a school together and makes it feel like a good place to learn, yet one might guess that the answer is somehow tied up in the informal cooperative relationships between principal and teacher, teacher and teacher, and ultimately between teacher and student. The legal standards for procedural fairness require a rationalized approach to teachers and their work. But the workself is not rationalized. Teaching machines have not replaced people; personal interaction seems crucial for successful schooling. Sorting, scoring, and ranking performance objectifies the relationships between teachers and administrators, just as it does those between teacher and students. In an institution that, at its best, promotes acceptance and inclusion, performance-based layoffs introduce competition and exclusion.

A central theme in Lortie's research was teachers' concern for "inclusiveness"—"reaching *all* students in one's charge (Lortie 1975, p. 111). The ideal teacher accepts all children as unique and having potential. He or she would encourage all children to succeed and reject no one who makes a serious effort. The comments of principals in this study suggest that they often regard teachers as the teachers regard students—as unique and capable of success. It seems that maintaining support for teachers may be essential if they are to continue to work effectively and enthusiastically with children. When teachers are treated impersonally, without regard for who they are and what they need, this may threaten the foundation of effective schooling.

It is ironic that the requirements for maintaining a superior teaching staff may violate basic notions of what should happen in schools. A practice that looks so right and so responsible from one perspective may look counterproductive from another. School administrators and policymakers might well approach strict performance-based layoffs with caution and a spirit of moderation, for in this instance, the interests of accountability and the interests of children may not coincide.

References

Deal, T.E., and L.D. Cellotti. "Loose Coupling and the School Administrator." Unpublished manuscript. Stanford University, 1975.

Dunkin, M.J., and B.J. Biddle. *The Study of Teaching.* New York: Holt, Rinehart & Winston, 1974.

Gage, N.L. *Teacher Effectiveness and Teacher Evaluation: The Search for a Scientific Basis.* Palo Alto, Calif.: Pacific Books, 1972.

Holley, W.H., and H.S. Feild. "The Law and Performance in Education: A Review of Court Cases and Implications for Use." *Journal of Law and Education* 6 (1977).

Johnson, S.M. *Declining Enrollments in the Massachusetts Public Schools: What It Means and What to Do.* Boston: Massachusetts Department of Education, 1978.

Lortie, D.C. *Schoolteacher: A Sociological Study.* Chicago: University of Chicago Press, 1975.

McNeil, J.D., and W. James Popham. "The Assessment of Teacher Competence." In *The Second Handbook on Teaching,* edited by R.M.W. Travers. Chicago: Rand McNally, 1973.

McLaughlin, M. "Implementation as Mutual Adaptation: Change in Classroom." *Teachers College Record* 77 (1976): 337-51.

Meyer, J.M., and B. Rowan. "The Structure of Educational Organizations." In *Environments and Organizations,* edited by M.W. Meyer. San Francisco: Jossey-Bass, 1978.

Meyer, J.W., W.R. Scott, S. Cole, and J. Intili. "Institutional Dissensus and Institutional Consensus in Schools." In *Environments and Organizations*, edited by M.W. Meyer. San Francisco: Jossey-Bass, 1978.

Murphy, J.T. "Title I of ESEA: The Politics of Implementing Federal Education Reform." *Harvard Educational Review* 41 (1971): 35–63.

National Center for Education Statistics. *Projections of Education Statistics to 1985–86.* Washington, D.C.: U.S. Government Printing Office, 1977.

Pressman, J.L., and A.B. Wildavsky. *Implementation.* Berkeley: University of California Press, 1973.

Rosenberger, D., and R. Plimton. "Teacher Incompetence and the Courts." *Journal of Law and Education* 4 (1975).

Rosenshine, B. *Teaching Behaviors and Student Achievement.* London: National Foundation for Educational Research in England and Wales, 1971.

Rosenshine, B., and N. Furst. "The Use of Direct Observation to Study Teaching." In *The School Handbook of Research on Teaching*, edited by R.M.W. Travers. Chicago: Rand McNally, 1973.

Stone, M., ed. *Arbitration in the Schools.* New York: American Arbitration Assoc., March 1970–December 1977.

Weick, K.E. "Educational Organizations as Loosely Coupled Systems." *Administrative Science Quarterly* 21 (1976): 1–19.

Williams, W., and R.F. Elmore, eds. *Social Program Implementation.* New York: Academic Press, 1976.

Wolcott, H.F. *The Man in the Principal's Office: An Ethnography.* New York: Holt, Rinehart & Winston, 1973.

23
Planning, Plotting, and Playing in Education's Era of Decline

Terrence Deal and Martha Stone Wiske

Administrative tasks of growth—building, adding, and hiring—are giving way to the onerous chores of decline—closing, cutting, terminating, and consolidating. Done wisely, decisions of decline may prune educational organizations to survive a lean decade. Done capriciously or haphazardly the decisions may leave schools misshapen and incapable of adapting to the conditions that lie ahead. How can research inform sound decisions or caution against the ill-advised?

To answer this question, we need to ask two others: (1) In what ways are the times hard for schools these days? and (2) What specific problems do hard times present for educational administrators? Answers to these subsidiary questions sketch the context in which research is being asked to provide assistance.

The label "hard times" emerges from a period in which schools face a formidable troika: resources are tight and shrinking, public confidence in education has waned, and, in many places, the morale of teachers and administrators is dropping below levels required for professional and personal stability or growth. These three conditions are related even though they do not originate from the same source. Each provides its own set of issues and problems. Together, they produce difficult choices for administrators.

Tight resources result from three developments. Over recent years, the population of elementary and secondary school-age children has declined. At the same time, the economy is being crippled by inflation, reducing the

---

Reprinted, by permission, from *Managing Schools in Hard Times*, ed. Stanton Leggett (Chicago: Teach 'Em, Inc., 1968), pp. 2–16.

value of the dollar. Finally, school systems in many states are facing a reduction in revenues because citizens have voted to cap public spending statewide or have refused outright to approve additional expenditures at the local level. Taken together, these three developments make for very tight school budgets.

But the financial crisis cannot be separated from what David Tyack describes as a society-wide "crisis of authority":

Future historians may regard the last twenty years as one of those great turning points in educational history comparable to the common school crusade of the mid-nineteenth century or the campaign for centralization and social efficiency at the turn of the century. Recent complex changes have called into question some of the legacies of earlier reforms: that education was the most potent means of creating equality; that schools should be "kept out of politics"; that the professionals could discover "the one best system" through specialized knowledge; and that public schools could create one society from many people—*e pluribus unum* [Tyack 1974, p. 18].

In a nutshell, confidence in public schools has hit rock bottom. The public doubts whether schools can serve as instruments of social reform; the public even doubts whether schools can handle the more limited task of teaching basic academic skills. Many states have recently passed competency testing programs, in an attempt to force schools to focus more attention on basic skills.

These twin crises—finances and authority—wreak havoc on staff morale. Educators face myriad blows to their professional confidence. Reductions put jobs in jeopardy as schools are forced to cut staff. Declining faith in schools makes administrators and teachers feel unappreciated and unsuccessful. Their insecurity and feelings of bewilderment or defeat are compounded further by the inherent uncertainties of educational practice.

If teaching or managing schools were certain, clear, and straightforward tasks, then educators could find a haven in a professional culture or technology. But education is an indeterminate enterprise. Its purposes and technologies are unclear. Its goals are diverse, diffuse, and disputed among various stakeholders. Why and how students learn—or whether they do at all—is hard to define, difficult to measure, and unlikely to be disentangled from multiple events that contribute to student growth and development. For all these reasons, teachers and administrators have a hard time knowing, demonstrating, or proving their effectiveness. As doubts and accusations mount from a public that has lost faith in schools, educators are strapped for responses. Their ambiguous answers reflect the reality of what they do; their self-doubts increase as the public presses for more certainty in a process that is inherently ambiguous.

The combined effects of dwindling financial resources, waning public faith and confidence, and ebbing professional morale creates an unfavorable environment for schools. Within this context, administrators are being asked to do the impossible: cut the school budget—eliminating people, programs, and schools—without disaffecting influential segments of the community whose continued support is essential and without further undermining staff morale. Nested within this basic dilemma are a number of specific problems.

What schools should be closed? Each neighborhood has a string of sensible reasons why its own school should not be the one to go. Cutting programs and closing schools inevitably involve staff transfers and dismissals. How can these personnel decisions be made without creating divisive squabbles and saddling survivors with guilt and grief? For school administrators, a typical day or week is now filled with such questions.

Stationed at the front line under the rapid-fire barrage of such problems, most administrators want answers to two questions: (1) What should I do? and (2) How should I do it?

Research and Answers

As administrators look to the research community for help, they often seek a scientific basis for deciding what to do. But, in the past, researchers have usually either dodged important questions or provided general answers that never seem to work under local conditions. These irrelevant or nonspecific results have shaped the perception administrators often hold of researchers: (1) They have theories that stimulate research but are of little practical use; (2) They have answers that are true under artificial experimental conditions but do not apply in the complex everyday world of schools.

A more contemporary response of researchers to administrators seeking assistance is: "It all depends." This answer leads administrators to dismiss researchers as fuzzy-minded, wishy-washy, and incapable of providing answers to the pressing questions confronting schools. But, behind the phrase "It all depends," lies some knowledge that administrators may find liberating and directly related to the onerous task of deciding what to do as resources decline. Research can never provide answers that apply directly and unconditionally except for mundane questions whose answers administrators already know. For this reason, administrators—not researchers—must play the role of expert as solutions are developed at the local level. The search for specific answers in research results in a futile one. Practitioners are the rightful owners of real wisdom about what to do in schools.

Research and New School Images

Research may not have answers but those researchers who study organizational phenomena have clarified new images of how schools work and have begun to explore how images affect administrative practice. Decisions about solutions and strategies under conditions of decline are heavily influenced by one's vision of schools as organizations.

Many administrators, at least those who paid attention in administrative training courses, tend to view their role in decisions as one who gathers information, weighs alternatives, and arrives at a sound, just, and acceptable decision through professional judgment and expertise. Problems are seen as having solutions. Administrators are seen as having a central role in finding both problems and solutions. Research is seen as providing sensible alternatives based on logical reasoning and empirical evidence. This perception of schools, decision making, and the role of research is based on a more general image of organizations as rational-technical systems. (See Table 23-1.) From this perspective, purposes can be reduced to performance criteria for both students and staff and outcomes can be prespecified and measured. Schools should be managed so as to achieve the highest output per unit costs where outputs are usually measured by student achievement test scores and costs are measured in dollars. The administrator's role in this view of schools is not unlike that of a chief executive officer or factory manager. The administrator attempts to plan ahead, to define performance or output criteria and to make decisions that maximize efficient use of resources and achieve desired outputs. In making decisions, a process is envisioned in which problems are identified and defined on the basis of objective information, alternatives are sought through logical analysis, and strategies are selected on the basis of tangible merits.

But there are other images that have begun to emerge from studies of schools as organizations. A second view emphasizes the political aspects of schools. This view focuses less on the goals and outcomes of schools and more on the process of contending with competing interests, agenda, and preferences that are important in attempting to administer schools. Policies and decisions must be able to win the support of a sufficiently powerful combination of constituencies. One of the administrator's chief concerns is to maintain enough power to stay in office. Longevity on the job may require the administrator to intimidate, collaborate, manipulate, bargain, bluff, and bully. Another concern is to form coalitions that will support desired directions. In trying to manage a school the administrator may feel more like a lion tamer or a power broker than a factory manager or chief executive officer. The process of deciding what to cut will involve the

Table 23-1

Three images of schools as organizations

	Rational/Technical	Political	Symbolic
Metaphor	Factory	Jungle	Temple
Emphasis	Goals	Power	Myth, ritual, and ceremony
Basis of Effectiveness	Quality of output	Satisfaction of constituencies	Faith and meaning
Key Administrative Task	Planning, decision making, and evaluation	Balancing interest groups and contending with conflict	Convening rituals and ceremonies; mastering myths and maintaining faith
Administrator's Role	Manager or chief executive officer	Lion tamer or power broker	Guru or High Priest(ess)
Main Concern in Hard Times	Maintaining quality of people, programs, and schools	Maintaining support of key constituencies	Maintaining faith, belief, and meaning among internal and external groups

activation of a variety of interest groups, who will form coalitions and bargain around specific interests. The outcome will be decided more on the basis of power than the merits of a specific proposal.

A third vision of schools emphasizes the importance of symbolic rather than technological or political aspects of school administration. The focus here is less on the functions of schools or on the political forces that make them work. Rather, the symbolic view emphasizes the meaning that schools and activities have for various participants. From this perspective, achievement test scores or political clout are not so important by themselves. What matters are the beliefs students, teachers, administrators, parents and citizens hold about the scores, political trade-off, or the effectiveness of schools. When schools are viewed symbolically, the administrator's role is to run the schools so that the various stakeholders experience schools as meaningful institutions worthy of their faith and support. This perception of schools as meaningful, effective, or worthy of support is influenced less by concrete evidence of effectiveness and efficiency than by public myths, values, and expectations. In the symbolic view, schools are institutions both based on and expressive of faith and shared community values. They are more like churches, temples, or community theaters than like factories or political jungles. The role of the administrator in such settings is more like a guru or high priest than a factory manager or liontamer. In this view, decisions about what to cut will be reached through a complex interplay of irrational forces. The process of this interplay is as important as the decisions it produces. In making decisions about what is to be cut in hard times, it is important that people have faith in the decisions, grieve about their losses, develop stories that explain why decisions have been made, and hammer out shared myths for future operations.

As administrators approach the difficult decisions of how to get along with less, they need to reflect on their own image of schools. How administrators view schools and their role will be a major factor in how they act in the face of hard times. Each view—rational, technical, political, or symbolic—illuminates different features of the complex organizations within which difficult decisions have to be made. Administrators who are able to view problems from several perspectives will probably avoid obvious pitfalls and see more opportunities than those who are locked into one view. Research is helpful to administrators in hard times by offering some alternative images of school organizations and by illuminating alternative pathways that might be followed in defining and solving problems within a particular district or school.

Research and What to Do

How can research help administrators actually decide which groups, programs, or schools to trim during hard times? The role research might play looks different from each of the three views of schools as organizations. (See Table 23-2.)

In the rational-technical view of schools, the chief role of research is to provide information for making decisions about which programs to cut, which personnel to dismiss, which schools to close, or how to reorganize. Answers based on "hard" research data should provide a sound basis for terminating or cutting back without undermining the efficiency and effectiveness of a school.

The main problem is that the ability of research to provide such definitive answers is limited. In determining which programs to cut, research studies suggest that priorities be given to maintaining classroom teachers and line administrators—the backbone of a system. Specialists and

Table 23-2

Image of organizations and the role of research in
deciding what to do in hard times

	Rational/ Technical View	Political View	Symbolic View
Key Problem	Quality	Interest groups v. general welfare	Faith, meaning belief
Use of Research	Provide criteria for making cuts without sacrificing quality	Provide external power base in advocating decisions for general welfare and contesting positions of interest groups	Provide shared justification for cuts that reinforces, reinterprets or replaces old myths, beliefs, and meanings
Desired Outcome	Quality is maintained or improved	General interests prevail	Belief and faith in schools are renewed, new myths are developed
Metaphor for Research	Answers or information	Shield or ammunition	Scripture

special administrators have little impact on classroom activities. What teachers and principals expect and do probably bears more relationships to how much students learn than anything else. Research studies would also suggest that increasing class size, reducing the budget for instructional materials, or de-emphasizing individualized instruction would not make much of a difference. The link between these variables and student learning are not that strong or consistent.

In trying to decide which personnel should be cut, some research studies emphasize the importance of evaluation systems with clear criteria, regular observations, clear explicit oral and written evaluations, and an objective basis for ranking personnel according to their competence. But other studies caution against the use of formal evaluations in making decisions about personnel. They suggest that relying on formal evaluations as a basis for such decisions may further undermine internal morale and create conflicts that jeopardize the bond of faith and confidence between schools and local communities. Competence is exceedingly difficult to pinpoint among professionals who work in schools. Using competence as a factor in dismissals usually creates tension with schools and produces conflicts among constituencies outside.

Similarly, the usefulness of research in deciding which schools to close or how to reorganize falls considerably short of providing the specific answers that administrators need. The relationship between physical facilities or instructional characteristics and student outcomes is tenuous at best. So is the relationship between organizational arrangements and their effects. Research provides very little evidence that various patterns of decision making, grade organization, or administrative structures will make a significant difference in how much students learn.

From a rational-technical view of schools, research is of limited use in telling administrators what to do in hard times.

Because research does not provide general or specific answers about what to do, administrators need to consider locally developed practices and standards of quality in making decisions. But, often, shared criteria are not available to guide systematic problem solving. Various interest groups will have their own positions to support or defend.

In such circumstances, research results can become political ammunition in debates about which programs are cut, which teachers or administrators are let go, or which schools are closed.

As interest groups struggle to gain a political toehold, they look for backing from external sources. Research findings are often cited as a source of external expertise. Isolated research studies can be found to support almost any position if one ignores methodological limitations or flawed analyses of results. Many interest groups will attempt to bolster their ideological positions by linking their claims to research findings.

There are two ways that administrators can use research politically as decisions are made about cutbacks. Administrators can cite research results in advocating their own position or that of groups or coalitions favoring the general interests. By conveying an appearance of rational analysis, research can add clout to an argument. As administrators reach closure about what needs to be cut—through intuition, political expediency, or divine revelation—they can use research to support or buttress their argument.

Administrators can also use research to combat the claims made by interest groups opposing general interests. When the claims of interest groups are supported by research evidence, contradictory findings can be used as a shield to protect the position that the administrator considers in the best interest of the general welfare. From a political view, decisions get made on the basis of which group has the most power. Research studies can be used as a source of power in political contexts. Research does not provide definitive answers. But it can provide a basis of authority that tips the balance of political influence.

From a symbolic perspective, the primary role of research is to cloak decisions with an aura of legitimacy, to provide a justification for decisions that promotes (or maintains) faith and confidence, and to cushion individuals and organizations from the anguish of loss. Like the political perspective, the symbolic view portrays research as providing little help in determining what should be cut. The political view sees research as power that can be used to increase the willingness of interest groups to support a particular decision. From a symbolic perspective, research is more like scripture. A proposal supported by research invokes a higher, almost divine authority that increases the likelihood that people will believe in its merits or utility. This authority or increased legitimacy helps people make sense out of new circumstances that result from a decision. In this way, research can smooth the disruption and can help generate new myths as old beliefs are challenged and undermined. For instance, when the myth of neighborhood schools is undermined by closing a school, parents need new justifications for sending their children to a faraway school. When young effective teachers are dismissed, people may find new meaning in ideologies that support the wisdom of experience. When cherished programs in music and art are cut, people may find solace in extolling the importance of the basics. In taking away schools, programs, or people, old meanings and beliefs are often undermined or ruptured. Research results can play an important role in legitimizing decisions or helping people find new meaning in the changed circumstances that hard times create.

As administrators turn to the research community for answers to the tough decisions in times of retrenchment, they will find few answers. Research findings do not provide explicit guidelines for what to do. At best, research results can be used politically to advocate or contest specific decisions or used symbolically to legitimize decisions or to provide a new foundation for beliefs that cutbacks damage or destroy. As administrators confront the decisions that hard times create, they will need to create their own answers. Research does, however, yield some suggestions about how administrators might approach the process of creating answers.

Research and How to Do It

Although research is of relatively limited assistance in helping administrators decide what they ought to do, it can be helpful in determining how such decisions should be approached. Research suggests three main options that administrators might consider. These options cluster around the three images of organizations. (See Table 23-3). A rational approach suggests that cutbacks may provide opportunities for school districts to cut programs, personnel, or facilities that are less effective than others. A political approach outlines a Machiavellian strategy in which an administrator plays a heavy-handed role in making cuts. A symbolic approach emphasizes the importance of negotiation and interaction among various constituencies as an avenue for building a shared justification for cuts and an opportunity for individuals to vent and to grieve. Each of these approaches is based on research. Each offers guidelines for the process of making decisions about which programs, individuals, and schools should be cut.

Table 23-3

Three images of how to make decisions in hard times

	Rational/ Technical	Political	Symbolic
Metaphor	Think tank	Coliseum	Theatre
Participants	Representatives from all constituencies	Administrator and interest groups	Key performers and audience
Process	Problem solving	Game playing	Role playing
Key Ingredient	Information	Power	Script
Primary Focus	Exploring	Winning	Performing
Intended Outcome	The best decision	An acceptable decision	New meaning
Role of Administrator	Analyst	Politico	Conductor, Director, or Choreographer

The rational approach to making decisions about what to trim as hard times hit schools is based on studies of innovation when resources were more plentiful. Berman and McLaughlin (1978) studied school districts that use federal funds to implement a variety of innovations. According to this research, districts struggling to make new ideas work went through three stages: mobilizing (planning and getting support), implementing (making plans operational), and institutionalizing (making the change permanent).

In each stage of innovation, districts experienced problems. The mobilization phase was marred by seeking funds for the wrong reasons and by poor planning. Many districts saw innovations as an opportunity to obtain money without addressing why the change was needed. In most districts, planning was short-term, crisis oriented, and dominated by administrators. Teachers and community representatives had little chance to make their views or concerns known. In the implementation phase, districts were swamped with conflict. The commitment of teachers and support of administrators was in short supply. The flow of information and the use of evaluation to pinpoint problems was absent. As a result, innovations rarely were implemented as intended and frequently left the districts basically the same as before the effort began. In the final phase—institutionalization—districts failed to make provisions for successful programs to continue after the external funding stopped. Programs were therefore allowed to "wither away" rather than being supported with funds from less successful efforts elsewhere in the districts. In sum, even under conditions of expanding resources, schools often were unable to manage change effectively. As a result programs were added or dropped without developing a rationale or confronting the conflicts that they inevitably created.

Berman and McLaughlin (1978) argue that in times of plentiful resources, districts were able to manage change loosely and to add something for everyone without asking hard questions. The result was a patchwork quilt of people and programs with new ones added willy-nilly on top of the old. In a period of decline, however, many of the problems of managing change under conditions of growth will need to be confronted directly. Otherwise, schools and districts will tend to make cuts in people, programs, and schools by retracing their steps. Those most recently added will be the first to be eliminated, thereby missing an opportunity to select the most effective and eliminate those that are weaker.

To avoid these pitfalls Berman and McLaughlin (1978) suggest that administrators should approach cutbacks with the following guidelines in mind:

1. Decisions about cutbacks should be based on long-range educational concerns rather than on short-term political or bureaucratic needs. Administrators need to develop a clear vision of present and future needs and to keep this version uppermost in deciding what is to be cut. Renting schools temporarily to assure that facilities will be available for future growth needs, keeping talented teachers aboard to anticipate the needs of shifting population changes, or maintaining a special-education program to deal with pressing issues three years away are examples of considerations that need to be taken into account in making decisions about cuts.

2. Base decisions about cutbacks on sound, reliable information. Administrators need to gather information which provides a clear picture of the time costs or tradeoffs of cutting particular staff,

programs, or schools. This information needs to be put in a form that allows people to see clearly what is being sacrificed in one area to meet the needs in another. Modern budget techniques that permit comparisons across programs or units are examples of information systems that need to be used in making cuts.

3. Arrive at decisions about what personnel programs or schools to cut through a comprehensive planning process that generates broad-based support from all constituencies in the community and provides an opportunity for individuals to observe directly the criteria, information, and considerations that go into a particular decision. Approach the problem of decline through a process that defines problems clearly, generates alternative solutions, and provides sound criteria for selecting and implementing the best and most workable alternative.

4. Involve the staff and community intensively in the planning process rather than keeping important decisions within the administrative realm. Carefully design structures that invite the participation of staff and community and make their involvement important and influential rather than token window dressing.

5. Ease the problems of transfer or reassignment by investing in in-service training that prepares individuals for new roles and new jobs. As programs are cut, jobs are eliminated, and schools are closed, individuals will often be asked to assume new responsibilities— many times in new and unfamiliar settings. Providing training gives people the skills and attitudes needed to meet these new challenges.

These recommendations exemplify a rational approach to decisions in times of decline. They emphasize the widespread participation of all important constituencies in a process that uses information, analytic tools, and a long-range vision of educational needs to determine what is to be cut. For administrators, the key is effective management of this process.

A political analysis of decisions during decline has been developed from case studies of successful attempts to terminate policies and programs in the public sector. The specific cases involved closing public training schools in the Massachusetts Department of Youth Services (see Behn 1975), and annulling the National Park Services commitment to a soil erosion project. (See Behn and Clark 1976.) This analysis is rooted in the assumption that public policies, programs, projects and organizations are rarely terminated and then only through a protracted and vicious political struggle. In these battles, the administrator is usually the loser or victim— witness the case of President Carter's 1977 decision to terminate several water resource projects or President Ford's 1975 decision to eliminate the office of telecommunications policy. Cutbacks always take place in a political context and powerful groups can mobilize pressure to protect their special interests. As a result, the administrator must take the initiative operating from a position of power and employing Machiavellian tactics that enhance the power. Otherwise, decisions about what to cut, if anything, will be decided by groups that can marshal the most power. Such factors may not consider the overall welfare of the organization. The following guidelines are for the administrator who takes the political approach. The guidelines are adapted from Behn:

1. Don't float trial balloons. Trial balloons are traditionally a valuable strategy for testing the direction and strength of political winds. But when the trial balloon is something to be cut, its release will quickly galvanize the opposition, produce questions that cannot be answered, and reduce the chance that the decision will ever get off the ground.

2. Enlarge the constituency favoring the cut. Every position, program, or organization has loyal supporters who will be galvanized by a threat to their interests. Such supporters can marshal the forces to prevent a cut unless they are opposed by the larger and more ardent group who favor the cut. Parents of a school to be closed, for example, can carry the day unless their position is opposed by an equally vocal group of concerned taxpayers or parents who are concerned about the continuation of the special-education program. Those directly affected by cuts are instantly activated. The administrator needs to develop a broader constituency whose interests are less directly affected by the cut or who favor an alternative program tied to supporting the decisions.

3. Focus attention on the negative aspects—or harm—of what is to be cut. Trying to eliminate anything on the basis of its inefficiency or ineffectiveness arouses only general concerns. General concerns provide little leverage in dealing with the specific issues that interest groups raise to keep a program alive. By calling attention to the harm done by an incompetent professional, an outmoded program, or time-worn facility, adequate support for their termination may be obtained.

4. Inhibit compromise. Compromise is one of the most successful strategies for survival. Any candidate for termination—individuals, programs, policies, or organizations—will have a group of supporters who propose compromise in order to survive. Responding to demands for compromise can undermine a decision to cut something. In making cuts, the issue may need to be cast in

"either/or" terms. Otherwise, interest groups may succeed in their strategies of defending their particular turf.

5. Recruit an outsider to terminate or make cuts. Insiders are often bound to past decisions and need to defend the status quo. Cutting successfully may require a change in administration or the retention of a special administrator or external consultant. Existing administrators may be so tied to special-interest groups that they cannot represent the general sentiment of an organization. Retaining someone to do the unpleasant chores and then moving on may be the only way that necessary cuts can be made successfully.

6. Avoid votes. Votes by representative groups, committees, or governing boards are dangerous because they rob the administrator of discretion and create opportunities for compromise. Governing bodies are especially vulnerable to pressure groups since incumbents are concerned about political points and reelection.

7. Do not encroach upon the prerogatives of policy-setting groups. Votes should not be avoided at the expense of encroaching upon legitimate prerogatives of policy-setting groups such as school boards, parent associations, or faculty councils. The administrator must push for as much discretion as possible without stepping on toes and creating other issues that undermine the effort. If the issue becomes procedural, any termination effort can be derailed. Even its supporters may rally in defense of following procedure.

8. Accept short-run cost increases. Often it may be more costly in the short-term to eliminate something than to continue it. Administrators may need to emphasize the long-range efficiencies of cuts in order to preserve their political viability in the more immediate political debate.

9. Pay off the beneficiaries. Short-run costs may be incurred mainly to make certain that those directly affected are not able to use personal discomfort and dislocation to undermine the main decision. Severance pay to displaced teachers, attractive retirement benefits to older individuals, career counseling to locate new job opportunities, or promises of different or better programs or facilities are short-term provisions that may protect needed long-term decisions.

10. Terminate only what is necessary. Making cuts can spawn a number of painful results. Reductions in programs may eliminate jobs. Closing schools may eliminate programs or positions. An effective administrator will focus on the cuts that are necessary, leaving others in the background. Every termination needs its justification. Scattering the rationale over many cuts will weaken the chances for the primary target.

The political approach to making cuts emphasizes the role of the administrator who must decide and protect needed decisions from the influence of groups that arise to protect specific interests. Behaving like Machiavelli may be necessary to carry off the tough decisions of cutting people, programs, or organizations. The key for the administrator is to decide in the interests of the general welfare and to employ political tactics to assure that the decision is not undone by the actions of pressure groups.

The symbolic approach to making decisions about what stays and what goes in hard times is based on several strands of research: studies of change in rural school districts, studies of loss among grieving widows and individuals displaced by urban renewal projects, and studies of planning. The basic premise emerging from this research is that change inevitably results in disorientation and loss among both active participants and outsiders who have some stake in the enterprise. Particularly when programs are being cut, people are being dismissed, schools are being closed, and roles and relationships are being reorganized, the sense of disorientation and loss becomes acute and widespread. Disorientation and loss shake faith, belief, and meaning and create tension and conflict.

Typically, however, disorientation, loss, tension, and conflict are not confronted directly in organizations. Instead, issues are avoided and smoothed over until they become intolerable. At that time coercive strategies pit one group against another until a winner emerges and the issue is eventually decided by power. Administrators are often the victims of such power struggles, although the use of coercive power typically leaves scars across groups within an organization or community. The scars take years to heal.

The symbolic view of organizations emphasizes the importance of shared values or beliefs as decisions are made. When resources shrink, groups are pitted against one another in a struggle for a fair share. While these struggles can become political bloodbaths, they also provide opportunities for diverse viewpoints and interests to be welded into a shared perspective that bonds participants together in a common effort, reduces disorientation, and cushions loss.

Most organizations have sagas—shared stories or myths—which illuminate distinctive characteristics or practices and condense these into cherished symbols which bind participants together in a meaningful collective effort. Sagas or stories will affect cutbacks in two ways: they can buttress resistance or help marshal acceptance. In organizations with strong sagas, making cuts will prove almost impossible—unless the ongoing saga can be revised to fit the new circumstances. In organizations where things cannot get much worse, new sagas often arise to meet the challenge. Hard times may therefore provide an opportunity for schools to revise sagas that are strong but obsolete or to create new ones where none exist. In response to Pearl Harbor or the Great Depression, for example, America developed powerful sagas or myths that bonded the country together and provided inspiration, initiative, and comfort. The saga also gave the president and congress enormous power to respond to the emergency.

While it is not clear how organizations develop sagas, the concept has some intriguing possibilities for how decisions of hard times might be approached. In this view, the arena for making decisions about what to cut becomes a theatre. Various individuals and groups have parts to play. An audience watches as the drama unfolds. The interplay of the various roles and voices permits an expression of important issues and dilemmas. The ending may contribute to a shared outlook, new meaning, or justification for decisions that need to be made, thereby uniting people and groups. As individuals and groups watch, they have an opportunity to mourn and to grieve openly the loss of things that are important to them—much as an audience watching a funeral or wake (Marris 1975). Each individual actor has the opportunity to play the part well and to be acknowledged. A script (explicit or hidden) influences how the plot develops and how the drama ends.

The symbolic and rational-problem solving approaches resemble one another in that both emphasize the active involvement of all constituencies in an open process. But the symbolic view focuses on the expression of beliefs and values, the playing out of scripts and roles, rather than on rational analysis of information or cost-benefit calculation. The symbolic approach shares with the political approach the importance of interest groups and power. But rather than seeing interest groups as forces to be squelched, they become integral voices or parts in a drama that ends with a justification or meaning that all can believe in and support.

The following guidelines provide administrators some direction for approaching difficult decisions in a novel and imaginative way:

1. Expect conflict as resources shrink. Decisions about what to cut will inevitably intrude on someone's turf. Both insiders and stakeholders will experience disorientation and loss as specific cuts are discussed and debated. Conflicts over decisions of what to cut creates dilemmas. These can be resolved only through myths, sagas, or stories that provide a justification everyone shares and believes. In organizations with strong sagas, sagas will need to be refurbished, relabeled, and renegotiated. In organizations without sagas, new ones will need to be created.

2. Identify the players. Decisions of decline and cutbacks will attract individuals and groups with specific interests to protect.

Administrators may have a role in casting the drama by trying to influence the selection of players in order to get the strongest actors involved. In addition, administrators may have to search actively for someone to play a part called for in the script that no one steps forward to fill. A student, representative from a parents' group, or spokesperson for the "silent majority" are examples of parts that are often left unfilled.

3. Create the arena and set the stage. Before the drama can go on a stage is needed to create an appropriate backdrop. Individual actors need some idea of the script—even though in many districts the play will undoubtedly be more improvisational than planned. Administrators can play an important role in designing the set with appropriate props, communicating the mood, and assuring that each individual actor has a general idea of the plot and the other players.

4. Orchestrate the drama. For the decision-making drama to proceed, each player needs to attend and to play the part well. The upstaging of an undeveloped character or a weak performance can impair the overall impact of drama—for both actors and audience. Administrators can orchestrate the process through prompting, delivering their own lines strongly, and altering their lines to encourage a stronger response from a player with stagefright, to reduce the overacting of a "ham," or to solicit a dramatic performance from an actor with a key role to play.

5. Keep the audience involved and attentive. The drama of decisions in hard times needs an involved and attentive audience. Every attempt must be made to get as many people in the theatre as possible and to keep them engaged in the drama—even as participants if the plot seems to move naturally in their direction.

6. Call attention to the dramatic aspects of the performance and interpret its meaning. Following a performance, administrators can use the media and other sources to highlight the key features of the drama and to provide a coherent interpretation of what the drama meant. The interpretation, like the review of a play, may involve influencing the critics, responding to critics, or trying to get publicity for those who seem to pull from the performance the central meaning.

From the symbolic view of organizations, the dilemmas of hard times will produce disorientation, tensions, and conflicts. These are unavoidable and many are not resolvable through rational analysis or political exchange. The key issue is to encourage the development of a shared myth, or saga, that bonds participants together and provides a shared justification for what needs to be done. One way to do this is to approach hard decisions as if the process were a drama and to encourage the drama to play itself to as large an audience as possible. The administrator cannot control the drama but in subtle ways can orchestrate it.

Research provides administrators with three very different options for how decisions that hard times create might be approached and managed. The conditions of each setting and the images and preferences of individual administrators will dictate whether a rational, political, symbolic approach—or a distinct blend—will be used. Research suggests the alternatives; administrators must make the choices.

Applying Perspectives to Decisions

There are two givens in the challenge of administering schools in the 1980s. First, decisions are going to be difficult and impossible to sidestep. Nearly all school administrators are going to preside over cutbacks in programs and personnel. Some may find creative ways to consolidate resources to reduce the number of cuts that are necessary. But eliminating programs, terminating staff, and closing schools are tasks that most administrators will have to tackle and tolerate. Second, the unique characteristics of schools create a setting that is ambiguous, uncertain, and highly charged politically. Lofty, diffuse goals produce few clear criteria for decisions. Specific criteria that are set forth will be quickly and hotly contested. A weak technology makes competence an illusive factor in decisions about dismissals and obscures educational soundness as a basis for deciding which schools are closed. Political vulnerability makes any administrative decision a target for special-interest groups to attack. These conditions are fixed, largely unalterable, and have frustrated nearly every effort of the past two decades to reform or to improve schools.

If administrators have any control at all, it is probably in how they respond to the challenge. Hard times breed inflexibility and encourage administrators to respond in ways they know best. If administrators search at all, the quest is for answers or foolproof recipes that carry the backing of the research community. But either relying on old approaches or following verbatim a pathway that new knowledge dictates is bound to fail. As administrators confront the decisions of hard times, they can resist the temptation to tighten and rigidify. Instead, they will need to play creatively with difficult situations and be willing to view problems from novel perspectives, bouncing their experience against new images that the research community provides. Administrators must develop the capacity to learn, to invent under conditions of uncertainty, and to transform problems into opportunities on a continuing basis. They must be able to use wisdom from past experience as a starting point without expecting it to provide an end point in their deliberations. Donald Schon has described how knowledge from past experience can be applied to current conditions:

The here-and-now provides the test, the source, and the limit of knowledge. No theory drawn from past experience may be taken as literally applicable to this situation, nor will a theory based on this experience be literally applicable to the next situation. But theories drawn from other situations may provide perspectives of "projective models" for this situation which help to shape and permit action within it [Schon 1971, p. 231].

"Projective models" are pictures or theories about the relationships among actions, conditions, and outcomes developed from experience. These models are projected onto new situations and shape the way that the situation is seen and the types of actions considered. As administrators confront the new situations of decline they will undoubtedly do so armed with projective models developed under conditions of growth. To succeed, however, administrators will need to develop new projective models. These will rise from experience and can be linked to the more general images that the research community has evolved from its wider vision of the past. While new images or projective models are not sufficient for administrators in dealing with the difficult problems of today, they are necessary, powerful, and one of the few aspects of the situation that administrators can control. As administrators resist the temptation to rigidify and tighten their perspectives and instead embrace the opportunity to play and to learn, they can be guided by the imperatives that Schon (1971) outlines:

—Learn to tolerate ambiguity and uncertainty.

—Seek to develop convictions and commitment while recognizing that beliefs and values are ways of looking at the world rather than objective truths.

—Engage with others.

—Pay attention to the process of your efforts as much as to the products, while accepting the values of those products that survive the test of being applicable in the here-and-now.

—Reject a literal view of the past, but accept the past as a projective model for present situations.

—Recognize that often we must act *before* we know in order to learn.

Conclusions

Hard times frequently set off a frantic search for the quick fix. The danger is that research will be expected to yield solutions that can be broadly applied as panaceas. Dewey has warned against the waste and possible harm of trying to use research results in this way. Research findings must ripen before their implications and applications to real problems can be wisely recognized.

Others (Schon 1971; McGowan 1976; Wise 1979; McDermott 1976) have cautioned against trying to hyperrationalize educational systems. To the degree that education is an indeterminate process, attempts to tighten administrative control over schools or to force strict adherence to some research-based policy are likely to backfire. When school practitioners are required to comply with overly rigid administrative directives, they are likely to spend their time on irrelevant or misguided activities or to ignore the policies entirely.

Given these constraints on the utility of research findings, research cannot be made to provide recipes. Research results seldom, if ever, spell out exactly what must be done to produce a particular outcome. Their less specific but nevertheless valuable purpose is more like that of a metaphor. They offer a way of thinking about problems in schools that can help administrators reconsider the jobs they are trying to do. But these practitioners must look to their own wisdom and experience to find the particular implications of the metaphor within the priorities and resources of their particular settings. In hard times research can expand the options available to administrators by providing their context and their tasks.

References

Behn, R.D. "Termination: How the Massachusetts Department of Youth Services Closed the Public Training Schools." Duke University, Working Paper 5752, 1975.

Behn, R., and M. Clark. "Termination II, How the National Bank Service Annulled Its Commitment to a Beach Erosion Control Policy at the Cape Hatteras National Seashore." Duke University, Institute of Policy Sciences Working Paper No. 1176, November 1976.

Berman, P., and M.W. McLaughlin. "The Management of Decline: Problems, Opportunities and Research Questions." In *Declining Enrollments: The Challenge of the Coming Decade*, edited by S. Abromowitz and S. Rosenfield. Washington, D.C.: The National Institute of Education, 1978.

McDermott, J.E. *Indeterminacy in Education*. Berkeley: McCutchan, 1976.

McGowan, E. Farrar. "Rational Fantasies." *Policy Sciences* 7 (1976): 439–454.

Marris, P., *Loss and Change*. Garden City, N.Y.: Doubleday Anchor Books, 1975.

Schon, D. *Beyond the Stable State.* New York: Random House, 1971.

Tyack, D. "Historical Perspectives of Educational Reform." *The Final Report and Recommendations of the Summer Institute on the Improvement and Reform of American Education.* Washington, D.C.: U.S. Government Printing Office, 1974.

Wise, A. *Legislated Learning: The Bureaucratization of the American Classroom.* Berkeley: University of California Press, 1979.

Additional Readings

Abromowitz, S., and Stuart Rosenfield. *Declining Enrollments: The Challenges of the Coming Decade.* Washington, D.C.: The National Institute of Education, 1978.

Adler, E. "School Effectiveness: The Relationship Between School Characteristics and Student Outcomes." Unpublished Qualifying Paper. Harvard Graduate School of Education, 1981.

Baldridge, J. Victor. *Power and Conflict in the University.* New York: John Wiley, 1973.

Behn, R. "Termination III: Some Hints for the Would-be Policy Termination." Duke University: Working Paper 577, 1977.

Bolman, L. "Organization Development and the Limits of Growth: When Smaller is Better Can OD Help?" Unpublished manuscript. Harvard Graduate School of Education, 1980.

Clark, B.R. "The Organizational Saga in Higher Education." In *Managing Change in Educational Organizations,* ed. J. Victor Baldridge and T. Deal. Berkeley: McCutchan, 1975.

Cohen, D.K., and B.H. Rosenberg. "Functions and Fantasies: Understanding Schools in Capitalist America." *History of Education Quarterly* 17: 2 (Summer 1977).

Cohen, E.G., T.E. Deal, W. Meyer, and W.R. Scott. "Technology and Structure in the Classroom: A Longitudinal Analysis of the Relation Between Institutional Methods and Teacher Collaboration."

Cohen, M., and J. March. *Leadership and Ambiguity.* New York: McGraw-Hill, 1974.

Coleman, J., et. al. *Equality of Educational Opportunity.* Washington, D.C.: U.S. Government Printing Office, 1966.

Deal, T.E., and C. Brooklyn Derr. "Toward a Contingency Theory of Change in Education: Organizational Structure, Processes, and Symbolism." This article is adapted from a paper prepared for the Stanford-Berkeley Symposium sponsored by the National Institute of Education, Finance and Productivity Division.

Deal, T.E., B. Neufeld, and S. Rallis. "Hard Choices in Hard Times: Evaluation in Schools." Unpublished manuscript. Harvard Graduate School of Education, 1981.

Deal, T.E. and S.C. Nutt. *Promoting, Guiding and Surviving Change in Small School Districts.* Cambridge, Mass.: Abt Associates, 1973.

Dewey, J. *The Sources of a Science of Education.* New York: Horace Liveright, 1929.

Dornbusch, S.R., and W.R. Scott. *Evaluation and the Exercise of Authority.* San Francisco: Jossey-Bass, 1975.

Edelfson, C., R. Johnson, and N. Stromquist. *Participatory Planning in a School District: A Study Using Three Theoretical Approaches.* Unpublished manuscript, 1977.

House, E. *School Evaluation: The Politics and Process.* Berkeley: McCutchan, 1973.

Johnson, S.M. "Performance-Based Staff Layoffs in the Public Schools: Implementation and Outcomes." *Harvard Educational Review* (May 1980).

Meyer, J.W., and B. Rowan. "The Structure of Educational Organizations." In *Environments and Organizations,* ed. M. Meyer and Associates. San Francisco: Jossey-Bass, 1978.

Weick, K.E. "Educational Organizations as Loosely Coupled Systems." *Administrative Science Quarterly* 21 (1976).

Weiss, C. "Measuring the Use of Evaluation." In *Utilizing Evaluation: Concepts and Measurement Techniques,* ed. James A. Ciarlo. Beverly Hills, Calif.: Sage Publishing, 1981.

24

Educational Reform: Retrospect and Prospect

David Tyack, Michael Kirst, and Elisabeth Hansot

Observers sometimes lament that educational reform is an institutional Bermuda Triangle. Intrepid change agents go out to the schools and never surface again. Whatever *did* happen to performance contracting, or airborne television instruction, or Program, Planning, Budgeting System? (Parker 1976). We admit that many educational panaceas have been abortive, but we argue that there is a long history of important changes in *educational programs,* in *governance,* and in *beliefs* about education. In this article we examine what some of these reforms were and why they persisted. We look at the diversity of attempted changes from Sputnik to the mid seventies. We suggest some strategies that may be learned from this history.

But we start with a caution: There is good reason to suppose that educational reform in the 1980s may be quite different from most educational change thus far. The reason is that many parts of the nation now face conditions unprecedented in educational history, except perhaps for the depression of the 1930s, for now we have declining enrollments, tax revolts, and shaky public support. Although public education has historically been an expanding and optimistic enterprise, today it is

Authors' note: We wish to acknowledge the support of the Institute for Finance and Governance at Stanford University, an agency financed by the National Institute of Education. The views expressed, of course, are those of the authors and not necessarily those of the sponsoring groups.

Reprinted, by permission, from *Teachers College Record* 81: 3 (Spring 1980): 253–269.

contracting. Morale is low in many districts as staff debate who is to walk the plank next. It is quite possible that present adversarial relationships between professionals and between educators and the public will grow worse, not better.[1]

Decisions to cut back or eliminate existing programs collide with conflicting goals and interests. It is much easier to be tolerant of differences when new functions are added than when they are swept away. It is one thing to disagree about where to place a new elementary school and quite another to decide which one to close. While reform by accretion often brings good feeling, retrenchment tends to produce accusations and hand-wringing. Fear and anxiety rarely prompt creative solutions to problems.[2]

Most ominous today for people who believe in public education—as we do—are signs of a declining loyalty to the ideology and institution of the "common school," the old term for public education. Like others, we have spent much of our professional lives criticizing the gap between the ideal and the actuality of public education. Now we are coming to feel rather like the railroad buff who complains about dirty cars, poor food, and bumpy roadbeds on Amtrak only to find others nodding and suggesting that passenger trains be abolished.[3]

Today there may be declining consensus that public education is a public good and an increasing tendency to see education as a consumer good to be purchased in the market. If the people most attuned to quality in schooling and most capable of acting on their choices begin to find alternatives like private schools and vouchers attractive, a danger exists that (in Albert Hirschman's [1970] terms) *exit* from the system of public schools rather than *voice* to improve it will become increasingly common. Thus it is imperative, we feel, to revive the sense of public education as a public good and to renegotiate the ideological contract Americans made long ago

---

[1]The question of public confidence in American institutions is, of course, somewhat tricky to judge, although available evidence suggests a drop during most of the 1970s. The October issues of *Phi Delta Kappan* include an annual poll on the public rating of public education. It demonstrates a decline every year for the last five. In a 1977 Field Poll of public attitudes toward 24 major institutions, 38 percent of respondents indicated that they had "not much confidence" in the public schools, second from the bottom in the entire list (above unions with 43 percent negative opinions) *(San Francisco Chronicle,* May 12, 1977). Rates of approval of local bond levies have declined—see, for example. Piele and Hall (1973).

[2]See Boyd (1979). The entire issue of *Education and Urban Society* 11:3 (May 1979) is edited by Boyd on the politics and economics of enrollment decline.

[3]For an analysis of the historic grounds for loyalty to the common school, see Butts (1978).

to use the common school to realize democracy. This will be no easy task, for school people in many parts of the nation today are in a state of shock, conflict, and overload, and citizens lack the kind of leadership that once gave focus and resonance to the aspirations of public education.

We begin this article with a discussion of reform waves from the 1840s to Sputnik, briefly analyzing changes in governance, in ideology, and in growth of programs by accretion. We argue that the common school of the nineteenth century was the product of a widely based social movement that shared a similar ideology. During the progressive era at the turn of the twentieth century, subtle and important changes began to take place both in decision making and in the normative bases for those decisions. School people and lay allies pressed for a centralization of power that increasingly turned over leadership to professionals who sought to elaborate and differentiate systems of public schools. Still talking about democracy, they redefined it to mean that public education was for the people but that it was best run by experts who could adapt the schools to the different needs and destinies of pupils in a complex industrial society. In recent years many new actors who have been skeptical about the wisdom of such established experts have entered the politics of education. Time has altered the balance of power in public schooling. In recent years several competing ideologies and programs have emerged as the earlier consensus eroded.

Over the decades the innovations in programs that have lasted were mostly structural in nature, were easily monitored, and responded to or created new constituencies. Examples of such changes include school lunches, vocational tracks, or classes for handicapped pupils. It was easy to monitor the existence of such structural reforms and to identify the people who had strong motives for retaining them. By contrast, reforms calling for new skills or added efforts on the part of existing staff have had a more checkered fate. Team teaching and the core curriculum are cases in point (Orlosky and Smith 1972).

The history of programmatic change in education is thus an ambiguous legacy for the present for several reasons. One is that it is precisely structural add-ons that will be unlikely during the next decade, while new efforts and new skills on the part of existing teachers could make a difference even in hard times. A second is that the creation of a fractionated system of specialized groups has clouded much of the older sense of common purpose and increased the possibility of internecine conflict over scarce resources. In addition, the erosion of a sense of a common ideology of public education and bitter conflicts over the governance of the system have made it difficult to recapture a sense of common purpose, of morale, and of loyalty to the common school as a public good.

Reform Movements, 1840–1958

Cheerful amnesia and lack of balance have often characterized educational reformers. Those with longer memories have often commented on the cyclical pattern of attempted changes in education, however. Periodically, people discover with alarm problems that have been with us for decades if not centuries: poverty, wayward youth, inadequate preparation for work, and rigid schools. Specific solutions are proposed with all the hype that advertisers invest in the "new" Old Dutch Cleanser, yet often these are recycled solutions from earlier eras: accountability and business efficiency, the career motive in education, or teaching the "whole child" (James 1969; Wirth 1972). When the difficulty of actually changing schooling becomes apparent, when the costs in effort and money become onerous, panaceas often fade, and little changes behind the classroom door.

Reaction to overpromising often brings unintended consequences. Some observers begin to find genetic explanations of "failure" convenient or persuasive. Others of more radical persuasion argue that only changes in the basic social and economic system can bring about lasting educational change. Both arguments undercut the case for gradual improvement of schools.[4]

As we have said, we believe that waves of reform do leave lasting deposits when they pass through the educational system, although not always the ones most desired. These deposits are legacies of what many historians see as three major periods of educational reform: the common school movement of the mid-nineteenth century, the progressive era in the early twentieth, and the great ferment of the last generation, which as yet has no generally agreed-upon name (though by the year 2000 historians will no doubt have found a label).

Viewed over a long time perspective, these three periods share certain common features. Each brought subtle and pervasive changes in the belief system that supported citizens' loyalty to public education; each questioned and altered existing patterns of educational governance; and each brought in its train substantial changes in the educational program.

The Common School Movement of the Mid-Nineteenth Century

The common school of the nineteenth century was the product of a vast social movement that spread a basically similar institution from coast to coast across a sparsely settled continent. In 1860, 80 percent of Americans lived in rural areas. There was at that time no United States Office of

---

[4]Katz (1968, pp. 216–18) has pointed out the drift to genetic explanations.

Education and only the tiniest beginnings of state educational bureaucracies (indeed, as late as 1890, the median size of state departments of education was two, including the superintendent). It was largely lay people who built and supervised the public schools and young, untrained teachers who instructed the pupils. Yet by the Civil War a pattern institution had emerged—the common school—that was already the mainstream of schooling in the United States. As advocated by Horace Mann and other school promoters, the common school was to be public in political control and economic support, was to include the children of all classes, sects, and ethnic groups, and existed to produce literate, numerate, and moral citizens. While theoretically nonsectarian and nonpartisan in politics, the common school often had a pan-Protestant and conservative slant, but apart from Catholics, most citizens found its teachings nonoffensive. Unlike the situation in other English-speaking countries, Protestants joined to support the public school and political parties did not differ in their educational programs to any significant degree (Tyack 1978).

The creation of such a system was a reform of immense magnitude— indeed, the greatest institution-building success in American history. It is hard today, when public education is so familiar a part of our lives, to recapture the ambience of the pre–Civil War era when the common school was still a tenuous experiment. Prior to the movement, Americans supported all kinds of schools with enthusiasm—private colleges and academies; charity schools; proprietary schools; schools based on class, sect, or ethnicity; and public schools (Katz 1971, chap. 1). But it was the genius of the common school crusaders to persuade citizens that American millennial destiny was best served by support of a common school. It was hundreds of thousands of such promoters from Maine to Oregon who accomplished this task, not a central ministry of education.

Unifying the common school movement were a basic system of similar beliefs and a common vision of their institutional embodiment. The promoters of public education were Victorian opinion-shapers, largely British-American in ethnic origins, bourgeois in economic outlook and status, and evangelical Protestant in religious orientation. They believed that a common school controlled and financed largely by local trustees and public taxation was essential to the realization of a millennial vision of a righteous republic. The Protestant-republican ideology embodied in this institution was vividly expressed by the *McGuffey Readers,* which were probably used by 200,000,000 school children of that period. The characteristic form of that institution was the one-room school of rural communities and the graded school of towns and cities. Neither type of school was highly differentiated, and both were designed to give pupils a basic elementary education to fit them for participating in political life and for entering the world of work (Wiebe 1969; Howe 1976, pp. 3–28).

The Progressive Era: Centralization of Control and the Elaboration of the System

At the turn of the twentieth century a new vision inspired many of the leaders of American public education. It was a time of rapid expansion and massive elaboration of the system around the central nucleus of the common school. A key political goal of educational administrators and their lay allies was to centralize control of urban schools in small boards of education elected at large, to destroy local ward boards, and to vest most decision making in appointed expert superintendents. They sought to use state legislatures and departments of education to standardize public education and to consolidate one-room schools into larger township or regional schools. Essentially they wished to "take education out of politics"—meaning, usually, away from decentralized control by lay people—and to turn "political" issues into matters for administrative discretion. In large degree they succeeded in centralizing structures of governance in cities (though the reforms did not always bring the results they hoped for) and in creating increasingly effective state regulation of schools, but it was not until after World War II that the campaign to eliminate small rural schools gained rapid momentum (Tyack 1974, parts 1, 4).

These reformers were simply exchanging one form of politics for another, of course, and the changes in educational governance were part of a larger shift of power in the society as a whole from local constituencies to large national organizations and professional groups. In arguing for these changes, reformers claimed that educational leadership was becoming an expert profession that deserved to be buffered from the vagaries of locally elected officials. In practice much of the actual direction of change came from nonelected and private individuals and groups claiming special competence to judge what was in the public good. In this way, psychologists devised intelligence and achievement tests that profoundly shaped the destiny of students; university professors at leading institutions like Teachers College, Columbia, trained and placed superintendents in major cities; educators from foundations and higher education made surveys of states and cities that told citizens what was approved practice and how well their schools matched this new professional wisdom; and accreditation agencies made such standards criteria for good standing. It was a time of great confidence in a new "science of education" that would reshape schooling in such a way that public education could engineer a smoothly running, "socially efficient" society. They believed that they were discovering the means of shaping social evolution; it was a heady dream, comparable in power to the earlier millennial ideology of Horace Mann.[5]

As the progressive administrators redefined the concept of democracy, the school systems they constructed were internally hierarchical and shielded from lay influence. The new school systems stratified and differentiated public education, particularly in cities, adding new layers and functions. Secondary education grew enormously until it became a mass institution. In junior and senior high schools educators added a plethora of new subjects and services: vocational classes, health education, physical education, guidance, classes for retarded children, programs for truants and delinquents, and revised curricula in older subjects like English or history. Whereas the older common school had provided only basic education in the three Rs and civic morality, now school people increasingly believed that they should prepare students directly for specific later roles in life and that schools should sort and train the young according to their future destinies. Equality came less to mean sameness of treatment and more a specialized training adapted to different abilities and careers. As compulsory attendance laws began to bring young people into schools for a longer span of years, and as employers increasingly attended to educational attainment, schools became more important as doorways to a specialized labor market (Krug 1964).

Like many other occupational groups, educators sought to use the power of the state to strengthen their position, as in certification requirements, better state funding, and standardization of facilities and curricula. Although there were disputes within the profession over child-centered pedagogical practices and over the emphasis to be given to such innovations as vocational training, by and large there was more consensus than conflict over the elaboration of the system and the attempt to buffer school politics. One reason was that the national and state educational associations were mostly dominated by administrators trained in the new education departments and schools. In times of expansion, there was little controversy over reform by accretion, and even in the retrenchment of the Great Depression there was relatively little infighting among educators, partly because the persistence of a common value system dampened factionalism (Wesley 1957).

As we shall suggest, however, many of the ideals and achievements of the progressive administrators have come under sharp attack during the last generation. The ideal of a "closed system" in equilibrium run by

---

[5]On the importance of private power, see Cohen (1978).

professional managers and their experts has been shaken by the entry of new groups into educational decision making: minorities pressing for desegregation and community control and jobs for their members; activists calling for black history or bilingual instruction; lawyers and judges demanding changes in assignment policies or student rights; state and federal legislators passing categorical programs or requiring new forms of accountability; and various other reformers both inside and outside the schools. Decentralizers in cities have sought to reinstitute something resembling the old ward boards of education abolished during the years from 1890 to 1920. Legal activists have challenged the use of an earlier reform, the IQ test. Professional associations have been torn by internal battles. Older loyalties were questioned, and the stage was set for an era when a fundamental institution was no longer seen as a self-evident public good (Ravitch 1977).

Reforms from Sputnik to the Mid 1970s: New Voices and Old Problems

The reform generation starting with Sputnik in 1958 and lasting to the mid 1970s had no single focus but changed kaleidoscopically. The federal government's role in education grew to include sixty-six categorical programs, while California alone mounted fifty-two reform initiatives from 1958 to 1975. To mention but a few reform efforts is to suggest how diverse they were in philosophy and program: new curricula in science and mathematics aimed at gifted students; compensatory education for "disadvantaged" children; ethnic studies courses; programs to eliminate sexual bias in athletics or vocational education; desegregation; bilingual, bicultural programs; performance contracting; head-start and follow-through programs; open classrooms; team teaching; minimum competency testing; affective education and sensitivity training; creation of alternative schools; legal protection of student rights; management by objectives; provision for the handicapped; and experiments in parental choice of education through vouchers. In many cases extravagant claims were made for the efficacy of the innovations, yet as soon as one was alleged to have "failed," another panacea quickly appeared on the horizon (Mann 1978).

Why was there such a rapid succession of attempted innovations? One reason is that schools today perform a variety of functions, themselves legacies of earlier reform eras, yet innovations usually focus on only a narrow range of purposes. People want schools to:

—give children basic skills and knowledge

—sort people out for future roles by grading and testing them; thus providing an apparently fair way to ration opportunity

—encourage personal attributes such as creativity, self-reliance, or interpersonal sensitivity

—provide daytime custody for children

—socialize children to core values of the society and provide a bridge between the home and the world of work and political participation

These are explicit functions. There are, of course, a number of implicit ones as well, like giving jobs to the administrators, teachers, aides, and others who work in schools (Bailey 1976).

While Americans have always argued to some degree about the purposes of education, in recent years there has been heightened factionalism over which functions are most important. At different times different weights were given to this range of purposes and this tendency has been reinforced by the "issue-attention cycle" in education, which has rapidly shifted attention from one feature to another—basic skills to creativity, for example, or the gifted to the disadvantaged (Downs 1972). People eager to enhance the standing of their particular group or identified with particular reforms often saw others as competitors for attention and funds. Few spoke and worked for balance; few worried about those who had not yet found a voice in the forum of educational politics.

Despite the many changes in educational rhetoric and the insistent claims of new squads of reformers, each with solutions ready, actual practices in the classrooms may not have changed markedly. Behind the classroom door teachers can sabotage the best-laid plans of systems analysts if they disagree with them or can unwittingly derail a reform if they are not helped to understand it. Regulations by the state, strictures of accrediting bodies, the influence of testing agencies, and garden-variety bureaucratic inertia often inhibit change. American education in recent years may thus be considered both faddish and resistant to change (Boyd 1978; Wirt and Kirst 1975, chap. 10). Patterns of governance in public education during this period became very complex and often contradictory. Rapidly the older ideal of direction by professionals buffered from the external environment gave way as new people entered educational politics. Successive groups banded together to influence the schools in a series of powerful social movements, triggered first by blacks in the civil rights movement and then joined by the women's movement, various ethnic groups, coalitions of the handicapped, and other people who believed that they had been excluded from influence. Such groups often turned to legislation and the state and federal courts to bring about changes. Certain innovations were also pushed by "professional reformers" in foundations, universities, and government who felt it their duty to represent the poor and disfranchised. A small network of lawyers and social scientists, for example, spearheaded school finance reform in many states, aided by funds and people from foundations (Kirst 1979).

One result of the new politics of educational reform was greatly increased regulation of local districts. There was an explosion of litigiousness as publicly financed lawyers pressured schools to guarantee rights to an enlarging number of categories of people. In consequence, part of the governance of education became increasingly centralized. A single federal judge could order a large city to desegregate its schools. A state legislature could mandate minimum competencies for all students. Fear of the cut-off of federal funds could impel districts to eliminate differentiation by sex in physical education or vocational classes. Courts could order educators to change their policies of tracking handicapped students (Wise 1977b).

But along with centralization came new pressures for lay participation at the local level. Federal and state laws required districts to set up school site councils. Large systems experimented with decentralization and community control. And some reformers called for parental choice, whether in the form of alternative schools within the public system or vouchers.

In the meantime, within the educational profession there were similar tugs-of-war between centralization of power and factionalism. Once weak, teachers' unions grew in numbers and influence, and state teachers' associations gained much greater clout in politics. Once anathema, strikes by teachers multiplied, while collective negotiations became mandated by law in most of the populous states. As teachers banded together to press their economic and political demands, they split away from administrators; conflict rent the once-unified National Education Association, for example. Principals and other middle managers were caught in the middle in the power squeeze and sometimes formed separate bargaining units of their own. Adversarial relationships became commonplace in a profession that once had prided itself on consensus (McDonnell and Pascal 1979).

The fate of programmatic educational reform amid this internal and external turbulence was confusing. As in prior history, the changes that were most likely to last were additive, structural, and supported by new constituencies. Thus programs in compensatory education or bilingual instruction, for example, created new positions such as coordinators of federal programs or remedial reading teachers. Many of the attempted reforms, however, were short-lived if they did not possess these characteristics. Reforms such as team teaching or the open classroom were often implemented only partially at best, and they were easy targets when the issue-attention cycle shifted "back to basics." Efforts at top-down curricular change, treating the school and the teacher as a neutral "black box," often were ignored. Federal program standards that stressed fancy business management techniques often met only symbolic compliance. Ambitious programs like President Nixon's Experimental Schools program that called for "comprehensive change" according to multiple, vague, and conflicting goals led to arm-wrestling matches between federal monitors and local educational agencies eager for funds. The rational model of bureaucratic change often espoused by government administrators ignored the organizational realities of actual school systems and the power of passive resistance, which teachers had mastered (Berman and McLaughlin 1978; Mann 1978; Herriott and Gross 1979).

The reform wave of the 1960s brought not only new programs but also important changes in governance and in attitudes toward education. New groups not previously heard in educational decision making now made their needs felt. Issues of social justice too long ignored became salient in the public mind. School people came more and more to understand that in a democratic polity, public education could never be "above politics." In important ways educators were forced by laws, by court decisions, by protest groups, and by their own changed consciousness to become more responsive to outcast groups.

But the new factionalism in school governance also had its unfortunate consequences. Amid the shock and overload of attempted reforms and new demands, the competition of new constituencies for attention, it was hard to remember that the public schools existed to serve all children, not simply those with vocal defenders. Amid the contests of single-issue reformers and special interest groups, it was easy to forget the broader purposes of the common school, the belief system that made the parts coherent (Peterson 1974; see also Mosher and Wagoner 1978).

Problems of the Late 1970s and Strategies for the 1980s

For all the conflict, the 1960s and early 1970s were heady years. Schools were rapidly expanding to accommodate the population bulge of pupils, funding grew at a rate unparelleled in history, and reformers found ready audiences and sponsors. In the early years of the war on poverty it seemed as if the traditional American faith in schooling had never been stronger. People talked of educational moon shots. Long-awaited reforms such as federal aid to education seemed to promise real solutions to old problems (see Bailey and Mosher 1968, esp. chap. 2).

In 1980 the educational universe looks far different. Now we confront declining enrollments and tax revolts. Some people talk of public schools as a declining industry and expect pathologies similar to those in the railroads: an aging work force, an overwhelming concern for job security and hence some featherbedding, the exit of ambitious and talented people, less willingness to take chances, a gradual deterioration of plant and equipment, and a public increasingly inclined to seek alternatives. Just as railroad passengers turned to the airlines and shippers to trucks, so some expect education-conscious parents to shift their children to private schools.

When an organization declines, people have various responses: *apathy*, as bystanders observing its demise; *exit*, the withdrawal of one's presence or support; *voice*, or the mobilization of forces to change the organization; and *loyalty*, a commitment so deep to the purposes and character of the organization that one must revitalize it and cannot contemplate alternatives.[6] We believe that loyalty is the appropriate response since public schools are major institutions for the continuous re-creation of democracy and social justice. These are freighted words not especially fashionable today. Now there is a retreat from funding of public services, a glorification of the market and individual choice, and a privatism that negates the common good. Educators, like many other civil servants, are often viewed as yet another interest group at the public trough—a perception in part magnified by infighting within the educational profession over declining resources and by the splintering of the common front of the profession during the 1960s. Today there is less optimism about education than has historically been the case. In part this may stem from real problems that people see in their communities such as violence and vandalism in the schools, and apparently dropping test scores. In part it may reflect widely publicized studies that purport to show that schools do not make much difference in the life chances of children. And some of the deflation of confidence may come from the angry and funereal tone of muckraking books like *Death at an Early Age*.[7]

So just when a traditionally expanding and optimistic enterprise—the public school—has entered an era of declining enrollments and unstable fiscal support, we face a crisis of public confidence and low morale in the profession. At such a time as this it is perhaps useful to ask if historical perspectives can give us some guidance and if we can learn from dead people as well as by experimenting on the living. We think that people can learn from the past—not specific courses of action in the present but a general knowledge of how past reforms have turned out and what those outcomes may imply for the present.

---

[6]See Hirschman (1970). For the scenario of schools as a declining industry, see Mayhew (1974, chap. 7).

[7]As a sample of the poor public press, see Cronley (1978).

Strategies about Program

It is unlikely that educational reform in the 1980s will proceed in the incremental fashion of old reforms, simply adding on new layers and functions around the existing ones. As we have seen, much of the innovation of the recent past has followed an issue-attention cycle (now the gifted, now the handicapped, now minorities, now ecology, now vocational education) that has tended to forget the need to balance the different functions of schooling and to set priorities for what schools can do well. Citizens and educators disagree about what is "basic" about education. They need to be reminded that all children need a rounded education. In addition, in order to gain attention for some favored change, reformers have often become Cassandras and snake-oil salesmen, making exaggerated laments and positive claims. In promoting a "new" reform, advocates have often forgotten what is to be learned from past similar experience or theory (the fans of open education might have read John Dewey with profit, and current promoters of accountability and management by objectives would have discovered the limits of rationalism by studying the fate of the "cult of efficiency" in the second decade of this century) (Callahan 1962). People are tired of overpromising, of crying with alarm. Now is a time for the balancing of functions, for realism in claims, for improving the way schools do what they can actually accomplish.

Strategies about Governance

There is a danger today that retrenchment will increase the factionalism and me-tooism that is apparent in many districts. One of the forces that makes a programmatic reform stick—the constituency it creates—could make cutbacks an intensely competitive process. It will be tempting simply to find targets of least resistance rather than to make decisions based on the interests of the children (to fire art teachers, for instance, or to close an innovative school in a low-income district rather than one in a silk-stocking district). Yet opportunistic administrative decisions belie the statesmanship required in public education, and factionalism among educators ultimately weakens the whole enterprise.

As we shall suggest later, what we most need now is a renewed sense of loyalty to the goals of public education. This is not a plea for a return to the older administrator-dominated professional associations, for their unity was often achieved at the expense of real voice for teachers and other interested people. Rather, it is a warning that factionalism could lead to the situation described by Benjamin Franklin: If people do not hang together, they will hang separately. There are signs today that educators do perceive the need for unified appeal and action.

The history of lay governance of education shows swings, both rhetorically and actually, between centralization and decentralization. We have suggested that the common school originally was created and governed by broad-based lay participation, that it became increasingly insulated from such direct lay control, and that during the last generation there have been conflicting pressures toward both centralization and decentralization. Power has migrated both up and down the system. It is time, we think, to ask which kinds of decisions can best be made at which levels. Many recent discussions on this matter tend to oversimplify the normative and technical issues (Sher 1977). We believe that some questions are best decided at the federal or state levels. Constitutional issues like the separation of church and state, student rights, and racial and sexual equity cannot be left to the opinions of local board members. Fiscal equity is probably best handled through federal and state legislatures (Hogan 1974; see also Berke 1974).

But the history of pedagogical reforms centrally imposed on teachers has not been an encouraging one. As Arthur Wise (1977 and 1978) and others have argued, we simply do not have a sufficiently solid technology of teaching to warrant the imposition of uniform methodologies or curricula. The search for the one best system has proved illusory. Most of the available evidence suggests that decisions about instruction require the active involvement of the teachers if they are to be successfully implemented. Effective programs are typically well adapted to particular groups of children. We believe that federal and state funds for instructional improvement should be channeled to individual schools and allocated by committees including both staff and lay residents. Instead of giving salary increments based on university course credits, pay increases might well be tied to in-service workshops coupled to such attempts to improve teaching (Herriott and Gross, chaps. 11 and 14).

Public schools have tended to respond to organized groups. This is the way politics typically operates in this country. Businessmen and unions, for example, have had impact on vocational education, patriotic groups on the teaching of history, and minority groups on the teaching of ethnic studies and hiring of staff (Boyd 1978; see also Wirt and Kirst 1972). In recent years formerly excluded groups have gained a needed voice in school affairs. But in a pluralistic society such as ours—one in which there are great differences of wealth, status, and political power—some groups or individuals will remain unrepresented. We do not advocate returning to an older paternalistic tradition in which wise experts supposedly took care of everyone—for that was a pious fraud—but we do believe that there is a danger in a me-tooism in which only the loud will be heard. There is a valuable tradition in public education, and one that should not be lost, that sees teachers as the trustees of all children. And this brings us to our next and final subject.

Loyalty

The issue of loyalty to public education as a public good is closely related to participation in governance. In a democratic polity, to be able to influence an institution helps to create loyalty to it. Loyalty without voice is blind; voice without loyalty can easily led to premature disillusionment and exit. Exit may make sense in some markets. If a soap manufacturer refuses to make a biodegradable product, a consumer might rationally shift to another brand. But public schools are not just a consumer good.

In recent years we have seen a large number of citizens seeking particular changes—a long line of petitioners or agitators, often with little communication between them about the central goals of the institution they sought to change. Many decision makers—school board members, legislators, educational leaders—have also lacked a coherent system of beliefs about public schooling and might help them to set priorities. Reforms have come and gone, and intellectual fashions have changed. An ardent integrationist of one period has become an equally ardent advocate of parental choice, private schools, and vouchers.

We do not believe that is is possible to find one narrowly defined set of principles that should underlie loyalty to public schools. Education so deeply involves basic values in tension—liberty and order, quality and equality—that each generation must renegotiate its own educational belief system. We welcome the notion of pluralistic and decentralized participation in school decision making, for it can create loyalty through voice. But we do believe that in the historic conception of the common school is a broad justification for a loyalty that could reestablish commitment to public education. In this view the public school was common not in the sense of vulgar, but common as the air we all breathe—a public good as vital to the commonweal as public health. As citizens we all depend on the civic competence, good will, and knowledge of others. The same is true of our economic interdependence, as the future of the social security system illustrates. It has been estimated that the ratio of workers to retired people will drop from five-to-one to three-to-one by the turn of the twenty-first century; surely those children now in school will need to be a highly trained labor force. The effective education of *all* children—not just those whose parents know how to find it—is a public good, for ultimately society pays for ignorance just as it pays for disease and crime. The fact that these are old arguments for public education does not destroy their cogency (Cremin 1951, pt. 2).

American society has invested less than most economically advanced nations in public goods and has made relatively few commitments to all citizens. Our vast system of public education, however, is an exception. More than any other nation in the world we have made extensive free education a right of all children and youth. Even when educators have criticized the shortcomings of our educational system, we have usually done so according to what Gunnar Myrdal called an American creed—one that stressed democracy, social justice, and equality. Most of our institutions—including public education—have fallen far short of that creed. It is foolish to believe that the public schools alone can bring about social justice or guarantee precarious democratic processes, but it is hard to imagine such goals without the public schools. We need to remind ourselves and the public forcefully and repeatedly of the principles that underlie the system. It was just such a forceful and repeated statement of ideology that helped to create the system in the first place.

Educators can no longer count on reform by accretion, nor can we do much directly about birth rates, oil shortages, stagflation, or other macro forces. What educators can do, however, is to rediscover and revitalize the images of potentiality of public education. The difficulties we face today are large, but by no means more awesome than those confronted by school people at the turn of the century, who coped with masses of immigrants in overcrowded classrooms in the cities and with grossly underfinanced rural schools. But then they had a deep faith in their task, a sense of almost millennial aspiration. "The community's duty to education," wrote an educator of that time, "is . . . its paramount moral duty. By law and punishment, by social agitation and discussion, society can regulate and form itself in a more or less haphazard and chance way. But through education society can formulate its own purposes, can organize its own means and resources, and thus shape itself with definiteness and economy in the direction in which it wishes to move." Once thus aroused, he believed, the community would give educators the attention and resources they needed. The writer was John Dewey (1929), who realized more than any other American of the last century how fully democracy and social justice need to be re-created in each generation.

References

Bailey, S.K. *The Purposes of Education*. Bloomington, Ind.: Phi Delta Kappan, 1976.

Bailey, S.K., and E. Mosher. *ESEA: The Office of Education Administers a Law.* Syracuse: Syracuse University Press, 1968.

Berke, J.S. *Answers to Inequity*. Berkeley: McCutchan, 1974.

Berman, P., and M.W. McLaughlin. *Federal Programs Supporting Educational Change, Vol. VIII: Implementing and Sustaining Innovations.* Santa Monica, Calif.: Rand Corporation, 1978.

Boyd, W.L. "The Changing Politics of Curriculum Policy-making for America." *Review of Educational Research* 48 (Fall 1978): 577-628.

Boyd, W.L. "Retrenchment in American Education: The Politics of Efficiency." AERA address, April 9, 1979.

Butts, R. Freeman. *Public Education in the United States: From Revolution to Reform, 1776-1976.* New York: Holt, Rinehart & Winston, 1978.

Callahan, R.E. *Education and the Cult of Efficiency.* Chicago: University of Chicago Press, 1962.

Cremin, L.A. *The American Common School: An Historic Conception.* New York: Bureau of Publications, Teachers College, Columbia University, 1951.

Cronley, C. "Blackboard Jungle Updated." *TWA Ambassador* (September 1978).

Cohen, D.K. "Reforming School Politics." *Harvard Educational Review* 48 (November 1978): 429-47.

Dewey, J. *My Pedagogic Creed.* Washington, D.C.: Progressive Education Association, 1929.

Downs, A. "Up and Down with Ecology—The Issue-Attention Cycle." *Public Interest* 28 (Summer 1972): 38-50.

Herriott, R., and N. Gross, eds. *The Dynamics of Planned Educational Change.* Berkeley: McCutchan, 1979.

Hirschman, A.O. *Exit, Voice, and Loyalty: Responses to Decline in Firms, Organizations, and States.* Cambridge: Harvard University Press, 1970.

Hogan, J.C. *The Schools, The Courts and the Public Interest.* Lexington, Mass.: D.C. Heath, 1974.

Howe, Daniel Walker, ed. *Victorian America.* Philadelphia: University of Pennsylvania Press, 1976.

James, H. Thomas. *The New Cult of Efficiency.* Pittsburgh: University of Pittsburgh, 1969.

Katz, M.B. *The Irony of Early School Reform: Educational Innovation in Mid-Nineteenth Century Massachusetts.* Boston: Beacon Press, 1968.

———. *Class, Bureaucracy, and Schools: The Illusion of Education Change.* New York: Praeger, 1971.

Kirst, M.W. "The New Politics of State Education Finance." *Phi Delta Kappan* 60: 6 (February 1979): 427-32.

Krug, E.A. *The Shaping of the American High School.* New York: Harper & Row, 1964.

McDonnell, L.H., and Anthony Pascal. "National Trends in Collective Bargaining." Education and Urban Society 11: 2 (February 1979): 124-51.

Mann, D. *Making Change Happen?* New York: Teachers College Press, 1978.

Mayhew, L. *Educational Leadership and Declining Enrollments.* Berkeley: McCutchan, 1974.

Mosher, E.K., and J. Wagoner, eds. *The Changing Politics of Education.* Berkeley: McCutchan, 1978.

Orlosky, D., and B. Othanel Smith. "Educational Change: Its Origins and Characteristics." *Phi Delta Kappan* 53 (March 1974): 412-14.

Parker, F. "Where Have All the Innovations Gone?" *Educational Studies* 7 (Fall 1976): 237-43.

Peterson, P.E. "The Politics of American Education." In *Review of Research in Education*, edited by F.N. Kerlinger and J.B. Carroll, vol. 2. Itasca, Ill.: Peacock, 1974.

Piele, P.K., and J.S. Hall. *Budget, Bonds, and Ballots.* Lexington, Mass.: Lexington Press, 1973.

Ravitch, D. "A Wasted Decade." *The New Republic* (November 5, 1977): 11-13.

Sher, J., ed. *Education in Rural America: A Reassessment of Conventional Wisdom.* Boulder, Colo.: Westview Press, 1977.

Tyack, D. *The One Best System: A History of American Urban Education.* Cambridge: Harvard University Press, 1974.

————. "The Spread of Schooling in Victorian America: In Search of a Reinterpretation." *History of Education* 7 (October 1978): 173-82.

Wesley, E.B. *NEA, The First Hundred Years: The Building of a Teaching Profession.* New York: Harper and Brothers, 1957.

Wiebe, R. "The Social Functions of Public Education." *American Quarterly* 21 (Summer 1969): 147-50.

Wirt, F., and M.W. Kirst. *The Political Web of American Schools.* Boston: Little, Brown, 1972.

————. *Political and Society Foundations of Education.* Berkeley: McCutchan, 1975.

Wirth, A.G. *Education in the Technological Society: The Vocational-Liberal Studies Controversy in the Early Twentieth Century.* Scranton, Penn.: Intext Educational Publishers, 1972.

Wise, A.E. "Why Educational Policies Often Fail: The Hyper-Rationalization Hypothesis." *Journal of Curriculum Studies* 9 (May 1977a): 43-57.

————. "The Hyper-Rationalization of American Education." *New York University Quarterly* 4 (Summer 1977b): 2-6.

————. "Minimum Competency Testing: Another Case of Hyper-Rationalization." *Phi Delta Kappan* (May 1978): 596-98.